Microsoft got it right with the latest 2003 version of its small business server software and nobody provides a better guide to installing, configuring and using it than longtime guru Harry Brelsford. His clearly written explanations and authoritative recommendations make this book an essential accessory for administrators and users of Small Business Server 2003.

Hugh "unclehughie" Anderson
Montreal Gazette

"Harry Brelsford extends his winning streak in delivering another useful book for resellers in the small business technology community. This book provides technical procedures to assure positive outcomes when implementing Windows Small Business Server 2003 for customers. We consider this to be required reading for SBS resellers!"

John Martinez, Publisher
Reseller Advocate Magazine
www.reselleradvocate.com

"How often do you run across a book that dishes out practical IT information *and* sound business advice? Besides the depth of Small Business Server 2003 technical help, Brelsford incorporates lessons he's learned in running a successful practice that you can use as a bible for your own small and medium-sized business."

Michael Domingo, Editor
MCPmag.com

"...arms length...hands on..."

Anonymous

"...legs length...paws on...

Brisker
English Springer Spaniel

HARRY BRELSFORD'S SMB SERIES

WINDOWS SMALL BUSINESS SERVER 2003 Best Practices

VOLUME ONE

Introduction & Intermediate

SMB Nation Press

SMB Nation Press
P.O. Box 10179
Bainbridge Island, WA 98110-0179
206-842-1127
Fax: 425-488-3646

10 9 8 7 6 5 4

Printed in the United States of America

ISBN 0-974858-04-8

Cover Design: Laura Zugsda
Editor: Vicki McCown
Indexing: Judith Gibbs
Interior Layout: Stephanie Martindale

Contents

Section One: Deploying SBS

Chapter 1

SBS Around The World

Section Two: Extending SBS 2003

Chapter 5

Section Three: SBS 2003 Administration

Section Four: SBS 2003 Premium Edition

Chapter 13

Chapter 14

Apendixes

Appendix A

About The Author

Involved with SBS since June 3rd, 1997, at 9:00am Pacific (true story!), approximately half a year before its commercial release, Harry Brelsford is a longtime SBSer. His SBS accomplishments include:

- Serving a wide and diverse group of clients, including Contra Costa Cardiology, Wallace Properties, EIS Group, the Peace Corps, and CainSweet.

- Founding the SMB Nation conference series (www.smbnation.com), which is focused on SBS. The 2003 annual conference was held in Indianapolis, Indiana, and the September 2004 annual conference will be held in Seattle, Washington. One-day SMB Nation Summits are held world-wide, including in Australia, New Zealand, India, Asia, the Caribbean region, the UK, Europe, the US, and Canada.

- Authoring numerous books and countless articles on SBS, including the Microsoft Press Small Business Server 2000 Resource Kit.

- Serving as editor and publisher of a free monthly SBS newsletter titled *Small Business Best Practices*.

- Serving the Microsoft SBS development team as a vendor, participating in setup videos, and acting as the subject matter expert for Course 2301a and the advanced SBS 2000 computer-based training (CBT) module.

- Training participants at the SBS hands-on labs during the fall 2002 and fall 2003 US tours.

- Delivering speeches frequently on SBS at numerous venues, including Puerto Rico Direct Access event (Spring, 2001), the Gateway/Intel/Microsoft Solutions Tour at ITEC (Fall 2001), and MCP Magazine TechMentor and SuperConference (accounting group, Chicago 2001).

Harry works from his home office on Bainbridge Island Washington. He holds two degrees (BSBA and MBA) and numerous industry certifications: MCSE, MCT, CNE-retired, CLSE, CNP. The author of eleven books on technology topics, Harry can be reached at harryb@nethealthmon.com.

Dedication

Dearly missed Dad (you da' Law Boss!) and my family: Kristen, Geoffrey, Harry, Brisker, and Jaeger. And let's not forget all the SBSers out there!

Acknowledgements

Where oh where to start!

I certainly would not be where I'm at today in the SBS community without the grace and goodness of the Microsoft Small Business Server marketing and development teams. I recently counted my Outlook contacts for these groups and had over 100 names (too many to list!). You know who you are and I thank each of you. Special thanks to Dean Paron, Eduadro Melo and Alan Billharz.

To HP/Compaq including my Houston buddies: Marc Semadeni, Andy Bauman.

The wonderful group at Hara Publishing helped immensely including Sheryn Hara, Vicki McCown, Stephanie Martindale, Judith Gibbs and Lisa Delaney. Good on ya. And from that experience, the new SMB Nation Press was born!

And I shan't forget those business people who prop me up daily. This includes my SBS buddies Burl Carr, James Rose and Ty Christiansen. And good friends like Fredrick Johnson. Plus there are a few folks that pitched in at the end of this book to make good things happen: Alan Shrater, Beatrice Mulzer, Kim Walker, Karen Christian, Kevin Royalty.

And all the rest (that's et. al. for y'all lawyers out there).

Foreword To Harry Brelsford's SMB Series

To live free, make an impact, enjoy your work, and make a profit. Those are the primary life goals of most any SMB consultant you are likely to meet. The trick is that an SMB consultant can't get too hung up on any one of those four issues, because the secret to happiness is to balance those often conflicting needs, rather than letting any one of them dominate at the expense of the other three.

Of course, this is all much easier said than done, so it takes an extraordinary individual to be a successful SMB consultant. Unlike their mercurial customers, the SMB entrepreneur needs to combine patience with business insight to help guide their customers through a labyrinth of technology choices that can easily aggravate a class of customers who are keenly aware "time is money."

The simple truth is the SMB owner is the most challenging customer in the IT industry because, more often than not, their business can flourish or expire thanks to the right or wrong technology decision. Alas, nothing in this industry is ever as straightforward as it seems, so a nervous SMB owner who is typically worried about making payroll can easily be led astray. And once that happens, a torrent of frustration and recrimination is quickly unleashed squarely on the head of the SMB consultant.

All too frequently this leads to the tarring of all SMB consultants in the same way a few bad lawyers or journalists can cast aspersions on an entire profession. Of course, there are times when the misstep of a consultant does lead to some debacle, but the root cause of that disaster is usually ignorance rather than malfeasance. All told, the vast majority of SMB consultants are a credit to the industry.

Whether an SMB consultant created their practice as a deliberate act to advance their careers or as an unintended consequence derived from events beyond their control, everybody needs a helping hand. So we at CRN applaud the publishing of a book that seeks to increase the number of savvy SMB consultants in the world, which will reduce the number of failed IT projects and consulting practices while simultaneously increasing the value proposition of technology itself.

It's important to remember that the technology industry as a whole would not exist as we know it today if it were not for the SMB consultants serving as its evangelists for countless products. More often than not, it is the SMB market leading the way in terms of bringing new technology innovations to market. That becomes even more apparent when you consider the challenges of the SMB owner. With fewer resources and people, the SMB owner frequently needs to compete for business against larger rivals by being more adroit. And in the absence of larger rivals, there's always the need to be more efficient, because the cardinal rule of business is "Revenue drives growth."

The only way to achieve those twin goals is to reduce the steps it takes to execute a business process and increase revenue per employee. And the quickest way to do that is to maximize a technological edge before any one else does.

Of course, most SMB owners are not technological gurus. So they turn to trusted SMB consultants to get them through the all-too-often daunting tasks associated with investing in technology. For the industry as whole, this means the SMB consultant is the primary way the word gets out about which products work and which don't. Without the guidance of the SMB consultant, billions of dollars spent on technology marketing would fall on the deaf ears of SMB owners too busy to appreciate the lasting impact any given technology can have on their business.

So here's a salute to the SMB consultant. For the most part, they make a good living and enjoy being masters of their own domain. But more often than not, they are typically underappreciated and undervalued by vendors who are more focused on the name on the check than the actual person who got them the deal.

We can only hope that with the publishing of more books such as this one, it will become easier for a larger number of people to form their own SMB consulting practices. Lest we forget, it is the SMB consultant who truly forms the bulwark of this industry and, as such, we are invested in their success.

Yours very truly,
Michael Vizard,
Editor In Chief, CRN

Michael Vizard joined CMP Media's CRN, the newsweekly for builders of technology solutions, as editor in chief in August 2002. In this role, Mr. Vizard is responsible for the strategic vision of the newsweekly, ensuring editorial coverage goals are met by evolving the reporting and editorial beats to accommodate readers' information needs.

Mr. Vizard has more than 15 years of computer technology and publishing experience. In 2001 and 2002, Mr. Vizard was voted one of the Top 30 Most Influential Technology Journalists by Technology Marketing. He was also named one of the Top 15 media influencers in the trade press category. Prior to joining CRN, Mr. Vizard spent seven years as editor in chief of InfoWorld Media Group, where he was responsible for managing strategic editorial partnerships, the day-to-day management of InfoWorld's editorial department, and leading the content of InfoWorld Online.

Prior to joining InfoWorld, Mr. Vizard had been an editor at PC Week, Computerworld, Digital Review, and ebn. Mr. Vizard holds a degree in journalism from Boston University.

Preface

Welcome aboard the SBS 2003 boat, mate! This book is a comprehensive guide to Microsoft Windows Small Business Server 2003 from a real world, third-party perspective. Embedded herein you'll find the following highlights

Methodology

Much care has been taken to develop a sample company storyline that is presented in each chapter. Over the course of the book, and I suspect several weeks of reading and practice, you'll successfully set up the SBS 2003 network for Springer Spaniels Limited (SPRINGERS), a 10+ employee fictional firm located on Bainbridge Island, Washington, USA. Fact of the matter is that, if you carefully follow each procedure, you'll be a bona fide SBSer within a short amount of time. All examples have been tested and include the implementation of third-party SBS solutions, such as virus detection. For example, after planning and setting up the SBS 2003 server for SPRINGERS, you'll download and install a trial version of Trend Micro's OfficeScan application. So, hang in there with me and this book, and you'll enjoy a completely satisfying SBS experience!

Real World

Part of the fun in writing a third-party book is that I can weave in real world scenarios, such as client war stories. Equally important, this book is written on the released version of SBS 2003 - plus a few months hands-on, in-the-field, ass-kicking, real-world experience. It's the type of computer book I've always wanted to write! Topping that off, Frank Ohlhorst, Technology Editor at *CRN*, has contributed a few "real world" columns to the mix.

Microsoft SBS Team Insights

To balance my real-world SBS-isms, I've asked for and received tons of feedback from members of the SBS marketing and development teams at Microsoft. It's a win-win situation for all. They've commented on my works so that inaccuracies are stopped from hitting the printing press. And my insights from real-world SBS consulting, expressed herein, help the SBS teams at Microsoft understand how we work with SBS.

Best Practices

Central to this book are my BEST PRACTICES. These odd SBS factoids are sometimes stranger than fiction. I attempt to divulge these hard-learned lessons and little-known nuggets from SBS 2003 between the covers of this book. As a rule, each chapter has several BEST PRACTICES.

Notes

I have instructed the wonderful page layout artist to insert Notes here and there on the pages of this book. That decision was made after looking at how readers have used my previous technology books. These books have become tattered, dog-eared daily references with hand written notes in the margins. I've now institutionalized that positive behavior by adding Notes sections on several pages per chapter. Go ahead and doodle away. Treat this book as your journal on your SBS 2003 journey.

Usual Stuff

Oh yes! This is a book with a start, middle, and finish. It features SBS 2003 planning, setup, deployment, administration and troubleshooting issues. Each SBS 2003 component is explored in-depth, including:

- Core operating system matters with Windows Server 2003
- Messaging with Exchange Server 2003
- Collaboration and document management with Windows SharePoint Services
- Remote Web Workplace
- VPN
- Standard security with Routing and Remote Access Services (RRAS) NAT/Basic Firewall
- Advanced security with ISA Server 2000
- Database management with SQL Server 2000
- SBS consoles and wizards

- Client computer setup
- Shared Fax Service
- Internet Connectivity
- Outlook 2003 and Internet Explorer
- And more...

Texas Accent

All authors like to think their books are unique, just as all homeowners feel their real estate is unique. While that's not true, one thing that helps make this book more unique than other technology tomes is my written Texas accent. I knew those days at summer camp in the Kerrville, Texas, hill country would some day, some way yield royalties (literally!). Seriously, my shtick is to present technology matters in a kind, nurturing, and sincere way that is friendly and affirming. Go ahead, thumb through a few pages now and see if my twisted Texas tongue doesn't tickle you!

Warning: HUMOR!

Let me try again to make one of my points from the last section. Consider this your first dose of expectation management. I've poured my heart, soul, and personality into this SBS 2003 tome. Ergo, you'll be exposed to a lot of humor along the way as you read my work. I look at the decision to include humor on a computer book as doing the greatest good for the greatest number. The feedback over the year about my irreverent technical writing style has been overwhelmingly positive. Seems the few people who don't like humor with their technology bought the wrong book. (These grumps are more than welcome to purchase books from my competitors, who I can assure you aren't nearly as joyful).

Organization

A lot of thought went in to the design of this book. I first looked at how I and other SBSers work in this business. I then looked at how my paying clients use SBS 2003. This resulted in four sequential sections.

Part 1: Deploying SBS

This is the planning and setup section. It all starts here. Time to rock and roar!

Part 2: Extending SBS

SBS 2003 is, in many ways, here to help organizations function better. This section shows you how to connect securely to the Internet and configure Exchange Server 2003-based e-mail to take full advantage of Outlook 2003. You will configure the SBS 2003 sample network for remote connectivity with Remote Web Workplace and faxing.

Part 3: SBS Administration

After you've set up an SBS network, you need to manage it! This section explores the recurring administration tasks (daily, weekly, monthly, and annual) plus a look at network monitoring.

Part 4: SBS Premium Edition

So, you want more out of SBS 2003, you got more! This section takes you to the next level with SBS 2003. It is here that you'll learn about ISA Server 2000 and SQL Server 2000. These are the premium components of the SBS 2003 product family and are an appropriate final two chapters for this book.

Appendix Matter

Not only are you pointed to some great SBS 2003 resources on Appendix A, but in Appendix B, the SBS 2003 upgrade issue is discussed. Because this book is based on SPRINGERS, the sample company that installs SBS 2003 fresh on a brand new machine, the upgrade discussion was better handled in Appendix B. Appendix C lists the materials you need to add SPRINGERS staff members to the SBS 2000 network. Appendix D discusses my experience working with VMWare and Microsoft Virtual PC in running SBS 2003. The final appendix, Appendix E, highlights the OEM version of SBS 2003.

And don't let me forget to mention there is a photo section in this book showing SBS around the world!

High Standards

This book should more than meet your needs, surpass your expectations, and be held to the highest standards. There should be no free pass here in SBS-land. I offer these measurements for judging how successful this book is:

- Save an hour, pay for the book. I believe that if this book has saved you one or more hours of SBS tail-chasing, it's paid for itself. At this basic level, the time and money you invested in this book should yield high dividends.

- Entertain you. Life's too short not to have fun with SBS 2003. Kindly accept my good humor in the spirit that it was written. You might find yourself laughing while reading a computer book, an oxymoron if I've ever heard one!

- "I didn't know that." Granted, there are many things you will already know in this book. However, I'm hopeful that just once (okay, maybe twice or even more) you'll utter "I didn't know that" while reading this SBS 2003 book.

- Next steps! This book picks up where other SBS resources end. That is, after surveying existing SBS resources and listening to feedback from other SBSers, I've handcrafted a book that flies higher, further, and faster than other SBS resources available to you.

Reader Feedback

As a writer, I welcome and relish reader feedback. I need your feedback and, more important, the world needs your feedback. Your feedback on my SBS 2000 book resulted in some big changes in this book. For example, I retained a superstar indexer to create a professional index.

Drop me a note or post your feedback, hopefully positive, as "Reader Reviews" at the following online book reseller sites.

- Amazon: www.amazon.com

- Barnes and Noble: www.bn.com

So - turn the page! It's now time to start SBSing.

Cheers........harrybbbbbb
Harry Brelsford
Bainbridge Island, Washington
harryb@nethealthmon.com
December 2003

PS - As an SBSer consultant and author, I live by referrals. If you like what you've read in this book, please tell friends, family, and, of course, fellow SBSers! Thanks!

Section One
Deploying SBS 2003

Chapter 1
Welcome to Small Business Server

Chapter 2
Small Business Server
Design and Planning

Chapter 3
Small Business Server Installation

Chapter 4
SBS 2003 Deployment and
Management Tools

Chapter 1
Welcome to Small Business Server

Howdy and welcome to Microsoft Windows Small Business Server 2003, better known as *SBS*. SBS, now in its fourth major revision, solidifies Microsoft's position in the small business space. In past editions of my SBS books, I wrote that Microsoft was starting to "get there" technically with early SBS versions and beginning to understand the small business space. With SBS 2003, such historical talk is exactly that: legacy chatter. It's time to look forward and not only appreciate the product maturity, but also appreciate its repositioning into two versions (standard and premium) with pricing that best meets the needs of different types of small businesses.

With the SBS 2003 release, it's safe to say it's NOW time—to borrow from crowd chants at NBA (National Basketball Association) games. It's NOW time to go forth and implement SBS 2003 without the hesitations you justifiably had with the younger SBS versions.

SBS clearly represents Microsoft's strongest commitment to the small business market, which, as you will see later in the chapter, represents the largest computing market when measured by sheer number of businesses. With a single Microsoft networking product such as SBS, it is possible to "right-size" a small business networking solution, and all with one reasonably priced and powerful personal computer known as a *server*.

> BEST PRACTICE: This will be one of the only "before SBS" points in this book. But, before SBS, trying to implement Microsoft's default business networking solution at a small business site was a frustrating exercise in budget creep, much like placing too big of an engine in a small car! I share this point with you because folks who look at implementing the full complement of Microsoft Server products at

a small business today are in many ways demonstrating pre-SBS Neanderthal business ways. Enough said. Go forth with SBS!

A properly set-up SBS network can improve the way you run your business (or the way your clients run their businesses if you're an SBS/SMB consultant), help lower computing costs, and, perhaps most important, make it easier for you, the technology consultant or SBS administrator, and your users to use and enjoy computers.

Defining SBS

Exactly what is SBS? Actually, there is more than one answer to that question. I like to think of defining SBS as akin to being a tax attorney: everyone's situation is different and tax codes can be interpreted differently by different people. Note this section speaks towards both the standard and premium editions of SBS. Specific SBS constituencies, further described below, include:

- Cost-effective, cost-efficient crowd
- Larger-than-life image crowd
- SBS feature creatures
- SBS Zen crowd
- The Big B crowd: Small BUSINESS Server
- Converters and others

BEST PRACTICE: As you delve deeper into this book, there is no better time to expand on my comment in passing above about the standard and premium editions of SBS. The premium edition most closely resembles the predecessor SBS 2000 release in both price and bundled features and applications. It includes everything! The standard edition is much cheaper and doesn't include Internet Security and Acceleration Server 2000 (ISA) or SQL Server 2000.

Table 1-1 below defines the components, and the premium edition is discussed much more in Section Four.

Cost-Effective, Cost-Efficient Crowd

SBS provides a cheap, robust, reliable, and easy-to-manage small business networking solution. The small business crowd wants to work with business applications, send and receive e-mail, print, and make sure the data is backed up and protected from viruses. Properly deployed, SBS scores high marks in these respects. SBS offers a cost-effective way of bundling full Microsoft Server applications and the Windows Server 2003 operating system. Here the emphasis in on bang-for-buck, and SBS is viewed as just a different Microsoft stock keeping unit (SKU).

Larger-Than-Life Image Crowd

Presenting a larger-than-life image is the goal of some SBS clients who use SBS to look more impressive and bigger than their small business size warrants. With a high-speed Internet connection and SBS, these businesses look and act as if they are much larger entities. More than once, customers who've conducted business with these small businesses, thinking they're engaging in transactions with a larger firm, are surprised to learn it's been just three buddies, a pizza, and an SBS network all along. And get out your digital camera, for when these customers visit such an SBS site, a photograph of the look on their faces when they discover the firm that appeared to be a big-time organization is just an incredibly efficient small business is priceless.

Another take on the larger-than-life crowd is keeping up with the Joneses. SBS is sexy and allows you to use and show off the latest Microsoft Servers products. You too can be part of the hip, happenin' SBS crowd on your block.

SBS Feature Creatures

Many view SBS as a set of mini-Microsoft Servers or "mini-me" (to quote from the popular Austin Power movie) and like to fully exploit SBS applications, such as Microsoft Exchange 2003 and SQL Server 2000. This group, the SBS feature creatures, are going to be most interested in Table 1-1, which is divided, as much as possible, into the server-side (the powerful computer that typically resides in a closet) and the client-side (user workstations) components. Almost to a fault, this group is sometimes more interested in SBS as a technology rather than as a device for running a more sophisticated and efficient business. That is a dangerous and ominous warning sign to beware, as any college business professor will tell you. Anytime you start to get more excited about the technology instead of your core business, then please set the book down and take a slight break. While the SBS technology is cool, it's still just a business tool.

Each SBS component is discussed further in later chapters in this book, so don't worry if you don't understand, much less master, each one right now. Such comfort levels and expertise will be developed over the next several hundred pages and in your career as an SBSer. For example, each server component is defined in great detail in its own chapter. Take Microsoft Exchange Server 2003. You'll learn much more about this e-mail messaging solution in Chapter 6.

Table 1-1: SBS Components at a Glance

Component	Description	Server or Client Component
Windows Server 2003	Microsoft's 32-bit network operating system. An operating system controls the basic functions of a computer, including security, storage, printing, user management, remote communications, and so on. Supports Active Directory, Terminal Services in remote administration mode (discussed below), Group Policy for homogeneous Windows Server 2003 networks, disk quotas, advanced security such as encrypted file system (EFS). Windows Server 2003 is necessarily discussed across many chapters in this book. Your greatest interaction with Windows Server 2003 will be during the initial setup and configuration of the SBS network.	Server
Microsoft Exchange Server 2003	E-mail messaging application used for communication and collaboration. Supports Outlook Web Access (OWA) Discussed in Chapter 6.	Server
Windows Sharepoint Services	An intranet portal and basic document management program discussed in Chapter 7.	Server

Microsoft SQL Server 2000	Powerful database application offered in premium edition of SBS 2003. Discussed in Chapter 14.	Server
Microsoft Internet Security and Acceleration (ISA)Server 2000	Firewall gateway application with the capability to store or cache frequently accessed Web pages and part of the premium edition of SBS 2003. Discussed in Chapter 13. Note the SBS 2003 standard edition security approach of Network Address Translation (NAT) and the Basic Firewall, provided by Routing and Remote Access Service (RRAS), is discussed in Chapter 5.	Server
Microsoft Internet Information Server 6.0	Internet server application that provides core SBS support for Web-related management. Discussed in Chapter 10.	Server
Shared Fax Service	A powerful faxing application discussed in Chapter 9.	Server
Microsoft Front Page 2003	An application that creates Web pages and can be used for desktop publishing. A single-license version can be installed on the server machine. FrontPage 2003 is discussed in Chapter 11.	Server
Additional Goodies	VALUEADD and SUPPORT folders contain useful tools and sample software.	Server
SBS Management Console	GUI-based management console, called Server Management, using powerful yet friendly administrative wizards. Server Management provides a central location to accomplish tasks. The Server Management console is discussed all across the book and specifically in Chapter 4. Note the Server Management console houses the infamous SBS To Do List.	Server
Microsoft Management Console 2.0 (MMC)	Provides the framework for creating management consoles to perform task management. The SBS consoles are based on the MMC. Discussed in Chapter 4.	Server
Server-based Wizards	Include the Add User and Computer Wizard, E-mail and Internet Connection Wizard, device and peripheral management. Also include numerous Windows 2000 Wizards. Wizards are discussed across the book.	Server

Health Monitor	Provides real-time network monitoring of critical performance variables. Has the ability to generate alerts. Discussed in Chapter 12.	Server
Server Status Reports	A tool that can be configured to send reports on system operations and third-party applications via e-mail or fax. Discussed in Chapter 12.	Server
Server Status View	Provides a view of critical event, performance counters, and services. Discussed in Chapter 12.	Server
Microsoft Connector for POP3 Mailboxes	Created with great pride by the SBS development team to allow small businesses to use existing POP3 e-mail services with Exchange Server 2003. POP3 accounts are mapped to internal e-mail accounts. Discussed in Chapter 6.	Server
Windows Terminal Services	Terminal Services is a multi-session solution in Windows Server 2003 that facilitates remote management of the SBS server by the technology consultant. Similar to remote control applications such as PCAnywhere or VNC. Discussed in Chapter 4 and 11.	Server
Online Guide	Robust online help for SBS administrators.	Server
Internet Explorer 6.x (IE)	Internet browser for navigating both the Internet and intranets. Installed on both the SBS server machine and SBS client's machine. Discussed across the book (for example, client computers on the SBS network are now added via IE) and in Chapter 10.	Client/ Server
Default Page Internet	Connects IE to the CompanyWeb as the default. Discussed in Chapters 7 and 10.	Client/ Server
Microsoft Outlook 2003	Client-based e-mail, client scheduling, and contact management application. Discussed in Chapter 6.	Client
SBS Fax Sharing Client	Faxing functionality and capabilities. Discussed in Chapter 9.	Client
SBS Firewall Client	Client-side ISA Server functions (WinSock redirector). Discussed in Chapter 13 as part of the premium SBS discussion.	Client

SBS Zen Crowd

Meanwhile, continuing with my broad definition of SBS, there is another group of SBSers who view SBS as a state of mind. While SBS is a full member of the Windows Server 2003 computing family, these folks view SBS as special, unique, and their life calling. As you might say in Texas, these folks "GET IT" when it comes to SBS. For them, unique SBS tools, such as the Server Management console, are what life is all about.

The Big B Crowd: Small BUSINESS Server

Another view on defining SBS is looking at it from a business perspective: that is, how does SBS support the mission of the business to be efficient and successful? The SBS wheel in Figure 1-1 addresses this point of view.

Figure 1-1
The SBS wheel allows you to view SBS using a business analytical framework for gaining perspective on core SBS applications.

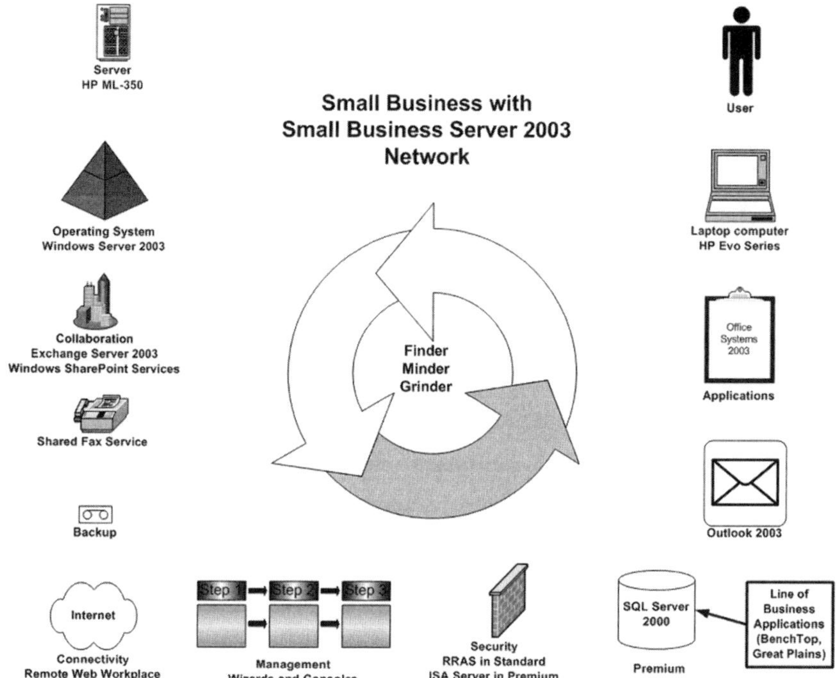

The left side of the wheel predominately speaks toward server-side components, such as Windows Server 2003, Exchange Server 2003, and the like. The lower portion of the wheel speaks to the management function via the SBS Server Management Console. The right side of the wheel speaks to the client-side applications, such as Microsoft Outlook 2003.

The "business"of SBS continues in a moment in the Finder, Minder, Grinder section on core business operations.

Converters

Finally, as part of the goal to define and segment the SBS customer population, consider the following. There are the conversion candidates for SBS:

- Linux Losers
- Peer-to-peer upgraders
- Windows NT and other Microsoft Servers
- Novell NetWare converters
- The soon-to-be newly networked: VIRGINS!

Linux Losers

So shareware's not your bag, at least when it comes to running a bona fide business operation. And the Linux user experience is just a tad too much on the bit twiddler side, eh? No hard feelings. Welcome back to SBS. And by the way, ever since the Microsoft FUSION conference in Anaheim, California, in July 2001 and forward, the Microsoft SBS team has gone to great lengths to compare (and compete) SBS to Linux. Turns out, according to a Microsoft study, the argument that Linux is free is misleading. When considering the total cost of operations in a computer network (labor, hardware, training, and operating system), the operating system is only 3 % of the total costs.

Peer-To-Peer Upgraders

As you may or may not know, peer-to-peer networks are workstations that have been cabled together into a quick-and-dirty network. This is a significant SBS customer group, because two factors are driving the upgrade decision: pain and gain. Peer-to-peer networks traditionally suffer from poor performance (that's the pain part) and many small businesses can easily see the gain a true client/ server network such as SBS can deliver (that's, of course, the gain part).

Windows NT and Other Microsoft Servers

Considered the low hanging fruit in the small business space, those firms running Windows NT-based networks are more than overdue to upgrade to SBS. A big part of Microsoft message and efforts with SBS 2003 centers on moving folks on NT-based systems up to SBS 2003. The performance gains alone justify the conversion.

Soon-To-Be Newly Networked: VIRGINS!

These are the last frontiers in networking left today. Networking consultants, acting as explorers, seek out this type of SBS customer with a vengeance. Why? Because we can put our stamp on their successful network, and it's likely this type of client hasn't yet had a negative networking experience (or negative experience with their network consultant). Great SBS customers if you can find them.

Novell NetWare Converters

This is perhaps historically one of the touchiest and most-difficult SBS customer groups to work with for several reasons. I know, I know, you're saying that NetWare is dead. Not so quick, my Missouri cousin! Why is it so many small businesses are running good old NetWare 3 even to this day? Granted, NetWare isn't the dominant force it once was, but it's a huge source of billable hours for me: converting NetWare to SBS. NetWare sites are prime to go to SBS 2003 in order to enjoy broad industry support for LOB applications.

Finder, Minder, Grinder

With respect to how SBS supports core business operations, let me take a moment to speak about the three major functions of nearly any small business: finder, minder, and grinder.

> BEST PRACTICE: I have a book called *SMB Consulting Best Practices* (ISBN: 1-887542-11-6) that is totally dedicated to viewing the SMB space and SBS specifically from the finder, minder, grinder perspectives. So I'll only touch on the business stuff here and encourage you to follow-up with my other text, which is more of a "pocket MBA" for SBSers!

Finder

A finder is a rainmaker: the person who markets and "gets" or develops business for the firm. In many firms, it is the owner, CEO, or president; in others, it is a salesperson. Whoever has this important responsibility can directly benefit from SBS in many ways.

There is electronic-based commerce. Electronic-based commerce includes everything from basic e-mail communications to elaborate Web pages that provide direct updates to your accounting system or electronic data interchange (EDI) with Microsoft BizTalk.

> BEST PRACTICE: Late breaking news! BizTalk will actually run on SBS 2003! In fact, teams at Microsoft are looking at making BizTalk part of SBS 2003 in some fashion.

At a minimum, a salesman in the early 21st century can benefit from using Internet e-mail, a feature supported by SBS with the Microsoft Exchange Server 2003 and Outlook 2003. A finder can benefit from Outlook in other ways as well. Outlook provides contact management and scheduling capabilities in addition to serving as an e-mail client. Outlook is discussed in Chapter 6. You will learn basic Outlook functionality, such as e-mail and using Company contacts, under Public Folders in SBS 2003. You will even learn how to run Outlook over the Internet, via Outlook Web Access (OWA). This allows you to check your SBS-based e-mail from a late-model Web browser from any Internet-connected PC in the world! Saying you're disconnected while vacationing in the Australian Outback is no longer an excuse with Outlook-based technologies.

So I end the finder section with a real world example. I know a CEO of the landscaping company in Issaquah, Washington, who uses SBS to increase his company's sales. His idea is to fax "spring cleaning" notices to past landscaping clients. SBS does this very well with its fax server support. Broadcast faxing is a breeze, and as an added bonus, this CEO found that he could fax directly to the names listed in the company-wide Outlook contact list. I'll talk more about faxing in Chapter 9.

What's really been said in this finder section is that SBS can offer you a competitive advantage over your competition.

Minder

There's one law of business that I've never seen broken: For every finder, there is at least one minder. Minders serve as office managers, administrators, COOs, and all-around nags. Bless 'em, because we need 'em. SBS was designed with minders in mind (please don't *mind* the pun!). Typically, when I've deployed SBS from a minder's perspective, it has been to implement a piece of industry-specific line of business (LOB) software. You will see in Figure 1-1 that I listed LOB applications. One such LOB application is BenchTop, a very powerful service management software application implemented on the SBS system at a client site I consult to. BenchTop, which uses premium SBS's SQL Server application for its engine, is very much a minder tool. This application brings control to the workflow and allows the manager (aka the "minder") to compile performance metrics specific to his industry. The minder at this site unknowingly benefits from SBS because SQL Server is included as part of the premium SBS bundle. All the minder knows is that BenchTop makes his job easier and he is more productive.

Also falling into the minder category with SBS is the whole business planning cycle plus cultural and organizational reengineering. Here's what I mean. When SBS is introduced into an organization like a small business, it often upsets the apple cart in a good way. Managers start thinking "We're gonna do things differently around here and we need a fresh business plan." And the collaboration of Outlook and Windows Sharepoint Services will improve communication and improve organization outcomes, etc. It's a management revolution inside each box of SBS! To some extent I make this point again in the grinder section that follows next.

Grinder

Grinders are the worker bees. These are the people who are typically task-oriented and look at the SBS infrastructure as a support system that makes them more productive. Grinders benefit from SBS in two distinct ways.

First, LOB applications such as BenchTop that run on top of premium SBS's SQL Server allow the repair staff to enter important job and task information. This helps track the flow of goods in the system and effectively lowers cost by allowing better control. Another business application that uses SQL Server is

Great Plains from Microsoft, a robust accounting application. I've had tremendous success installing this on SBS machines, and I can attest that the worker bees—typically accounting clerks, bookkeepers (and yes, beekeepers)—have been able to complete their work in an efficient and reliable manner. Most important, in both cases with BenchTop and Great Plains, the grinders trust that SBS allows them to better do their work. Such has not always been the case with worker bees, known for coining such pithy phrases as "The #@%$!&* computer network is not working again!" in the early days of computer networking (and during the first two releases of SBS in the late 1990s—OUCH!).

Second, basic communication applications, such as Outlook e-mail, contacts, and scheduling, have allowed grinders to improve the quality of their work, which translated into greater productivity for the firm. Many times SBS is introduced into business environments that have no prior network or e-mail service, often fundamentally changing how people do their work and, in its own way, reengineering workflow. The improvement in e-mail communications is but one example. Throughout this book many more business workflow improvements are presented hither and yon.

SBS Philosophy 101

It is difficult to overlook the sheer numbers of small businesses that could benefit from an SBS-type networking solution. Such was the idea behind SBS. Microsoft recently found SMB religion and has made SBS a cornerstone of its push into this relatively virgin small business space. The numbers speak for themselves when it comes to measuring the number of small businesses. Although you can easily say that there are only 1,000 companies in the Fortune 1000 list, conversely you might be surprised to know that there are over 22 million small businesses in the United States, according to the U.S. Small Business Administration. Can't you just see the marketing wheels at Microsoft turning and the marketing staff dreaming of an SBS installation at every small business? You betcha.

In this section, I'll present SBS philosophy from three views: that of the small business, the SBS consultant, and Microsoft.

The Small Business

Understanding that small businesses are fundamentally different from larger enterprises, the SBS product literally sells itself when positioned by SBS consultants as a tool to help small business run better, with less effort, and, ultimately, more easily. You could say that SBS is nothing more than a return to the original LAN paradigm that both Apple Computer and Novell rode in the 1980s. This LAN paradigm, with a few modifications to accommodate SBS, is anchored by these key tenets:

- **Sharing:** The major justification for implementing SBS in the small business is the ability to share information. Sharing information, such as cost accounting data at the construction company, allows staff to work together with less redundancy (multiple entries are eliminated). Owners get better information about their operations. Staff works together as a team.

- **Security:** Like the enterprise, small businesses demand that reasonable levels of security be provided to protect sensitive information from competition and from loss or casualty. SBS provides regular Windows Server 2003-based security (and there's a lot of security features there, let me tell ya) in the standard SBS edition, plus the security afforded by Microsoft ISA Server in the premium SBS edition.

- **Cost Effectiveness:** Relatively speaking, SBS is cheap. The standard version of SBS, a very popular option, can be purchased on the street starting for under $600 USD. In fact, there are some major hardware manufacturers that have seen fit to send you out the door with the standard SBS edition and a capable server for $1,000 USD! Man is that a change from the not-too-distant days past of $5,000 server machines for the small business. So tack on a few $500 USD capable workstations and another $1,000 USD for necessities (virus protection suite, hubs, wireless cards, etc.) and you're up and running on a pauper's payroll, not that of the prince! Note you might find you will need a mid-range server when you look closely at your needs. Such a server runs $1,500 USD standalone as of this writing.

BEST PRACTICE: When amortized, for accounting purposes, over the typical five-year holding period seen in many small businesses (versus the more aggressive three-year holding period typically seen at the enterprise-level), SBS is really cost-effective. After the basic installation, allowance for training (say, a one-time $500 USD per user outlay) and technology consulting fees, an SBS network easily costs less than $500 USD per user per year. THIS IS $1.38 USD PER USER PER DAY, FRIEND! (Yes, I'm shouting for emphasis.) That's less than my subscriptions to the *USA Today* and *Wall Street Journal* newspapers! That's less than my first cappuccino!

If you've ever worked at the enterprise level, you'd be viewed as kooky if you told someone you had lowered your annual IT costs per user to less than $500 (more likely at the enterprise-level it would be over $5,000 USD per user per year).

- **Efficiency:** After an initial period of negative productivity (measured in hours) while everyone is learning the new SBS network and its powers, company-wide productivity for the firm quickly soars to a level exceeding pre-SBS days. One example of this is the use of broadcast e-mails and faxes instead of making lots of telephone calls.

- **Better Work, New Work:** This includes fewer mistakes because of better communications, such as e-mail with staff, vendors, and customers; better scheduling with Outlook's calendar, etc.; and new work, such as winning new contracts because your work is of higher quality (proposals with accurate financial information derived from staff, and so on). In fact, as an SBS site starts using more and more SBS features, I've seen these small businesses dramatically increase their business. Back at the ranch, oops, I mean the previously mentioned landscaping company client, you will recall that SBS's faxing capabilities are used to fax "Spring planting announcements" to its clients resulting in increased sales. Small businesses, enlightened by the powers of SBS, have also been known to enter into new business areas, knowing they have the network infrastructure to back up promises. Need more convincing? A small construction company I worked with, confident that SBS-based e-mail and remote communications solutions wouldn't fail them, took on work in other cities.

- **Bottom Line:** How does SBS sum up? Properly implemented, SBS can help small businesses enjoy higher-quality work and get more work finished with the fewer resources:

  Land — Office space is used more efficiently, as older office machines, file cabinets, and the like are eliminated. Hell, with the Remote Web Workplace feature I'll explain in Chapter 8, the whole darn office space can nearly be eliminated and everyone sent to Starbucks coffee shops to use Wi-Fi to do their business!

  Labor — Existing staff works more efficiently, allowing owners to squeeze out more productivity. But fear not that SBS will result in staff downsizing. I've worked with a variety of SBS sites and have never seen a layoff or firing related to SBS. In fact, the opposite tends to occur. Small businesses get excited very quickly with SBS when they understand it and see it working. In short order, additional (and unplanned) work requests roll in. For example, several of my small business clients who barely knew what the Internet was prior to the SBS installation call back and ask for Web home page development assistance. I typically refer an intern from the local college to these clients, allowing them to save on Web page development costs and giving a starving college kid the chance to earn some money. And guess what! More often than not the college intern becomes a full-time employee, actually increasing headcount at the client site as a result of the SBS implementation.

  Capital — Not to understate the initial capital investment in getting an SBS network up and running, but, after that outlay is made, the general consensus is that SBS delivers a positive return on investment (ROI) by increasing the firm's productivity and mitigating additional large capital outlays for the foreseeable future. One example of this is the reduced wear and tear on photocopiers. A client of mine who has aggressively exploited SBS features now stores documents electronically and faxes directly to vendors. By doing so, this customer found it could forego the purchase of a new, expensive photocopier.

SBS Consultant

To paraphrase from my *SMB Consulting Best Practices* book, SBS is a "consulting practice in a box." It's a structured setup with an assured positive outcome; it's a To Do List and a Server Management console that is used at each site; and it's about making every customer implementation exactly the same to contribute to consulting success. SBS is a consultant's dream, and I'll leave it there as my other tome uses over 600 pages to express these sentiments.

Microsoft

So what does Microsoft think? Well, Microsoft extends this SBS paradigm specifically by adding these design goals:

- **Ease of Use/Simplicity:** The idea was to make everything easy, easy, easy. And when compared to the old command-line interface of NetWare 3.x (which a surprisingly high number of small businesses are still running, having foregone the opportunity to upgrade to NetWare 4.x, 5.x), you could say that SBS is easier to manage and use. For example, Dawn, who works at an athletic club I've assisted, took many years (appropriately so) to master NetWare. When Dawn was confronted with the decision to upgrade to the newly released NetWare 5.0, I loaned her a training machine that had SBS installed. One week later, Dawn was confident and had even confirmed that her narrow market vertical applications would run on SBS. Not surprisingly, Dawn and her firm became another SBS success story.

  But *easy* is in the eye of the beholder. Whereas Dawn was coming from a more complex networking environment, allowing her to enjoy the ease of SBS when compared to NetWare, SBS has sometimes fallen short for small businesses that have never been networked. These firms, accustomed to working manually with file cabinets, fax machines, and basic word processing, are often disappointed with SBS initially when they (a) can't believe installing a network is so difficult and (b) don't understand why servers don't work perfectly all the time (for example, blue-screen crashes or applications stop responding). So take Microsoft's SBS ease of use argument with a grain of salt.

However, if it is usability that you are measuring, clearly SBS wins when compared to other NOSs such as NetWare and Linux. With its superior graphical user interface (GUI), SBS encourages even those on-site power users unaccustomed to managing a network server to feel comfortable using the Start button, menus, mouse, and so on. Score one for SBS for high usability. Of course, I'm assuming the SBS consultant has asked for and approved the power user's help.

- **Making Decisions for the Customer:** In the context of having an automated setup and implementation process ("just add water"), SBS (in Microsoft's view) reduces the research, engineering, and guesswork that goes into making the networking decision. Microsoft correctly asserts that users do not have to decide whether the SBS machine should be a domain controller (it should, because it controls the operations of the network) and whether to install Active Directory. Active Directory is the directory services database used to store user and computer account information.
- **Designed for Success:** This point speaks to the SBS consoles I've previously discussed. The idea is that SBS administrators should enjoy a "simple, stupid" networking management experience and not really have to perfectly plan what they intend to do. Adding a user is a click away in the Server Management console. Simple.

BEST PRACTICE: Here again, I must interject a few clarifying comments regarding the pro-Microsoft comments. For new users and NetWare administrators coming over to SBS (such as Dawn), I've found the SBS cool tools—such as the management console and wizards—are great and really aid the SBS learning process. So on that count, Microsoft is correct with its ease of use, automatic decision making, and successful design assertions. But for old-school Windows Server gurus with headstrong ways of doing things, the SBS consoles are sometimes more of an enemy. These Windows Server gurus begrudgingly use the SBS Server Management console (interestingly, the native tools are exposed in the Server Management console, removing the need to drop down and use the Administrative Tools folder). I'll say it now and most assuredly say it again: Do everything from the SBS Server Management console (and its wizards).

Microsoft has another view of SBS with its Go To Market (GTM) methodology (visit www.microsoft.com/partner and select **Windows Server** under the **Server** family product on the left). GTM is a four-step methodology:

Learn About It. Microsoft views its partners' success with SBS as a function of how much knowledge they have about the product. Microsoft offers SBS hands-on labs (online and in-person), Microsoft Official Curriculum (MOC) courses specific to SBS and other training tools.

Sell It! There is no shortage of resources when it comes to supporting your SBS sales efforts. Logos, canned PowerPoint presentations, and the like are all accessible from the Microsoft Partner site referenced above.

Build On It! Here the idea is to add value by bundling SBS with additional services and products. For example, you might implement the Microsoft Great Plains solution on top of SBS as your package. You might also sell and deploy a LOB application such as those discussed earlier in the chapter.

Deploy It! Ah, the good stuff—installing and configuring SBS. This is considered the most fun part of the entire SBS equation by many.

Deciding Whether SBS Is for You

Early in your decision-making process to either install a new network or upgrade the existing network at your business, you need to decide whether SBS is for you. SBS has several practical limitations that you should be aware of.

> BEST PRACTICE: In consulting, we call this frank assessment "expectation management." You should manage your expectations up front about what SBS can and can't do (especially the "can't do" part). That way, later on, you won't suffer severe disappointments.

User and Client Machine Limit

Only 75 users can be logged on at one time with SBS. And on a legal licensing note, only 75 client access licenses (CALs) may be attached to the Small Business Server network. (Please read the license agreement in your SBS packaging for more details.) Microsoft imposed this 75-CAL limit as the break point between SBS and the full Microsoft Servers products.. Typically, businesses that are growing rapidly and have over 65 users today need to consider the full Microsoft Servers product family instead of SBS as the correct networking solution. The upgrade path to the full Microsoft Servers product family via the SBS migration kit retains your existing settings so that you don't have to do a complete reinstall of your network from what we call "bare metal." Also note that more than 75 users can be entered into SBS as users (technically "user objects" in Active Directory), but only 75 may be logged on at any time. This preceding discussion assumes that you have the user licenses in place for a 75-user SBS network. And under no circumstances may you have more than 75 CALs attached to your SBS network.

> BEST PRACTICE: SBS is often undersold by the people who love it most, the true blue SBSers. That is, SBS is a great servant in larger organizations, such as the Alaskan fishing company with 900 employees that has only 25 client computers connected to the network. All of the other worker bees reside on factory trawler boats off the west coast of Alaska! If you didn't dig deep enough, you might have assumed SBS wouldn't work for this medium-sized company, but clearly it does. Remember that size doesn't matter.

There is another point to make in the concurrent-user-limit discussion: license enforcement. Suppose that you have a five-user license for SBS. Perhaps you won it at a Microsoft TS2 event (www.msts2.com), where you learned about SBS and other SMB solutions from Microsoft. That would mean the sixth user is locked out and is unable to work on the SBS network. In order for the sixth user to log on, you would need to purchase and install additional SBS CALs.

> BEST PRACTICE: For those of you who've been around SBS for a while, you be delighted to know that SBS CALs are now much easier to obtain. This is accomplished via the Licensing link in the Server Management console. Heck, you can even purchase your SBS CALs online direct from the SBS server machine over the Internet. And CALs come in two flavors: device and users.

Four Walls

Please promise here and now that you'll honor the following point as you evaluate whether SBS is for you: four walls. In its heart of hearts, SBS was designed to serve as the server on a local area network within the four walls or confines of a bona fide small business. It's not designed to act as a branch office solution connecting multiple offices. It's certainly not designed to act as a departmental server for an enterprise. You get the point. Used outside of four contiguous walls, SBS becomes a defrocked fallen IT solution.

> BEST PRACTICE: Not that folks haven't tried to take SBS above and beyond what it's designed for. I've seen it firsthand and "fired" two clients who wanted me in my role as SBS consultant to take SBS into the no-can-do zone! If your needs are that of a branch office or departmental server, please DO NOT USE SBS. Use the full Microsoft Server products. I'll be happy and you'll be much happier!

One more point on the four walls matter. In the SBS 2003 release, Microsoft has clouded the waters by delivering the super-cool Remote Web Workplace tool. This would appear to suggest you function outside of four walls with SBS. But a key distinction for now is that Remote Web Workplace is designed for occasional, dial-on-demand usage. It's not positioned as a permanent WAN solution to connect multiple offices. More on Remote Web Workplace in Chapter 8.

One Business, Two Businesses, Three Businesses, Four

A popular implementation of SBS is in a shared-office space scenario where tenants rent executive suites or sublet space. SBS can support multiple Internet domain names, allowing each tenant to have an appropriate Internet identity. In fact, some executive suites implement SBS and then recoup their costs by charging tenants a monthly "networking" fee. This form of SBS implementation—supporting multiple business entities—might not be apparent at first blush, but is possible.

Single Domain, No Workgroups

SBS is limited to a single domain and must be the root of the Active Directory forest. (A domain is an administrative unit in a Windows Server 2003 environment.) This limitation is a hindrance if your organization is part of a larger enterprise that has other Windows Server 2003 machines and typically uses Active Directory's implicit two-way "trust relationships" to interact with other domains. Don't forget this SBS rule: SBS trusts no one!

> BEST PRACTICE: A quick Active Directory primer for you: First, contrary to the rumors circulating in late 1999 and early 2000, domains are still with us in Windows 2000 and 2003. In fact, there are two domains: the traditional NT-like NetBIOS domain name typically associated with the internal network domain and the Internet domain (ye olde dot-com) type. A forest is a collection of trees and a tree is a collection of domains. Whew!

Workgroups are not really allowed in the SBS networking model because SBS must act as something called a *domain controller* (*DC*). A DC is the central security authority for the network. It is responsible for logging you on, auditing usage if so configured, and whatnot. Workgroups do not use such a robust security model, and interestingly, many small businesses upgrading to SBS have been using peer-to-peer networks built on the workgroup model. This change from workgroups to domains is often startling to the small business and requires extra care and planning. Why? For one reason, domains by their nature are a much more centralized management approach; workgroups are decentralized. So people who were comfortable with the workgroup sharing model are often put off by the heavy-handed centralized management domain view. Be careful here, especially if your working with peace-loving hippies from the 1960s!

Real SKUs

Don't let the name "small" in the SBS title fool you. The components of SBS 2003 are the "real" Microsoft Servers products or stock keeping units (SKUs). This is "really" Windows Server 2003 standard edition (although see my following Best Practice) and it's the "real" Exchange Server 2003 product. SBS detractors in the past have tried to paint SBS as having "lite" versions of Microsoft Server SKUs. Some from the enterprise space sneered that SBS was really "baby BackOffice" Not true, buddy boys. SBS is the real McCoy and you can go forth with confidence in your small business infrastructure implementations.

BEST PRACTICE: In the next breath, I must warn you there are exceptions to the rule, as tax attorneys like to say. First, I've cited the trust relationship limitation in the prior section above. I am also honor-bound to mention, that while it's truly the Windows Server 2003 standard SKU in SBS 2003, it's also limited to two processors to help define the SBS 2003 product. The unbound standard version of Windows Server 2003 allows up to four processors. Details, details!

Cost/Benefit Analysis

Another SBS consideration is cost. The standalone version of Windows Server 2003 is actually more expensive than a comparably licensed version of SBS 2003 standard edition. While I've lost SBS consulting opportunities in the past, when the underlying NT operating system was cheaper than the legacy SBS 4.x versions, such is not the case in the new world of SBS 2003 standard edition. Today the situation is that SBS 2003 standard edition will pass any cost/benefit test applied to it! So how does the argument work for SBS 2003 premium edition. If the firm needs the increased features and functionality provided by the SBS 2003 premium edition, they should be willing to pay for it (otherwise the SBS 2003 standard edition will satisfy the budget of this low-end customer segment).

So to summarize the "goodness of fit" SBS discussion presented in this section, consider the following. Not honoring these limitations might cause you to make a bad decision concerning your firm's computer network. The key point is to make sure that SBS is the right fit for your organization. And if SBS doesn't fit, PLEASE DON'T USE IT! Use the full Microsoft Servers products.

Business Reasons for SBS

Ultimately, it's a dollars-and-cents decision. How does SBS contribute to the bottom line? Does SBS have a favorable ROI?

It has been my experience in working with SBS and small businesses that the business software application typically drives the SBS decision (although there are exceptions that I'll mention in a moment). Other business reasons for migrating to SBS include cost-effectiveness. This has previously been highlighted in the prior section on Cost/Benefit Analysis. Basically, in a nutshell, we're talking apples are cheaper by the dozen or bundled applications are cheaper than the standalone price.

Believe it or not, politics will sometimes have a role in selecting SBS. In a case of "eating your own dog food," as Microsoft likes to say, I implemented SBS for a very senior Microsoft executive who had just purchased a 100-room oceanfront lodge outside of Seattle as an investment and Microsoft getaway. This executive was more familiar with the Microsoft consumer software that his division managed and was personally new to SBS. Upon his real estate transaction closing, it became apparent that the existing NetWare network would have to be tossed. Enter SBS and a major win politically for the SBS development and marketing teams with a most senior Microsoft executive. He knew what SBS was from that day forward!

Finally, more and more SBS purchases are being swayed by the increasing catalog of SBS-specific applications entering the market. First and foremost in this category are SBS-compliant and enhanced ISV-based tools and applications. Software vendor Veritas has released an SBS suite of its Backup Exec product. Columbia Software from Portland, Oregon, has an SBS-specific version of its document management system that is noteworthy (visit www.documentlocator.com).

Guest Column

The SBS 2003 Advantage

By Frank J. Ohlhorst

With the launch of Small Business Server 2003, Microsoft has empowered consultants with the ability to provide enterprise class solutions to the smallest of businesses, those with less than 75 users. The products rich feature set, ease of installation and low cost offer significant advantages when bringing a small business into the world of networking.

In the past, consultants and VARs had to rely on proprietary server appliances to meet the value equation required by small businesses. While server appliances met those initial needs, consultants found that the inherent simplicity and low cost offered by the devices often led to dead ends or incomplete solutions. That forced many consultants to move over to either traditional networking solutions or pursue the trail of never ending upgrades, much to the angst of their customers.

Simply put, a server appliance is an all in one system running an open source operating system on low cost hardware. Most server appliances cover the basics by providing a browser based configuration and management interface, along with basic user security, file and printer sharing, and in some cases email and web server capabilities.

Where these devices often fall short is in customization, compatibility and remote access, all areas well addressed by SBS2003. First off, a server appliance offers limited growth and services potential, the devices are designed to be a basic plug and play solution that can be forgotten about, simplicity is the rule of the day here.

While that may sound initially appealing, consultants often find themselves addressing needs by installing stand alone applications on client systems, instead of a centralized server. That increases costs in both materials and time and can often break a small businesses budget. Key examples range from databases to antivirus to antispam software. In cases where a server appliance vendor offer those solutions, they tend to be expensive and complex to install and manage. The very nature of SBS2003 being built off of the Microsoft platform creates choices. Consultants can choose from several solutions on the market to build added functionality to the SBS2003 based network, dozens of software vendors offer applications that will run on SBS2003 with little or no fuss, that allows consultants to tailor what works best for their customers, a real win-win situation.

Another advantage offered by SBS2003 is hardware compatibility, while server appliances often use proprietary hardware, SBS2003 runs on most any windows compatible hardware that meets the products minimum requirements; which offers numerous advantages. For instance, if a server appliance fails, technicians may have to wait for proprietary replacement parts, ranging from complete units to individual specialized components. With SBS2003 the flexibility of supported hardware offers technicians the ability to swap out similar components, ranging from motherboards to ram to hard drives, and then get a failed system up and running quickly. What's more, with SBS2003, technicians have the option of reinstalling SBS2003 on another server and restore data to that unit to quickly bring a failed network up and running. Major server vendors also offer same day service contracts to resolve problems that much more quickly, an option not often found with server appliances.

While many of the above elements solidify the argument of choosing SBS2003 over server appliances, consultants will find that this only scratches the surface of what SBS2003 offers their customers. With the erosion of hardware prices and the availability of add on products, consultants will quickly find that the advantages once offered by server appliances no longer make much sense once SBS2003 is considered.

Notes:

Microsoft SBS Design Goals

There is no argument that Microsoft's primary SBS design goals were to serve a well-defined small business market. That said, something that I've learned and heard from other SMB consultants is that serving the small business customer is dramatically different from serving the enterprise. Because of this observation, I'd like to spend a few pages presenting these differences and defining the small business market. Such discussions are bound to make you more successful in your SBS implementations as either a consultant or business person. In fact, if you are a small business person seeking to set up and use SBS, discover whether you don't see a little of yourself in these forthcoming section (although I make many comments that pertain specifically to SBS consultants).

Defining the SBS Market: The Small Business Model

Now that I've installed over 100 SBS networks, I can wax poetically as an SBS elder statesman about the small business firm. Small businesses are very different from the enterprise in three areas:

- Attitude
- Affluence
- Expertise

Attitude

Small businesses are more concerned with delivering goods and services than focusing on the technology being implemented, and rightly so. In fact, many small business people have a hostile attitude toward computers, viewing them as a drain on time and financial resources. Remember, these are the firms that complain long and loud when you purchase an unplanned network adapter card for $40!

Such antagonistic attitudes can be overt, such as criticizing your efforts, or more covert, like not sending staff (including the owner) to basic computer training. Don't forget that the real measure of success of the SBS network one year hence will be a function of training. Are the users using the SBS network? Have they taken advantage of many of the SBS features, such as robust Internet connectivity, faxing, and the Windows Sharepoint Services? If not, the significant investment of time and money in implementing the SBS network will be viewed unfavorably.

And even when you find and help a technology-friendly small business, you can't help but see that the owner and manager really should leave the SBS networking to you, the SBS consultant. Their energies are best allocated toward running their business, not running an SBS network.

I have one client, Marc, who is the owner of a small, middleman distribution firm. Marc is from a decent technical background that includes knowing his firm's technical products and building and flying model airplanes! It's been my observation Marc has been successful because he's moved himself into executive management and has become less focused on technology. One of the critical success factors in Marc's transformation from butcher, baker, and candlestick maker to president and CEO was his shift from doing the work to managing the work. It's arguably as difficult a shift as any small business founder will ever have to make, and Marc is no exception. The point is this: When I arrived as Marc's SBS consultant, I inherited a large case of boundary definition and expectation management, because Marc wanted to participate in the SBS administration, troubleshooting, and whatnot. But better business senses prevailed, and Marc reluctantly did the things that presidents and CEOs do: go out and get the business.

This next point is a case of "fear not." Many times the negative attitude that is demonstrated by small businesses toward technology, such as SBS, is based on fear. We all get defensive when confronted with the unknown, and small business people fear that SBS might make them look stupid. As an SBS consultant, you need to wear their moccasins for a moment and be a buddy and a mentor.

> BEST PRACTICE: I have found that a fear-based negative attitude toward SBS by the small business person is really a cry for more information. In the absence of sufficient information about SBS, small business people manufacture their own information.
>
> What's my recommendation? Overcommunicate with the small business person about SBS. Once he or she is educated, expectations are kept in line, and you can chalk up another SBS victory. In fact,

I've taken to communicating to my clients in writing, either via e-mail, fax, or mailed letter every time I perform SBS-related work at their site. What's cool about this method is that, months later when both you and the SBS customer have forgotten something technically related, you can easily go back to your files and look up the facts (and, here again, prevent SBS misinformation).

BEST PRACTICE: Be sure to keep your own attitude in check. I can directly trace SBS failures more times than not to an enterprise "know-it-all" arrogance imposed on the small business person. In many cases, the small business person has a perceived negative notion about arrogant computer people. Don't validate that perception. Remember that you're typically serving as both a technical consultant and a business consultant. At the small business level, you wear multiple hats. It's hard to do, and few MCSE-types really do it well. But a few random acts of kindness go a long way with the SBS clientele (even though your enterprise experience frowns on such openness).

What's my solution to this alleged attitude problem from the SBS consultant side? I now have more communicators on my consulting staff than I did in the past. Yes, there is still a role for tech heads who are appreciated for their expertise, but I've enjoyed great success with the SBS product line by taking liberal arts majors, training them on SBS, and having them score wins with my SBS clients. So, leave that big league Microsoft Servers attitude outside the door when working with SBS!

Affluence

One of the earliest lessons learned with SBS was that the small business isn't the enterprise. And remember that the small business truly watches dollars closer than the enterprise ever will. Remember the example at the top of this section regarding $40 network adapter cards? The enterprise-level Windows Server 2003 site probably has a half-dozen network adapter cards stacked in the server room ready for use. An enterprise-level Windows Server 2003 administrator wouldn't think twice about getting another network adapter card from the pile. But that cavalier attitude pales against the dollar-conscious small business that disapproves so greatly of unnecessary SBS-related expenditures that I've witnessed:

- A small firm struggles with an older network adapter card for hours instead of buying a new card for $40 or less.

- A small firm didn't hook up an HP laser printer directly to the network (via the built-in HP JetDirect card) because it didn't want to run to the store to purchase another strand of CAT 5 cable. (Instead, this high-priced printer was attached to the SBS server via a parallel cable, which, of course, had significantly lower performance than a direct network connection.)

Expertise

One of the great consulting opportunities today in the world of Windows Server 2003 is SBS. When performing SBS engagements, I've found that I'm a large fish in a small pond. That's opposite of the typical enterprise-level Windows Server 2003 engagement at the Boeings of the world where, even as a know-it-all, you're really nothing more than a cog in a huge networking machine. So I guess you could say that rank has its privileges. Working with small businesses and helping them implement SBS can be tremendously rewarding.

The expertise coin has another side, however. As the SBS guru, you will be relied upon in more—often unexpected—ways than you might be at the enterprise level. Here is what I mean: When working with Windows Server 2003 at the enterprise level, you likely benefit from having someone on staff who can walk through a series of steps to solve a problem (often while you're speaking via telephone from a different location). But at the small business level with SBS, this may not be the case. Here you are interacting directly with paralegals, bookkeepers, cashiers, clerks, and owners—not necessarily in that order! Not only do these people often lack the technical aptitude to assist your SBS troubleshooting efforts, but they usually become intimidated and nervous when working with you, the SBS guru.

So, while there may be a bona fide expertise gap when you work with SBS sites, your commitment will be certainly no less than the commitment you make to regular Windows 2000 Server sites. Just ask a friend of mine, who, as he approached the front of the long line for the ferry to Washington's fabulous San Juan Islands, was paged by a small business site. Apparently, this SBS site was unable to connect to the Internet. Without in-house technical competency, the SBS site doomed my friend to drive back to the city and assist it. Bummer! When you're the guru, you do the work when called. Haughty enterprise-level folks coming down to SBS will learn quickly that there is no staff to delegate to except you!

Defining the SBS Market: The Small Business Model

While I dwell on market definition in my *SMB Consulting Best Practices* book, let me share the following at-a-glance statistics for you about small businesses.

- There are 22 million "businesses" as defined by the U.S. Small Business Administration (SBA at www.sba.gov).

- Under the SBA's definition of "small business," consider the following breakdown: There are 16,000 businesses with 500 employees or more. There are 100,000 businesses with over 100 employees. This would suggest the bulk of businesses (say 21.9 million) have fewer than 100 employees. And let's assume that all of these firms with fewer than 100 employees don't allocate a computer to each employee because of the nature of the firm's work (e.g., construction). Thus many 100-employee firms might only have 25 to 50 computers, placing it well within SBS licensing limits. This is a huge SBS marketplace opportunity for you.

- Small businesses contribute 39% of the US Gross Domestic Product.

- Small businesses create two out of three new jobs.

- More than half of the technological innovations come from small businesses.

- An older IDC study (late 1990s) reported that 74% of small businesses have one or more PCs. This number should be adjusted upward now.

- The same study reported that 30% of small businesses are networked. Again, this number is out of date and should be adjust upward.

Microsoft's SBS partner page (www.microsoft.com/partner/sbs) offers the following interesting statistics for consumption.

- 4.1 million small businesses in the United States have more than one personal computer with no network installed, providing a strong market opportunity for Small Business Server as first and primary server.

- Microsoft Small Business Server sales are rapidly growing over 30% per year.

- Nearly 1.65 million servers are expected to ship into the worldwide small business market this year.

BEST PRACTICE: Just between you and me, you need to engage in a little expectation management here. Based on a collection of conversations around Microsoft, I believe that much of the growth in SBS is from overseas in international markets. The USA isn't driving SBS; rather it's hanging on to the tail and being wagged along. Hats off to the Aussies and others for banner years with the SBS product. Have a pint on me, mates!

Notes:

SBS Architecture

SBS is essentially a trimmed-to-fit version of the Microsoft Servers family. SBS can be viewed as a complex circle, as shown in Figure 1-2.

Figure 1-2
SBS architecture presented from an easy-to-understand "circle" perspective.

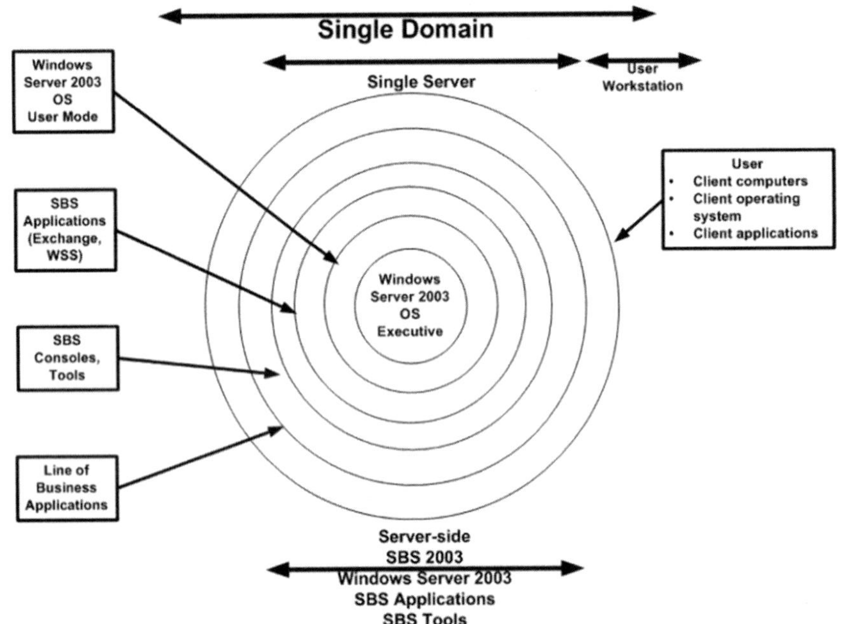

Let's discuss the SBS architecture model by starting with discussing a single domain (in a tree in an Active Directory forest, but more on that in a moment) and ending at the Windows Server 2003 operating system kernel. Note as you read the next few pages, it's to your benefit to refer to Table 1-1, which not only lists the SBS components but makes a distinction between server-side and client-side components (Figure 1-1 might also help).

Root of Forest and a Single Domain

SBS must be the root of an Active Directory forest, which effectively prevents SBS from being another server (say a branch office server) in an enterprise-level Active Directory domain infrastructure. In other words, practically speaking, you would say that SBS operates in a single-domain environment. As mentioned earlier, the SBS architectural model does not provide for multiple domains or explicit NT-like trust relationships. An Active Directory forest is a grouping of domains. A domain is an administrative or logical grouping of computers that participate in a common security model. This domain model manages the user accounts and security. Such security includes providing logon authentication for valid user accounts.

A Single Server

Only one computer on an SBS network can act as the root domain controller (DC). Out of the box, the SBS architectural model is to have one server, with the SBS machine acting as a root DC, per network. It is possible to have additional servers on the SBS network acting as domain controllers or non-domain controllers (aka "member servers").

Another DC on the SBS network will host a replica of the DC's Active Directory database. Such a machine can verify a user's logon credentials; however, in my experience, it is extremely rare to have another DC on an SBS network. That's because additional DCs are typically placed on either a larger LAN or across slow WAN links on an enterprise-level network (two qualifications that typically aren't met with SBS).

A popular additional server on an SBS network is a member server. Member servers, often known as *application servers*, typically run one or two specific LOB applications that can't run satisfactorily on the SBS root DC. Take the example of an animal service organization where I installed an SBS network. After installing the SBS server machine, I discovered that the fundraising software would run best on its own server. This software, known as Raisers Edge, has its own SQL engine separate from SBS-included Microsoft SQL Server. Raisers Edge's SQL engine proved itself to be quite a resource hog, necessitating the need for a standalone application server on this SBS network.

Because the components included with SBS can't be installed on separate member servers, it is critical that you purchase a machine with sufficient horsepower to optimally run SBS.

> BEST PRACTICE: Be advised that any additional servers on an SBS network may not be installed with the SBS product. Only one SBS server is allowed per network. But when discussing additional servers, note that I've worked on SBS networks where a NetWare server acted as a file/printer/application server on an SBS network (and did fine running a large Computer Associates business accounting application). The wilderness advocacy organization I assisted kept the Sun UNIX-based servers as application servers so that the GIS specialists could continue using their high-end GIS/mapping software.

End-User Workstations

Assuming you have the full licensing allowed for SBS (75 CALs), you know by now that up to 75 user workstations can be attached and concurrently logged on to the SBS network at any time. SBS natively provides full support for six Microsoft operating systems: Windows XP Professional (not Home edition), Windows 2000, Windows ME, Windows NT Workstation 4.0, Windows 98, and Windows 95. By *native support* I mean that the SBS client setup routine is fully supported.

SBS provides extremely limited support for other clients, including older versions (pre-4.0) of Windows NT Workstation, Windows For Workgroups, Windows 3.x, Macintosh, UNIX workstations, and LAN Manager Clients 2.2c. SBS does not offer support for OS/2 clients.

Notes:

User Applications

This area typically includes Microsoft Office, a suite of applications including Microsoft Word for word processing, Microsoft Excel for spreadsheets, and Microsoft PowerPoint for presentations. Other user applications include narrow vertical-market software, such as WESTMATE by Westlaw if you are an attorney, Timeslips if you're a professional who bills for your time, or QuickBooks if you are the bookkeeper in small company. You get the picture.

SBS Client Components

This includes many of the things listed as client components in Table 1.1 like common applications, such as Microsoft Outlook 2003 (discussed in Chapter 6), but also SBS components, such as the Shared Fax Service (discussed in Chapter 9). For a fully compliant SBS network, all SBS client components should be installed on the user's workstations.

Be advised that after the initial setup of SBS, the majority of your time will be spent dealing with users, client workstations, end-user applications, and the like. This isn't much different than any small network, but clearly Figure 1-2 isn't drawn to scale with respect to the time commitment you will ultimately make to end-user workstations, user applications, and SBS client components.

Server-Based Business Applications

Next in the SBS architecture in Figure 1-2 is server-based business applications, such as BenchTop and Great Plains Dynamics, two applications that use SBS's SQL Server as their engine. To reiterate, it is this layer of the SBS architectural model that is so important. Powerful business applications, typically server-based, will drive the purchase decision to implement an SBS-based solution. Every industry has its own narrow vertical-market application that the small business seeks to implement. It is critical to assess that the SBS architecture will faithfully support such an application.

Server Management Console

The SBS Server Management console represents the server-based graphical user interface (GUI), from which the vast majority of your SBS management duties are performed. When a Server Management console option is selected, an easy-to-use wizard is typically launched. This wizard often completes complex tasks without the user's knowledge. I discuss the SBS consoles in detail in Chapter 4.

Microsoft Servers Applications

SBS includes several traditional Microsoft Servers applications, such as Microsoft Exchange Server 2003, ISA Server 2000 (SBS premium edition), and SQL Server 2000 (SBS premium edition), which are listed in Table 1-1. As previously mentioned, some trimming, mainly licensing, has occurred when the SBS application suite is compared to the full Microsoft Servers products. Each of these applications is discussed in this book, often in a chapter dedicated specifically to that topic.

Windows Server 2003

As you might recall, Windows Server 2003 can be cleanly divided between user mode and kernel mode. Figure 1-2 reflects this division.

User Mode

This is where services and applications run in protected memory (Ring 3) environmental space. To make a long story short, that means an individual application or service can not explicitly crash the operating system. Each application enjoys its own protected memory space.

Kernel Mode

This contains the Windows Server 2003 executive, hardware abstraction layer (HAL) and third-party device drivers. More advanced discussion regarding user and kernel modes can be found in Microsoft's TechNet library (www.microsoft.com/TechNet). Further discussion here is beyond the scope of this book.

Bringing It All Together

So a lot of great information about SBS 2003 has been presented here to kick off your SBS experience. Granted, if you are new to SBS, you have much to digest and perhaps a good night's sleep is needed before jumping into Chapter 2 , where you meet the Springer Spaniels Limited methodology (the fictional company for which you will create an SBS network as you work through this book).

But allow me one last opportunity to shed light and impart knowledge on the SBS experience. This viewpoint, while oriented more towards technology consultants who implement SBS solutions, speaks towards an underlying foundational issue about why SBS is here (and why we're here using it). So here goes.

My clients (and perhaps yours too) are business people who first and foremost care about running their businesses profitably so that they can accumulate wealth in the long run. This is standard Economics 101 stuff from college. At the far upper left of Figure 1-3, the business person asks a simple enough question: "How can I run my business better?" This is a question that I encounter early and often with my SBS clients as I help them work through the decision to implement SBS. Such discussions usually lead to the business person understanding that more and better information is needed. Take the example of an accounting report he hasn't been able to receive before. Granted, this need for better information may not manifest itself as a better account report. It might well be another type of business report he hasn't been able to compile prior to the introduction of a network such as SBS or, equally likely, a report that can be compiled faster (the information was always available but took too long to obtain). Now let me throw a quick twist at you. In order to get the superior accounting information in my example, the business must upgrade its accounting package (e.g., Great Plains) to the latest version that runs best on Windows Server 2003, the underlying operating system in SBS 2003.

Notes:

Figure 1-3
The business purposes of an SBS network: running the business better!

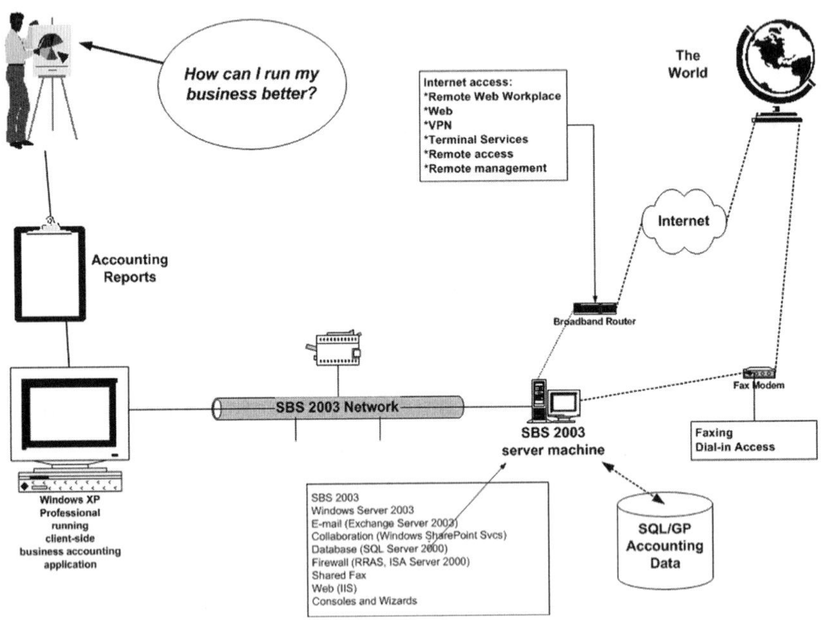

In the fictional example above, all the business person knows or cares about is (and perhaps you have a real world situation in your life that you can relate to this) that the report is obtained by running the accounting client-application on his or her workstation. That's it. Anything between the workstation through the network wall jack in the wall to the machine running SBS and even out to the Internet are of little concern. This is where the SBSer technology consultant kicks in. We (you, me, and the other SBSers out there) know that the workstation has to be connected to the network via cabling, and cabling is typically connected to a hub in order to manage the network media. Also connected to the hub is the machine running SBS and the all-important accounting application (e.g., Great Plains). This last point is something that will perk up the business person's attention as you mention accounting applications again.

Well, in order for Great Plains Dynamics to run in my example, it needs SQL Server 2000 as its database engine, which is provided as part of SBS 2003 (premium edition). And yes, once asked, the business person agrees that he needs internal and Internet e-mail capabilities, such as those provided by Exchange Server 2003 in SBS 2003. And heck, if we're going to be connected to the Internet for e-mail, we better facilitate Web browsing (with Internet Explorer) and insure security with firewall protection (with ISA Server in the premium SBS 2003 edition). Oh yeah, and before I forget, the business person also sees value in other SBS features, such as the Shared Fax Service, the ability to work remotely via a secure VPN session (via RRAS), and the ability to work remotely (via Remote Web Workplace). Lastly, the business person responds favorably when you mention you can perform some of your network consulting duties remotely, using Terminal Services, and better yet, keep an eye on the server machine with the built-in Server Status Reports. Whew! That's a long list of SBS success factors.

But understand what exactly has occurred here over the past few paragraphs. We've brought it ALL TOGETHER from the point a business person expressed a desire to run his business better down to the nitty gritty details of SBS 2003. So as you can see, SBS really can help someone run his or her business better!

Competitive Analysis

No SBSer should blindly accept the awesome virtues of SBS 2003 without doing the necessary homework. By this I mean it's a healthy exercise to look at what competes with SBS 2003. By observing the competition, you can, of course, affirm the decision you've made to purchase and install SBS 2003. You'll eliminate any doubts you've had and answer any lingering questions. There are three primary competitors to SBS, near as I can tell:

- **Microsoft and Windows 2000 Server/2003.** Good old, bare-bones Windows 2000 Server and standalone Windows Server 2003 is a competitor for SBS 2003. This may be all you need, especially if you're using a POP3 mail account for your e-mail needs. God bless you is this is the case. Understand that you're missing out on so many other features of SBS by selecting this alternative.

- **Windows XP Pro Peer-to-Peer.** This is the "micro" solution recommended for two-person offices (up to 10 people). Give the devil his due: Windows XP peer-to-peer is a competitor of SBS.

BEST PRACTICE: Another take on this: When you are as large as Microsoft, you're gonna compete with yourself. Remember this as you consider SBS as a consulting platform (for the consultant reading this book). Your biggest competitor is Microsoft!

- **Novell Small Business Suite (NSBS).** This is the closest bona fide competitor to SBS 2003 on the market. It darn near matches, feature for feature, the components in SBS 2003 (including consoles, wizards, and even remote management). However, NSBS doesn't have a robust database solution (SBS 2003 premium edition has SQL Server 2000) and doesn't provide robust health monitoring. The pricing is comparable. NSBS is shown in Figure 1-4.

Figure 1-4
Novell's small business offering can be found at www.novell.com.

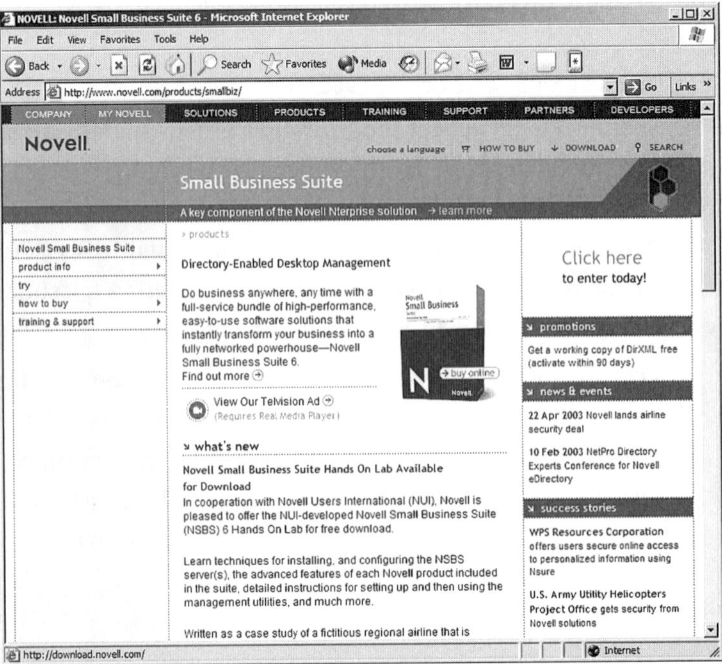

Oh, and did I mention that NSBS is based on the NetWare operating system, which, while robust, is considered more difficult to work with and, more important, doesn't have the "mind share" or positive political support it once did in the business and technology communities (something to consider when looking at the investment you will make in a networking solution). The point I'm trying to make here is that business application developers, all things being equal, will typically develop their releases for a Windows Server 2003-based solution (SBS 2003) before a NetWare-based solution (NSBS).

SBS 2003 Product Launch

A very special moment in SBS history occurred when SBS 2003 was launched in New Orleans on October 9, 2003! It was at that moment that all the words in this book truly came to life. You could go forward, create the Springer Spaniels Limited sample network over a few weeks to a month, and call yourself a true SBSer! Photos from the SBS 2003 launch are included in the photo section of this book. Note I also include photos of the SMB Nation, a conference held just prior to the launch of SBS 2003 in late September 2003 in Indianapolis, Indiana, (hosted by yours truly).

The Future of SBS

There are two angles to this discussion. First is the SBS product itself. Microsoft, and more important, the marketplace, have given every indication that SBS is here to stay. SBS has crossed some significant financial thresholds inside Microsoft so that it positively contributes to the bottom line of the Mother ship.

SBS 2003 will undoubtedly be followed by future SBS upgrades, each one providing more functionality and stability. While we all hope SBS 2003 has a long life, it's a fact of life that future upgrades will occur.

Notes:

And because SBS 2003 is a full member of the Windows Server family, it's here to stay! Past versions of SBS weren't much more than a black sheep distant cousin to the full Windows Server family and didn't enjoy overwhelming respect! That's changed and SBS 2003 finally has a seat at the family dinner table.

The second dimension addresses what your future with SBS is. Ideally, if you have a growing business, SBS is merely a stepping stone to implementing the full Microsoft Servers products, and this path is certainly in alignment with Microsoft's view. If you can use SBS as an incubator to help you expand your business, Microsoft will be more than happy to upgrade you to the full Microsoft Servers products at a future date!

Summary

This chapter fulfilled several roles and met some very important goals. The first part introduced you to SBS with a brief introduction of each component and described SBS's capability to deliver a single-server comprehensive networking solution that is relatively simple for the small business to implement and maintain. A key tenet to SBS—business application support—was emphasized. The second part of the chapter defined the small business market for SBS and provided an in-depth look at SBS's underlying architecture. The future of SBS was discussed in closing.

The chapter also provided you, in passing, with an overview of where this book is headed and how it is organized. Several topics were briefly described in Chapter 1 and cross-referenced to future chapters where the topic area or feature will be covered in more depth.

You are now ready to proceed to Chapter 2. And before you know it, a short time will have passed, and you will be a competent SBS professional. Or as we say in the trade, SBSer!

Chapter 2
Small Business Server Design and Planning

Welcome to Chapter 2, where you will proceed with specific planning tasks, all of which increasingly work forward to the actual hands-on activity of implementing SBS 2003. You are also introduced to Springer Spaniels Limited, the blessed sample company in this book.

Planning is considered an upstream function in a technology project. It tends to be less hands-on and more general than the actual setup and maintenance tasks that follow, these last two task areas being known as a downstream function. While it is easy to consider planning as an intuitive process that doesn't require much of a time commitment from the SBSer or business person, such an assumption is a fallacy. Indeed, planning is typically considered to be the best use of time in a technology implementation. In fact, you really can't escape planning. You can perform it upstream at the start of the technology implementation in an orderly and well-behaved way, or you can perform your planning it downstream—the hard way—when you find your self re-installing SBS multiple times, realizing with each passing installation that you'd like to change the way you did things. Ouch!

Springer Spaniels Limited

First off, let's take a moment to meet Springer Spaniels Limited (SPRINGERS), the company for which you'll implement a complete and successful SBS-based networking solution throughout the remainder of the book. You will often hear me refer to the SPRINGERS methodology when I walk you through steps in a setup sequence. Understand that the context of my references to the SPRINGERS methodology is this: While there are numerous ways SBS can be implemented (for example, partition sizes can vary after the minimum requirements are met, company names and Internet domain names will most certainly vary, etc.), by following the SPRINGERS methodology, you will find the experience very educational, consistent, and even fun!

There are some very important reasons to work with an imaginary company the first pass through this book. It has been my experience with SBS (and life in general) that you know much more after you've done something once. It's another way of saying that hindsight is 20/20, a well-accepted old saw.

Such is the case with SBS. Typically, you set up SBS based on some assumptions that are made early in the planning process. Such assumptions might include the domain name you create, and so on. But fast-forward in the process, perhaps a few weeks. More than once an SBS administrator has commented to me that, now that she knows what SBS really is, she would have set it up differently. Those observations about getting it right are analogous to creating the chart of accounts when installing accounting software. You make some early decisions that you have to live with the rest of your life.

Now back to SPRINGERS. By using this company for the remainder of the book, you have the chance to learn SBS, warts and all, before installing it for real. These methods also allow you to avoid the scenario mentioned previously, wherein weeks after your "real" SBS install, you might lament that you would have done a few things differently if you had the chance to do it over again. With SPRINGERS, I'm providing you that chance at a very low cost.

By completing the activities in the remaining chapters, you will learn what works for you and what doesn't. When you go to install SBS for real, with live company data, you will have your feet on much more solid ground. That will result in a successful SBS install for you and your organization.

SPRINGERS, for these purposes, is a small company with 10 users and 30 employees. Please note that not every employee uses a computer (many clean kennels and so forth). The company breeds, raises, and shows prize-winning springer spaniels. SPRINGERS is headquartered on Bainbridge Island, Washington, on a converted apple orchard. The SPRINGERS operations and prize Springer Spaniels named Brisker and Jaeger are to be seen in the photo section in the middle of the book. SPRINGERS has six departments in addition to the executive offices, as shown in Figure 2-1.

Figure 2-1
Springer Spaniels Limited (SPRINGERS) organizational chart.

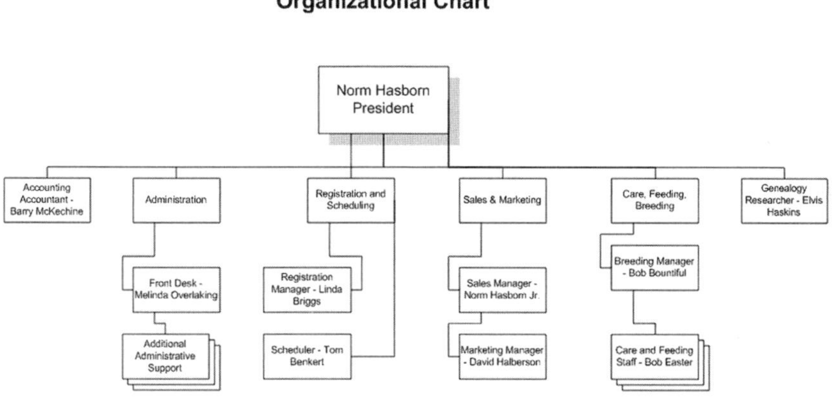

As you will see, SPRINGERS benefits from SBS in many ways, including its robust built-in Internet connectivity. How? Since canine breeders everywhere are worried about genetic variety in breeding (that is, they want to avoid inbreeding), the Internet is used to find suitable breeding partners. And I'm not talking about anonymous Internet chat rooms full of lonely Springer Spaniels looking for love in all the wrong places. Rather, SPRINGERS intends to search sophisticated and legitimate breeding databases around the world (if you are not aware, the Springer Spaniel breed is well-respected for its diversity in breeding, which is a kind way of saying the breed hasn't been ruined by inbreeding).

SPRINGERS also benefits from other easy-to-use SBS features, such as the Server Management console that will be featured in detail in Chapter 4. As the chapters pass in this book, I will divulge more details of SPRINGERS as needed. Periodically, you will enter SPRINGERS information into SBS to complete exercises if you are following this book chapter and verse. It's the well-planned SPRINGERS methodology that is the foundation and backbone of this book.

Not surprisingly, I do want to tip my hat of acknowledgement to those of you who may not follow the exact steps of the SPRINGERS methodology, as you may be using this book as a quick primer to sharpen your SBS 2003 skills before building your own server (or the server of a client if you are a consultant). Right on! And for those of you who aren't dog lovers and find it hard to get excited about Springer Spaniels, I can appreciate that too. This book isn't a monument to dogs or the Springer Spaniel breed; rather the dogs and SPRINGERS serve as a convenient metaphor for telling a story and teaching you SBS 2003. So no e-mail from non-dog lovers please!

BEST PRACTICE: Now is a great time to start your own *needs analysis* for your SBS project. A needs analysis typically involves looking at the ebbs and flows of business activity in your firm, often for the first time. Start by creating your own organizational chart similar to Figure 2-1. From that, you may discover that your company and SBS users are organized in ways that might not have been apparent. I have found that, early in the SBS planning process, many people use the SBS computer project as an opportunity to reorganize their businesses. In fact, an SBS consultant is often a management consultant as well.

SBS Project Management

You should never undertake an SBS project without sufficient planning. In fact, I typically spend a day or more with an SBS client doing nothing more than planning for the new SBS network. I can't emphasize enough how important planning is with an SBS implementation. These upfront hours are certainly some of the best you spend.

An SBS project can be divided into five phases. These phases, which will be described in detail, follow:

1. **Planning Phase:** The logical and physical design of the SBS network occurs here as well as some early expectation management to avoid future disappointments.
2. **Server Installation Phase:** The SBS server is installed.
3. **Workstation Installation Phase:** The workstations are installed and configured.
4. **Follow-up Phase:** Over the course of several weeks, new SBS features are introduced. This mirrors the layout of this book as later

chapters present additional SBS features as well as general trouble-shooting, user support, and network optimization.

5. **Celebration Phase:** Projects create stress, and an SBS installation is no different. Phase five is an opportunity to not only release some tension but also solicit feedback from SBS network stakeholders. This phase applies to both in-house SBS installations as well as those SBSers serving as consultants.

Planning Phase

For anyone considering SBS, the earliest planning exercises involve identifying and communicating why you want to implement SBS in your organization. That can be accomplished by answering the following questions. You will note that appropriate responses from SPRINGERS have been entered.

Early Planning Questions

I've got a secret for you about planning. To be honest, planning is very much about asking questions about the firm's existing and future situation with respect to technology and then actively listening to the responses given. It's harder than it looks. You might well find it easy to ask a lot of questions, but are the questions appropriate or effective? Do you have good listening skills and incorporate the client's feedback into your planning process?

Here are some sample planning questions to get things going:

Q: List the three reasons you plan to use SBS.

A: (1) Ultimately to install our accounting system, Great Plains Dynamics, using Microsoft SQL Server 2000 (which is included with SBS 2003 premium edition). (2) To have a secure and robust Internet connection for communications (e-mail) and Web-based research purposes. (3) To lower our information system costs by performing much of the ongoing administration ourselves via the friendly SBS Server Management console.

Q: What is the time frame for implementing SBS?

A: We intend to set up, install, troubleshoot, and train everyone on the network over a 10-week period starting in four weeks when the new computer equipment arrives. (And after you've finished reading this book!)

Q: How have you arranged for training for the new SBS network?

A: *The SBS consultant will train those responsible for network administration. The SBS administrators will show the users how to log on, print, and save information. These users will also attend three half-day training sessions on the following topics: Windows XP Pro, Office Systems 2003, and Outlook.*

Q: What roadblocks or problems can you identify today that might make the SBS project more difficult to complete?

A: *First and foremost would be staff turnover. If our accountant leaves, not only would we have lost the individual we've identified as the SBS administrator, but we will have also lost our Great Plains Dynamics talent. To combat this potential problem, we plan to have the receptionist assist with the SBS setup and administration so she can act as a backup SBS administrator in an emergency. A second possible problem is the bank financing for our computer equipment purchase. We anticipate that the lending process will take only two weeks and the equipment will arrive roughly two weeks later. With the SBS deployment being a critical path item, any bank financing to pay for the work would delay the start of the SBS installation.*

Existing Network Layout

Early on in the planning process, it is incumbent on SBS consultants and small-business owners alike to know exactly what they have when it comes to computer hardware and software. This baseline measurement allows you to determine what must be ordered, replaced, repaired, and so on. This information is typically gathered by inventorying the network and presenting your findings in a spreadsheet table or a network diagram. My preference has been to use a network diagram because its graphical display facilitates ease of understanding.

These network diagrams are typically drawn by hand, or with a network diagramming software application such as Microsoft's Visio, resulting in a schematic or drawing of your existing network. More information on Visio is available at www.microsoft.com. Visio can be purchased for under $500 USD retail or as part of the Microsoft Action Pack ($299 USD). Such a drawing might look similar to the drawing created for SPRINGERS in Figure 2-2.

Figure 2-2
Existing network for SPRINGERS.

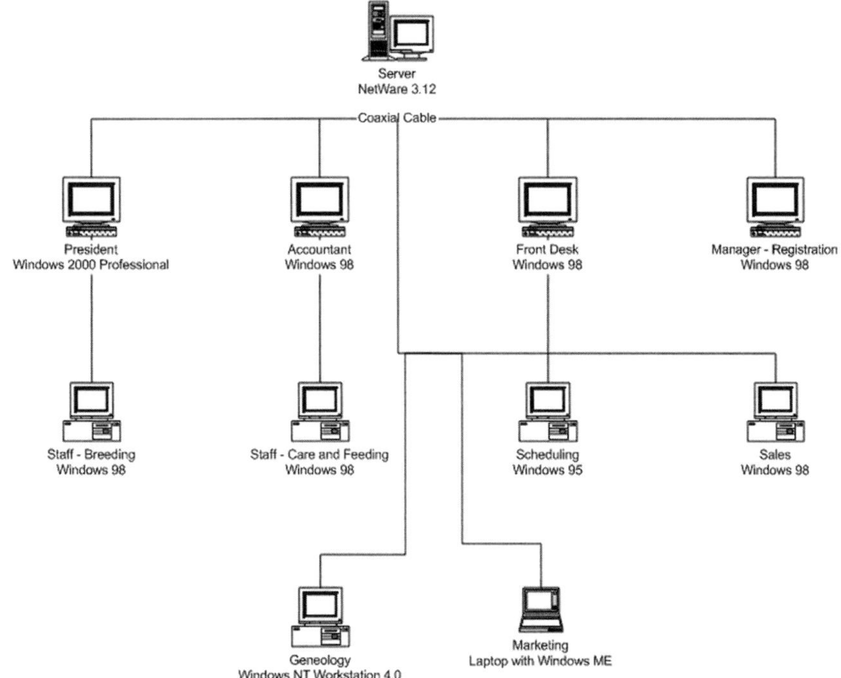

Check Existing Infrastructure

Assuming a network diagram has been created, you need to gather a little more information for SBS planning purposes. Take a tour of your existing physical site and make notes regarding the following items: cabling, hubs, and wall jacks. Table 2-1 shows the existing infrastructure information for SPRINGERS.

Table 2-1: Existing Infrastructure

Item	Condition/Notes
Cabling	Need to implement Category 5/6 10/100BASE-T, Ethernet-type cabling at site. Existing coaxial cabling will not work.
Hubs	Will purchase and install dual-speed hubs.
Wall jacks	Each office will have one wall jack plus extra wall jacks in hallway.

Cabling

In the case of SPRINGERS, you will note in Figure 2-3 that the existing cabling media is coaxial, which is considered inferior to the more modern Category 5, 10/100BASE-T, Ethernet-type cabling (5/6). Because SPRINGERS intends to replace the cabling, it is so noted on the proposed network layout (see Figure 2-4) later in the chapter.

Hubs

A hub is a central gathering point for network cabling. Many people today who are using the Category 5 cabling described previously are opting for high-speed 10/100 hubs to replace older, slower hubs. Thus, when designing your SBS network, consider the more expensive, faster, dual-speed 10/100 hubs over the 10Mbps hubs. With an eye on the future and getting the best long-term value from your SBS network, you will be glad that you did.

> BEST PRACTICE: Why the dual-speed hub? Some older machines on a network, such as older laptops that use a parallel port-based network adapter, might not be able to run at 100Mbps (the new, higher network speed). If such is the case, you might need a dual-speed hub that supports both the older 10Mbps and the newer 100Mbps speeds.

Wall Jacks

It is common when planning an SBS project to discover that you will need to increase the number of wall jacks at your site. This typically occurs for two reasons. The first is that additional networked workstations will be added as part of the SBS implementation. This is very common. More often than not, when a new network is installed, so are additional workstations. These additional workstations typically are purchased for new hires, suggesting company growth is a driving factor in implementing a new SBS network. Or, the additional workstations might be for existing employees—formerly reluctant players—now stepping up to the table to join the networked world.

Here is what I mean. At a property management firm I serve, the commissioned-based real estate agents must contribute financially to join the SBS network. That is, they have to buy a node on the network. Prior to introducing SBS, the old network was based on a NetWare server, something that didn't thrill many of the agents. Thus, several agents went without network connectivity in the past. Enter SBS, and these do-withouts became more excited about networking, especially with SBS's Internet connectivity. Thus, existing standalone computers were added to the network when the SBS network was up and running.

Another cause for ordering additional wall jacks is the pervasive use of network-connected printers. A popular setup is the Hewlett Packard (HP) laser printers connected directly to the network with a JetDirect card. These network printers are typically connected directly to the network using one of the wall jacks. Many firms use the SBS network project as an opportunity to upgrade their existing printers or add more printers, so it is very common when planning an SBS network to order additional network wall jacks.

> BEST PRACTICE: Attaching printers to the network in no way affects your user count with respect to SBS licensing. Some of you from the old NetWare days might recall that network devices, such as printers and Shiva LanRover modems, could and would consume one or more of your network logon licenses. Such is not the case with SBS. You can have as many network printers as you'd like.

Assuming you're going wired, it's a given that you probably need to order wall jacks for your SBS network, so be sure to over-engineer the number of wall jacks ordered. I like to order up to 25 percent more wall jacks than I anticipate needing. These extra wall jacks are typically placed in the conference room where training occurs or temporary employees work. In my book, you can never have enough wall jacks. Plus it is cheaper to install them all at once rather than have the cabling specialist make return visits.

List of SBS Stakeholders

Another important SBS planning item is to create your list of SBS stakeholders. Stakeholders include yourself, any consultants, service providers, and so on who have a role on the SBS project. And because everyone today has multiple telephone numbers (work, work-private, work-fax, home, cellular, pager, and so on), I highly recommend that you add each stakeholder's telephone numbers and e-mail addresses to your SBS stakeholders list.

Notes:

Table 2-2: SBS Stakeholders

Name	Role	Contact Information
Tom Jagger	SBS Consultant	SBS Staffing, Inc. 123 Main Street Redmond, WA 98000 W: 425-555-1212 Fax: 425-123-1234 Home: 206-222-2222 Cellular: 206-333-3333 Pager: 206-123-0987 Ski Condo: 503-200-1999 tomj@sbsrus.com
Jane Unionski	Cabling Specialist	Unionski Cabling Box 3333 Unionski, WA 98111 W: 222-333-4455 Cellular: 222-444-3344 Pager: 222-123-4567 union@cablespec.com
Bob Easter	Manager, SPRINGERS	Springer Spaniels Limited 3456 Beach Front Road Bainbridge Island, WA 98110 W: 206-123-1234 Fax: 206-123-1235 Home: 206-111-1234 bob@springersltd.com
Roni Vipauli	Lender, SBS	Small Business Savings 123 Small Business Blvd. Small Town, WA 99882 W: 425-111-8888 Fax: 425-SBS-LEND roni@smallbusinesssavings.com
Ted Rockwell	Sales Associate	Overnight Warehouse PO Box 8855 Acorn, WA 98234 1-800-111-0000, ext. 334 ted@sales.overnight.now.com

BEST PRACTICE: The users contained in Table 2-2 will be amongst the first names entered into the company contact list in Microsoft Outlook 2003.

User List

Next in the general planning process under the SPRINGERS methodology would be creating a user list for your SBS network, those people you intend to allow to use the SBS network. It's not as easy as it sounds. First, you have to typically think through who needs SBS network access, as not all users do. Once it is decided who will be allowed on the network, you need to take extra care to spell each user's name correctly on the network and have an initial password to use. Each user's name at SPRINGERS (10 users) is shown below. These names will be entered into the SBS network in Chapter 4.

First: Norm
Last: Hasborn
User Name: NormH
Password: Purple3300
E-mail alias: NormH
User Template: Power User
Computer Name: PRESIDENT

First: Barry
Last: McKechnie
User Name: BarryM
Password: 2Reedred
E-mail alias: BarryM
User Template: User
Computer Name: ACCT01

First: Melinda
Last: Overlaking
User Name: MelindaO
Password: Blue33
E-mail alias: MelindaO
User Template: User
Computer Name: FRONT01

First: Linda
Last: Briggs
User Name: LindaB
Password: Golden10
E-mail alias: LindaB
User Template: User
Computer Name: MANREG01

First: Bob
Last: Bountiful
User Name: BobB
Password: Bish4fish
E-mail alias: BobB
User Template: User
Computer Name: BREED01

First: Tom
Last: Benkert
User Name: TomB
Password: Whitesnow101
E-mail alias: TomB
User Template: User
Computer Name: SCHEDULE01

First: Norm
Last: Hasborn Jr.
User Name: NormJR
Password: Yellowsnow55
E-mail alias: NormJR
User Template: User
Computer Name: SALES01

First: David
Last: Halberson
User Name: DaveH
Password: Grenadine2002
E-mail alias: DaveH
User Template: User
Computer Name: MARKET01

First: Elvis
Last: Haskins
User Name: ElvisH
Password: Platinium101
E-mail alias: Elvis
User Template: User
Computer Name: GENE01

First: Bob
Last: Easter
User Name: BobE
Password: dogcatcher1
E-mail alias: BobE
User Template: Power User
Computer Name: CAREFEED01

Security

Not surprisingly, small organizations have many of the same computer network security needs as larger enterprises. The owner of a small business typically has confidential information that should not be widely distributed.

Security is a recurring theme in this book as different SBS components are discussed, such as Microsoft SQL Server and ISA Server. But for your initial SBS planning purposes, the first security issue to address is membership in the Administrators group. Administrators are the functional equivalent of Admins and Supervisors in NetWare or the super user account in a UNIX environment. Thus, it behooves you to select carefully who should have "full control" as an administrator over your SBS network. Typically, this membership group is limited to the organization's leader (owner, CEO, President), the day-to-day SBS administrator, and perhaps the SBS consultant you've retained.

Notes:

Project Schedule

The next step is to create an SBS project schedule. Because of the nature of SBS projects—working with small organizations—it is not necessary to use Microsoft Project to create complex Gantt/Pert/CPM charts. These high-end project-scheduling applications are better left for putting pipelines across Alaska.

However, I do recommend that you create a simple calendar-based schedule for your SBS project. Microsoft Outlook has a calendar that works fine. The project schedule for SPRINGERS is shown in Figure 2-3.

Figure 2-3
SBS project schedule for SPRINGERS.

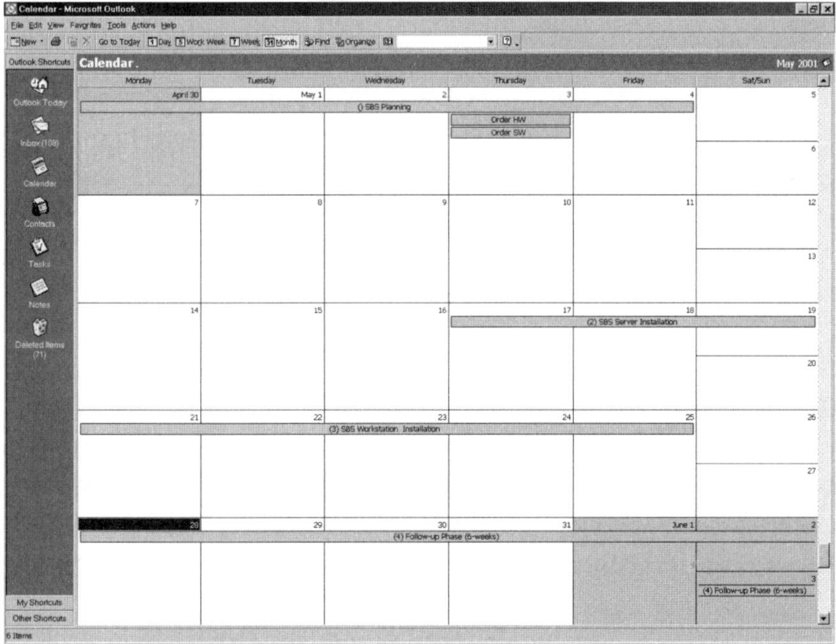

Addressing Hardware, Software, and Services List and Budget Needs

You must now create the hardware, software, and services lists for your SBS network as the next planning step in the SPRINGERS methodology. The list shown Table 2-3 is the desired outcome. Regarding the hardware area, a new server and new hub are being purchased by SPRINGERS. With respect to software, SBS, sufficient user licenses, and additional software are being purchased by SPRINGERS. Several types of services will be required, including additional telephone lines for the new Internet connection and new wiring, because a new star topology based on the Ethernet standard has been selected. A *star topology* occurs when each workstation and the server is connected to the hub in a "spoke and hub" configuration similar to a bicycle tire. You will also see that, by adding an additional column in Table 2-3 for costs, the list not only serves as your purchase specifications, but also your budget. Note that I describe hardware, software, services, and budgets in much more detail later in the chapter.

Table 2-3: Hardware, Software, and Services List for *SPRINGERS*

Item	Description	Cost
Hardware	HP/Compaq ML-350 Server for SMB/SBS, tape backup unit, 1 GB RAM, 60GB HD, HP Laser Printer (HP 5M), UPS backup power.	$2.500
Software	SBS, Add'l Software (third-party tape backup, antivirus client/server suite, software).	$3,500
Services	SBS Consultant, wiring with wall jacks, telephone line hookup, Internet service.	$5,500

Proposed Network Layout

The next step is to create a drawing of the proposed network. The proposed network for SPRINGERS, shown in Figure 2-4, graphically depicts many of the items discussed previously in the section "Addressing Hardware, Software, and Services List and Budget Needs." The old NetWare server will be "retired."

Notes:

Figure 2-4
Proposed SBS network for SPRINGERS.

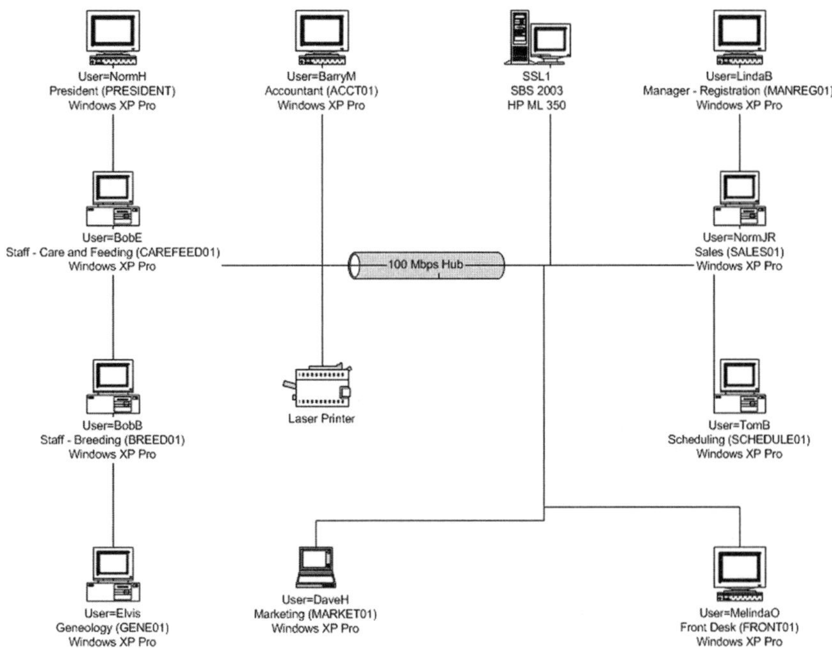

Final Planning Activities

Three items remain as part of the SBS planning process: ordering, walk-through, and documentation.

Ordering

A "critical path" item in your SBS project is the need to order your hardware, software, and services. Why? Under even the best of conditions, it can take 10 or more business days to receive your new server machine. Services such as scheduling your SBS consultant and ordering additional telephone lines can take even longer (especially when the telephone company is involved).

BEST PRACTICE: If you use an SBS consultant, consider having her attend the calls placed when you are ordering ("you" being the business person in this case). Typically I sit in a conference room with my SBS customer on "order day." The vendors are placed on the speakerphone, allowing for all parties to speak up and clarify anything. I've found that, by clarifying purchase specifications on order day, I save the client significantly more than my hourly consulting fees. Consider it another win for my SBS customer.

Walk-Through

Now that you are near the end of the planning phase, I highly recommend that you once again walk the floors of the site that will house the new SBS network. By taking a fresh look at the site where the SBS network will be installed, you might notice a few things you initially missed. Items that have caught my eye on this final walk-through include:

- Server placement: Where will the actual server reside? Is it near power outlets? Have you coordinated the extra telephone lines, some of which are used by SBS, to terminate at or near the SBS server machine?

- Workstation accessibility: Can you easily reach each workstation on the network? Is there enough room between the desks and walls to allow the cabling specialist to install wall jacks?

- Building access: Do your service providers have access codes and keys to perform after-hours work on the SBS project? Believe me, you can count on some unexpected late-evening visits from members of the SBS team!

Documentation and Loose Ends!

It is essential that you take a few moments to gather the letters, e-mails, bids, drawings, yellow sticky notes, and the like and organize these in an SBS project notebook. The SBS project documentation serves several purposes.

First, if you should leave the organization, you properly share your SBS knowledge with your SBS successors via the SBS network notebook. In effect, people who follow you don't have to start from the beginning. You, of course, would appreciate the same courtesy.

Second, because of the demands a small organization places on its staff, it's unlikely that you will remember the finer points of your SBS installation several months hence. Thus the value of an SBS network notebook.

> BEST PRACTICE: As you'll see in later chapters, SBS 2003 is "self-documenting" if you simply click a link on the completion page of each wizard and save the configuration information as a file. I don't want to tell you much more right yet, but the SBS development team made it real easy to create your network notebook with SBS 2003.

Loose ends run the whole spectrum of SBS computing. You name it, and I've probably seen it. Some doozies in this category include:

- Sufficient quantity of telephone cable. Lesson learned: Do you have enough telephone cabling to hook up the modems? And in this day and age, that might include DSL modems with its special cabling.

- Length of telephone cable: Lesson learned: Are the telephone cables long enough?

- Environmental controls. Lesson learned: Do you need a fan to help keep the server cool (because the work area is too warm)?

Another loose end to consider while planning your SBS network is training. One of the keys to success with an SBS network is to over-train your users! It's a theme worth repeating (and I do so several times in this book!). Training can take several forms, all of which are discussed in Chapter 11.

> BEST PRACTICE: Note the SBS project planning phase is typically 10 to 15 hours of consulting work if you are planning on doing it "right." If you are undertaking your SBS project without a consultant, budget for one to two days of your own planning time.

Server Installation Phase

The big day arrives. Sitting in your workspace are large boxes on a pallet, representing the new server, monitor, and additional networking accessories (hub, modems, UPS, and so on.).

The server installation phase includes:

- Unpacking and physically building the server.
- Physically installing the network accessories, such as the UPS, modems, and hub.
- Reseating the existing adapter cards that might have come loose during shipping.
- Installing SBS.
- Installing server-based applications, such as virus detection utilities, third-party tape backup applications, and so on.
- Performing several post-server installation tasks, such as creating the emergency repair disk (ERD), sharing folders, mapping drives, installing printers, and verifying security. This also includes completing SBS To Do List items (such as adding SBS licenses) and running SBS wizards from the SBS consoles.
- Configuring SBS 2003 applications. Typically Microsoft SQL Server must be configured for use. By itself, with no configuration out of the box, Microsoft SQL Server isn't especially useful. It is also common to configure Microsoft Exchange above and beyond its basic configuration to accommodate public folders, etc. This step may also include running wizards from the SBS consoles.
- Installing applications such as Great Plains Dynamics (accounting software).

It is important to have a server installation worksheet similar to Table 2-4.

Table 2-4: Server Installation Worksheet for *SPRINGERS*

Item	Description	Completed
Server Name	SPRINGERS1	
Internal DNS Domain Name	SpingersLTD.local	
External Internet Domain Name	SPRINGERSLTD.COM	
Initial SBS Registration Name	Bob Easter	
Organization	Springer Spaniels Limited	
Installation Codes	Small Business Server (use from product ID sticker on disc sleeve)	
Area Code	206	
Address	3456 Beach Front Road	
City	Bainbridge Island	
State/Province	WA	
Zip	98110	
Country	United States of America	
Business Telephone	206-123-1234	
Business Fax	206-123-1235	
Initial Administrator Password	Husky9999!	
Hard disk	SBS operating system and applications partition is 10GB. Data partition is approximately 20GB. Both partitions are formatted NTFS. Server has a RAID-5 configuration. If you have only a single hard disk or mirrored drives (but not RAID 5), you may continue for the purposes of learning SBS 2003 via the SPRINGERS methodology. However, you'll want to consider RAID 5 or mirrored drives in the real world.	

Item	Description	Completed
	NOTE: In Appendix D I'll introduce the setup configuration on Microsoft Virtual PC (the virtual emulation environment) that would allow you to configure an SBS network (server and client computers) on a single machine for learning and demonstration purposes. I often set up SBS networks that way on my laptop to demonstrate the product.	
Time Zone	Pacific	
User Accounts	Administrator (password= Husky9999!)	
Printers	Install new HP Color LaserJet 5M printer on network with HP5 share name.	
Registry	No known Registry modifications needed in SBS. However, if you plan to set up SPRINGERS on Microsoft Virtual PC, there is a Registry modification needed on the host operating system (e.g., the Windows XP Pro operating system on your super-duper laptop) that is necessary in order for Virtual PC to emulate two network adapter cards (this is detailed in a KBase article: 825374: How to Configure a Guest PC to Emulate More Than One Network Adapter). Note this applies to Virtual PC version 5.2 and might be fixed by the time you are reading these words.	
Folders	Create additional folders on Data partition: **Accounting** (this is where Great Plains Dynamics will be installed along with the storage area for the accounting data) **Backup** (this folder will contain on-the-fly backups of company data between tape backups, such as internal SQL Server database backups)	
Shares	Create **ACCT** on the **Accounting** folder. Everyone allowed change rights. Full control rights to NormH, BarryM.	

Item	Description	Completed
Internal IP Addressing	Use the default 192.168.16.2 IP address and the 255.255.255.0 Subnet Mask.	
External IP Addressing	Use the following: IP: 207.202.238.215 Subnet Mask: 255.255.255.0 Default Gateway: 207.202.238.1 Preferred DNS: 209.20.130.35 Alternate DNS: 209.20.130.33	
Misc.	Windows Server 2003 operating system to be installed on C:. SBS components (Exchange, etc.) to be installed on C:. Will approve all licensing questions with "Yes."	

Regarding partitions, SBS requires that the partition containing the operating system (typically the C: drive) be formatted as NTFS to operate correctly. NTFS (NT file system) is the partition scheme that allows advanced security and file management. The other partition selection is FAT32. FAT32 is the successor to FAT from the file allocation table world of the MS-DOS days of old. FAT partitions are less protected and considered less robust. The Microsoft Web site at www.microsoft.com provides extensive information on NTFS and FAT. Further discussion here would be beyond the scope of this book.

Workstation Installation Phase

The workstation installation phase is really the work that occurs in Chapter 4 when you will connect a workstation to the SBS 2003 network. That said, there are a few key steps in the workstation installation stage worth listing:

- Complete the SBS workstation installation sheet. That information is found on my Web site for download at www.smbnation.com.
- Physically unpack and construct workstations.

- Reseat the existing adapter cards that might have come loose during shipping.
- Complete installation of client operating system if necessary.
- Complete the Add User/Setup Computer Wizard to create the configuration information for the workstation to join the SBS network. Then at the workstation, launch the IE Web browser and point to the http://SSL1/ConnectComputer to launch the over-the-wire process for joining a workstation to the SBS network. Bye-bye Magic Disk from prior SBS releases. Very nice touch.
- Perform basic SBS client component tests, answer user questions, and so on.
- Enable and demonstrate network file sharing from client PCs.
- Enable and demonstrate network printing from client PCs.
- Enable and demonstrate basic *internal* e-mail via Outlook and Microsoft Exchange.
- Set a date to return to fully configure Outlook (shared calendar, shared contact list).
- Propose a date for network (logon, printing, saving) and Outlook training.

The middle steps involve testing the setup. Those are key steps in the success of attaching and using an SBS workstation. Too often I've observed homegrown SBS networks where the connectivity wasn't fully tested. In effect, the SBS network never did completely work. In fact, at one site, the users jokingly called it an SBS notwork! Unfortunately, those SBS networks that forego workstation testing usually discover such things (gremlins) later rather than sooner.

And it shouldn't be lost on you that training is mentioned as the last step of the workstation installation phase. Again, training is important.

Follow-Up Phase

As far as this book is concerned, the follow-up phase encompasses the balance of the SBS installation and administration experience. Why? It is the follow-up phase where additional SBS functions, such as faxing, and applications, such as SQL Server, are introduced. There are important reasons for staging the introduction of many SBS features as separate, discrete tasks contained within a phase separate from server and workstation setup.

It has been my experience with organizations implementing SBS that the mere introduction of a computer network is enough to start with. The users need to become familiar with the basic Windows networking environment that is the foundation of SBS. In fact, for many users, being able to log on, save a file, and print are features enough to start out with.

Even network-experienced and computer-savvy organizations cannot absorb too many features too early. For example, e-mail is a great early candidate to introduce on the SBS network. But I have often found that even the best users aren't ready to tackle SQL Server (SBS 2003 premium edition) and its strengths too early, so this speaks to delaying the heavy stuff for a while on your SBS networks.

Lastly, there is the Christmas-morning emotional response. Given a pile of wrapped toys, a child will eagerly attack, opening each and every gift until, several hours later, the child is overstimulated and sobbing in a corner. Such is the case with many SBS sites. Users want to do everything *right now* on the first day the network is available. But by the end of the day, the same users are bewildered, frustrated, and, worst of all, have negative feelings toward the new SBS network. You, the SBS administrator, don't want and can't tolerate such an early defeat. Be smart. Stage the rollout of SBS features over time.

Celebration Phase

Yee-haw! Call it an opportunity to get a free lunch, but one of the most successful things I've accomplished is gathering user feedback that might not readily reveal itself during day-to-day SBS network use. And, based on user feedback, I can offer the opportunity to provide additional meaningful services that my SBS customer might not have initially considered. Five additional services, beyond core out-of-the-box SBS functionality, have proven popular with customers:

- **Windows Sharepoint Services (WSS) customization** — You can achieve the highest and best use of your SBS system by using the powers of WSS! Consider using it as a basic document management package.

- **Public folders** — Many users, when they become addicted to e-mail, want additional help implementing public folders (shared resources) in Microsoft Exchange.

- **Microsoft Outlook customization** — When users start to use the contact list in Microsoft Outlook, the follow-up requests to create custom forms can be expected.

- **SQL Server tables** — The really hard-core SBS sites (using the premium version) know that SQL Server can handle their most demanding database challenges, but few of these SBS sites actually know how to execute SQL queries and so on.

- **Web page development** — Last, but certainly not least, the discussion over the pizza lunch inevitably turns to Web pages and electronic commerce.

SBS Expectation Management and Perception

Avoiding disappointments is perhaps job one for an SBS administrator and certainly an SBS consultant. Recall that, in Chapter 1, I set the framework for understanding what SBS actually is. Disappointment can be avoided early, for example, by understanding that you will need to purchase a third-party virus scanning application because SBS is devoid of such a critical goodie.

BEST PRACTICE: Something to consider before you get too far along is the assured outcome of the SBS 2003 original equipment manufacturer (OEM) stock-keeping unit (SKU). Here, HP will just about completely install SBS on one of its SMB server machines (e.g., the ML 350 model used in this book as an example). When you start up, you'll complete a mini-setup process that constitutes the personalization of your server machine and accepting the license agreement. I'll discuss the OEM SKU more in Appendix E, but what's important to understand here is that the SBS 2003 OEM SKU is a rapid setup methodology with an assured outcome (and a positive outcome at that).

Scope of Work

If you are using a consultant, a scope of work should be defined, largely based on much of the planning work accomplished previously. In my firm, the scope of work is typically delivered as a detailed proposal that describes how the work will be accomplished. Likewise, the engagement letter, which refers to the proposal for scope items, is a contract between my consulting firm and the client. An engagement letter typically covers items such as terms and conditions of payment, how disputes will be resolved, and so on.

BEST PRACTICE: Here is an additional thought for SBS consultants about the scope of work and engagement letters. Many SBS consultants ask how you get paid for your planning efforts if you haven't yet created a scope of work or gotten the client to sign the engagement letter.

The answer is you should contract with the client for 10+ hours of your consulting time to assist with planning. Perhaps this consulting time could be evidenced with an engagement letter separate from the SBS project engagement letter you intend to present later. It has been my experience that if the customer is not interested in paying you for 10+ hours of your planning time, that customer isn't very serious about having a successful SBS installation. Also, if the SBS customer is cautious about the planning phase, explain that the scope of work you create with 10+ hours of planning time can be easily converted into a request for proposals (RFP) that could be distributed to other consulting firms and resellers.

The thought here is that you can get 10+ hours into your SBS project with this customer, and either one (or both) of you decide that you don't care to work together anymore. This approach provides an out for all involved.

The scope of work would likely contain the following items:

- **A detailed proposal**
- **A schedule**
- **A budget**
- **A project task list or checklist**

Notes:

Overcommunicate

Another theme to this book is that of overcommunicating before, during, and after your SBS project. It is very easy to do. You can do it in person via periodic SBS network meetings, pizza lunches, and the like. You might consider sending out an SBS project update e-mail, such as presented in Figure 2-5.

Figure 2-5
SBS e-newsletter.

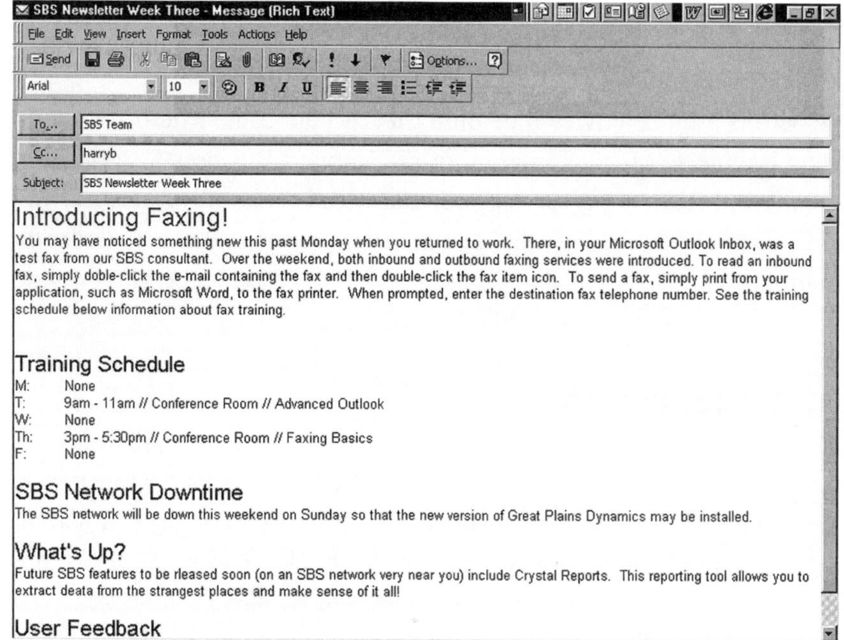

Selecting SBS Service Providers

Another planning issue is that of selecting the service providers for products and services for your SBS network. There are several types of SBS service providers:

- SBS consultants
- Hardware and software resellers
- Wiring and cabling contractors

- Telcos
- Internet service providers (ISP)

First, a comment regarding service providers. In general, the very best way to retain a service provider is via referral of a mutually respected third party, typically a friend at another organization that has used a service provider he is pleased with. Acquiring or avoiding a service via this avenue is greatly recommended. In fact, as an SBS consultant, one of my key motivators to perform at the highest level is the prospect of getting referrals from my existing SBS client base!

Now here is a bit of advice they didn't teach you in the Microsoft Certified System Engineer (MCSE) program or the Harvard Business School, for that matter. Avoid retaining a service provider based on an advertisement in the media, telephone book, and other outlandish promotional venues. Under these circumstances, it is very difficult to ascertain the quality of a service provider's work, communications style, and other critical factors.

SBS Consultants

Of course, one of the earliest and most important decisions you will make relates to whether you will engage the services of an SBS consultant. I wrote this book so that you could indeed implement an SBS network on your own with both study and practice (the two key tenets to this book). But many of you might want to extend the SBS best practices in this book by having an SBS consultant on your team for all or part of the SBS project. Furthermore, many of you are reading this book with the thought of becoming an SBS consultant.

Assume that you indeed plan to use an SBS consultant. You need to consider a few things up front. First, many Windows Server gurus have bestowed the title of SBS consultant on themselves because the shoe appears to fit. Such is not the case for reasons I presented in Chapter 1 that underscore how different SBS is from Windows Server. So what's my advice to you, the SBS customer? Avoid being the early training grounds for tomorrow's SBS guru (unless you're getting a significant discount on the billing rate being charged by the greenhorn SBS consultant, a point I surface in the next paragraph).

However, SBS gurus are in relatively short supply right now, so what should you do if all you have to select from are SBS newbies? At a minimum, negotiate a training rate that is significantly less (perhaps 50 percent) than the consultant's normal fees. I also recommend that, armed with this book, you work side-by-side with the SBS consultant to make it right!

Those consultants who are SBS gurus tend to be nichers. Like a medical specialist, true SBS gurus basically live and breathe SBS all day long. You'll potentially pay extra for this level of expertise (perhaps a 50 percent premium over the bill rates of a general practitioner), but it's typically considered to be well worth it.

> BEST PRACTICE: SBS consulting is something I cover in much more detail in my SMB Consulting Best Practices book. However, if you're looking for an SBS consultant, be sure to check Microsoft's SBS page at www.microsoft.com, where an SBS consulting partner locator tool is maintained. That'll help you locate an SBS guru in your area.

Hardware and Software Resellers

To be brutally honest, when purchasing for SBS networks, I've found the very best hardware and software buys on the Internet and via 800 numbers. My short list of select vendors that I've used via this approach include the following:

Hardware

- HP/Compaq. (www.hp.com and its HP small business page at www.hp.com/sbso/index_evo.html?jumpid=go/business-evo that I show in Figure 2-6)

Notes:

Figure 2-6

No hardware manufacturer has made a bigger commitment to the SBS 2003 market than HP!

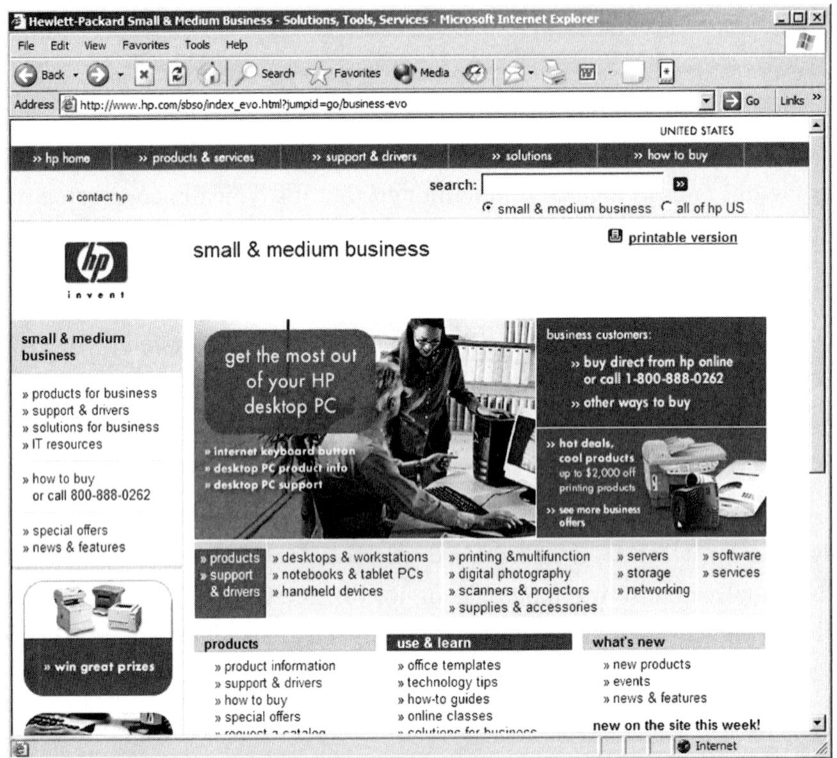

Software

- CDW. (www.cdw.com)

BEST PRACTICE: If you are an SBS consultant, you may well want to resell software and hardware as another revenue source. While I personally don't do this, you should look at this possibility. For software sales, one firm has made it easy for the small business consultant to become a software reseller and make a little pocket change at the same time. The firm, License Online, can be reached at 1-800-414-6596 or www.licenseonline.com. Good luck!

I've advised clients to be cautious about using resellers to perform the installation work, because these organizations, often storefront retail establishments, typically lack SBS-specific expertise.

> BEST PRACTICE: Hardware and software resellers can be a good source of free consulting as long as you keep in mind that you get what you pay for. For example, if you call HP to order your server, the sales consultant can serve as a reality check regarding the number of processors, amount of RAM, and hard disk storage to order. That second opinion is of value and can be obtained for free.
>
> The online help system via the Server Management console in SBS 2003 also speaks to hardware requirements.

Wiring and Cabling Contractors

Here again, getting a reference is a great way to locate a competent wiring and cabling service provider. You might check with the property management firm that manages your office space. They most likely use one or two such firms when building out office space.

> BEST PRACTICE: Be sure to have the wiring and cabling contractor test and certify his work (network cabling, wall jacks, and so on). Faulty network cabling can wreak havoc on an SBS network, and you should have some type of recourse against the contractor. A cabling and wiring certification provides the documentation you need to seek relief.
>
> One of my SBS jobs, at a mortgage brokerage, suffered from faulty wiring. After trying to troubleshoot the software, server, other hardware, and so on, it was finally discovered the wiring was the culprit. So, beware. Bad cabling happens.

Telcos

Here my options are limited for giving advice. You might not have the ability to select from multiple telephone companies (telcos) that can provide you with the additional lines needed for your Internet connection, faxing, and remote access. Increasingly though, many areas now have local telco competition, so choice is increasingly becoming available.

> BEST PRACTICE: Whenever working with a telco on any matter related to your SBS network, be sure to allow plenty of lead-time for the delivery of the services that you are requesting. Due to a booming demand for telephone lines, backlogs in filling service orders can be measured in weeks in many locations.

Internet Service Providers

Aside from using an ISP referral that you deem trustworthy, you have great flexibility in working with any old ISP you might stumble across. The E-mail and Internet Connection Wizard (EICW) in SBS 2003 is open to working with existing ISP accounts, large ISPs, small ISPs, even your dog's ISP (just a little Springer Spaniel humor there). The EICW is displayed and discussed in Chapters 4, 5, and 6. In the planning phase of the SPRINGERS methodology, it behooves you to be a prudent purchaser of ISP services and shop around. Look at ISPs that best meet your technological needs and budget. For example, you might well find an ISP that is hurricane- and earthquake-proof (having backup batteries on-site that will run for weeks and other features), but such an ISP might be very expensive to do business with.

SBS Trivia: Did you know that the first release of SBS (SBS 4.0) had an ISP referral tool? It's true!

Advanced Planning Issues

This part of the chapter presents more details on software and hardware issues surrounding your SBS project. I offer a few comments with respect to SBS budgeting and the purchasing process.

Software

SBS ships in a variety of configurations. It's important that you check the SBS 2003 product SKUs at the SBS page at Microsoft (www.microsoft.com/sbs), as these SKUs occasionally change to reflect market conditions (e.g., a competitive upgrade SKU being introduced), changes in pricing, or a new build (e.g., a service pack is slipstreamed into a SKU). You want to pick the right SKU for the right job. For many people, that'll be the OEM SKU for SBS 2003, as they'll be upgrading a server machine at the same time that SBS 2003 is being installed. For others, it'll be the retail SKU of SBS 2003, because it'll fit better if your reusing an existing server machine.

> BEST PRACTICE: I'm not trying to cop-out here and shorten my typing in this chapter by not going into painful detail on product SKUs, part numbers, and a review of the legal agreement. Rather, in my past books when I've dedicated 10 pages to pricing, licensing, SKUs, and the such, I've found my writing is out-of-date six months later when Microsoft makes significant changes in the product category. Ergo, I'm not kidding when I say visit Microsoft's SBS Web page at www.microsoft.com/sbs for the very latest. No book could stay current in this area!

There's even an SBS 2003 SKU that is, in effect, a time-bombed trial version. This evaluation SKU (Part Number X10-04043), typically given away at Microsoft events such as TS2 (www.msts2.com) will allow you to run SBS 2003 for 180 days before you must purchase and install the "real" SBS SKU. That good news is that the evaluation SKU can be upgraded in-place, and you don't need to FDISK or perform a complete reinstall to apply the "real" SBS SKU.

Don't forget part of your SBS 2003 software purchasing process involves securing sufficient client access licenses (CALs).

> BEST PRACTICE: There is an exception to the rule, just like US Tax Law (where there always seems to be an exception to the tax code). If you add another Windows Server 2003 server machine to your SBS network (perhaps to work as an application server and run an accounting application), you will NOT need to purchase Windows Server 2003 CALs (which are a different type of license from SBS

CALs) for each user who intends to log on to the new Windows Server 2003 machine. That's because the SBS 2003 CAL converts to per-seat for the network operating system component in that case (the Windows Server 2003 operating system). This was done to encourage the appropriate use of additional servers on a SBS 2003 network and not penalize the customer.

And just to throw another twist at you, SBS CALs are not bona fide Terminal Services CALs. For your information, Terminal Services CALs are very expensive and a separate product from anything else that we have discussed here in this chapter. Learn more about Terminal Services and its CALs at www.microsoft.com/servers.

Other Software

It is not uncommon to purchase other software to run on the server machine running SBS. I have found that SBS customers typically purchase:

- Third-party tape backup applications, such as Veritas Backup Exec for Small Business Server
- Virus detection applications, such as Trend Micro's OfficeScan Suite
- Accounting applications, such as Great Plains
- Other business applications

The key point is that SBS is rarely purchased and installed in a software vacuum. There is typically a supporting cast of other software applications running on the SBS machine to provide an organization with a complete computing solution.

Notes:

BEST PRACTICE: Don't forget that no software discussion is complete without considering what to deploy on the client computers. As of this writing in late 2003, the choice is clear with respect to workstation operation systems: Windows XP Professional. Throw on the latest Microsoft Office 2003 software family and you've got a rootin', tootin', wild workstation ready for some serious business!

Hardware

With respect to hardware, you name it, and it has probably been run on an SBS network. Why? Because smaller organizations often have lots of legacy equipment that they want to continue using on their SBS network. And small businesses aren't known for overspending.

Microsoft has a set of recommended hardware specifications for the server and client workstations on an SBS network. These specifications can be found at—you guessed it—www.microsoft.com/sbs. Here again, I've elected not to list the specifics found on Microsoft's Web page because its SBS hardware specifications are periodically updated to reflect real-world improvements, cost reductions in storage and memory, and good old-fashioned customer feedback.

BEST PRACTICE: So a few real-world tidbits to share. First, as of late 2003, I'd recommend 1GB of RAM memory, 50GB or higher of hard disk space, and dual processors (say Intel P4 in the 3 GHZ range). My words will fall on deaf ears a year after the book is written, of course, as memory and disks drop in price and processors become more powerful!

SBS Cheapskate, Beware!

Don't poor-boy that SBS hardware purchase. I've seen people scrimp several ways with SBS-related hardware, none of it acceptable. Here are three examples.

First, small businesspeople have attempted to recycle older monitors from retired workstations so that they didn't have to purchase a new monitor with the new server (a cost savings of perhaps $150). The problem is that older monitors can't provide the screen resolution you need to work with the Server Management console. In fact, if you can't create an 800x600 screen resolution on the server during the setup of SBS 2003, you'll receive a blocking message that doesn't allow you to continue.

Second, I've observed small businesses that wanted to use the SBS server machine as a workstation for one of its users. At a land development company, the president (the heiress to a well-known Pacific Northwest retail empire) ran Microsoft Word, Outlook, and CompuServe right on the SBS server machine. The performance was unacceptable. Several months later, the president purchased a workstation, allowing the SBS server machine to do what it does best: act as a dedicated server. Needless to say, both the president and I were much happier from that point forward in our SBS relationship.

Finally, there is the case of the green machine. Here, a paving contractor decided to save a few bucks by using a workstation as an SBS server, resulting in some strange behavior. In this case, the BIOS-level energy-saving function couldn't be turned off, so each night, when the server had several hours of inactivity, it went to sleep. Well, the underlying network operating system in SBS didn't like that one bit, forcing the general manager at the paving company to reboot every morning. I finally solved this problem by creating artificial server activity every 15 minutes (I ran a ping program called PingPlotter that you can learn about at www.nessoft.com).

> BEST PRACTICE: Better yet, leave the hassles of the cheapskate world behind and buy an honest-to-goodness name-brand server, such as those from HP, to run SBS and avoid many of the problems described above.

Notes:

Hardware Necessities

It goes without saying that you should purchase the tape backup unit—once listed as "optional" in Microsoft's server requirements (in the SBS 2000 time frame)—to back up your valuable data. Some form of backup, often tape based, is hardly optional and the Microsoft SBS 2003 development team is well aware of that (you'll learn about backup improvements in both Chapter 4 and Chapter 11). Other necessities include an uninterruptible power supply (UPS) to protect your system and properly shut it down in a power outage. UPS devices from American Power Corporation (APC) ship with a free copy of PowerChute.

> BEST PRACTICE: Another item to consider is a Zip- or Jaz-type drive with removable cartridges. I've used these in one specific case with great success in an SBS scenario. That case is SQL Server. SQL Server allows you to run an on-the-fly database backup separate from the SBS-based tape backup you typically perform at night. This internal backup to SQL Server typically runs at midday, so you get a fresh SQL Server database backup between tape runs. I like to drop these internal SQL Server backups down on a Zip or Jaz drive or CD/DVD burner so that the tape drive is not disturbed. It's something to consider if you are working with SQL Server on your SBS network. And, as an aside, if you ever hear a grinding sound with a Zip or Jaz drive, beware, as trouble is looming on the drive.

Hardware Compatibility List

One of the final hardware issues to be discussed is hardware compatibility. The good news is that SBS 2003 is much less finicky about the hardware you select for use on the server machine compared to prior releases. Here is what I mean. If the hardware runs and is supported on Windows Server 2003, it'll work with SBS 2003! Hardware devices that have been tested for Windows Server 2003 are listed on the Hardware Compatibility List (HCL) at www.microsoft.com/hcl. This list should be honored under all circumstances. More important, if you don't select hardware from the HCL, it is likely you won't receive official Microsoft support when you have problems. And it's a sure bet that noncompliant hardware won't have the cute Windows seal of approval on its retail box!

BEST PRACTICE: Please honor hardware as a critical supporting actor on your SBS 2003 network. I've become partial to name-brand network adapter cards, such as Intel. With modems, I can truly say you get what you pay for. If you're serious about the Shared Fax Service in SBS 2003 (to be discussed in Chapter 9), then you need to purchase a robust and capable modem, such as the v.Everything model from US Robotics/3COM. Such a modem, known to sell for around $250 USD, delivers your basic five 9s or six sigma of outstanding performance.

SBS Budgeting

And as the corner is turned on Chapter 2 with its focus on planning, don't forget to keep an eye on the financial farm, that is the SBS budget. I've seen many a good SBS project fail not for technical reasons, but because business basics, such as creating and adhering to a budget, were ignored.

BEST PRACTICE: When budgeting for your network, be sure to consider the following budget tip: If you're eyeing a more powerful server than you planned on purchasing and are concerned about its cost, perhaps the more powerful one isn't as expensive as it first appears. For example, let's say a server with more processors, RAM, and storage would cost you an additional $1,500. Now, assuming you recover your costs or depreciate the server over three years, that incremental amount ($1,500) adds up to an extra $500 per year, or roughly $1.50 per day in aggregate for the entire company. So ask yourself this: For an extra $1.50 per day, shouldn't I purchase the server I really want? In all likelihood, you will probably enjoy more than $1.50 per day in increased network performance, as measured by your staff's ability to get more work accomplished. Think about it!

Summary

You've now completed two chapters of SBS definition, needs analysis, and planning, and you know what? It's now time to move on and actually install SBS 2003.

Chapter 3
Small Business Server Installation

The time has come to actually install SBS! The argument could be made that installing SBS is nothing more than swapping four SBS discs and performing a few reboots along the way. However, such an oversimplification of the SBS installation task is incorrect. You have already invested significant time defining what SBS is, performing a needs analysis, and planning in the prior chapters.

> BEST PRACTICE: As you might have guessed from the last chapter, you will implement SBS 2003 based on the SPRINGERS methodology. That is how this chapter is constructed, after many hours of editorial design. By way of a disclaimer, let me say that your specific SBS implementation may vary slightly based on machine types, components installed, and so on. Furthermore, after I walk you through the step-by-step installation process under the broad jurisdiction of the SPRINGERS methodology. I then present some advanced setup topics in the second part of the chapter. If you are an advanced SBSer who is interested in these advanced topics, you may look at those now before you start the setup process or, preferably, follow the setup process under the SPRINGERS methodology, and then read the advanced setup topics, taking into account the advanced knowledge that will be imparted for your future real-world SBS setups.

I assume that you are using a new server machine for SBS. If you are using an old server machine that will be redeployed as an SBS server, many of these steps, such as unpacking the server, do not apply. Ditto for same-server machine

SBS upgrade scenarios. In the case of SPRINGERS, the firm has purchased the following hardware and software shown in Table 3-1. The following table is used to verify that everything ordered was indeed received.

Table 3-1: SPRINGERS Hardware and Software

Item	Description
Server	HP/Compaq ML-350 Server for SMB/SBS, tape backup unit, 1 GB RAM, 60GB HD, 17" VGA Monitor, SCSI-based internal tape backup device, internal CD drive
Modem	US Robotics 56K External
Network Adapter Cards	Intel Pro 100+ PCI EthernetBCM5730 Gigabit Ethernet
Printer	HP Color LaserJet 5M with HP JetDirect Card
Other Hardware	APC UPS with PowerChute
Software	Microsoft Small Business Server (SBS) version 2003 5-user version, 5-user SBS client access licenses (CALs) , Veritas Backup Exec Small Business Server Suite (tape backup program), Trend OfficeScan Suite.
Miscellaneous	Modem cable, extra CAT5 patch cables, telephone cable, power strip/power tree

BEST PRACTICE: Note that Appendix D contains information on how to set up SBS 2003 on a Compaq laptop (e.g., Evo N800c) using Microsoft Virtual PC or VMWare. This would allow you to have the entire SPRINGERS network on a laptop for learning and demonstration purposes. It's very cool!

All of this required hardware adheres to the Windows Server 2003 hardware compatibility list (HCL) discussed in Chapter 2. You can find updates to the Windows Server 2003 HCL at www.microsoft.com/whdc/hcl/default.mspx. If you are an SBS consultant who regularly installs SBS for different clients, you are encouraged to monitor this site regularly and look for changes to either the

HCL or System Requirements. If you are a business person or otherwise a non-SBS consultant installing SBS as a one-time discrete event, which it typically is for a single system at a single location, just initially verifying the hardware you intend to use for the SBS installation at www.microsoft.com/hcl is sufficient.

Note that you should acquire the most current Windows Server 2003 drivers you will need for the SBS installation. One example of this is to make sure you have on hand any needed SCSI or RAID drivers which will be needed if your SCSI or RAID controller isn't supported natively by the underlying Windows Server 2003 operating system. At the first step in the character-based setup phase (later in the chapter), you will be provided the opportunity to select the F6 key and provide these mass storage SCSI or RAID controller drivers (a very important step if it applies to you).

If you have a RAID-based system you would need to perform the computer manufacturer's steps to prepare the hard disks in the RAID array for use by the operating system. In the case of my server, this is accomplished by selecting CTRL-M when instructed by the computer during the character-based POST setup phase of the computer boot cycle. This process will vary by manufacturer and computer model, so kindly use your very best judgment and consult the documentation that accompanied your computer.

Also note that while a SCSI-based tape backup device is the preferred hardware option, non-SCSI tape backup devices are supported via the ATAPI device driver in Windows Server 2003. But be advised that non-SCSI tape devices run much slower than SCSI tape devices. Ouch!

Notes:

Preinstallation Tasks

You need to perform several tasks before the actual setup process commences. Failing to perform these tasks will certainly result in failure.

Unpack and Connect

Assuming that your infrastructure, such as cabling, is in place and the server you have ordered has arrived, it's time to unpack the server and its components from the shipping boxes. If you haven't built a computer before from boxes, it's quite simple. Many name brand servers have color-coded guides so that you know which port the keyboard and mouse attach to. If you are still unsure of yourself, don't hesitate to hire a computer consultant to help you attach and build the computer. In fact, consider hiring a competent high school or college student who is both computer literate and seeking a few extra dollars. Again, putting together the computer from boxes is quite simple.

After physically building the server, make sure the following items are properly attached to the server box:

- A monitor or screen (be sure to attach the monitor to a power source). In the case of SPRINGERS, this is a 17-inch monitor.
- A keyboard
- A mouse
- A power cable
- External modems (if applicable; your modem might be an internal version, which, by the way, isn't recommended by myself – nor do I recommend USB modems either)
- A tape backup device (could be internal or external). Remember SCSI-based tape backup devices deliver higher performance.

- Other external devices that connect directly to the server (printers, Zip- or Jaz-type drives, scanners, and so on; and, if applicable, don't forget to gather the needed drivers before starting setup)
- A network cable (attach the network cable to both the network adapter card port and the wall jack; this connects your server to the network)
- Uninterruptable power supplies (UPS) (you can connect the power cables to the UPS, but do not connect the serial cable from the UPS to the serial port on the server yet; see my BEST PRACTICE next on this matter)

BEST PRACTICE: If you have a UPS, do not attach it to the server at this time. UPS devices are attached to the SBS machine via COM ports (the same type of port used by modems). However, SBS tests each COM port as part of the installation of modems. Granted, modems are now an optional installation component during the setup of SBS (the Shared Fax Service will install without a modem attached). What I'm getting at is this: If you elect to install a modem as part of the SBS setup, an attached UPS can cause the SBS machine to become confused during this installation period. Bottom line: After SBS is installed, you will hook up the UPS.

If you are interested in developing expertise as a hardware technician to supplement your SBS consulting practice or skills as an SBS administrator, you might also consider studying for and taking the A+ certification exam. The A+ certification is oriented towards computer maintenance from a technician point of view. It is a well-regarded designation created and managed by the Computer Technology Industry Association. For more information on the A+ certification, see www.comptia.com.

BEST PRACTICE: Assuming the power is off and unplugged from the computer and external devices, and you are wearing a grounding strip on your wrist to discharge any built-up static electricity (before you touch an electronic component), take a moment to open the SBS machine and reseat all of the adapter cards. It has been my experience that a new server shipped across the country can arrive with loosened cards, cables, and even memory chips! That's not to be critical of my friends at HP, but such loose cards have wreaked havoc with some of my early SBS installs when the internal network adapter card couldn't be detected during setup because it had become partially dislodged from its slot. Another experience I have had when working with new computers is that the ribbon cable located inside the server machine (used to connect internal devices to cards or the motherboard) can come loose. If you need to reattach a ribbon cable, remember this rule of thumb: the side of the ribbon cable with the red line always points to the power supply.

After you've completed the check on the system, plug in the power to the computer and the devices in order to proceed with the setup. And don't forget to verify (sorry to be a pest by mentioning this again and again) that you have sufficient power protection through surge protection power strips and UPS.

Check the Network

Has the cabling been properly attached to the hub? Perhaps this was a task that you assigned to the cabling specialist who installed the cabling at your site. If it hasn't been done, do that now.

To verify the fitness of your network, you must perform the "green light" test. After everything has been plugged in properly to the network, including the network hub, do the following:

1. Turn on the network hub.
2. Briefly turn on the server computer.
3. Observe whether a port light on the hub turns on. (This typically illuminates as the color green).
4. Observe whether the network adapter card connection light on the back of the server illuminates. (Again, typically green).
5. If you see green lights at both the hub and network adapter connection, you're green lighting!

Perform Server Quick Tests

So you've put the computer together and connected it to the network. Now is the time to turn on the computer for a few moments to see whether the BIOS information is correctly displayed on the screen during the power on startup test. (This is called POST and is a term used in the technology community). This quick-and-dirty test is important for several reasons. It will check:

- **Video card** — If you see no information displayed on the computer monitor, it is possible that the video card has failed. Such was the case during an SBS class I once taught. Not only was the computer unusable for the SBS class, but valuable time was wasted trying to determine exactly what the problem was. At first and second blush, it wasn't entirely clear that the video card had failed, as this type of problem can disguise itself.

- **Component attachment** — Did you know that if a ribbon cable between the computer motherboard and floppy drive is incorrectly attached, the computer might fail to start, leaving you with only the sound of a failed start up: three quick beeps? This is but one example of how incorrectly configured internal components in your server can prevent you from having success with your computer. These are exactly the type of issues that you want to catch immediately, before you try to install SBS.

- **Hidden partition server tools** — First, of all, let's just get this out in the open. SBS 2003 works fine with hidden system partitions (you may recall SBS 4.5 had a distinct problem with this, requiring you to delete the hidden system partition). Now for the next point. Starting up the computer also allows you to determine whether the computer manufacturer's server tools were correctly installed on a hidden partition on the hard disk. When manufacturers ship their servers to you, they might or might not install their server tools (e.g., HP/Compaq's SmartStart). Typically, the paperwork received with the server remains unclear on this point. The best way to test that is to look for language at the top of the screen during machine startup. In the case of an HP/Compaq server, such language instructs you to hit the F10 key to launch SmartStart.

BEST PRACTICE: If the manufacturer's server tool hasn't been installed to a hidden partition on the server, it is essential that you do this now. Failure to do this at this point would mean that you would forever be prevented from installing these wonderful and helpful tools designed to configure and manage your server. That's because after the operating system and SBS are installed, you cannot go back and install the manufacturer's server tools on a hidden partition.

To install the manufacturer's server tools on your system, be sure to follow the setup instructions for the specific tool. In the case of HP/Compaq's SmartStart, it is very simple. Because a Compaq server is designed, by default, to boot from the CD drive, you simply place the SmartStart CD in the CD drive and restart the computer. On startup, and with no further fuss, you are presented with the SmartStart installation screen. Several minutes and one reboot later, SmartStart is installed on your system. Again, tools such as SmartStart provide the capability to configure your server properly, create driver disks, monitor your server's health, and so on.

- **BIOS operation** — There is simply no better test to make sure the computer's all-important BIOS is functional than to turn on the machine and observe that the BIOS information (copyright, date, storage device configuration, and so on) is displayed on the screen. Common BIOS names are American Megatrends and Phoenix.

BEST PRACTICE: It is very common for BIOS manufacturers to release upgrades shortly after the original BIOS has been shipped to market. These upgrades typically consist of bug fixes and the like. So consider downloading the BIOS upgrade and prepare to install or flash the BIOS upgrade. But be extremely careful about applying a BIOS upgrade to your server. If you've applied the incorrect BIOS version to your server, the server can be rendered inoperable or become unreliable. See the BIOS discussion on upgrades, installation, and flashing at your BIOS manufacturer's home page. And if you are at all uncomfortable with this, consider hiring a qualified technician or consultant to research and implement a BIOS upgrade for your server.

- **Operating system status** — By performing the quick power-up test, you can determine whether any operating system has been installed on the computer. It is common for clone-makers to both format and SYS (apply basic MS-DOS files) the primary drive (C: drive) of the server. If no operating system has been installed, you will see a character-based error message that indicates the operating system is missing. If you purchased a name-brand server and elected to have SBS preinstalled (OEM style!) as discussed in Chapter 2, you will notice the SBS setup process launches after the initial POST phase terminates.

BEST PRACTICE: Note that in the SBS 2000 time frame, I recommend running the Windows 2000 Readiness Analyzer Tool. I've searched high and low in the SBS 2003 time frame and haven't found a like tool to recommend for you to run. Perhaps your guide for "readiness" should be the Windows Server 2003 logo on your components. This signifies the component has been tested to work with Windows Server 2003.

Notes:

And no discussion about assessment and fitness is complete without pulling out a third-party tool. I've used CheckIt Professional Edition, a relatively low-cost computer assessment application from SmithMicro Software. For more information, visit www.smithmicro.com. This is shown in Figure 3-1.

Figure 3-1
CheckIt is a long-standing favorite of technicians to peer inside their systems. It's been around for years and is now owned by SmithMicro Software.

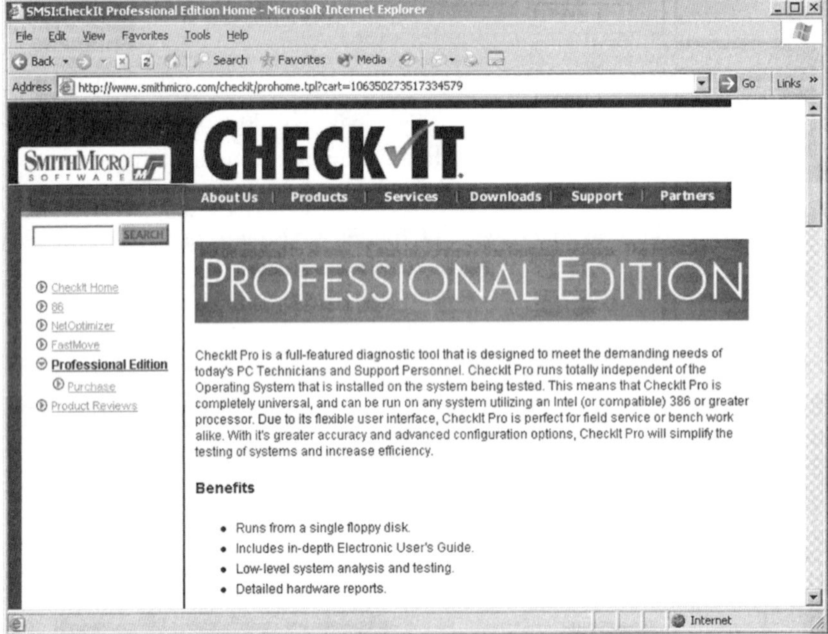

Backup Data

With SPRINGERS, you are installing SBS on a brand-new HP/Compaq Proliant server as part of our sample company setup. The company's data initially remains on the old NetWare server until it will be transferred over the wire or across the network to the new SBS server. That said, the data backup precautions are nothing out of the ordinary: Last night's backup should be verified.

But let's trade places for a moment and present a different scenario: reuse of an existing server machine. This assumes you are like many small businesses and hope to reuse your existing server for SBS. So one of the first things you are confronted with is major data backup issues. That is, how do you transfer data, via a single machine, from your previous operating system (say NetWare or NT) to SBS?

> BEST PRACTICE: Please carefully read the following scenario and appreciate that is an advanced topic for guru SBSers. First and foremost, I do assume that the foreign environment you are migrating data from has a tape backup device attached to the server, the tape backup device works, and you know how to make and verify a tape backup on the foreign system. My example uses Novell NetWare as its foreign system from which the data will be migrated to the new SBS system. But to be honest, you'll likely see more Windows NT scenarios out there than NetWare.

Assume that you are converting from a small Novell NetWare network to SBS. Also assume that, to save money, you plan to reformat the hard drive on your existing NetWare server and install SBS. Thus, your first challenge is to make darn sure that you've completely protected the business's data located on the existing NetWare server prior to reformatting its hard disk. If not, let's just say there aren't enough hours in the day to re-create the data you've lost!

The challenge here is that the tape created on a NetWare server using an NLM-based tape backup application isn't readable by the SBS's native tape backup application. In fact, relying on such a strategy results in an error message regarding a foreign tape when you try to access the tape under the native backup routine in SBS.

So what can you do? I've performed the following work-around to transfer this data from NetWare to SBS server-based environments. What makes this work-around so SBS-specific is that you can play this trick in a smaller environment, the kind of environment that SBS caters to. Obviously, this trick wouldn't be possible in larger enterprise environments that the full versions of Windows Server 2003 cater to.

First, copy the NetWare-based data to a second server or even one or two client workstations. As you know, today's workstations have huge hard drives that are often larger than those found on older servers in smaller companies. In my case years back, I pursued both strategies. I literally copied the firm's data from its existing NetWare server (2.5GB of data on a NetWare partition) to a loaner NetWare 4.11 server that I brought from home. I also copied the same data to a subdirectory of a robust workstation. After I completed my SBS installation, I (of course) copied the data back to the newly created SBS server from the client workstation. Using the data copy stored on the workstation, I saved a lot of time by not dropping under the hood on SBS and performing a somewhat nasty Win2K-ism of installing Gateway Services For NetWare (GSNW) to retrieve the data from my loaner NetWare 4.11 server.

> BEST PRACTICE: I've done the same thing with an SBS installation converting from a Linux server to a new SBS server. In this case, I wasn't interested in wasting the time to perfect the ICE.TEN terminal emulation connection between the Linux box and the SBS server. Thus, I copied the data from the Linux box to a workstation and back to the new SBS server.

Read Release Notes

Take my advice and open the README.HTM which points you to four documents:

- Small Business Server 2003 Release Notes
- Getting Started
- Restoring Your Server (this is very cool and something I speak to in Chapter 11 of this book and my forthcoming advanced book for SBS 2003 that will be released in mid-2004).
- Windows Server 2003 Release Notes

Using these onboard resources, you can find many of your questions regarding SBS and its limitations will be answered.

SBS Site Review

Humor me and quickly walk around the site where the SBS 2003 network will be installed and make sure that there is no existing DHCP Server (either another server machine or a router-type device). Suffering from fatigue, I didn't do this at one of my SBS installations a while ago, and sure enough, it came home to bite me bad. It turns out, as this story goes, the client site (a law firm) was a sublease from a former dot-com enterprise gone dot-bomb. Upon moving in, the law firm used much of the technology equipment, including the DSL router, from the former tenant. It turned out the DSL router, which no one had the password to, was acting as a DHCP server and issuing internal 10.x.x.x network IP addresses to workstations. When installing the SBS server machine, I found this condition violated one of the cardinal laws in SBS land: SBS must be the one and only DHCP server on the network.

So the outcome of all this was that the SBS server didn't complete its setup. I manually had to add the DHCP Server service and configure the default scope, add the Windows Internet Naming Service (WINS) and also re-run the SBS Setup Wizard in order for the licensing manager to work properly. (Initially the licensing manager wasn't accounting for logged off workstations, causing it to reach its limit of ten workstations very quickly.) The lesson learned, even though this was actually with the SBS 2000 release, was that more planning would have prevented this foolish error. My embarrassment is clearly your gain.

SBS Installation Overview

Allow me to take a moment to outline the SBS installation process for you. Understanding this setup blueprint is important because, if your setup fails somewhere along the line, you can quickly assess at what stage your setup failed. That failure assessment is extremely beneficial in troubleshooting any setup problems you might be having. Your understanding of the setup process will also help you communicate with your SBS consultant (a.k.a. SBSer guru) or Microsoft support.

BEST PRACTICE: These setup steps assume that you have purchased SBS as a standalone retail software package. These are not the same steps undertaken by the preinstalled (or OEM) version of SBS. The SBS OEM preinstallation approach is discussed later in the chapter and Appendix E.

The SBS installation process can be divided into six discrete steps (shown in Figure 3-2).

Figure 3-2
SBS installation overview.

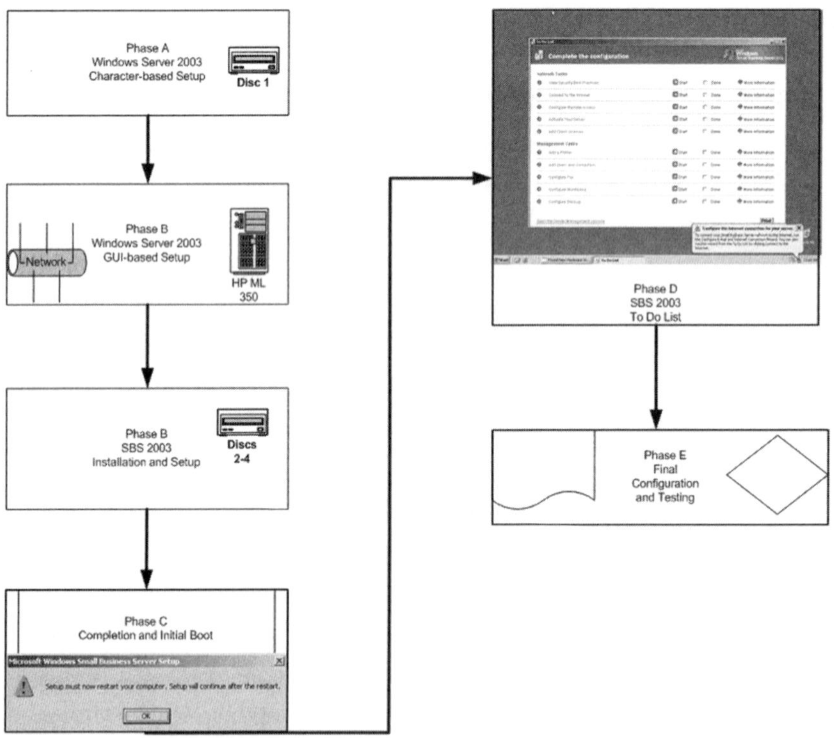

Windows Server 2003 Character-Based Setup (Phase A)

This phase consists of inserting the first SBS CD (Microsoft Windows Small Business Server 2003 Disc 1) when requested.

> BEST PRACTICE: Please ensure you are using a modern server machine with a bootable CD drive to install SBS 2003 using the SPRINGERS methodology. SBS 2003 also ships in a DVD format, which is very desirable as it results in performing the installation from a single disc. But speaking only for myself, few of my clients actually have a DVD in their server machine.

You must answer questions regarding welcome and licensing. Create and format a hard disk partition of sufficient size. Extensive file copying occurs at this stage from Disc 1. The computer reboots once.

> BEST PRACTICE: Also note that Windows Server 2003, acting as the underlying operating system in SBS, no longer requires an emergency repair disk or a unique boot disk created for recovery efforts. Recovery is now supported via the recovery console accessed by selecting the "R" keystroke early in the boot phase of Windows Server 2003.

Windows Server 2003 GUI-Based Setup (Phase B)

After the second reboot, you are presented with a Windows-like graphical user interface (GUI) to complete the installation of Windows Server 2003. Provide a user name for registration purposes and an organization name. Either accept the automatically created computer name or provide your own computer name. Provide the administrator password.

Observe the networking components being installed. Select the correct time zone for the SBS computer. The correct computer monitor settings are tested and, after additional Windows Server 2003 files are copied over, the SBS computer reboots.

SBS 2003 Installation and Setup (Phase C)

The computer automatically restarts and performs an autologon. The Microsoft Small Business Server Setup Welcome dialog box appears, and you answer many, if not all, of these setup questions regarding the following topics:

1. Software licensing
2. SBS Product Key entry
3. Proof of ownership for upgrades
4. Active Directory domain name
5. NetBIOS domain name
6. Computer name
7. Installed network adapters
8. Company information
9. Administrator's password to facilitate automatic logon
10. Applications to install (after the mid-point Windows Configuration reboot) and the path to install those applications
11. Data folder path

After you provide the information in steps 1 through 9 above, Active Directory and its required services, such as DNS, are installed and configured in the Windows Configuration stage. Additional Windows Server 2003 services, such as DHCP and Terminal Services, are installed. One reboot later and the true-blue SBS components (management consoles) and applications (Exchange Server, and the like) are installed. During this phase, you insert SBS Discs #2, #3, and #4 when requested (the fourth disc is really Outlook 2003). At the end of this phase, you need to click **Finish** in a dialog box indicating the SBS setup process has completed. The SBS computer asks you to approve a reboot.

BEST PRACTICE: Regarding the SBS installation process, actual installation time varies greatly. It can take anywhere from 90 minutes to over four hours depending on the speed of your disc drive, hard disk, and CPU microprocessor and the installation selections that you made. The amount of RAM also affects setup times. Believe me, I've seen both the fastest time and the slowest time listed here and everything in between!

SBS 2003 Completion and Initial Boot (Phase D)

Assuming you have successfully installed SBS 2003, this phase represents the first logon to the underlying Windows Server 2003 operating system. Log on with the administrator user account and password.

> BEST PRACTICE: Carefully note that the context of my discussion herein assumes you are starting with a clean machine (as I alluded to in the paragraph above. Upgrading from SBS 2000 requires a slightly different process and is covered in Appendix B: Upgrading. The reason I've placed the upgrade discussion in Appendix B is that the beloved SPRINGERS storyline centers around the use of a new server machine with no prior operating system installed. Understandably, your specific real world situation may vary.

SBS 2003 To Do List (Phase E)

When you first log on to the SBS computer after completing the installation, you are presented with a To Do List of tasks to complete on a screen titled **"Complete the configuration."**

> BEST PRACTICE: The To Do List in SBS 2003 is different from SBS 2000. The To Do List has been divided into two broad categories: Network Tasks and Management Tasks. SBS 2000 had no such functional distinctions. You will complete much of the SBS 2003 To Do List in Chapter 4.

Notes:

Network Tasks

1. **View Security Best Practices.** This is a screen with important security information.
2. **Connect to the Internet.** This is the E-mail and Internet Connection Wizard. Very powerful!
3. **Configure Remote Access**. This wizard is a big improvement in SBS 2003, as it replaces what was a manual process in SBS 2000. More on this later.
4. **Activate Your Server**. In the Windows Server 2003 time frame, Microsoft requires activation as an anti-piracy measure. This is the link to activate your SBS 2003 server.
5. **Add Client Licenses**. Client access licenses (CALs) are necessary to add users to your SBS network after the initial installation. These are purchased online now and a CAL diskette is not required. This is a big improvement over SBS 2003.

Management Tasks

1. **Add a Printer.** This is where you add printers.
2. **Add Users and Computers.** This is the improved Add User Wizard that chains to the Setup Computer Wizard.
3, **Configure Fax.** This wizard is a dramatic improvement in SBS 2003 as the fax configuration process in the SBS 2000 timeframe was manual (ouch!).
4. **Configure Backup.** Big-time improvements here with the backup configuration wizard (more details later).
5. **Configure Monitoring.** The SBS monitoring capability is a jewel and this is the link to configure it.

Microsoft created the To Do List with the idea that you would complete each step in order (according to members of the SBS development team who shared this public information with me directly over the years). I agree with Microsoft on this point, that the SBS To Do List should be completed in order, because it's part of the SBS methodology for being successful (I spend hundreds of pages addressing this topic in my *SMB Consulting Best Practices* book). Understand that nothing prevents you from either following the To Do List step-by-step or using an ad-hoc To Do List approach. As with the execution of any task on a computer, always think before acting and use your best judgment.

BEST PRACTICE: You can return to the To Do List at any time, not just the first time you log on to the SBS computer. This is accomplished by clicking the To Do List selection in the console pane on the System Manager console.

Final Configuration and Testing (Phase F)

This phase resolves loose ends, including attaching and making operational the uninterruptible power supply (UPS) that I discussed in Chapter 2. You also check the event logs to ensure that the SBS installation went well (from the Windows Server 2003 event logs via the Computer Management (Local) snap-in in the found in the Advanced Management section of the Server Management console). You also perform some basic SBS system tests so that you know you're ready to proceed to Chapter 4 with confidence. Also during this phase, a tape backup of the system would likely be made to preserve your setup and configuration, and you might install third-party applications, such as a virus protection application at this phase.

BEST PRACTICE: I'll have you run Windows Automatic Update in Chapter 5 in order to have the latest patches, bulletins, security fixes and the like applied before being "live" too long online and subjecting your computer to the badness of the Internet, such as worms!

Ready, Set, Go

Make sure you're familiar and armed with the numerous SBS setup sheets from Chapter 2. If this is your first pass through the book, these sheets, which reflect setup information for SPRINGERS, have been completed for you. If this is your second pass through the book, and you're installing SBS for real, gather blank setup sheets from my Web site at www.smbnation.com. Much of the information on the setup sheets will be called for in the next section.

You are now ready to install SBS 2003.

BEST PRACTICE: Let's take a deep breath at this point to reflect and meditate for a moment on exactly what is going on here. The planning and installation presented to date, and the forthcoming setup steps, are based on the viewpoint of SPRINGERS. Why? Because this book has been written with the idea in mind that, if you invest some of your limited time and you follow each step in this book, you will be a bona fide SBSer with a functional network for SPRINGERS. That is the underlying paradigm to how I wrote this book, and as you might imagine, I jealously guard my SPRINGERS methodology for quality assurances purposes.

Now, granted, your situation may be dramatically different if you install more than one SBS network (particularly if you are an SBS consultant). For example, one client site may use an IDE-based disk system on an older computer as the server machine. Another site may use a SCSI-based computer as the server machine. And yet another site may use a SCSI or IDE RAID array hard disk storage system. Variations in SBS implementations will exist, depending on your unique situation. Another area of variation is data migration. You may or may not have data to migrate from another machine, another partition of the existing machine that you are installing SBS on. Talk about an area where things can vary on a case-by-case basis, that area would be in data (some data is comma separated value, some is text, some uses XML, etc.)

So what's the bottom line? Stick with me and follow this methodology exactly and you'll have a functional SBS network for SPRINGERS after completing this book (I'm assuming it would take you about a month to complete the book from start to finish). But in the very next breathe, I'm not as tough of an old Angus bull as I first appear. If you are reading this book for pleasure and do not care to follow SPRINGERS rhyme and verse, God be with you and it's likely you'll still derive great value from these pages. But back to the SPRINGERS methodology. As an example, I have a printer installed on the SBS network later in the chapter, but you might not have a printer in the real world of SBS implementations. While it's unlikely you don't have a printer, SBS can be implemented without incident without a printer. Heck, you can even install the Shared Fax Service without a modem attached!

Vary from this specific methodology and you're on your own. (Sorry, mate!) And again, I do try to accommodate different scenarios as much as possible (such as the upgrade discussion in Appendix B). Thanks!

The first step assumes that you have a server machine that will boot from the CD drive. You are then sufficiently equipped and ready for the next section that commences the step-by-step setup procedure.

SBS Setup

Ladies and gentleman, it's time to rock and roll, SBS 2003 style!

1. Insert the Microsoft Windows Small Business Server 2003 Disc 1 in disc drive and turn on your computer. Boot from the disc (typically pressing any key will do) to do this. The POST stage will complete and the setup character-based setup phase commences (numerous setup files will load for several minutes).

BEST PRACTICE: Immediately after the character-based setup commences at this step, you will note language at the bottom of the screen that asks you to "Press F6 if you need third-party SCSI or RAID driver."

There are several issues concerning this message. First, if you are using an unsupported SCSI or RAID disk controller, you would indeed press F6 at this point and provide the manufacturer's driver on a floppy disk. This is straightforward enough. However, I've installed SBS 2003 on HP/Compaq systems which had SCSI and RAID controllers without having to hit F6. How can this be, you ask? Easy. The SCSI or RAID controllers were supported by the underlying Windows Server 2003 operating system with its native drivers (many of which were supplied by leading hardware manufacturers and burned on SBS CD Disc 1). This can also be a function of the OEM setup process used by major hardware manufacturers such as HP/Compaq.

Also note that I assume you have configured the hard disk to be used by the RAID subsystem as I discussed earlier in the chapter. (This is where you add the hard disks to the array using the steps provided by the computer manufacturer during the POST startup in the computer boot phase.)

Note when I installed SBS 2003 on the HP ProLiant ML-350, it had native support for SBS 2003 and pressing F6 was not necessary.

2. On the **Welcome to Setup** screen press **Enter** to setup the server for SPRINGERS.

    Welcome to Setup.
    This portion of the Setup program prepares
    Microsoft Windows to run on your computer.
    * To set up Windows now, press ENTER.
    * To repair a Windows installation using Recovery Console, press R.
    * To quit Setup without installing Windows, press F3

3. The **Windows Licensing Agreement** screen appears. After reading this license agreement, press **F8** to agree to the license and continue. If you don't agree to the licensing, the setup will terminate.

BEST PRACTICE: At this point, if you are installing on a machine that has a previous edition of Windows Server 2003 installed on it, you would receive a message that you could quit the installation (by pressing F3,) repair the Windows installation (by pressing R), or hit the escape key (ESC) to not perform a repair and proceed.

In the case of SPRINGERS, you would not be confronted with this screen as I assume you are starting with a new server machine that had not previously had Windows installed on it.

4. Assuming you have a new hard disk, you see the following hard disk partitioning screen. The actual space value (MB) varies depending on how large your hard disk is. In this case with SPRINGERS, the hard disk is a 34 GB RAID array. You will create two partitions based on the configuration information from Chapter 2 (see Table 2-4). The partition for the operating system and core applications will be 10 GB and denoted as Drive C. The data partition (Drive D) will be 20 GB. As you religiously follow the SPRINGER methodology, note how you can vary the partition sizes to reflect your hard disk capacity (which might be different from my setup). Also – later on after you've completed this book and the SPRINGERS methodology, you'll want to evaluate that partition sizes work best for you in the real world. I'd always have a 10 GB system partition or larger to accommodate growth, service pack installations and so on. Meanwhile, back at the SPRINGERS methodology, click **C** to create a partition (you will first create the 10 GB system partition).

```
The following list shows existing partitions and
unpartitioned space on this computer.

Use UP and DOWN ARROW keys to select an item in the list.
*  To install Windows on the selected item, press ENTER.
*  To create a partition in the unpartitioned space, press C.
*  To delete the selected partition, press D.

 — — — — — — — — — — — — — — — — — — — — — —
 | 34493 MB Disk 0 at Id 0 on bus 0 on scsi (MBR)   |
 | Unpartitioned space          34493 MB              |
 — — — — — — — — — — — — — — — — — — — — — —
```

5. On the screen below, enter **10000** (that is ten thousand) in the **Create partition of size (in MB):** field. Press **Enter**.

   You have asked Setup to create a new partition on
   34493 MB Disk 0 at Id 0 on bus 0 on scsi (MBR).

   - To create the new partition, enter a size below and press ENTER.
   - To go back to the previous screen without creating the partition, press ESC.

   The minimum size for the new partition is 8 megabytes (MB).
   The maximum size for the new partition is 34493 megabytes (MB).
   Create partition of size (in MB): 10000

6. On the screen below, press C and create a 20 GB partition which will be the DATA partition (basically repeat the step above to do this). Upon returning, select the new C: drive partition and press **Enter** to install Windows Server and (in several steps) SBS on the newly created 10GB (approximately) system partition.

   The following list shows existing partitions and
   unpartitioned space on this computer.

   Use UP and DOWN ARROW keys to select an item in the list.
   * To install Windows on the selected item, press ENTER.
   * To create a partition in the unpartitioned space, press C.
   * To delete the selected partition, press D.

```
 - - - - - - - - - - - - - - - - - - - - - - -
|34493 MB Disk 0 at Id 0 on bus 0 on atapi          |
| C: New (Unformatted)        10001 MB              |
| D: New (Unformatted)        20001 MB              |
| Unpartitioned space           491 MB              |
 - - - - - - - - - - - - - - - - - - - - - - -
```

7. Select **Format the partition using the NTFS file system** on the screen that appears and press **Enter**. The formatting process will commence and take several minutes. Setup files are then loaded, a reboot occurs, and the character-based phase of the setup commences.

   The partition you have chosen is not unformatted.
   Setup will now format the partition.

   Use the UP and DOWN ARROW keys to move the highlight
   to the file system you want and then press ENTER.

   If you want to select a different partition for Windows,
   press ESC.

   Format the partition using the NTFS file system(Quick).
   Format the partition using the FAT file system (Quick).
   Format the partition using the NTFS file system.
   Format the partition using the FAT file system.

BEST PRACTICE: Because you are following the beloved SPRINGERS methodology, you will indeed have seen the screen in step #7 above. However, if you were installing SBS in a scenario where you installed to an existing formated hard disk partition, you would not see the screen in step #7 because it would not be necessary to format the partition.

Setup now formats the hard disk partition you have just created. This formatting process takes several minutes. Feel free to get a cup of coffee to pass the time. After the formatting is complete, the computer's hard disks will be inspected for hard disk errors.

After the initial partition formatting has been completed, numerous Windows Server 2003-related files (.inf, .exe, .dll, .wav, .sys, .fon, .hlp) are copied over to the newly NTFS formatted partition. A screen will appear briefly, communicating the newly copied files are bein initialized.

8. An autologon occurs and the GUI-based Windows Server 2003 phase commences as seen in Figure 3-3. At this point, user input is not required.

Figure 3-3
You will notice the traditional Windows Server 2003 setup is the same in SBS 2003 as other Windows Server 2003 SKUs.

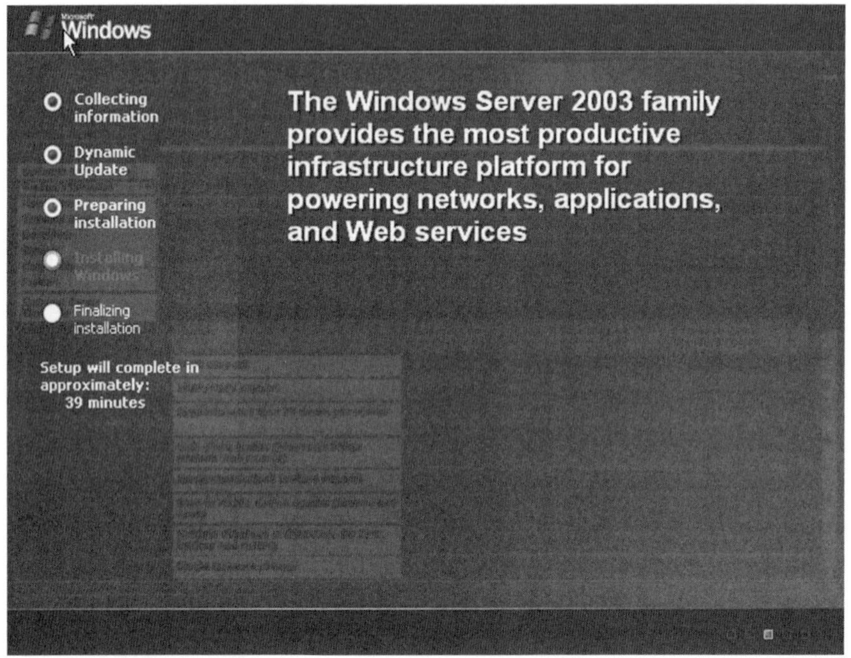

9. On the **Regional and Language Options** page, accept **English (United States)** and **US keyboard layout**. Click **Next**.

10. On the **Personalize Your Software** screen, type **Bob Easter** in **Name** and **Springer Spaniels Limited** in **Organization** as seen in Figure 3-4. Click **Next**.

Figure 3-4:
Enter the SPRINGERS information taken from Table 2-4 to complete the personalization information.

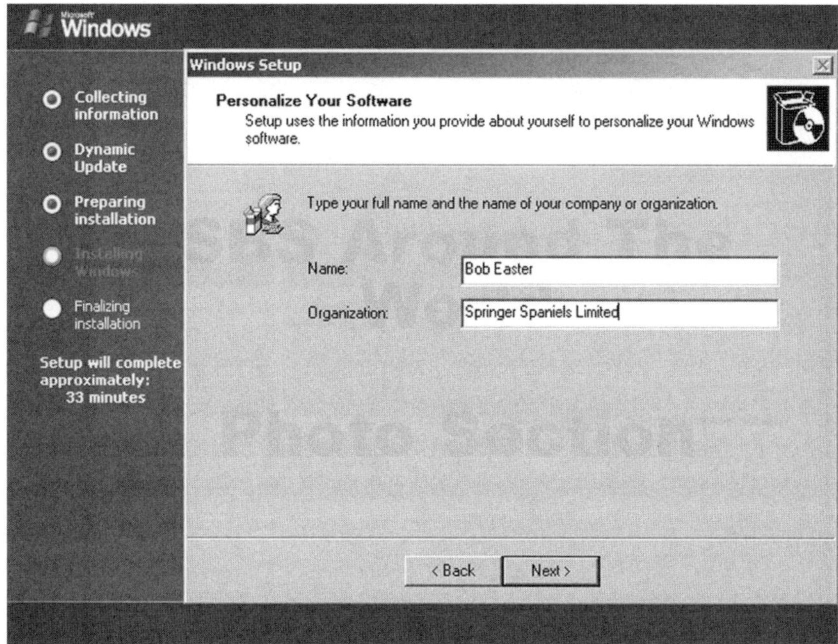

Notes:

11. Complete the **Product Key** field on the **Your Product Key** page (you will need to supply the product key provided on the disc case (it is a 25-character code on a yellow sticker). Your screen should look similar to Figure 3-5. Click **Next**.

Figure 3-5
Complete the product key field correctly as it is used to hash out a code for activating your server in Chapter 4.

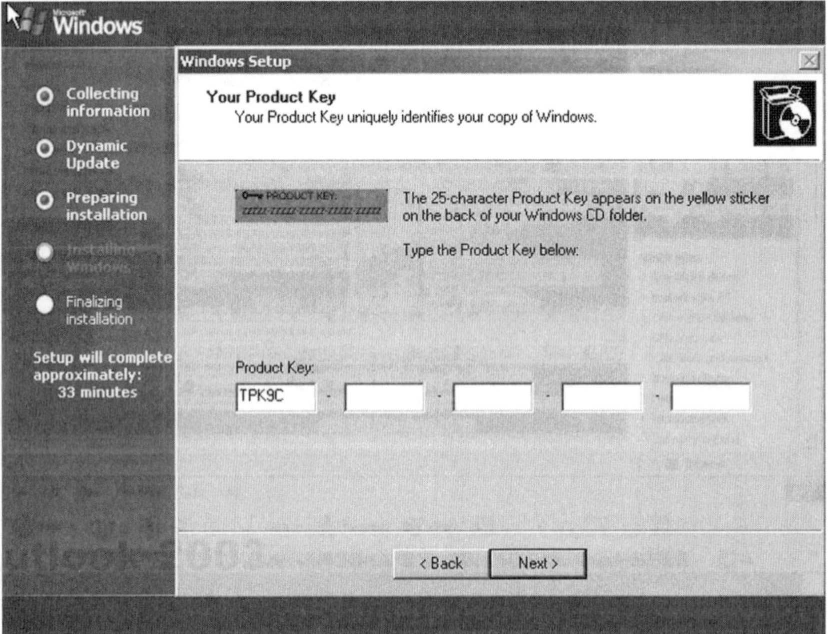

Notes:

12. The **Computer Name and Administrator Password** screen appears (Figure 3-6). Provide the computer name (**SPRINGERS1**) for SPRINGERS in the **Computer name** field and the Administrator password (**Husky9999!**) in both the **Administrator Password** and **Confirm Password** fields. Click **Next.**

Figure 3-6
You will initially name the server machine here and provide the administrator password.

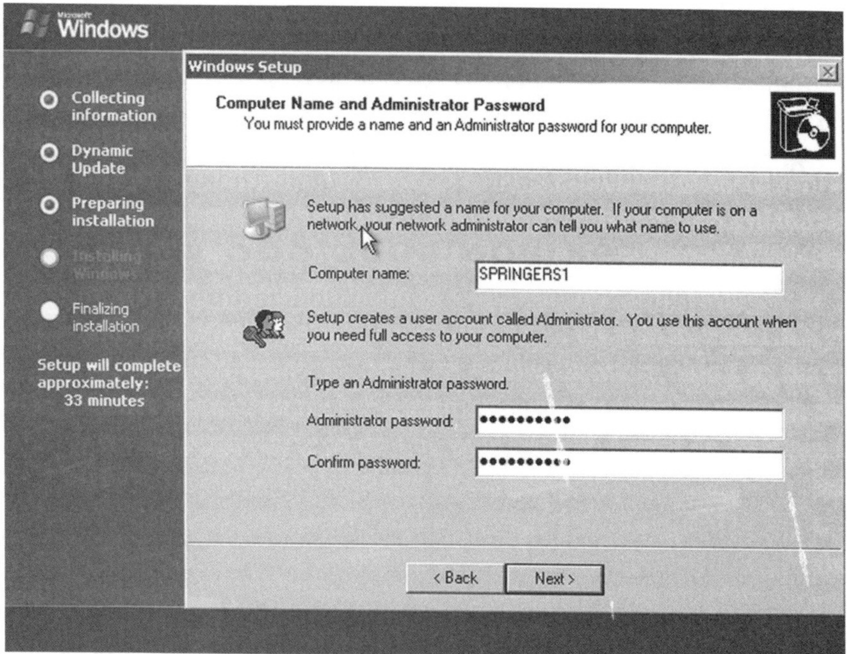

BEST PRACTICE: You will note that a computer name has been automatically suggested in the Computer name field (e.g., SPRINGERSPA-B3KU6G), but your suggested name may vary. There are several issues surrounding the suggested computer name.

First, the suggested computer name is typically long and difficult to remember. There are still applications that require you to manually type the server computer name during a setup screen or to map a drive via a uniform naming convention path (UNC). In this case, a simpler machine name is desirable for spelling purposes.

Second, the SPRINGERS methodology used throughout this book demands you name the machine SPRINGERS1 in order to successfully complete the examples herein this text.

Third, while you should put care and thought into naming the computer at this point, you actually have one more chance to change the machine name in the SBS setup routine. This last chance to change the computer name occurs later in what I defined as Phase C: SBS Installation and Setup (this is just prior to the **Windows Configuration** screen in the SBS 2003 setup wizard). There is a screen in the SBS setup routine at that time that allows you to modify the computer NetBIOS name.

BEST PRACTICE: Microsoft has eliminated a screen right here in SBS 2003 that appeared in the SBS 2000 product. The screen was titled Windows 2000 Components and allowed you to select server-side components before continuing.

13. Assuming you are adhering to the SPRINGERS story line and have a modem attached (as specified earlier in the chapter), the **Location** screen appears (Figure 3-7). Complete the **What country/region are you in now?** drop down box (for SPRINGERS, select **United States of America**), the **What area code (or city code) are you in now?** field (for SPRINGERS, enter **206**), and the **If you dial a number to get an outside line, what is it?** field (for SPRINGERS, leave blank). Select between **Tone dialing** or **Pulse dialing** under **The phone system at this location uses:** and click **Next**. I am, of course, assuming you can find out all of the answers to the questions above relatively easily for your own real-world use (for example, many businesses dial "9" to reach an outside line and use tone dialing). If you don't have a modem attached, the **Location Information** screen will not appear and you will go immediately to the next step for date and time settings. Remember that the SPRINGERS methodology assumes you

have a modem attached. It's not a true showstopper if you don't, but understand the faxing chapter (Chapter 9) will play out slightly differently for you without a bona fide modem attached.

Figure 3-7
Completing the modem setup via the Location Information screen. Note this assumes you are using a modem that has been automatically detected and installed, which is the usual case.

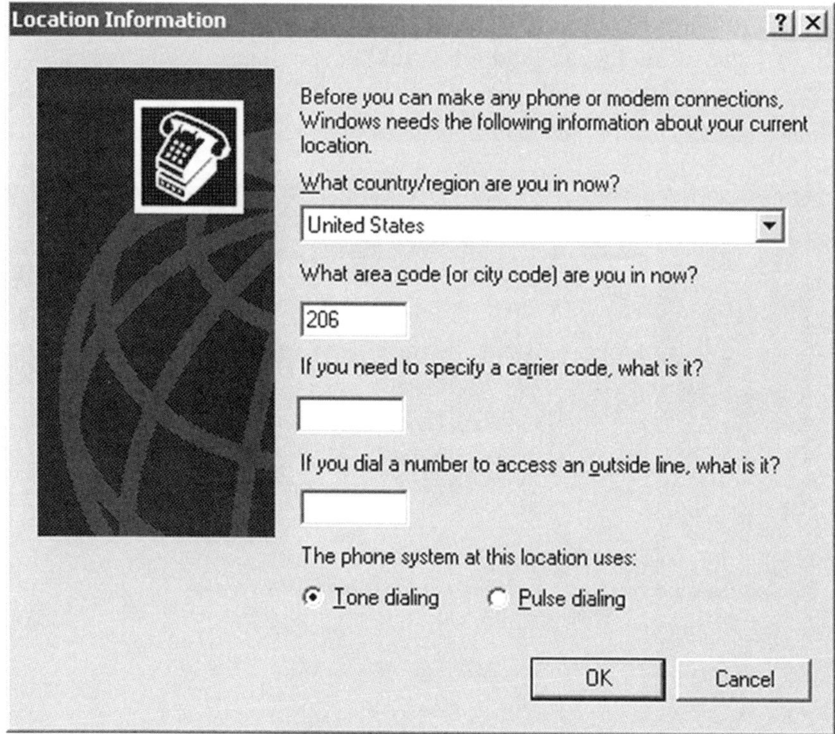

BEST PRACTICE: Note that SBS 2003 supports multiple modems if you have busy, active faxing needs. Perhaps one modem would be for executive usage and the other modem for faxing activity generated by the worker bees.

Also, you get what you pay for with modems and if you're serious, consider the V.Everything modem from US Robotics/3COM.

14. Select your date, time, and time zone when presented with the **Date and Time Settings** screen (Figure 3-8). For SPRINGERS, select **(GMT-08:00) Pacific Time (US & Canada), Tijuana** in the **Time Zone** drop-down field. You can enter whatever day and time you desire (and this can be changed via the Control Panel when the server machine is up and running after setup) in the **Date & Time** drop-down fields. Click **Next**. Note that for SBS sites in the United States, it makes sense to select the **Automatically adjust clock for daylight saving changes** checkbox to automatically adjust your server time in the spring (ahead) and fall (back).

Figure 3-8
Complete the date and time configuration.

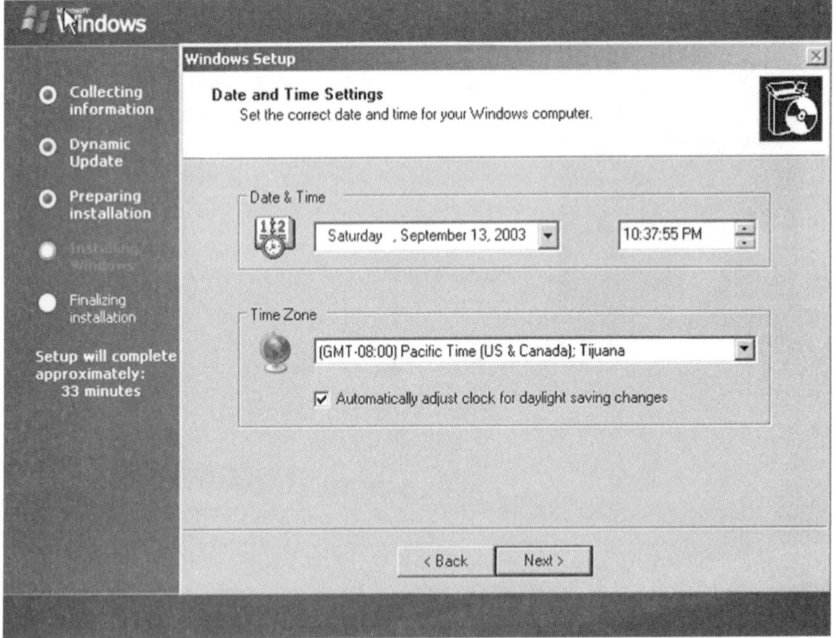

15. Additional computer files are copied and installed and more configuration activity occurs. The installation is "finalized" as shown in a bullet point on the left in Figure 3-9.

Figure 3-9
The underlying Windows Server 2003 installation autopilots at this points and completes the operating system installation.

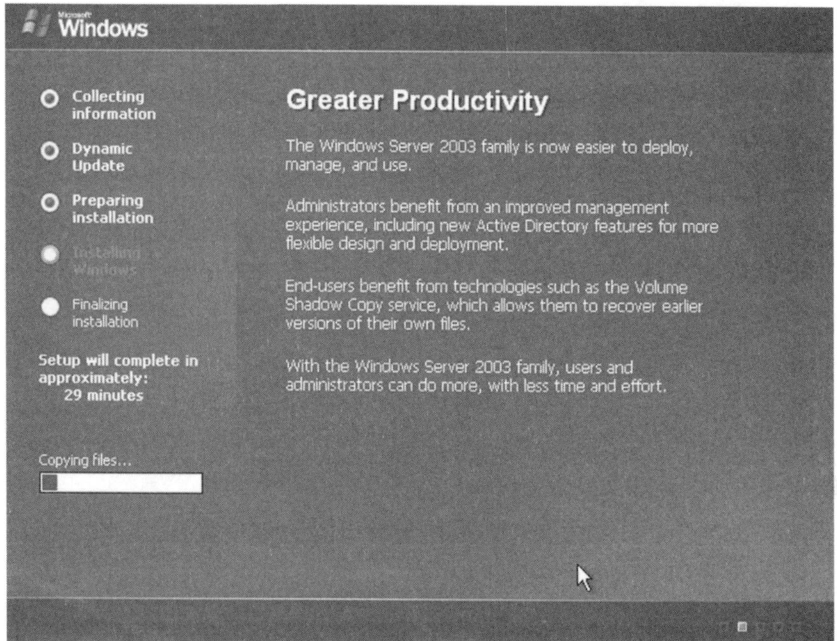

16. You are instructed to press **Ctrl-Alt-Delete** at the **Welcome to Windows** dialog box. The **Log On to Windows** dialog box appears. After you log on as **Administrator** (remember the password is **Husky9999!**), a dialog box will appear advising you that setup files are being copied to a temporary directory, followed by another dialog box communicating that 40 separate installation components are being loaded. A few minutes later, you are greeted by the initial SBS setup screen that is titled **Continuing Microsoft Small Business Server Setup,** Click **Next** (but first read and honor the next two BEST PRACTICES).

Figure 3-10
The SBS 2003 installation continues.

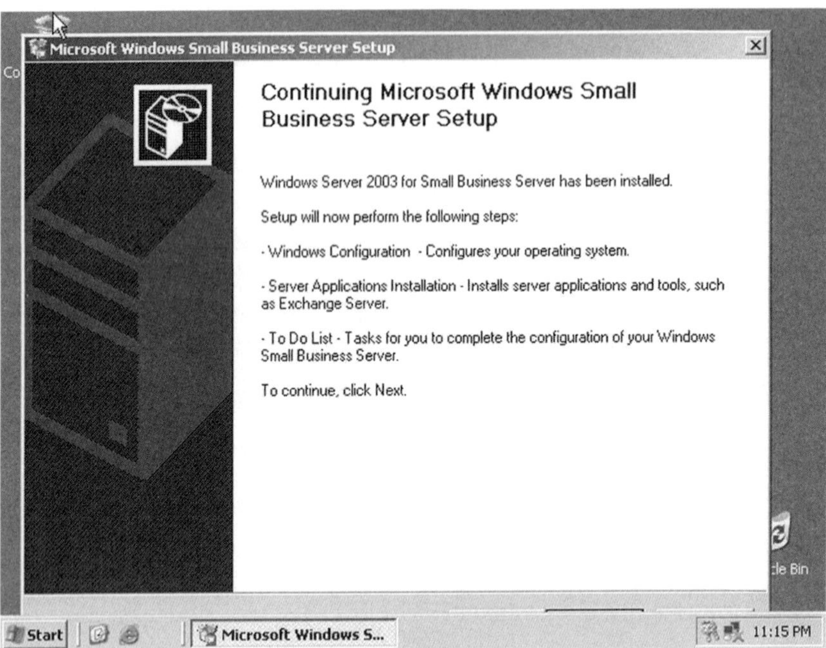

BEST PRACTICE: Depending on the hardware you have installed on your system, such as a USB device, plug-and-play device, or PCI-based device, you might see the Add New Hardware Wizard. If such is the case, complete the wizard and return to the screen in Figure 3-10.

BEST PRACTICE: You now need to configure the second drive area (Drive D) for storing data. In order to do this, click **Start**, **Administrative Tools**, **Computer Management**, expand **Storage**, and click **Disk Management**. Right click on the **D:** volume and select **Format**. The **Format D:** dialog box appears. Name the volume **DATA** in the **Volume Label** field, confirm **NTFS** as the default file system, keep the **Allocation unit size** as **Default** and select **Perform**

a quick format. Click **OK**. Click **OK** on the warning notice you receive. Take a few deep breathes while the formatting completes and then close the **Computer Management** window.

An interesting historical note for you: In SBS 2000, you had to format Drive D no later than this point (you could have also formatted it back in the character-based phase at the partition screens). But SBS 2003 is more forgiving! I've found that you can configure Drive D as late as after the reboot after the Windows Configuration stage (in several steps) and have it be recognized by the Microsoft Windows Small Business Server Setup wizard. That improvement reflects the fact the setup wizard remains much more dynamic (and less static or fixed) in SBS 2003 compared to the predecessor SBS 2000 version. Jolly good show!

So perhaps you're feeling unwelcome in SBS 2003 at this point. In the step above in SBS 2000, you received a "Welcome" notice instead of the word "Continuing." So perhaps SBS 2003 isn't as warm and fuzzy during setup, but don't let that prevent you from marching forward! OK—when you see the belated SBS 2003 "Welcome" message, click **Next**.

Notes:

BEST PRACTICE: At this point, you might well receive an informational, warning, or a blocking message on the **Setup Requirements** page (Figure 3-11) indicating your machine doesn't satisfy some SBS setup requirement. First and foremost, understand that such messages appear depending on machine settings, so one SBS setup on a specific machine might vary from another SBS setup on another machine (the point being you might receive a warning or blocking message on one machine and not the other).

Figure 3-11
Messages are displayed which must be addressed.

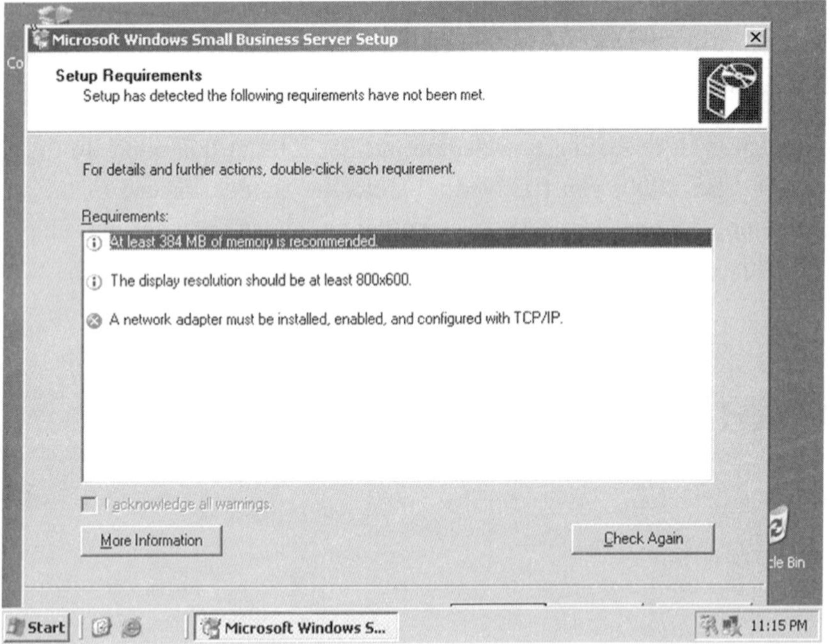

As a general rule, a warning message does not stop the SBS setup routine and can be cured immediately. A blocking message is typically more severe and will require more extensive remedial action on your behalf. In Figure 3-11, a network adapter isn't present and the installation can not continue. This must be fixed.

Just for giggles, I show another **Setup Requirements** screen I encountered that relates to supported processors in SBS 2003 (Figure 3-12). You will recall that SBS 2003 supports two physical processors and that is the configuration on the HP/Compaq ML-350 at SPRINGERS. But the ML-350 server machine also supports hyper-threading, defined in the next paragraph.

Figure 3-12
A warning message communicates to you that only two processors are supported.

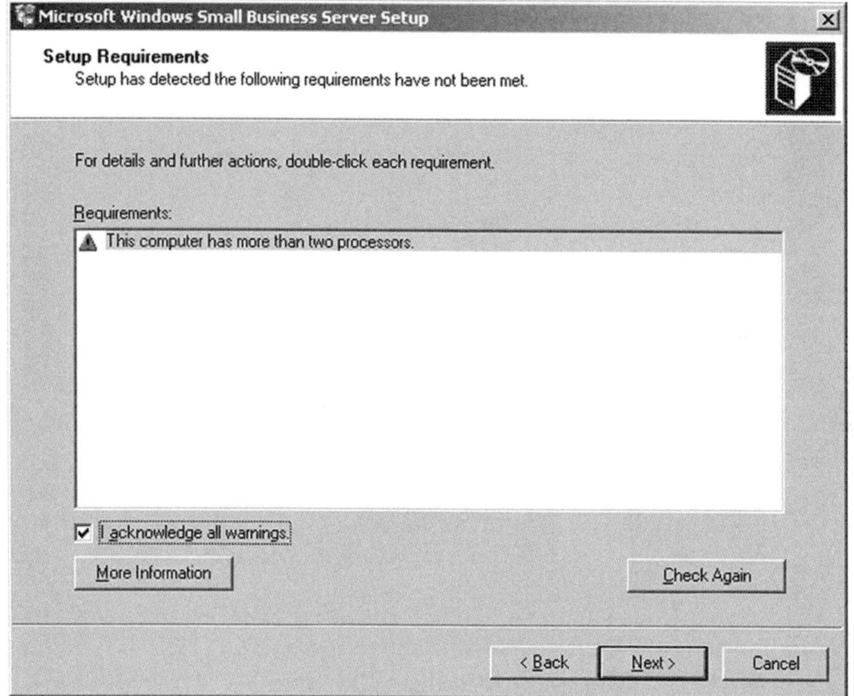

Hyper-threading allows a single processor to act as two processors. When you install SBS 2003 on a machine with two physical processors that support hyper-threading (in effect telling the operating system you have four processors), you'll receive the error message in 3-12. This is unique to SBS 2003 because it uses the standard version of Windows Server 2003 (which natively supports four processors), but then caps the processor support at two. The hyper-threading issue kinda throws SBS 2003 into a mild tizzy and it generates the two processor warning message.

But, just to add fuel to the fire, even though you received a warning message on a two processor machine using hyper-threading (causing SBS 2003 to believe you have more physical processors), SBS 2003 will actually exploit and use the two physical processors and the two "virtual" processors. I prove this by showing you Figure 3-13 where all "four" processors are active.

Figure 3-13
The Performance tab on Windows Task Manager (select from right-clicking Start task bar) shows four busy processors on the SPRINGERS SBS 2003 server machine.

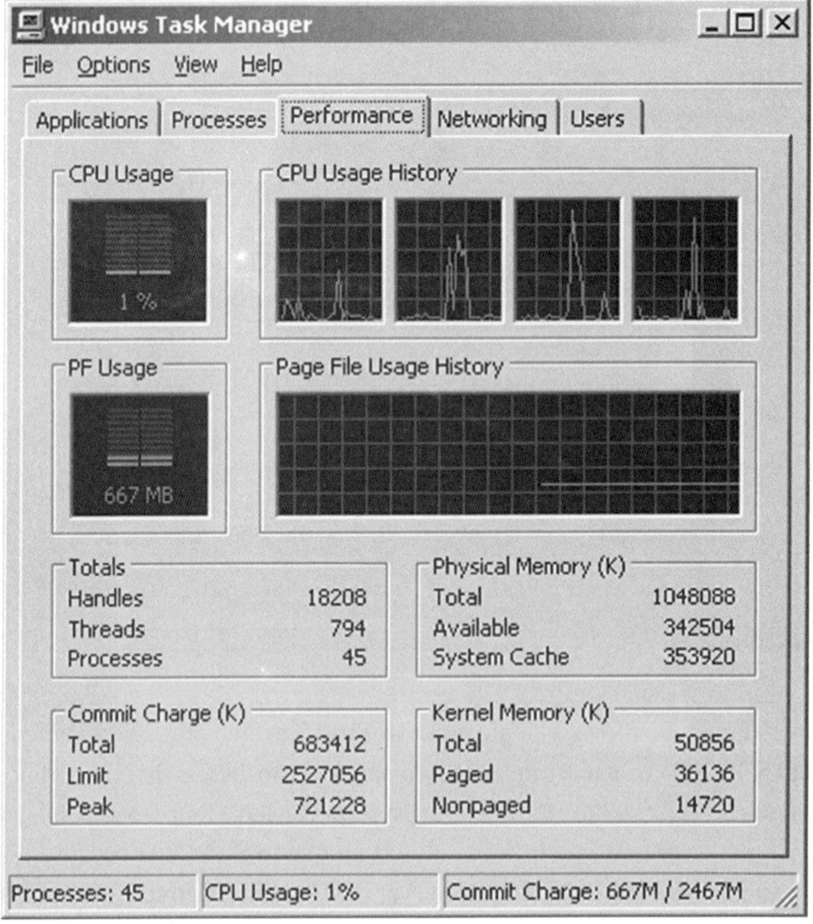

Finally, SBS 2003 has a warning message if you only have one network adapter card installed. That is because Microsoft, in its endeavor to promote security best practices everywhere, wants you to have two network adapter cards to take advantage of the basic firewall capabilities included in SBS 2003. More on that topic in Chapter 5.

And, of course, if you did not receive a warning or blocking message, you will proceed with the setup.

17. Complete the **Company Information** page with the information contained in Table 2-4 (prior chapter) for SPRINGERS. Your screen should look similar to Figure 3-14. Click **Next**.

Figure 3-14
Complete the Company Information screen to match what you see here.

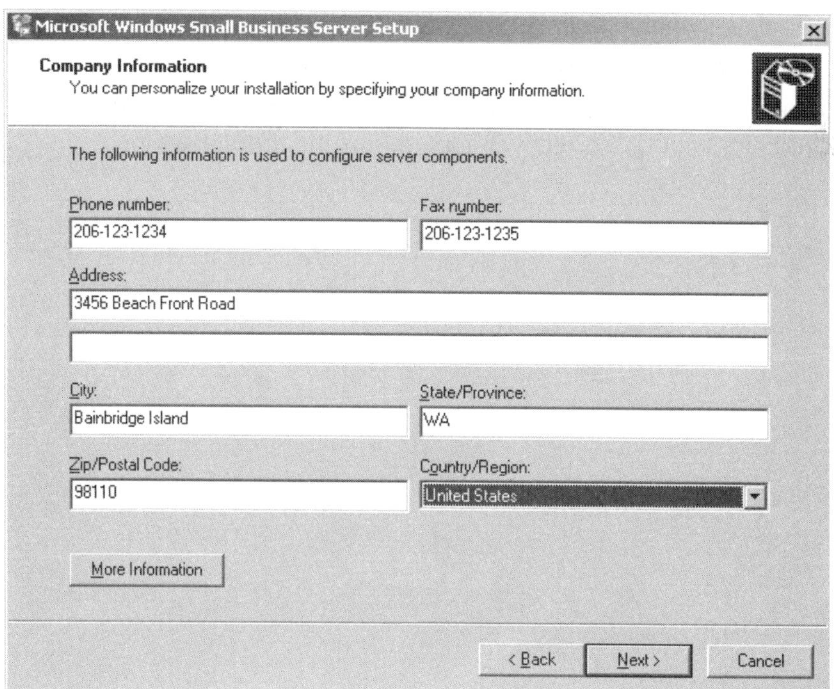

BEST PRACTICE: Complete as many fields as possible on all SBS setup dialog boxes when you set up your own SBS machine. Much of this information, known as *metainformation*, is used in other places within SBS for the life of the system.

Note that in SBS 2003 the **Company Information** screen contains telephony information. In SBS 2000, a separate telephony screen would have followed. SBS 2003 has eliminated the Product Information screen at this point, which required you to reenter the registered user name, the company name, and the product key. This is now accomplished in the Windows Server 2003 GUI setup phase.

BEST PRACTICE: You should be aware of the More Information button at the lower part of each page. Click **More Information** and you are presented a worksheet and a help topic for the screen being displayed. Initially introduced in SBS 2000, this is a big improvement over SBS 4.5, where only a few screens had the More Information button. More important, the More Information buttons help you install SBS 2003 correctly if you are unsure about a setting.

Notes:

18. Be careful on the **Internal Domain Information** page to overwrite the default naming information to reflect SpringersLTD.local as the internal domain name in the Full DNS name for internal domain field. In the NetBIOS domain name field, type **SPRINGERSLTD**. Leave the computer name as SPRINGERS1. Your screen should look similar to Figure 3-15. Click **Next**.

BEST PRACTICE: You may read a doctoral thesis on internal and external domain naming by clicking the More Information button on the Internal Domain Information screen.

Figure 3-15
Carefully complete the fields on the Internet Domain Information screen as you will commit these names in a moment.

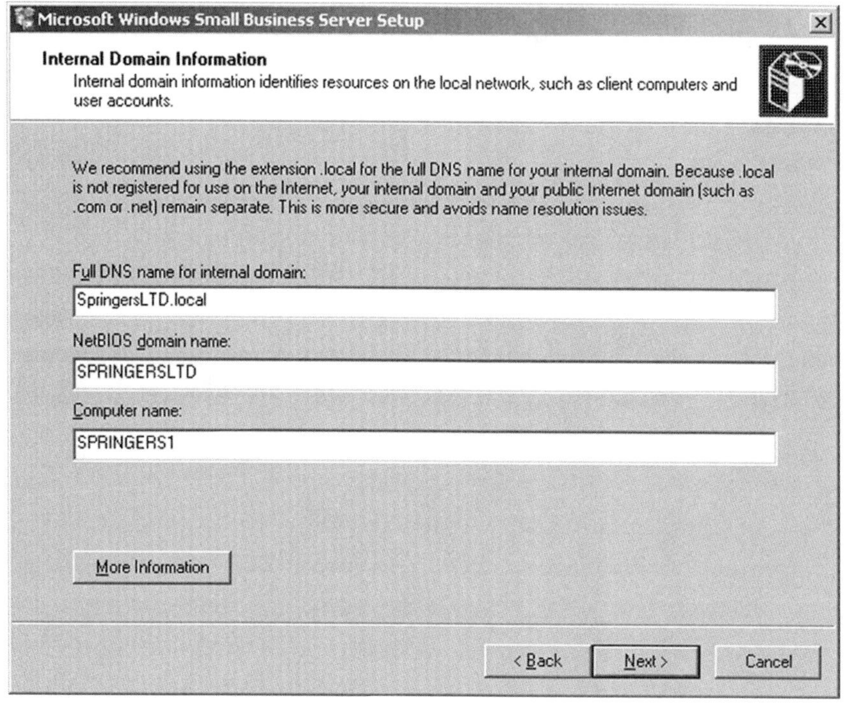

19. On the **Local Network Adapter Information** page, select the network adapter card that you want to be the attached to the local area network. This is shown in Figure 3-16. Click **Next**.

Figure 3-16
Select the network adapter card you want to use for the local area network. The other card is temporarily disabled.

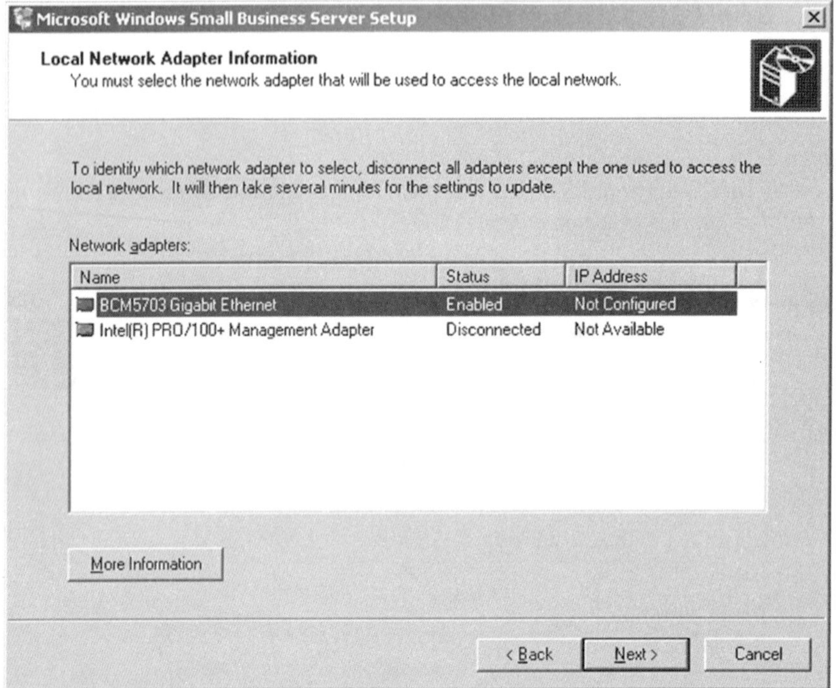

Notes:

20. Accept the default **IP address** (192.168.16.2) and the Class C (255.255.255.0) subnet mask on the **Local Network Adapter Configuration** page. This is shown in Figure 3-17. Click **Next**.

Figure 3-17
Verify your information matches on this Local Network Adapter Configuration page before proceeding.

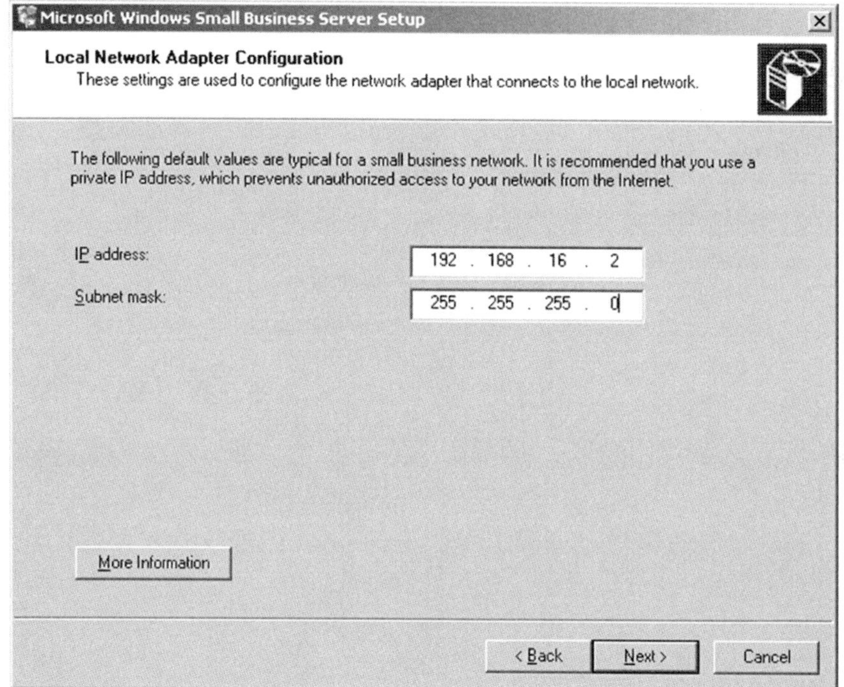

BEST PRACTICE: Here again I weave in a pocket MBA SBS/SMB consulting best practice that each of your SBS networks should be the same (even if you only have one!). One place to make each network the same is screen in Figure 3-17 where you accept the default IP addressing.

21. Accept the default selection of **Log on automatically** and type **Husky9999!** in the **Password** field on the **Logon Information** page. Click **Next**. This allows you to walk away from the two reboots of the SBS 2003 server machine during setup and have the setup process continue automatically.

22. The **Windows Configuration** page appears alerting you that the next configuration stage may take up to 30-minuntes to complete (Figure 3-18). Click **Next**.

Figure 3-18

The Windows Configuration approval screen.

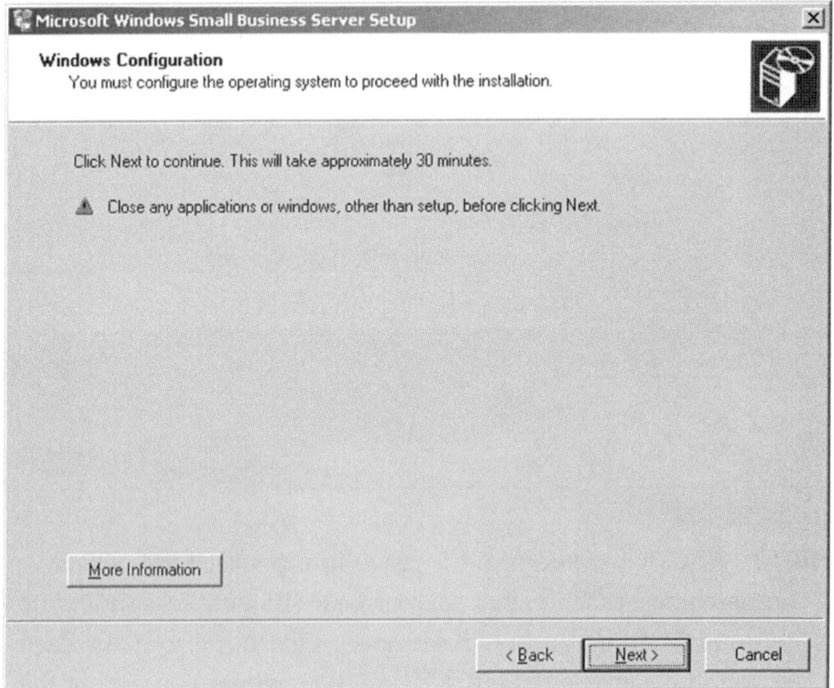

BEST PRACTICE: This Windows Configuration stage SBS 2003 replaces the Baseline Scenario stage in SBS 2000. At this stage, you've committed the computer name and the domain name on the server machine. Instead of taking 30 minutes, completing this stage takes closer to 15 minutes. So go get a strong cup of coffee!

Figure 3-19
Observe the progress of critical foundation components being installed for SBS 2003 on the Component Progress screen.

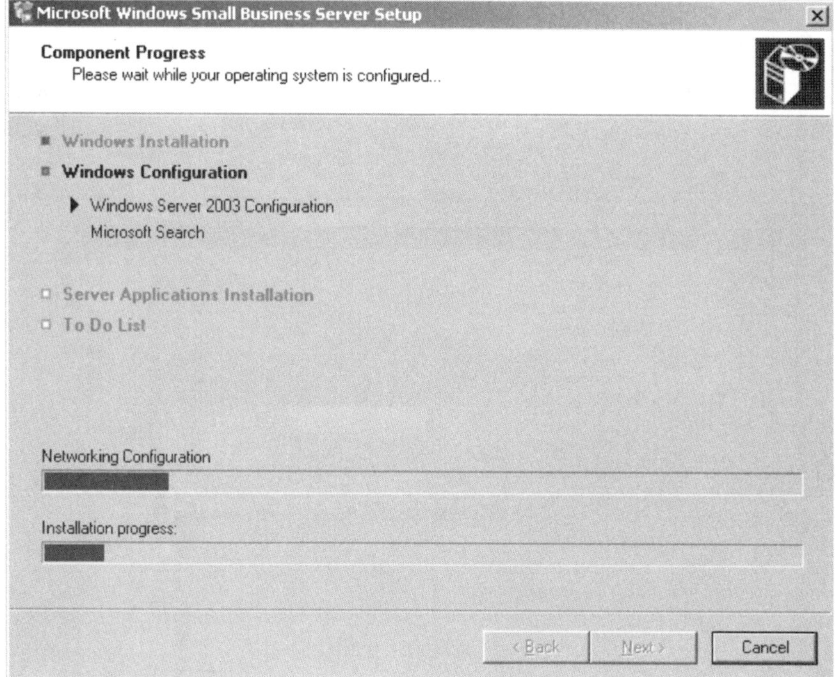

23. After a reboot and some final configuration activity, the **Component Selection** page appears as seen in Figure 3-20. Note that you could redirect the installation path for the applications if you so desired. Click **Next**.

Figure 3-20
This is your chance to make decisions about the installation location of the core SBS applications.

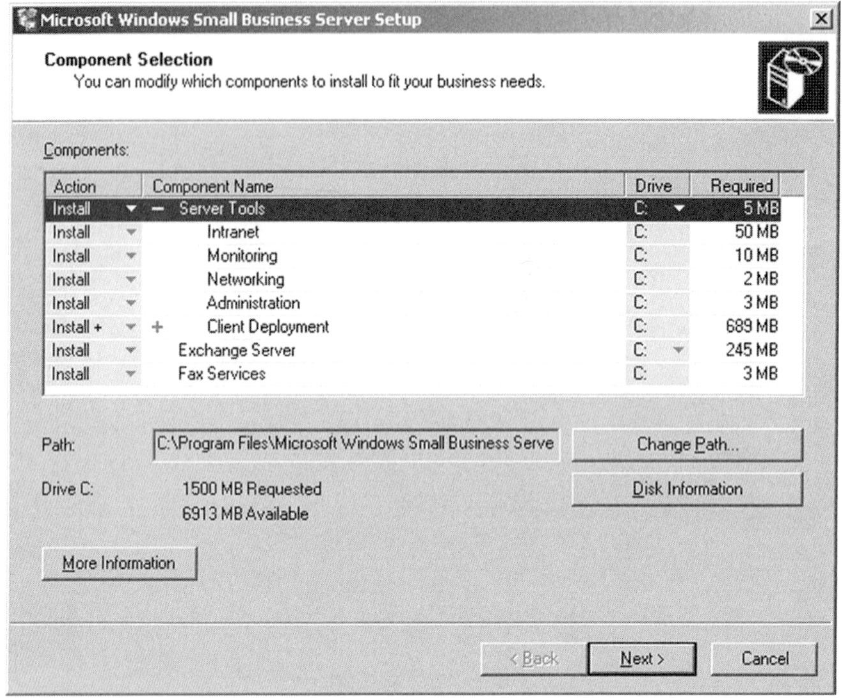

BEST PRACTICE: Revisit Table 1-1 in Chapter 1 if you need to refresh your memory about what each SBS component is and does. For example, Microsoft Exchange Server 2003 is the messaging program in SBS.

BEST PRACTICE: Did you notice the Shared Fax Service was selected by default and installed whether or not you have a modem attached? This is true in SBS 2003 and a major improvement compared to past

SBS 4.x releases where a modem detection issues could kill the whole party (this great *sans* modem capability also existed in SBS 2000).

And the older-timers would again notice the Shared Modem Service is absent (it's no longer part of SBS 2003).

24. Next up is the **Data Folders** screen. You will redirect some of the components to Drive D as part of the SPRINGERS methodology. The User Shared Folders, Sent Faxes, and Exchange Store will be redirected to Drive D. But the Microsoft Data Engine (MSDE), Client Applications folder, and Exchange Transaction Logs will remain on Drive C. Note that I consider the Exchange Transaction Logs to be part of the application and not the data. Your screen should look similar to Figure 3-21. To change the location of a folder, select **Modify Location**, erase the first term **"C"** on the far left of the path in the **Enter the path below** field, and replace it with the term "**D**" for Drive D. Click **OK** and when you receive a notice that the path doesn't exist and a question as it whether it's okay to create it, click **Yes**. After redirecting the data folder paths, click **Next**.

Figure 3-21
Redirect data paths.

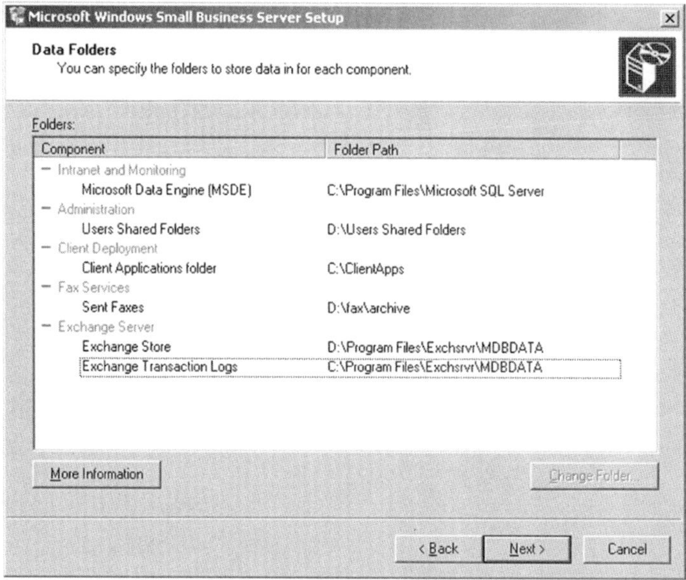

BEST PRACTICE: By the way, there is a school of thought that the Exchange store and transaction logs should be on two physically separate drives as a recoverability best practice. This is more enterprise thinking than I need to delve into here, but the point is well taken and you should consult some of the great advanced Exchange texts at your local technical bookstore. Note that my having you redirect the Exchange store to Drive D is not technically the equivalent of separating the Exchange store and transaction logs. Why? Because drives C and D are simply partitioned on the same RAID 5 array and aren't truly separate physical disks.

25. The **Component Summary** page appears, allowing you to confirm or change your settings one last time (Figure 3-22). Click Next. The heavy lifting on installing SBS 2003 occurs here as the application installation process takes off, displayed in Figure 3-23.

Figure 3-22
This is your last chance to make changes to your selections before the heavy lifting commences.

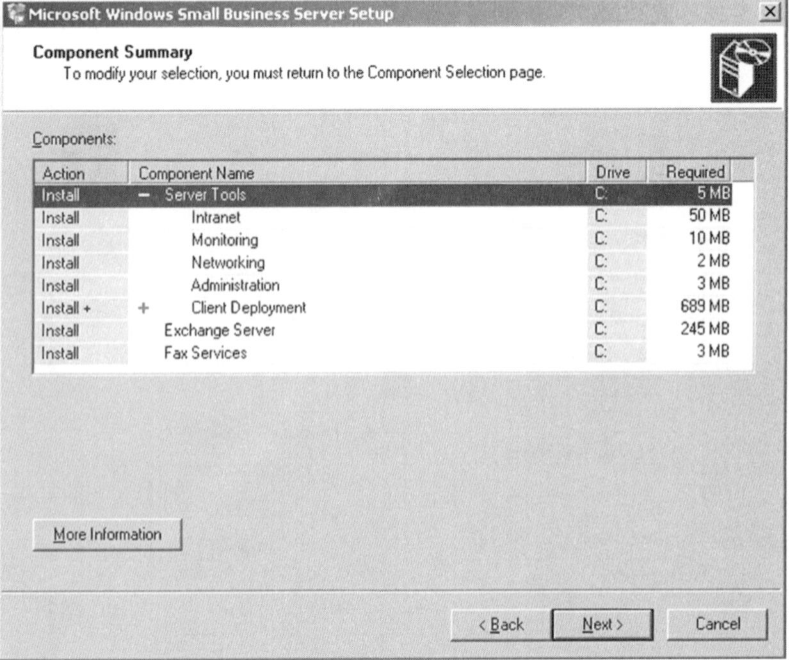

BEST PRACTICE: Those of you who are "old-timers" should recognize that the last few steps of the SBS setup process are much leaner than SBS 2000, where there were several more screens. Some of this has occurred because wizard pages have been consolidated. This also appears to be the case because ISA Server 2000 and SQL Server 2000 weren't installed by default (this chapter is demonstrating the standard edition of SBS 2003). In the last section of the book, which is dedicated to the premium edition of SBS 2003, I speak to installing the premium applications. Also—my Advanced SBS 2003 text due in mid-2004 will address the premium edition in much greater detail.

Figure 3-23
This is the heavy lifting!

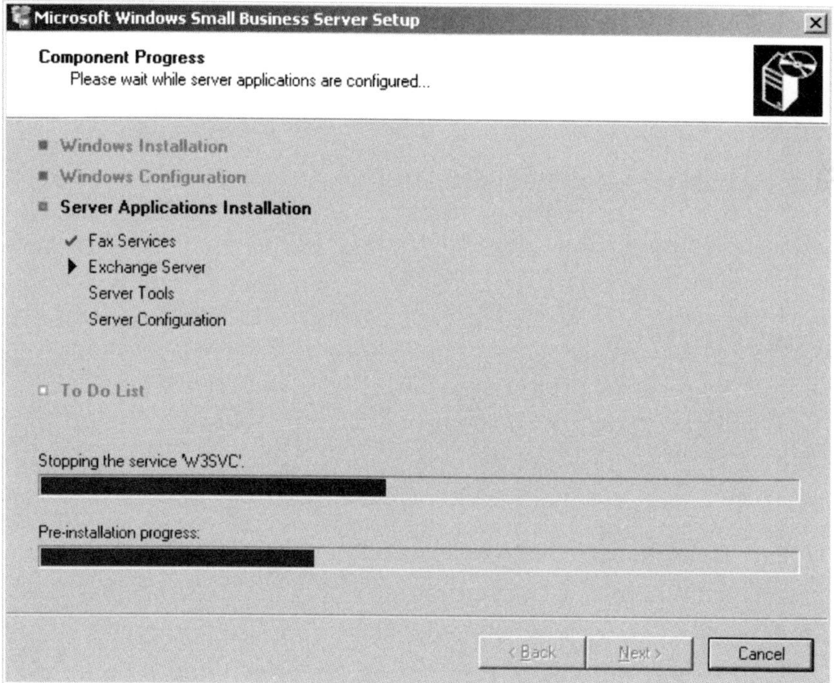

26. When requested, insert Disc 2. Click **OK**.

BEST PRACTICE: Now go to lunch, friend! Disc 2 in the SBS 2003 setup process is primarily focused on Exchange Server 2003 and the Active Directory modifications can take upwards of 30 minutes in an unattended mode! This is shown in Figure 3-24. See you back here soon.

Figure 3-24
Exchange modifies Active Directory here during setup.

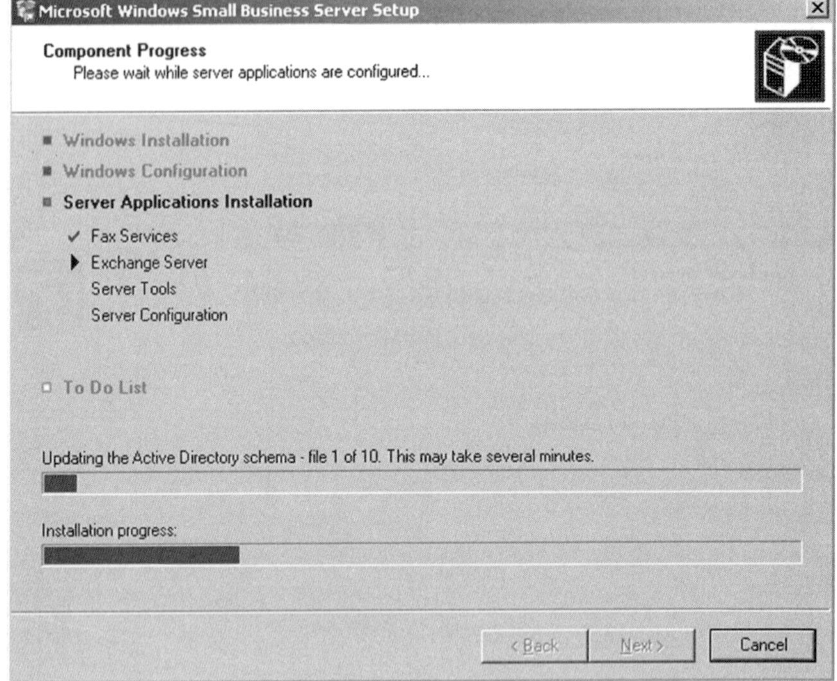

Okay, so you're back. Note when you return it's likely that the server machine console was "locked" as a security best practice, because there was no mouse or keyboard activity for a significant amount of time. Perform the logon sequence (Ctrl-Alt-Del) and type in the Administrator's password of Husky9999!.

27. When requested, insert Disc 3. Click **OK**.

28. When requested, insert **Microsoft Office Outlook 2003 CD** (which is effectively Disc 4) and click **OK**. This is shown in Figure 3-25.

Figure 3-25
This is the fourth disc from the SBS 2003 disc media.

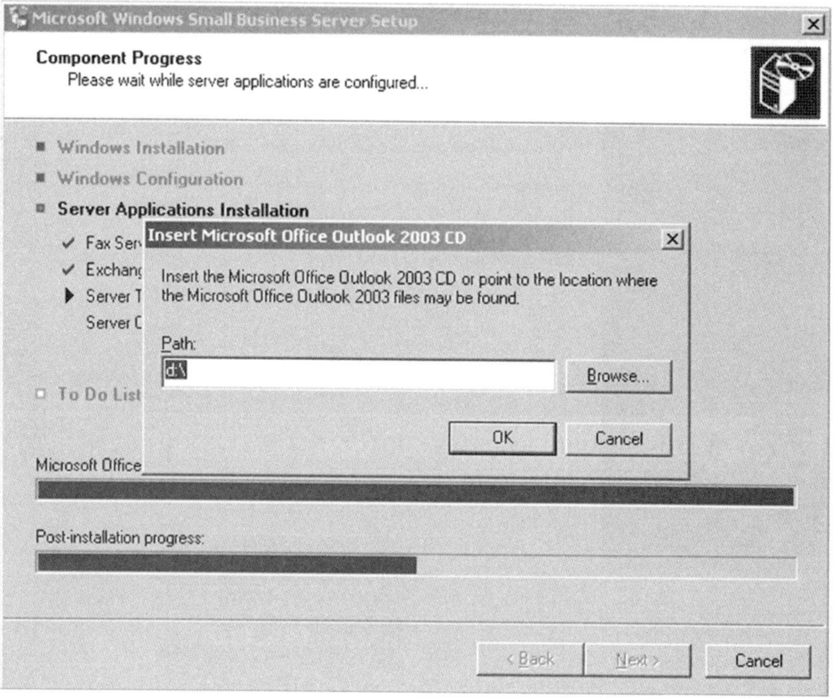

Microsoft Windows Small Business Server Setup

Component Progress
Please wait while server applications are configured...

Windows Installation
Windows Configuration
Server Applications Installation
Fax Ser
Exchan
Server T
Server C
To Do List

Insert Microsoft Office Outlook 2003 CD

Insert the Microsoft Office Outlook 2003 CD or point to the location where the Microsoft Office Outlook 2003 files may be found.

Path:
d:\

Browse...
OK Cancel

Microsoft Office

Post-installation progress:

< Back Next > Cancel

Notes:

29. The **Finishing Your Installation** page will appear as seen in Figure 3-26. Click **Finish**.

Figure 3-26
You're basically finished and just about to start the configuration of SBS 2003.

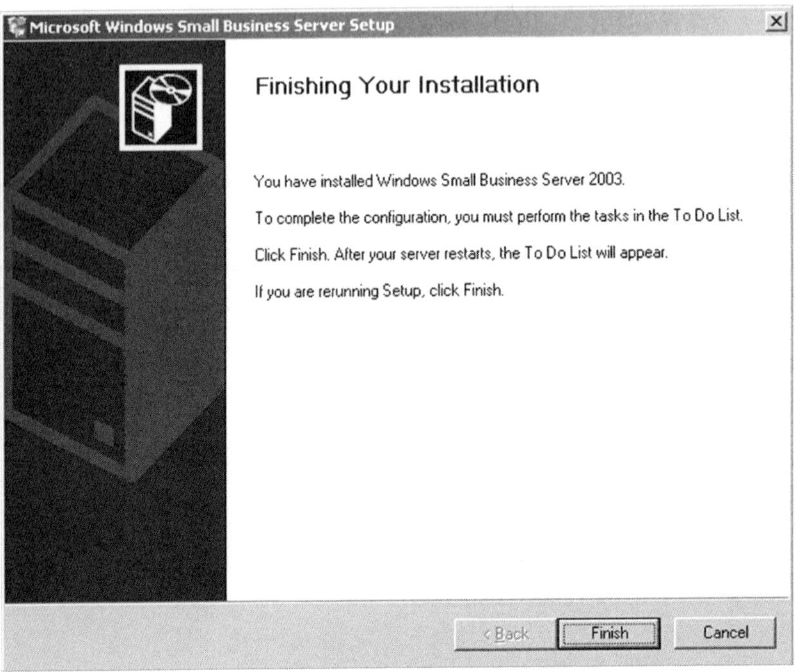

BEST PRACTICE: If for some reason you've had a faulty installation with failed components, the **Components Messages** screen will be displayed describing the failure. After reading this screen, click **Next** to continue.

If your SBS installation was unsuccessful, you must stop and troubleshoot the failed components. Typically, a reinstallation of the failed components will cure the problem. However, I've had to call Microsoft's Product Support Services (PSS) in the past to solve the really tough ones!

Specific to SBS 2003, I had a failed installed in a test lab where the second disc wasn't detected correctly and Exchange didn't install on the first pass. I reran the SBS 2003 setup and Exchange correctly installed on the second pass. But shortly thereafter, I noticed that the new cool company-related Public Folder (Springer Spaniels Unlimited Archive) and the company contacts (Springer Spaniels Unlimited Contacts) weren't created because the script to create those apparently doesn't run on a second pass of the SBS 2003 setup wizard. So I manually created these Public Folder objects (which I discuss much more in Chapter 6) and all was well. The only other setup oddity I've experienced to date derives from this same second pass scenario. Apparently, the Shared Fax Service, which did correctly install on "round two" wasn't completely whole. When I clicked the Configure Fax link from the To Do List, the fax configuration wizard failed because it said the Shared Fax Service wasn't installed (even though it was installed and running at the time). I share these insights with you so you'll not fall victim to your own imagination if you encounter setup problems (that is, you're not imaging what is happening to you because it might have happened to me!).

30. Click **OK** when notified that setup must restart your computer. The core SBS 2003 setup is now complete. Take a bow!

BEST PRACTICE: Be sure to remove the fourth disc from the disc drive at this point and store it safely with your other SBS 2003 media.

So assuming otherwise that all went well, let me be the first to say congratulations! You have now completed the base installation of your SBS server machine using the SPRINGERS methodology. Now, more configuration items await you.

BEST PRACTICE: After the computer restarts, SBS performs some background housekeeping duties. Don't be alarmed. These are one-time configuration events.

SBS is completely installed. When the logon dialog box is displayed, provide your username (**Administrator**) and password (**Husky9999!**).

Time Flies (Not!)

The basic SBS setup process from Phase A to the end of Phase D should take anywhere from 90 to 240 minutes, depending on the speed of your computer. I've noticed installation time breaks down as follows:

Phase A — Windows 2000 Server Character-Based Setup: 15 percent

Phase B — Windows 2000 Server GUI-Based Setup: 20 percent

Phase C — SBS Installation and Setup: 60 percent

Phase D — SBS Completion and Initial Boot: 5 percent

Guest Column

CRN Test Center Review: Small Business Server 2003

By Frank J. Ohlhorst

With the release of Small Business Server 2003 expected on Oct. 9, Microsoft has fired a shot across the bow of the SMB server appliance market. The new, slimmed-down version of SBS 2003 standard edition offers everything most small businesses would need, and at an attractive price point, making the product an alternative to low-priced, proprietary server appliances.

Microsoft has gone to great lengths to integrate key back-office applications into SBS 2003, without overly complicating the product, reducing initial setup to less than 15 minutes when purchased with OEM server hardware bundles. Aggressive hardware bundling deals from leading server vendors should bring the overall cost of a new five-user SBS 2003 standard edition server to less than $1,500, while the reduction in administrative and setup chores helps to greatly reduce installation costs.

SBS 2003 standard edition combines Windows Server 2003 with Exchange 2003, Share Point Services, networking, faxing, a network health monitor and several other components aimed at easing administration and setup. The premium edition adds ISA Server, SQL Server and a specialized edition of BizTalk 2004. Both versions of SBS 2003 are limited to single-server installations and 75 users.

CRN Test Center engineers put SBS 2003 standard edition through its paces and were impressed with the improvements offered. Starting with an HP Proliant server configured with an OEM install of SBS 2003 standard edition, Test Center engineers were able to set up a basic SBS 2003 network in less than 45 minutes, including configuring Internet access, VPN connectivity and five user accounts.

The basic installation process shows that Microsoft has accepted the fact that many businesses now use broadband connections that leverage broadband routers.

The Test Center used a D-Link DI-624 broadband router connected to a cable modem as the interface to the Internet. SBS 2003's installation wizard recognized that router using universal plug and play and then offered several scenarios to best integrate the device into the network. Test Center engineers chose to have DHCP assignments remain with the D-Link router and then configured port forwarding on the router to pass specific services on to the SBS 2003 server.

The key advantage offered by that setup is that solution providers can leverage an existing hardware firewall, without overcomplicating the deployment of an SBS 2003 network. Furthermore, solution providers could choose to integrate a broadband security appliance into the mix to perform content filtering, ant-virus filtering and antispam technology. In the past, most of those services were installed directly on the server, impacting performance and further complicating deployments.

Setting up VPN access was just as easy. Test Center engineers simply used the "configure remote access" wizard found on the setup "to do" list to add VPN functionality. That wizard offered to use DHCP assignments from the D-Link router, further simplifying setup. The only caveat concerned setting up appropriate port forwarding on the router to pass PPTP VPN traffic on to the server.

Solution providers looking to support SBS 2003 networks remotely will appreciate not only the ease of VPN setup, but also the inclusion of remote desktop support. That feature can be set up to work with or without VPN functionality. Furthermore, SBS 2003 offers the ability to establish remote desktop connections to Windows XP professional workstations located on the network. That feature adds the ability to establish a remote workforce or to remotely troubleshoot desktop options. Microsoft could have scored big if that connectivity could have been extended to Windows XP's Remote Assistance capability, a true remote control application suitable for remote training and support. For those wanting true remote control, products such as PCanywhere or GotomyPC will be required.

One of the limitations often encountered by broadband users is the lack of a static public IP address. That limitation prevents the registration of public domain name that can be assigned to the SBS 2003 server. Test Center engineers overcame that problem by using Tzolkien's TZO service, a Dynamic DNS provider. That service runs as a small client application on the server and associates a domain name with the assigned public IP address and updates that association whenever an ISP issues a new IP address to a broadband connected device. For those looking to host Web sites, or use services remotely, Dynamic DNS becomes a key add-on element.

Simplicity abounds throughout SBS 2003. Wizards to add users, set up shares, modify security and many other tasks ensure that even a technician with basic knowledge can deploy SBS 2003. The product's enhanced simplicity does come at a cost for solution providers: a reduction in billable installation and configuration hours, along with a reduction in billable support costs. But, that is also the case with most server appliances on the market at this time.

For most businesses, the combination of the standard edition of SBS 2003 and a broadband router should be adequate and offers probably the best platform for business tasks. Solution providers should only consider the premium edition if there is a distinct need for SQL Server or if it is possible to leverage business-process management chores using BizTalk. All things considered, SBS 2003 hits the nail on the head when it comes to networking small businesses.

The To Do List Lives!

After you successfully log on for the first time, the SBS To Do List, on a page titled "**Complete the configuration**" shown in Figure 3-27 automatically appears.

Figure 3-27
To Do List is your starting point for the SBS deployment experience.

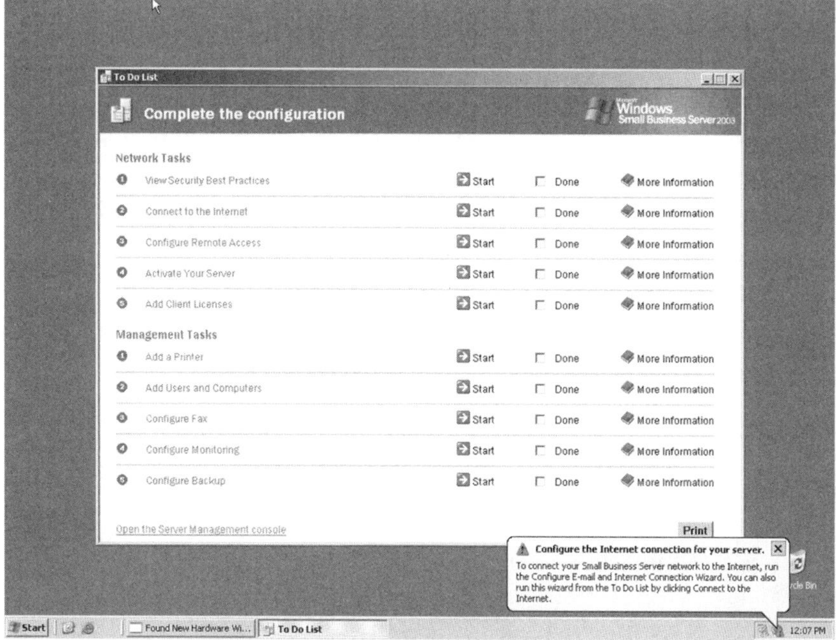

BEST PRACTICE: Also at this stage, a "balloon" appears in the lower right advising you to configure the Internet connection for your server. This is the second link on the To Do List titled "Connect to the Internet," which we'll do in just a moment. You may close the lower left balloon.

In the Chapter 4 I pick up the SBS deployment process using the SPRINGERS methodology. You will also complete the To Do List and learn about the Server Management console.

Advanced SBS Setup Issues

After you've installed SBS several times, you'll likely recognize many of the following advanced SBS setup issues. It's also likely you'll see a thing or two not mentioned here. If so, be sure to share your wisdom with some of the SBS newsgroups and mailing lists listed in Appendix A, "SBS Resources." Let's face it—SBS is an evolving culture (oh, and an evolving product too), so you'll some day, some way, have something to share with the SBS community.

OEM Setup Scenario

Microsoft is perhaps most proud in the SBS 2003 time frame of its improvements to the Original Equipment Manufacturer (OEM) Prenstallation Kit (OPK). SBS 2003 can be set up out of the box in about 15 minutes because of an Active Directory improvement that allows for renaming the computer and domain post-SBS installation. Needless to say, this might change how you view SBS 2003's deployment both as a customer and a consultant. See you in Appendix E where I discuss the OEM approach more (with screenshots!).

BEST PRACTICE: Okay—last mention of my *SMB Consulting Best Practices* book, but I truly go into the consulting ramifications of the shorter SBS 2003 setup cycle in said text and how to make money at it as an SMB/SBS consultant. 'Nough said!

One Source for Source Media

Two topics, not part of the detailed SPRINGERS methodology, are nonetheless of interest to the SBSer. First, you can copy all four SBS 2003 CD Discs to a partition on your server (e.g., Drive D) and perform the installation from this location. Why would you do this? Because this prevents you from having to swap the discs during the later steps of the SBS setup process. And just how did I learn this, you ask? Let's just say necessity is the mother of invention. When developing a training course whereby students would actually perform the installation, I concluded that the SBS 2003 source installation files should be located on a second partition. Why? Because this prevented delays in the class when students forgot to swap discs (e.g., students take a coffee break and the machine simply waits for the next disc). Also, hard disk input/output (I/O) is significantly faster than CD disc I/O, resulting in a faster, in-class SBS installation experience. (This is important when you're trying to teach SBS 2003 in a one-day course format, let me tell you!)

Second, if your server is a late-model cream puff, to borrow terms from the automotive industry, you might be able to use the DVD media that ships with SBS 2003. This single DVD disc contains all of the SBS source installation media at a single source. Unfortunately, most of my small business clients don't drive such cream puffs, but you get the point here: A late model server machine may well have a DVD device installed, saving setup time.

The Exchange Server 2003 Pre-Prep Maneuver

Another hidden hook in the SBS 2003 setup process is to save time in the later steps by "pre-preparing" Active Directory for Exchange Server 2003. You may recall that one of the longest phases in the later part of the SBS 2003 setup process was the amount of time Exchange Server 2003 took to modify the Active Directory schema. This time can be minimized (but not completely eliminated) by running a command after the Windows Configuration routine early in the SBS 2003 setup phase completes. Here are the steps to run this command that modifies the Active Directory schema for Exchange Server 2003 before the SBS Setup Wizard proceeds to install the applications.

1. Place SBS Setup Disc #2 in the CD drive on the SBS server machine.
2. Assuming you are logged on as the Administrator, click **Start**, **Run**, **Browse**.
3. Navigate to the following location: **\exchsrvr65\setup\i386\setup.exe**. Click **Open** to close the **Browse** dialog box.
4. In the **Open** field of the **Run** dialog box, append the command with **/Forest Prep**, so the total command would appear as **\exchsrvr65\setup\i386\setup.exe /Forest Prep**.
5. Click **OK** and the command will execute. The Active Directory schema will be prepared for Exchange Server 2003.

So the big question is, why would you do this? Simply stated, you would do this if you wanted to save time during the last part of the SBS setup process. I've done this so that when I demonstrate the SBS setup process to clients and students, we don't have to spend up to (or more than) 30 minutes watching Exchange Server 2003 prepare the Active Directory schema. Let me tell you, when you are in front of a crowd, those minutes seem like hours!

Unsupported Devices

Every SBS installation has a right way and a wrong way to do it. There is the easy way and the hard way. There is the "follow the rules way" and the "break the rules" way. Surprisingly, you're likely to try, suffer, cheer, celebrate, and curse all approaches during your tenure as an SBS guru. So far, I've demonstrated only the SPRINGERS methodology for installing SBS (which I believe to be a "best practices" methodology for installing SBS). Now, and I'm addressing the most advanced guru SBSers amongst us, let's break the rules and understand why you would do so.

Without question, one of the greatest SBS installation challenges today is that of managing your library of current drivers from third-party vendors. By that I mean, when you install and maintain SBS, you have the latest drivers from the vendors of the components attached to your system. This is extremely important because operating systems are built and released at a certain point in time. Although the periodic release of service packs allows the operating system to refresh its library of drivers, in no way can an operating system hope to ship with the latest and most current drivers from all of the third-party vendors. It's a common and daunting challenge that confronts system engineers everywhere.

What's the bottom line? If you have unusual or new drivers, you need to specify **F6** when installing SBS in the early character-based setup screen (immediately after the character-based setup process commences, which would be while disk 1 is still in the floppy drive if you selected to set up SBS with the four disks instead of booting directly from the CD disc) when you are asked to specify additional controller and adapter cards. And when you communicate that you want to specify drivers, you often have to specify the drivers for existing controller and adapter cards, because the setup's auto-detection has not been stopped. That is, once you press **F6**, you'll likely have to specify all controller and adapter cards, not just the unsupported one you were trying to add.

BEST PRACTICE: So of course there must be a Texas tale to accompany this section, and here it is. There I was on a sweaty summer Saturday afternoon installing SBS (prior version, but example still applies here) at an accounting firm called "CFO2Go" in Bothell, Washington. For some strange reason, the SBS installation kept "hanging" or stopping right when the networking components were being installed. It was all very strange and I tried the setup a couple of times. No luck. I even tried installing the DNS, DHCP, and WINS services manually thinking something was hung up there. Heck, I even tried manually installing Terminal Services in Remote Administration Mode. Lo and behold, it turns out the SCSI card was an older Adaptec brand card that had been misidentified by the underling Windows operating system during setup (this was actually Windows 2000 Server). Once I downloaded the correct and supported Adaptec driver for Windows 2000 Server, it worked just fine and I was able to sail right past my blockage. Clearly this isn't an SBS 2003 example, but is included here for reference purposes to help you think how you might solve some setup failures (if any should occur) in SBS 2003.

Upgrading to SBS

No setup chapter would be complete without a tip of the hat to the upgrade process. Because it's not explicitly part of the SPRINGERS methodology, I've moved that discussion to Appendix B of this book. I'll see you there!

Troubleshooting Setup Errors

In your career as an SBS professional, you will possibly have occasion to troubleshoot setup errors. These errors come out of left field, but the Readme.htm document contained on Small Business Server 2003 Setup Disc 1 discusses a surprisingly large number of setup errors and the suggested resolution steps (I discuss this document early in this chapter). Hats off to the SBS development team for shipping this timely resource in time!

You may also want to consult the SBS resources listed in Appendix A to stay current with SBS 2003 setup issues. Heck, don't hesitate to throw in your own two cents in the discussion group and news list (listserv) mentioned.

And consider simply rerunning the SBS setup, as I discussed earlier, as your first line of attack in curing a problem.

BEST PRACTICE: And don't forget that a book is outdated the day I type its final words. The technology world changes quickly and you'll want to visit the Microsoft TechNet page to stay current with all the latest and updated knowledge related to SBS 2003. So no flames, masking as reader replies on Amazon.com, saying that my book doesn't discuss some future issue you encounter in the Year 2005 with SBS 2003.

Summary

As you reach the end of the SBS server machine setup and installation discussion, remember to go forward keeping a healthy perspective. Often I witness SBS professionals spending hours troubleshooting some setup- or installation-related problem. In many cases, that is not a good use of time. Remember that it often takes less than three hours to do a complete SBS server machine reinstall. Believe me, I've done plenty of fresh SBS installs and come out hours ahead. Just a thought!

Chapter 4
SBS 2003 Deployment and Management Tools

Congratulations to you, good friends! You're well on your way to a completed, functional, and optimally performing SBS 2003 network. But a few important deployment and management tasks remain, including completing the items on the To Do List and discovering the powers of the Server Management console. This task area shouldn't be marginalized. Whereas you possibly performed the SBS 2003 server machine setup out of sight (and hearing range) from your end users, you don't have that same luxury with the final deployment tasks and the workstation setup phase you are about to undertake. Your role will be very public, and so will the users' feedback. So, slow down, pardner, and take the extra time needed to get it right.

BEST PRACTICE: Let me take a moment to reiterate a key point to our time together in the SBS tome. As you work through this and other chapters, understand that the book is based on the SPRINGERS methodology (the sample SBS client based on Bainbridge Island, Washington).

The idea is that you spend the time upfront with this book creating a successful SBS network for a sample company following every keystroke in every chapter. It is paramount you try to follow through with each example and task. At the end of the book, you're a bona fide SBSer as far as I'm concerned. I also understand that your real world SBS experience will be slightly different from mine with my beloved dogs. You'll work on different equipment under different conditions. In fact, Microsoft reports that the majority of SBS sales are international, so you're likely setting up SBS in a different country than I or my Springer Spaniels live in. (And, by golly, perhaps your country favors different breeds of dogs - cool!)

More important, where possible I try to compare and contrast different SBS features and functions, but sometimes I'll bypass some esoteric alternative path to accomplish a task in the spirit of maintaining the purity of my SPRINGERS methodology. All I can say is that some excellent advanced resources that explore every conceivable SBS feature and function, starting with the online help system, exist for your academic researching pleasure. Thanks in advanced for your understanding (and no flames on Amazon, please, as I've taken this moment to manage your expectations). Long live SPRINGERS!

Meet Server Management Console

Microsoft has changed (okay - improved) the management console concept in SBS 2003 compared to prior SBS releases. What has occurred is that, based on experience and tons of feedback from SBSers like you, strong emphasis is placed on completing all network deployment and management tasks from the Server Management console, which is displayed in Figure 4-1.

Notes:

Figure 4-1
Meet the Server Management console. Play nice as you'll be using this interface forever more to manage your SBS-based network.

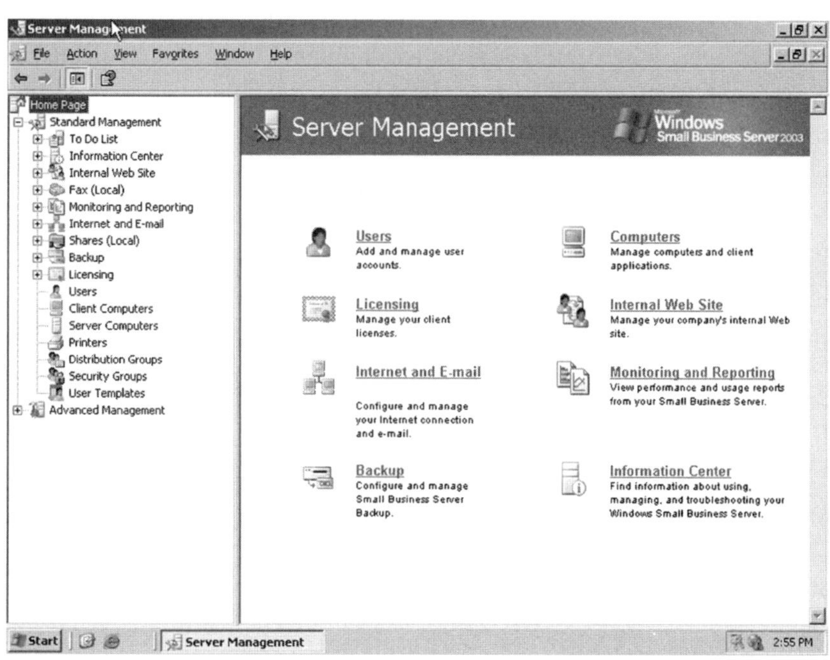

In a past SBS book, I took tens of pages to describe the SBS console in its various forms and functionality. But in writing these words, I discovered I can quickly convey what the console is all about in far fewer pages, a true testament to the SBS development team trying to simplify the console experience for the SBSer. I liken it to this. I can now describe the Server Management console in a short elevator ride. Let's now take that elevator ride together as I present the Server Management console by discussing its two major divisions: Standard Management and Advanced Management.

Standard Management

Consider this both the "noun" and the "verb" of the Server Management console. The objects listed here are "things" you do such as faxing. What's important to understand here is that you are not exposed to the application name at this time (e.g., Exchange). Microsoft has, in its wisdom that I respect here, elected to be task-oriented, such as Backup (i.e., Backup is something that we "do"). The components of Standard Management are described below.

- To Do List. This is covered in extensive detail in the next section but cuts to the heart of the SBS 2003 deployment methodology. Read on whilst I write on.

- Information Center. This is your SBS portal for seeking help or more information. You can click over to Microsoft update site, view internal documentation, click over to the SBS public product Web site at Microsoft and commence an online technical support request.

- Internal Web Site. This allows you to manage your Windows SharePoint Services internal Web site. I'll feature many of the links on this page in Chapter 7.

- Fax (Local). This obviously relates to the SBS 2003 faxing function which is awesome. I cover this area in Chapter 9.

- Monitoring and Reporting. Covered in more detail in Chapter 12, this relates to configuring the Server Status Report and the Health Monitor tool in SBS 2003.

- Internet and E-mail. This is the page for all matters related to Internet connectivity and e-mail. We'll spend some time here in Chapters 6 and 10.

- Shares (Local). Not surprisingly, this page displays the folders that are shared on the SBS server including administrative (hidden) shares that end with the dollar sign ($) in the share name. I'll mention it in Chapter 11 again, but be advised that the View Connected Users on this page is the easiest way to discover who is currently logged on the network.

- Backup. WOW! Much improved in SBS 2003, this is where the backup and data protection experience commences. Lots of discussion on this in Chapter 11.

- Licensing. A few changes here that I think you'll like. No longer is client access licensing information hidden on an "About..." dialog box (as it was in SBS 2000). No sir! It's now presented front and center on the Manage Client Access Licenses from the Licensing link.

BEST PRACTICE: Client Access Licenses (CALs) have really changed in SBS 2003. First, there are two types of CALs: devices and users. Long-time SBSers are familiar with device-based management, where a certain number of client computers are allowed on the network (say 55 PCs based on the number of CALs you have purchased for the SBS 2003 network).

User-based licensing is new to us SBSers and might be implemented under a scenario where device-based licensing doesn't make sense. For example, imagine a small software development company with ten employees using SBS 2003. Each employee has four PCs for development and testing purposes (for a total of 40 devices). Here the customer is better off by using the user-based licensing and purchasing ten CALs.

So you want more licensing chatter? You can mix and match device and user-based licensing to optimize the amount of bucks you drop on CALs, pardner! And remember that the licensing model is EXACTLY THE SAME as Windows Server 2003 which helped me when I had to learn about SBS 2003 licensing and then proceed to go out and give speeches on it. So in addition to the licensing discussion found at the main SBS 2003 Web page (from the Information Center link above), you are highly encouraged to view the traditional Windows Server 2003 CAL licensing discussion at www.microsoft.com/windowsserver2003/howtobuy/licensing/caloverview.mspx.

Other licensing tidbits include the online purchase of CALs and the elimination of the CAL licensing diskette (thank you). You purchase CALs by the five pack (as was the case in the SBS 2000 time frame).

Note in my advanced SBS 2003 book, due mid-2004, I'll delve deep into the depths of SBS licensing, but for the purposes of this book and SPRINGERS, this is far enough for now! Also be advised that I won't have you add more CALs to the SPRINGERS network as part of this step-by-step book (even though you add ten users later in the chapter). That's because I never have you log on more than one user at a time as we work through this SBS tome.

- Users. This link displays the Manage Users page where much of the support and configuration for users can occur.
- Client Computers. This link displays the Manage Client Computers page.

BEST PRACTICE: Aside from your performing client computer management duties here, this is the one place that you can start the Setup Computer Wizard (SCW) natively without having to rerun the Add User Wizard (to which the SCW is chained). Huh? Say that again and don't use ten dollar words?!?! Okay - what I meant to say is that if you have a user, let's call her "Sally," and she purchases a new HP laptop, you really only want to run the SCW to add existing user Sally's new HP laptop. You don't need to run Add User Wizard to get to the SCW to configure Sally's new HP laptop. If this still doesn't make sense, it will later in the life of SBS when users start to replace client computers. Trust me.

BEST PRACTICE: Each release of SBS has a "paradigm" combined with a "raison d'etre" (which I'll call a "paradigm d'etre"). In the first releases, SBS was the BackOffice bundle at a competitive price. The SBS 2000 time frame had "server-side stability" as its reason for being. SBS 2003 has a couple of paradigm shifts and I'll share one here: client computer setup. Here's what I mean. In the SBS 2000 time frame, there was such an emphasis on the server-side that the client computers were much ignored. The damn Define Computer Applications link from the SBS 2000 To Do List basically didn't work. And the SBS 2000 To Do List and consoles didn't natively take advantage of Group Policy Objects (GPOs). That's all changed in SBS 2003 where client computer setup, configuration, and management received much attention! The results show.

I'll share another SBS 2003 paradigm d'etre in just a moment.

- Server Computers. This is the interface for the management of server computers.

BEST PRACTICE: There is nothing like timing in business. As I was writing this chapter, I was working with my client, a cardiology clinic, who wanted to move to SBS 2003. In the planning phase, the managing doctor (that's Dr. Paul to you) held the belief that SBS can be the only server on the network. Such is not the case, as you have member servers and even other domain controllers on the network (as I discussed earlier in Chapter 1). However, you can have only one SBS 2003 server machine on the network.

So, assuming you might have additional server computers on an SBS 2003 network, how might you manage them? From the Server Computers link we're discussing right here, right now!

- Printers. Printers are printers (what can I say?). Once the primary reason we even had networks in small businesses (to share printers), printers are managed here. This is also where you manage the fax device that we treat like a printer.

- Distribution Groups. You use distribution groups to send e-mail to a specific set of people. By default, everyone you add to the SBS network will appear in the default distribution group named after the information you provided in the Organization field in Figure 3-4 earlier in this book (when you were in the GUI-based phase of the Windows Server 2003 setup). In the case of SPRINGERS, the default distribution group would be called Springer Spaniels Limited.

- Security Groups. This relates to grouping users together for the purpose of granting permissions. For example, the folks in the bookkeeping department might belong to a security group called Accounting that has specific permissions related to the Timberline accounting folder. Please click over and view all the security groups created by default in SBS 2003. (Hint: There should be 22 security groups by default which would make a great exam question.)

BEST PRACTICE: You might not have known that security groups are actually e-mail enabled by default in SBS 2003. You would care about this because, for instance, the Accounting security group example I mention above might be the same group of people whom you want to receive an important e-mail about a Timberline accounting upgrade, etc., and you wouldn't need to plop all these folks in a new distribution group to accomplish this. Rather, you could simply e-mail the security group (which should be security@springersltd.com by default once you create such a security group).

- User Templates. User templates are really nothing more than a disabled user account that has certain settings you want to easily apply to new user accounts you are creating. Each of the templates is self-explanatory by reading the Description field on the Manage Templates page that appears. However, what is interesting is the addition of the Mobile User Template to provide remote access support for worthy users.

BEST PRACTICE: Time for another paradigm d'etre! So another big deal in SBS 2003 is the support for mobile worker bees. The Mobile User Template is only the start of how this paradigm d'etre plays out, and I continue the mobility discussion in Chapter 8.

BEST PRACTICE: Around when SBS 2003 was being released in October 2003, I was teaching a hands-on lab in Orange County, California, when a student, totally enthusiastic about SBS 2003, asked if he could fine-tune a user template on his SBS 2003 network and then deploy it in its exact form at his customer SBS network sites. That is, suppose he sold a customer relationship management (CRM) application that required specific settings, could it be created once and cloned over to his customer base? The answer is yes. You'd create a user template on the master network and use the Export Templates link (to launch the Export Templates Wizard) and get the configuration out to a floppy disk (the export function assumes Drive A: by default) or a USB hard disk key (my favorite approach to transfer information in the 21st century!).

To import the user template at the customer site, just reverse the process - click the Import Templates link and complete the Import Templates Wizard.

Notes:

Advanced Management

It is under Advanced Management that the "native tools" you need to interact with SBS 2003 are exposed. For those of you who worked with SBS in the 4.x era, you'll recall that it was more difficult to utilize the native tools (and some native tools even crippled SBS 4.x!). That, of course, changed in the last two SBS releases, wherein native tools are placed front and center for your benefit. The components of Advanced Management, as listed on the left panel of Figure 4-2, are described below.

Figure 4-2
The focus in this figure is the Advanced Management components.

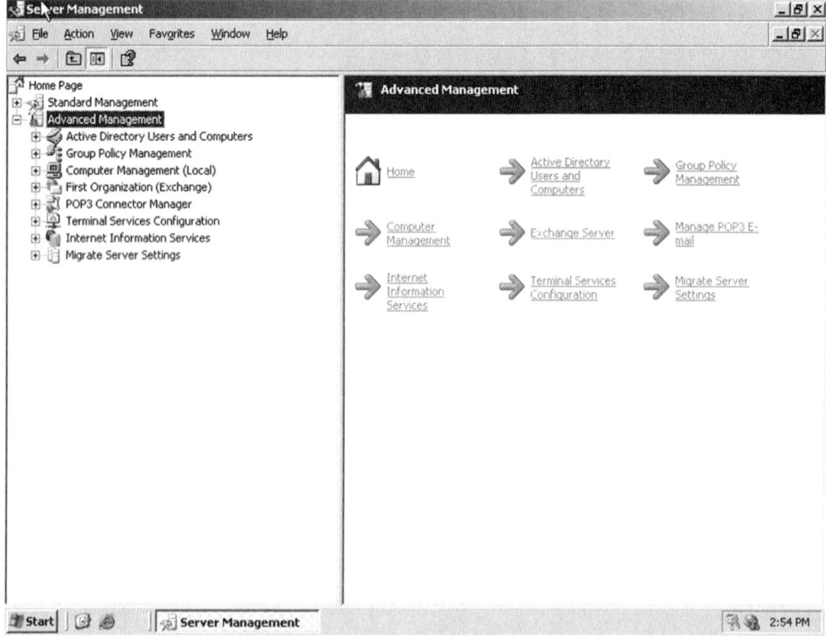

- Active Directory Users and Computers. Ah, every MCSE certification candidate has likely committed to memory this tool that is the primary interface for managing objects in Active Directory such as users and groups.

BEST PRACTICE: A hands-on lab instructor for whom I have the utmost respect has an interesting take on Active Directory Users and Computers. He believes that it is the primary approach to managing the messaging function on a server computer with Exchange Server 2003 installed. What? I'll explain this more in Chapter 6, but take a moment to look at the Exchange-related tabs that appear when you view a user object in **Active Directory Users and Computers** when you've selected **Advanced Features** under the **View** menu. You'll see four Exchange-related tabs. Then ask yourself where you do most of your Exchange-related management on a day-to-day basis. I do believe you'll agree that you do it here, pardner!

- Group Policy Management. Remember that paradigm d'etre we discussed earlier about support for client computer configuration? Yep! That is again manifested by the Group Policy Management page.

- Computer Management (Local). Lots of great reasons to get to know this object, including the ability to manage your hard disks and start and stop services. I'll explore this tool more in Chapter 11.

- First Organization (Exchange)/SPRINGERSLTD (Exchange). This is System Manager in Exchange Server 2003, where I can't deny many Exchange-related tasks are performed. Let's hold off further discussion until Chapter 6.

- POP3 Connector Manager. Hail to Charlie, a senior member of the SBS development team who owns the POP3 Connector Manager in SBS 2003. This allows you to download e-mails from POP3 servers (typically located at your ISP). This is discuss more in Chapter 6.

- Terminal Services Configuration. This tool could be used to modify the default Terminal Services configuration in SBS 2003 (which is in Remote Administration Mode). I'll discuss Terminal Services more in Chapter 11.

- Internet Information Services. Yes - Internet Information Services (IIS) is alive and well in SBS 2003 and the focus in Chapter 10, so I'll wait until then to dive into the details.

- Migrate Server Settings. This page brings together all the cool settings you can migrate between SBS 2003 servers. This would, of course, benefit an SBM/SBS consultant who has perfect settings that he wants to easily share with customers. More on these settings in Chapter 11 and 12.

BEST PRACTICE: For a real good time, look at the menu shortcuts in the Server Management console. Click Favorites from the upper toolbar and look at the Standard Management and Advanced Management menu items. You might be surprised by what you see, such as the Sessions and Open Files items.

BEST PRACTICE: Don't forget that the Server Management console in SBS 2003 is based on Microsoft Management Console (MMC) 2.0 and that customization is possible. How? Simply place the Server Management console in Author mode and add a snap-in, such as the SQL Server Enterprise Manager. The location of the Server Manager console on which you would want to perform your modifications is:

%System Drive%\Program Files\Microsoft Windows Small Business Server\Administration\itprosbsconsole.msc

You would right-click the above file and select **Author** from the secondary menu to make your edits.

By the way, a little SBS culture here. Really, really early looks of SBS 2003 had the console being based on SharePoint technologies (e.g., Windows SharePoint Services). But in the final product, it's all MMC 2.0, baby!

Power User Console

And just when you thought they'd taken away the Personal Console from SBS 2000 days, I have news for you. If you really must have your "Personal Console," which is a dumbed-down version of Server Management called Server Management for Power Users, you can find it at the following location:

%System Drive%\Program Files\Microsoft Windows Small Business Server\Administration\mysbsconsole.msc

Personal console, I mean Server Management for Power Users, is automatically launched when a Power User logs on remotely via Terminal Services to perform server management tasks (this is shown in Figure 4-3). Note the Power User is totally locked into using Server Management for Power Users. If said Power User closes this console, they are immediately logged off the SBS server machine. Period.

Figure 4-3
A power user at SPRINGERS logs on to perform server-related work and uses Server Management for Power Users.

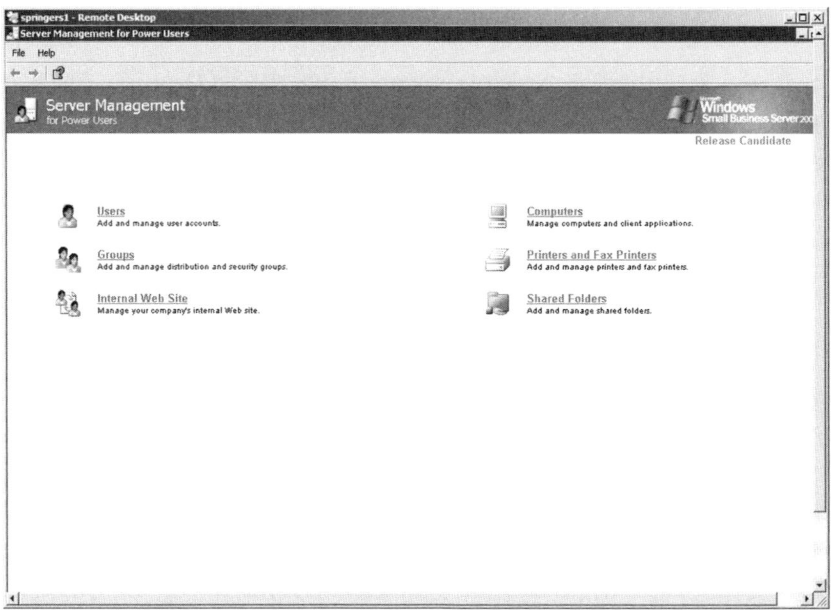

To Do List: In Order!

So with the finer points of Server Management console behind us, it's time to get down tonight! Let's start by planning the SBS 2003 Methodology ballad. Few things in the deployment of SBS exemplify the notion that SBS is a ready-made network in a box (or SMB consulting practice in a box for us consultants) than the existence and brilliance of the To Do List. We'll spend tons of time walking through the To Do List here.

But back to the brilliance part. The To Do List has been engineered to be your deployment approach for all of the SBS servers you'll ever install. You start at the top and work your way to the bottom. This structured approach, whether you install one or 1000 SBS server machines, should be honored. Don't be like a Boeing IT employee here in Seattle who likes to say, while installing SBS 2003 at her church over a weekend, "I don't use the To Do List or the Server Management console at Boeing, so we're not going to use it here on this holy site!" Such pompous thinking is truly short-sighted in successfully deploying SBS 2003 and can result in an unsatisfactory outcome. But BY FOLLOWING THE TO DO LIST, you can be assured of a positive outcome each and every time when you set up SBS 2003. You heard this breaking news here first!

So that said, let's start at the top and work down the To Do List. You'll start by noticing the To Do List is divided into Network Tasks and Management Tasks. That's because the SBS development team, in its wisdom, determined that folks wanted to see it play out that way with task sets divided between network and management.

> BEST PRACTICE: Note that you and I will indeed complete the To Do List in order as part of the SPRINGERS methodology. You would expect this. However, I don't have to walk through the entire To Do List in this chapter; instead, I'll take you through the first seven links. I leave the Configure Fax, Configure Monitoring, and Configure Backup links to be completed in order in later chapters.
>
> Remember the mantra, mates: Always complete the To Do List in order!

Network Tasks

There are five items under Network Tasks on the To Do List that we'll walk through right now.

View Security Best Practices

Talk about a future book! You could clearly write a thick tome on security on small business networks, but I'll leave that for another day. Rather, I point you to this link as a "primer" on top-of-mind security best practices to consider as you move forth in deploying your SBS network. In fact, it'd be good to visit this link with each SBS server you deploy so that you don't overlook a security best practice. When you select View Security Best Practices, you'll read details on the following 16 topics:

1. Protecting your network from the Internet by using a firewall
2. Configuring password policies
3. Configuring secure remote access to the network
4. Renaming the Administrator account
5. Implementing an antivirus solution
6. Managing backups
7. Updating your software
8. Running security tools
9. Granting access permissions
10. Educating users
11. Not using your Windows Small Business Server as a workstation
12. Physically securing the server
13. Limiting user disk space
14. Keeping up-to-date on security information
15. Auditing failed logon events and account lockouts
16. Using monitoring tools

BEST PRACTICE: Regarding item #13 above, you would want to know that SBS 2003 implements a disk quota for users in the Add User Wizard. Specifically, for a user the disk space is limited to 1024 MB and a warning is sent at 900 MB. This can be manually modified later.

When you complete reading this list, please close the Small Business Server Help and Information screen that is open and return to the To Do List. Check the **Done** box next to **View Security Best Practices** (you check off each To Do List item as its completed, which is a nice touch!).

Connect to the Internet

Continuing our way down the list, we actually have to "pause" on the list in the case of SPRINGERS, because we have a second network adapter card installed on our server machine that needs to be configured. You'll recall that two network adapter cards were present back when you installed SBS 2003 in Chapter 3. To configure the network adapter card, before continuing with the Connect to the Internet link, please perform the following tasks.

1. Log on as **Administrator** on **SPRINGERS1** with the password **Husky9999!** and click the **Start** button.
2. Click **Control Panel, Network Connections** and select **Network Connection**. This is the second network adapter card because the primary local network adapter card is called Server Local Area Connection by default. A Network Connection box will appear informing you the card is being enabled.
3. When notified by another Network Connection dialog box that the network adapter card can be configured by the E-mail and Internet Connection Wizard, click **Cancel** to not launch such a wizard, and allow the network adapter card to be configured manually.

BEST PRACTICE: So exactly what gives in Step #3 immediately above? Here's the deal. If you click Yes in the prior step, the E-mail and Internet Connection Wizard starts as you would expect. Then, when you get to the fourth screen of said wizard, the darn second network adapter card has been automatically enabled to receive its IP address dynamically. Truth be told by me to you, but it's unlikely in most cases that you'd want to acquire your IP address dynamically on the wild-side NIC (aka second network adapter card). Rather, you are far more likely to input a static IP address that your Internet Service Provider (ISP) gave to you for use on your SBS 2003 network. And that's the scoop, mates!

4. This is where the strange get weird. You've clicked Cancel, which killed the process underway from the steps above. Please repeat Step #2 again to select the **Network Connection** from the **Network**

Connections option in **Control Panel**. The **Network Connection Status** dialog box will appear.

5. Click **Properties**. Network Connection Properties will appear.
6. Select **Internet Protocol (TCP/IP)** and click **Properties**.
7. Complete the **General** tab of the **Internet Protocol (TCP/IP) Properties** sheet to reflect the following information (as shown in Figure 4-4). **IP address** is **207.202.238.215**, **Subnet Mask** address is **255.255.255.0** and the **Default Gateway** address is **207.202.238.1**. Make the **Preferred DNS** server **209.20.130.35** and make the **Alternate DNS** server **209.20.130.33**. Click **OK**.

Figure 4-4
Correctly configuring the second network adapter card for the SPRINGERS SBS network.

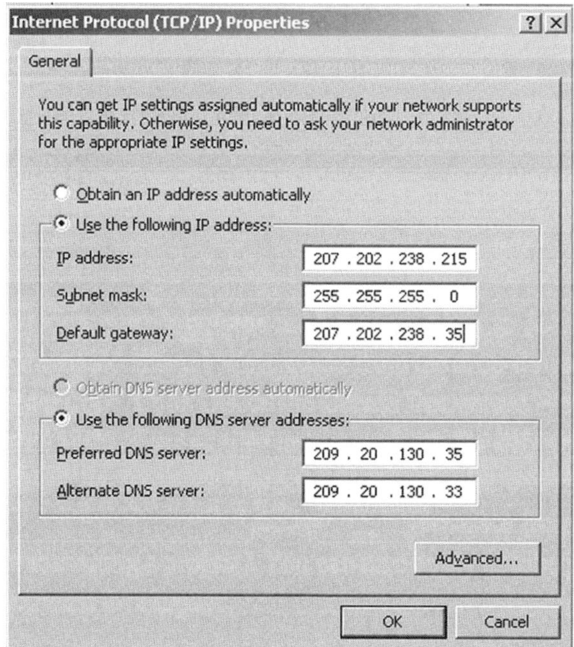

Note on page 4-21 I will explain how the Preferred DNS server field is reset to 192.168.16.2 by the EICW overriding your settings in Step #7 above.

8. Click **Close** twice (to return to your desktop).

It's now time to configure the e-mail and Internet connectivity capabilities in SBS 2003. Perform the following:

1. Click **Connect to the Internet** from the To **Do List** in **Server Management**.
2. The **Welcome to the Configure E-mail and Internet Connection Wizard** page appears. Take a moment to read about the information that is required to complete this wizard by clicking on the **Required Information for Connecting to the Internet** link (then close the help screen that appears). Click **Next**.
3. On the **Connection Type** screen, select **Broadband** and click **Next** as seen in Figure 4-5.

Figure 4-5
Select the Broadband choice on the Connection Type screen.

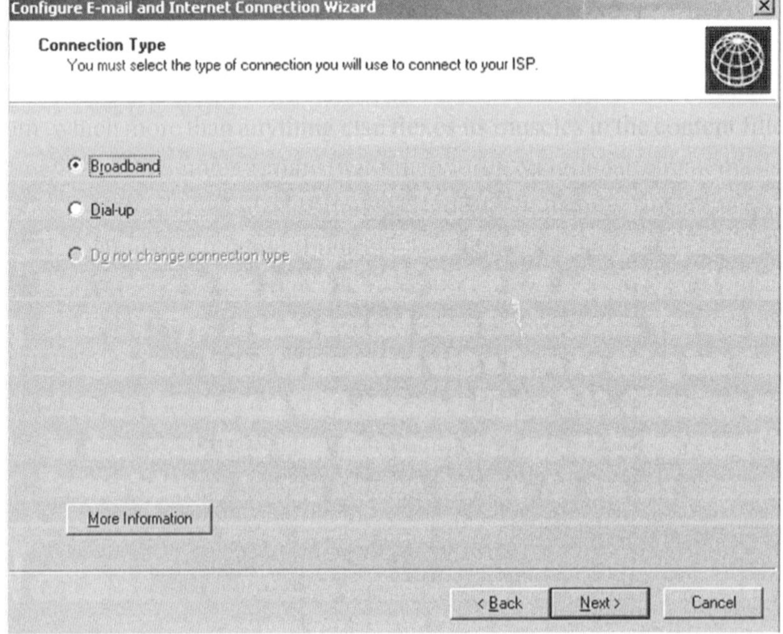

4. Select **A direct broadband connection** beneath **My server uses:** on the **Broadband Connection** page. Click **Next**. See Figure 4-6.
5. On the **Network Connection** page that appears, confirm that the ISP network connection reflects Network Connection with the IP address

of 207.202.238.215. Confirm the Local area network connection reflects the IP address of 192.168.16.2. This is shown in Figure 4-7. Click **Next**.

Figure 4-6
You will select a direct broadband connection for SPRINGERS.

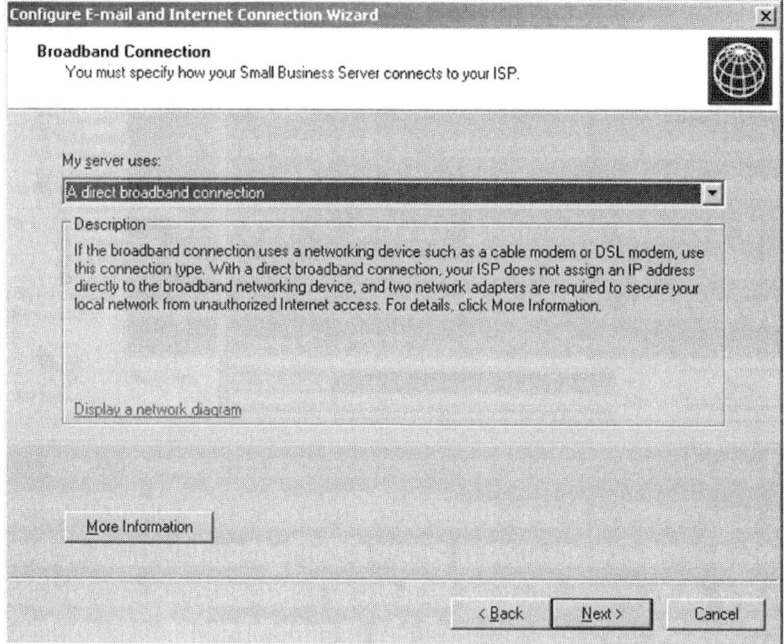

Figure 4-7
Take an extra moment to confirm your page looks like this figure. This is where you define the local area network connection (the "inside") and the outside Internet network connection (the "wild side").

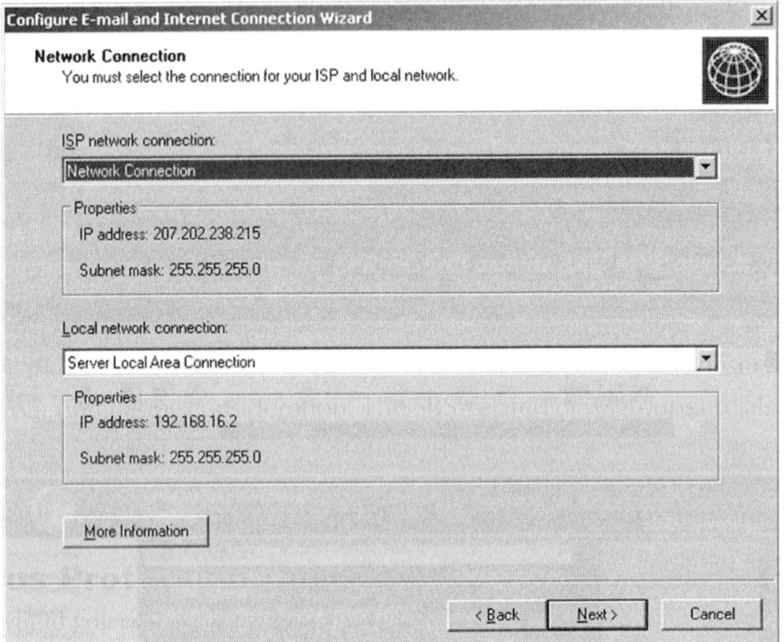

6. The Direct Broadband Connection page appears. Confirm your screen looks similar to Figure 4-8 and click **Next**.

Figure 4-8
The bottom three fields are editable on the Direct Broadband Connection page.

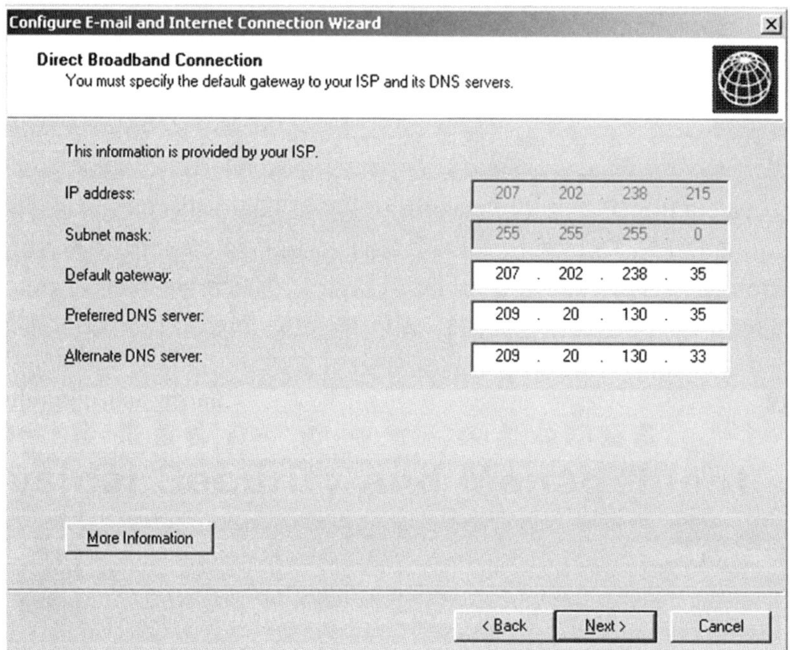

BEST PRACTICE: So even though my advanced SBS 2003 book won't be out until mid-2004, a few gurus are reading this book and might ask this question after reviewing the Direct Broadband Connection page in the EICW: "Why do you accept the ISP DNS IP address settings and not point it back to 192.168.16.2 to utilize the DNS service in SBS 2003 as a well-known TechNet article states?" The same question was asked by an angry student whom we'll call Jeff in Dallas, Texas, at a late-September 2003 SBS 2003 hands-on lab. Turns out Jeff thought he was being duped by the EICW because he wanted to point the wild-side NCI cards back to the DNS of 192.168.16.2. Fair enough. But Jeff, you might be surprised to know that the EICW does this internal referral thingy after running, because it's the darn EICW that configures the DNS in SBS for forwarding out to the ISP's DNS servers.

7. Select **Enable firewall** on the **Firewall** page and Click **Next**.
8. On the **Services Configuration** page, select **E-mail, Virtual Private Networking (VPN) and Terminal Services**, and **FTP**. This is part of the SPRINGERS methodology and something you might not do for every customer site in the real world. Your screen should look similar to Figure 4-9. Click **Next**.

BEST PRACTICE: When you select the VPN-related checkbox, you'll receive a notice that the server is not configured for remote access through VPN. You will further be advised that you'll need to run the Remote Access Wizard in order to do this. This message is normal, helpful, and actually points to the very next link on the To Do List that you and I will complete for SPRINGERS in the next section.

Figure 4-9
Selecting what services will be accessible via the Internet.

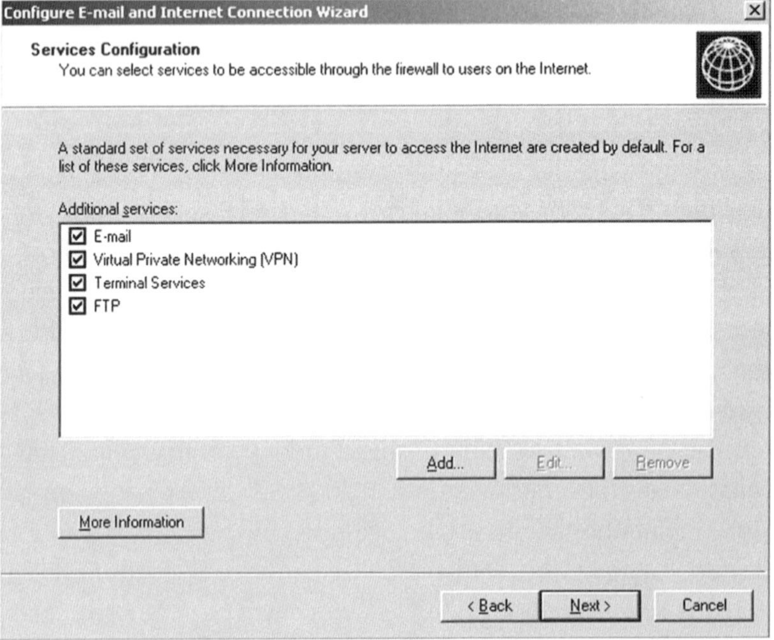

9. The Web Services Configuration page appears. This is where you'll select which Web services are externally accessible. In the case of SPRINGERS, we'll select the radio button titled **Allow access to only**

the following Web site services from the Internet and select everything EXCEPT Business Web site (wwwroot) and click **Next**. This has effectively selected all of the checkboxes you see in Figure 4-10.

Figure 4-10
Completing the Web Services Configuration page.

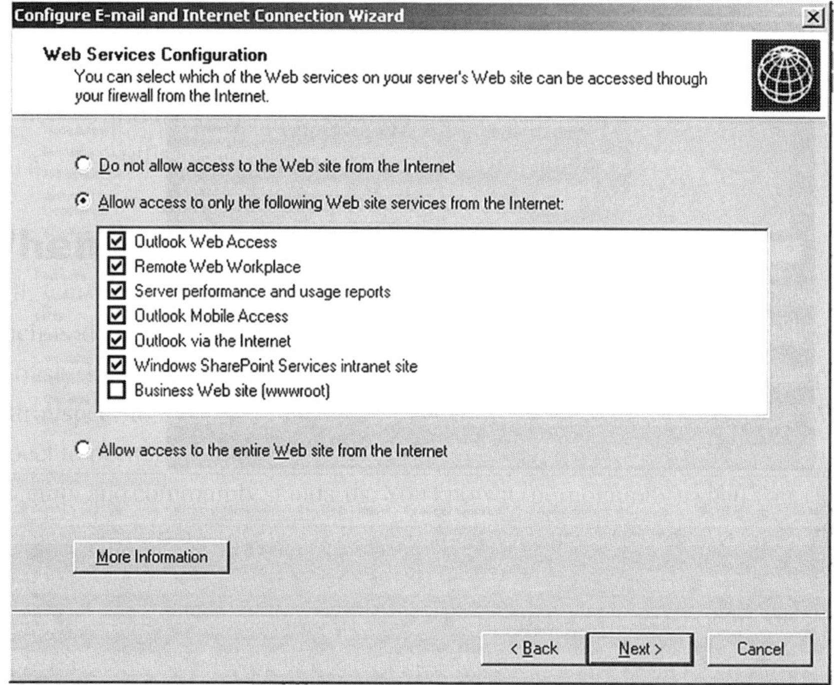

BEST PRACTICE: Call it a case of Miami madness or "mean season" malfeasance, but there I was delivering the SBS 2003 hands-on lab in Miami, Florida in early October 2003 and being blamed by a student that an exercise involving Remote Web Workplace didn't work. How could this be? If you look closely in Figure 4-10, the default settings on the Web Services Configuration page include the Outlook Web Access and the Remote Web Workplace screen. What gives here?

The student didn't append the URL with /remote. You'll learn more in Chapters 8 and 10 on this topic.

And now for the rest of the story. Microsoft and I agree that you do not want to expose your root page to the Internet - EVER - unless you are going to host a Web site. Because the SPRINGERS methodology does not include Web site hosting, you've made the correct selections in Figure 4-10.

10. Approve the dialog box that advises you that the site will be accessible via the Internet. To do this, click **Yes**.
11. On the Web Server Certificate, select **Create a new Web server certificate** and complete the **Web server name** field by typing **springers1.springersltd.com**. Your screen should look similar to Figure 4-11.

Figure 4-11
Creating the full Internet name for external clients to receive security certification.

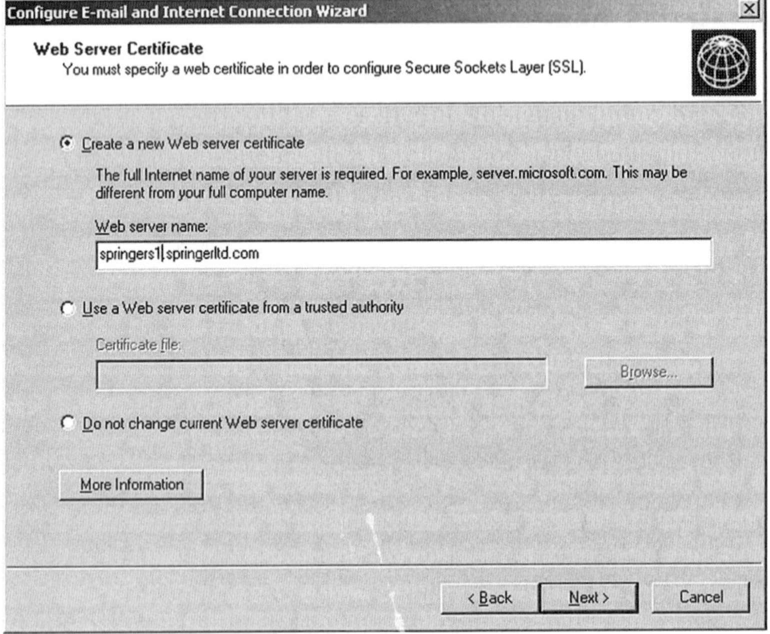

Notes:

BEST PRACTICE: What you've done in Figure 4-11 is provide the fully qualified domain name (FQDN) that can be accessed directly over the Internet. Remember, you'll need a resource record ("A" record) registered in the DNS at your ISP which points to the IP address of your wild side network adapter card to make the FQDN functional in this scenario. In the case of SPRINGERS, the IP address 207.202.238.215 would point to springers1. springersltd.com via an A record at the ISP. Whew!

Oh - another war story. Perhaps you completed the original online SBS 2003 hands-on lab that was released in mid-July 2003 with the release candidate software (microsoft.granitepillar.com/partners). In that hands-on lab, there was an exercise where you completed the EICW. On the Web Server Certificate page of the EICW, you configured the Web server name field with Denver.woodgrovebank.local. So what's wrong with that picture? The *.local domain extension as part of your FQDN entry can't be referenced externally. So that would be a mistake. One way that you could satisfy your own curiosity about this matter would be to click the More Information button. The first sentence that describes the first option (Create a new Web server certificate) spells it out clearly by saying "...access your server from the Internet.").

12. Select **Enable Internet e-mail** on the **Internet E-mail** page and click **Next**.
13. Select **Use DNS to route e-mail** on the **E-mail Delivery Method** page and click **Next**. This is the most common setting when using Simple Mail Transport Protocol (SMTP)-based e-mail, and it is indeed part of the SPRINGERS story line.

Notes:

14. On the **E-mail Retrieval Method** page, select **Use Exchange** and verify that **E-mail is delivered directly to my server**. Click **Next**. This is shown in Figure 4-12.

Figure 4-12
In the case of SPRINGERS and in the real world, you typically have your e-mail delivered directly to the SBS server machine.

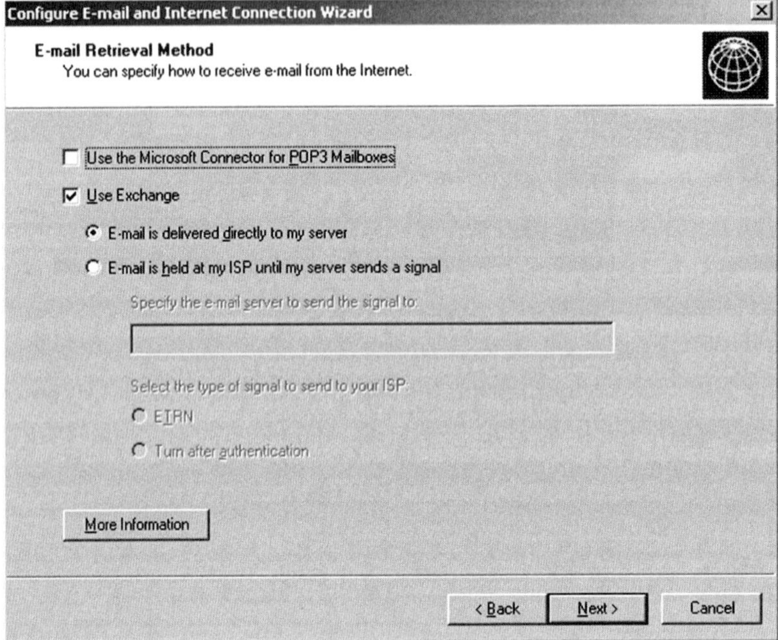

Notes:

15. On the **E-mail Domain Name** page, type **springersltd.com** in the **E-mail domain name** field. This is shown in Figure 4-13.

BEST PRACTICE: Here again, if you took the online SBS 2003 hands-on lab available after mid-July 2003 (microsoft.granitepillar.com/partners), you might recall that you were instructed on the E-mail Domain Name screen to enter a third-tier domain name (e.g., denver.woodgrovebank.com). There is a problem with this instruction in that you only want to enter a second-tier domain name (e.g., woodgrovebank.com).

Figure 4-13
Enter springersltd.com for the register Internet e-mail domain name.

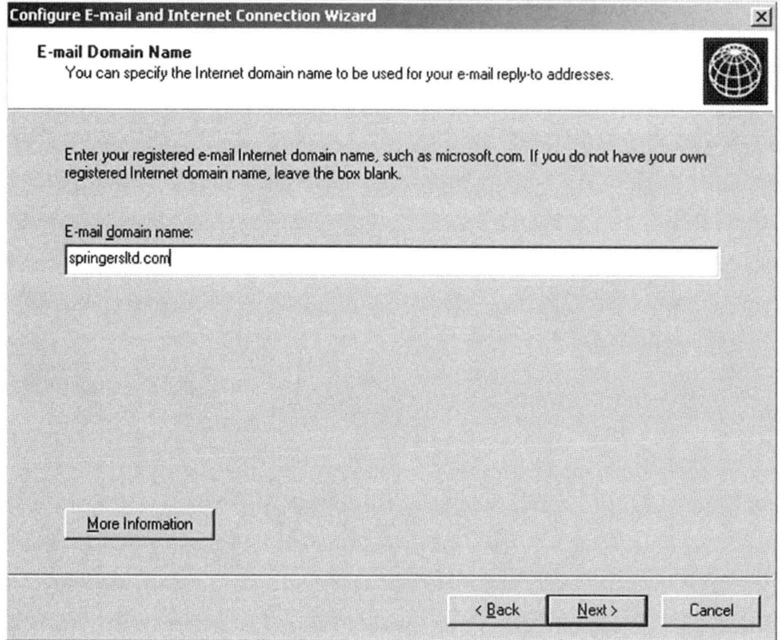

Notes:

16. On the **Remove E-mail Attachments** page, confirm that **Enable Exchange Server to remove Internet e-mail attachments that have the following extensions**. Then observe that all of the file name extensions are selected. This is shown in Figure 4-14. Click **Next**.

Figure 4-14
This is a really cool new feature in SBS 2003: the ability to block harmful e-mail attachments!

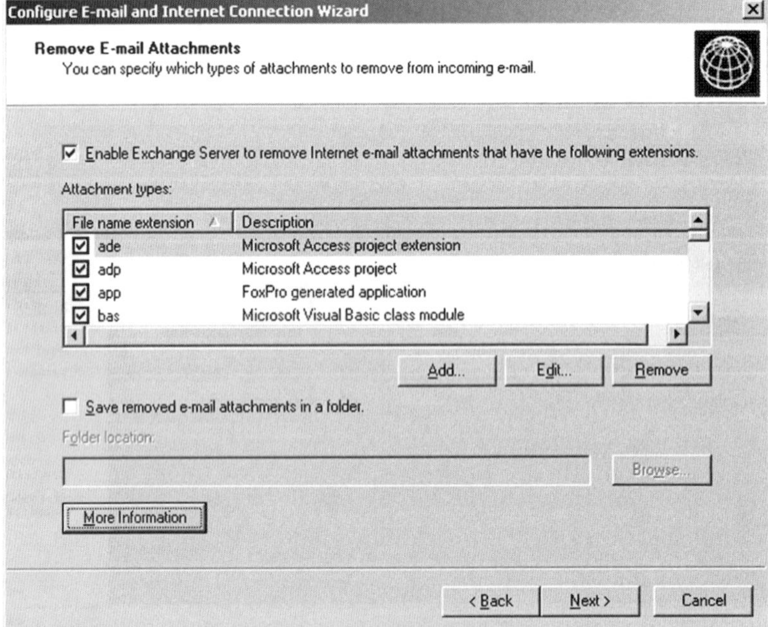

BEST PRACTICE: Exactly what are these harmful e-mail attachments, anyway? And how are they blocked? Are the attachments blocked on POP3 e-mail in addition to SMTP e-mail? The answers to all your questions can be found by clicking the **More Information** button on the **Remove E-mail Attachments** page. Take a moment to do that now.

17. On the **Completing the Configure E-mail and Internet Connection Wizard** page, click the link at the bottom titled **here**. You will proceed to create a network notebook.

18. As seen in Figure 4-15, a Web page displaying the EICW configuration information appears when you select the "here" link in the prior step. Select **File, Save As** and save the file as **EICW Configuration.htm** in the default location (My Documents). Click **Save**.

BEST PRACTICE: A few comments about this "network notebook" capability in the SBS 2003. First, major hats off to the SBS development team for adding this capability, because every SBS and SMB consultant I know worth their salt has always wanted to do a better job of documenting their network! More important, if you're the second SBS consultant at a customer's site, you'll be mighty appreciative if your predecessor had taken the time to perform this type of documentation.

Second, at the end of any native SBS 2003 wizard, you are presented with a "here" link to facilitate the creation of this network notebook. So, no excuses for not taking an extra moment to literally click "here" and document that network!

Third, look at the default naming in Figure 4-15 below. Notice it's a sorta hokey looking file name. That's why you rename the file to be more descriptive in Step 18 above. Fourth, you're going to plop all of these network notebook files in a folder that becomes your de facto notebook binder.

Oh - you can still follow my advice from my prior book (*Small Business Server 2000 Best Practices*) and simply select the configuration information via your mouse on the completion page (Step 17) by typing **CTRL-C** to copy it to the operating system clipboard and then selecting **CTRL-V** to paste it into a text document (say in WordPad).

Notes:

Figure 4-15
Displaying network configuration information.

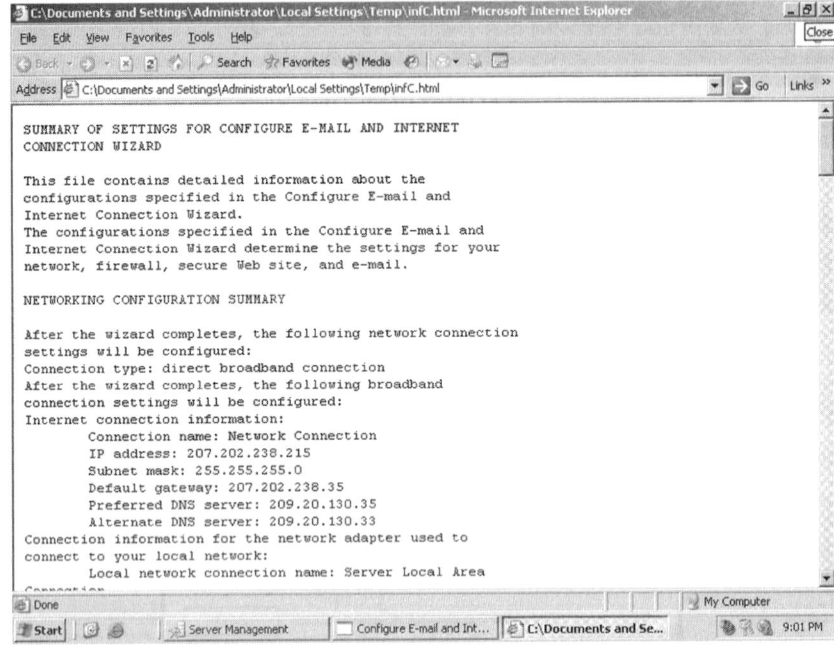

19. Close the Web page displaying the configuration information and click **Finish** back on the completion page. The EICW configuration process will take several minutes. Click **Close** at the end of the configuration process.
20. A dialog box will appear notifying you that password policies have not been enabled on the network. Let's go ahead and do that now, so click **Yes**.

21. Select all checkboxes on the **Configure Password Policies** dialog box (Figure 4-16) and click **OK**.

Figure 4-16
Implementing meaningful password policies reflects security improvements in SBS 2003.

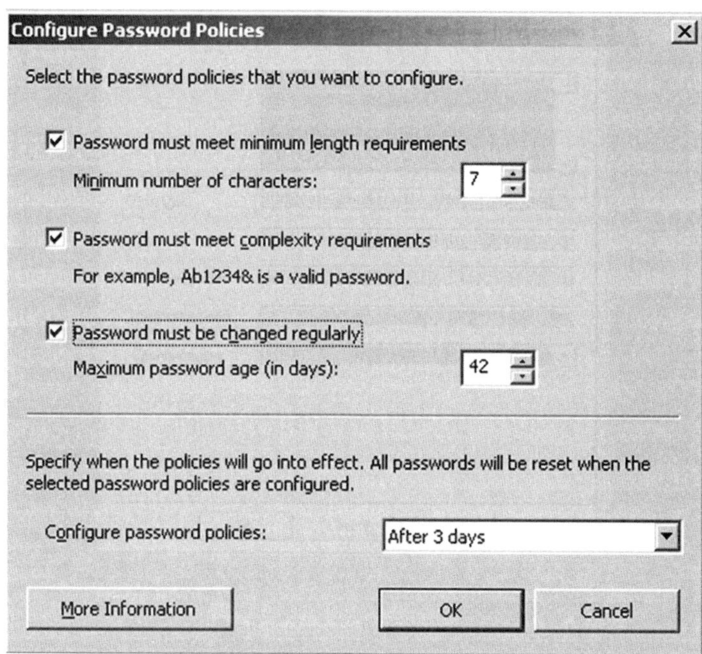

22. Click **OK** when notified that your server is connected to the Internet and immediately apply the latest critical and security updates. This is a great reminder and much appreciated. In the real world, you would do exactly what is being suggested (with SPRINGERS, I'm assuming you're building this on a test network possibly without a real Internet connection, so please make the necessary adjustments). When you click OK, Internet Explorer will attempt to connect to the Microsoft update site. In the case of SPRINGERS (assuming you aren't truly connected to the Internet) simply close the Web page. I discuss the updating process in Chapter 5.

BEST PRACTICE: By the way (BTW), if you launch Internet Explorer on the SBS 2003 server machine (SPRINGER1) prior to launching and completing the EICW, you will see the Web page displayed in

Figure 4-17. Interestingly, it is a Web page describing the process of how to complete the EICW.

Figure 4-17
Internet Explorer encourages you to complete the EICW when you first launch it on an SBS 2003 server machine.

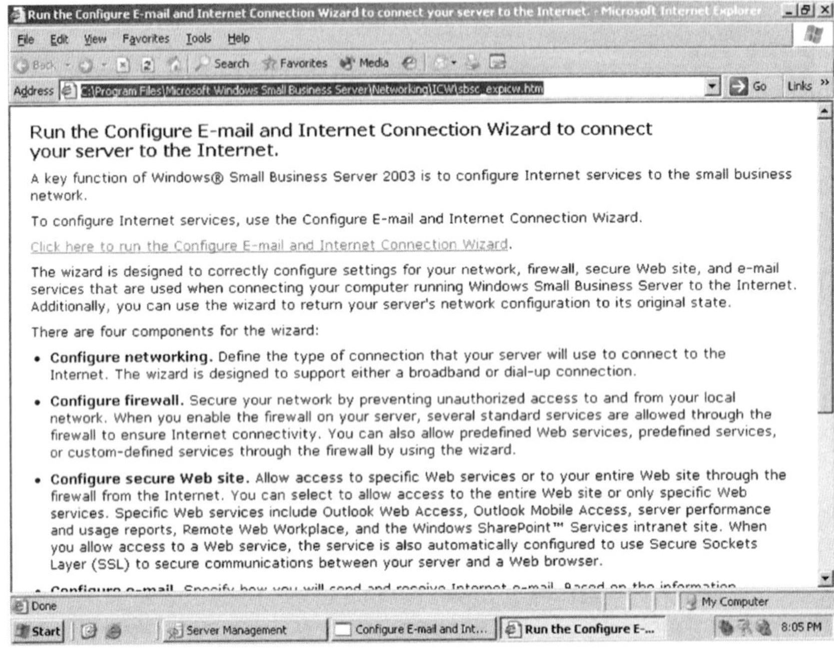

After your run the EICW, the default Web page programmatically changes to CompanyWeb, as seen in Figure 4-18. Note that it'll take a moment the first time you launch Internet Explorer post-EICW, as some background page-building activity will occur.

Figure 4-18
Post-EICW, the default Web page becomes CompanyWeb.

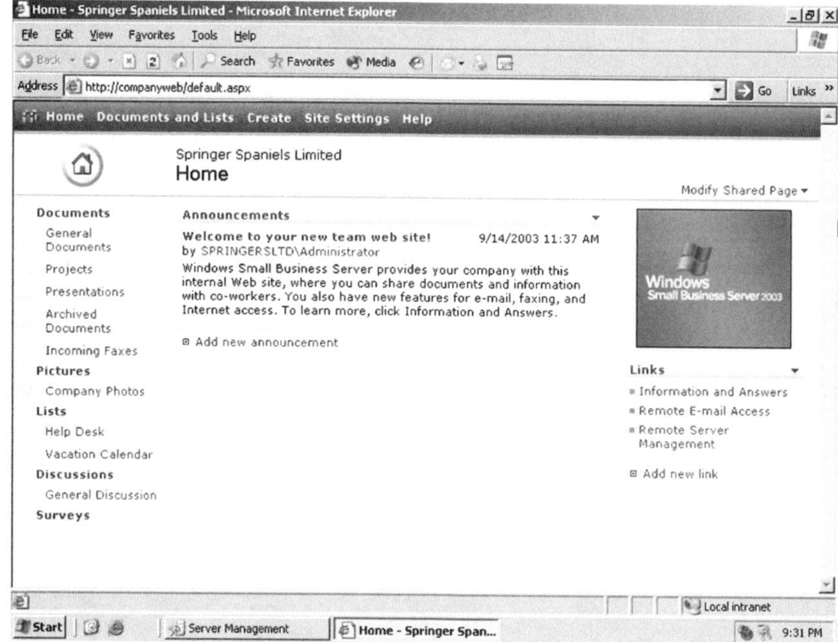

It's been a long haul so far in this chapter, and we've got a long way to go. Take a break and I'll see you back here after a cup of coffee.

Configure Remote Access

Welcome back. Time for more step-by-step.

1. Click on the **Configure Remote Access** link.
2. Click **Next** at the **Welcome to the Remote Access Wizard**.
3. Verify that **Enable remote access** is selected and **VPN access** is checked as shown in Figure 4-19. Click **Next**.

Figure 4-19
This is the magic moment for facilitating VPN remote access.

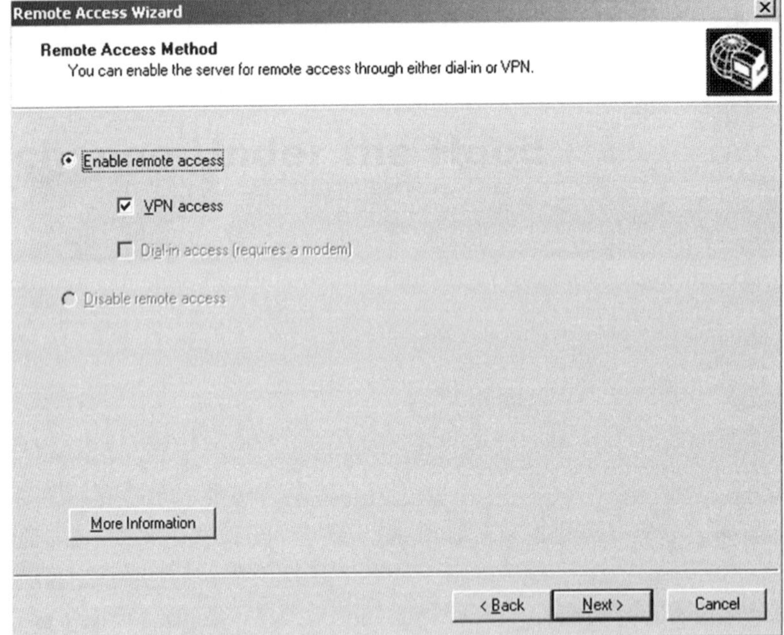

4. On the **VPN Server Name** page, the **Server name field** is automatically populated with **springers1.springersltd.com** (this information was extracted from the EICW). After confirming you screen looks like Figure 4-20, click **Next**.

BEST PRACTICE: So, do you always have to VPN in via the FQDN you're entering in Step 4 above? No! You can also ring up the SBS server machine by simply typing in the wild-side IP address to commence a VPN session. In the case of SPRINGERS, this would be 207.202.238.215.

Figure 4-20
You are defining the FQDN that allows access to the server over the Internet.

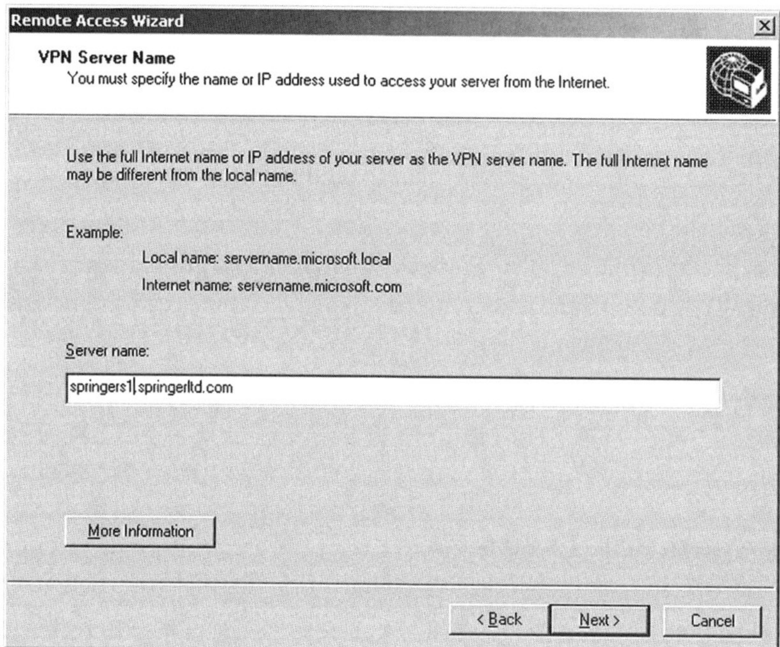

5. Click the **"here"** link on the **Completing the Remote Access Wizard** and save the configuration as **VPN.htm** in the **My Documents** folder (similar to the steps you undertook at the end of the EICW). Click **Finish**. After a few minutes the remote access configuration process will be completed, at which time you will click **Close**.

BEST PRACTICE: Before you and I become forgetful, please select the **Done** boxes on the **To Do List** for the **Connect to the Internet** and **Configure Remote Access** tasks.

Activate Your Server

In the real world, you would now click the Activate Your Server task on the To Do List and complete it. Because you are creating an imaginary network for SPRINGERS, let's not do that and say we did! Seriously, when you make a second pass at your SBS network, you will, of course, complete this task.

Server activation can occur online or via the telephone. Server activation is required because your server will otherwise become inoperable 14 days after creation if it isn't activated.

Add Client Licenses

Here again, in the real world, you'd likely add more client access licenses (CALs) in order to support the full staff at your small business site. Earlier I spoke to licensing and its improvements (purchase online, device and user CALs, etc.).

In the case of SPRINGERS, we're gonna keep it simple and not dig deeper into your hip pocket to make you purchase CALs. Remember, this is a sample network to learn SBS 2003. Later, when you're "live," you'll proceed to purchase the required CALs you need.

> BEST PRACTICE: Now select the **Done** checkbox on the **To Do List** for the two tasks discussed immediately above.

Management Tasks

The SBS development team drew a demarcation line between network tasks and management tasks to delineate the type of work you perform on the To Do List. Whereas the tasks performed above tend to be one-time in nature, the tasks that follow in this section, such as adding users and computers, might be repeated. Thus, the SBS development team created a "management" category.

Add a printer

What can I say. Adding a printer is all about adding the physical printer and publishing it to Active Directory. We'll do so now because you might remember from Table 2-4 in Chapter 2 that SPRINGERS has a HP Color LaserJet 5M laser printer (with the share name of HP5).

1. Assuming you are still logged on as **Administrator** on the server machine **SPRINGERS1**, select **Add a Printer** from the **To Do List**.
2. Click **Next** at the **Welcome to the Add Printer Wizard**.
3. On the **Local or Network Printer** page, accept the default setting of **Local printer attached to this computer**. But please deselect **Automatically detect or install my Plug and Play printer** (in the real world, you might very well select that automatic detection option,

but under the SPRINGERS approach, let's face it, we're kinda playing make-believe here to learn the product). Click **Next**.

4. Select **LPT1: (Recommended Printer Port)** in the **Use the following port:** field on the **Select a Printer Port** page. Click **Next**.
5. On the **Install Printer Software** page, select **HP** under **Manufacturer** and **HP Color LaserJet 5M** under **Printers**. Click **Next**.
6. On the **Name Your Printer** page, type **HP5** in the **Printer name** field. Click **Next**.
7. Accept the default share name of **HP5** on the **Printer Sharing** screen and click **Next**. This name was obviously extracted from the **Name Your Printer** page and in all cases has the 15-character NetBIOS naming limit.
8. Type **Main Office** in the **Location** field on the **Location and Comment** page and click **Next**.
9. Select **No** when asked if you want to print a test page on the Print Test Page. Click **Next**.
10. Click **Finish** on the **Completing the Add Printer Wizard** page. Note that there is no "here" link to add this information to your SBS network notebook I'm encouraging you to complete. Why, you ask? Because the Add Printer Wizard is not a native SBS wizard and thus doesn't incorporate that functionality.

Add Users and Computers

Now for the good stuff. We're going to add all of the users for SPRINGERS, using the new bulk capability to add users. This is different from SBS 2000 when users were added in a linear, one at a time fashion. Time is a wastin', so let's get started by first reviewing the time-tested tasks of preparing the workstation to be added to the network. After that, you'll perform the actual step-by-step tasks to add users and computers and connect the client computer to the SBS 2003 network.

Workstation Installation Plan

The following tasks are necessary to be completed prior to performing the SBS hands-on workstation configuration tasks, such as adding users and setting up the workstations. These tasks include the following:

1. **Setting up a staging area.** Be sure to find a place to set up the workstations if you purchase new workstations for your SBS network.

This workstation staging area is typically a conference room. If you are converting from an existing network, or the users already have their workstations in place, you probably won't need a workstation setup area.

BEST PRACTICE: If you indeed use a workstation staging area, it is very helpful to have a network hub (connected to the SBS network) in the center of your work area. That way, as you build each workstation, you can complete the workstation setup tasks in a good ol' blue-collar assembly line-like fashion. It's very efficient.

2. **Building the new workstations.** If you have new workstations, physically build the workstation by unpacking all the components from the shipping boxes (monitor, computer, and keyboard). Be sure to reseat each adapter card inside the new workstation in case it came loose during shipping. After connecting all the workstation components, turn on the power and verify that the workstation is functional. I recommend that you check the workstation BIOS settings similar to how the server BIOS was observed in Chapter 3. (You typically press the Delete key during the power-on phase to see the BIOS settings.)

BEST PRACTICE: Be sure to confirm that the workstations you specified and ordered while you read Chapter 2 are the same as the workstations now in your possession. And does each workstation have a network adapter card as specified and ordered?

Whether the workstation is new or not, take a moment to confirm that your workstation meets the minimum system requirements specified by Microsoft for participating on an SBS network (see Chapter 2 for discussion on this). In particular, make sure that you have enough hard disk space to accommodate the SBS client applications you intend to install in a few moments. The most popular SBS workstation setup error I've witnessed is a shortage of hard disk space on the client workstation. Unfortunately, you aren't always advised of such space shortage problems until well into the SBS client workstation setup process. The workstation space requirements in SBS have grown to over 300 MB if you install each client component.

3. **Completing the installation of the workstation operating system.** New workstations typically have no operating system completely installed. As of this writing, the workstation would likely have a partial installation of Windows XP Professional. This is typically the case when you purchase from name-brand manufacturers, such as HP. With true clone workstations (sometimes called "white boxes"), such as the PC that your Uncle Chas built, it might or might not have any operating system (here it varies on a case-by-case basis). Regardless, it is essential that each workstation have a functional operating system, such as Windows XP Professional (my bias). So now is the time to make sure that each of your workstations indeed has a supported operating system installed and ready to run. In fact, the SBS client applications and networking functionality cannot be fully installed on a workstation until a supported workstation operating system is installed. Recall from Chapter 2 that SPRINGERS has standardized on Windows XP Professional for its workstation operating system on a company-wide basis.

BEST PRACTICE: Be sure to check the SBS site at Microsoft (www.microsoft.com/sbs) for which client operating systems are supported by SBS 2003. Because this list changes over time and will not stay current as of this writing, I'm simply directing you to the Web site.

However, I do feel secure sharing with you that the following operating systems are not supported by SBS 2003 in any way, shape, or form: OS/2, CP/M, Apple DOS, and Apple ProDOS. If you have such a workstation, do yourself a favor and strongly consider purchasing an Intel-based workstation running one of the supported operating systems so that you can participate on the SBS network.

And perhaps the "wild card" in this whole workstation equation will be XBOX from Microsoft. Wouldn't it be cool to have XBOX as a client computer on an SBS 2003 network?

4. **Testing the workstation's network connectivity.** Perform a workstation-level green light test: Plug a network cable (that is, CAT5

10BASE-T cable) into the workstation's Ethernet network adapter card jack. Make sure the other end of the network cable is connected to an active hub connection (for example, the hub in your workstation staging area). Much like the testing you performed on the server in Chapter 3, make sure that both the hub and workstation network adapter card jack have a green or active light.

If you use existing workstations on an existing network, you can also perform this test with little effort. Simply turn on the existing workstation and see whether the network adapter card jack is green or active. Then trot over to the network hub and confirm the same.

5. **Completing the workstation installation worksheet.** Be sure to revisit the SBS network user list shown in Chapter 2 (see the "User List" section and complete the Workstation Installation Worksheet for each user. The Workstation Installation Worksheet has been completed for Norm Hasborn, SPRINGERS president (see Table 4-1). The entries for the remaining employees are provided in Appendix C.

BEST PRACTICE: Remember that it is far better with SBS to populate each wizard page field, even if that means you enter N/A (Not Applicable or Not Available) because you don't have valid data to input. That way, you know at a later date that you didn't overlook any user and computer setup configuration field. Also, SBS user and computer setup configuration information is used in other areas of the SBS network, making it important to complete each and every user and computer setup configuration field.

Notes:

Table 4-1: SBS Workstation Setup Sheet

Setup Field	Input/Value/Description	Where Used
User's Full Name (First, Last)	*Norm Hasborn*	Add User Wizard
Logon Name	*NormH*	Add User Wizard
Telephone	*206-123-1234*	Add User Wizard
Password	*Purple3300*	Add User Wizard
E-mail alias	*NormH (default)*	Add User Wizard
Exchange Server	*SPRINGERS1 (default)*	Add User Wizard
Exchange store	*Mailbox Store (SPRINGERS1) (default)*	Add User Wizard
Description for User	*Founder and President*	Add User Wizard
Allowed to change password (Y/N)?	*No*	Add User Wizard
SBS User Template	*Power User*	Add User Wizard
Workstation NetBIOS	*PRESIDENT*	Set Up Computer Wizard
SBS Programs to Install	*Complete:* *Internet Explorer* *Outlook 2003* *Shared Fax Client*	Set Up Computer Wizard
Operating System	*Windows XP Professional*	Set Up Computer Wizard
Verify available workstation hard disk space based on SBS Programs to install listed immediately above (for example, 300 MB required)	*Yes*	Misc
Turn off programs at work-station such as anti-virus programs.	*Yes/No?*	Misc
SBS server-based Shared Folders this user will access.	*NORMH* *USERS* *COMPANY* *ACCOUNTING* *OLD* *APPLICATIONS*	Misc.
Printers	*HP5*	Misc.

Network Protocols	*TCP/IP*	Misc.
IP Address (Static or Dynamic)	*Dynamic*	Misc.
Mapped Drives	*S: SPRINGERS1\NORMH* *T: SPRINGERS1\USERS* *U: SPRINGERS1\ ACCOUNTING* *V: SPRINGERS1\OLD* *W: SPRINGERS1\ APPLICATIONS*	Misc
Workstation Shares (shares on workstation)	*N/A*	Misc.
Additional Applications to install (for example, Great Plains Dynamics accounting):	*Great Plains Dynamics client* *FRX Report Writer*	Misc.
Special configuration issues	*Triple-check security. This is the president's PC.*	Misc.
Comments	*Complete this one last after all other workstations.*	Misc.
Tested Logon (Y/N)	*No*	Misc.
Repairs/Reconfiguration Needed		Misc.

BEST PRACTICE: Remember that the workstation name is typically based on job title or function. Thus, the workstation names associated with the users at SPRINGERS are closely related to the user's job title. This naming convention is helpful when you have staff turnover, but the jobs remain the same.

Another useful practice, although not used with SPRINGERS, is to name machines after something neutral, such as fruits. A former client, Larry P, did this because he observed that while people change jobs, machines don't. The same job titles typically keep the same machine. Or sometimes you have people leave and the job is restructured with a new title. You get the point. Hey, if I'm going to have a machine named after a fruit, I want the machine named KUMQUAT01!

Note that for all users, access to the Internet is allowed by default just as it was in SBS 2000 (such wasn't the case in SBS 4.5).

SBS Workstation Setup Process

The SBS workstation setup approach is a four-step process, and compared to the SBS server machine installation, it is relatively simple. Another interesting point is that, whereas you perform the SBS server machine setup only once, you perform the SBS workstation setup multiple times. I've found that such repetition breeds familiarity; your comfort level increases with this process.

Of the four steps, the first two (running the Add User Wizard and then the Set Up Computer Wizard) are performed on the SBS server machine via the To Do List. The last two steps are performed on the SBS workstation. Run the setup program over the wire via a Web browser and install the client applications. This process is detailed in Figure 4-21.

A quick SBS 2003-specific comment for you: If you have worked with SBS in the past, say SBS 4.5, you will be very pleased to see that SBS 2003 has greatly simplified the add user and computer processes. This was accomplished in part by adding the bulk entry capability, using user account templates, and eliminating the "magic" setup diskette. All this and more will be displayed and discussed in a moment.

Figure 4-21
SBS Workstation setup process.

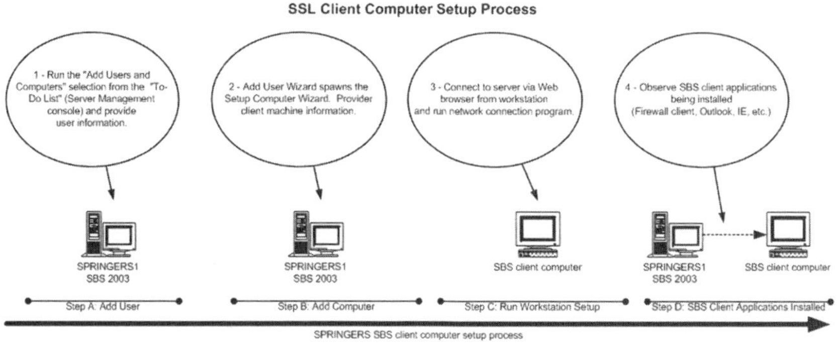

The step-by-step process for adding users and client computers commences right here, right now!

1. Again, assuming you're logged on as the **Administrator** at the server machine **SPRINGERS1**, you will click the **Add Users and Computers** link from the **To Do List**.
2. Click **Next** at the **Welcome to the Add User Wizard**.
3. On the **Template Selection** screen, pick **Power User Template**, as seen in Figure 4-22 and click **Next**.

Figure 4-22
There are several templates to select from, including the new Mobile User Template.

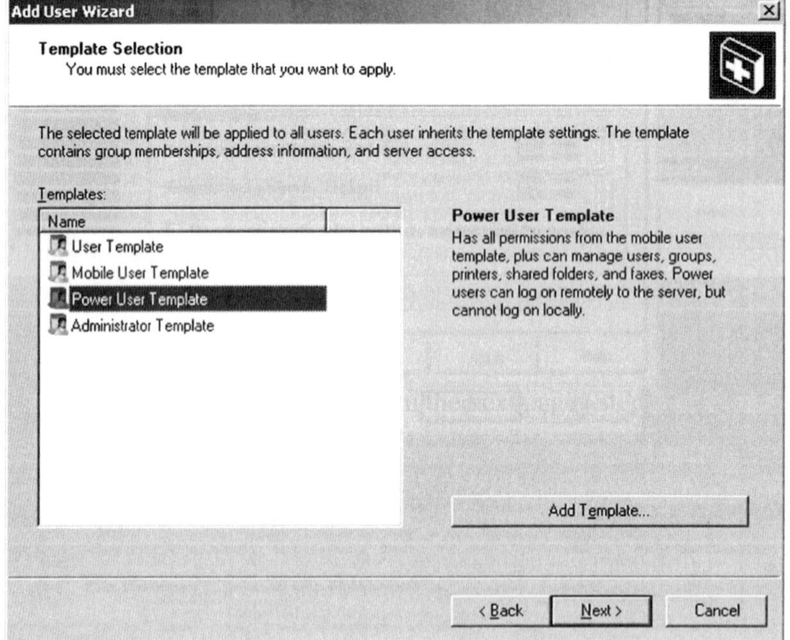

BEST PRACTICE: There is an interesting design feature in the bulk add capability that relates to the Template Selection screen in Figure 4-22 above. If you look closely, the language clearly states that the selected template will be applied to all users. Furthermore, each user inherits the templates settings (as you would expect). But, we've got a slight problem if you were lead to believe that, using the bulk addition capability, we could add all of the SPRINGERS users all at once. Such is not the case, because if you revisit the User List in Chapter 2, you see that two users are "power users" and the rest of the users are "users." This translates into the following: You will need to run the Add User Wizard twice in the SPRINGERS methodology in order to add users that fall into two template categories.

Oh - and fear not that I'm ignoring the Mobile User Template. I elevate a user's template-based permissions to that level in Chapter 11 using a cool new role transfer wizard.

BEST PRACTICE: You may look at the specific properties for each of these user templates to answer any questions you have. Such questions are often focused on exactly what settings are being invoked by selecting one template as compared to another template. However, viewing these properties can only be done when running the Add User Wizard in single-user mode (not bulk-add mode, which is the default from the To Do List). So you would click the **User object** under **Standard Management** in the **Server Management** console followed by a click on **Add a User**. Then select **Display selected template's default settings** in the wizard checkbox on the **Template Selection** screen. You should do this while adding at least one of your users, so you better understand the background process that is occurring.

Interestingly, you can create your own user templates for use in SBS. This would make sense where you want to model a particular group of users around an application or function. For example, you might want to give users in the bookkeeping department access to the shared folder containing the data. This is done by selecting the **Add Template** button on the **Template Selection** screen (this button appears in the **Add User Wizard** in both single user and bulk add mode). The Add Template Wizard will commence. To learn more about adding a template and even importing and exporting templates between SBS server networks (e.g., multiple SBS customer sites), click **User Templates** under **Standard Management** on the Server Management console.

Finally, just when you'd have enough template talk, I draw your attention to the fact that you are not required to use a template at all when running the Add User Wizard in single-user mode (select **Do not use a template** to define user settings on the **Template Selection** screen). When running the Add User Wizard in bulk-add mode, you must select a template (there is no option for bypassing template usage).

4. On the **User Information** screen, select **Add**. Complete the **Specify the user information** dialog box that appears in Figure 4-23. Click **OK**.
5. Click **Add again** on the **User Information** screen and complete the **Specify the user information** dialog box for Bob Easter in a manner similar to the above step. Click **OK** when complete.

Figure 4-23
Adding the first power user, Norm Hasborn.

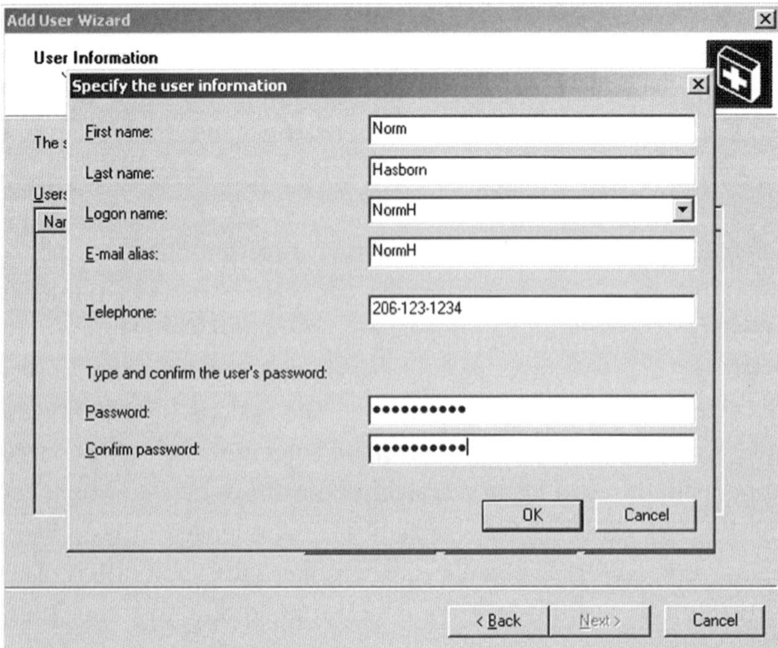

6. Click **Next** after you've completed the entry of the two power users on the **User Information** page.
7. Select **Set up computers now** on the **Set Up Client Computers** page. Click **Next**.
8. Add the computer names **PRESIDENT** and **CAREFEED01** by typing one name at a time in the Client computer name field on the **Client Computer Names** page and clicking **Add**. Click **Next**.
9. Accept the default selection of all client applications being selected on the **Client Applications** page. Select the **After Client Setup is finished, log off the client computer** checkbox as shown in Figure 4-24. Click **Next**.

Figure 4-24
Accepting all of the settings on the Client Applications page.

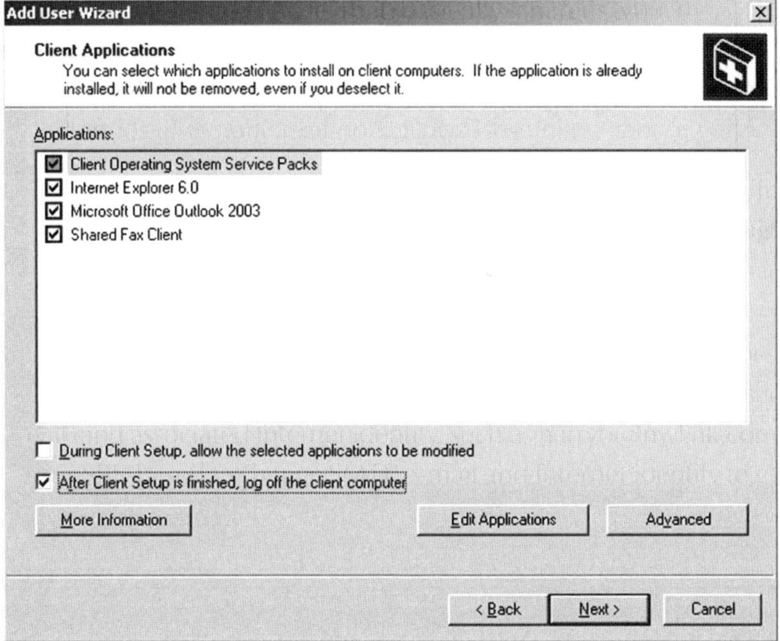

10. Click **Next** on the **Mobile Client** and **Offline Use** page. Although this functionality isn't part of the SPRINGERS methodology, you might consider these capabilities in the real world (functionality described under More Information). Click **Next**.

11. On the **Completing the Add User Wizard** page, be sure to click the **here** link and name the configuration page Add **Users1.htm** as part of your network notebook exercise. Click **Finish**.

BEST PRACTICE: Speaking of documenting the SBS 2003 network, there are a two other logs you would want to know about right now. These are located in \%System Drive%\Program Files\Microsoft Windows Small Business Server\Support\

*add_user_wizard.log. This log documents how users were added to the SBS 2003 network.

* scw.log. This log documents how client computers where configured for the SBS 2003 network.

A more technical log, SBSClientApps.log, can be viewed at \%System Drive%\Program Files\Microsoft Windows Small Business Server\Tools\. This log reports on internal application execution milestones.

Notes:

12. CAREFULLY read the **Finishing Your Installation** dialog box and click **OK**. This is shown in Figure 4-25.

Figure 4-25
A dialog box that hints at a next step you will perform on a client computer.

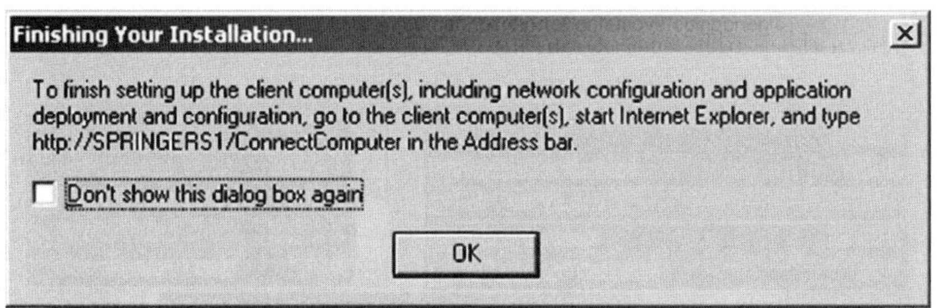

BEST PRACTICE: When you read the dialog box in the step above, you'll note that you're not being asked to actually go to the URL of http://SPRINGERS1/ConnectComputer at this time. Rather, the dialog box is telling you to go to a client computer and perform this action. I've seen people read this information far too rapidly and launch Internet Explorer on the SBS server machine and type in the URL to connect the computer. This happened repeatedly in the SBS 2003 hands-on lab tour in the US in the fall of 2003. You can not successfully run the connect computer command on the server machine, because the server is already connected to the network.

13. Click **Close**.

Now repeat the above steps to add the remaining SPRINGERS users (listed in Chapter 2 in the User List) in one more pass using the User Template (this is the common template for all of these users). You will answer **Yes** when asked if you want to run the Add User Wizard again to add more users. Figure 4-26 displays the User Information screen you should have as part of this process.

Notes:

Figure 4-26

Now you can really see the "bulk-add" capabilities in the Add User Wizard with all of these names displayed!

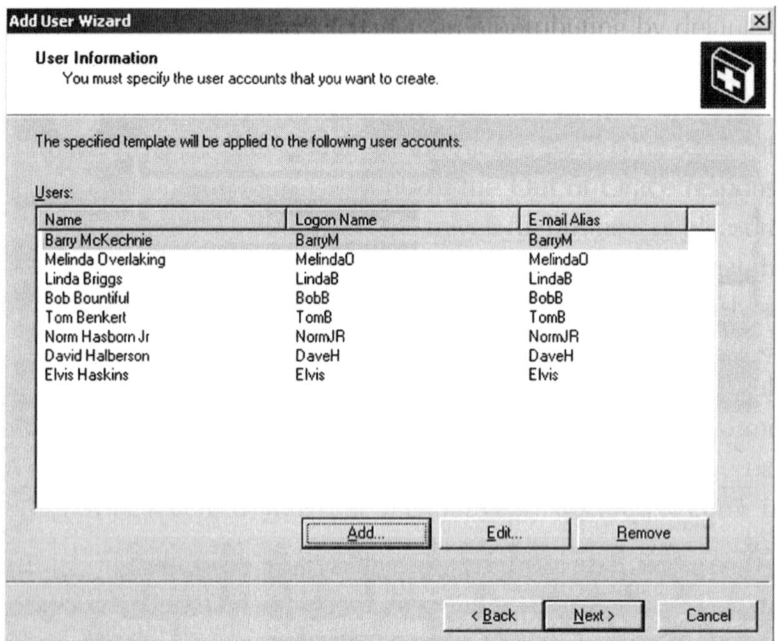

BEST PRACTICE: Note an interesting tidbit as you add all of the users for SPRINGERS. When you get to the Client Computer Names screen, there will be many client computers listed that have already been auto-named for you. This is typically the user name followed by "01" (e.g., BarryM01). Of course, this isn't what we intend for the workstation naming with SPRINGERS (the User List in Chapter 2 provides that names), so you will use the Remove button to remove those names and then add the proper client computer names (SPRINGERS names computers by job function and then places 01 at the end).

So, let's finish discussing the To Do List and then proceed to attach the client machine to the SBS network.

Configure Fax

This selection will launch the wizard for Fax Configuration Wizard. Over the course of several steps you will complete in Chapter 9, you will configure the Shared Fax Service to benefit SPRINGERS.

Configure Monitoring

The Monitoring Configuration Wizard is launched from this link on the To Do List. This will implement the awesome monitoring capability in SBS 2003 and will be discussed in detail in Chapter 12.

Configure Backup

The Backup Configuration Wizard is launched from this link and commences the configuration of the massively improved backup process. More on this in the SBS administration chapter later in the book.

> BEST PRACTICE: Because the last two To Do List items have only been discussed and not completed here, be sure you do not select the Done checkbox for these items. That wouldn't make sense as you've not completed the tasks. Later, once the relevant work is completed, you'll mark these tasks as done.

> BEST PRACTICE: You can print out the To Do List which makes for a nice checklist to work with as you run around as an SBSer. Simply click the Print button in the lower right.

Third-Party Interaction

So what's missing in this lengthy walk through of the Server Console and To Do List? It's third parties taking advantage of the ability to add their own buttons, links, and objects. You would have to go back to SBS 4.5 to really recall the last time a major independent software vendor (ISV) bothered to add their link or button to the To Do List or console. And can you guess who that ISV was? It was Veritas with its Backup Exec Suite for SBS.

Attaching the Client Computer

So now for one of the more interesting updates in the SBS 2003 time frame: adding the client computer. In prior SBS releases, you'd use a client computer setup diskette (e.g., Magic disk) at each workstation to configure it for an SBS network. Word is that the diskette not only went the day of the dinosaur, but somehow didn't pass Microsoft's internal security audit of the SBS 2003 product (as part of Microsoft's internal security code review).

You will now launch your client computer from a power on state (that is, turn on the computer!). Assuming the computer is physically attached to the local area network that houses the SBS server machine (and receives it IP address dynamically), then follow these steps:

1. Log on to the client computer (this would be a local logon).
2. Launch **Internet Explorer** from your **Start** menu. Type **http://: springers1/connectcomputer** in the **Address** field. It is this URL address that will display a Web page that allows you to connect the client computer.
3. The **Network Configuration** screen appears as seen in Figure 4-27. Click **Connect to the network** now.

Notes:

Figure 4-27
The new and very cool client computer setup process commences right here. Read the screen carefully about receiving a security warning notice (which you would approve to continue).

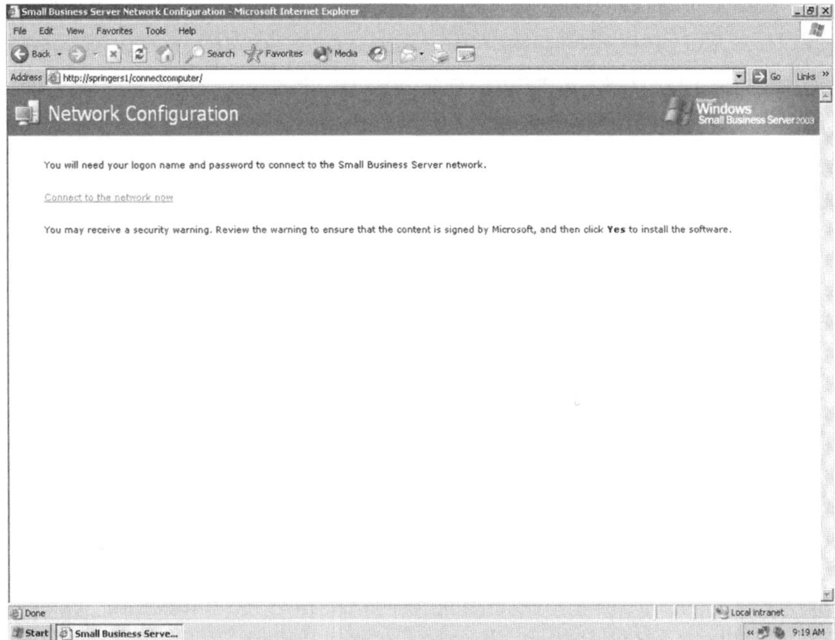

4. The **User Account and Password Information** page appears in the **Small Business Server Network Configuration Wizard**. Type **Administrator** in the **User name** field and **Husky9999!** in the **Password** field. Click **Next**. This step is necessary to provide domain-level administrator credentials to allow the machine to be joined to the domain (we need a God-like account to configure the machine, which makes sense).
5. On the **Assign users to this computer and migrate their profiles** page, select **Administrator** and **NormH** under **Available Users**. Click **Add** and these two user names should appear under **Users assigned to this computer** as seen in Figure 4-28. Click **Next**.

BEST PRACTICE: Three points to surface here.

(A) This step is effectively adding the user as a local administrator in order to install software on the local machine. At the Worldwide Partner Conference hosted by Microsoft in New Orleans in October 2003, CEO Steve Ballmer entertained a question from a concerned attendee that this seemed like a case of very generous security to grant a mere mortal (agreed!).

(B) At a future date, if you want to add more users (such as new users) as being assigned to this machine, you'll need to do it manually. So one attendee in the October 2003 hands-on lab in New York City (Sharon Tirosh, who is well known on the SBS Yahoo! Group) suggested that you manually add a security group (e.g., from the domain to the local machine) to the local machine and then put the additional users in that security group. Note that you CAN NOT do this security group addition trick from the **Assign users to the computer and migrate their profiles** page. So, this is not native to SBS 2003, but can be performed under the hood.

(C) Click the **More Information** in Figure 4-28 and learn more about the ability to migrate profiles from existing workstations. This capability invokes a process that searches the local machine for existing profiles (e.g., a local profile in an existing peer-to-peer network scenario) and displays the found profiles in a drop-down under **Current User Settings**. You would then select one of the profiles (obviously the profile that is the best fit) to migrate that profile to the domain membership for a user and preserve his settings. In lecture, I typically refer to this as the grandchild capability wherein the business user can arrive Monday (Humor Zone: That's Tuesday in Australia, as they are one day ahead of the US!) and still see the grandchild's photo that is the local machine desktop. Hell hath no fury like a user who can't see her grandkid's photo after joining an SBS network!

Note: I'll investigate these above points in greater detail in my advanced SBS 2003 book in mid 2004.

Figure 4-28
Assigning users to the local machine. Note that you aren't creating domain user account here (this was accomplished earlier on the server machine via the Add User Wizard).

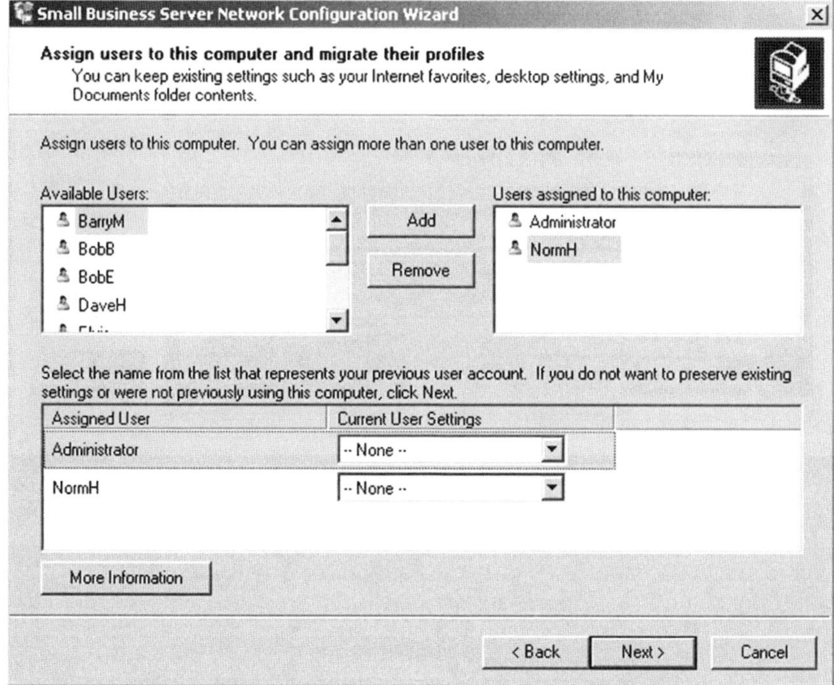

6. On the **Computer Name** page, select **PRESIDENT** and click **Next**.
7. On the **Completing the Network Configuration Wizard** page, click the **here** link and proceed to save the configuration on the local machine (much like you've created your network notebook on the server machine). Click **Finish** to start the network configuration process. A reboot will occur immediately to join the machine to the domain.
8. After the first reboot and automatic logon, additional domain joining activity occurs and there is a second reboot.
9. After the second reboot, log on as **NormH** with the password **Purple3300**.

10. Then the client computer configuration process continues when you click **Start Now** on the **Client Setup Wizard**.
11. Click **Next** on the **Welcome to the Client Setup Wizard** page.
12. The **Application Setup Process** page appears and the core SBS client-side applications are installed (Outlook 2003, Shared Fax client, operating system updates). This is shown in Figure 4-29.

Figure 4-29
Observe the setup of the applications.

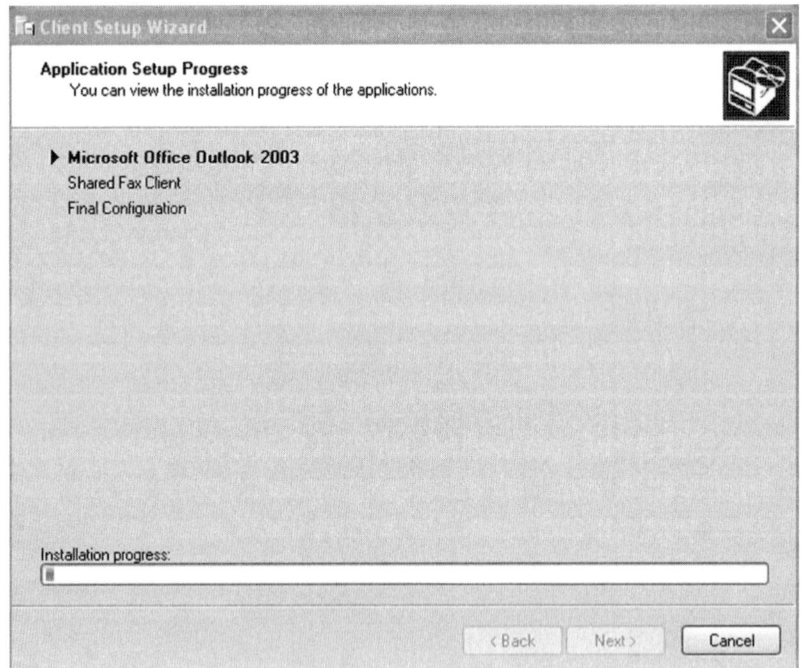

13. The machine reboots (again!) and you will log on as **NormH** again (password is **Purple3300**). The setup process is now complete and you've officially added a client computer in our beloved SPRINGERS methodology.

BEST PRACTICE: If for some reason the client computer applications, such as Outlook 2003, didn't completely install correctly, there is a manual workaround. Simply navigate to \\SPRINGERS1\ClientApps (this is the UNC path back to the SBS server machine) and launch the appropriate native setup routine (e.g., setup.exe) for the applications you want to install on the client machine.

Guest Column

Another Take On Internet Connectivity

By Frank J. Ohlhorst

With broadband connectivity becoming commonplace for most any small business, consultants will need to carefully consider the implications of high speed internet access for their customers. SBS2003 does a great deal to leverage those broadband connections ranging from the ability to share the connection with client PCs to hosting web based services to incorporating remote access. But consultants will find that there are some limiting factors when it comes to today's broadband connections.

The first problem encountered often revolves around the lack of a static IP address assigned from the broadband purveyor. Most cable companies and a good portion of DSL providers supply a dynamic IP address for the broadband connection device (DSL Modem or Cable Modem), that prevents a friendly URL from being assigned to the SBS2003 network in question. In other words, consultants can not offer their customers the ease of using "mysbs2003-network.com" as a solution for connecting to the customer's network. Simply put, dynamically assigned external IP addresses have the net effect of eliminating many of the advantages offered by SBS2003 for remote users. Luckily, consultants can turn to a Dynamic DNS service to solve that connectivity problem.

Dynamic DNS services are available from several vendors, with key players being Tzolkien's TZO service (www.tzo.com), Dynamic DNS Network Services' DynDNS (www.dyndns.org), No-IP.com's No-IP service (www.no-ip.com), and Deerfield's DNS2go service (www.dns2go.com). All of those vendors share a common concept and functionality, the service works by running a small client application on the SBS2003 server, which is then used to inform the Dynamic DNS provider with the public IP address of the network. That information is then used to associated a URL with the public IP address and is updated whenever the IP address is dynamically changed and viola, the site now has a valid URL.

Simplicity is the key for keeping Dynamic DNS working, most of the services on the market rely on a small client application that can be quickly installed and configured, that client application should also be configured to run as a service and auto launch on startup. Some further configuration is often needed, for sites running a firewall or ISA server, it may be necessary to open some ports to allow the Dynamic DNS service to work.

Another option is to not use a Dynamic DNS client at all, how is that possible? Many of the broadband routers coming onto the market are now building Dynamic DNS clients in. Key players there include Linksys, D-link, SMC, Buffalo, Zyxel and several others. That offers the advantage of moving the client software off of any servers or PCs and eliminates the need for opening additional ports, also it brings the advantage of being able to remotely administer the router if desired.

Once the URL dilemma is solved, there may be some other issues to contend with, namely blocked ports. Many ISPs are now blocking incoming and outgoing TCP/IP ports, effectively eliminating the ability for broadband users to host websites, host email servers and the like. That becomes a significant problem for those looking to leverage those very features found in SBS2003.

The solution to that problem can also be found with the Dynamic DNS service providers, some of which support port redirection or forwarding. Simply put, if an ISP blocks port 80 (HTTP web traffic), simply redirect that traffic to another port, say port 81. That feat is accomplished by the dynamic DNS service provider capturing port 80 traffic at their site and redirecting it to a port of your choice.

Port redirection does require some integration work, namely modifying applications to listen for traffic on different ports than normal, for example you would have to "instruct" IIS to look for traffic on port 81, instead of the default of port 80. For those using broadband routers, that whole process can be simplified if the router supports port redirection, then the router can be instructed to listen for traffic on port 81 and then redirect that traffic to port 80 on the server's internal IP address. The same goes for Email, FTP and other services.

The moral of the story here is not to let an ISP's restrictions or lack of features prevent consultants from providing customers with all of the features SBS2003 has to offer. By using a Dynamic DNS service, the two major problems associated with broadband are easily overcome, blocked ports and dynamic IP addresses are no longer a brick wall for leveraging key features of SBS2003, such as remote access, email and hosting.

Summary

Whew! You've made it through four demanding chapters and your reward is a functional and operational SBS 2003 network. In this chapter, you greeted the Server Management console and completed much of the To Do List. This included important wizards to connect to the Internet, configure remote connectivity and adding users and computers. This "stuff" was foundation and allows you to confidentially continue forward with the SPRINGERS methodology. And most important of all, you started to completed the To Do List in order, something that is very important in the SBS world. I started earlier by offering you congratulations and I end on the same note. The next chapter is the all-important security topic!

SBS Around The World

Photo Section

SBS Around The World
Photo Section

Some readers may elect to make this book a coffee table book. For that and other reasons, such as building community and excitement around SBS, I've included a photo section in a computer book (yes – you've read correctly!). Enjoy a good chuckle!

Three-day SBS 2000 Course
Australia, December 2002

Figure P-1
The hands-on at Microsoft Australia's Sydney office.

Figure P-2
The Saturday "executive MBA" lecture on SBS and SMB consulting at the downtown Sydney Intercontinental Hotel.

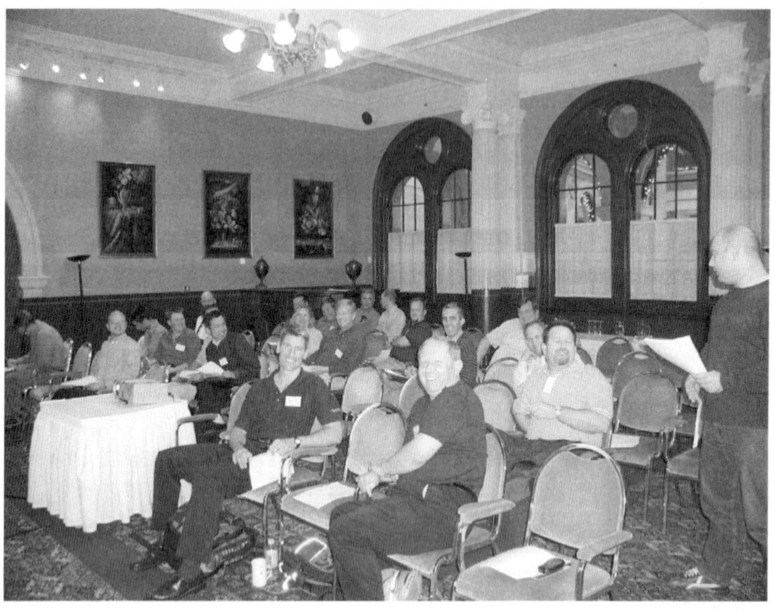

Figure P-3
The Saturday afternoon class field trip in Sydney. SBS MVP Wayne Small in the foreground (left).

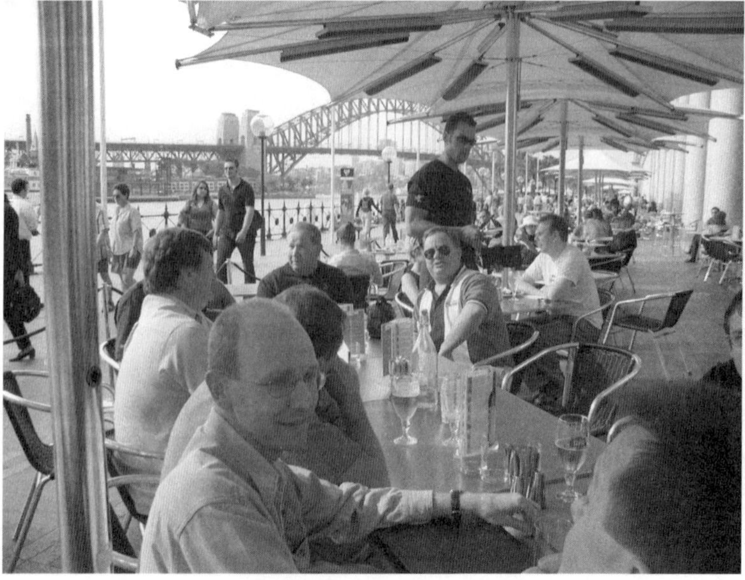

Figure P-4
The hands-on session in Melbourne.

Figure P-5
The other hands-on session Melbourne!

SBS 2003 RTM Party

Redmond, WA September 16, 2003

Figure P-6

The author giving the "thumbs up" to the symbolic RTM product box! It was signed by all members of the SBS development team.

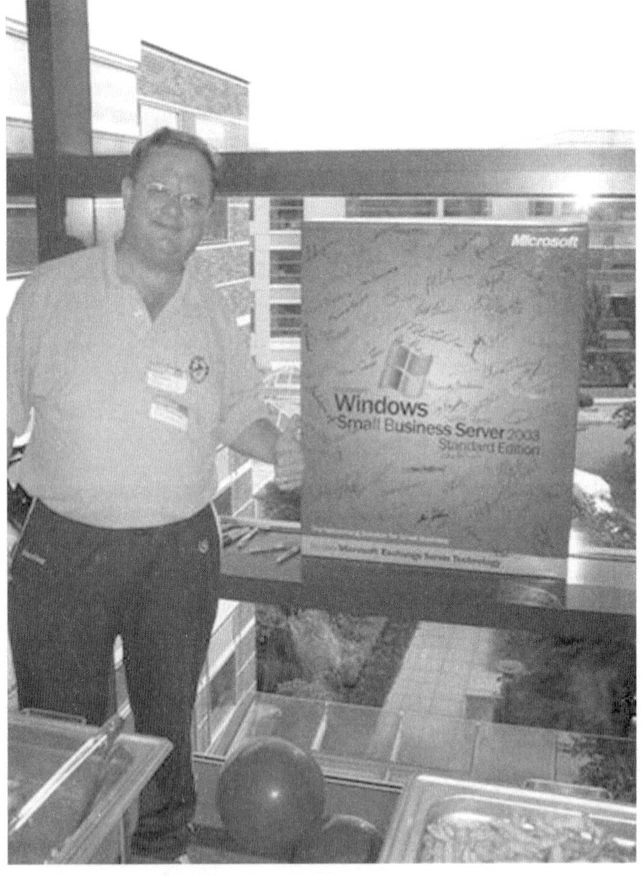

Figure P-7
The RTM cake.

SMB Nation 2003

Indianapolis, IN, September 2003

Figure P-8
Curtis Hicks from Detroit, MI (left) and other SMB Nation attendees enjoy the Indy 500 track tour.

Figure P-9

Bob Hood from Chicago, IL (right) talks SBS with Dave and Conchita Bryner at the Indy 500 BBQ event.

Figure P-10

Dean Paron, program manager on the SBS development team, delivers the keynote speech on Friday night at SMB Nation.

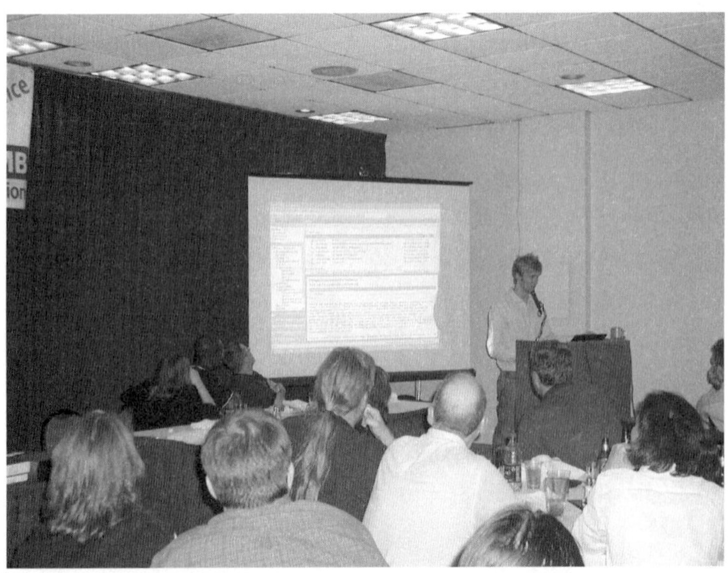

Figure P-11
Roger Otterson, president of the San Diego California SBS Users Group, walks the trade hall at SMB Nation and learns more about Geekcorps.

Figure P-12
Robert Osbrone of Microsoft delivers one of the most popular topics ("...how Microsoft can help you make money with SBS 2003") at SMB Nation in a break out session.

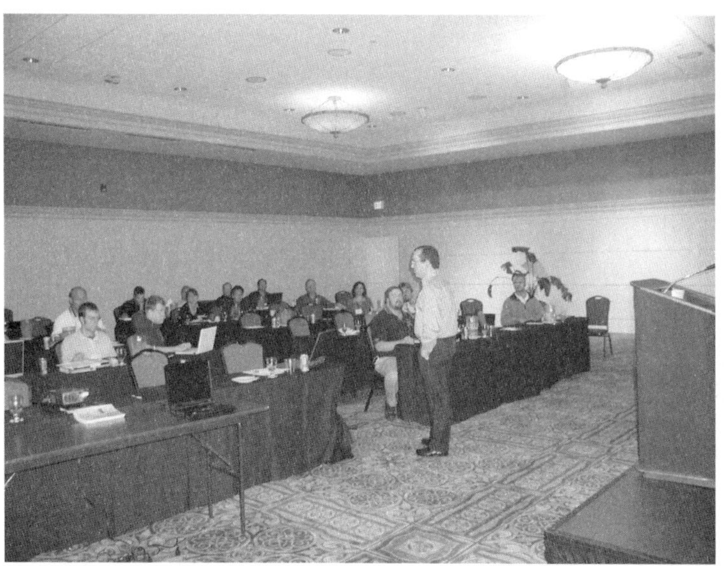

Figure P-13
SBS MVP Susan Bradley was the highest rated speaker of the entire conference. Here she presents "A Google a day keeps the BSOD's away: Support tools that get results fast!"

Figure P-14
Roger Otterson (left), Scott Colson (center) and John Washenberger (right) sneak out of a presentation to visit in the common area. Participants regarded the social interaction and relationship building as seen here as one of the highlights of SMB Nation.

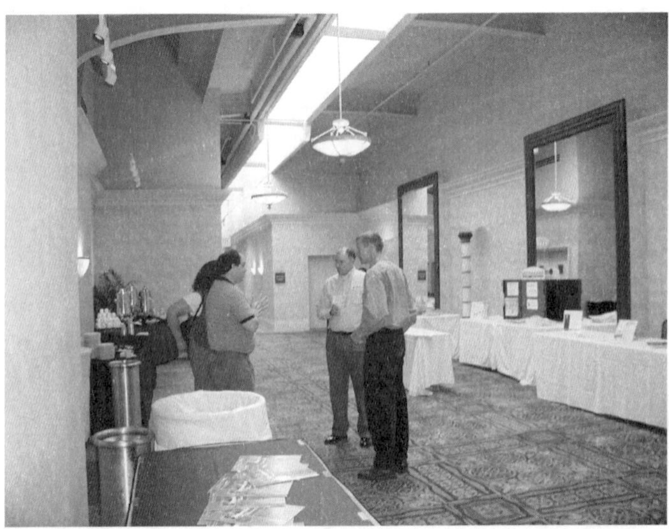

Figure P-15
SBS Mobile at Monster Garage Night "before!" Evening coordinator Gregory Martin from Palm Springs, CA exits the driver seat.

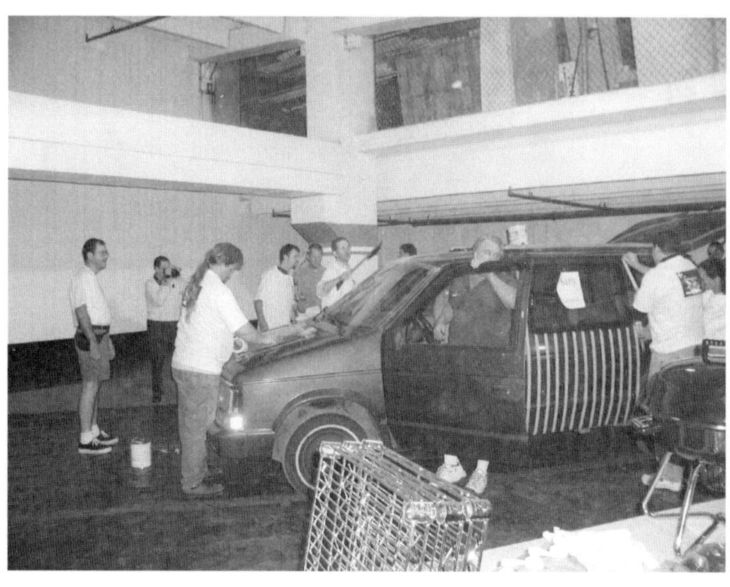

Figure P-16
SBS Mobile "during" the event. Marc Semadeni (left) and Andy Bauman paint the HP logo.

Figure P-17

SBS Mobile "after" with banner being held by SBS MVP's Wayne Small (left) and Andy Goodman (right).

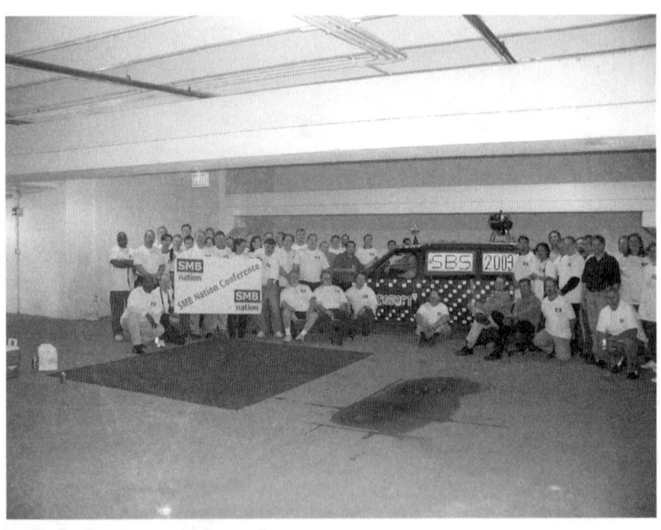

SBS 2003 Launch

New Orleans, LA, October 2003

Figure P-18

A New Orleans jazz funeral procession proclaims Microsoft Live Meeting is alive. This was part of the "Welcome Walk" herding attendees into the SBS 2003 launch.

Figure P-19
Orlando Ayala (left) and Katy Hunter (right) launch SBS 2003!

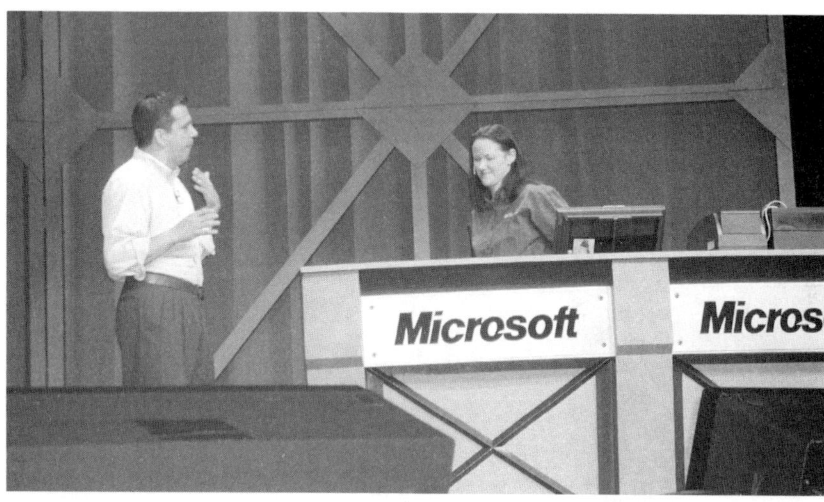

Figure P-20
One of many SBS 2003 booths on the trade show floor. This booth featured HP.

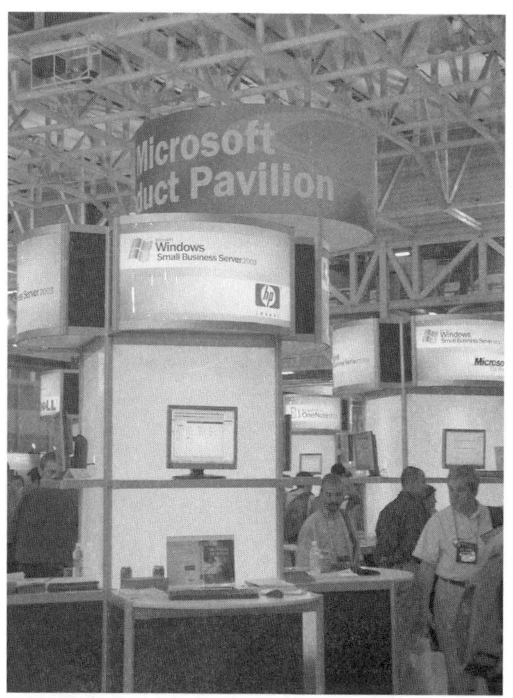

Figure P-21
Attendees watching Duran-Duran at the SBS 2003 launch party!

Figure P-22
SBS Product Manager Dean Paron (left) and Ross-Tek President Fred Johnson (right) enjoying the SBS After Party.

SBS Development Team

Redmond, Washington

Figure P-23

Harry Brelsford Jr. (center) hands Dean Paron (left) a copy of SMB Consulting Best Practices. Geoffrey Brelsford (right) hand a copy to another member of the SBS development team. This was book gift day in building 43 at Microsoft's Redmond campus.

SBS 2003 Hands-on Labs

USA, India

Figure P-24

The author teaching the SBS 2003 hands-on lab in San Francisco, CA (October 2003).

Figure P-25
Attentive students in New Delhi, India learning SBS 2003 (November 2003).

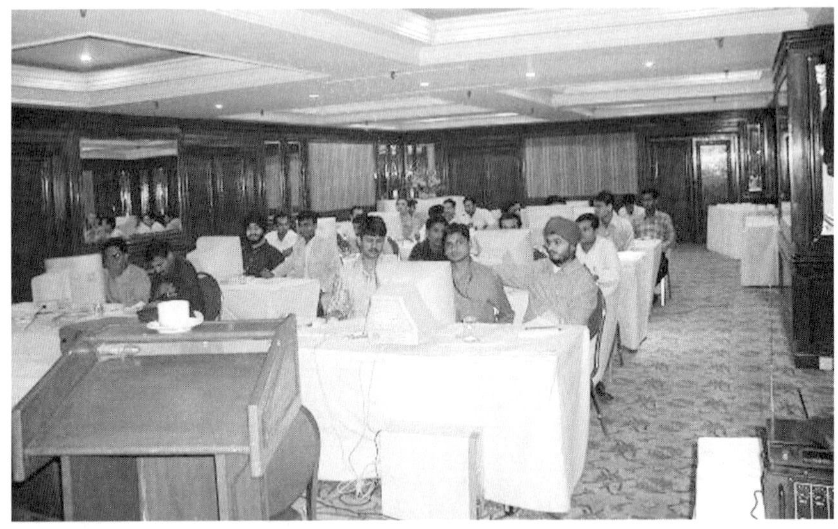

Figure P-26
SBS 2003 students in Bangalore, India. Bangalore is a very technology-oriented city. (November 2003).

Figure P-27

These students attended the SBS hands-on lab in Bombay/Mumbai India.

Springer Spaniels Limited

Figure P-28

Welcome to Springer Spaniels Limited at South Beach on Bainbridge Island, WA. The SPRINGERS world headquarters to right. This will be the site for the SMB Nation 2004 retreat day and concert evening.

Figure P-29
Prize dogs Jaeger (right) and Brisker (left) exercising at the Springer Spaniels Limited facility.

Figure P-30
Brisker (right) and Jaeger (left) enjoying retirement and taking in ABC Monday Night Football.

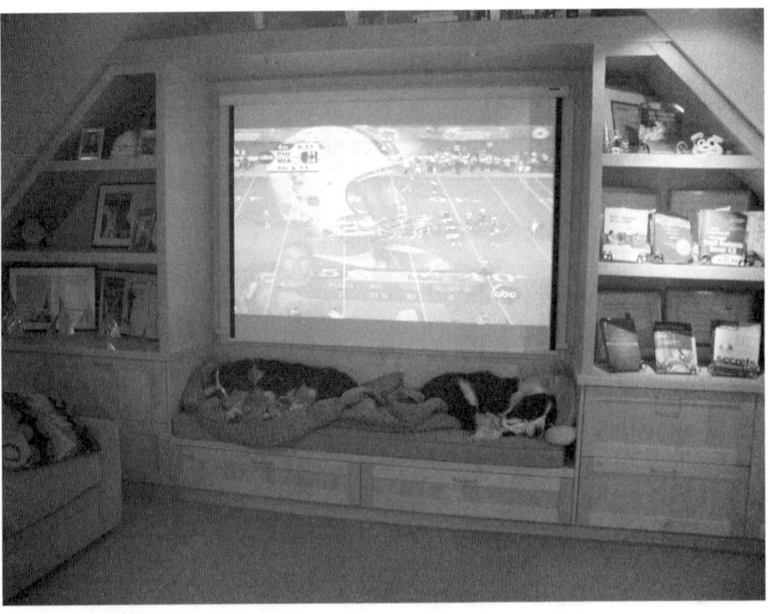

Figure P-31
The author writing this book.

Figure P-32
The author as SBS guru!

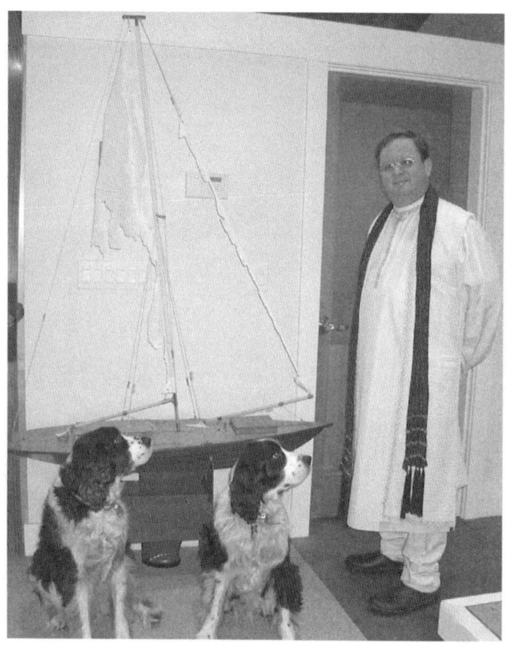

Figure P-33
Springer Spaniels Limited is powered by HP! This is the HP ML-350 server running SBS 2003 premium edition.

SMB Nation Summits Around The World

Figure P-34
Bangalore, India

Figure P-35
London, UK: Geoff Cox (left) and David Croudass (right)

Figure P-36
Singapore

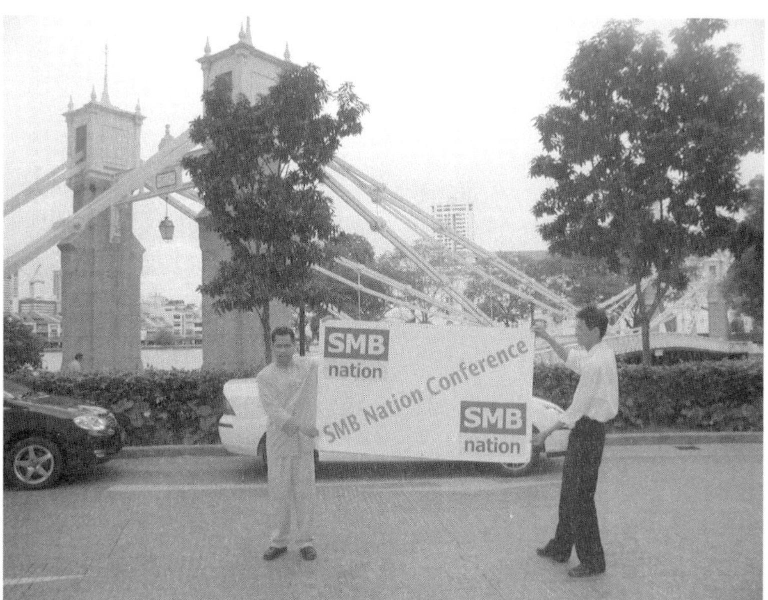

Section Two
Extending SBS 2003

Chapter 5
Standard SBS Security

This chapter honors the all-important security discussion. Up until most recently, every year was dubbed the "Year of Security" by the popular media. That moniker has finally been retired with Microsoft announcing this as the "Year of SMB" with the launch of SBS 2003 in October 2003 at the Worldwide Partners Conference (WWPC) in New Orleans, Louisiana, USA.

BEST PRACTICE: With the completion of your basic SBS 2003 network for SPRINGERS over the last few chapters, if might be easy to believe your job as the SBSer is largely complete. But in reality your job has only begun! Did you know that the moment you completed the deployment of your SBS 2003 network, it was already badly and sadly out of date! "What?!" you say. Don't be angry - this isn't personal. SBS 2003 standard edition was released to manufacturing (RTM) on Tuesday, September 16, 2003, at 11:00am Pacific Standard Time. And SBS 2003 premium edition RTMed on Wednesday, October 1, 2003. On those respective dates, both products instantly started to age and become out of date from a patch management point of view. That is, a patch released on October 7, 2003, (as an example) would never be included out-of-the-box at startup in either of the original RTM SBS 2003 editions. You need to apply this update.

More encouraging words. This isn't about working yourself out of a job when it comes to SBS, but rather about the fact that more work lies ahead of you than behind you. Most security tasks in the chapter are typically performed on an ongoing basis over the life of the computer network.

Of course this chapter continues the SPRINGERS methodology whereby you are deploying an SBS 2003 network for the imaginary Springer Spaniels Limited company.

Introduction

So many folks in the SBS community equate security with a firewall it's scary! If you were do conduct a focus group and engage in a word association game whereby you said the word "security" to a panel of SBSers, you'd be shocked, awed, amazed, and dazed at how many would utter the word "firewall."

Truthfully, security is much more like a multi-headed Hydra beastie from Greek methodology. Certainly a firewall is one component of security, but it only joins other security elements as listed below:

- **Computer**. Obviously much security attention will be devoted to making the computer system as secure as possible, including completing a secure setup, keeping all devices updated with the latest patches, using the security features and best practices that ship with SBS, and even supplementing SBS security with additional tools. All of this is discussed in the chapter.

- **Physical**. Later in the chapter, the physical element of security is discussed whereby you might find yourself running to secure your SBS server machine (which someone could easily walk away with).

- **Management practices**. Do you have a written security policy so that employees are educated on what workplace behaviors are acceptable or unacceptable?

- **Personal practices**. I'll only mention this here, but look at how you conduct your own affairs. Do you use a 900MHZ cordless telephone that neighbors can hear over a baby monitor (especially when you read your credit card)? Do you allow a minimum-wage valet to park your luxury car (and perhaps plant a "bug" from your business competitor)? Get paranoid right now about your personal security. Be aware of your surroundings. Enough said.

Security is an evolving, ongoing concern that you "did" yesterday, "do" today, and "will do" tomorrow. It never ends and at no time can you become complacent and utter that our small business is completely secure. In fact, at the end of this chapter, I only point you to more intense security resources to march forward with.

BEST PRACTICE: Truth be told, achieving complete security on your SBS network is never truly possible, as my friend security author Roberta Bragg has reminded me. But a high level of computer security can be achieved by just turning both the server machine and client computer off (although Roberta cautions that wake-on LAN technologies might work around even this approach). The next level down on the security food chain would be to simply unplug the SBS server machine from the Internet. But since most of us live in the real world, are merchants of some trade, and seek to conduct business and consummate transactions, we have to be reasonable and practical and find a balance between security and business functionality. That might be a different experience for different people, but I want to set the framework for that decision making.

SBS Setup Revisited

Believe it or not, you've already taken significant steps so far in making your SBS network secure. For example, you have deployed the SPRINGERS network with two network adapter cards (aka network interface card or NIC) that will create something of a "Great Barrier Reef" (GBR) to create a division between good and evil (Figure 5-1). The GBR will make even more sense in a few more passages when you explore the Routing and Remote Access Service (RRAS) basic firewall capability in SBS 2003.

Notes:

Figure 5-1
This figure shows at a high-level how two network adapter cards work in conjunction with SBS 2003.

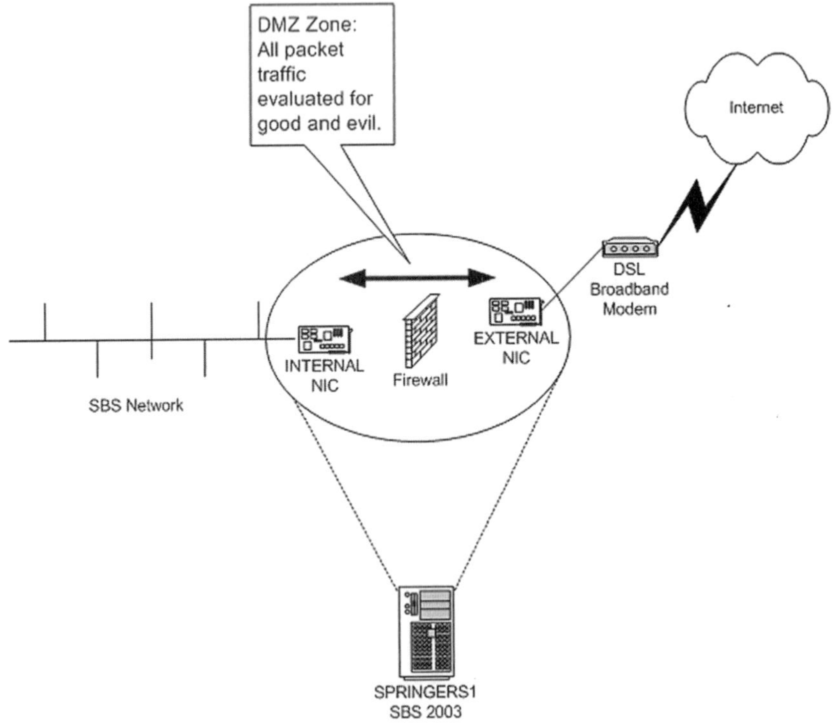

BEST PRACTICE: You'll recall that the two network adapter cards were suggested during the SBS setup at mid-point via a setup warning message. This was discussed in Chapter 3. And I'm honor bound to comment that while the two network adapter card method is much preferred, remember that the crown jewels are sitting atop the "reef," to follow my analogy. You have been so advised.

Another task you completed in the SBS 2003 setup phase was naming the internal domain (SPRINGERSLTD.LOCAL). This act laid the foundation for having separate DNS domains and creating separation from the outside world. Read on to the next paragraph to "hear the rest of the story" on this.

You also completed the E-mail and Internet Connection Wizard (EICW) in the prior Chapter (Chapter 4). It was necessary to complete that wizard, which applied many security configurations to SBS 2003, in that particular chapter to maintain "order" in the SPRINGERS methodology. In the EICW, you referred to and configured SBS 2003 to realize and recognize the external domain (SPRINGERSLTD.COM). So between the SBS 2003 setup process and completing the EICW, you effectively created domain separation, which is a good thing. Why? Because you've shielded the internal domain from external viewing. But heed this disclaimer: The outsiders can still see the external IP address of the wild side network adapter card on the SBS server machine.

Whether you knew it or not, basic auditing was turned on as part of the SBS setup process so that logons are recorded in the Security log under Event Viewer (this is located under System Tools beneath **Computer Management (Local)** under **Advanced Management**). My forthcoming advanced text on SBS 2003 will cover auditing in much more detail.

And finally, you completed the password policies settings, read the security best practices stuff from the To Do List, completed the remote access configurations (which inherently have security in mind), and so on. So you're not new to security in SBS.

Updates!

With SBS 2003, as soon as you're connected to the Internet, you need to RUN, NOT WALK to implement the very latest patches. This will make your machine "fit" for service, and should be done given the speed in which gremlins travel on the Internet. As elegantly pointed out by Microsoft CEO Steve Ballmer at the SBS 2003 launch at the WWPC, the time between identification of vulnerability and acts that exploit said vulnerability has been dramatically compressed. Waiting only minutes prior to implementing the latest patches clearly exposes your "naked" SBS 2003 server machine to worms and other bad stuff. And if your SBS server machine is located in New Delhi, India, be sure to immediately secure it physically so it's not attacked and stolen by monkeys! (An almost-true story here as told to yours truly).

Automatic Updates!

Because this is such an easy step, it's easy to overlook. In fact, overlooking this task is one of Microsoft's great fears and was the subject of extensive media coverage in the fall of 2003. Why? Because Microsoft, as displayed by Ballmer in his WWPC keynote address, has typically released a patch to correct a vulnerability *before* someone exploits that vulnerability (e.g., Microsoft released its SQL Server Slammer patch before the worm was released in the wild). But the problem is that folks don't take the time update their computers. So while the patch existed, in many cases it hadn't been applied. That certainly reflected some "dark days" in the world of network administration and exposed some of us to be less than competent at our SBSer job.

This specific issue about getting folks to update their system has spawned significant debate in the technology community and media. One side believes that Microsoft should automatically update your system as its default, out of the box configuration. Others are concerned about the privacy issues involved in allowing Microsoft to collect machine configuration information (so it can decide what to apply!). You are encouraged to follow popular journals such as CRN (www.crn.com) to monitor this technical/social/political debate.

Note that you will remember in Chapter 4 the automatic update function started to run at the conclusion of the E-mail and Internet Connection Wizard (EICW). However, I elected to defer the in-depth updating discussion until this chapter to make it "fit" the security discussion.

You might be amazed at how easy it is to actually update your SBS 2003 system with the latest patches. Follow these steps.

1. Log on to your SBS 2003 server machine (e.g., SPRINGERS1) as **Administrator** (which in the case of SPRINGERS would use the password **Husky9999!**).
2. Click **Start, All Programs, Windows Update**.
3. Click **Next** at the **Automatic Updates Setup Wizard** page where you are welcomed.

BEST PRACTICE: Perhaps the socio-political discussion earlier in this section hit home with you. On the Automatic Updates Setup Wizard page, there are links that allow you to learn how automatic updates impact your licensing agreement and how Microsoft's privacy policy affects you when Automatic Update is run.

4. The **Notification Settings** page (Figure 5-2) allows you to configure the Automatic Update settings. This relates to the degree in which you want the update function to be automatic. For example, are you interested in having the updates automatically updated and applied? Probably not, as I'll explain in the next Best Practice. The default selection regarding downloading updates automatically and notifying you is the preferred method (this is advisory mode).

Figure 5-2
For SPRINGERS, please make your screen look similar to this figure.

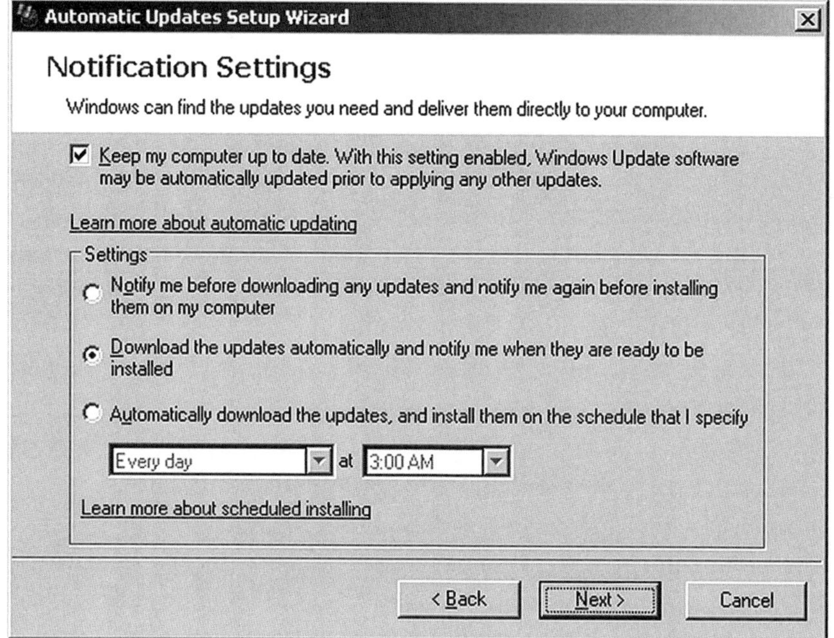

BEST PRACTICE: Civil liberties and privacy concerns aside, you want some control over how your updates are applied and the automatic deployment of updates is typically frowned upon. Why? Because you may well want to test the updates on a sample network (e.g., SPRINGERS with a live Internet connection on a test server) before applying the updates to a real production machine. Once in a blue moon, a patch will fix one thing and break two (that statement isn't to fault Microsoft, but rather speak the truth and appreciate the complexities of software interaction).

So test and verify whenever possible before deploying patches on a production server machine!

5. Click **Finish** on the **Completing the Automatic Updates Setup Wizard** page. Note there is no link titled "here" to save this as part of your SBS 2003 network notebook, because this isn't a native SBS 2003 Wizard.
6. An Internet Explorer Web browser will launch and connect to Microsoft's automatic update site (http://v4.windowsupdate.microsoft.com/en/default.asp). Note in the case of your imaginary implementation of SPRINGERS, it may well be that you aren't truly connected to the Internet. But in the "real world" you likely would be connected to the Internet and could complete this task as expected.
7. Approve the request from Microsoft to download a component called "Windows Update" to analyze your machine by clicking **Yes**. It is this process that will assess what patches are missing and need to be applied. Oh, and you may select the checkbox to **Always trust content from Microsoft Corporation**.
8. On the **Welcome to Windows Update** page that appears, click **Scan for updates**.
9. A screen of suggested updates will be displayed next (titled **Pick updates to install**). Click **Review and install updates**.
10. The actual updates to approve and install are shown in Figure 5-3 on the **Total Selected Updates screen**. You may remove updates at this point that you do not care to install. Because this book, being written in the fall of 2003, is only as current as the day on which I wrote it, I can't even hope to recreate a figure that displays the update you're likely to see at a future date. Bear with me. Assuming the suggested updates are acceptable, click **Install Now**.

Notes:

Figure 5-3
Carefully review each update before proceeding. If in doubt, remove the update and reconsider it at a future time (don't wait too long though, but be careful nonetheless).

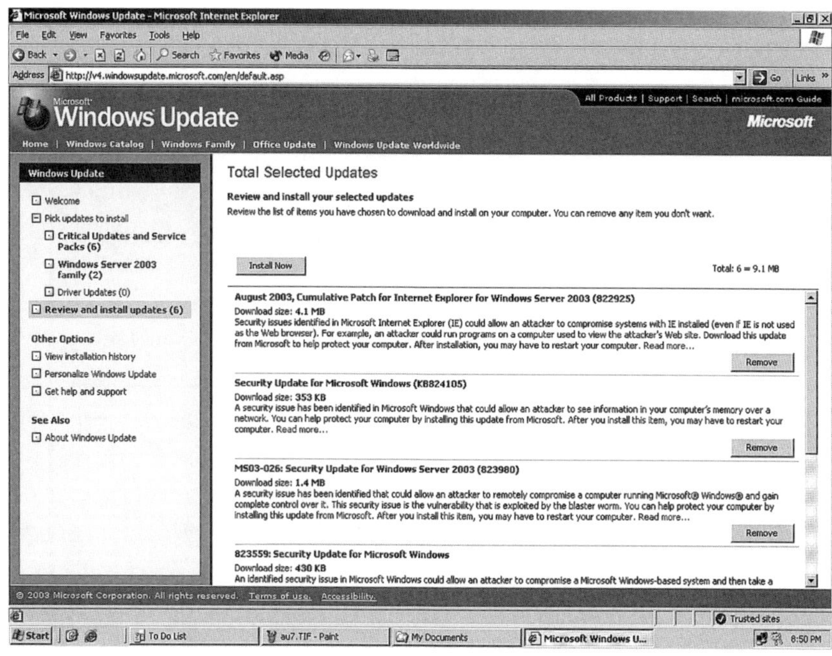

11. You will likely need to approve a license agreement for one or more of the updates being applied. Such an agreement might look like Figure 5-4. Click Accept.

Figure 5-4
Accept any necessary license agreements so that you can proceed.

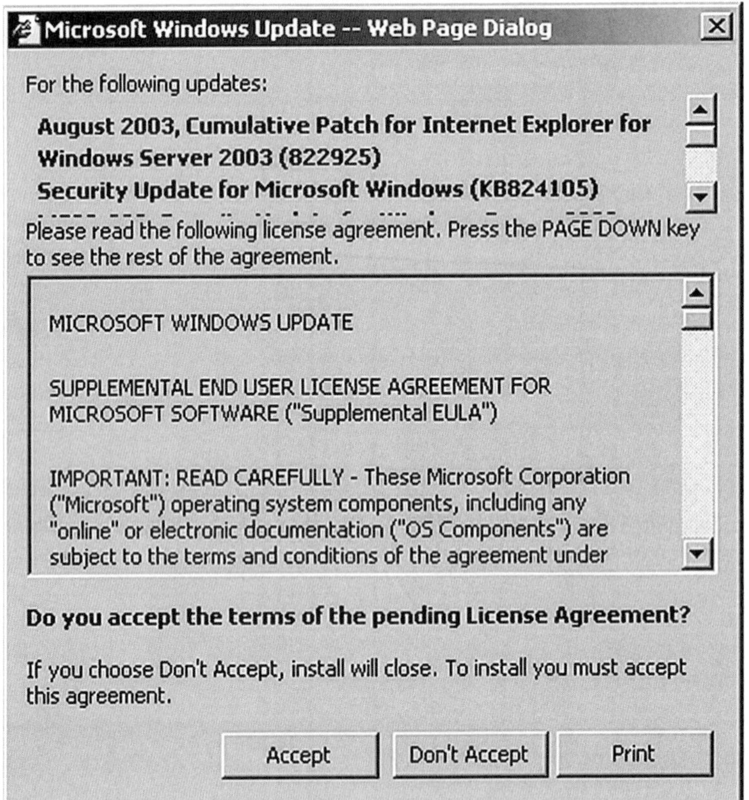

Notes:

12. A component progress dialog box will be displayed similar to Figure 5-5.
13. You will arrive at the **Installation Complete** page seen in Figure 5-6 and you will likely be asked for a reboot at this stage. This is normal; see my further discussion under patch management.

Figure 5-5
You can monitor the status of the updates being applied.

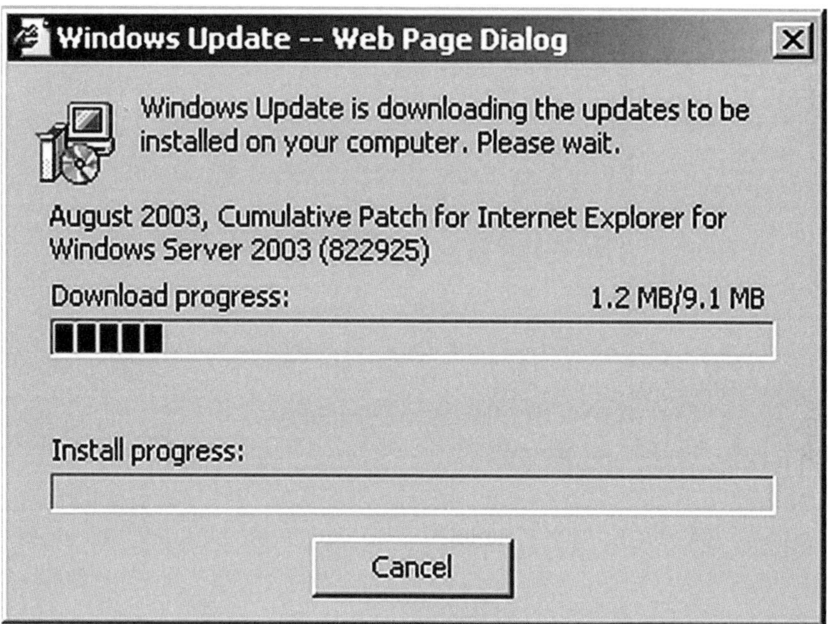

Notes:

Figure 5-6
Success followed by a reboot.

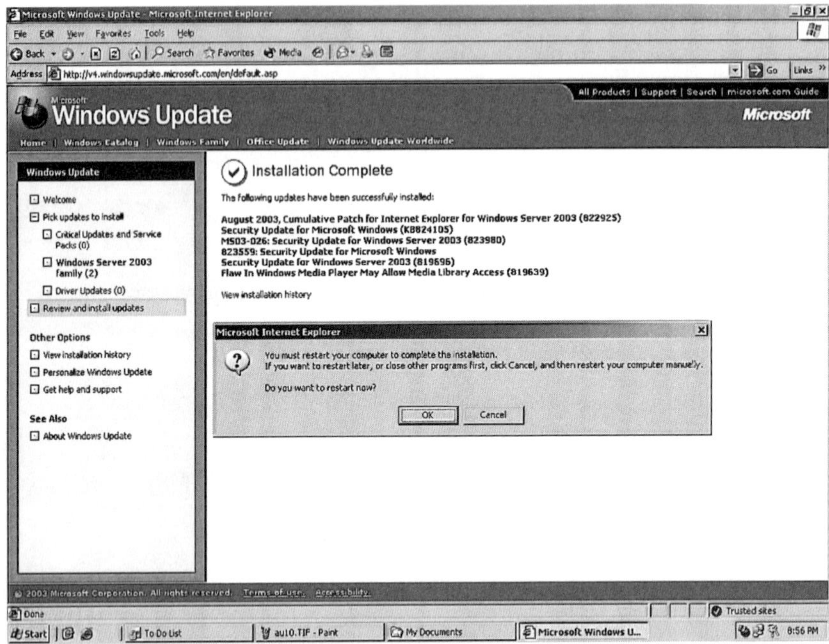

BEST PRACTICE: Don't forget to run Automatic Update on *all* of your workstations. These individual workstations on the SBS network need to stay-ship shape as well!

BEST PRACTICE: Sometimes you'll have a configuration that is slightly different from what Automatic Update expects to see and what it can report. For example, perhaps Automatic Update isn't the best way to keep your legacy NetMeeting application patched because it doesn't necessarily know about, care about, and have the smarts to deal with that application. So some updates are applied manually by visiting the Microsoft security Web site at www.microsoft.com/security.

Of course the above paragraph only begs the question: HOW WOULD YOU KNOW TO GO TO THAT SITE AND CHECK FOR

MANUAL UPDATES? Calm down! You can subscribe to my SBS newsletter wherein I'll announce such updates and you can subscribe to the Microsoft security bulletins at the aforementioned site to receive similar notices. See the resources section near the end of this chapter for more information.

Microsoft Baseline Security Analyzer

In the world of biotech, a double-blind test is often run to validate research results. While I'm not going to suggest you go out and get a grant from the Springer Spaniels Limited Medical Research Foundation to accomplish this, I am going to suggest you take another update step to cover your backside as an SBSer.

While I'm a big fan of the Automatic Update capability in SBS 2003, I still sleep better when I also download, install, and run the Microsoft Baseline Security Analyzer (MBSA). This tool is similar to Automatic Update in that you analyze and apply suggested updates. You can download MBSA from www.microsoft.com/security (a file titled mbsasetup.msi as of this writing). Note you might be asked to install Microsoft XML Parser 3.0 Service Pack 2.5 which can be obtained from www.microsoft.com/msdn.

Software Update Service

A lot of noise is being made in the infrastructure community about Software Update Service (SUS). As of this writing, many of us in the SBS community have been "playing" with the first release and learning it along the way. I've found success in using it to update SBS server machines, but neither Burl (a gentleman who works for me) nor I have found out how to efficiently use SUS to support a wide and diverse range of workstations on a network. This is where the promise of SUS version 2.0 resides (and unfortunately was not available at press time for testing).

Notes:

But back up just a second. What is SUS? The SUS experience is shown in Figure 5-7 and described step-wise below.

Figure 5-7
A well-worn Microsoft presentation slide has been recast and is shown in an SBS scenario.

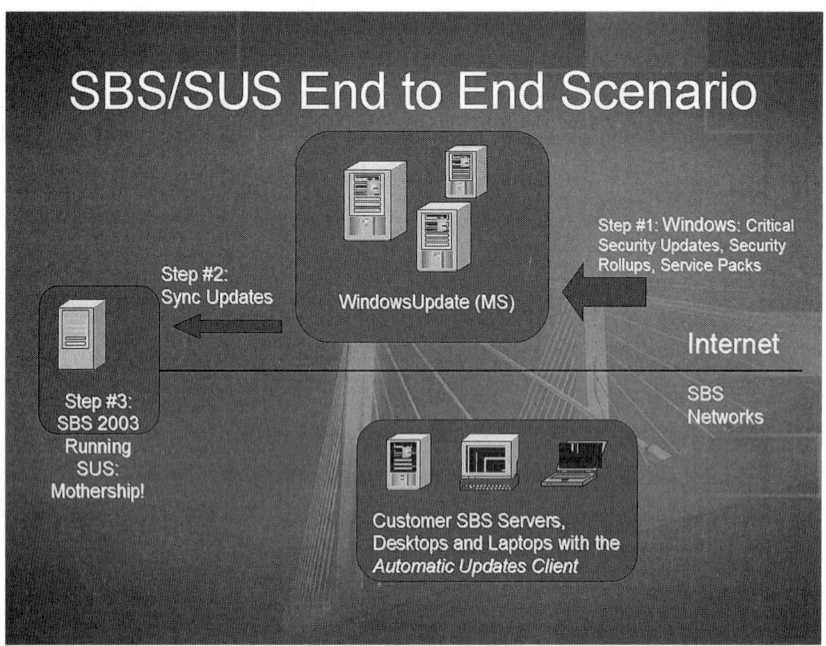

The SUS / SBS process is as follows.

Step #1: Microsoft develops and releases security updates, security rollups, and service packs to its Windows Update site.

Step #2: The SBS 2003 server machine you've configured with SUS rings the Windows Update site to receive these updates.

Step #3: You approve selected updates and apply them on your mothership SBS 2003 server machine.

Step #4: Your customers' sites have SBS server machines configured via Automatic Update to "phone home" to the mothership server and receive the approved updates. Again, as of this writing, this process works well at the server level and should be improved soon at the client computer level. (Note the Windows XP and

Windows 2000 releases are reasonably well supported here, but the process comes up short with Windows 9x workstations.)

BEST PRACTICE: Did you know this piece of SUS trivia? Upon its initial release in the second half of 2002, SUS wouldn't work with SBS. That's right! At that time, SUS wouldn't work on a domain controller and the SBS server machine is a domain controller. But in late 2002, right around Christmas, Microsoft released SUS Service Pack 1 that fixed this shortcoming and allowed SUS to forever more run on an SBS server machine.

A few more comments on SUS and SBS include:

- Erin Bourke-Dunphy and SMB Nation (www.smbnation.com). Erin, a long-time program manager on the SBS development team, recently joined the team that has ownership of SUS. She graciously spoke at my SMB Nation conference in Indianapolis, Indiana, USA (September 2003). An interesting point in her excellent presentation was the fact that SUS was being positioned to serve the SMB, not enterprise space. And SBS plays, of course, in the SMB space. Enterprise sites would use System Management Server (SMS) with the SUS Feature Pack. Her speech, which covered a lot of ground and will be presented in its entirety in my advanced SBS 2003 book due out in mid-2004, brought out one point I want to share now: support for additional content. SUS version 2 will support updates for Office 2003 and other Microsoft server-based applications, such as Exchange and SQL Server. As of this writing, SUS is really about updating the networking infrastructure.

- Steve Ballmer and the WWPC. I don't know if it was irony or what, but if you review the transcripts of proceedings for the SBS 2003 launch at WWPC, you'll see that SUS essentially was the warm-up band to the launch of SBS 2003. That's right! Ballmer concluded his speech focusing on security topics and after a short question and answer session, followed by a break, SBS 2003 was launched! So SUS and SBS 2003 will always be married in time.

Patching Best Practices

If you've been looking for an area in the technology sector that hasn't fully matured and offers lots of promise for good work, consider patch management. If you run your own SBS network, add "patch management" on your skill set list. Microsoft is giving intense focus on patch management to make its systems more and more secure. This is a welcome trend. One example of this is the "chaining" of updates to reduce reboots, as seen in a slide from a recent Microsoft partner "Go To Market" slide deck (Figure 5-8).

Figure 5-8
In the Windows Server 2003 time frame, which is the underlying network operating system in SBS 2003, SBS server machines experience fewer planned reboots and thus higher reliability because of chaining updates (see upper right).

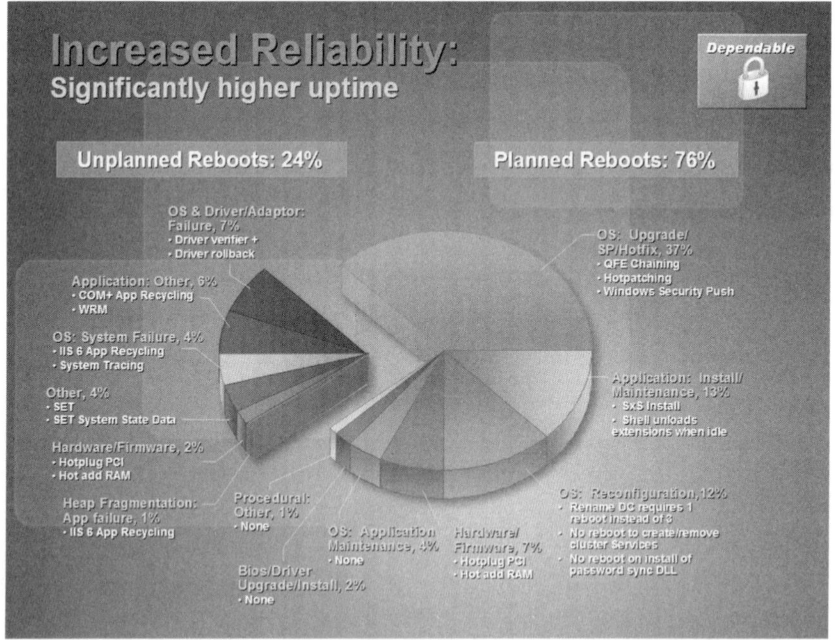

One leading SBSer in New York City, Michael Klein, looks at patch management as a significant portion of his profitable SBS consulting practice. He can use the remote management capabilities in SBS 2003 to "terminal services" into his customer sites and perform patch management, saving an on-site visit. Another

SBSer, a highly rated instructor on the USA SBS 2003 hands-on lab tour in the fall of 2003 named Quinn Guiteras, has a tale to tell about patch management. He likens a lot of technology consultants, including SBSers, to being rejected firemen (we wanted to be fireman, but didn't have the body). Some of us in the technology field are into the thrills of putting out network fires, even at the SBS level. But Quinn, a forward thinker, believes that yesterday's frustrated fireman is today's Smokey the Bear! That is, with the evolution of patch management, prevention is now the paradigm to embrace and should be the focus of network managers everywhere.

I hope this section on patch management has you convinced that preventative medicine is a preferred best practice.

RRAS Unplugged

So now that you're all patched and updated, let's do some meat and potatoes. That is, let's delve into the firewall component of SBS 2003 standard edition: RRAS's NAT/Basic Firewall. I'll essentially repeat Lab 7 from the afternoon of the USA SBS 2003 hands on lab tour that I both wrote and delivered in fall 2003. The intent of the lab was this: After a long day together of SBSing, some folks had unanswered questions about security and exactly what voodoo do you do when you complete a native SBS Wizard. Oops - I went Ragin' Cajun on you for a moment there. What I meant to say was SBSers sometimes wonder what real settings they affect when the complete a pretty wizard.

It's important, before proceeding, to remember that you completed both the EICW and the Remote Access Wizard in the prior chapter in order to maintain the sanctity of our SPRINGERS methodology. So, in effect, you've already implemented the security related to firewall protection in SBS 2003 standard edition.

The key pages in the EICW that relate specifically to the security we'll discuss in this chapter (and future chapters) are EICW page 7 (the Firewall screen where you enable the firewall), EICW page 8 which relates to services that will be accessible across the Internet (see Services Configuration in Figure 5-9), EICW page 9 (Web Services Configuration that I really discuss more in Chapters 8 and 10) and EICW page 10 (Web Server Certificate) that I discuss more in the next section.

Figure 5-9
Revisiting the Services Configuration page.

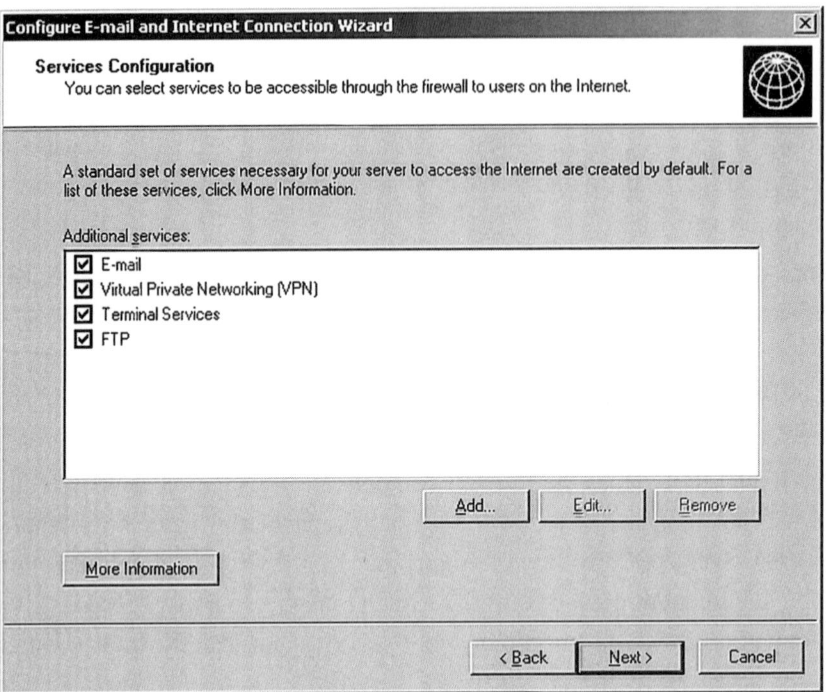

BEST PRACTICE: You'll increasingly learn and be comfortable with your own situation best. Remember that the SPRINGERS methodology is a pass across SBS 2003 using a story line that works. On the Services Configuration page as part of SPRINGERS, we made some selections in the last chapter.

But what if your real-world needs are slightly different? Perhaps you'll need to allow some other services, read port openings, be accessible via the Internet. How would you do that in Figure 5-9? Just click the **Add** button and type in the service name and port information.

In the next procedure, you'll not only see where your Service Configuration settings are implemented, but you'll get a peek at the additional services you could select from. Please be advised that the following procedure, which is basically a look and see, is here so you can appreciate where some of the security settings you select in the EICW are truly "set."

1. Log on to **SPRINGERS1** as **Administrator** with password **Husky9999!**.
2. Click **Start, Server Management, Advanced Management, Computer Management**, and **Services and Applications**.
3. Select **Routing and Remote Access, IP Routing** followed by **NAT/ Basic Firewall**.
4. Right click on **Network Connection** and select **Properties** from the secondary menu, (and then see my figures).
5. Observe the **NAT/Basic Firewall** tab sheet (Figure 5-10) that depicts the selections for NAT and Basic Firewall. These were selected when you enabled the firewall on page 7 of the EICW. I'll discuss the concept of NAT and Basic Firewall in just a second.
6. Click the **Services and Ports** tab. Observe the services that you can select.

Figure 5-10
This is where the NAT and Basic Firewall selections are made.

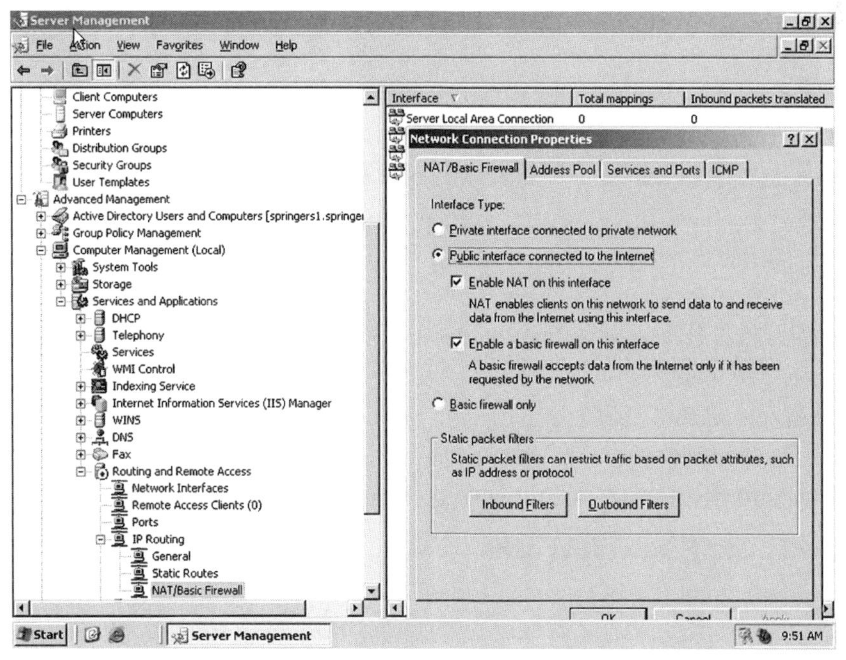

Figure 5-11
This is where the Internet-accessible services were selected.

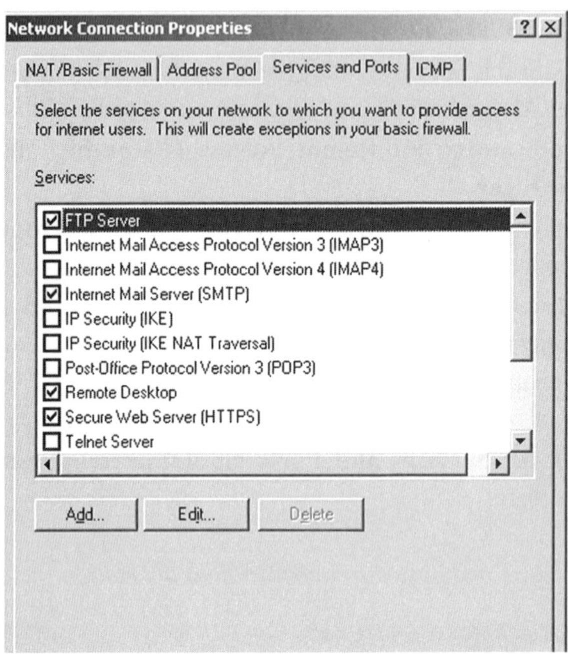

7. Click **OK**.

Defining Basic Firewall/NAT

Meanwhile, back in the lecture hall, it's time to lay one down on you about NAT and the Basic Firewall. You can use Basic Firewall to help secure your network from unsolicited public network traffic, such as traffic sent from the Internet. People who send such traffic might be trying to access your network without your permission. You can enable Basic Firewall for any public interface, including one that also provides network address translation (also known as NAT, an Internet Protocol (IP) translation process that allows a network with private addresses to access information on the Internet for your network).

How Basic Firewall Works

First of all, what is a firewall? Quoting directly from the online help system in SBS 2003: *A firewall is a combination of hardware and software that provides a security system, usually to prevent unauthorized access from outside to an internal network or intranet. A firewall prevents direct communication between network and external computers by routing communication through a proxy server outside the network. The proxy server determines whether it is safe to let a file pass through to the network. Also called a security-edge gateway.*

Next, the Basic Firewall provided via RRAS in SBS 2003 is a stateful firewall which combines dynamic packet filtering of network traffic with a set of static packet filters. Said Basic Firewall monitors traffic that travels through the interface for which Basic Firewall is enabled. If the interface is configured for private network traffic only, Basic Firewall will route traffic among the computers on the private network only. The Basic Firewall will route traffic between a private network and virtual private network (VPN). I define a VPN below in the advanced section.

If the interface is configured for private network traffic and to provide NAT, each packet's source and destination addresses are recorded in a table. All traffic from the public network is compared to the entries in the table. Traffic from the public network can reach the private network only if the table contains an entry that shows that the communication exchange originated from within the private network. In this way, Basic Firewall prevents unsolicited traffic from a public network (such as the Internet) from reaching a private network. This is a key point, pardner: We're keeping the bad guy out here.

Service Accessibility

Perhaps you noticed earlier in this RRAS section that adding the additional services by name and port was as easy as dropping beneath the hood and simply selecting from the bevy of services contained on the Services and Ports screen (which you observed in the last step-by-step procedure above). The services on the Services and Ports screen are listed here.

- FTP Server
- Internet Mail Access Protocol Version 3 (IMAP3)
- Internet Mail Access Protocol Version 4 (IMAP4)
- Internet Mail Server (SMTP)

- IP Security (IKE)
- IP Security (IKE NAT Traversal)
- Post-Office Protocol Version 3 (POP3)
- Remote Desktop
- Secure Web Server (HTTPS)
- Telnet Server
- VPN Gateway (L2TP/IPSec - running on this server)
- VPN Gateway (PPTP)
- Web Server (HTTP)

And if you insist, you can always add different services via the Add button on the Services and Ports tab just like you could back in the EICW.

Get Certified!

A cool feature that is managed by the Web Server Certificate page in the EICW is the ability to easily install a self-signed certificate on your SBS 2003 server machine.

> BEST PRACTICE: Note the self-signed certificate is not the same as installing and configuring Certificate Services to create a certificate authority. (You can see via Control Panel, Add/Remove Programs, Windows Components that Certificate Services HAS NOT BEEN INSTALLED and configured after the Web Server Certificate page in the EICW is complete.) As author Roberta Bragg put it to me, it's "kool" but it's not Certificate Services. This is important to understand and perhaps you'd want to proceed to install Certificate Services for other purposes such as e-commerce. That suggestion begs the next point.

So, do you need to continue to pay the SSL King (Verisign) his ransom in the world of SBS 2003? The answer is perhaps not if you were using Certificate Services as your certificate authority. So, save those dollars to be spent on something more meaningful like taking your spouse/partner out to dinner (a real nice dinner in Vegas with your Verisign savings!).

Real world speaking, this self-signed Web certificate will be most noticeable in two ways to users. First, the address in a Web browser (known as the URL) will start with the prefix HTTPS. Second, you'll typically need to approve the certificate when a security dialog box appears as a user commences a Web session on the SBS 2003 server. And how do you explain this to the same real-world users? Tell them this is akin to logging on to their bank (e.g., Wells Fargo) or brokerage firm (e.g., ETrade).

BEST PRACTICE: The Web Server Certificate page in the EICW is dramatically reducing the number of keystrokes you had to perform in the SBS 2000 time frame to achieve the "nearly" same kind of security-related functionality (granted, I'm comparing apples to oranges here for a few minutes, but go with it). Again, a self-signed certificate and Certificate Services are not the exact same thing.

In my now retired Advanced SBS 2000 Workshop, I demonstrated the keystrokes necessary to (1) install Certificate Services from Control Panel, Add/Remove Programs, Windows Components, (2) create a self-signed certificate, (3) apply the certificate to the appropriate locations (e.g., root of the default Web site in SBS 2003 that houses OWA), and (4) apply the SSL setting to child objects (e.g., the Public folder under IIS). Note these steps, in the SBS 2000 time frame, were documented in the following documents:

- a white paper titled "Step-by-Step Guide for Setting Up a Certificate Authority"
- the following *KBase* article: "Turning on SSL for Exchange 2000 Server Outlook Web Access" (Q320291)

- *KBase* article: "How to Force SSL Encryption for an Outlook Web Access 2000 Client" (Q279681)

This kinda stuff is now handled via the Web Server Certificate page in the EICW (at least as far as the typical SBS network is concerned). Note the enterprise security folks reading this book would of course beg to differ and point out huge differences in a self-signed certificate and Certificate Services, such as the ability to issue certificates for IPSec (which our little ol' self-signed certificate can't do). Enough said.

Advanced SBS Security Topics

No chapter worth its security salt could be devoid of a few advanced security topics even though said topics are beyond the scope of this introductory volume on SPRINGERS! While my future advanced SBS 2003 text will delve deeper and fly further on a single tank of gas, try on a few of the following advanced security topics for size. Security is of such importance that this is one time we can clearly take a respite from the SPRINGERS story line and explore:

Hardware-Based Firewall

Yes, Virginia, there is native SBS 2003 support for hardware-based firewalls. It's kosher as well and you'll be accepted in the open and affirming SBS community. Best of all, when you select the router option in the EICW as you set up the network connection (see the third screen regarding connection type in the EICW), you'll be able to take advantage of a really cool SBS 2003 feature: It automatically configures hardware-based routers as part of its wizardry! Say what? This isn't a misprint. What occurs is this. If your hardware-based firewall is Universal Plug and Play (UPNP) compliant (this is an industry standard) and you provide sufficient credentials (that allow you to configure the hardware-based firewall itself), then the EICW will open the correct ports to support the services you've selected that need access from the Internet.

Dual-Firewall

Another popular configuration with SBS 2003 is to implement a dual firewall. In this case, you'd use the built-in firewall capability in SBS 2003 and then supplement that on the network border with an additional firewall. Note this additional firewall is typically hardware-based, but could very well be a software-based firewall from another vendor. A view of a dual firewall scenario is shown in Figure 5-12.

Figure 5-12
This is your road map for implementing a dual-firewall scenario with SBS 2003.

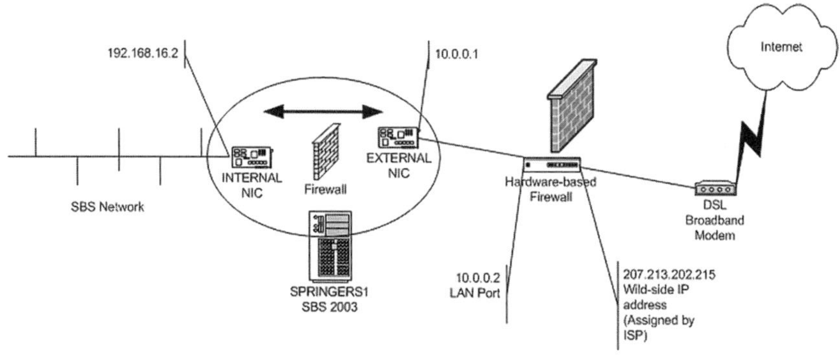

BEST PRACTICE: You could implement a dual firewall scenario with either SBS 2003 standard edition (with the RRAS NAT/Basic Firewall) or SBS 2003 premium edition (with ISA Server 2000 discussed later in Chapter 13).

What Is a VPN?

No, this isn't a trick question. Many readers of this book might not actually know what a VPN is. Don't believe me? Then you should have been there during the filming of an SBS setup video at Microsoft Studios on 158th Ave NE in Redmond the day we forgot to define VPN in the script. An important marketing manager discovered this omission and we had to play some Hollywood magic to splice in a short lecture on VPN connectivity in the post production phase. Needless to say, this drove up the video costs and since that day, I've never forgotten to add this lecture in any chapter where it makes sense.

Here is the official definition of a VPN taken from the online help system in SBS 2003: *The extension of a private network that encompasses encapsulated, encrypted, and authenticated links across shared or public networks. VPN connections can provide remote access and routed connections to private networks over the Internet client computers. However, computers that are part of a private network will not be able to detect computers outside of the private network, and computers that are not part of the private network will not be able to detect computers that belong to the private network.*

Relating VPN connectivity to security is the next step. You might be saying "Who cares?" at this point. Both you and I care. When the shoe fits, establishing a VPN connection using either the point-to-point tunneling protocol (a poor man's encryption method) or layer-two tunneling protocol (a rich man's encryption method that requires a certificate authority) creates a secure link between a remote computer and the SBS 2003 network. Essentially, you can compute with less worry from afar.

BEST PRACTICE: I'll touch on VPN connectivity in Chapter 8 again with step by step procedures. And don't forget you actually configured server-side VPN connectivity in Chapter 4 when you completed the Configure Remote Access link. Be advised much deeper discussion is beyond the scope of this introductory SBS 2003 volume. Look for richer VPN discussion in my advanced SBS 2003 text due in mid-2004.

Black Hat Thyself

So, you think you're an SBS security hot shot? Perhaps you are. One way to validate whether you're "hot or not" is to black hat yourself on the inside and outside. That'll tell you exactly how super you are. In a nutshell, you'd download a port scanner such as GFI's LANGuard Network Security Scanner (www.gfi.com) and run it against yourself. Figure 5-13 shows how such a scan on the internal LAN might look (revealing tons of information) and Figure 5-14 shows how such a scan might look when run over the Internet, showing only the ports you opened via the EICW. (Talk about a great way to validate your work!)

Figure 5-13
Black hattin' on the inside.

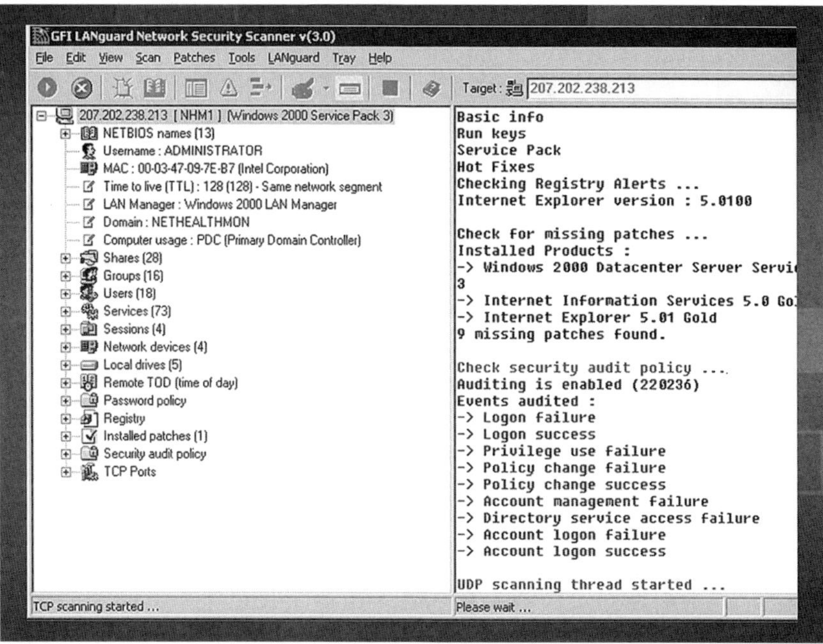

Notes:

Figure 5-14

Black hattin' on the outside.

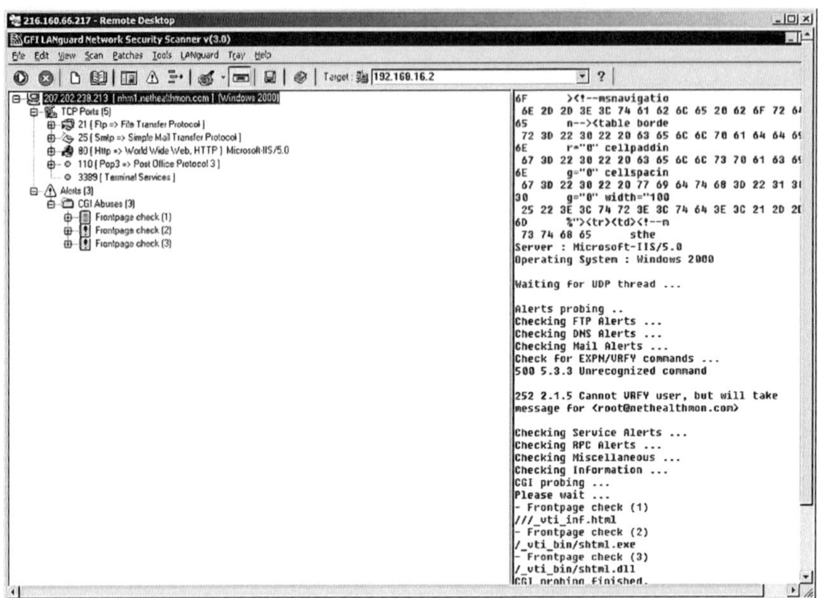

BEST PRACTICE: Perform this activity on each SBS network you work on (even if it's only one). Hopefully, you won't be too surprised by the outcome (in general, SBSers don't like to be surprised in this area). If you're a consultant, share the outcome of this black hat exercise with your clients.

Packet Sniffing

Talk about an MCSE-level exercise that works for us SBSers as well: packet sniffing. Here you would install the Network Monitor tool that is native to the underlying Windows Server 2003 operating system, but not installed by default, and then sniff around. To install the tool, perform the following procedure:

1. Log on as **Administrator** on **SPRINGERS1** (password is **Husky9999!**).
2. Click **Start, Control Panel, Add or Remove Programs**.
3. Select **Add/Remove Windows Components**.

4. Select **Management and Monitoring Tools** in the **Windows Components Wizard**.
5. Select **Network Monitor Tools** and click **OK**.
6. Click **Next**.
7. Insert Disc #1 when requested.
8. Click **Finish**.

In Figure 5-15, you can see what the results of a packet sniffing session might look like. This tool can be used to troubleshoot network problems (such as logon problems) and to search for rogue devices (such as another server running network monitoring on your network without your knowledge).

Figure 5-15

The three-finger salute of TCP/IP session establishment is shown here in a Network Monitor session. Look closely at the source and destination address columns (packets 31-33).

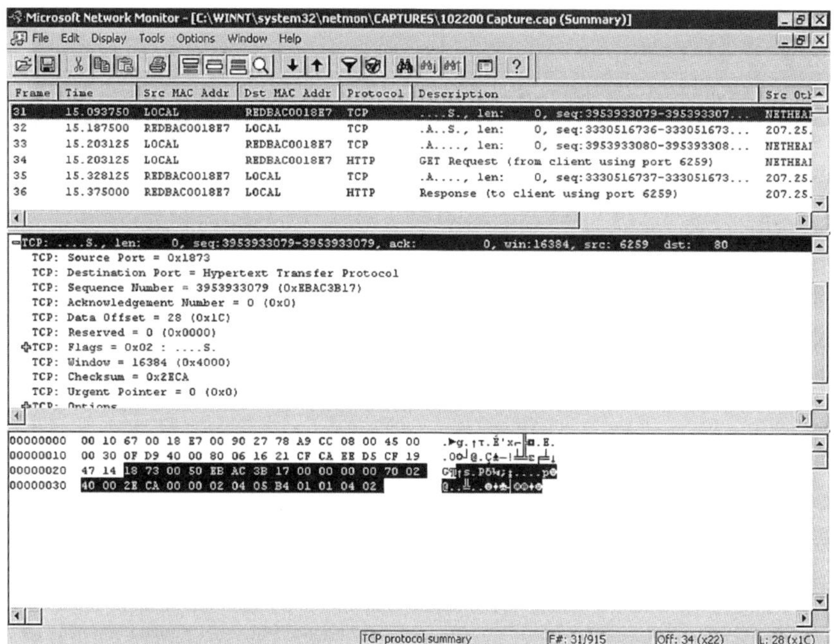

BEST PRACTICE: I used this tool once in early 2003 to investigate whether Microsoft automatic update sessions were actually going out into the ether. A client, a well-known Seattle-based author (not me!), believed said updates where going to an offshore site not controlled by Microsoft. The packet analysis facilitated by the Network Monitor tool showed the fears were unfounded. The client then rested easy and allowed his workstation to be automatically updated. I kinda felt like one of the central characters in an old US movie called *Ghosbusters* and Network Monitor was my tool!

Spam Blocking

Spam blocking fits in the security chapter as well. The malady of "spam" is well known to readers of this book as unwanted e-mail traffic. In fact, the perception of excessive spam on an SBS 2003 network can create unwarranted criticism about SBS 2003 itself, which just isn't fair.

Spam blocking can be divided into two discussion areas: content filtering and attachment blocking.

Content Filtering

I've enjoyed great success using the GFI's MailEssentials spam blocking program, which more than anything else flexes its muscles in the content filtering department. For example, e-mails with the word "Viagra" are treated as spam and processed accordingly, which might include deletion, move to another folder, etc. MailEssentials is shown in Figure 5-16.

Notes:

Figure 5-16
Meet MailEssentials from GFI. Note that this product is very aggressive out of the box and will sometimes go too far, filtering out legitimate messages.

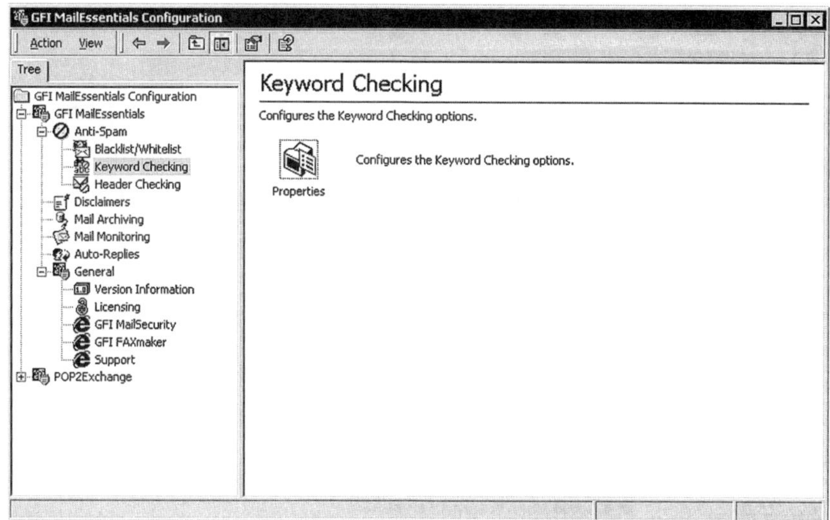

BEST PRACTICE: Because of the false positives and positive negatives in the world of filtering junk e-mails, the oft-cited security author Roberta Bragg insists that I tell you to send filtered mail to a junk mailbox, instead of deleting it! Right on, Roberta!

Another way to easily engage in a form of content filtering is to utilize the junk mail feature in Outlook 2003. This is a MAJOR IMPROVEMENT in Outlook 2003 and is discussed in Chapter 6.

Attachment Blocking

Of course, the simplest way to invoke attachment blocking is to complete the 15th page of the EICW titled "Remove E-mail Attachments." I'll discuss that more in Chapter 6 when you and I look deeper at Exchange Server 2003.

But meet GFI's MailEssentials once again. Assuming you own this application for its effectiveness in the content filtering area, then consider using it as your attachment blocking tool.

BEST PRACTICE: The above statement raises the question about which attachment types to block if you're using a third party tool such as MailEssentials. This list is easily created by looking at and copying the list from the Remove E-mail Attachments page in the EICW.

And yet another attachment blocking tool is contained within Outlook 2003 itself. Since I don't want to spill the beans on Chapter 6 yet, I'll wait to discuss it there. Similarly, you can use the SMTP application filter in ISA Server 2000 to engage in both content filtering and attachment blocking (discussed in Chapter 13).

BEST PRACTICE: I only cite GFI's spam fighting tool because I know it. The infamous Stu at Sunbelt Software in Tampa FL (www.w2knews.com) markets effective spam blocking tools ("I Hate Spam") that deserve your purchasing consideration. The SBS-related newsgroups are also a source of information for third-party spam fighting applications (see Appendix A for this information).

Virus Protection

So, would you consider virus protection a germane security topic? You betcha! I'll discuss this much more in Chapter 11 with some step-by-step procedures using Trend Micro's OfficeScan suite solution, but I'd be remiss to have a security chapter without emphasizing the importance of virus protection as part of your comprehensive approach to security on your SBS 2003 network.

BEST PRACTICE: I'll say it here and again later on. Virus protection is only valid when the data files are up-to-date. More later.

SpyWare

If you want to be humbled in a hurry, download the spyware detection applications from www.BulletProofSoft.com. Install its SpyWatch and SpyWare Remover programs and then, when no one is your witness, run these programs. You might be shocked to see what's been camping out on your SBS network without your knowledge. Thanks to a student from the Louisville, KY hands-on lab for that tip! Many apparently harmless Web sites accessed by your users are really implementing click counters and other spyware nasties. One of the all time greats (or "worsts") was Gator. An instructor with whom I've previously worked on another tour had actually worked for Gator during the dot-com boom and he sends his profound apologies!

FTP Site Notification

And now from the hallowed halls of the Harvard Law School! Did you know that if you dig deep enough into the legal treatise of USA jurisprudence system, you'll find that long ago, a hacker got off the hook because an FTP site at a company said "Welcome!" Apparently the hacker claimed that he felt invited in to poke around and destroy things. The legal lesson learned here? Prevention! Make the introductory screen of your FTP site say "Authorized Users Only!" or something just as strong.

Physical Security and Management Practices

Just when you thought all security was computer-related in the world of SBS, here comes a paradigm shift wherein we'll discuss the real, physical world! The reason for broader security discussion is to get you to once again leave the bits behind for a minute and put that business hat back on. As an SBSer, you can't help but be involved in business matters such as physical security and management practices.

Let's Get Physical!

After reading this section, walk around your office and see if any of the following don't ring true or otherwise apply to you:

- Is the server physically secure? Or is it placed in the open where a large gorilla (or heck, in this day and age, a guerilla) could swoop it up and ship it to a chop shop.

- Lock down time. Locking down the disk and disc drives (that's the floppy and CD/DVD variety) can go along way to preventing the introduction of malware. Don't forget USB ports!

- Assuming the server isn't sitting out in the open and is placed in a room or closet, are the doors to this area locked? Who has the keys?

- Speaking of key management, how many people have key access to your office space? Any keys still in the hands of disgruntled ex-employees?

Management

- Is there a written security policy for the use of the SBS 2003 network? Refer to Appendix A for SBS resources, such as the Yahoo! Groups that include posted documents such as security policies.

- A traditional bookkeeping matter to think about: Are the company's business checks secure? There's nothing like an employee with a gambling problem writing a check to stall Bruno, the mob enforcer.

- How do you feel about employee background checks? Remember some of the biggest crooks are the brightest people and have the most engaging personalities!

- Beware of psychological warfare. Kevin Mitznick and Frank Abagnale, two renowned white-collar criminals, used a form of social engineering to talk their way into profitable illegal activities—hacking into computer systems and stealing money via check fraud respectively. Mitznick would ring an employee of a company and harvest that person's user name and password to then penetrate the company's networks. Abagnale used things like wearing pilot uniforms to earn free flights. Both have written well-received books about their exploits and the power of social engineering.

BEST PRACTICE: Perhaps you've got a war story about social engineering and psychological warfare yourself that underscores the power of this penetration method and its associated security risks. I've got a quick one to share. Traveling home from the WWPC in New Orleans in October 2003, I used my red press pass badge holder (a conference badge holder that hangs around your neck) to carry my passport identification and airline ticket. Once I cleared security, I stopped in a restaurant for a bite to eat. When it came time to pay my bill, I received a 10 percent discount because, with my red badge holder, I was mistaken for being an airport employee (in a secure area nonetheless) and granted the employee discount. I took the 10 percent savings and ran and didn't further cause mayhem in the secure airport terminal with my newfound identity! The point is that you or I could impersonate someone else and gain access and favors we're not entitled to. And just try having a firewall service setting block that attack!

When Do You Need ISA Server?

Well, you'll certainly need ISA server 2000 by the time your reach Chapter 13, which is dedicated to this application in the SBS 2003 premium edition. But, seriously, ISA Server 2000 fits my favorite analogy about shoes and pornography. With respect to shoes, you'll use ISA Server 2000 when said shoe fits. With respect to pornography, simply recall the famous US Supreme Court opinion on obscenity and community standards: You know it (pornography) when you see it. Translation: You'll know when you need ISA Server 2000. But enough teasing.

This chapter was written to demonstrate the security in SBS 2003 standard edition. Period. If you want to peek at Chapter 13 to learn more about ISA Server 2000 usage, go for it. I'll see you back here.

BEST PRACTICE: Keep this in mind. If you purchase the premium edition of SBS 2003 and deploy ISA Server 2000, you will not configure and utilize the security features supported by RRAS. You would let ISA Server 2000 do the heavy lifting.

Security Resources

Given by now we all agree that security is a fluid, dynamic concept and not static, you need to take a long coffee break and go learn more about the following security resources:

- Microsoft security site. First and foremost would be to spend a few hours poking around the Microsoft security web site at www.microsoft.com/security. Enough said.

- Read Ballmer's WWPC keynote. Believe it or not, it might be valuable for you to read the keynote given by the CEO of the richest company on earth at the October 2003 WWPC conference. There are tons of details on Microsoft's view of security and that's something you should know. Click over to www.microsoft.com/presspass to find the transcripts of his speech.

- Roberta and Thomas. Can't say enough about the security books by Roberta Bragg and Dr. Thomas Shinder. Read all about it by searching on these author names at Amazon (www.amazon.com). See Roberta's excellent article titled "Giving The the Small Business" discussing SBS 2003 security at www.mcpmag.com/columns/article.asp?EditorialsID=630.

- Small Business Best Practices. Be sure to sign up for my SBS newsletter at www.smbnation.com where I'm honor-bound to present to you the latest SBS-related security matters.

- Review security in the To Do List in SBS 2003. Believe it or not, a great use of time right now would be to read, print, and read again the information contained beneath the View Security Best Practices link on the SBS 2003 To Do List. Note that we'll walk through a few of these suggestions you'll see when we get to Chapter 11 and discuss SBS 2003 administration.

Next Steps

Before you get to the summary and move on, a few final thoughts.

Security is all about next steps. It never ends. Some days you're just trying to stay one step ahead of the bad guys. Other days the bad guys are one step ahead of you. Be active, be diligent, and never rest for a mere second.

More advanced topics to be covered either later in this book and/or in my forthcoming advanced SBS 2003 book include:

- Auditing (I hinted at this earlier)
- Time synch with Internet clock
- Group Policy stuff and its mysterious powers
- Software restrictions policies
- IPSec
- More details on Network Monitor (Roberta Bragg's fave)
- The dangers of encrypted file system (EFS).
- Learn about the Microsoft software asset management program at www.microsoft.com/samservices.

So stand by and hold your horses!

Guest Column

Leveraging Security Appliances

Frank J. Ohlhorst

Spam has become the scourge of every business. Today, almost every mailbox is clogged up with unwanted content, becoming both a space hog and a drain on productivity. Unsolicited email can be more than a nuisance; some spam messages contain viruses or worms which can do incredible damage to Windows based systems.

Small Business Server 2003 includes very little in spam and virus fighting capabilities, although the latest version of Microsoft Outlook does offer some malicious code protection and spam filtering capabilities, most users will not find it enough when it comes to optimally controlling the problem. What's more, relying on desktop applications for virus control and spam is far from ideal, after all, messages and files are still passed through the SBS server via Microsoft Exchange. The real key here is to prevent viruses, worms and spam from getting to the server in the first place.

Salvation comes in the form of hardware based security appliances. Those units, which are firewalls with added features, come in all shapes and sizes; complicating what makes a good fit for a SBS 2003 network. Those security appliances offer additional valuable features, ranging from content filtering to web caching. Once the gains in productivity are considered by eliminating spam and malicious code, security appliances become quite affordable. What's more, additional savings can be had by choosing SBS2003 Standard Edition over Premium Edition, after all if a hardware firewall is in place, why bother with the cost and management overhead of ISA server.

Although plenty of software products exist that integrate with ISA server to handle critical security concerns, integrators will find moving those tasks off of the server will net increased performance and reduce complexity. SBS2003 is a single server solution, that prevents integrators from economically moving ISA server off to another server to reduce the overhead created by firewalls and add on products.

The key is to look for a unit which acts as a proxy for internet traffic and examines every incoming data packet. Those requirements will help to thin the heard a little when selecting a unit. Several vendors offer units that are tuned to small business needs, those looking for strong antivirus and content control should consider units from Fortinet (www.fortinet.com), which makes a whole host of scalable solutions for the SOHO/SMB market. Sonicwall (www.sonicwall.com) is another vendor that creates comprehensive hardware security solutions for the SMB market. In some cases it might be advisable to go straight to the source for strong firewall and security features; which is where CheckPoint (www.checkpoint.com) excels with their S-Box line of security appliances.

Regardless of what vendor's product is implemented, integrators need to consider more than just the feature set. Ease of management and adding options should be at the top of the list, especially if ISA server is to be eliminated. Here is where browser based interfaces rule and setup wizards show their value.

Both Fortinet and Sonicwall strive to ease the administrative burden. Ideally, the selected unit should also offer remote management capabilities, which allows integrators to remotely tune and update the appliance, eliminating the need for a site visit. Another key feature to consider is automatic updating of virus signatures and spam lists, most of the products on the market successfully handle those tasks.

All things considered, spam and virus concerns only strengthen the argument for adding a hardware firewall. The trick is to select an economical product that can grow with networking needs by offering expansion options, such as content filtering, VPN or dialup failover support.

Summary

Okay - we've done the drill on security. This chapter focused on the standard version of SBS 2003 and the RRAS-based security features at the bits level. But really, this chapter was much more than service port openings in a firewall. Security is a multifaceted matrix of endless threats. These threats are both bits and business, virtual and physical. It's kinda like a popular Western belief in God: Security will never end!

Meet me in the next chapter to explore Exchange Server 2003 and, later on, in Chapter 13 to discuss security once again as part of the SBS 2003 premium edition and ISA Server 2000.

Ciao!

Chapter 6
Messaging with Exchange Server 2003 and Outlook 2003

Take a bow. Why? Because even before you start reading this chapter on Exchange Server 2003 ("Exchange") and Outlook 2003 ("Outlook"), you really know more about these two messaging applications than you might admit in public. As the first part of the chapter will show, you've darn near completed the configuration of Exchange and Outlook just by deploying SBS 2003 over the past several chapters. So accordingly, I start with what you should likely already know up to this point. And after you finish the chapter and work more with Exchange in the real world, you'll really know these products inside and out from an SBS 2003 viewpoint.

By the way, this chapter isn't as SPRINGERS-centric as my other chapters are. This is in part because the SPRINGERS storyline doesn't need a lot of direct interaction with Exchange Server 2003 for proper SBS 2003 network deployment to occur. So bear with me as I provide you a Texas-size buffet of Exchange and Outlook matters you're like to lasso up in the real world.

What You May Already Know About Exchange Server 2003!

This section of the chapter should inspire confidence as you'll likely comment "I already knew that" about certain Exchange matters. Let's get started.

- **Core SBS component installation.** Just prior to the Windows Configuration phase outlined in Chapter 3, the setup routine "harvests" the information on the Company Information page (revisit Figure 3-14 in Chapter 3 to see this) for later use in creating Exchange Global Address

List (GAL) entries (Figure 6-1). This same company information also populates the properties for an Active Directory user object on the Address tab (Figure 6-2).

Figure 6-1
Viewing a Global Address List entry in SBS 2003.

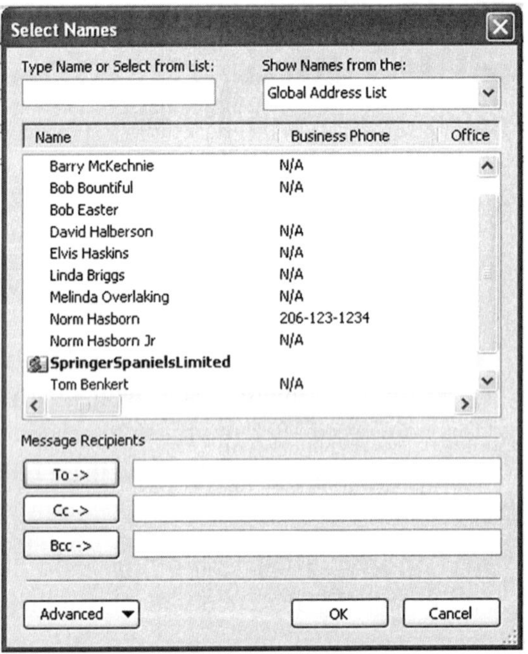

Notes:

Figure 6-2
Viewing the address information in Active Directory for a user.

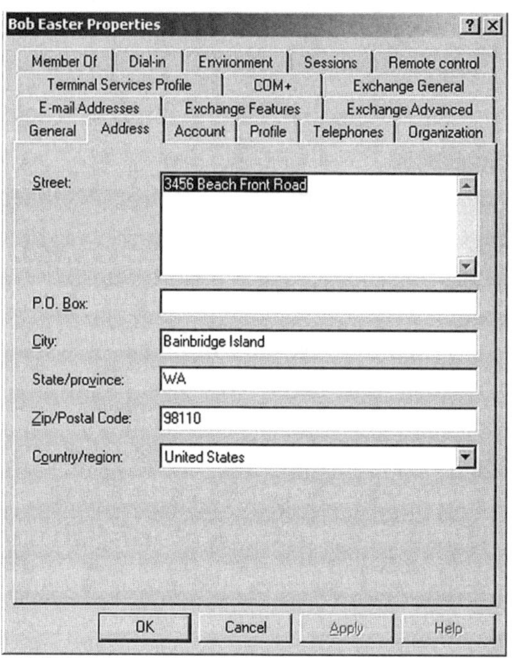

BEST PRACTICE: Call it a missed opportunity, but this company information would have been great for creating an Outlook contact record for each user that is added to the SBS 2003 network. Said Outlook contact record could then be used by fellow workers to list your home and cellular telephones, making it possible to reach you with ease! Heck - such an Outlook contact record could be synchronized to your personal digital assistant (PDA), such as a sassy HpCompaq iPAQ, allowing you to find co-workers when you're out of the office. As it stands today, the company information is used to populate the screens in Figures 6-1 and 6-2, but few of us in the small business arena truly get excited about GALs and AD user objects! This good stuff also could have been (but isn't) used to create a cool list in Windows SharePoint Server (see Chapter 7 for more).

- **SBS application setup information.** You will recall, after the Windows Configuration reboots at mid-point during the SBS setup phase, you completed a wizard page titled Data Folders (see Figure 3-21) where you redirected the location of the Exchange data (you also had the option to redirect the Exchange logs, but we didn't). This is an especially cool capability in SBS 2003 because back in the SBS 2000 era, the same screen (see Figure 3-20 in my legacy *SBS 2000 Best Practices* book) gave you no opportunity to redirect Exchange data and logs. Rather, in the old days, you had to manually redirect Exchange data and logs following the steps in KBase article Q257184.

- **Core SBS application installation phase.** Who could forget the 20+ minutes you spent during the SBS installation process when you inserted Disc 2 and Exchange Server 2003 modified the Active Directory Schema-surely you remember the 1 of 10, 2 of 10, 3 of 10 messages? (You can see this in Figure 3-24 back in Chapter 3). And when Exchange itself was installed at this step, the Company archive public folder and the Company contact object were created inside the Exchange public folders.

- **E-mail and Internet Connection Wizard (EICW).** Of course, the EICW greatly affected Exchange Server 2003 when you completed it in Chapter 4. It was there that you elected to use the built-in firewall and allow e-mail services to flow through the firewall (see the **Services Configuration** page). The firewall-related page that followed, titled **Web Services Configuration**, allowed you to invoke **Outlook Web Access**, **Outlook Mobile Access**, and **Outlook via the Internet** (in-depth description of each of these sections are available by clicking **More Information** on that page). Next up, you selected **Enable Internet e-mail** on the Internet e-mail page. On the **E-mail Delivery Method** page, you selected **Use DNS** to route e-mail. **The E-mail Retrieval Method** page followed that allowed you to elect **SMTP-based e-mail** (in effect, you turned Exchange "on" for use). You didn't configure the POP3 Connector for Exchange (a native SBS 2003 tool that I discuss later in the chapter) on this page because it's not part of the SPRINGERS storyline in this book. This was followed by the **E-mail Domain Name** page where you provided the Internet domain name you wanted to use for your SMTP-based external messaging. (Note that a BIG ASSUMPTION exists here that you've worked closely with your ISP to point a Mail Exchange (MX) record in DNS to your SBS 2003 server to successfully deliver the SMTP e-mail. If you haven't, please contact your ISP immediately.) Finally, something I'll discuss later is the e-mail attachment removal process that you implemented on the Remove E-mail Attachments page.

BEST PRACTICE: Actually, this is more humor than serious, but after all the details in the bullet points above about Exchange functionality in the EICW, I kinda feel like I'm listening to the patriarchal parent of the bride in the *My Big Fat Greek Wedding* movie who claims every word has a Greek origin. Here, after the exhaustive EICW play-by-play above, you might start to think every piece of SBS functionality originates in Exchange.

- **Add User Wizard (AUW).** Not to be outdone, the AUW holds its own in the Exchange configuration department. Exchange and the AUW are related in the following ways. First, the AUW creates the user object in Active Directory which also creates the Exchange mailbox. The template you select for the user in the AUW would also affect Exchange e-mail functionality. A mobile user would need the Mobile User Template to remotely access e-mail. The Power User Template provides sufficient permissions for the endowed user to create other users with an Exchange mailbox on the system via the Power User Console.

What You May Already Know About Outlook 2003

You probably know more about Outlook, including the 2003 version, than you give yourself credit for. Consider the following.

- **Pervasive usage.** Perhaps the question to ask here is "Who *hasn't* used Outlook?" A show of hands would yield a very small data set. Just about everyone on Planet Earth has in some way or some how used Outlook. In fact, for that reason, a change from my past books is that I'll not show you how to send an e-mail message, as I'll assume you already know this basic function.

- **Setup Computer Wizard (SCW).** When the AUW spans Setup Computer Wizard (SCW), you assign users to the computer for whom Outlook will be available. You also make the decision to install the Outlook application itself. And finally, you may elect to install Active Synch 3.7 which will synchronize Outlook information with your personal digital assistant (which I'll demonstrate and discuss more later).

Exchange Under the Hood

Before you trot off believing you know everything there is to know about Exchange, pull up for a moment and read this section on peeking and poking around under the hood. Granted, you'll likely know some of what is presented below, but perhaps you'll find a gold nugget along the way that you hadn't seen in prior sluicing runs.

Okay - What Is Exchange Server 2003?

A good instructor will always encourage even the most basic of questions by promoting a learning culture of "No question is stupid; the only stupid question is the one you don't ask." So it's fair game to ask, "Exactly what is Exchange Server 2003?"

Back in time, when SBS 4.0 was released in late 1997, the Exchange application was considered to be an e-mail program. It quickly became a popular e-mail program in an era where folks were relatively new to e-mail and all of its wonderfulness. Fast forward a few years-and running around getting excited about e-mail is not only "legacy" but it's so yesterday! Later on, the marketing message and positioning for Exchange was altered to reflect more noble goals, such as messaging, communications, and collaboration. A contemporary view of Exchange is that it's a robust message application with collaboration being better handled by SharePoint technologies (which you meet in the next chapter).

To some extent, even the communications tag line is now deemphasized with the introduction of the Microsoft Real Time Communications server product.

But this section isn't placed here to reiterate what you likely know about Exchange production positioning. Rather, I wanted to weave in a neo-Exchange viewpoint served up by a fellow instructor on an SBS hands-on lab tour in late 2002. This gentlemen proposed the thesis that Exchange is really nothing more than a set of messaging tools and functionality that resides atop Active Directory. Huh? I'll tease you with this hypothesis herein until the next section, where what appears to be a ridiculous riddle is solved.

Really Managing Exchange

Once installed with SBS 2003 and configured with the EICW, Exchange Server 2003 doesn't really require you to do much on a day-to-day basis. The damn thing just works! But there are three primary management tools you should know about: the Manage Internet and E-mail page, Exchange Server 2003 System Manager, and the Active Directory Users and Computers snap-in.

Manage Internet and E-mail

First and foremost, you should utilize the Manage Internet and E-mail page, accessed by clicking the Internet and E-mail link under Standard Management in the Server Management console. This page provides numerous links that include forcing a connection to the your ISP to retrieve mail (see the Synchronize E-mail link). Take a moment to look at the options on that page.

Notes:

Exchange Server 2003 System Manager

Remember your walk down the Server Console in Chapter 4? Under the Advanced Tasks section, you were exposed to the System Manager tool. It's shown in expanded view here in Figure 6-3.

Figure 6-3
Like the alluring Venus flytrap plant, Exchange Server 2003 System Manager is fully exposed in its attempt to lure you in deeper and deeper.

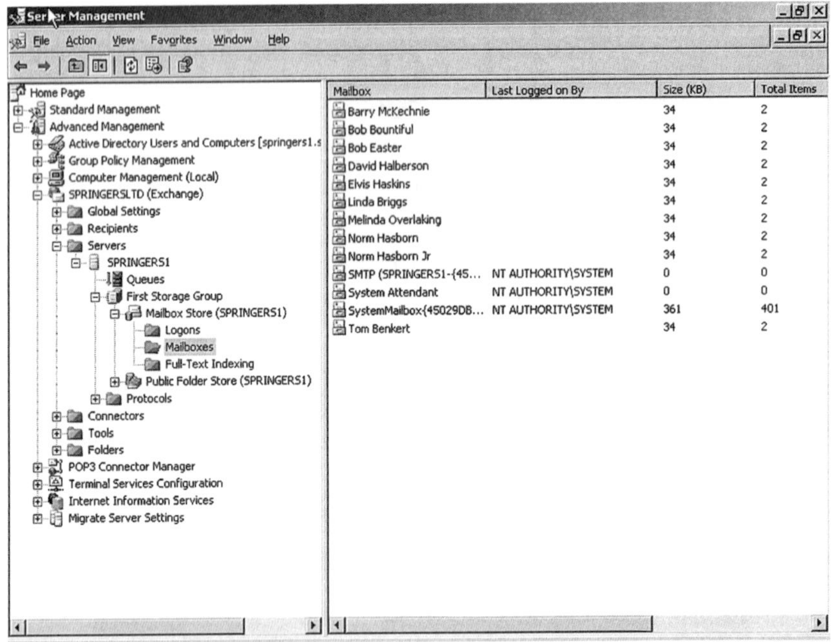

When nature calls and you simply have to perform some heavy server-side configuration procedures in Exchange Server 2003, you'll use System Manager, plain and simple. But it's not likely that you'll interact with System Manager on a day-to-day basis.

BEST PRATICE: I'll weave in very specific and narrow surgical strikes in System Manager in the remaining part of this chapter, so for now simply hop and skip around this tool. Go ahead and dig deep. Drill down into the countless child objects layered in this surprisingly powerful management tool. Later, when you're commanded to perform a procedure, your comfort level with System Manager will be high.

Active Directory Users and Computers

Time to solve the riddle from a few minutes ago. The solution set is this: You're gonna perform most Exchange administration from Active Directory, using tools such as the Active Directory Users and Computers snap-in. The following tabs are shown on a user property sheet (see Figure 6-4 below as well):

- **Exchange General.** This identifies the mailbox store, alias delivery restrictions, delivery options, and storage limits.

- **E-mail Addresses.** This lists e-mail addresses associated with this user, including Custom Address, X.400 Address, Microsoft Mail Address, SMTP Address, cc:Mail Address, Lotus Notes Address, and Novell GroupWise Address.

- **Exchange Features.** As seen in Figure 6-4, this displays the Mobile Services that are configured plus protocol status information.

- **Exchange Advanced.** This provides settings for changing the simple display name, hiding the account from the Exchange address list (more on this later), setting custom attributes, configuring an Internet locator service, and modifying mailbox rights.

Notes:

Figure 6-4
The Active Directory user object property sheet showing the Exchange Features tab.

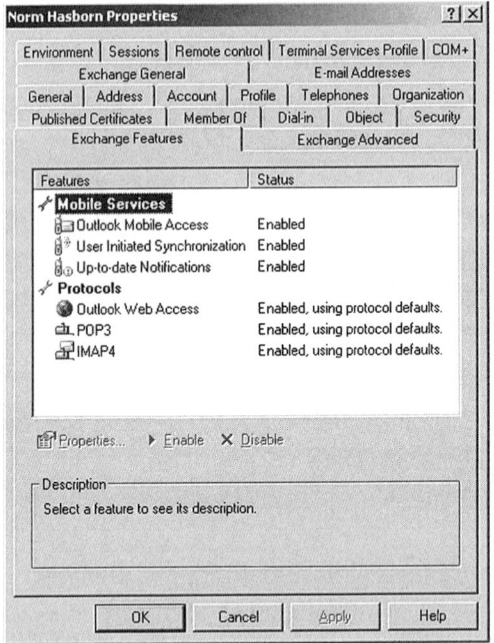

BEST PRACTICE: In the legacy SBS 2000 time frame, you did not see the Exchange Advanced by default on an Active Directory user object property sheet. You had to select Advanced Features under the View menu in Active Directory Users and Computers snap-in for this to appear. Also, the Exchange Features tab in the SBS 2000 time frame was very different and addressed the Instant Messaging configuration. Such is not the case in SBS 2003 (I discuss Instant Messaging later in this section).

While we're talking about Active Directory, let's add a little fuel to the fire. Remember that it's Active Directory providing several forms of critical support to Exchange Server 2003, such as:

- Active Directory provides a directory of all Exchange objects
- Exchange uses Active Directory for all authentication and access control

- Active Directory provides replication and the Global Catalog (GC). Exchange clients depend on the GC.

- Exchange makes irreversible Active Directory schema changes. I hinted at this earlier in the chapter with the "1 of 10" setup comment where Exchange was preparing the forest and domain before installing itself.

BEST PRACTICE: While this chapter won't turn into a book on Exchange, you are, of course, encouraged to read more in books dedicated to Exchange. For example, you should learn more about Active Directory distributions groups. (SBS 2003 creates a default distribution group that includes all added users named after the organization name you typed in the Windows Server 2003 GUI setup phase-for example, Springer Spaniels Limited.) Also, you might be interested in knowing that Active Directory security groups are e-mail enabled, so that if you created a security group titled "Accountants" at our sample company, you could easily send an e-mail message to its membership with the following SMTP e-mail address: accountants@springersltd.com.

Remember that distribution groups and security groups can be managed via their respective icons under Standard Management in the Server Management console.

Notes:

Internet Information Server

Exchange is dependent on Internet Information Server (IIS). IIS provides Web store support. IIS provides support for Outlook Web Access (OWA) and Outlook Mobile Access (OMA). This is shown in Figure 6-5.

Figure 6-5
Viewing the IIS supporting role for Exchange (this is being viewed in the Server Management console).

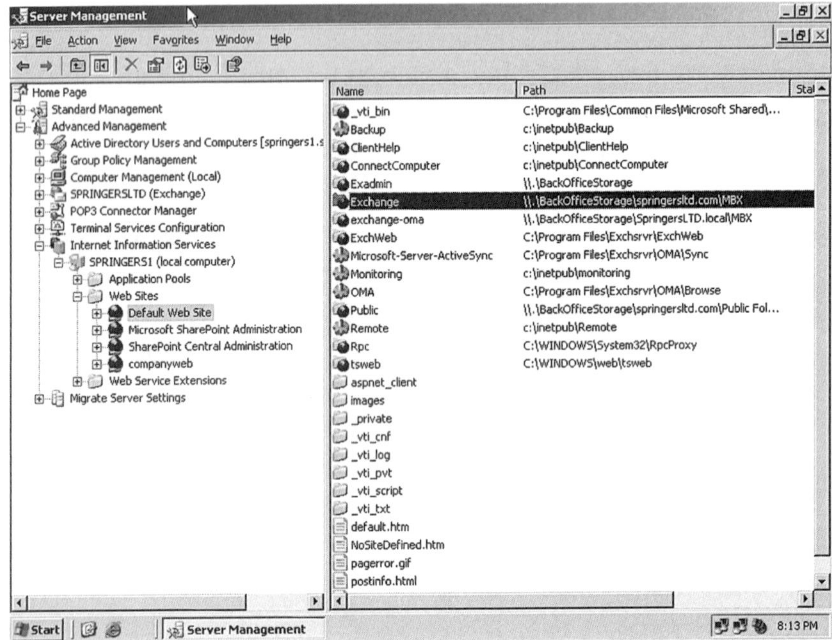

BEST PRACTICE: Wanna test Exchange's dependence on IIS? A trick I've played in past Microsoft hands-on labs to confound the Doubting Thomases who can't draw out an Exchange/IIS relationship is the following: Simply turn off the World Wide Web Publishing Service in Services (in the Server Management console, this is under Advanced Management, Computer Management (Local), Services and Applications, Services). Then launch a Web browser (e.g., IE) and try to access OWA. You'll error out every time with the World Wide Web Publishing Server turned off. Turn this service back on and OWA will work just fine.

Blocking Attachments, E-mails, and Content

There are some interesting capabilities that you might not know about in Exchange in SBS 2003 relating to attachment and domain blocking. Content filtering is another matter I'll close this section with.

> BEST PRACTICE: CRN reported in "Rivals Face Challenge As Microsoft Extends Its Antispam Technology" (http://crn.channelsupersearch.com/news/crn/46130.asp) that Microsoft will offer stronger anti-spam technology in Exchange Server 2003 in the first half of 2004. No other details available at press time but monitor Microsoft's Exchange and TechNet sites for updated information. CRN at www.crn.com should be monitored as well.

Attachment Blocking

You likely recall the Remove E-mail Attachments page (Figure 4-14) in the EICW from Chapter 4. The function it performs is relatively straightforward: remove e-mail attachments of a certain type. But a question that continually arose during the fall 2003 hands-on labs for SBS 2003 concerned where this setting was being made in the background. Students asked if they could see where the EICW was setting this.

So I researched this by consulting with the Microsoft SBS program manager who owns this functionality and found that:

- An SMTP "sink" is trapping the attachments and handling them according to the rule you set on the Remove E-Mail Attachments page.
- There is no user interface (UI) to "see" where these settings are made or where this activity is occurring (other than the outcome, such as the attachment being removed or saved to a folder).

And don't forget that we have Outlook 2003 as a backstop to also block common attachments in e-mail. This is covered later in the Outlook 2003 section of this chapter.

Junk E-mail Blocking

Another popular question is what native ability Exchange has to block offensive e-mail domains as a poor man's form of spam blocking (that is, using it instead of purchasing a third-party spam blocking tool). This is most easily accomplished by select and configure the Connection Filtering and Sender Filter tabs on the Message Deliver Properties dialog box that you see in Figure 6-6 (right-click **Message Delivery** and select **Properties** under **Global Settings in the Exchange System Manager** under **Advanced Management** in the **Server Management console**).

Figure 6-6
Get to know the Message Delivery Properties sheet if you want to engage in basic e-mail blocking inside of Exchange.

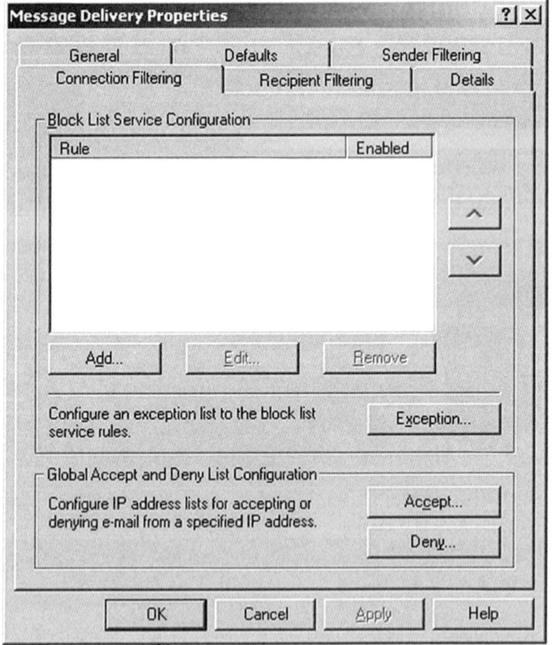

This e-mail blocking can also be accomplished painfully by creating an Active Directory contact object that has the offending e-mail name (such as player@gamblinggreen.com) and then adding it via the Delivery Restrictions tab (click the **Add** button beneath **Reject messages from**) on the Small Business SMTP connector Properties screen.

BEST PRACTICE: Of course, I saved perhaps the best junk e-mail blocking discussion for last. Near the end of the fall 2003 SBS 2003 hands-on lab tour in the US, a few students, already having worked with SBS 2003 at that point, waxed poetically about the effectiveness of the Outlook 2003 spam blocking capability. The consensus was it just works. A Microsoft employee echoed the same sentiment as "your Microsoft Research division dollars at work." Couldn't have put it better myself!

Content Filtering

Now for the bad news. Content filtering-as many of us know it in third-party spam filters that eliminate offensive e-mails selling Viagra and Vicodin-is not natively available in Exchange (but should be around mid-2004 as per the Best Practice earlier). Don't be confused because some might think that the Content Restrictions tab on the Small Business SMTP connector Properties screen (Figure 6-6 above) is really performing a filtering function. It is not. It is allowing e-mail of different priorities, etc.

Note that I'll cover spam blocking in it various forms (attachment blocking, e-mail and domain blocking, and content filtering) more in Chapter 11. You'll recall that I briefly mentioned spam in Chapter 5. Stand by!

Exchange Interaction With SBS Backup

Later in this book in Chapter 11, you'll complete the Backup Configuration Wizard to configure the backup capabilities in SBS 2003. So while I'm jumping the gun a little, let me share with you that you'll affirm Exchange's deleted item retention capability to store deleted e-mail. The default setting, which is actually in place before you run the Backup Configuration Wizard, is 30 days. (I'll have you increase it to 60 days just to be extra safe.) This is a very useful approach for quickly retrieving a piece of e-mail that a user might have deleted (later in the chapter in the Outlook discussion I'll share with you the procedure for this). The setting for deleted item retention is shown on the Limits tab of the Mailbox Store Properties screen (seen in Figure 6-7).

Figure 6-7
Observe that the ability to recover deleted e-mails is much more "foreground" in SBS 2003 with its Exchange Server 2003 application. In the SBS 2000 era, this capability wasn't as widely known and utilized.

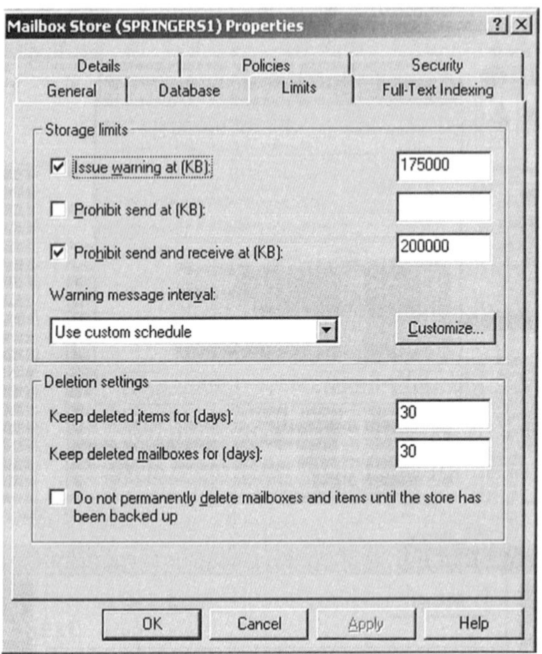

BEST PRATICE: Interestingly, the deleted item retention setting that you can set via the Backup Configuration Wizard only applies to the Mailbox Store and not the Public Folder Store. The Public Folder Store is set automatically to seven days to retain deleted items. I recommend you set this to 60 days on the Limits tab of the Public Folder Store Properties screen. And why do I recommend that? Later in the chapter when we look more closely at Outlook 2003, you'll see the crack SBS development team implemented two public folder objects based on the organization name you inputted during the SBS setup phase. Translation: You are being encouraged to use public folders for storing important information.

The backup store gets even more interesting when discussing Exchange interaction with the native backup program in SBS 2003. Essentially, what occurs is that the Shadow Volume Copy Restore capability in the SBS 2003 backup approach takes a two-second snapshot of the Exchange information store and then makes its backup from said snapshot. That allows Exchange to function without noticeable interruption.

> BEST PRACTICE: Note that the SBS 2003 backup approach is not backing up Exchange at the "bricks" or mailbox level. For that form of backup, you might need some of the third-party backup software (provided by Veritas, Computer Associates), which I'll discuss in Chapter 11. By the way, this whole discussion area of whether to use the native SBS 2003 backup program versus a third-party backup solution was asked in each city in the late 2003 SBS 2003 hands-on lab USA tour (a very common question).
>
> But note that you can effectively simulate a really low-level backup capability (even lower than bricks level) by taking full advantage of the deleted item retention capability in Exchange to recover an individual piece of e-mail some 60 days out as discussed in the prior section.

A final point related to Exchange backup activity concerns Exchange transaction log growth. Without fail, I have client whom I hear from only when something goes wrong (and usually at all the wrong times like when I'm enjoying a sunny summer day off). One case related to Exchange shutting down and not allowing e-mails to be sent or received. Upon close examination, the culprit was excessive Exchange transaction log growth. What occurred was this el cheapo client wasn't getting successfully backed up (and wouldn't pay us for monitoring to know whether they were getting sufficiently backed up, etc.). When Exchange isn't successfully backed up, it continues to build transaction logs that are basically 5MB in size each as a form of self-preservation. Not surprisingly, over the course of 300 days, with the logs growing in multiples of 5MB at a time, the system drive was consumed and it ran out of room. When Exchange tries to operate on a drive with less than 10MB free space, it shuts down. And that's how this client learned they weren't getting good backups: All of the disk space had been consumed by excessive Exchange transaction log growth.

BEST PRACTICE: Don't forget that you had the option to direct where the Exchange transaction logs should be stored when you initially ran the SBS 2003 Setup Wizard and viewed the Data Folders Redirection screen. But simply placing the Exchange transaction logs on a huge hard disk to let them grow like weeds is no substitution for having beautiful bona fide backups!

POP3 Connector

It's with great pride that the SBS development team created the POP3 Connector that allows external POP3 e-mail to be downloaded on a schedule and "mapped" to an Exchange SMTP account. Translation: You're using POP3-based e-mail at your ISP today (say my POP3 account of harryb@nwlink.com) and you want that mail delivered seamlessly to your SBS network e-mail (in my case, harryb@nethealthmon.com). It's the POP3 Connector that facilitates this mapping between disparate e-mail accounts (and account types) and performs the download delivery function.

Configuring the POP3 Connector in SBS 2003 is much simpler than prior SBS 2000 releases, because it's now got a direct link in the Server Management console! In the Server Management console, click **Internet** and **E-mail under Standard Management**. Then select **Manage POP3 E-mail** followed by a click on the **Open POP3 Connector Manager** link. The result is displayed in Figure 6-8.

Notes:

Figure 6-8

The POP3 Connector is configured on this property sheet via the Mailboxes and Scheduling. Because it's not really part of the SPRINGERS storyline, this figure is a simple "look and see."

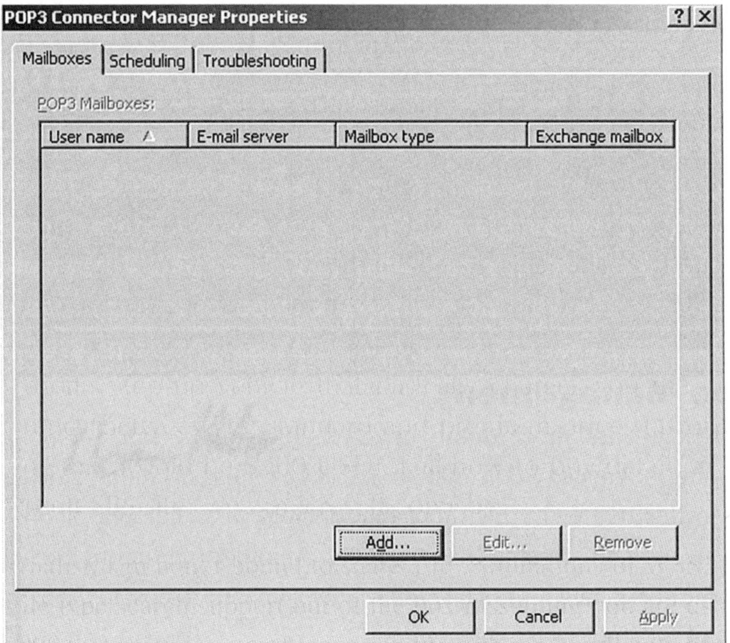

BEST PRACTICE: In its heart of hearts, the POP3 Connector is best used as a transition tool to help you migrate your POP3-based e-mail (and associated Internet identity, such as harryb@nwlink.com) to your SBS-based Exchange SMTP e-mail and Internet identity (e.g., harryb@nethealthmon.com). There is much power in having an Internet identity that closely relates to the name of your organization and isn't a generic e-mail domain name (e.g., JUNO and other large ISP identities). In fact, one of the slides in the Microsoft Partner PPT in late 2003 widely circulated in the public SBS 2003 hands-on labs and other venues cites hosting your own SMTP e-mail as a true benefit to SBS 2003. It's the POP3 Connector that can help facilitate this transition.

But hey - that's not to say that some folks don't use the POP3 Connector on a permanent basis to maintain POP3 e-mail on an on-going basis. This can be done without harm, without foul.

I know across this book I sound like a broken record, but I'll delve deeper into the POP3 Connector in my advanced SBS 2003 book.

BEST PRACTICE: Oops. I almost forgot a late-breaking discovery regarding the POP3 Connector. There I was in late 2003 teaching a bunch of attentive and smart Microsoft Partners in Bangalore, India, when I was asked the following question: Can the POP3 Connector be configured to leave a copy of the e-mail on the e-mail server at the ISP? After horsing around with it, the answer appears to be no.

Queue Management

While I'll go into more detail on Exchange queue management in my forthcoming Advanced SBS 2003 book, I'd be remiss if I didn't at least pay lip service to this matter in this more introductory text. Inbound and outbound e-mails awaiting processing live in queues. A point of failure in Exchange can occur at the queue, and it's not uncommon for someone to post to the newsgroups that e-mail is "stuck in the queue."

BEST PRACTICE: As an example, when outbound e-mail gets stuck in the queue, it can slow down the entire SBS server machine. One cause for this can be that spammers have sent e-mail into your Exchange organization to a nonexistent e-mail account (say superuser@springersltd.com) and you have somehow configured Exchange to send a nondeliverable report (NDR) back to the spammer (over the Internet) that basically says said user doesn't exist in your organization. Well, when the spammers return e-mail address is itself fake, Exchange will try and try again to deliver the NDR and queue blockage will result.

Pardon me while I shout, but NDRs are ENABLED BY DEFAULT IN SBS 2003! This could create the above situation out of the box on your SBS 2003 network. So, clearly the point of the above story and shouting is to turn off NDR delivery that will go out over the Internet. This occurs by deselecting the **Allow non-delivery reports** checkbox on the **Default Properties** dialog box (this is the property sheet for the Default object under Internet Message Formats under Global Settings in the Exchange System Manager under Advanced Management in the Server Management console). This is shown in Figure 6-9 after the correction has been made.

Figure 6-9
Please promise you'll turn off the Allow non-delivery reports checkbox here to prevent queue build-up.

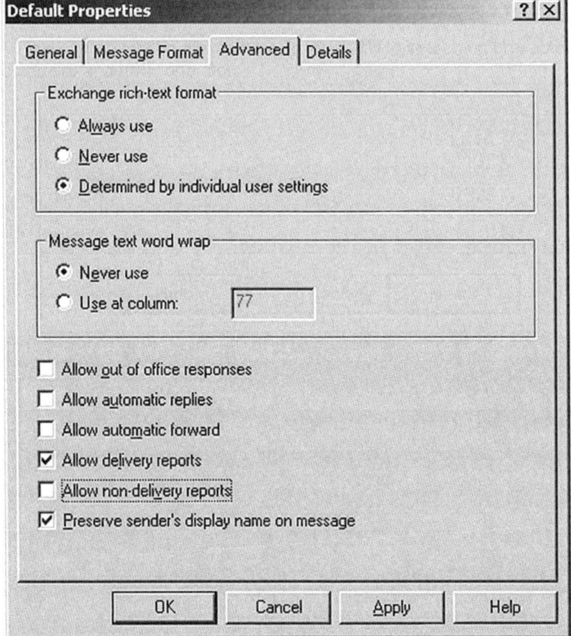

Possibly you're a reader from Missouri (the "Show Me" state) and you need to see e-mails in the queue to better understand what we're talking about here. Or perhaps you're sinister and want to see to whom users are e-mailing messages (this is SPYING and could be considered bad behavior). That is accomplished by drilling down from **Server Management**, **Advanced Management**, selecting the **Exchange System Manager**, selecting the **SPRINGERS1** domain object, and clicking **Queues**. Then select the queue of your choice, such as **Messages**

queued for deferred delivery followed by clicking the **Find Messages** button. You'll see the messages that exist in that queue.

BEST PRACTICE: One last point about Figure 6-9 above. Did you know that SBS 2003 and Exchange are contributing by default to the health, welfare, and safety of your home? That is accomplished by an ounce of prevention. What? Look closely at Figure 6-9 and notice that Allow Out of Office responses are disabled by default. That way, if one of your users utilizes the Out of Office response capability in Outlook 2003 when he travels for business or pleasure, the bad guys who spam said user don't receive notification that the user is out of town and his home is wide open for theft! Seriously, an Out of Office response that is sent over the Internet is an open invitation for bad guys to rip you off! If you think that's bad, it could be worse, as a woman real estate agent once pointed out to me. What if you were using your vacation time at home and the bad guys, having received your Out of Office reply, decided to come by for a quick burgle. Her point was that she'd rather get ripped off while not at home than to risk personal harm when the bad guys appear. A valid point!

16GB Store Limit

Something that really freaks out some SBSers is the fact that Exchange Server 2003 standard edition, which is the SKU placed in SBS 2003 (both standard and premium edition) has a 16GB data storage limit for all stores combined. In the old days, 16GB was a ton of space, but now with a mailbox approaching 1 GB or more per user, you can easily see how you might overtax Exchange's storage limitation at the information store level. Why have mailbox sizes increased so much in the early 21st century? Well, a generation ago, the Church Lady (played by Dana Carvey) on Saturday Night Live (a popular US comedy show that won't die) would have blamed...SATAN! I'd rather put my faith in the fact that folks are using their Exchange-based mailboxes as filing systems to manage their business information. In this case, the Outlook application accessing the Exchange-based mailbox has replaced traditional NTFS-folders viewed from Windows Explorer as the information repository of choice. Yours truly is truly guilty as seen in Figure 6-10, where the offline data storage file for Outlook (OST file), which is representative of my Exchange mailbox, is approaching 1.2 GB in size!

Figure 6-10
All you would need is 16 users like Harry (that's me) in your organization with SBS 2003 to exceed the information store-level storage limit in Exchange. Ouch!

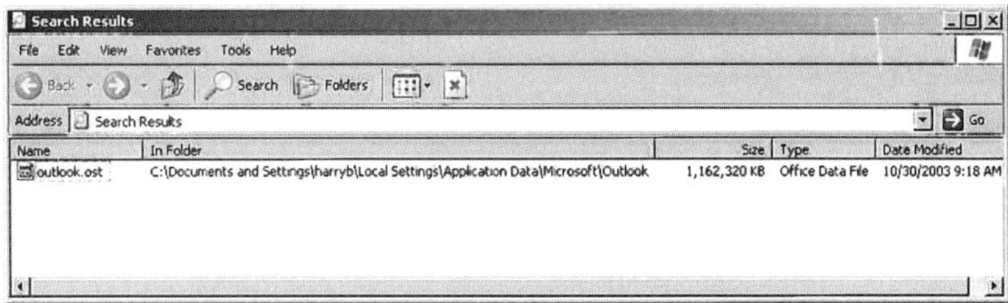

Respecting the Dearly Departed

A network administration trick as old as the origins of NetWare and ArcNet (some of you probably join me going back to the early days of local area networks) is the idea that you disable but not delete user accounts when someone departs from a organization (such as leaving a job). Later, at a future date when you're convinced the individual won't return, you can delete the user account that you've previously placed on disabled status.

So here is the dilemma. One day, I received a call from a client complaining that an employee who had been terminated recently still appeared when the To: button in a new Outlook e-mail message was selected and the GAL was

displayed. I was accused of not addressing a client request to "eliminate" this user. Further investigation revealed that a user account, once disabled, still appears in the GAL. To hide a dearly departed but disabled user from the GAL, you would need to select the **Hide from Exchange address lists** checkbox on the **Exchange Advanced** tab on a user's property sheet, as seen in Figure 6-11.

Figure 6-11
This figure suggests that Norm Hasborn, the owner of SPRINGERS, has been terminated. This is highly unlikely, of course, but does allow you to see how to hide a user from the Exchange GAL.

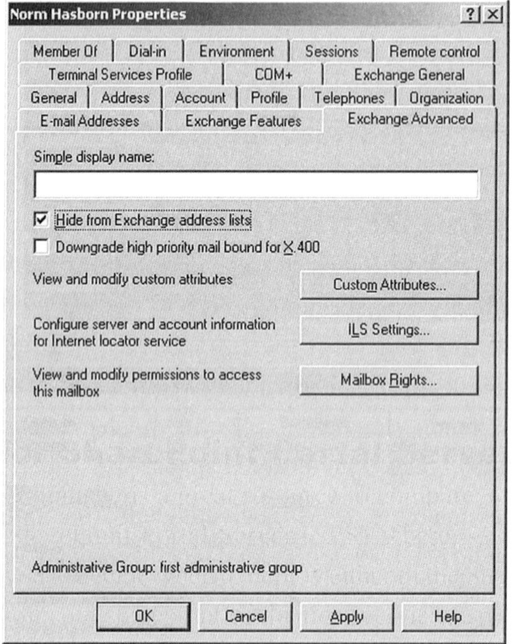

BEST PRACTICE: Why on earth did my telephone ring again from this client accusing me a second time of not terminating the terminated employee from the system? I had correctly selected the checkbox listed above. It turns out the secretary at this client site had double-checked my work very shortly after I reported I'd fixed the situation. The lesson learned is this. If you hide a user from the GAL, there is a propagation period before the change takes effect.

But there is a way to accelerate the propagation period. Figure 6-12 displays the Update Now secondary menu option on the Recipient Update Service (SPRINGERSLTD). Selecting this would make the change take effect immediately and you would then escape the wrath of the somber secretary I've shared with you here.

Figure 6-12
If you look closely at this figure, especially on the left, you can see where Recipient Update Services is located under the Advanced Management part of the Server Management console.

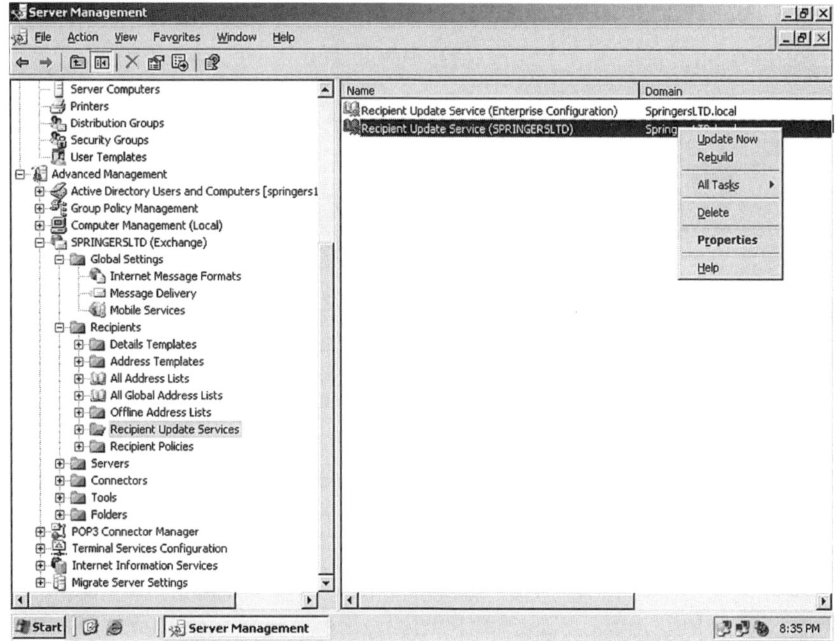

Mail Bagging and Multiple MX Records

No, this isn't a paragraph that will replay a tale of sassy Samantha (a lead character on HBO's popular program *Sex in the City*) having a racy encounter with a postal worker. Rather, this is about having a backup location for your e-mail to flow to when your SBS 2003 server machine (properly running Exchange for SMTP e-mail) is offline. Instead of the senders in the "offline SBS 2003 server machine" situation receiving an NDR or bounced e-mail message, these incoming e-mails can temporarily reside on another mail server. Later on, you would retrieve and properly distribute these e-mails using a tool such as the POP3 Connector in SBS 2003 that was discussed above.

BEST PRACTICE: If you think you might like to have this form of messaging redundancy, consult with your ISP to arrange it. Your ISP, who I assume is holding your DNS records, will need to enter a second MX record with a lower priority that points to a backup mail server (typically maintained by the ISP).

I'll cover this topic more, including more procedural steps, in my forthcoming advanced SBS 2003 book due in mid-2004.

Exchange Migrations

This topic, another one way outside the SPRINGERS story line, merits mention nonetheless. You might find yourself in a situation where you need to move Exchange data because of an upgrade or migration. While I discuss upgrades and migrations more in Appendix B, the point is that you'll possibly encounter such a scenario and you need at least some basic guidance.

The tools that you'll use to migrate Exchange data is the ExMerge tool. For the latest discussion on the use of ExMerge, visit www.microsoft.com/technet and search on the "exmerge" term. You'll see the page in Figure 6-13 that advises you to download the Exchange 2003: Mailbox Merge Wizard (ExMerge) tool.

BEST PRACTICE: Yes - you read correctly. The ExMerge tool is now downloaded. In the SBS 2000 time frame, it was found on the SBS setup disc that contained the Exchange application. Such is not the case in the SBS 2003 time frame.

Notes:

Figure 6-13

Go here for the ExMerge tool to migrate your all-important Exchange data.

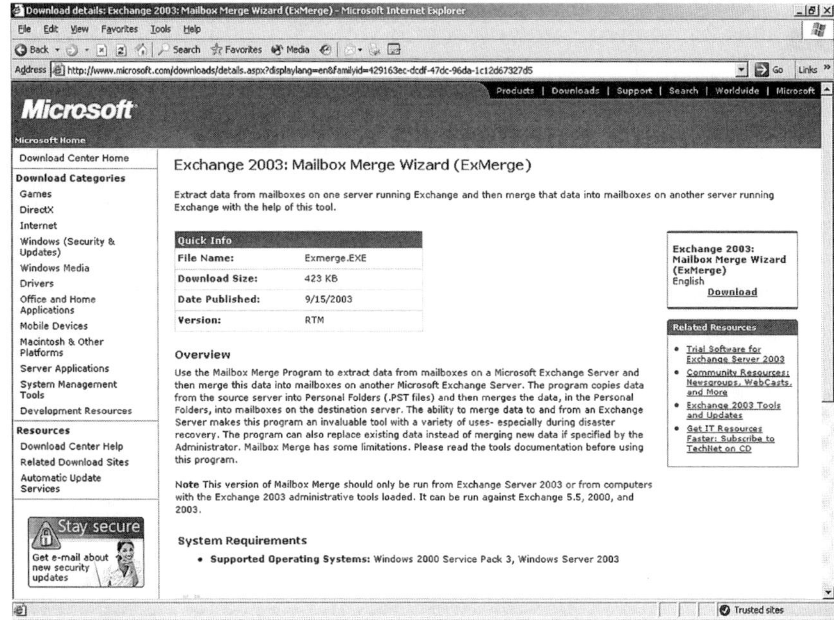

So a few pointers to send you forward with respect to Exchange's ExMerge tool:

- This version of ExMerge requires an "ExMerge" user account with administrator-level permissions to function correctly. This wasn't the case in the SBS 2000 timeframe.
- ExMerge can be run against older versions of Exchange (5.5, 2000) and thus serves as an effective migration tool.
- ExMerge interacts with mailboxes, not public folders or Internet favorites. This interaction is basically import and export capabilities. You will need to manually import and export the content of public folders using the Import and Export option on the File menu in Outlook. Internet favorites, accessible from Outlook and considered by some to be part of the messaging migration mix, can be either manually migrated or migrated by using the profile migration capabilities of the Add User Wizard that was explored in Chapter 4.

BEST PRACTICE: There is a key, public folders point to make about that bullet above. As you'll learn later, the SBS development team has dramatically increased the visibility of public folder usage by creating company-related objects in SBS 2003. So it's a reasonable assumption that you will put important data in the company-related public folder objects (such as maintaining a company-wide customer contacts). Given that, you will need to manually migrate such data.

- If ExMerge fails with a mailbox (this can happen when a PST file you're working with has been flagged to read-only and would occur if you moved a PST file by writing it to a CD disc), then you can always revert back to the manual import/export capability in Outlook as described in the bullet above.

BEST PRACTICE: Microsoft has posted additional migration guidance at www.microsoft.com/exchange. As of this writing, there is a scenario for migrating from Exchange 5.5 to Exchange 2003.

Instant Messaging - NOT!

It's unfortunate but true in SBS 2003 that the Exchange Server 2003 component has removed the instant messaging capability that many of us enjoyed in the SBS 2000 time frame. Many readers will recall that my prior book, *Small Business Server 2000 Best Practices*, provided the procedures for configuring this wonderful cool tool.

In the SBS 2003 time frame, you will now need to supply Instant Messaging functionality differently. You can purchase Microsoft's new Live Communications Server, starting at $1,059 with five CALs (your rich SBS CALs do not cover this server application). Live Communication Server information is shown in Figure 6-14.

BEST PRACTICE: A member of the SBS development team has confirmed that Live Communications Server does install and function for internal messaging in SBS 2003. However, users will need to logon to the instant messaging client with their internal name (e.g. Normh@springersltd.local). There will be a white paper out that will teach you how to intregrate SBS 2003 and Live Communications Server (no publication date available at my press deadline).

Figure 6-14
Those SBS legacy sites that utilize Instant Messaging will need to strongly consider Live Communications Server to deliver the same functionality in the SBS2003 time frame.

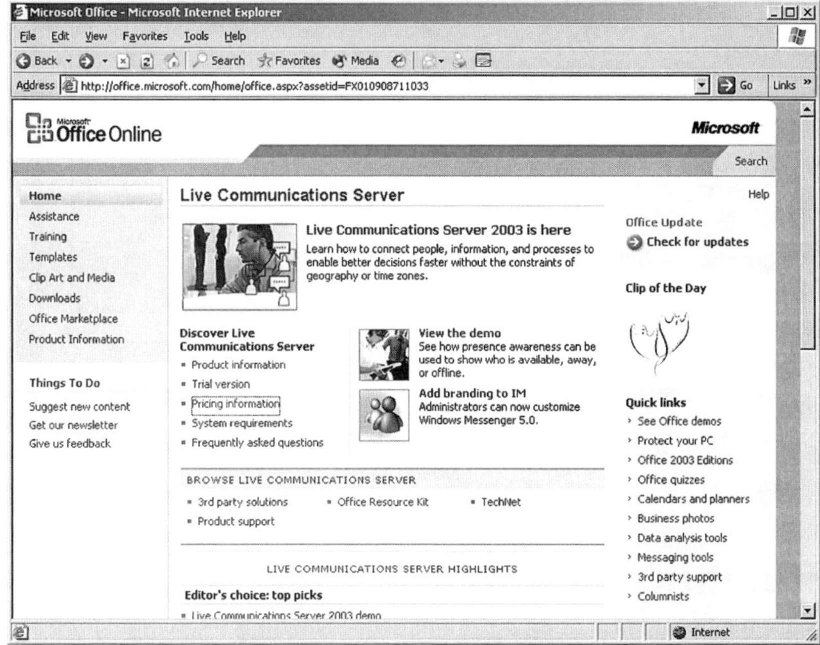

BEST PRACTICE: There is a poor man's way to deliver instant messaging on an SBS 2003 network: Use MSN. That's right! The Internet-based MSN instant messaging capability, described in Figure 6-15, may be just the cheapo ticket you're looking for. Visit www.msn.com/people, but be advised one drawback of this approach is that your chat traffic will result in increased Internet traffic, and there is a huge assumption that you have Internet connectivity!

Note that some readers have reported that they prefer the instant messaging solution from Yahoo! at www.yahoo.com.

Figure 6-15
Consider MSN to restore basic instant messaging (called IM by some folks) to SBS 2003.

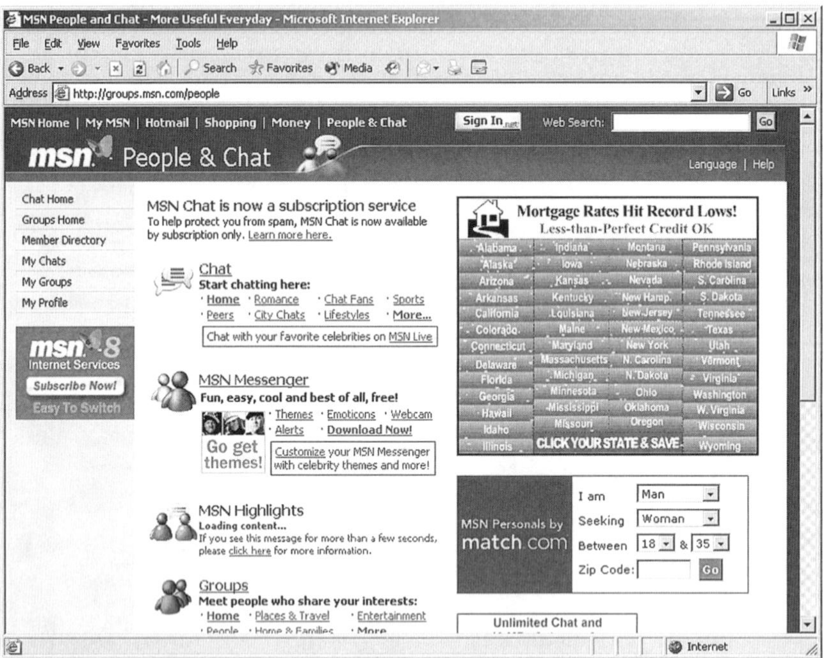

Extending Exchange

Some topics fit better under a heading about extending Exchange, rather than peeking under the hood as the last section did. In this section, I'll share some thoughts about implementing Exchange in SBS 2003 on a storage area network (SAN), support for multiple Exchange servers, and use of Exchange Conferencing Server.

Storage Area Networks

The consultants and trainers in the readership of this book will appreciate the following sentiment. Because of your numerous customers, you see and hear a lot of things you might not otherwise think of yourself. Such was the case recently in Phoenix (the city, not the bird) where a keen student attending the SBS 2003 hands-on labs asked about redirecting the Exchange Store database to a SAN during the setup of SBS 2003. The answer is that this is supported. On the SBS 2003 Setup page that speaks towards data folder redirection (see Figure 3-21), you would redirect the Exchange Store to a SAN via a Uniform Naming Convention (UNC) path such as \\server2\storage\exchange.

Multiple Exchange Servers

This is the type of paragraph I like to insert in a book such as this for the SBS gurus out there who aren't happy with a text until the find something they don't know. Then these same gurus are your friends for life. So here is such an opportunity. You CAN have multiple Exchange servers on the same SBS 2003 network. You might want do this to shoehorn SBS 2003 into a multiple office scenario or to gain some form of messaging database redundancy. This would be accomplished by purchasing a second copy of Exchange Server 2003 (standard edition) and installing it on a second server running Windows Server 2003 (which you would also need to purchase). You would then link the Exchange servers together as part of the Exchange Server site.

The bottom line for introducing another Exchange server machine into your SBS 2003 network? You'd be out the following "hard costs":

- Exchange Server 2003 standard edition: $699 USD
- Exchange 2003 User CAL: $67 USD/each user
- Windows Server 2003: $999 USD
- HP ML 350 Server Machine (adequately equipped): $1,500

If you total the above figures, you'll see that you'll pay a handsome price to introduce a second Exchange server machine in the small business. But it can be done.

> BEST PRACTICE: Having a need to discuss the use of multiple Exchange servers might really be a customer's cry for more information about whether SBS with its Exchange Server 2003 SKU is really the best fit. Consider visiting the comparison chart of all Exchange Server 2003 SKUs (including SBS 2003) at www.microsoft.com/exchange/evaluation/Mail_compare.asp as

seen in Figure 6-16 below to answer your own Exchange right-sizing questions.

Figure 6-16
Use this page to, at a glance, line up Exchange features and better understand what the capabilities and limitations are in SBS 2003.

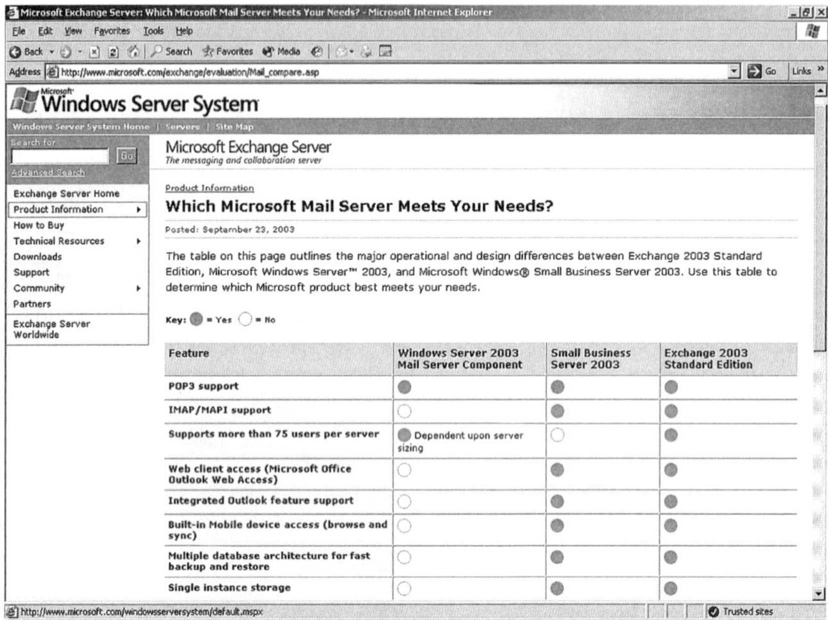

Microsoft Exchange Server
The messaging and collaboration server

Product Information

Which Microsoft Mail Server Meets Your Needs?

Posted: September 23, 2003

The table on this page outlines the major operational and design differences between Exchange 2003 Standard Edition, Microsoft Windows Server™ 2003, and Microsoft Windows® Small Business Server 2003. Use this table to determine which Microsoft product best meets your needs.

Key: ● = Yes ○ = No

Feature	Windows Server 2003 Mail Server Component	Small Business Server 2003	Exchange 2003 Standard Edition
POP3 support	●	●	●
IMAP/MAPI support	○	●	●
Supports more than 75 users per server	● Dependent upon server sizing	○	●
Web client access (Microsoft Office Outlook Web Access)	○	●	●
Integrated Outlook feature support	○	●	●
Built-in Mobile device access (browse and sync)	○	●	●
Multiple database architecture for fast backup and restore	○	●	●
Single instance storage	○	●	●

Exchange Conferencing Server

For some, discussing "extending" Exchange translates into adding value. One way to add value on an SBS 2003 network is to implement Exchange Conferencing Server. This allows multicast video and audio conferencing utilizing the Exchange Server product in SBS 2003 (yes - this will run on SBS 2003). The benefit to small businesses might be similar to what my client with several offices in the USA and Canada enjoys. Instead of having face-to-face meetings around the continent, he uses Exchange Conferencing Server to reduce travel time and expenses while still providing the look and feel of an in-person meeting. Of course, you'd need to reduce the air travel costs by at least $4,500 US, as that is the baseline price for this add-on.

You'll want to access the Exchange Conferencing Server web site at Microsoft at www.microsoft.com/exchange/techinfo/conferencing/default.asp for more information on this product, to download a trial copy and for technical deployment white papers. Some long-time readers will recall that I provided the step-by-step procedure for implementing this solution in Chapter 11 of my *Small Business Server 2000 Best Practices* book.

BEST PRACTICE: Another conferencing alternative for the small business is the use of Microsoft Office Online Live Meeting. This is a cost-effective way to purchase video and audio conferencing on a per-use basis using Microsoft's Internet-based conferencing capabilities. Access Office Live information from www.microsoft.com/office and select the **Microsoft Office Online** link (see Figure 6-17).

Note the photo section of this book shows the New Orleans Jazz Band/Funeral Procession that entertained 5,000 Microsoft Partners at the SBS 2003 launch event at the Worldwide Partners Conference (WWPC) in October 2003. The photo, which shows band members wearing T-shirts saying "Live Has Arrived," was taken only hours before SBS 2003 was launched! This was an excellent way to get jazzed about Live Meeting.

Notes:

Figure 6-17
It's been said every girl has her bag of tricks! Accordingly, every SBSer needs a bag of tricks and Live Meeting should be one such trick.

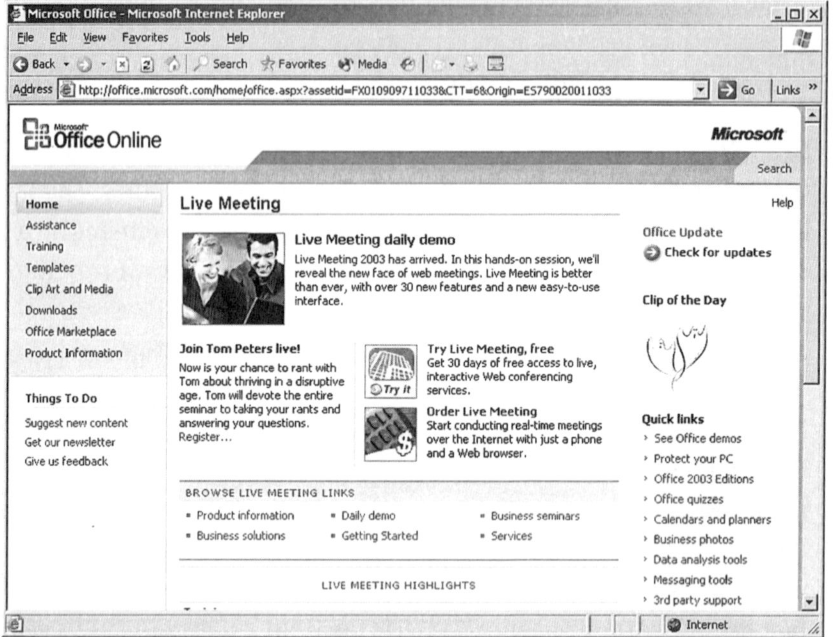

Outlook 2003

Now for the good stuff. Whereas I touted you might not confront server-side Exchange management issues daily, you will likely use Outlook each and every day (and perhaps all day!). This section starts by revisiting the SPRINGERS methodology where you will send an e-mail, enter contact records, and perform other such tasks.

Sending an E-mail

Time for some step-by-step to have NormH send an e-mail to all employees at SPRINGERS.

1. Have **NormH** log on to **PRESIDENT** with the password **Purple3300**.
2. Click **Start**, **E-mail**. This will launch Outlook 2003. Because this is the first time that you've launched Outlook 2003, you'll see a dialog

box titled Configuring Outlook that automatically completes the configuration of Outlook accounts and generates the Welcome message.

BEST PRACTICE: You will also see a notice in the lower right that Outlook is setting up a local copy of your mailbox. Why is this occurring? Because back in Chapter 4 you might recall a BEST PRACTICE that displayed the advanced client computer settings, one of which related to the Outlook profile creation. This profile also configured local caching so you can use Outlook offline when you're not attached to the network.

By the way, if you want another way to see the Outlook profile setting configuration option (post-setup), go to SPRINGERS1 and log on as **Administrator** (password is **Husky9999!**), select **Client Computers** under **Standard Management on the Server Management** console, then select **PRESIDENT** in the right pane. Click the **View Computer Settings** link and expand **PRESIDENT** in the **View or Change Client Computer Settings** dialog box that appears. Expand **Client Setup Configuration Options**. Observe the **Configure Outlook Profile Information** entry. This is where the Outlook profile configuration settings reside that relate to the setup of this computer.

3. You should have two e-mails in your Inbox. One will welcome you to Microsoft Office Outlook 2003. The other will welcome you to Windows Small Business Server 2003. Please open and read each of these as they contain important information on Outlook and SBS 2003 features and functionality that I won't repeat here. An example: The Outlook 2003 welcome message discusses the Junk E-mail filter (very cool and spooky smart).
4. Click the **New Mail Message** button on the Outlook toolbar to create a new message.
5. In the **To:** field, type **Springers** (in a moment, this entry will automatically resolve to **Springer Spaniels Limited** distribution list entry which is basically sending out a message to everyone in the company). In the **Subject:** field, type **Ideas for forthcoming Dog Shows!**

6. Click in the text body portion of the message and type the following message: **G'day folks! I need your input on which dog shows we should attend this year with which dogs. Thanks!** Your screen should look similar to Figure 6-18.

Figure 6-18

Your sample message should look similar to this figure. This is how you create an e-mail message.

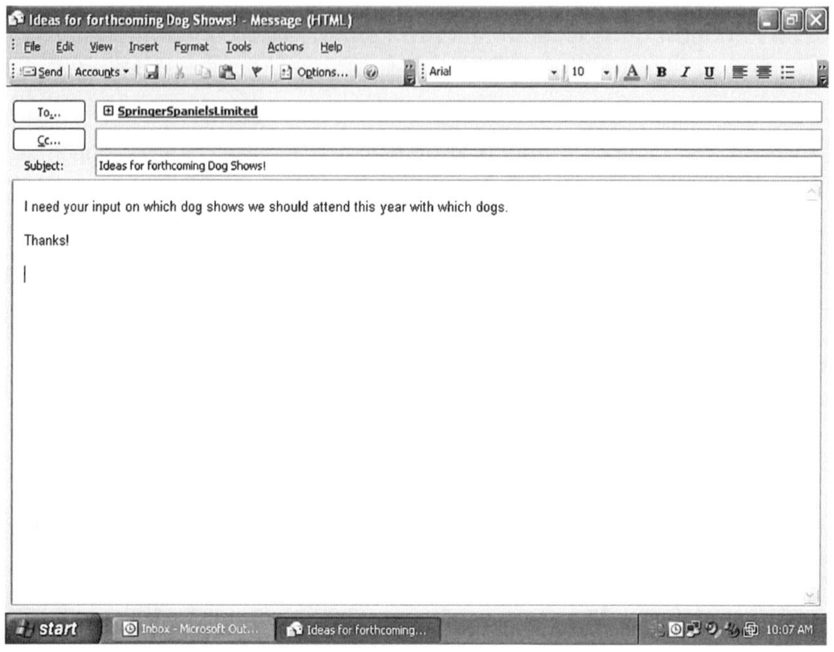

7. Click **Send** on the message toolbar to send the message. The message should now appear in your Inbox (Figure 6-19).

Figure 6-19

Congratulations! You've sent your first e-mail message as part of the SPRINGERS methodology.

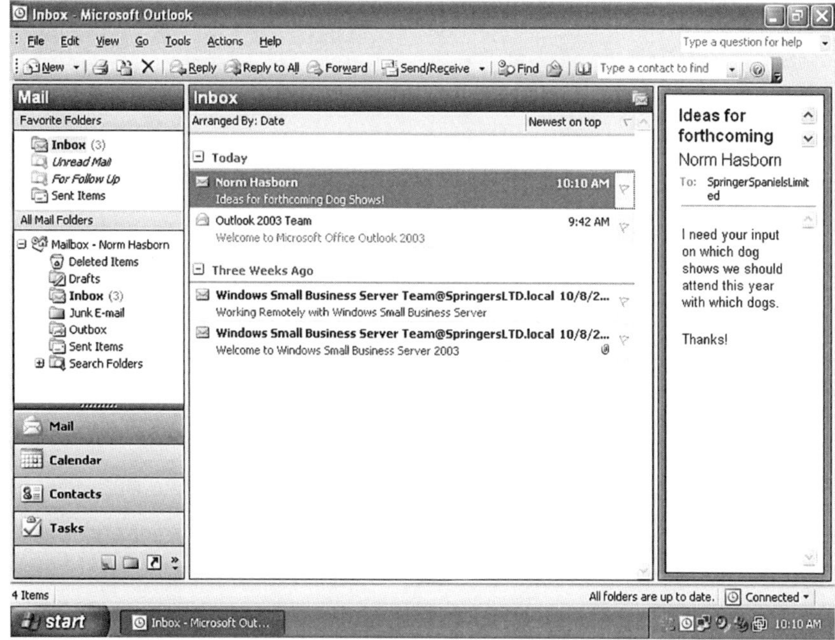

Creating an Appointment

Now you will create an appointment in NormH's calendar. It concerns the very important matter of Brisker's mental health (you'll recall from Chapter 2 and the photo section of this book that Brisker is one of the lead dogs at SPRINGERS).

1. Assuming you are logged on as **NormH** on **PRESIDENT** with Outlook 2003 open, select **Calendar** in the left pane.
2. Click the **New Appointment** button on the left of the upper toolbar.
3. An **Untitled - Appointment** windows appears. Type **Take Brisker To Therapist** in the **Subject**: line. Type **Dog Psychiatrist** in the **Location** field. Select **Must Attend** under **Label**. Select a **Start time** of **October 9, 2004 1:00pm** and an **End time** of **October 9, 2004 3:00pm**. In the text field, type **Report on Brisker's hypnosis progress**. Your screen should look similar to Figure 6-20.

4. Click **Save** and **Close**.

Figure 6-20
Again - congratulations! You've created your first appointment.

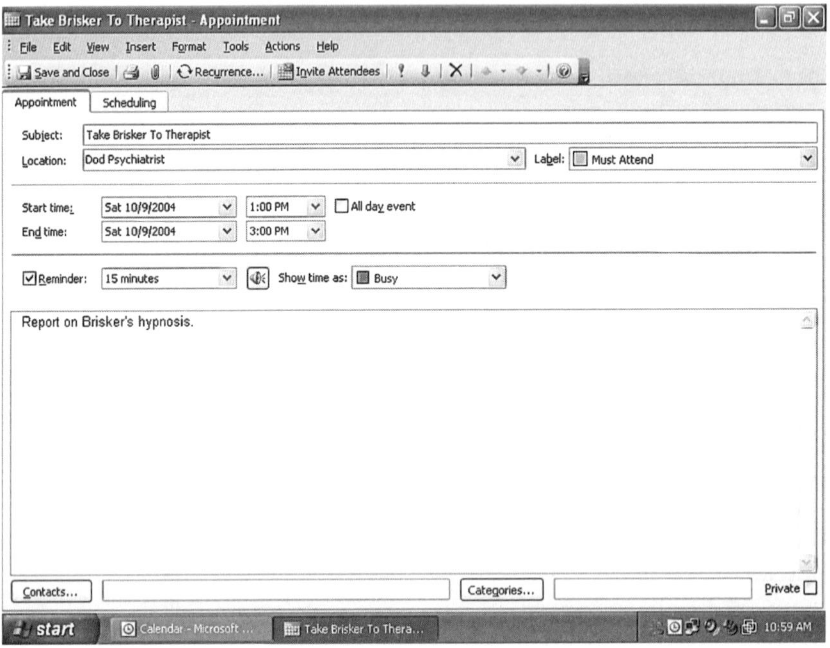

Creating Contacts

You will now use one of the coolest capabilities in SBS 2003: the built-in company public folder contacts. By creating these public folders objects, this information will appear in everyone's Outlook 2003 client computer-side application and with this increased visibility, hopefully be used more than prior SBS releases. Let's start the procedure to enter SPRINGERS stakeholders as contact records.

1. If necessary, have **NormH** log on to **PRESIDENT** with the password **Purple3300**. This, of course, shouldn't be necessary, because you should still be in Outlook on PRESIDENT as NormH from the last procedure.
2. Click the **Folder List** icon on the bottom left toolbar (it looks like a yellow folder). Alternatively, you could click **Ctrl-6**.

3. The center under **All Folders**, scroll down and expand **Public Folders**. Then expand **All Public Folders**. Notice two SBS 2003-specific objects in the SPRINGERS story line: **Springer Spaniels Limited Archive** and **Springer Spaniels Limited Contacts**.
4. Select **Springer Spaniels Limited Contacts**.
5. Click the **New Contact** button on the upper toolbar, far left.
6. You will enter all of the SPRINGERS stakeholders that are listed in Chapter 2, Table 2-2. The entry of a single contact record should look similar to Figure 6-21 and the complete list of stakeholders should look like Figure 6-22. Remember that you click **Save** and **Close** after each contact record is populated and then repeat Step #5 above.

BEST PRACTICE: You might see the Location Information screen for a modem connection appear as you enter this information on PRESIDENT. Why would that be? Because you're entering telephony information on a machine that hasn't previously been configured for such.

Figure 6-21
A record has been entered.

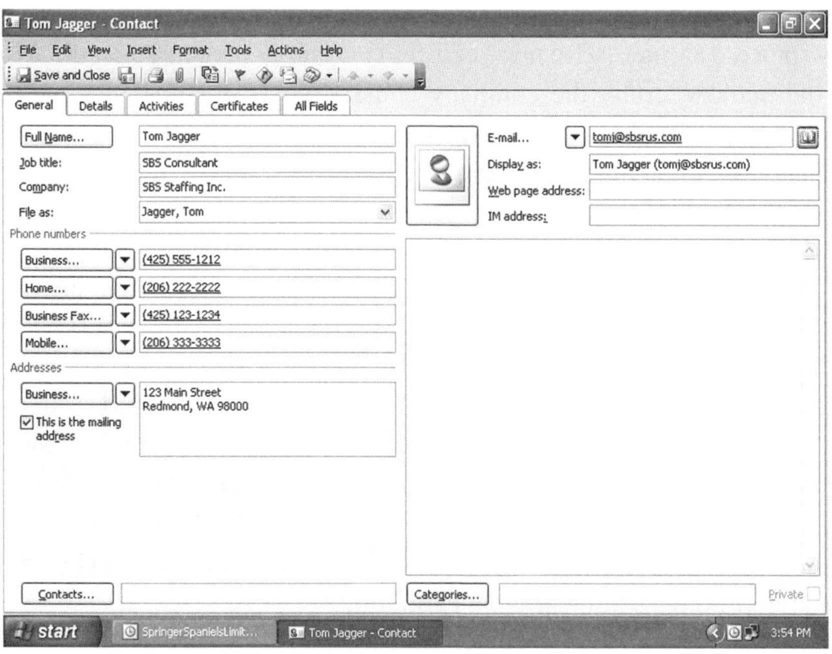

Figure 6-22
All records have been entered and are displayed here.

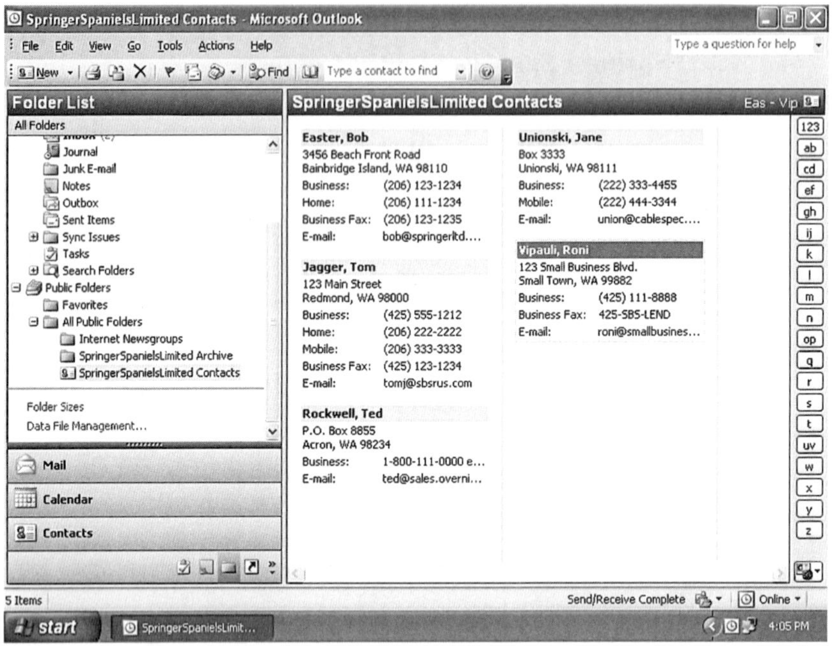

Now proceed to enter each employee in the company as per some prior discussion in the book whereby the company contact would include SPRINGERS employees to be meaningful. All SPRINGERS employees are listed in Chapter 2 under the section titled User List.

BEST PRACTICE: If the two company public folder objects, Springer Spaniels Limited Archive and Springer Spaniels Limited Contacts don't appear, it reflects an incomplete SBS 2003 setup. This can occur if for some reason you stopped the SBS 2003 setup at mid-point and then restarted. The problem is that the "restarted" setup didn't complete the script to create those company-related public folder objects. You can easily cure this by manually creating these objects. And exactly how do I know this? On one of the builds of the SBS 2003 hands-on lab master, the setup routine was stopped at mid-point, and I learned all about it.

Public Folder Procedure

Before we go too much further, I need you to create a public folder called "fax" so that we can direct the faxes to this public folder a few chapters down the road. Because your screen should show the public folders at this point (from the completion of the procedure above), please right-click **All Public Folders** and select **New Folder**. Make the folder configured for **Mail and Post Items**. Click **OK** to complete the setup. You've just created something we both need in the faxing chapter to complete an example.

By the way, that "fax" public folder object you just created is SMTP mail enabled as fax@springersltd.com automatically. Very cool.

Attachment Blocking

Something folks love and curse is the native attachment blocking in Outlook 2003. They love it because it protects them from harmful e-mail attachments. They curse it because, in the heat of business battle, you can't get to your darn tootin' attachment that is mission-critical. But let's fight fire with facts here.

There are two levels of attachment blocking in Outlook 2003. Level 1 is fixed, can't be changed, and includes the following attachments (these are the file extensions): ade, adp, app, bas, bat, chm, cmd, com, cpl, crt, csh, exe, fxp, hlp, hta, inf, ins, isp, js, jse, ksh, lnk, mda, mdb, mde, mdt, mdw, mdz, msc, msi, msp, mst, ops, pcd, pif, prf, prg, reg, scf, scr, sct, shb, shs, url, vb, vbe, vbs, wsc, wsf, wsh, xsl.

> BEST PRACTICE: These file types are defined when you type "attachment blocking" in the Outlook 2003 help system and select the Attachment file types blocked by Outlook link.

Level 2 is more liberal and prompts the user to save the file type to a hard disk. An Exchange administrator can allow a file type to be moved from Level 1 to Level 2 to allow this saving (the Exchange administrator can also modify the above list of Level 1 files). Note that the native SBS 2003 attachment blocking capability discussed earlier in this chapter will come into play interacting with Outlook on the network and the most conservative attachment blocking list will win between Outlook and SBS 2003.

BEST PRACTICE: You can get an offending attachment around the blockade by simply renaming it to an acceptable file format, such as *.doc (for a Word document). Then rename the file type back to its original name once you've saved it to your C: drive. This is commonly done with file attachments ending in *.exe because this attachment type might be a legitimate business program that need to be received.

Junk E-mail

Microsoft has one of the largest research and development (R&D) budgets in the corporate world. Sometimes, shareholders get a little fussy with billions being spent on R&D because they want to see things that immediately contribute to current earnings. One positive R&D payoff is the sophisticated junk e-mail management approach built in to Outlook 2003 (this was actually spelled out as one of the points in the Outlook 2003 welcome e-mail you were asked to read earlier). Since I won't sit here and retype the online help system in Outlook 2003, if you'd like to learn more about the Junk E-mail capability at a deep level, simply search on the term **"Junk e-mail"** in **Outlook 2003 Help** and select the **About the Junk E-mail Filer** link.

Back to the real world. You're probably interested in knowing how to configure the Junk E-mail capabilities in Outlook 2003. It's simple. Just select **Tools**, **Options**, **Junk E-mail in Outlook 2003**. The **Junk E-mail Options** dialog box will appear, as seen in Figure 6-23. You can then change the default setting (Low) to a different level.

Notes:

Figure 6-23
This figure shows all of the settings on Junk E-mail Options. But, equally important, look over to the left and observe the Junk E-mail folder under the Folder List. This is where e-mails are moved.

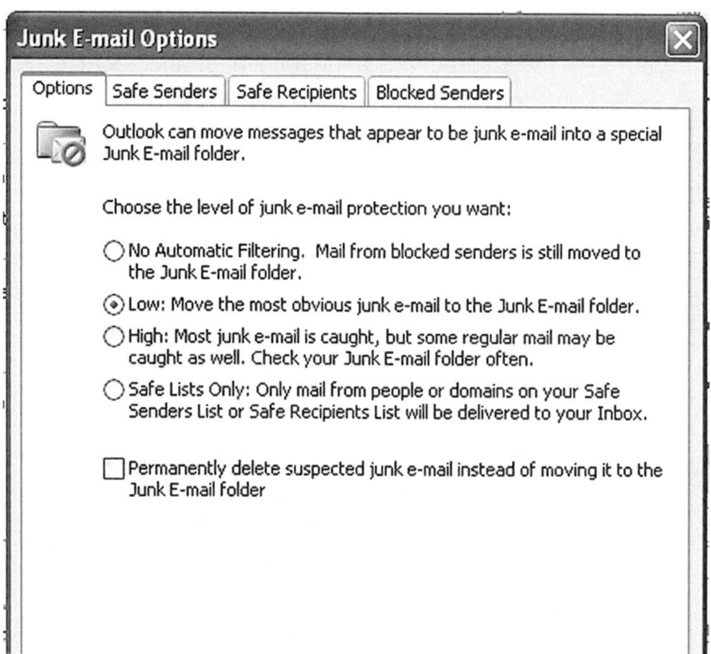

So if you're a Microsoft shareholder, now you know how your R&D dollars are being spent!

> BEST PRACTICE: You simply must read this white paper/analysis on the internals of Outlook spam blocking. I first learned of this from the *W2KNews* newsletter (www.w2knews.com) that goes out to about a half-million readers (as an author, I can tell you that is a very large number of readers!). So click over to http://www.mapilab.com/articles/outlook_spam_filter.html and see the report from MAPI Lab. Excellent!

Junk Users

Maybe you can relate to the following situation. I'm on an e-mail list that has some annoying and verbose members. For business purposes, I can't leave the list, but I often become frustrated with the quantity of e-mails (often of a soap opera nature) that clog my Inbox. Because I'm committed to staying focused on core business operations, and I'd rather review these distracting e-mails at a future decade (I mean date), I use a rule to move them to a folder titled "Much Later, Dude."

If you'd like to implement a similar approach in the management of your e-mails (or perhaps your SBS users would like to do this), then select **Rules and Actions** from the **Tools** menu in Outlook 2003. Then select **New Rule** and click **Move messages from someone to a folder** under **Stay Organized** (Figure 6-24).

Figure 6-24
This is the first step to bringing better management to many of the e-mails you receive from known babblers!

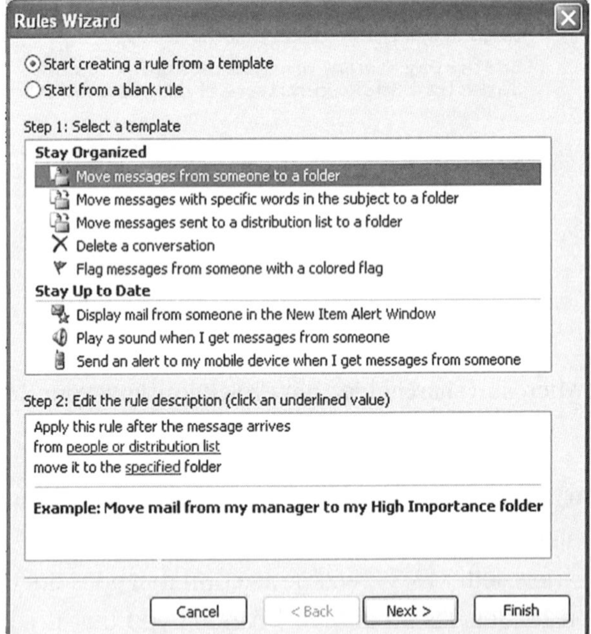

You would then click **Next** and complete the **Rules Wizard** where you'll configure e-mails from certain people to be moved to a folder and out of your Inbox (for example, you'll enter the e-mail address of folks whose e-mail you want moved).

BEST PRACTICE: Perhaps you're just discovering this cool capability later in life and you've got an Inbox full of distracting e-mails you want to move. On the final page of the Rules Wizard, you have an option called **Run this rule now on messages already in "Inbox"** so that, post-hoc, you can improve the quality of your Inbox life.

Recovery Movement

No, this isn't about a battle with the bottle. Rather, this is how to recover deleted e-mail and move it back into the Inbox or the folder of your choice. To learn this capability using Exchange's delete item recovery capability (set to retain e-mails for 30-days by default in SBS 2003), complete the following procedure:

1. If necessary, have **NormH** log on to **PRESIDENT** with the password **Purple3300**.
2. In Outlook 2003, delete the e-mail from Norm Hasborn by dragging it to the **Deleted Items** folder.
3. Right-click the **Deleted Items** folder and select **Empty "Deleted Items"** Folder. Select **Yes** when asked in the Microsoft Office Outlook dialog box if you really want to delete the item. Observe the **Deleted Items** folder is now empty and would appear you've lost this e-mail forever.
4. Now you will recover the deleted e-mail by selecting the **Deleted Items folder** and then selecting the **Recover Deleted Items** menu option under the **Tools** menu.
5. NormH's e-mail appears in the **Recover Deleted Items from Deleted Items** dialog box that appears (Figure 6-25). Make sure this e-mail is highlighted and click the **Recover Selected Items** button. The e-mail will be returned to the **Deleted Items** folder.
6. Move the e-mail from **Deleted Items** back to **Inbox**.

Notes:

Figure 6-25
E-mails that have been deleted within the retention period (30-days by default in SBS 2003) will appear here.

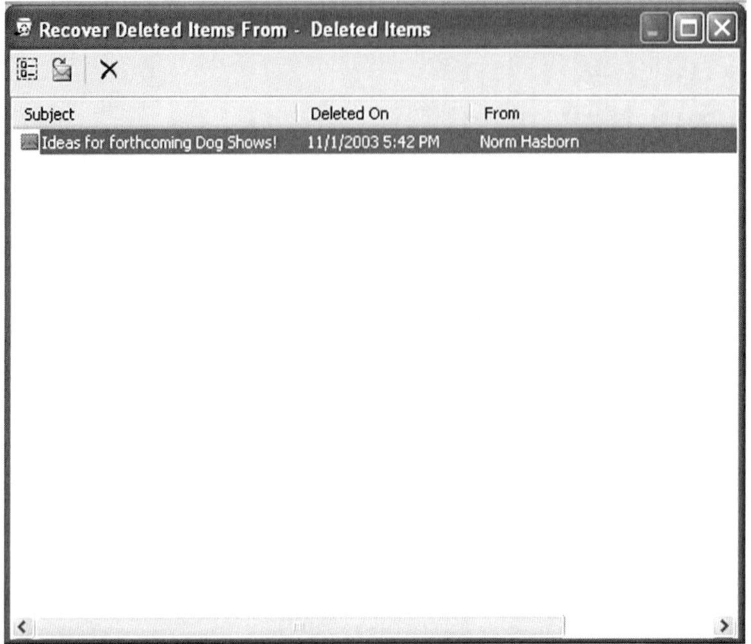

Forwarding E-mail to Your Mobile Telephone

Something that is increasingly popular is the ability to forward e-mails to your telephone. That's because numerous technologies are converging and breaking down functional and feature barriers. Heck - many brands of mobile telephone now include cameras, so why not e-mail too?

The key would be to forward the e-mails to your telephone. Of course, you'd want to keep a copy of it in your server-based mailbox, because telephones aren't a good permanent repository and reading a large attachment on a telephone is darn near impossible! So here are the steps you'd take to forward e-mails to your mobile telephone (using the SPRINGERS methodology of course).

1. If necessary, have **NormH** log on to **PRESIDENT** with the password **Purple3300**.
2. In Outlook 2003, select **Rules and Alerts** from the **Tools** menu.

3. Select **Send an alert to my mobile device when I get a message from someone** and click **Next**.
4. Under the **Step 1: Select conditions** list, deselect the default selection of "**from people or distribution list**" and select "**where my name is in the To or Cc box**" and then click **Next**. This will effectively forward all e-mail sent to you.
5. On the following **Select actions** page, keep the default selection of "**forward it to people or distribution list**" and click **Next**. On the lower part of this page, click the **people or distribution list** hyperlink
6. The **Rule Address** dialog box appears. Type the e-mail address of your mobile telephone in the **To ->** field. For example, you might type something like 2065551212@tmobile.com. Click **OK**.
7. Click **Finish** followed by OK to close **Rules and Alerts**.

BEST PRACTICE: Related to the forwarding concept, note that I've used the Active Directory contact object forwarding capability when a customer has a remote office that uses (and will continue to use) POP3 e-mail. The good folks at the home office, seeking to create a uniform e-mail organization/image, will create an Active Directory user for the employee at the remote site. That allows the internal employees to e-mail the remote employee directly from the GAL in Exchange and so on. But this remote employee also has an associated Active Directory contact object that is really the e-mail address for their POP3 account. And voila, the forwarding occurs from the Active Directory user to the Active Directory contact object. How? On the property sheet for an Active Directory user (let's say Norm), click the **Exchange General** tab, click the **Delivery Options** button, and complete the **Forwarding address box**. Be sure to leave a copy on the server!

Cached Exchange Mode

Something you'll readily appreciate in Outlook 2003 will be Cached Exchange Mode that is set by default for all SBS 2003 users. This allows you to work offline with Outlook 2003 when Exchange is down for maintenance, you are traveling, or you have a slow link (56K modem) connection back to the server. What's cool is that this is implemented by default and removes a task that you and I performed manually at each user machine in the past: configuring offline storage (OST files). Bottom line: You can work with Outlook 2003 very effectively while on a plane, train, automobile, or "no-tell" motel room full of swimsuit models!

Microsoft does a dandy job of explaining Cached Exchange Mode at http://office.microsoft.com/assistance/preview.aspx?AssetID=HP052516521033&CTT=98 (this can also be found by drilling down into Outlook from www.microsoft.com/office and then clicking the **Assistance** link). I encourage you to read more about this.

It's Client, Not Server!

If you completed the initial online SBS 2003 hands-on lab offered at www.microsoft.granitepillar.com/partners in the early fall of 2003, you would recall that the Part #3 of that courseware had you run Outlook 2003 on the SBS 2003 server machine and click past an important warning message. The point I want to make is that you should not run Outlook 2003 on the SBS 2003 server machine, and that warning message you receive, seen in Figure 6-26, is to be honored. Bottom line: Run Outlook 2003 on the client computer, not the SBS 2003 server machine.

Notes:

Figure 6-26
This message discusses why Outlook 2003 should not be run on the SBS 2003 server machine. There are TechNet KBase articles that also discuss this issue you might want to read.

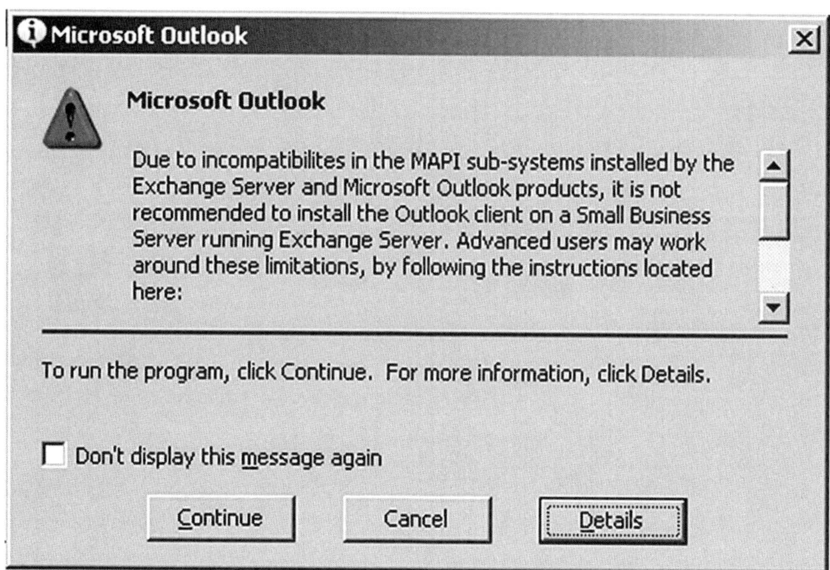

BEST PRACTICE: Some of you will recall that, in my *Small Business Server 2000 Best Practices* book, I had you run Outlook 2000 on the SBS 2000 server machine to save time. I was wrong, and I didn't do it again!

Extending Outlook

In this section, you will learn a few ways to further extend your use of Outlook 2003 in an SBS 2003 environment. These approaches are taken directly from the real world and reflect the reality you're likely to confront and embrace! Let's start with Outlook PDA synchronization, followed by using Outlook Express with IMAP and ending with a totally cool add-on called Outlook Business Contact Manager.

Outlook PDA Synchronization

You might recall the Mobile Client and Offline Use page when you ran the Add User Wizard/Set Up Computer Wizard late in Chapter 4 (this page is shown below in Figure 6-27). It was here you elected to install ActiveSync 3.7 on the client computer. This is a required application to synchronize Outlook 2003 between a personal digital assistant (PDA) and the client computer machine.

Figure 6-27
This is the critical path step to install ActiveSync 3.7 on the client computer.

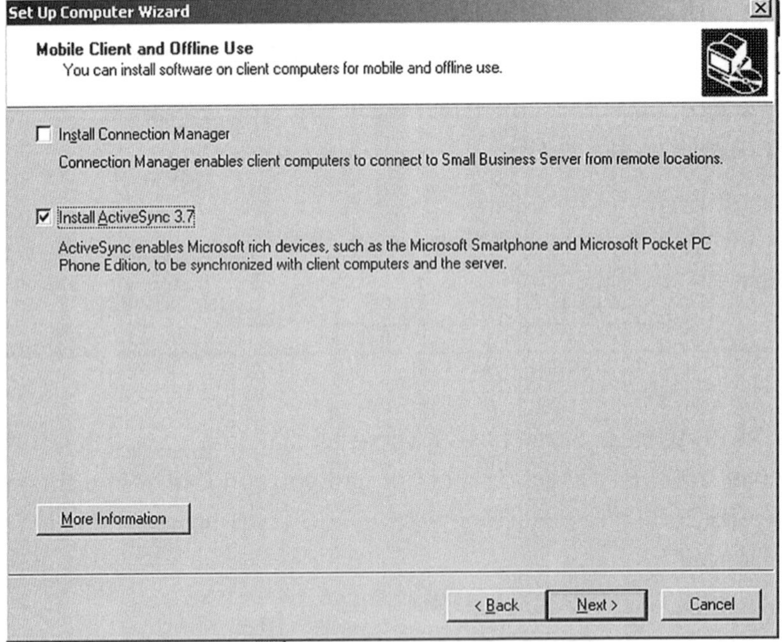

This is a VERY POPULAR SOLUTION with business people who want to carry Outlook information with them such as e-mail, contacts, and appointments on their PDA. This is how people work in the real world and they demand that this type of information be at their finger tips at any time. The way in which Outlook 2003 on the client computer will synchronize with the PDA using ActiveSync 3.7 is as follows.

ActiveSync 3.7 is installed on the client computer and ready for use. Assuming you use the Compaq/HP iPAQ PDA, you attach the cradle to the USB port on the client computer. You place the iPAQ in the cradle and launch ActiveSync 3.7 from Start, All Programs, Microsoft ActiveSync on the client computer. You complete the wizard to create a partnership and elect what Outlook 2003 objects/data you want to synchronize. You then proceed to actually synchronize the data and resolve any conflicts (e.g., double bookings on your calendar with the exact same appointment). The process is shown in Figure 6-28.

Figure 6-28
An early and assured win with business customers and SBS users is to deploy ActiveSync 3.7 to synchronize Outlook 2003 data with a PDA, such as the IPAQ shown here.

BEST PRACTICE: The whole Outlook 2003/PDA synchronization matter exposes a weakness in SBS 2003 that you'll need to utilize a third-party tool to correct: public folder synchronization. The problem is this. The SBS 2003 team is rightfully proud about creating the company-related public folder object discussed earlier in this chapter. For example, the contact list can be used as a company-wide contact list that eliminates duplicate lists of customers circulating about the firm. But how would you get this great contact list to your IPAQ PDA? Not natively, but with some of the third-party synchronization tools reviewed at SlipStick: www.slipstick.com/addins/olpda.htm#wince. You'll learn about products such as Pocket Lookout that performs this important function.

You can also use a Microsoft tool, the Outlook 2002 Add-in: Pocket Contact Synchronizer 1.2, which will take the contact information in the company contact folder and synchronize it to your mailbox-based Contacts, which would then synchronize to your PDA via ActiveSync 3.7. Granted - it's an additional step, but this shoe may well fit.

BEST PRACTICE: I just love late breaking news. The wonderful Susan Bradley, an MVP in the SBS and security areas, recently shared that Infoware - Team Contacts for Outlook at http://www.infoware.ca/content/tcon.asp and http://www.infoware.ca/content/infoframe.htm?tcon.asp synchronizes user contact lists with a central contact list in an Exchange public folder. This automatically merges changes when two users update the same contact in their personal Contacts folder.

Ride the Outlook Express With IMAP

I have a client who travels extensively for business and pleasure. Back in the SBS 2000 era, she complained that using Outlook Web Access (OWA, which I discuss in Chapter 8) was too bulky, slow, and awkward. Now granted, in just a few chapters I'll show you why OWA has improved and should be the remote e-mail access mechanism of choice. But for some, there will still be a chance to use Outlook Express with the IMAP protocol to access e-mail. As you know, Outlook Express is typically installed when Internet Explorer is installed, making it a near universally available e-mail client (in Internet cafés in Spain and so on).

When you launch **Outlook Express**, you'll need to configure the client machine to connect back to the SBS 2003 server, be authenticated, and use the IMAP protocol. This is accomplished by running the **Outlook Express Internet**

Connection wizard. This third page (**E-mail Server Names**) is the tricky one. You need to drop down the protocol list and select IMAP and then complete the server connection information (**Incoming, Outgoing**) with either an IP address or a fully qualified domain name. You provide logon authentication information on the **Internet Mail Logon** page (this would be your user account and password on the SBS 2003 network). And then all that is left would be to click **Finish**.

So why IMAP? Haven't we been throwing around the word POP3 in this chapter? SBS 2003 configures Exchange Server 2003 to support the SMTP, POP3, IMAP, and HTTP mail protocols. But IMAP offers the opportunity to efficiently download just the e-mail headers (but not the full e-mail). That would allow my client to scan the e-mails she wants to read and delete less worthy e-mails. The point is that the full e-mail isn't downloaded until the e-mail is opened. This is a nice touch when working from an Internet café! Note that POP3 is going to download the entire e-mail to the client.

> BEST PRACTICE: While Exchange Server 2003 installs and supports IMAP and POP3 natively, you'll need to start these protocols in Exchange. For example, to turn on the IMAP protocol, you would drill down into the **Exchange System Manager** under **Advanced Management** in the **Server Management** console. Expand **Servers**, **Protocols** and open the **IMAP4** protocol folder. On the right pane, right click **Default IMAP4 Virtual Server** and select **Start**. You're now ready to use the IMAP-based e-mail in Exchange Server 2003 (and ergo, SBS 2003).

Notes:

This is an IMAP security setting that you need to make. If the RRAS NAT/ Basic Firewall method is your Internet security method (as per SBS 2003 standard edition), you would select the Internet Mail Access Protocol 4 (IMAP4) as seen in Figure 6-29 on the Services and Ports tab in the Network Connection Properties dailog box. This will allow IMAP-related traffic to flow baby!

Figure 6-29
Selecting the IMAP4 port opening on your SBS 2003 server. When asked which private IP address to map to, enter 127.0.0.1 (a dialog box will ask this when you select this service).

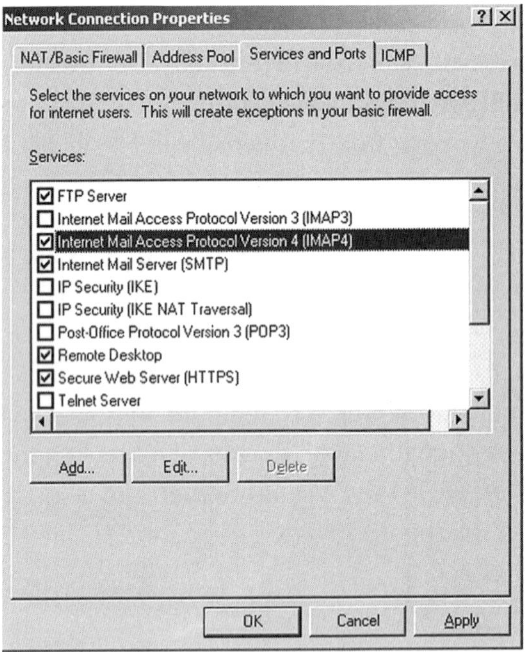

If ISA Server is your Internet security method (as per SBS 2003 premium edition), you would create a packet filter. You will do exactly that in Chapter 13, so hang on to your hat!

Outlook Business Contact Manager

This is known in some circles as customer relationship management (CRM) for da' little guy, whereas Microsoft's full CRM product is positioned for the firms between 25 and 500 employees with at least of $5 million in sales. Outlook Business Contact Manager is an Outlook 2003 add-on to help small business people improve sales management. A comparison between Business Contact Manager and CRM is shown in Figure 6-30.

BEST PRACTICE: Be well aware that Business Contact Manager is SINGLE USER ONLY. That's some good old expectation management up front and in your face because you might conclude that restriction will limit the functionality of this cool tool. Whereas the business public folders created by SBS 2003 would seem to promote hugging and sharing, Business Contact Manager would tend to do just the opposite and create an island of information in the small business. These two strategies are at odds.

Figure 6-30

Comparing Business Contact Manager and Microsoft CRM at a glance.

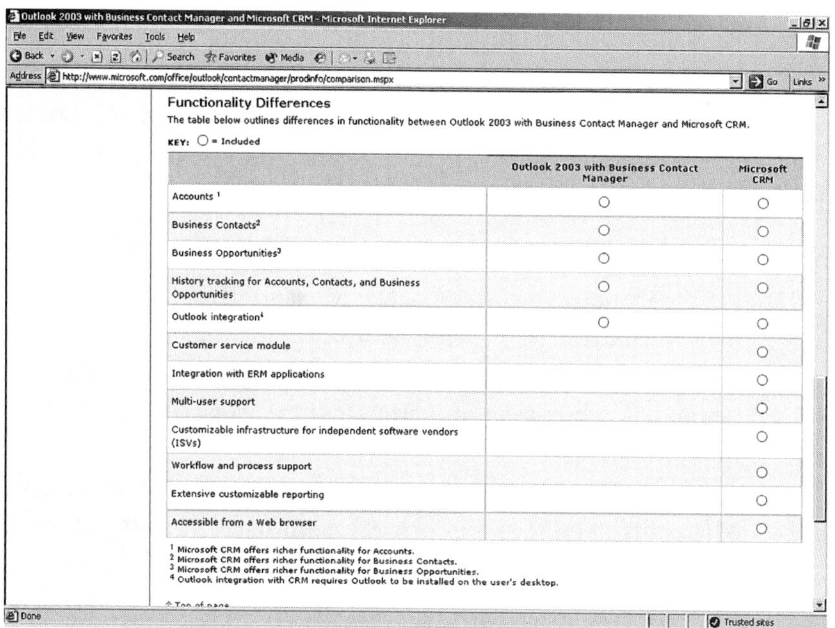

Functionality Differences

The table below outlines differences in functionality between Outlook 2003 with Business Contact Manager and Microsoft CRM.

KEY: ○ = Included

	Outlook 2003 with Business Contact Manager	Microsoft CRM
Accounts [1]	○	○
Business Contacts[2]	○	○
Business Opportunities[3]	○	○
History tracking for Accounts, Contacts, and Business Opportunities	○	○
Outlook integration[4]	○	○
Customer service module		○
Integration with ERM applications		○
Multi-user support		○
Customizable infrastructure for independent software vendors (ISVs)		○
Workflow and process support		○
Extensive customizable reporting		○
Accessible from a Web browser		○

[1] Microsoft CRM offers richer functionality for Accounts.
[2] Microsoft CRM offers richer functionality for Business Contacts.
[3] Microsoft CRM offers richer functionality for Business Opportunities.
[4] Outlook integration with CRM requires Outlook to be installed on the user's desktop.

BEST PRACTICE: As of this writing, Microsoft is launching a promotion that bundles SBS 2003 and CRM 1.2. The details are found in a CRN article at: http://crn.channelsupersearch.com/news/

crn/45066.asp. The good news is that Microsoft is looking for ways to extend SBS with tools such as CRM 1.2 (and I'll cover this pairing in my future advanced SBS 2003 book).

You acquire Business Contact Manager from Office 2003 (enterprise, professional, and small business editions). I'm not going to delve much deeper into the definition of Business Contract Manager but rather encourage you to take a short pause here and read more at www.microsoft.com/outlook. When you return, we'll start the step by step to install Business Contact Manager and make a couple of entries as part of the SPRINGERS methodology.

Note that I assume you've already installed Office 2003 on the PRESIDENT workstation. If not, do so now with the normal or most common components installed.

BEST PRACTICE: Late breaking news again! Please run an update that allows BCM to function properly with Exchange e-mail profiles on SBS 2003 by visiting the Microsoft download center at www.microsoft.com/downloads and searching under Office Outlook and the keyword Business. There is a quick fix you'll run prior to performing the procedure below.

1. Log on as **NormH** with the password **Purple3300** on **PRESIDENT**.
2. Put the Outlook Business Contact Manager Disc in the CD drive of the PRESIDENT and launch **Setup.exe**.
3. Click **OK** when the **Business Contact Manager for Outlook 2003** Setup dialog box asks for permission to detect and install the .Net framework 1.1.
4. Agree to the Microsoft .Net license by selecting **I agree on the Microsoft .NET Framework 1.1 Setup** screen and click **Install.** This setup can take several minutes. Click **OK** when the .NET Framework 1.1 is complete.
5. Click **Next** on the welcome page for Business Contact Manager.
6. On the **End-User License Agreement** page, select **I accept the terms in the licenses agreement** and click **Next**.
7. Accept the default destination on **C:** drive on the **Destination Folder** page and click **Next**.

8. On the **Ready to Install the Program** page, click **Install**. You will be advised of the installation progress on the status bar.
9. Click **Finish** on the **Wizard Completed** page. You've now completed the installation of Business Contact Manager.

In the following procedure, you'll launch Outlook and use Business Contract Manager.

1. Launch Outlook from **Start**, E-**mail**.
2. Observe and read the **Welcome to Microsoft Outlook with Business Contact Manager** e-mail. I'm counting on you to read this to learn more about the product as I won't repeat it here.
3. Select **Business Contacts** from the **Business Tools** menu. Complete the screen, similar to Figure 6-31, for a fictional customer (e.g., Mrs. Jones). Click **Save and Close** to close the record.

Figure 6-31
Adding a business contact.

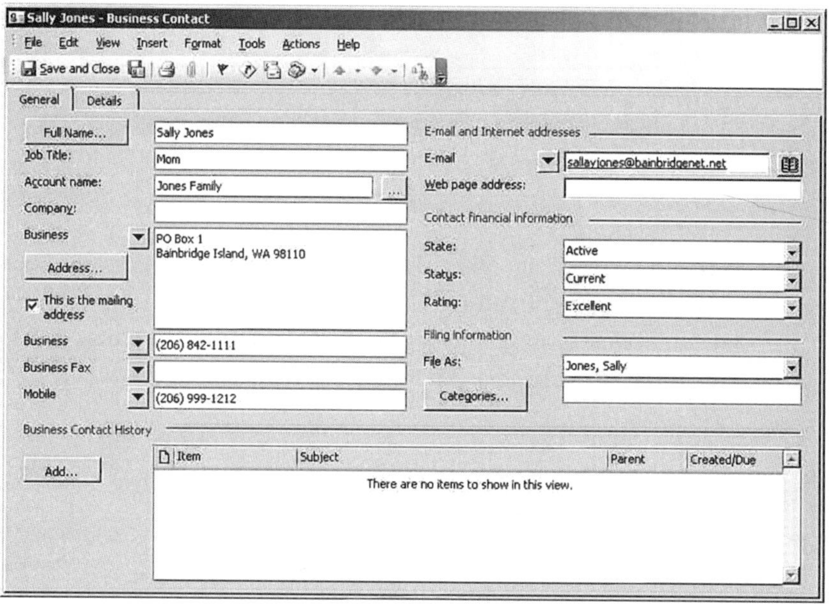

4. Select **Accounts** from **Business Tools** and complete the screen similar to Figure 6-32 with fictitious information. Be sure to add a business note and link Sally Jones. Click **Save and Close**.

Figure 6-32
Creating an account in BCM. You're putting the pieces in place for a CRM system.

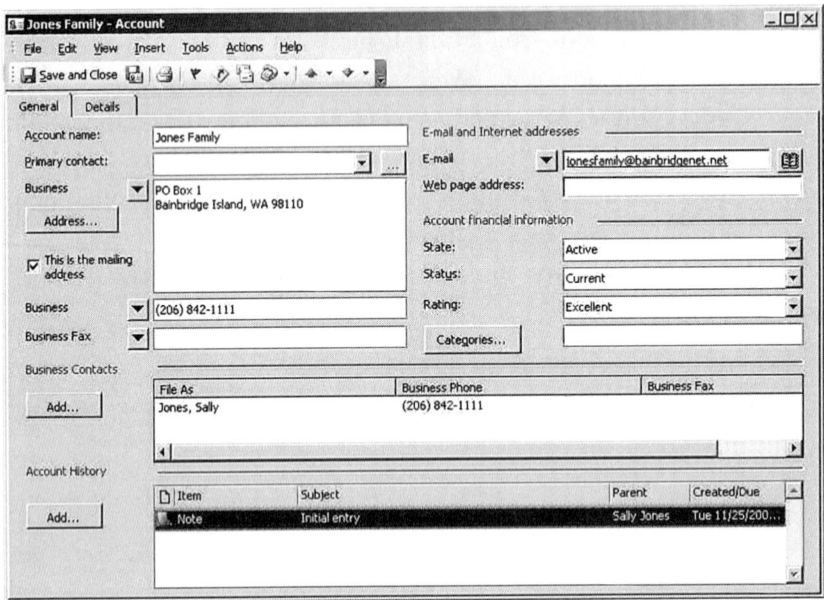

5. Next up, explore the other **Business Tools** menu options and create an **Opportunity**, **Product List** and, if connected to the Internet to launch a Web browser, select the **Business Tools** link that will take you to the BCM page at Microsoft for the latest updates.

6. Finally, play around with the **Reports** option under the **Business Tools** menu. One such report is shown in Figure 6-33.

Figure 6-33
The fictitious information is shown in the Account List with Business Contact report.

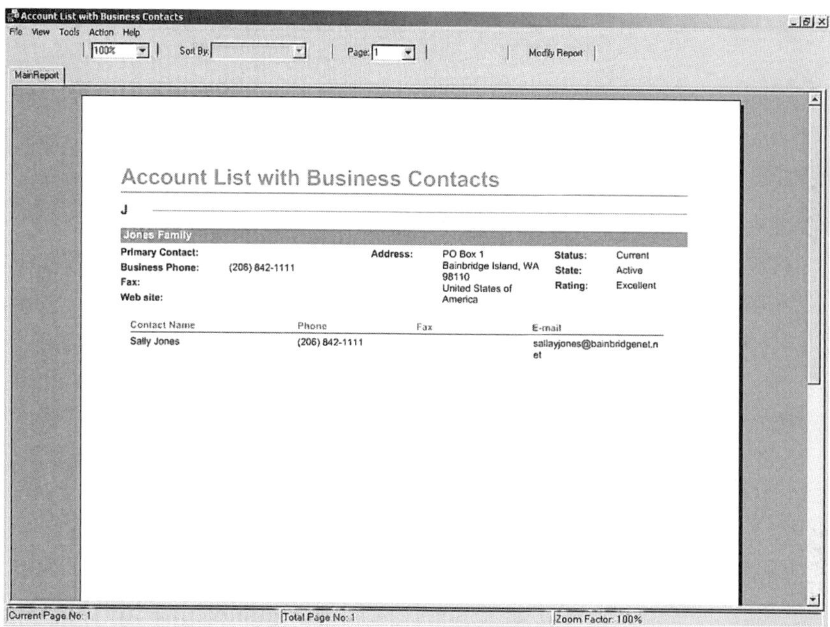

Note that my intent isn't to teach mastery of BCM but rather turn you on to this cool tool. Perhaps a full chapter in a future book will be dedicated to this tool for your reading pleasure.

BEST PRACTICE: BCM is a great start at delivering CRM to the "rest of us." I encourage you to learn it, use it and provide feedback on it to Microsoft (the Outlook newsgroups are sufficient to do this). However, it's necessary to understand that there are a couple of limitations for this, including that the BCM data doesn't really play well with native Exchange mailbox data. That is, a contact record format in BCM is different than the traditional Exchange contact record format. Also, BCM kinda has this "island of information" mentality and this isn't shared information. Rather, you should picture it as each salesperson in a company keeping their own CRM system that is separate from everyone else's. That is bothersome to me and at odds with attempts to centralize business information for the benefit (and profitability) of all.

I personally look for this limitation to be satisfied in a future BCM release, which is why I highly recommend you play with it today in anticipation of a better tomorrow.

Next Steps!

There are some next steps you can take that go above and beyond this chapter on Exchange and Outlook.

- Visit Microsoft Web Sites: Exchange and Outlook. Your very next step is to visit the sites at Microsoft for Exchange (www.microsoft.com/exchange) and Outlook (www.microsoft.com/office and select the Outlook link). Microsoft posts much of its technical resources to its sites and has created this treasure chest of current information on their products that this book can't hope to keep up with!

- Read Exchange and Outlook Books. While this book covers the full suite of products in SBS 2003, there are many excellent (and thick) books dedicated to Outlook and Exchange. I can recommend the Outlook and Exchange Administrator's Smart Pak (TechRepublic) with more information at https://techrepublic-secure.com.com/5106-6242-26-12333.html?part=tr&subj=12333.

- Use Microsoft TechNet to learn Exchange command line utilities. The second disc of the SBS 2003 media contains Exchange command-line utilities that help manage and recover the database. You should visit www.microsoft.com/technet and search on **"Exchange"** to learn more about these.

- Sign up for Sue Mosher's RSS feed for Exchange and Outlook issues: http://www.slipstick.com/rssnews/rssnews.aspx.

- Read current articles on Exchange and Outlook. There is an interesting InfoWorld article on the role of Outlook 2003 and SBS 2003 (Enterprise Windows: Oliver Rist, November 7, 2003, www.infoworld.com).
- Learn more cool Outlook features. This chapter is only the start, not the end of your time with Outlook. Please go forward and educate yourself on the vCard capability to mail your contact record to others, the mail merge capability, and the automatic meeting planning tool.
- Read Chapter 8 of this book. I've not forgotten OWA and other remote Outlook connectivity approaches (such as Outlook Mobile Access, Outlook over RDP, etc.). These are covered in the remote connectivity chapter.

Late Breaking News! EICW Support Matter

Just when you thought it was safe to go out in the neighborhood again, Karen Christian of the North County Technology Group (www.nctg.com) sent in this nugget for your consumption. This involves both the EICW (which Karen calls the CEICW below) and remote access. As such, it serves as a great transition to the remote connectivity chapter you'll read soon (Chapter 8).

11/11/2003

Here are the results of a couple calls to MS support and a couple TS sessions to my server in the last 24 hours.

We could not connect via HTTPS from the Internet for OWA or Remote Web Workplace and wanted to get this resolved. This server was SBS2000 w/ISA upgraded to SBS 2003 Basic/Premium. (Still have to install SQL via the Premium CD......think I'll take a breather first.)

MS tried rerunning CEICW and did not get the desired results. They manually configured DNS, ISA and IIS and got it working late last night. Today they wanted to get the wizard to do its job the way it was intended. It required some manual cleanup first which was not expected on their part. Guess this is another 'feature' we have to keep in the back of our minds.

Steps Performed:

1. Removed the Web Server Cert.
2. Removed the ISA Incoming Web Listener Cert
3. Removed the Web Publishing Rules
4. Removed the Destination Sets
5. Reran CEICW, and waited for services to restart. Services take a few minutes to restart, so ISA does not immediately show the changes. We are now able to connect as expected.

The expectation is that CEICW would have done all the updates and repair work needed but it didn't work as anticipated.

BEST PRACTICE: When you run the CEICW that comes with SBS2003 Standard edition (Premium edition is just another CD and we didn't have to install ISA as it was there from SBS2K already), you are given an opportunity to create a certificate if desired. You enter the Internet name (ie: servername.domainname.com). I found out today that the wizard process creates two certificates in the process. On my server it created one for nctgdc1.nctg.com and one for publishing.nctg.local. One is for the SSL session to ISA from the Internet and the other is for the SSL session from ISA to IIS. This problem originated when I created a certificate called nctgdc1.nctg.local which is incorrect. Still one would expect that rerunning CEICW would take care of this when you enter the correct certificate name.

Karen Christian

Thanks Karen!

Summary

I end how I started. You know more about Exchange Server 2003 and Outlook 2003 than you've likely given yourself credit for in the past. You probably know about 80 percent of the functionality of the programs and it's the remaining 20 percent that'll take much longer to master. And, hopefully, after reading this chapter that dug deep in Exchange and Outlook, you feel you know much more than prior to reading all this stuff (of course I've left out some other advanced Exchange and Outlook topics that I'll address in a future book down the road - keep reading!).

Chapter 7
Collaboration with Windows SharePoint Services

Perhaps you're seeing the other side of 40 and you remember a popular band called "Tower of Power" from the 1970s. This funky band had a well-received song called "What Is Hip?" That had jive, man! So one thing that's hip in SBS 2003 with tons of jive is Windows SharePoint Services (WSS). Thus, it gets its own chapter and my guarantee (or I'll eat a floppy disk) that you'll find this one of the coolest things in SBS 2003. Get out your boogie shoes and get ready to do the WSS dance.

> BEST PRACTICE: Expectation management time again! Remember that this SBS 2003 volume, dedicated to introductory and intermediate readers, is covering one heck of a lot of ground. And it's doing so at a specific point in time (current as of the book print date). For that reason, I show you appropriate (and cool) uses of WSS in SBS 2003. But the footer on the bottom of each page points you to the SMB Nation and the Microsoft TechNet for updates to any SBS feature that have occurred since this book was penned. I also think that the resources section at the end of the chapter sends you forth with more resources to dig deeper into WSS than I have the page count to do here.

What Is Windows SharePoint Services?

I'll start the WSS definition at the 50,000-foot level and descend to sea level (where you perform some procedures). At the broadest level, you could say WSS means different things to different people. It's a "beauty is in the eye of the beholder" thang. This section will divide the discussion between technical and business.

Technical Definition

The official party line is that WSS is a collaboration application. You'll see this "message" by observing the collaboration language (along with team hugs) in Figure 7-1. Note that collaboration in this context primarily means an intranet portal page.

Figure 7-1
An overriding theme on Microsoft's public SharePoint site is collaboration, collaboration, collaboration!

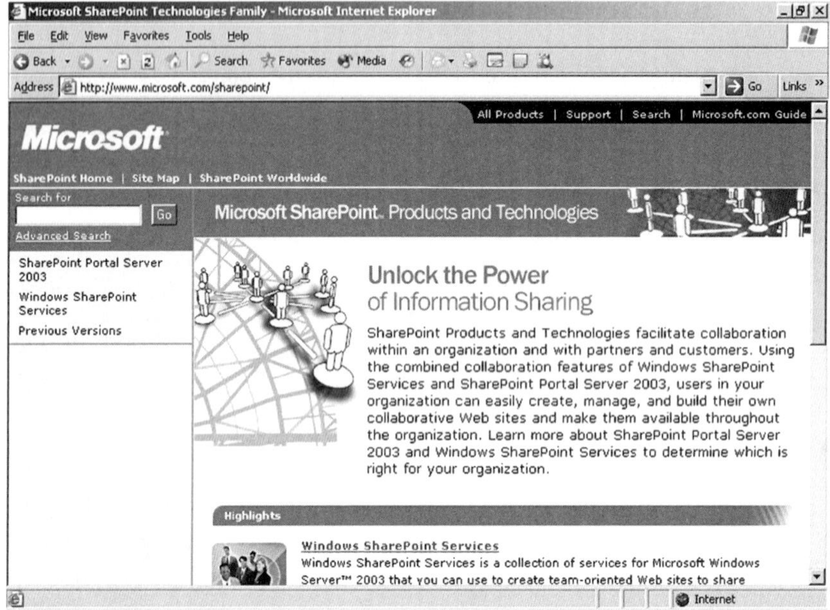

BEST PRACTICE: I wouldn't accuse Microsoft of speaking with forked tongue, but it currently refers to other robust applications as supporting collaboration: Exchange public folders, Microsoft Project Server's Project Central, bCentral's Web Collaboration (www.bcentral.com), and previously Outlook Team Folders. Your challenge here is to separate the wheat from the chaff and decide what collaborative solution best meets your needs. In the SBS 2003 space, clearly WSS is going to be the most efficient and effective collaborative environment to deploy.

So one term you didn't observe in Figure 7-1 above was "document management." When I was teaching SharePoint as part of the Spring 2003 Go To Market hands-on labs, the emphasis was on collaboration (much like the language on the Microsoft site) and not on document management. But, just because Microsoft publicly deemphasizes document management doesn't prevent me, as a third-party author, from doing just the opposite. The one thing getting me and my small business customers JAZZED on WSS is, in fact, the document management capabilities.

Why? you ask.. In Fall 2003, as I showed off the SBS 2003 Release Candidate to clients, they thought having an intranet page was cute, such as in announcing the annual company picnic. But they were sold on SBS 2003 when they saw the document management capability with their very own eyes! Finally, these small business owners believed they could bring order to the abyss of document management in their little fiefdoms. WSS presented an opportunity to extract themselves from the quagmire of mismanaged information. In short, my client, Mr. Wallace, could finally organize all of the existing real estate leases in his realty company. He's been wanting to do that for years!

Business Purpose

WSS is an MBA's dream come true. It represents, better than any other component in SBS 2003, the marriage of bits and bucks. It's the intersection of income and interface, accounting and ActiveX. You get the picture. But, just in case you didn't: WSS IS WHERE YOU WILL ADD REAL BUSINESS VALUE ON THE SBS 2003 NETWORK.

> BEST PRACTICE: I'm not going to repeat 625 pages of business stuff from my *SMB Consulting Best Practices* book here. I'm just planting seeds that WSS has a technical and business dimension to it and you'll want to read that other book for more of the business discussion.
>
> You should also take in Microsoft's top 10 reasons to use Windows SharePoint Services at www.microsoft.com/windowsserver2003/techinfo/sharepoint/top10.mspx. I'll save some "timber" and not rewrite those reasons here, so you'll need to surf over to read 'em.

Acquiring WSS

The logical follow-up question to defining WSS is how to acquire it. There are four ways to acquire WSS:

- SBS 2003. Relax and take a deep breath. You already have WSS in SBS 2003.
- Windows SharePoint Services site. You can simply download WSS from www.microsoft.com/windowsserver2003/techinfo/sharepoint/wss.mspx (if for some reason this link changes, simply select Downloads from the WSS site at Microsoft).
- SharePoint Portal Server (SPS). Fact of the matter is WSS is buried on the SPS media.
- bCentral. Using an application service provider (ASP) model, you can use WSS via the Web at bCentral (www.bcentral.com).

Installing Windows SharePoint Services

Take a bow. By this point, following the SPRINGERS methodology, you've already installed WSS. It was all part of the SBS 2003 setup process. But there are a few interesting things to share with you.

During the SBS setup phase, there are two areas in which you make decisions that affect WSS. Revisit Figure 3-20 at this time and observe the second line entry under Component Name column.

> BEST PRACTICE: First things first. The WSS problem is solved and the fix is in. I'm talking about the infamous late November 2003 WSS hiccup in SBS 2003 (details on the five o'clock news and in the paragraph below). What occurred was a critical WSS-related component, a dynamic link library (DLL), failed if the installation occurred after November 24, 2003 (WSS failed to correctly install as a result).
>
> So your solution can be simply stated: implement the fix as per Kbase article 832880 (see at Microsoft TechNet at

www.microsoft.com/technet and search on the article number). If you're reading this book and have acquired SBS 2003 after February 1, 2004, the fix has likely been imbedded on Disc 3. If you ordered the SBS 2003 product previous to February 1, 2004, you'd be advised to order the updated Disc 3 at https://microsoft.order-4.com/sbsrtmcd. More information on the WSS matter and fix at Microsoft's SBS site: www.microsoft.com/sbs.

Also - the fix is "in" on the Windows Automatic Update site as of mid-December 2003, so when you correctly update your system on a regular basis, this fix will be incorporated. NOW WOULD BE A GREAT TIME TO RUN THE AUTOMATIC UPDATE PROCESS WE DISCUSSED IN CHAPTER FOUR!

Hmmm. I guess an original dynamic link library (DLL) that WSS relied on didn't want to work past the end of Ramadan or had some problem with the pending Thanksgiving holiday in the US or who knows what? Anyway, please read the above referenced article if you have this problem in order to cure it.

So back to Figure 3-20 and the Component Name column, the entry, titled Intranet, relates to the installation and configuration of WSS. Revisit Figure 3-21 from the SBS setup chapter to see how you could redirect the location of the Microsoft Data Engine (MSDE).

BEST PRACTICE: What is really occurring is you are installing the SQL Server 2000 Desktop Engine (Windows), which is technically known as WMSDE. WMSDE does not have the 2GB data storage limitation or the five user logon limit of MSDE.

Clearly another WSS setup issue relates to some stuff in Chapter 4. Go back and look at Figure 4-10. That effectively configured WSS to be accessible from the Remote Web Workplace portal (which I discuss Chapter 8) across the Internet. Then there is the issue about setting the default home page for Internet Explorer

(IE) browser to the WSS intranet page. On the server, revisit the discussion surrounding Figures 4-17 and 4-18 to learn how to set the browser default home page (basically prior to running the EICW you won't see the WSS Home page). On a client computer, the default home page is set in (IE) when you run the Setup Computer Wizard (SCW). You typically encounter the SCW when you add a user (via the Add User Wizard) because the SCW is chained to the end of the add-user process. Specifically, in the SCW, there is an advanced screen found by clicking the Advanced button in Figure 4-24 that results in the Advanced Client Computer Settings dialog box seen in Figure 7-2. It is here you can see where the first entry, titled Internet Explorer Settings, will set the default home page to CompanyWeb (which is the default WSS portal in SBS 2003).

Figure 7-2

*This is where the WSS intranet settings for http://CompanyWeb are constructed. Click **More Information** on this dialog box to learn more.*

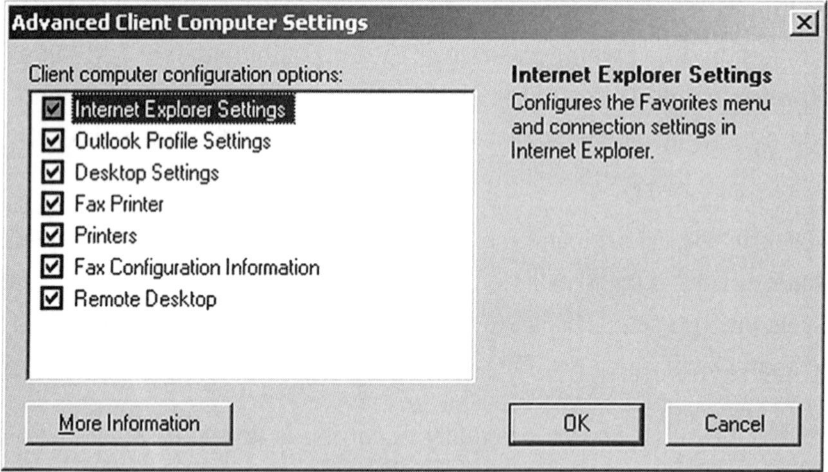

Document Management

Because I'm in charge here, we'll start with the document management definition followed by getting our hands dirty with WSS document management functionality (I'll get to the intranet stuff a little later). Specific to defining document management, here are common needs, concerns, and characteristics any organization will encounter:

- **Organizing the documents used in the business.** The methods used to establish storage locations can differ from one group to another within an organization, introducing unwanted complexity.
- **Finding documents in the business.** It can be very difficult to locate the documents you need.
- **Workers collaborating on documents.** Gathering and merging information from several coworkers into a single document can be a challenge.
- **Updating and tracking notifications.** It is difficult and very time-consuming to keep track of updates to content sources you are using.
- **Implementing approval processes.** It can be difficult to accommodate different approval scenarios and receive sign-off on documents in a timely manner.
- **Securing documents in the business.** It can be difficult to control access to documents and important content can be lost when documents are overwritten.
- **Accessing documents.** Accessing content from more than one local source can be difficult, making large amounts of information unavailable.
- **Providing scalability and the ability to grow.** When companies and knowledge bases are growing rapidly, it can be difficult to keep servers responding quickly and to ensure enough disk space exists for documents.

BEST PRACTICE: That last point on storage requirements is an important one. You should look at the excellent SMB storage guidance as part of a series of Microsoft Partner IT Solutions Guides for SMB. Read Mary Jo Foley's take on it at www.microsoft-watch.com/article2/0,4248,1399877,00.asp and the posting at the Microsoft Partner site at http://members.microsoft.com/partner/

solutions/additional/ITinfrastructure.aspx. I discuss this great resource more at the end of Chapter 11.

Now it is time to march forth, using the SPRINGERS methodology, to learn the document management capabilities of WSS at the keystroke level. You will first create a document storage structure, upload a document, perform check-in and check-out of the document, apply some settings to the document management function, and so on. Let's get going.

Document Storage Structure

As promised, you'll first create the document storage structure.

1. Log on as **NormH** on **PRESIDENT** with the password **Purple3300**.
2. Launch Internet Explorer from **Start**, **Internet**. The Springer Spaniels Limited Home page will appear (which is the WSS default portal).
3. Select **Documents** and **Lists**.
4. Click on the **Create** button and the Create Page will be displayed.
5. Select **Document Library**.
6. The New Document Library page will appear. Type **Clients** in the **Name** field. In the **Description** field, type **This is a data storage area for clients of Springer Spaniels Limited**. Verify your screen looks similar to Figure 7-3.
7. Make sure the **Yes** radio button is selected beneath **Display this document library on the Quick Launch bar** in the **Navigation** field.
8. In **Document Versions**, please CAREFULLY read the description text and then select **Yes** beneath **Create a version each time you edit a file in this document library**. Go ahead and accept the default settings under Document Templates.
9. Click on **Create** to create the document library. The document library has been created.
10. Click on the **Home** button on the right-side of the WSS tool bar.

Notes:

Figure 7-3
Creating the document library for SPRINGERS.

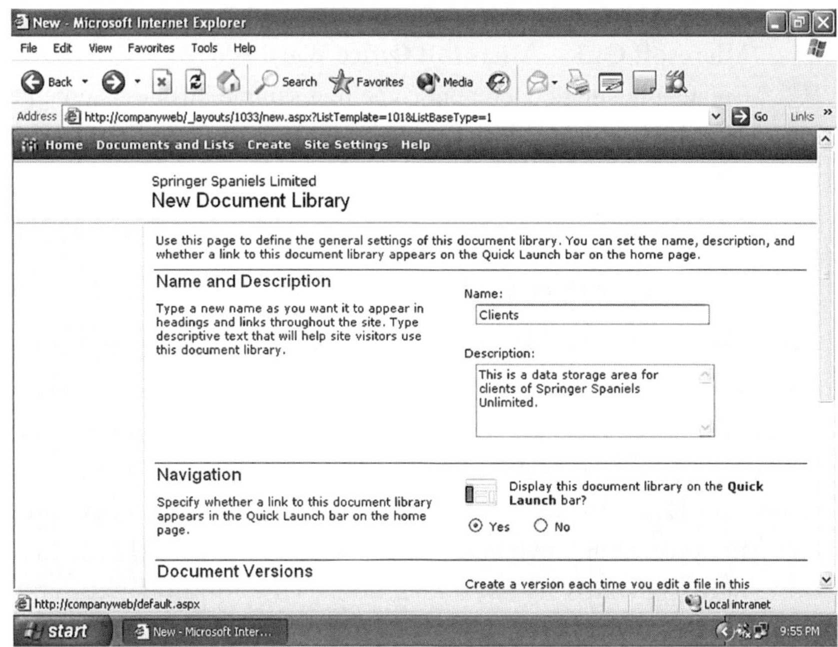

Next, you'll create the folder structure for some SPRINGERS customers. I assume you are still on the PRESIDENT computer and at the WSS Home page.

1. Select **Documents and Lists**.
2. Select **Clients** under **Documents and Lists**.
3. Select **New Folder**. Name the folder: **Walters Kennels**. Click **Save and Close**. Repeat this step to create another folder for **Jones Family**.
4. Minimize Internet Explorer (keep it open) but stay on the Clients page (where you should be at this point).

Create and Upload a Business Document

You will now create a business document on the PRESIDENT machine that you'll then upload into the WSS document management system. Note that I assume you have installed Microsoft Office 2003 on this workstation (as per the discussion in a prior chapter in the context of Business Contact Manager). If such isn't the case, you should install Office 2003 now before proceeding. You need Office XP or

Office 2003 to exploit all WSS functionality. You could sorta follow this example using WordPad to create the document, but it won't be the same.

1. Still logged on as NormH on PRESIDENT, click **Start**, **All Programs**, **Microsoft Office**, **Microsoft Office Word 2003**.
2. Create a business document (type in a sample business agreement, etc.). Then save the file to the My Documents folder as **Breeder1.doc**. **Close Microsoft Office Word 2003**.
3. Maximize **Internet Explorer** and click on the **Jones Family** folder visible on the **Clients** page.
4. Click **Upload Document**.

BEST PRACTICE: There is an even cooler way to upload the document that I'd encourage at this juncture. While in Word 2003, select File, Save As. Then select My Network Places on the lower left. Observe the SharePoint folders that have been published (General Documents on companyweb, Jones Family on companyweb). Drill down into the Jones Family folder and save the document (perhaps as Breeder2.doc). This method exploits SharePoint's deeper integration with Office 2003 and more nifty features are enabled. This would be the preferred way to add a document.

5. Click **Browse**, select **Breeder1.doc**, and click **Open**. Then click **Save and Close**. Your screen should look similar to Figure 7-4.

BEST PRACTICE: So you want to upload multiple documents at once, not one at a time as this example would suggest. It's easy! Notice below in Figure 7-4 that there is a select on the far left column titled Explorer View. Simply click that and you'll see the document corpus presented in a traditional Windows Explorer-like view. You can now drag and drop multiple documents from another Windows Explorer session into this window to upload multiple documents at once. Cool!

So time for something even cooler. Use the Import Files Wizard (select from Server Management, Standard Management, Internal

Web Site, Import Files) to not only import in bulk but also import deep file structures. Pretend you had a folder named Ralston that had many sub folders beneath it (project, accounts, training, etc.). Each sub folder has many documents. You would use the Import Files Wizard and point to Ralston (the parent folder) to import everything at once (all sub folders and files). This is very efficient and the ultimate preferred approach in a migration.

Figure 7-4
You've successfully created and uploaded the document in WSS at this point.

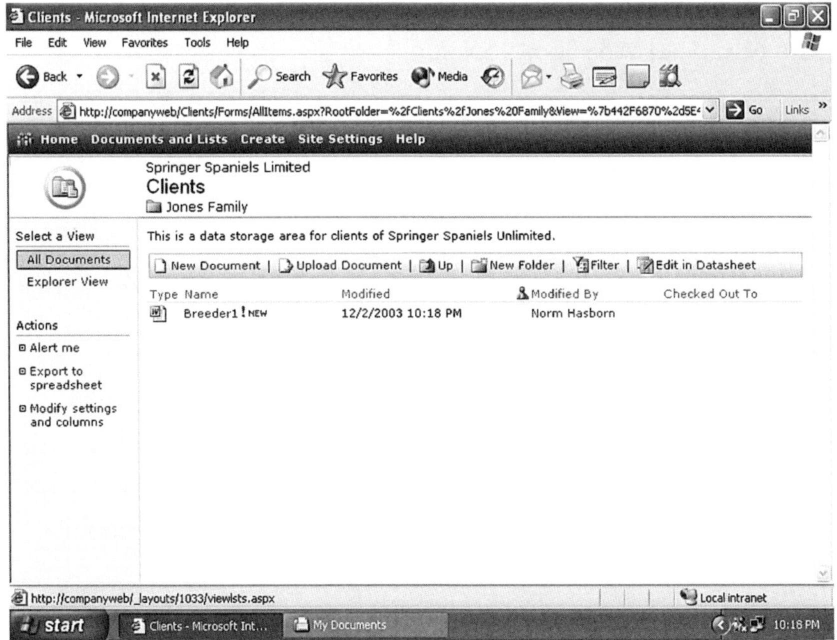

BEST PRACTICE: Taking a second to discuss the storage mechanism in WSS, you should know that the data files, such as Breeder1.doc, are being stored in a SQL Server-type database file. That effectively negates the coolness of Volume Shadow Copy Restore in Windows Server 2003 to individually recover a single file (such as Breeder1.doc). Rather, you'll have to access said file via WSS (where you could argue the cool versioning capability effectively acts like Volume Shadow Copy Restore for all practical purposes).

Speaking of recovering an individual document in WSS, you need to assume, too, that predecessor applications, such as Internet Information Server (IIS), are also running for WSS to function correctly. But don't let that discourage you from using WSS because, as you'll see in a moment, the versioning capabilities of WSS outweigh such minor concerns (in my humble opinion). And many document management systems on the market have similar dependencies, so this isn't just a WSS issue. I discuss WSS backup and restore later in the Advanced WSS Topics section.

Another take on the embedded object in the database matter worth discussing here. Students in the SBS 2003 hands-on labs have in the past asked, "Where is the document stored?" and "Let me use Windows Explorer to go find the document." The thing is that you can't go find the individual document using Windows Explorer after you've uploaded it into WSS. Case sorta closed.

The exception to the "law" I just laid out above is that you can use My Network Places to navigate to the Web folders (also known as a "network place") like Jones Family and retrieve your documents from a Windows Explorer-like interface. The enabling technology for this is Webdav.

You also need to consider the following storage fact. When you uploaded the document in the above procedure, it copied the document into the WSS database. It did not really move this file but rather kinda copied it. The risk is this: Users, accustomed to seeing the file at its original location (and still new to WSS), might inadvertently bypass WSS and open the original file. This would negate your good efforts to get everyone to use WSS. Ergo - once you upload the file into the WSS system (e.g., into the Jones Family), you need to move the original file (in the procedure above, it was in the My Documents folder) to another folder so those rascal users can't find it. You need to force them to use WSS!

Go ahead and delete Breeder1.doc from the My Documents folder before proceeding.

6. Now, carefully select the drop-down context menu for Breeder1.doc in the Jones Family folder. This is shown in Figure 7-5 (the reason for this screenshot is that many students had difficulty finding the drop-down context menu in the fall 2003 SBS 2003 hands-on labs that toured the US).

Figure 7-5
Viewing the drop-down context menu for the Breeder1.doc document.

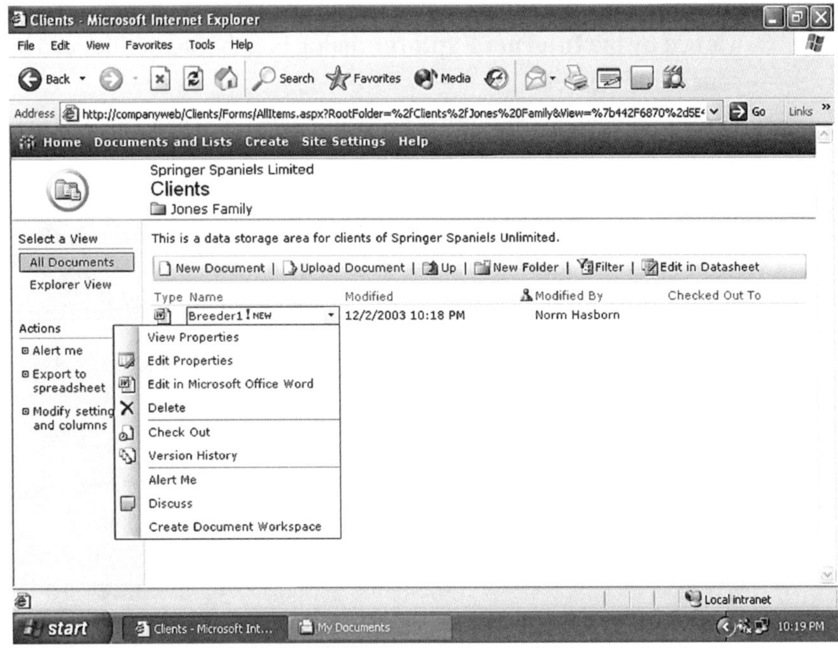

7. Select **Check Out** from the drop-down context menu shown above in Figure 7-5. The name **Norm Hasborn** now appears in the **Checked Out To** column.

BEST PRACTICE: You have now checked out the document, and any other user attempting to access the document will only have a read-only copy (they would know you have the edit version). This is the essence of the document management system in WSS: VERSION CONTROL, baby! It is akin to how programming code is managed using the library function in Microsoft Visual Source Safe (VSS) in the developer's world. Think long and hard about this BEST PRACTICE the next time you're in a quandary about which document is "most current" (like when you're writing an SBS book and managing chapter revisions - let me tell ya!).

8. Now select **Edit in Microsoft Office Word** from the drop-down menu seen in Figure 7-5 above to open the document. Note this edit menu option is only available with Office XP or higher. Click **OK** when warned by the **Internet Explorer** dialog box that some files can harm your computer, etc.
9. Modify the document with a few sentences such as that seen in Figure 7-6.

Figure 7-6

Note the WSS specific stuff in the right column of the Word document (this is the Shared Workspace area I discuss later in the WSS and Office 2003 section). This is a great example of how Office 2003 better exploits the full capabilities of WSS.

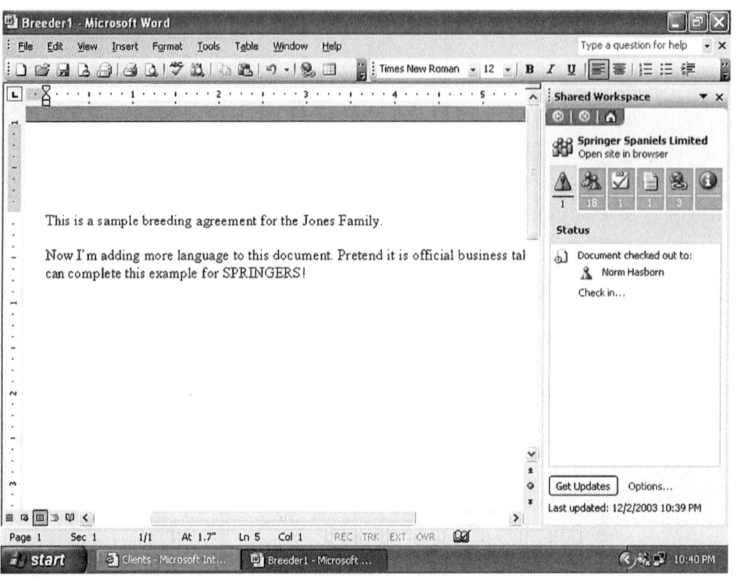

10. In the far right column, click **Check-in** under **Status for NormH**. Complete the **Check-in Comments** screen similar to Figure 7-7 and click **OK**.
11. Close the document in Microsoft Word.

Figure 7-7
The Office 2003 check process is much more elegant than using an older application where different steps would be required for checking in a document.

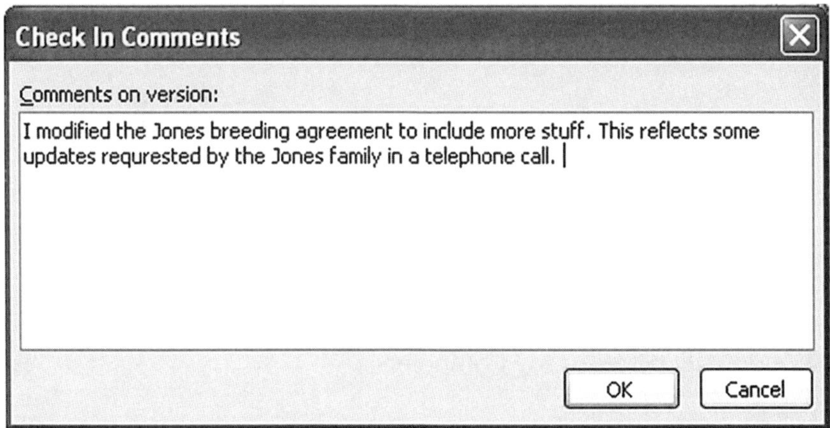

BEST PRACTICE: I know what you're likely thinking here. It's kinda weird that you could check in the document yet the document remained open and could be edited. I find it odd as well. Consider also that a document can be opened in WSS without being checked out. Sadly, I've confirmed with Microsoft in doing my book research that out of the SBS 2003 box, there is no way to enforce that a check-out must occur before a document is opened.

The above observations present two challenges. First, there will be a huge training opportunity for SBSers implementing WSS in an organization to get them to use it properly and consistently (that's aptly called a management consulting opportunity). Second, these observations are why I call WSS a basic document management package, something that Microsoft wouldn't dispute. It may well be that WSS will ultimately sell a lot of real document management systems like the SBS version of DocumentLocator from Columbia Soft (www.documentlocator.com).

Still want to talk through these limitations? Okay. Consider a discussion I had with a SharePoint expert in doing research for my book. On the one hand, you can argue that WSS can't be everything to all people. Two examples of a couple of limitations are:

- Access Control List (ACL) limitations. WSS doesn't use ACLs but rather uses permission controls at the document library level.
- Offline Access limitations. This is simple. There is no offline access in WSS.

But on the other hand, WSS has alerts that aren't present in the NTFS file system. And Microsoft found that in the SMB space, using the Web browser interface to manage files was more intuitive than Windows Explorer or My Computers.

The lesson learned is that there are always two stories to each side.

Notes:

12. Return to Internet Explorer where you should be in the Jones Family data storage area. Click on **Breeder1.doc** so that the drop-down menu appears. Select **Version History**. Your screen should look similar to Figure 7-8.

Figure 7-8
This is the screen that would allow you to roll back to a prior version of a document. This is VERY POWERFUL stuff!

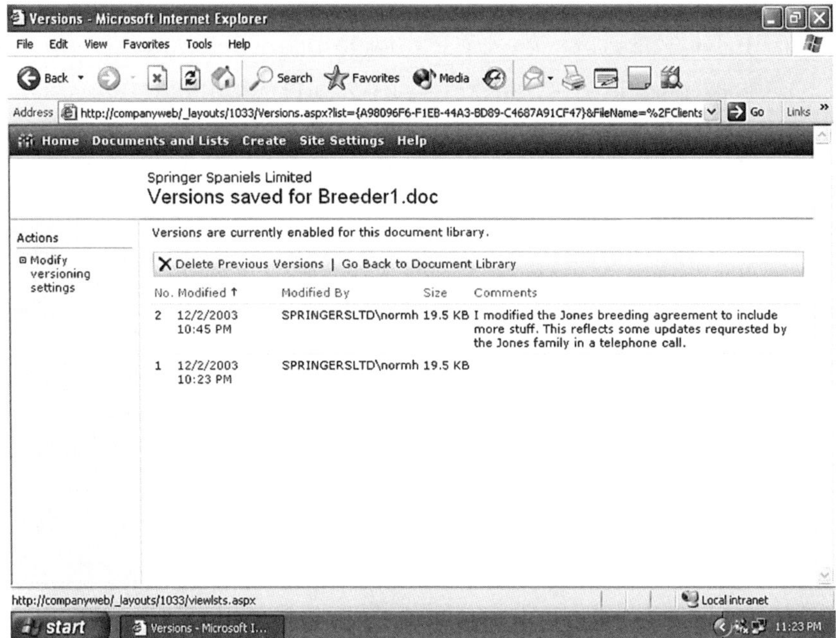

13. For more fun, click the **Modify versioning settings** on the left (under **Actions**) on the **Versions saved for Breeder1.doc** to page to learn about more settings. Select **Yes** under **Content Approval** so that a user with the Manage Lists right has to approve items submitted to this list. Click **OK**.

Notice that after you select the content approval setting above, there is a new option in the left column titled **Approve/reject items**.

BEST PRACTICE: So does Norm Hasborn have the Manage Lists permission? Let's find out by clicking **Site Settings** on the WSS tool bar. Then click **Manage Users** under **Administration**. Note on the list that appears, Norm Hasborn and Bob Easter are Administrators and the remaining users are simply Web Designers.

So how did those two users get to be members of the Administrator site group in WSS? It's simple. Back in Chapter 2 in the User List (just after Table 2-2), you'll recall that Norm and Bob were added with the Power User Template. That's what did it!

But I haven't answered the basic question. Prove that user NormH has the Manage Lists permission. Click on **Site Administration**, click **Go to Site Administration** under **Administration**. Click **Manage site groups** under **Users and Permissions**. Click on **Administrator under Manage Site Groups**. You will now see an Administrator membership list (with Norm and Bob on the list). Then click **Edit Site Permissions**. Notice that in Figure 7-9, they have the Manage Lists authority.

So, one more twist. Hit the **Cancel** button at the bottom of the page. Then select **Go Back to Manage Site Groups**. Then click on **Web Designer** (the site group everyone else belongs to) followed by a click on **Edit Site Group Permissions**. Notice that the Web Designer site group also has the authority to manage lists. So everyone you added from the user list in Chapter 2 (you actually added them in Chapter 4) could have the Content Approval permission!

Notes:

Figure 7-9
Administrators have the Manage Lists right.

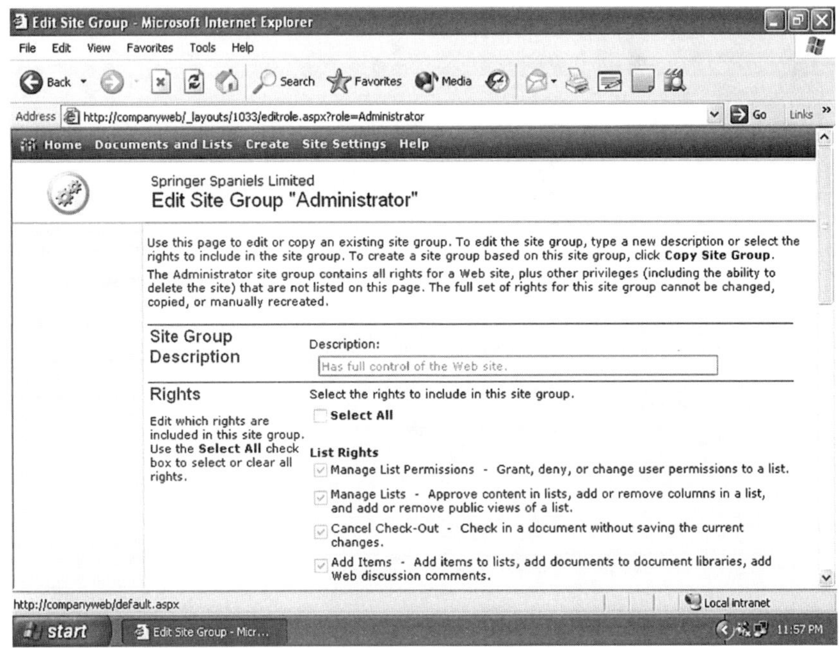

More Document Management

Had enough in the document management realm? No? Good. Let's do more. In this section, you'll explore alerts, adding a discussion item and creating a document workspace plus more! It all starts with a deftly placed click on the Breeder1.doc drop-down context menu (remember Figure 7-5) under Jones Family.

- **Alert Me.** Select this menu option. View the suggested settings on the **New Alert: Clients: Breeder1.doc** that appears (Figure 7-10). Click **OK** to implement this cool functionality.

Figure 7-10
Implementing alerts should be considered a powerful component of the basic document management capability of WSS.

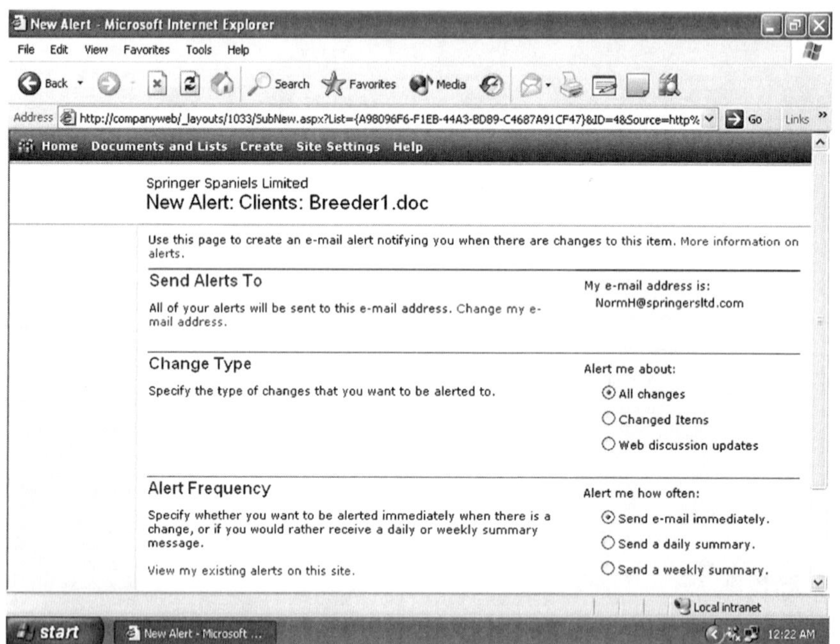

- **Discuss.** This is similar to the "yellow stickies" you might have used with Adobe Acrobat. It's actually based on the discussion object in Internet Explorer. Click on the **Discuss option** and then click **Open** on the **File Download** dialog box that appears. The document opens. Observe the Discussion tool bar that appears at the bottom. With the icons on this toolbar, you only have the option to have a discussion about a document (and not make the discussion part of the document). The ability to insert a discussion item into the actual document is disabled. Complete the **Discussion subject** and **Discussion text fields** and click **OK**. Your screen should look similar to Figure 7-11. Select the **Home** icon in Internet Explorer to return to the WSS home page for SPRINGERS.

Figure 7-11
Having a document discussion is another great way to use WSS for document management.

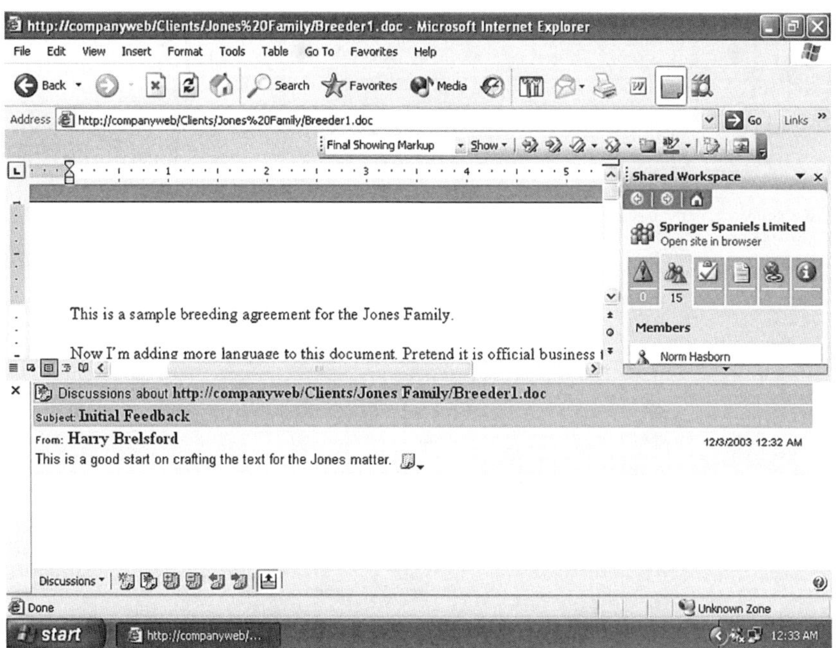

- **Create Document Workspace.** Navigate back to Jones Family and select **Create Document Workspace** from the drop-down context menu for Breeder1.doc. Click **OK** on the **Create Document Workspace** page. The result will appear similar to Figure 7-12. So why would you want a document workspace? The idea is that you're creating a new site where you can create a collaboration area separate from the main site (say for managing a project). You can also apply unique permissions to the Document Workspace.

Figure 7-12
Using the document workspace capability in WSS.

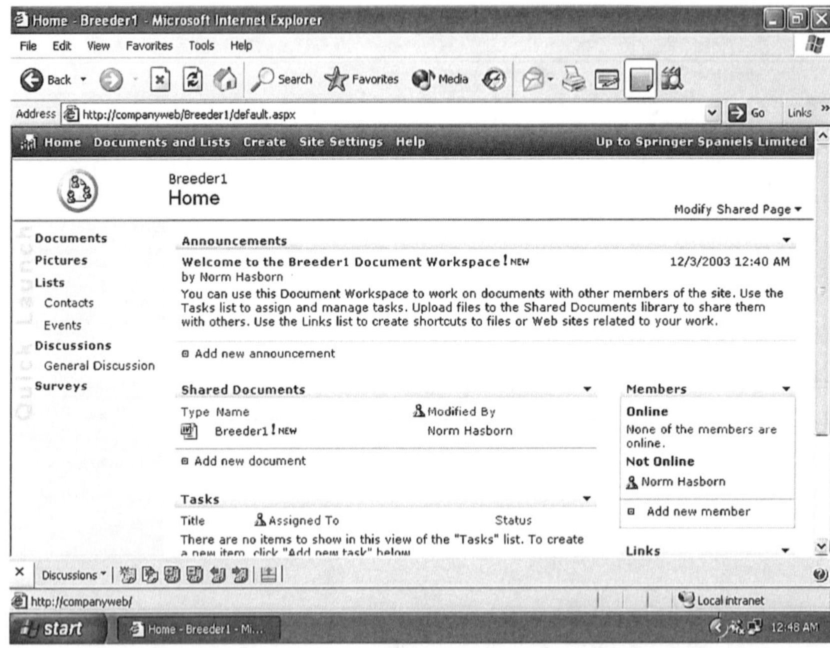

- **New Document Creation.** Click on **Up to Springer Spaniels Limited**. Return to the Jones Family folder and select **New Document**. Click **OK**. Type in some text and close the document. You will be promoted to save it and be presented with a **Save As** dialog box that will place the document in WSS, as seen in Figure 7-13. Click **Save** to save the document. This new document will appear in the same list as Breeder1.doc.

Figure 7-13
Creating a new document the WSS way!

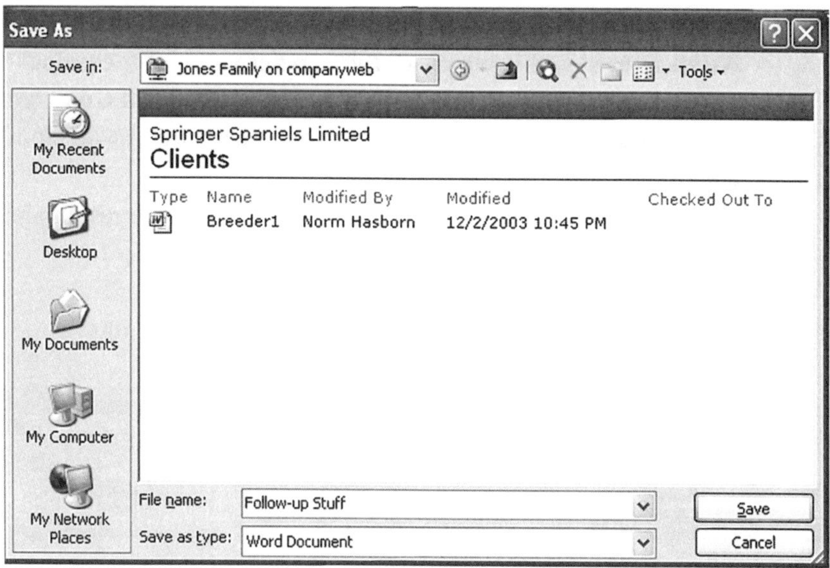

Intranet Collaboration

This section honors the roots of WSS: both its intranet and collaboration heritage. You will add an announcement to the SPRINGERS Home page, add a Web part, and create a "subweb" page to add financial data from Microsoft Excel. What I hope you'll draw out from this section is you'll see the Digital Dashboard roots of WSS. (If you worked with Digital Dashboard, you'll be right at home with WSS.)

Announcements

This is simple to accomplish. You will add an announcement to the Home page for SPRINGERS. Perform the following procedure.

1. If necessary, log on as NormH to **PRESIDENT** with the password **Purple3300**.
2. Launch Internet Explorer from **Start**, **Internet**. The Springer Spaniels Limited Home page appears.
3. Click on the **Add new announcement** link. The **Announcements: New Item** page appears.

4. Complete the following fields. In the Title field, type **AKC MVP Awards Announcement!** In the Body, type: **Great news from the AKC. Our beloved Curtis, Fredrick, and Ross were selected by the judges to be AKC MVP dogs and will join the AKC Hall of Fame. Needless to say, this increases the market value of these dogs significantly, which is what the MVP award is all about! Congratulations to our favorite dogs.** Go ahead and play around with the fonts and formatting.
5. Click **Save and Close** to return to the Home page. Your results should look similar to Figure 7-14.

Figure 7-14
The announcement is all positive for SPRINGERS and the AKC MVP awards.

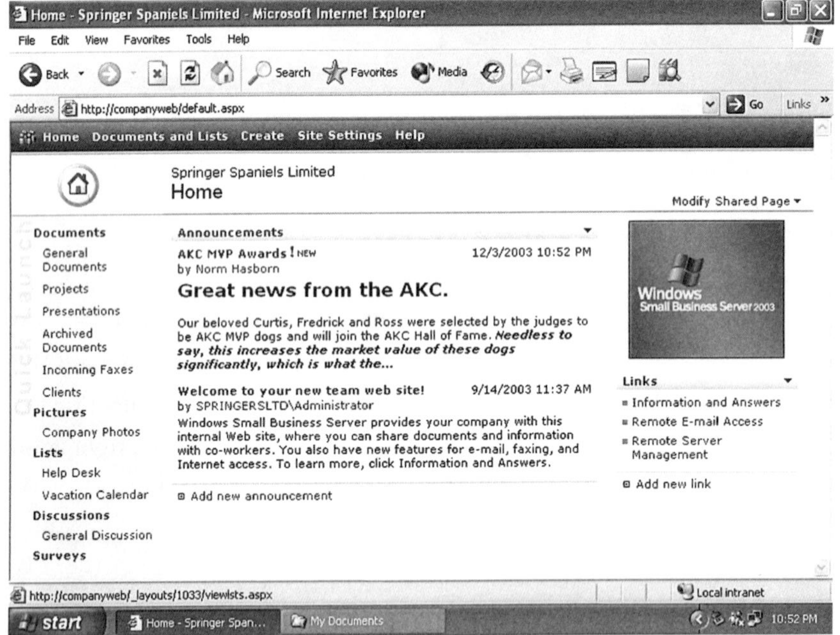

Subweb

You'll now create a subweb. This allows you to build up the WSS site structure into a rich intranet portal. Most commonly, you'll see a team on a project create a subweb to manage its communication, project-related documents, coordination and so on. It's a mini-Home page for a specific purpose if you will. You will create a Web Part Page here and then in the next section, add a Web Part.

1. The assumption is you are still logged on as NormH to PRESIDENT and Internet Explorer is displaying the Springer Spaniels Limited Home page.
2. Click **Create**.
3. Scroll down to the bottom to Web Pages and click **Web Part Page**.
4. On the New Web Part Page, type **SPRINGERS Cool Stuff** in the **Name** field. Accept the default layout and the location to save. Click **Create**. The result should look similar to Figure 7-15.
5. Click **Home**.

Figure 7-15
You have created a subweb page to house Web Parts for SPRINGERS.

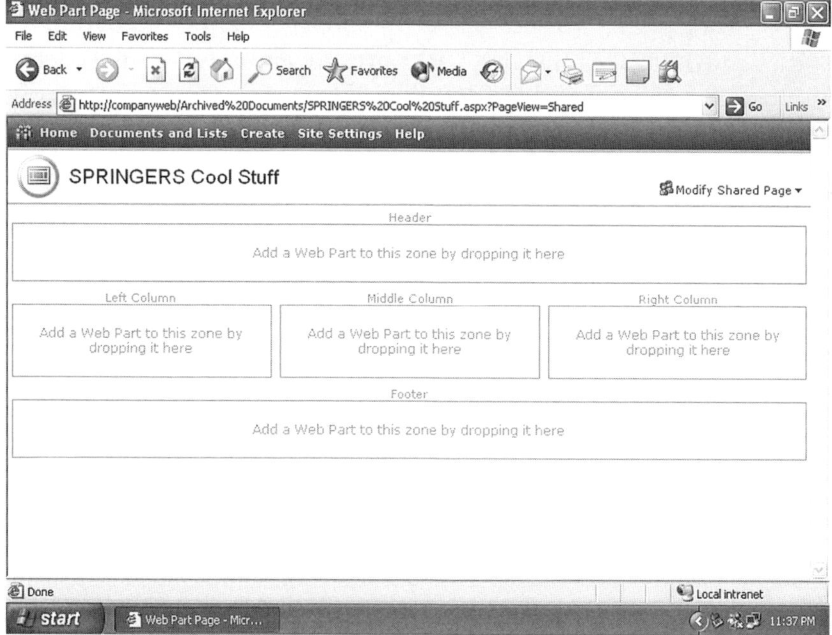

Links

You will now link the SPRINGERS Cool Stuff page to the Home page. And you'll link the Breeder1 workspace from earlier in the chapter as well.

1. The assumption is you are still logged on as NormH to PRESIDENT and Internet Explorer is displaying the Springer Spaniels Limited Home page.

2. Click **Documents and Links**.
3. Select **Archived Documents** under **Document Libraries**.
4. Select **SPRINGERS Cool Stuff** and then carefully highlight and copy (CTRL-C) the URL in the **Address** field. You'll need this exact address in a moment.
5. Click **Home** and then click **Add new link** under **Links** on the right side at mid-page.
6. Click in the URL field on the **Links: New Item** page and paste (CTRL-V). Complete the **Description** field: **SPRINGERS Cool Stuff**. Type text in the **Notes** field if you so desire.
7. Click **Save and Close**. Observe the new link.
8. You will now repeat the process to create a link for the Breeder1 workspace. This is easy to do by simply clicking **Add new link** and providing the following **URL: http://CompanyWeb/Breeder1**. Be sure to type a description for the link, such as Breeding Workspace. Your Springer Spaniels Limited Home page should look similar to Figure 7-16.
9. Test both links.

BEST PRACTICE: Note that the during the Fall 2003 SBS hands-on lab tour, many people confused the Links user interface element for the Links selection in the upper right (which is part of Internet Explorer, not WSS). Please don't make that mistake here.

Notes:

Figure 7-16
Linkage baby! Notice the link you created on the lower right side.

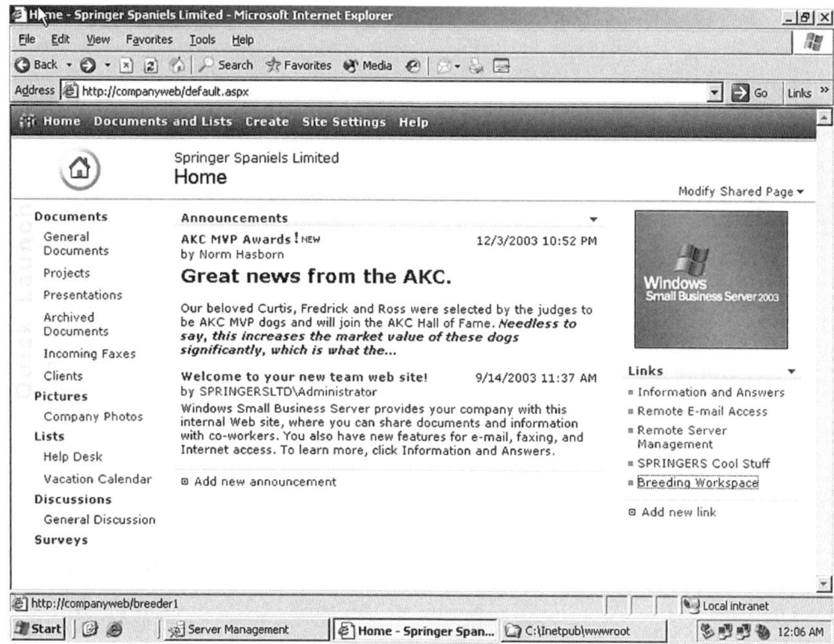

Web Parts

This is really cool. You'll add a Web part from Microsoft's Web part library to the Springer Spaniels Limited Home page in WSS.

1. Logon as **Administrator** on the **SPRINGERS1** machine with the password **Husky9999!** Launch Internet Explorer from **Start**, **Internet**. The Springer Spaniels Limited Home page should be displayed.
2. Also assuming your computer is connected to the Internet, launch another Internet Explorer session (**Start**, **Internet**), and browse to www.microsoft.com/sharepoint/downloads/components/default.asp (**SharePoint Products and Technologies Web Component Directory**). I selected **Top 5 Components** under **Component Downloads** on the right side. I then selected the **Web Part to view RSS Newsfeeds** (which can be accessed directly at www.microsoft.com/sharepoint/downloads/components/detail.asp?a=336). Click **Download Now** and **I Agree** on the license page (**Component Disclaimer**) that follows.

When the **File download** dialog box appears, save the file (RSSFeedReaderSetup.msi) to **My Documents** by selecting **Save**. You will import this Web part into your site in a moment. Click **Close**.

BEST PRACTICE: Have a pleasure moment and surf around the Microsoft Web Part Gallery. There is some cool stuff here that you'll likely want to add to your own WSS pages on your real-world SBS networks.

And why did I not take you to the built-in online gallery of Web parts in WSS (from Modify Shared Page, Add Web Parts, Browse)? Because on two SBS 2003 server machines that I built for this section of the book (according to exacting SPRINGERS standards), I found that the online gallery didn't completely install. Other SBS 2003 server machines I've worked with did not have this problem. There doesn't seem to be any rhyme or reason as to why the Web parts install on some machines and not others. Hmmmm. Further discussions with Microsoft resulted in their agreeing to look into this behavior but I have no update to share with you as of press time.

3. Double-click on the Web part - **RSSFeedReaderSetup.msi-** and install it by clicking **Next** several times, agreeing to the license and **Close**.
4. Click on the **Modify Shared Page** in the upper right of Springer Spaniels Limited Home and select **Add Web Part**, **Browse**.
5. Select the **Virtual Server Gallery** and select **RSS FeedReader** under **Web Part List**.
6. Click **Add** on the lower right. The Web part is added and a RSS FeedReader entry is made on the Home page at the top (you'll see the end result in a moment). Your result should look similar to Figure 7-17.
7. Click the **open the tool pane** link under **RSS FeedReader**. I'm going to have you add a technology news feed but you could certainly go out and find the RSS news feeds of your choosing (even dog breeding news!).
8. Launch another copy of Internet Explorer (**Start**, **Internet**) and visit W2KNews at www.w2knews.com. Copy its RSS feed links:

http://www.w2knews.com/rss/index.xml and **http://www.winxp-news.com/rss/index.xml** and paste into **RSS Feed URLs** text box on the right side in WSS. Click **OK**.

9. Enjoy the technology news that will now stream across your screen!

Figure 7-17

Welcome to the wonderful world of Web Parts in WSS. Congratulations on your first implementation. There are hundreds of cool Web Parts out there.

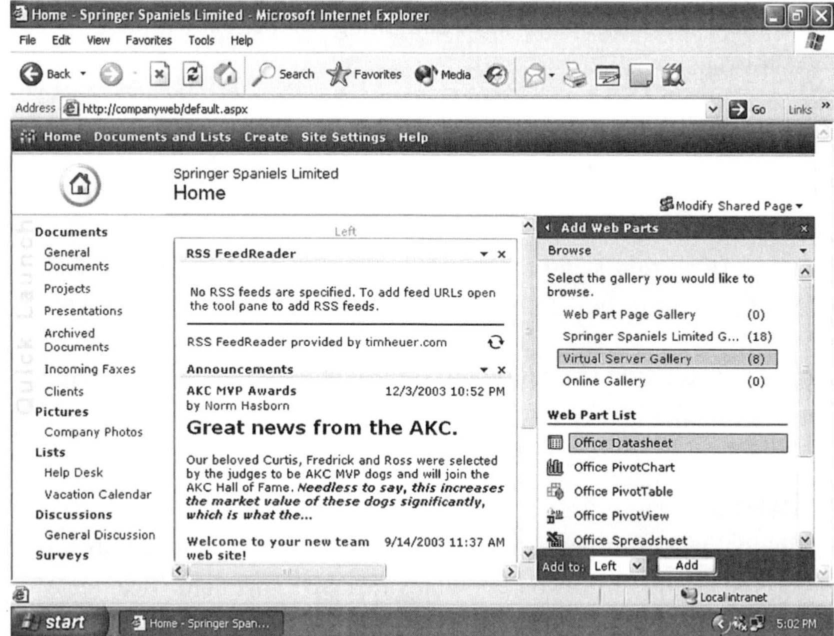

BEST PRACTICE: I've now given you enough ammunition to go forth and add real business value on the SBS network. My advice here would be to really learn about all the business-related Web Parts out there and create an Executive Information System (EIS). If you're not aware, an EIS is a business tool that was popular in the late 1980s for giving executives push button clicking to their financial information. EISes were typically based on the green light, yellow light, red light metaphor. In modern times, the Oracle Small Business Suite, based on NetLedger, is an example of this concept. But not to be outdone, you can create a kick-ass EIS in SBS with WSS. Go forth in the pursuit of profits!

Additional WSS Cool Stuff

Enough SPRINGERS step-by-step for a now. I want you to, in your free time, click around WSS and explore the following cool features (I will drill deeply into these areas in my advanced SBS book, so consider this a sneak peek!). You will want to use some or all of these cool things in the real world of SBSing to truly add value.

Documents

Granted, you've already worked a lot with documents in this chapter, but I highly recommend you delve deeper into the documents area to learn more. By clicking on **Documents and Lists**, you can see the types of documents that are suggested for storage in WSS. You will appreciate the descriptive text.

BEST PRACTICE: The incoming fax archive and its functionality to the fax service (more in Chapter 9) is unique to SBS 2003.

Pictures

This link defines itself but you might use this area as a photo archive. On the Fall 2003 SBS 2003 hands-on lab tour, super SBS instructor Beatrice Mulzer from Cocoa, Florida, turned out to be a major shutterbug. She snapped photos in each city and built up quite a collection. The business purpose was to document the events. This is exactly the business purpose I want to emphasize with respect to photo archives. Beatrice can be seen at work in Figure 7-18.

Notes:

Figure 7-18
Delivering the SBS 2003 hands-on lab in New York City!

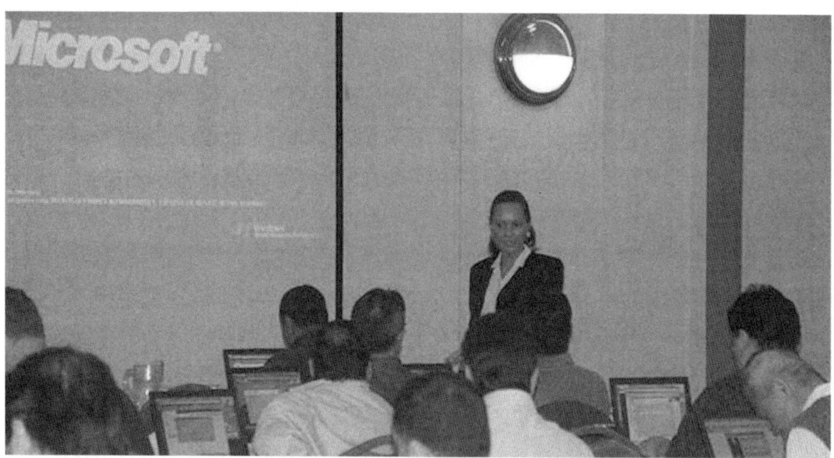

BEST PRACTICE: Another SBS client I have who is starting to greatly benefit from WSS is a real estate company with a HUGE photo library of commercial real estate properties. Keeping the photos organized was historically a major problem and one that WSS has solved in a single stroke of the proverbial pen. And we didn't have to deploy Adobe's new Photoshop Album 2.0.

Lists

Business people are slaves to lists! So the inclusion of built-in common lists, such as announcements, will sit well with the business folks using the SBS network. You can create your own lists to meet your specific needs, which is the beauty of the list paradigm in WSS.

BEST PRACTICE: That is a key point I don't want you to miss: creating custom lists. Whereas Microsoft masters on the SBS development team have made sound decisions about the common lists required in a business, they can't hope to know the unique requirements you face. Ergo, you can to add massive business value in WSS by creating lists that meet your specific needs. These could be needs that were never even anticipated by Microsoft (or even me!).

Pay particular attention to the Help Desk list. This is unique to SBS 2003 and is a really cool technology management feature. It is shown in Figure 7-19 with a user request that I've added (Elvis can't print...). Please create a similar request now. I'll relate this to the Administrator's view of Remote Web Workplace in the next chapter.

Figure 7-19
A user needs help!

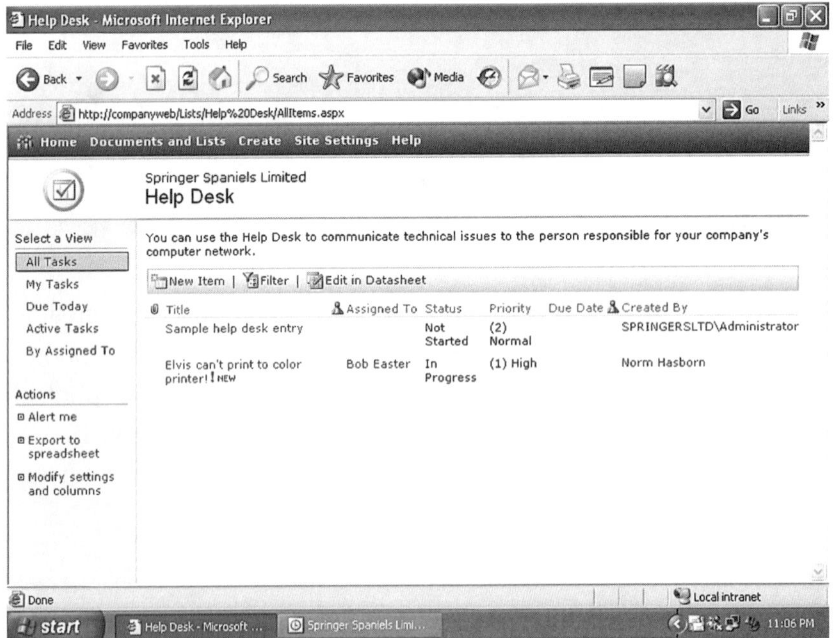

I highly recommend you also horse around with the Vacation Calendar (also unique to SBS 2003), as seen in Figure 7-20. This provides a centralized calendar for employees to make entries for out-of-office experiences, including vacation. My concern here is that you might be creating an "island of information" outside of Microsoft Exchange Server 2003 (Chapter 6). You do have the ability to link it back to Outlook by clicking Link to Outlook (you'll then reply **Yes** to a request to add a folder to Outlook 2003). By doing so a SharePoint Folders object is added to the Exchange Server 2003 organization and a calendar object titled Springer Spaniels Limited - Vacation Calendar is created (Figure 7-21).

BEST PRACTICE: So said vacation calendar concerns so noted, how about some perspective on why the SBS development team added this to WSS in SBS 2003. What the SBS development team members found with numerous customer site visits is that most small companies maintained a manual vacation calendar on the wall of the kitchen. The vacation calendar in WSS is intend to replace the manual calendar. It's not meant to compete with Public Folders.

While you and I are this topic of what was presented to you (vacation calendar), let me share with you what wasn't presented in SBS 2003. The SBS development team decided not to present WSS contacts and tasks (which you'd see in the full WSS on a non-SBS 2003 implementation) in order to prevent small business confusion. You should use the Springer Spaniels Limited Contacts in Public Folders for your contact sharing needs. Shared tasks could also be a Public Folder object.

Figure 7-20
NormH is getting away for a few days of skiing, according to the vacation calendar at SPRINGERS!

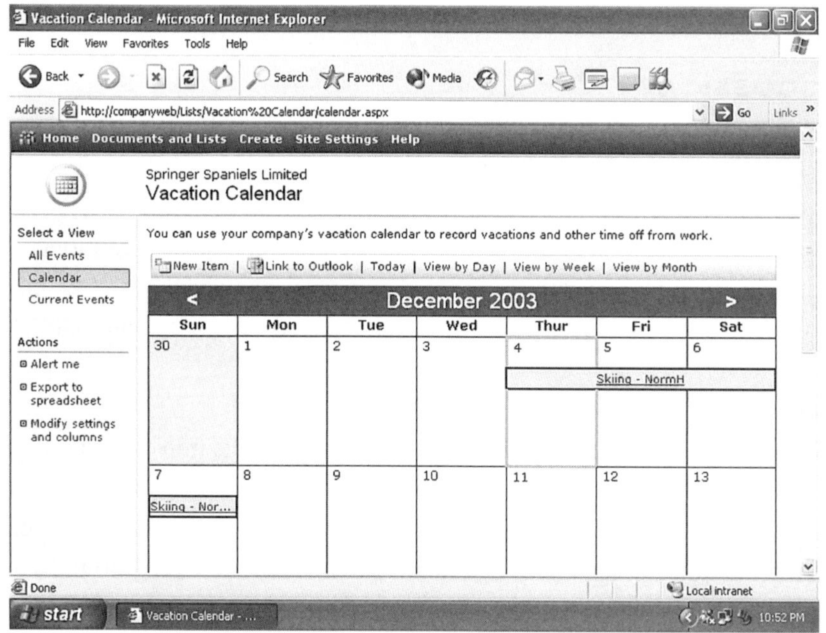

Figure 7-21
The ability to populate a calendar object in Exchange/Outlook assists in overcoming an "island of information" fear about using the vacation calendar in WSS.

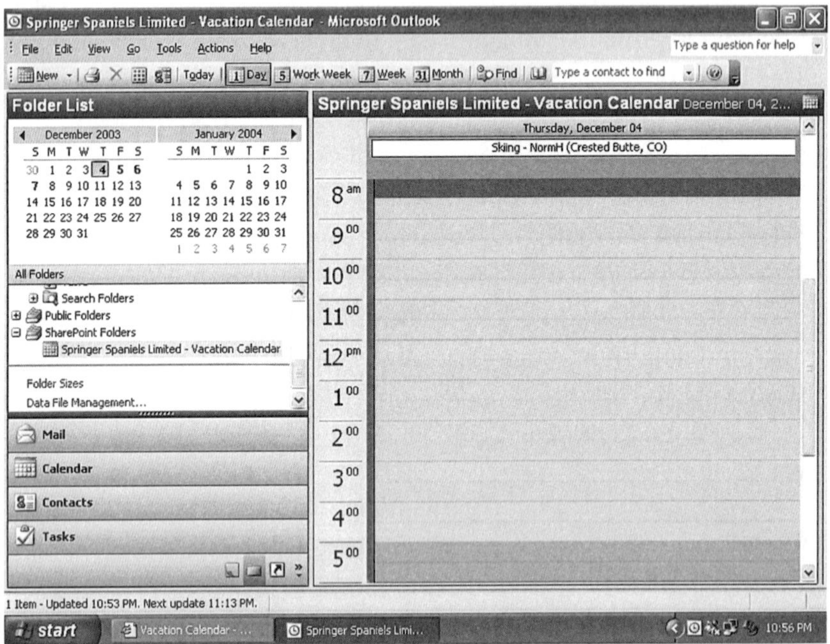

Discussions

The newsgroup meets SBS 2003! This is your chance to internally deploy a threaded newsgroup discussion in the organization running SBS 2003. This can be a more effective way to communicate business matters versus e-mails, because it's easier to preserve the discussion over time. That way, a new employee who "didn't get the e-mail" is able to follow the important business discussion. Just promise me that you will actively manage the newsgroup to minimize DRAMA!

Surveys

Why not? Why not create a survey to find out what folks think about business, technology, or event politics at the small business? There are entire management texts dedicated to business communication, facilitation, feedback, and sampling, so I'll just plant the seed here and make you aware that a very simple survey vehicle exists for your use. USE IT!

BEST PRACTICE: Much of the SBS-specific cool stuff in WSS I've highlighted so far is the result of the insight, wisdom, and fortitude of a Microsoft SBS program manager named "Dean" (we'll use AA rules here to protect his full identity). Dean "owned" WSS in the SBS 2003 time frame, and he had the vision to see both the business and technical dimensions to this tool kit. Please point your positive vibes towards Dean! And Dean, take a bow!

Advanced WSS Topics

I'm still planting WSS seeds for you to march forward with, and this section cultivates a garden of advanced SharePoint topics. These include meeting and greeting the options on the Modify Shared Page menu, learning how to use the management and statistics, server-side stuff and Office 2003 integration and using SQL Server with WSS.

Modify Shared Page

You've actually already peeked at this option in an earlier procedure, but this area warrants more discussion. Here I'll explain each of the options.

- **Add Web Parts.** You're quite familiar with this option because you added a Web Part earlier in the chapter.

- **Design this Page.** It's human nature and certainly the nature of SBSers to fiddle around. The SBS development team has provided a great start with the default Home page, but experience has shown that SBSers ask the following question early and often: "How can I modify the Home page?" Obviously, adding Web Parts (above) is one way. The other is to fiddle with the design via the option. Go ahead and play with it under the SPRINGERS methodology, as you can't do any real harm.

- **Modify Shared Web Parts.** This option is to modify existing Home page elements, including the announcements, site image, and link.

BEST PRACTICE: A popular modification right here amongst SBSers is to modify the site image. You can make the page better reflect the company's image by displaying the company logo instead of the Windows Small Business Server 2003 logo. See the default site image (Windows Small Business Server 2003) in the upper right corner of Figure 7-16.

- **Shared View.** This reveals the shared view that you are accustomed to at this point. A change made to the Home page is observed by everyone. This is the default view in SBS 2003.

- **Personal View.** There is some real power in WSS in creating personal views, where different users have a different WSS experience. Remember earlier when I spoke to the EIS creation process to report financial information. This is how you might do that, allowing executives to see sensitive financial information that isn't appropriate for the rest of the staff.

Management and Statistics

Another thing to learn all about is the Management and Statistics area. From the home page, this is easily accessed from clicking **Site Settings** followed by Go to **Site Administration** under **Administration**. You will now see the Top-level Site Administration page. The Management and Statistics section has a link that allows you to view site usage data, which provide the metrics that let SBSers know how effective their efforts are in delivering a compelling business portal. This is analogous to some Web monitor tools (e.g., hit counters) that are used in the world of e-commerce.

WSS Backup and Restore

There was a very interesting and timely discussion on the Yahoo! SBS newsgroup in mid-December 2003 that discussed backup options for WSS in SBS 2003. This is a dialog between two leading SBSers (note the following public discussion is unedited):

SBSer #1 thoughtfully comments with the initial posting:

```
Generally, if we restore an individual SharePoint file,
we need to have a file-based backup image of your
SharePoint documents. As I know, there are two ways to
```

perform file-based backup for your SharePoint database. For your convenience, I included the methods below:

Method 1. Use NTBackup.
=====================
According to our test, we can map the folders under \\companyweb
<file://%5C%5Ccompanyweb> as network drives now. Thus, we can use NTBackup to back up or restore the files in these folders (network drives) directly. To do so, please follow the steps below:

1. Map the \\Companyweb\Foldername <file://%5C%5CCompanyweb%5CFoldername> folder as a network drive
2. Run NTBackup and back up the network drive.
3. When you need to restore one file in this folder, simply run NTBackup to restore

Method 2. Use Stsadm.exe.
=====================
If you have enabled the recovery of SharePoint files, you can recover a
file or list item by restoring the entire site from a backup to a subsite of http://companyweb, selecting the file or list item that you want to restore, extracting it, and uploading it to its original location. To enable the recovery of individual SharePoint files, please use the following procedure:
1. Click Start, click Control Panel, click Scheduled Tasks, and then click Add Scheduled Task.
2. Click Next on the first page of the Scheduled Task Wizard.
3. Click Browse, go to %SystemDrive%\Program Files\Common Files\MicrosoftShared\Web server extensions\60\Bin, and then double-click Stsadm.exe.
4. Select how often you want this task to run, and then click Next.
5. Select the time you want to run the schedule, and then click Next.

6. Enter administrator credentials, and then click Next.
7. Select the Open advanced properties when I click finish check box, and then click Finish.
8. On the Task tab in the dialog box that appears, in the Run box, type "%SystemDrive%\Program files\Common files\Microsoft shared\Web server extensions\60\Bin\Stsadm.exe" -o backup -url http://Companyweb -filename target path -overwrite, where target path is where you save the backup of your internal Web site. Click OK. You must type the quotation marks.

If you have enabled this before, you can follow the steps below to restore the missing files:
1. Click Start, click Command Prompt, and then type "%SystemDrive%\Program files\Common files\Microsoft shared\Web server extensions\60\Bin\Stsadm.exe" -o createsiteinnewdb -url http://companyweb/sites/RestoredSite -ownerlogin DOMAIN\administrator -owneremail administrator@DOMAIN.local <mailto:administrator@DOMAIN.local> -databasename STS_RESTORE, where DOMAIN is your server domain and administrator@DOMAIN.local <mailto:administrator@DOMAIN.local> is your administrator¡¯s e-mail address. Include the quotation marks as part of the path. Press ENTER.

2. Type "%SystemDrive%\Program files\Common files\Microsoft shared\Web server extensions\60\Bin\Stsadm.exe" -o restore -url http://Companyweb/Sites/Restoredsite -filename target path -overwrite, where target path is the location where you chose to save your SharePoint backup. Include the quotation marks as part of the path. Press ENTER.
3. Open Internet Explorer, and in the address bar, type

http://Companyweb/Sites/Restoredsite. The site that appears is the same as your company Web site.
4. In the restored site, navigate to the missing file.
5. Right-click the file, select Save Target As, and then select a location to which to save the file.
6. Repeat steps 4 and 5 for all missing files.
7. Open your company Web site, navigate to the location where the missing files should be, and then on the SharePoint toolbar, click Upload Document.

NOTE: The second method is provided in the SBS Server help. You can find this by the following steps:
1. Open Server Management.
2. Click Standard Management->Backup.
3. Click Restore Sharepoint files in the right pane.
However, if you have not performed either method above to enable file-based backup, I am afraid that we may have to restore the entire database.

SBSer #2 thoughtfully replies:
Just realize that there are certain things to be aware of regarding method #1:
1) it is not a method supported by the SBS Dev Team
2) you need to have a separate network place on your server pointing to the each sharepoint document library, etc. you want to back up individual files from. Note that you cannot have a single network place just pointing to companyweb
3) NTBackup will not restore files back into the Sharepoint database. You will have to restore to an alternate location, then manually upload the file back into Sharepoint.

SBSer #1 reverts back and ends the thread:
Have to laugh though... that's a cut and paste from a Microsoft support
person posting.... but I have heard that #1 is not the preferred method. Thus my comment about using #2.

BEST PRACTICE: Be sure to catch the comment about the Restore SharePoint Files link under Backup (Server Management, Standard Management). Right now, please click over and read the Small Business Server Help and Information page (that appears upon click) on this topic.

Server-Side: SharePoint Central Administration

Much of what we have discussed so far has been on the client computer-side. You've interacted with WSS from Internet Explorer from NormH's PRESIDENT machine. But there is a server-side to WSS you should know about. In this section, you will observe the file types that are blocked from uploading and learn about the native antivirus protection. You will correctly use SharePoint Central Administration to do this (see my Best Practice in a moment about the best server-side tools to use).

1. Log on as **Administrator** to **SPRINGERS1** with the password **Husky9999!**.
2. Click **Start**, **Administrative Tools**, **SharePoint Central Administration**.
3. On the **Central Administration** page, select **Manage blocked file types under Security Configuration**.
4. Observe the default file extensions that are blocked. You can add or delete file extensions to this list. These are file types that can not be uploaded into WSS. Click **OK**.

BEST PRACTICE: Compare the list of blocked file extensions here compared to SMTP sink blocked file types discussed in Chapter 6 (see the attachment blocking discussion) and shown back in Figure 4-14 when the E-mail and Internet Connection Wizard (EICW) was completed.

5. On the **Central Administration** page, select **Configure antivirus settings** under **Security Configuration**.
6. Click the **Show me more information** link and read about the requirements for virus protection in WSS. You can then click the **About virus protection** link to learn even more. Close the help window.

7. Select the following antivirus settings: **Scan documents on upload**, **Scan documents on download**, **Attempt to clean infected documents**.
8. Click **OK**.
9. Close the **Central Administration** page.

BEST PRACTICE: In Chapter 11, you will be strongly encouraged to download and install a trial version of Trend Micro's PortalProtect for SharePoint, a WSS compliant application that will exploit the antivirus settings you just configured.

BEST PRACTICE: When I was teaching SharePoint technologies on the Spring 2003 GTM hands-on lab tour, a common challenge for students was to keep it all "straight" and remember where they were in WSS. You've already seen at least four ways to interact with WSS:

- Springer Spaniels Limited Home page when you launch Internet Explorer on a client computer
- Server Management console on the SBS 2003 server machine (see Internal Web Site under Standard Management)
- SharePoint Central Administration on the server. USE THIS ONE for administrative management of WSS.
- Microsoft SharePoint Administrator. BEWARE: this is FrontPage Server Extensions management, not truly WSS. **DO NOT USE THIS ONE**. This is a distant sister technology to WSS.

There is actually a fourth way to interact with WSS: Web folders. To see this, go to a client machine (e.g., PRESIDENT) and launch My Network Places from the Start button. Observe the Web folders related to CompanyWeb (the default WSS virtual server in SBS 2003). At this point, you should see General Documents and Jones Family.

SBS 2003 Integration with WSS

Those "dev dudes" on the SBS 2003 development team slipped in a few points of integration between SBS 2003 and WSS that need to be highlighted.

- Remote E-mail Access (under Links). This allows you to view your Exchange-based e-mail via Outlook Web Access (Chapters 6 and 8 discuss this area more).
- Remote Server Management (under Links). This spawns a Terminal Services session to manage the SBS 2003 server machine (Chapters 4, 8, and 11 discuss this functionality more).
- Add User Wizard/Add Template wizard. Adding users and templates automatically get WSS roles
- Client and Server home page setting
- EICW: publishing intranet takes care of publishing the intranet virtual server in IIS
- Import Files Wizard from Import Files link from the Internal Web Site.

Office 2003 Integration with WSS

Something I plan to emphasis during the SMB Nation Summit worldwide tour in 2004 (www.smbnation.com) is the integration of Office 2003 with SBS 2003. Nowhere is this integration more apparent than how Office 2003 ties into WSS. In this section, I'll discuss Shared Workspace, metadata promotion, and Meeting Workspaces and give examples of Access 2003 and FrontPage 2003 integration.

Note that I won't dwell on another integration feature, Document Workspace sites, because that's what we've basically been working with in this chapter. But for the record, Document Workspaces are clearly an Office 2003/WSS integration point.

Shared Workspace

You have already seen one such tie-in already. Revert back to Figure 7-11 and observe the Shared Workspace element on the right-side of the Word document.

This is one major way Office 2003 and WSS interact. A workspace is an area, hosted on a server (read SBS 2003), where colleagues can share documents, information, and hugs. The features of a shared workspace include document libraries, task lists, links lists, members list, and e-mail alerts. All shared workspace tasks can be performed in Office 2003 applications.

> BEST PRACTICE: The Shared Workspace task pane opens automatically when you open an Office 2003 document that is stored in a WSS document library. In addition to displaying Web site data in the Members, Tasks, Documents and Links tabs, the Shared Workspace pane provides information about the active document on the Status and Document Information tabs:
>
> The Status tab is pretty darn cool. It lists important information such as whether the document is up to date, in conflict with another member's copy, and whether it is checked out. The Document Information tab tells you stuff like modified date, etc.

Metadata promotion

Another Office 2003 integration point with WSS is metadata promotion. To understand the context of this discussion, consider the following. In a traditional document management solution, each document has a profile. The document profile consists of descriptive fields with information about the document (i.e., what the document is about). These fields are called metadata.

> BEST PRACTICE: You've likely worked with profiles and metadata at the document level for a long time and not necessarily even known it. How? Simply open any existing document from any Microsoft Office product (e.g., Word) and select File, Properties. The document property sheet that appears is a profile and the data in the fields (such as your name in the Author field) are metadata.

In a WSS document library, the columns of the document library (list columns) are the fields for the document profile. If you wish to add a field to the document profile for the library, you simply add a column to the WSS document library. The user-created columns of metadata fields automatically become populated fields in the file properties of the document. It's that easy! Whenever a user uploads a document to the library, she will be prompted to complete the metadata for the document. Note if you upload a document and make some off-line changes to the file properties of the document, said changes will be added as metadata in the document profile on the WSS document library.

> BEST PRACTICE: I'm really starting to cross a boundary here and move into a discussion on InfoPath, an Office 2003 family member. InfoPath is an editor that looks kinda like Word and is a backend application that manages forms. These forms are akin to the file properties for a document except these forms use the data via XML to create much more meaningful metadata (a property sheet in Word just sits there).
>
> For example, a company uses InfoPath and has a forms library with expense reports. The employee opens the new expense report form, enters data and saves it. This structured data is extracted by the accounting system.
>
> More on this with specific procedures in my advanced SBS 2003 book.

Meeting Workspaces

A Meeting Workspace is a Web site for centralizing all the information and materials for one or more meetings. Prior to the meeting, attendees use the workspace to publish an agenda, attendee list, and relevant documents. During or after the meeting, the workspace can be used to publish meeting results and track tasks. A user is typically invited to the meeting via an e-mail request and they click a link to join. You will recall from the SBS 2000 Best Practices book in the Exchange Server chapter when I turned you on to Exchange Conferencing Server that this type of invitation with a link capability was present in that conferencing environment.

There are five types of Meeting Workspace templates in WSS:

- **Blank Meeting Workspace**. Requires customization to meet your requirements

- **Basic Meeting Workspace.** Includes all the basics elements to plan, organize, and track your meeting. Predefined lists (and associated Web Parts) include: Objectives, Attendees, and Agenda.

- **Decision Meeting Workspace.** Similar to the Basics Meeting Workspace but also focuses on the ability to review document and record decisions during the meeting. Additional lists beyond the "basics" include Document Library, Tasks, and Decisions.

- **Social Meeting Workspace.** Oriented toward planning parties and social events. The lists include Attendees, Directions, Image/Logo, Things to Bring, Discussions, and Picture Library.

- **Multipage Meeting Workspace.** This is the same as the Basic Meeting Workspace but allows multiple pages.

You can create a Meeting Workspace either in WSS or via Outlook 2003. From WSS, simply click **Create** (from the top link bar) and select **Sites and Workgroups** beneath **Web Pages**. Then complete the information for the workspace site you want and click **Create** (when writing this I created a monthly meeting site for SPRINGERS and I encourage you to do the same). Then select a template on the **Template Selection** page (I selected the Decision Meeting Workspace). Click **OK**. And that's it, Your screen should look similar to Figure 7-22.

Notes:

Figure 7-22
Something not widely emphasized in other SBS 2003 learning avenues, like the hands-on labs, is the Meeting Workspace capability of WSS. Use it!

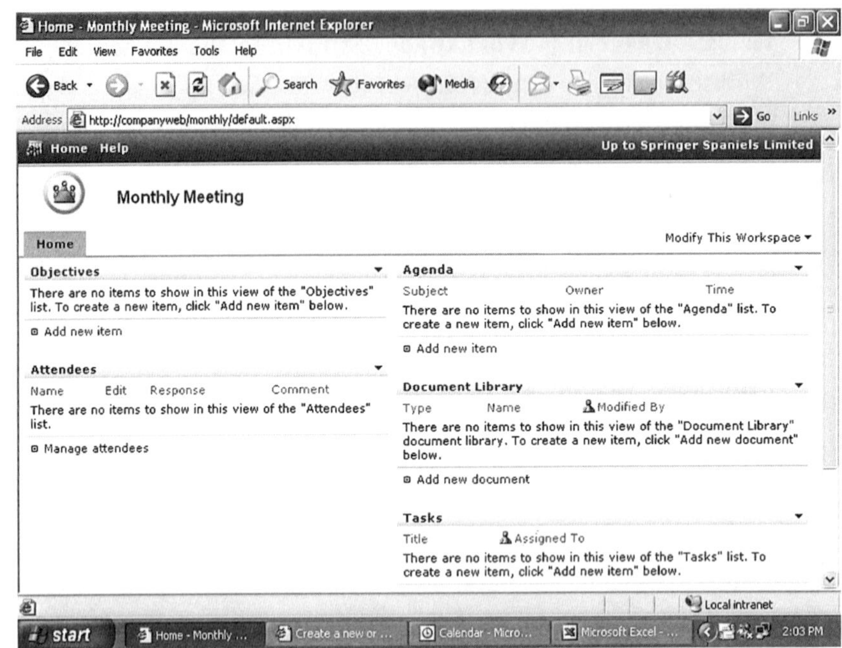

BEST PRACTICE: The online help in WSS has excellent support for Meeting Workspaces and I encourage you to delve deeper here.

Access 2003 Integration

First off, it's big assumption time. I'm assuming that you've run (not walked) and installed Office 2003 on your client computer to track with me (you heard me mention this in other chapters such as Chapter 6 in the Exchange and Outlook discussion). That said, let me explain how one of the killer applications, Access 2003, integrates with WSS.

There are five integration points between Access 2003 and WSS:

- **Export to WSS.** Here you simply specify a site during the Access 2003 export keystroke sequence and the fields are mapped automatically.
- **Import from WSS.** This is a wizard-driven import of Lists and Views of Lists from WSS.

- **Read/Write live link to WSS.** Think of this as revisiting Dynamic Data Exchange (DDE) and Object Linking and Embedding (OLE).

- **From WSS to Access 2003.** WSS exports stuff to Access 2003. Access 2003 then creates a linked table and reports.

- **Lookup field support.** Full support for the database lookup function in WSS.

Excel 2003 integration

Something that'll excite many readers is the simplicity with which you can send Excel 2003 data to a WSS list. You'll do that right here, right now.

1. Log on as **NormH** at **PRESIDENT** with the password **Purple3300**.
2. Start Microsoft Excel 2003 from **Start**, **All Programs**, **Microsoft Office**, **Microsoft Office Excel 2003**.
3. In Excel 2003, create a simple spreadsheet with financial information. As you'll see in a moment, I created a quick-and-dirty DuPont ratio model (if you don't know what that is, no worries - it's an MBA thang!).
4. Select **Data**, **List**, **Create List**. The data is converted to a list.
5. Select **Data**, **List**, **Publish List**. As seen in Figure 7-23, on the **Publish List to SharePoint Site - Step 1 of 2 pages**, complete the **Address** field to point to the Breeder1 site you created earlier (http://companyweb/breeder1) and then select the **Link to the new SharePoint list** checkbox. In the **Name** field, give a descriptive title such as **SPRINGERS DuPont Ratio Model** and under **Description** type something like **It's Norm's MBA in action!**

Notes:

Figure 7-23
You are creating the list to publish to WSS.

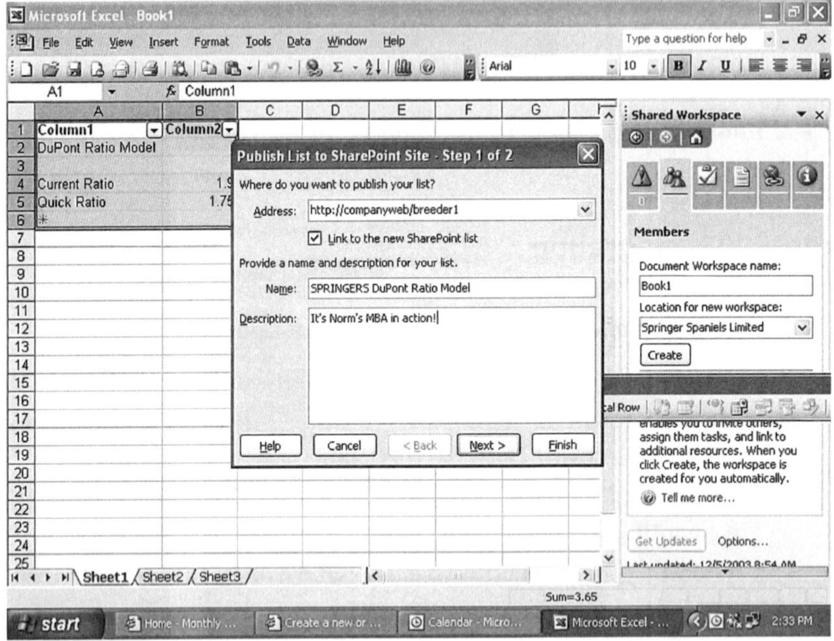

6. Click **Next**.
7. Confirm the column format on the next page (Step 2 of 2) and click **Finish**.
8. Click **OK** when the **Windows SharePoint Services** dialog box notifies you the list was successfully created.
9. Launch Internet Explorer from **Start**, **Internet**. The Springer Spaniels Limited Home page appears.
10. Click **Breeding Workspace** under **Links**. Click **Lists** in the left column. Select **SPRINGERS DuPont Ratio** model under **Create List**.
11. Observe the list in Figure 7-24. This is Excel 2003 data being presented in WSS and it's active. Go ahead and horse around here. Change values, insert a row, add data, and see how it affects the list in WSS and Excel 2003. Yee-haw!

Figure 7-24
This is a great way to integrate Office 2003 and WSS in SBS 2003. This example could be the basis for you to go forth and create an EIS (discussed in this chapter) on the SBS network.

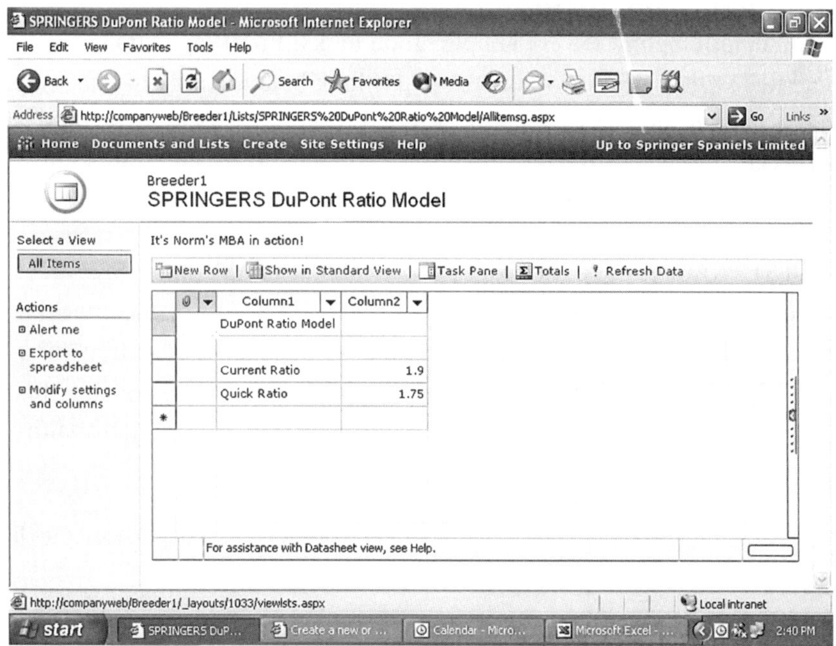

BEST PRACTICE: Another cool SBS 2003 WSS and Office 2003 integration point involves looking at a list in a data sheet and copying and pasting stuff from Excel. Here is what I mean. Create a data sheet in WSS and click the **List in Datasheet** option. Then open Excel 2003 and create a business spreadsheet populated with business data. Then right-click on your Start toolbar and select **Tile Windows Vertically**. At this point, the data list in WSS and the business spreadsheet in Exchange will be lined up. Then drag and drop the business data from Excel into the data list in WSS. This integration method, only possible with Office 2003 or higher, is another way to transfer data and is very efficient.

An individual I know who uses this approach likes it because it allows you to see the Excel-based business data line up correctly in the WSS data list. Seeing is believing.

FrontPage 2003 integration

This integration point is very simple: good looks! FrontPage 2003 can best be integrated with WSS is to make the pages look better. Kinda like the popular American television show Extreme Makeover meets WSS in SBS 2003! More conservative folk would say it allows you to create professional-looking, high-quality pages. Enough said.

BEST PRACTICE: To the extent practicable, PLEASE try to have all of your client machines upgrade to Office 2003. I propose that the integration of WSS with Office 2003 is the "killer application" or a sufficient reason to undergo this upgrade. Am I all wet on this proposition? Then voice your opinion to me at sbs@nethealth-mon.com!

Note my advanced SBS 2003 book will have much more discussion on Office 2003 and even SBS-specific integration with WSS! Stay tuned.

SharePoint and SQL Server 2000

And you thought I'd wait until the final section of the book to delve into SBS 2003 premium edition matters (fooled ya). There is a little bit of horse and cart going on here. I can't really wait until the SQL Server 2000 chapter to address WSS and SQL Server, so here goes.

The Big Advantage

There is a building consensus in the SBS community that WSS will sell a helluva lot of SBS 2003 premium edition. Why? Because SQL Server 2000 is contained with the SBS 2003 premium edition. And with SQL Server 2000, you can do more stuff with WSS. The big advantage of using SQL Server 2000 with WSS relates to the searching capabilities.

BEST PRATICE: In other words, and I stress, the searching capabilities ARE NOT available if WSS is deployed with WMSDE/MSDE (which is the configuration in SBS 2003 standard edition). WSS without the searching capability could be considered a half-baked Alaska without the flame!

There is little debate that the SBS premium edition is the better fit for organizations serious about WSS. Think about it. How enthusiastically would WSS be embraced if users hit a limitation on searching the document corpus? It would be a show stopper!

BEST PRACTICE: So you're now completely sold on the SBS 2003 premium edition. But what if you purchased the SBS standard edition first and are just now coming to appreciate the mystical powers of SQL Server 2000? How can you get from point A (standard edition) to point B (premium edition) without raiding the piggy bank and spending the lunch money? Simple. Use Microsoft's step-up vehicle that basically charges you the delta difference between the standard and premium prices (as of this writing that would be $900 USD). Full how-to-buy details at the Microsoft SBS site: www.microsoft.com/sbs.

As a journalist, I'm honor bound to share a few limitations of WSS. There is limited file type search support out of the box (assuming you are using SQL Server 2000 that provides searching capabilities). Search will only be natively performed against the following file types.

- .doc
- .xls
- .ppt
- .txt
- .htm

In a moment, I point you to some iFilters to extend WSS's document support.

Another limitation is that you can't search sub-site content from a top-level site. And only one language per database is supported. The language issue is especially important to SBSer as the majority of SBS sales are overseas (where mulitiple languages are often spoken in a single country).

SQL Server 2000 Configuration

To use SQL Server 2000 with WSS, you'll first need to install it using the installation guidance provided to you from the How to Install link (which launches a document titled "Completing Setup for Microsoft Windows Small Business Server Premium Technologies") on the SBS 2000 premium edition fifth Disc splash screen. (Chapter 13 of this book is also an ally of yours installing this database application.) You'll perform the actual installation by clicking the **Install Microsoft SQL Server 2000** and **Install SQL Server 2000 Service Pack 3a** on said fifth Disc splash screen.

If you have the SBS 2003 premium edition, you're welcome to install SQL Server 2000 at this time or wait until you've read this book and return to this page to implement WSS with SQL Server (remember to dog ear this page - get the SPRINGERS pun!?!?).

After SQL Server 2000 has been installed, you need to configure it for WSS. This is also documented, starting on page four, of the "Completing Setup for Microsoft Windows Small Business Server Premium Technologies" document. Specifically, you will complete the steps to:

- Upgrade the instance of MSDE used for Windows SharePoint Services (page 4). See Figure 7-25 for a key configuration page in this configuration process.

- Install SP3a to the SHAREPOINT instance of SQL Server (page 5). Be sure to catch the note at the bottom of page 5 for stopping the MSSQL$SHAREPOINT service when you upgrade the instance (you really have to do this). Don't forget to restart this service (and the MSSQLSERVER service) after you complete this configuration step.

- Review the SQL Server Collation Settings discussion (page 9).

Notes:

Figure 7-25
Selecting the Full-Text Search option is critical to invoking the advanced search capabilities in WSS when combined with SQL Server 2000. Please don't miss this step.

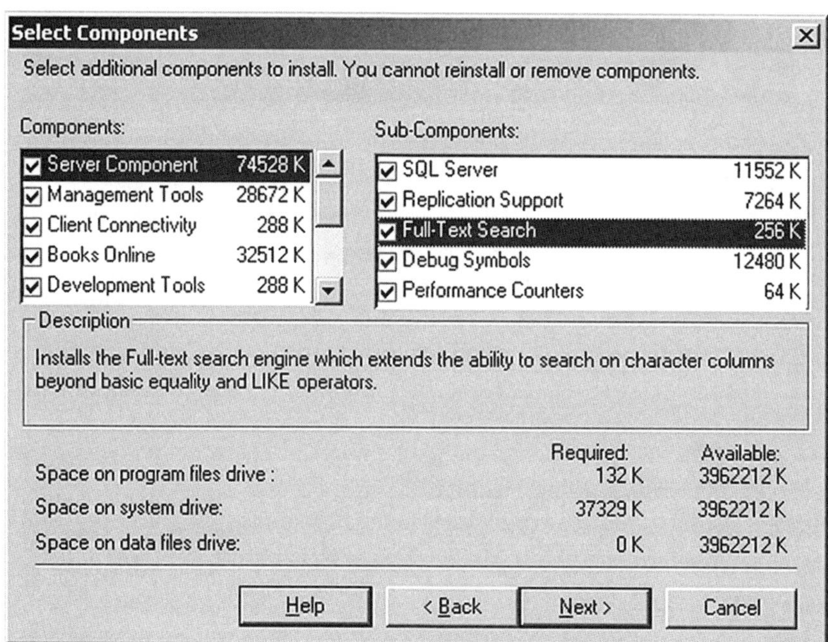

So how about a before-and-after view (like weight loss ads in general interest magazines). Before you installed SQL Server 2000, if you went to SharePoint Central Administration on the SPRINGERS1 server machine and tried to configure full-text searching, you received the message seen in Figure 7-26. But as you can see in Figure 7-27, after SQL Server 2000 was installed configured, SQL Server 2000 is now providing the default engine for WSS, Full search capabilities are now enabled. Right on!

Notes:

Figure 7-26
Before. Look at the message on the far right column.

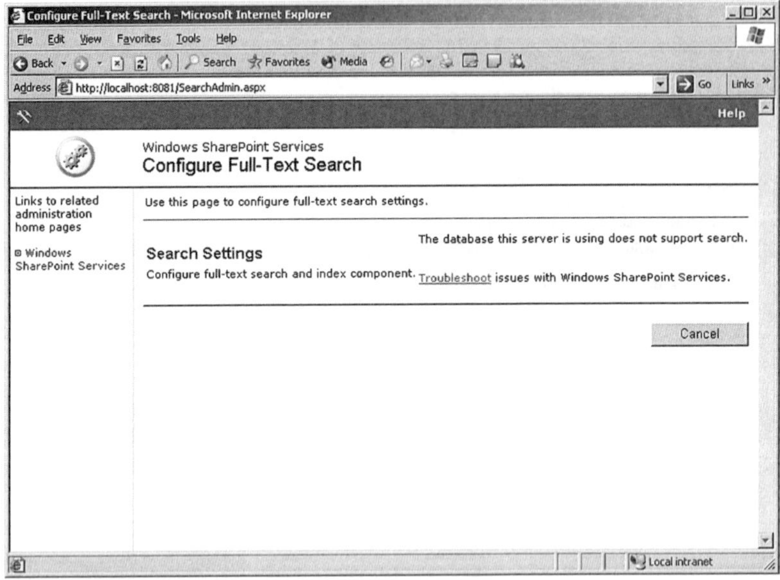

Figure 7-27
*After. It's SQL Server 2000-based search time, baby! When you click **OK** here, you will get a progress screen as the change is made.*

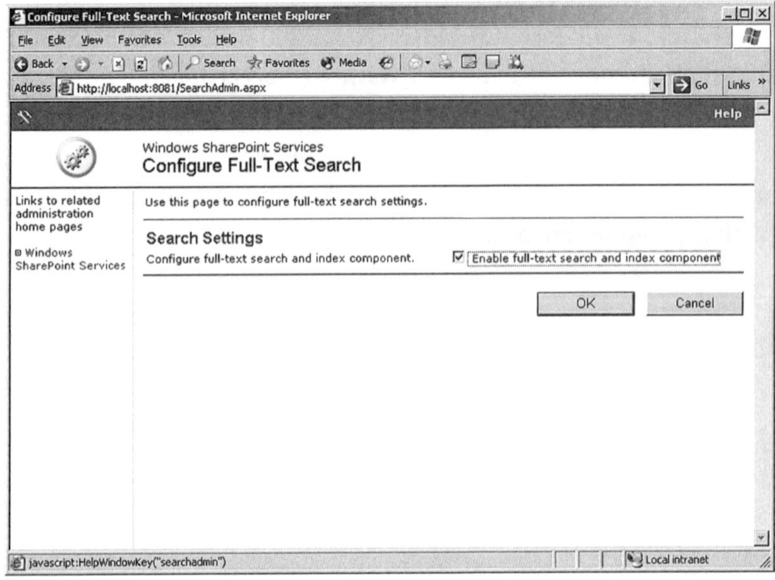

Advanced Searching Topics

So now that you're using the search capabilities of SQL Server 2000 with WSS, you might be interested in more factoids.

- **Mechanics.** WSS allows SBS users to search all Web site content on a virtual server basis. In SBS 2003, the WSS virtual server is titled "CompanyWeb." Subwebs inherit the search settings from parent sites.

- **Home page search field.** When you integrate SQL Server 2000 with WSS, a new search field appears on the Home page in the upper right. This search field is not present prior to integrating SQL Server 2000 with WSS.

- **IFilters.** Did you notice a few pages back that the document search capabilities were Microsoft-centric (e.g., a Word document with the .doc extension). What would you do if you needed to search a third-party document such as an Adobe Acrobat PDF file? You would go to www.sharepointknowledge.com (a resource I discuss in the next major section) and click the **IFilters** link on the left. You would then see the **IFilters and Protocols** page (Figure 7-28) where numerous IFilters for Abode, AutoCad, WordPerfect, and lots of other file formats are listed (even ZIP files).

Notes:

Figure 7-28
This is your "go to resource" for IFilters that allows different document types to be searched in WSS when SQL Server 2000 is installed and configured.

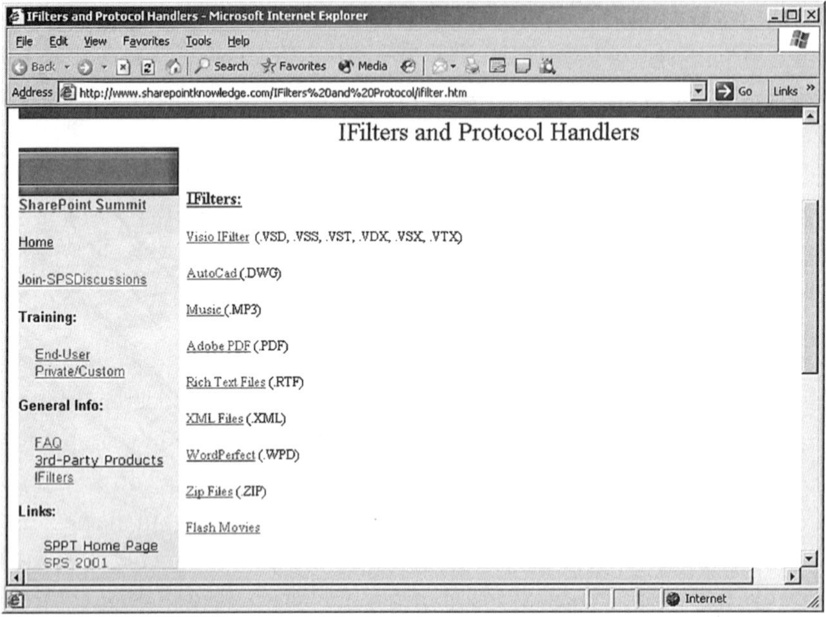

The Case for SharePoint Portal Server

Microsoft's SharePoint site is a great resource to compare WSS versus its big brother product, SharePoint Portal Server (SPS). There is an excellent white paper that allows you to decide when to deploy either of the SharePoint offerings. Visit www.microsoft.com/sharepoint/evaluationoverview.asp and download and read SharePointEvaluate.doc.

BEST PRACTICE: Time for a tad of plain Texas talk. WSS is going to be the best fit for SBSers in 99 percent of the cases. Why? Because SPS is really more oriented toward the enterprise with multiple sites, etc. SPS costs a lot of money ($5,619 USD) which is several times the cost of SBS 2003.

There was a time, in the spring of 2003, where it looked like the cool stuff (like searching and robust document management) was only going to be available with SPS. But Microsoft changed its mind and put much of the cool stuff, the stuff important to SBSers, down into the WSS product. Amen!

Current Topic: SharePoint versus Content Management Server

During the Spring 2003 GTM hands-on labs, students asked what some of the differences were between SharePoint and Content Management Server. Aside from pointing out feature and user interface differences, I replied that the difference was philosophical. SharePoint (WSS, SPS) can be viewed as an internal tool (although as you'll see in Chapter 8, it can be accessed externally with Remote Web Workplace) and Content Management Server is focused externally to rapidly post content to public sites.

In mid-October 2003, CRN published an article that discusses the Content Management Server team joining the SPS group. If you'd like to read it, visit http://crn.channelsupersearch.com/news/crn/45155.asp. Synergy between the two products is another key point in that article.

Resources

Here are some pointers to some additional SharePoint resources. This chapter, while capable for launching you into using WSS in SBS 2003, is only a start. You have much work ahead of you to master WSS!

Bill English books

Buy anything written by Bill English, a leading SharePoint consultant and author (he is also a SharePoint MVP). You can search on his name and the word "SharePoint" at Amazon to find his latest offerings. As of this writing, his current book, *The Administrator's Guide to SharePoint Portal Server 2001* (Addison-Wesley), is being updated.

By the way, a quick search on Amazon on the term "SharePoint" resulted in a shocking lack of books on this super cool application area (as of late 2003). I'm sure that'll be remedied within a few weeks as more books hit the stands.

And how could you forget that I'll provide more and more SharePoint secrets in the context of SBS 2003 in my forthcoming advanced SBS 2003 book. Keep monitoring www.smbnation.com for details.

SharePoint Web sites

Because I'm such a fan of Bill English books, you can't be too surprised that I'd recommend his excellent SharePoint Web site: www.sharepointknowledge.com. Microsoft's own site for SharePoint is excellent at www.microsoft.com/sharepoint. Searching on Google with the term "SharePoint" resulted in numerous hits including www.sharepointtips.com, www.sharepointcode.com, www.sharepointsample.com, and many other sites! Many of these sites are excellent resources (and the most current resources available).

SharePoint courses

During the depths of the technology recession in the early 21st century, some members of the SBS development team whispered in my ear that I should take the Microsoft Official Curriculum course for SharePoint. And given that it was August (read slow dog days of summer) and my billable hours were down, I went back to school to learn SharePoint. I was led to believe I'd be glad I did once SBS 2003 shipped. The advice was well-founded, because once SBS 2003 hit the streets, I felt I knew WSS reasonably well. You should heed the same advice and go take some courses on SharePoint. As of this writing, the SharePoint curriculum is being revised and you are encouraged to check the Microsoft training site at www.microsoft.com/traincert for the most current course listings. For the record, I took course 2095: Implementing Microsoft SharePoint Portal Server 2001, and I was very pleased (note this is the old SharePoint product).

Bill English delivers SharePoint courses and workshops. Check www.sharepointknowledge.com for his latest offerings. As of this writing, Bill is offering a summit (a four-day course typically in Orlando, Florida, or Anaheim, California, for $2,495) at www.sharepointsummit.com (Figure 7-29).

Notes:

Figure 7-29
Take in some sun in Orlando, Florida to attend the SharePoint Summit!

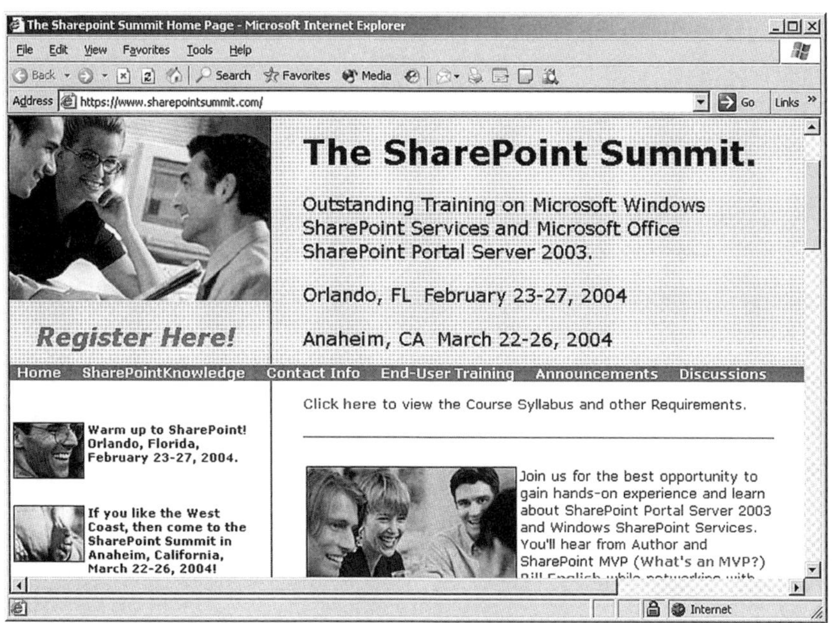

There is also a SharePoint Boot Camp offering in the US. Visit www.sharepointexperts.com for details.

Summary

This chapter had both a technical and business message focused on WSS. On the technical side, you worked with many primary elements of WSS including the document management and Intranet portal features. On the business side, you were exposed to some value-added thinking about how WSS can extend the SBS network and provide real solutions to real business problems, such as managing information inside a small business. WSS is one of the more important and popular features in SBS 2003, so you should use it to deliver your services as an SBSer to end users in the organization.

Chapter 8
Mobility and Remote Connectivity

Something that is huge in SBS 2003 is the emphasis on mobile computing or mobility. Such emphasis is well founded. Why? Because it's mobile computing that's almost single-handedly leading us out of the early 21st century "tech wreck" that followed the late 1990s boom in the dot-com and Y2K eras. Read for yourself in the article titled "PC Shipments Rise 15 Percent, Driven By Notebook Sales" (W. David Gardner, CRN, http://crn.channelsupersearch.com/news/tech/45278.asp) and "Study: Notebook Sales Surpass Desktops In Retail Market" (Edward F. Moltzen, CRN, http://crn.channelsupersearch.com/news/tech/43012.asp). I think you'll agree that the evidence is proof positive that the era of the mobile worker has arrived. And the SBS development team is spot-on for recognizing the application of this trend in the small business space and making mobility a huge part of SBS 2003. This chapter reflects that mobility paradigm as it's implemented in SBS 2003. A special emphasis is placed on Remote Web Workplace (RWW), which will start the chapter and move into exploring Outlook Web Access, Outlook Mobile Access, remote use of full Outlook, and VPN connectivity. Along the way, I'll weave in the Springer Spaniels Limited (SPRINGERS) methodology and toss a few best practices your way.

Mobility and SBS 2003 Sizzle

Starting in early July 2003, you, I, and everyone else were allowed to start playing with SBS 2003 (in its release candidate form). I built a few machines with SBS 2003 (including virtual machines running VMWare that I discuss in Appendix D) and started giving public speeches and demonstrations to clients. Something that sparked my audiences was the sizzle surrounding mobility. My prize client, a real estate company, approved the upgrade to SBS 2003 on the spot after seeing only a few screenshots of Remote Web Workplace. The company owner, having just opened a new office in Phoenix, Arizona, (the main office is in Bellevue, Washington), was impressed by the simplicity of RWW. Similar reactions have been observed when people first see the mobility components of SBS 2003. See let's move on and take a look.

What You Already Know About Remote Connectivity

Go easy on yourself, mate! You're completed just over 50 percent of this book and you probably are stronger in SBS 2003 than you're willing to admit. So take a bow and kindly accept my virtual honor bow directed your way. You've already been configuring the remote components in SBS 2003 as per the following list.

- Windows Configuration during SBS 2003 setup. Peek back to Figures 3-18 and 3-19 and recall the early part of the Microsoft Windows Small Business Server Setup wizard. It was here that critical networking components facilitating mobility in SBS 2003 were laid down. An example is the implementation of the Remote and Routing Access Service (RRAS) . Figure 3-20 in the setup chapter displays more mobility stuff that is occurring, including the installation of remote client connectivity components which will be used later.

BEST PRACTICE: By the way, now is as good of time to have a little chat about Texas terminology as any. While I refer throughout the book to the EICW, the folks at Microsoft in Redmond prefer to use the ten dollar acronym version and call it the CEICW for Configure E-mail and Internet Connection Wizard. That's just too much for me to pronounce, but we're talking about the same thing. To each her own!

- Remote Access Wizard. Revisit Figures 4-19 and 4-20 to see the short but sweet Remote Access Wizard in action. It was here you configured the server-side VPN settings. VPN connectivity is discussed a tad later in this chapter.

BEST PRACTICE: Remember that you can rerun the EICW and the Remote Access Wizard again and again. You're not locked into a "mistake" if, after reading this chapter and working with the mobility and remote access capabilities of SBS 2003, you decide you might try something different in the real world. One example of a change you might make is to re-rerun the Remote Access Wizard to allow direct dial-in access, because you have since added a modem to the SBS server machine (said modem wasn't present when you created the SBS server machine). This dial-in setting was revealed back on Figure 4-19.

- **Add User Wizard/Set Up Computer Wizard.** You should certainly know these wizards by now and readily recall that you had a few mobility and interaction points. First, some users you have created may have been set up with the way cool Mobile User Template (although in the SPRINGERS methodology, you set up simple users and power users - read the BEST PRACTICE below).

  Note when the user will add a user member of the RWW group (which includes all templates by default), you receive a welcome message that describes RWW. You also have the election to deploy the Connection Manager VPN package to clients during the client computer setup (Connection Manager is discussed in a different section later in the chapter).

- **Remote Assistance.** You may have already explored a tad and discovered client-side capabilities such as Windows XP Professional's Remote Assistance capability. This is the "cry for help" button that users can push to ping you and have you take over their desktop in a "PCAnywhere-like manner" to solve their problem. I discuss PCAnywhere later in the chapter.

Mind if a little advanced Remote Assistance (Windows XP Pro) discussion is interjected here? Remote Assistance uses Remote Desktop Protocol (RDP). Windows Messenger sets up the remote assistance session using the server-based session invite logic. Because of this, there is an issue with NAT addresses. So Remote Assistance includes additional logic to deal with the NAT scenario.

This logic simply tries to complete the TCP connection from both clients. This way, if one of the clients is behind a NAT, the connection can still be created and remote assistance occurs. If both clients are behind a NAT, the connection will not be established. You can read more on this issue with three TechNet KBase articles: Q301527, Q301528, Q301529.

BEST PRACTICE: Fear not if you've set up users via the simple User Template back in Chapter 4 and you want these users to take advantage of the cool mobility features at a later date. There is a way to elevate the privileges for these users. See the discussion in Chapter 11 about the Change User Permissions Wizard (you'll use this as part of the SPRINGERS methodology).

Remote Web Workplace

Not only does travel, which is "remote" by its very nature, allow you to learn firsthand the mobility solutions in SBS 2003, it affords the opportunity to meet SBSers worldwide who have different viewpoints to contribute. Across this book, such diverse insights have been interjected in a technical realm. Every day, SBSers worldwide are thinking of ways to work with SBS 2003 not imagined by the SBS development team in Redmond, Washington, or yours truly on Bainbridge Island. In this case, the insight is humorous, wherein some SBSer known only to the SBSers above, started pronouncing RWW as "arrr-wuuu-wuuu," an admittedly silly saying that seems to have found traction.

BEST PRACTICE: Rumor has it that, in Redmond, this area is called RUP (rhymes with pup, like puppy). If you call Microsoft Product Support Services (PSS), you could say RUP and arrr-wuuu-wuuu, but your coworkers who overhear the telephone call might look at you kinda funny.

BEST PRACTICE: Two initial thoughts on RWW are important to carry forward. First, when you access the external Web page that is exposed on the external interface of your SBS server machine, it is a Welcome Web site that greets you. This assume you opened Port

80 by selecting Business Web on the Web Services Configuration page in the EICW (not recommended). This is NOT RWW at this point. Rather, you select RWW from the Remote Web Workplace link from the Welcome Web site. Better yet, you can access RWW by addressing it via the FQDN/remote (discussed more later). Second, a point of confusion amongst SBS 2003 hands-on lab attendees in the Fall of 2003 was that RWW offers only the ability to take remote control of your desktop at work. That's only part of RWW. This will be revealed herein, but it's good to have this little chat first. Forward!

RWW Procedure: Daze and Amaze!

As you start this procedure, there is a big assumption you will introduce a remote computer into the SPRINGERS scenario (so far you've worked with the SPRINGERS1 server machine and the PRESIDENT client computer). A favorite way to describe the mobility area in SBS 2003 time frame is to say you're using a laptop over WIFI from a Starbucks coffee shop to access the office network!

What you need is a client computer that is not part of the SBS 2003 network and could be considered as being on the "outside" (not on the 192.168.16.x subnet). In Appendix D, you'll receive guidance for setting this up as a virtual network using either VMWare or Virtual PC from Microsoft. To facilitate this, I created a Windows XP Pro workstation in a workgroup called HASBORN (the machine name is NormLap). I assigned the static IP address of 207.202.238.225 with a Class C subnet to this external client computer. The naming isn't as important here as the concept of having an external client computer up and running in the SPRINGERS storyline.

1. Log on as **NormH** to the remote computer (in my case, **NormLap**) with the password **Purple3300** (in this case, Norm is a local user in the Windows XP Pro workgroup model). Also - please make sure the PRESIDENT workstation is powered on and running. And I guess the SBS 2003 server machine (SPRINGERS1) better be running too! That'll make this procedure infinitely easier to complete!

BEST PRACTICE: Later on, when you attempt to connect to PRESIDENT from NormLap, you'll appreciate the following. If PRESIDENT were not powered on and attached to the network in our case, you'd receive an error in the Remote Desktop connection process the reads: "Connectivity to the remote computer could not be established. Ensure that the remote computer is on and connected to the Windows Small Business Server Network."

2. Launch Internet Explorer from **Start**, **Internet**. Type in the following address in the **Address** field: **springers1.springersltd.com**.
3. If you did not select the Business Web on the Web Services Configuration page in Chapter 4 when you ran the EICW, you'd receive a 403 error saying that the page could not be displayed. If you did publish the root page by selecting Business Web on the Web Services Configuration page, the Welcome page appears as seen in Figure 8-1. You will now plow through each link. But notice that the address line reads "http" at this point. This is important as you progress through the examples.

Figure 8-1
The external public Web page on an SBS 2003 server machine. It kindly welcomes you aboard! This occurs when you publish the root Web page over port 80 in SBS 2003 (which is not recommended).

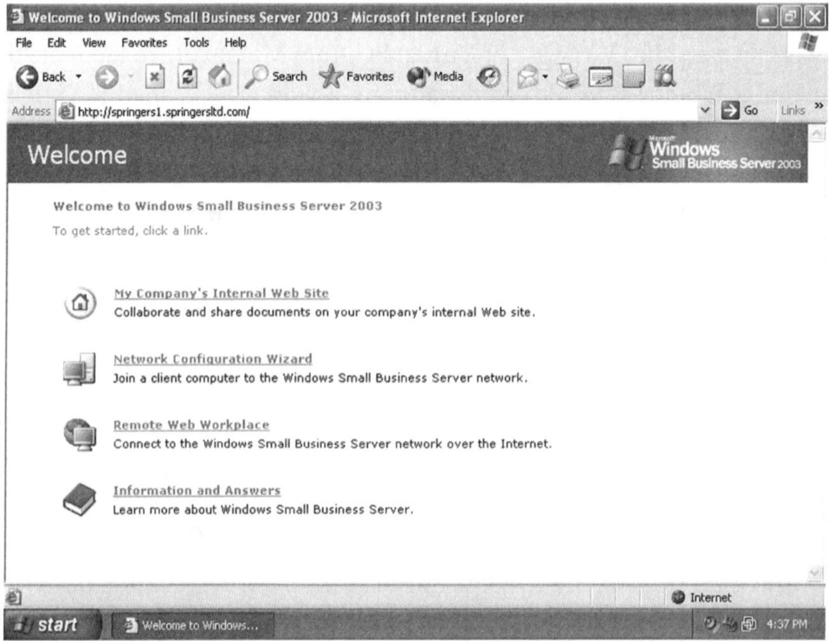

BEST PRACTICE: Slow down there, pardner! How did a FQDN address resolve itself in our simple SPRINGERS methodology when I didn't point you to an authoritative DNS server to resolve the address? Did I brain hiccup on ya there? Nope! I got sneaky and entered the following HOSTS file entry on the NormLap workstation:

207.202.238.215 springers1.springersltd.com

Note the host file on a Windows XP Pro is located by default at: c:\windows\system32\drivers\etc

4. Click **My Company's Internal Web Site** and nothing will happen. This was designed to be a simple placeholder for you to place a link to your company's Web site. It will not access the internal Web site despite the name of this link (the command being executed is http://companyweb which is an internal, not external reference). Click **Back** to return to Welcome.
5. Click **Network Configuration Wizard**. This is an internal LAN process to join the computer as an Active Directory object on the network. This certainly has a time and place, but you're going to defer on the opportunity to do this now because I want to maintain the sanctity of my methodology whereby NormLap is truly an external client computer. In fact, this wont' work externally. Click **Back**.
6. If you clicked **Remote Web Workplace**, you'd access RWW from the public root Web page. But read on.
7. So now I want to reverse course and do things properly! In the **Address** field, type **springers1.springersltd.com/remote** and click **Go**. You've commenced your connection to RWW.
8. Click **OK** when you see the **Security Alert** dialog box.
9. Another **Security Alert** dialog box appears and relates to the self-signed security certificate described in Chapter 6. Click **View Certificate** and select **Install Certificate**. Click **Next** when the **Certificate Import Wizard** launches. Click **Next** on the **Certificate Store** page (the default selection is **Automatically select the certificate store based on the type of certificate**). Click **Finish** followed by **OK**. Click **OK** to close the **Certificate** dialog box. So what did you just do? You installed the certificate in Internet

Explorer on the external client computer. Finally, click **OK** to clear the Security Alert dialog box that greeted you at the start of this step.

BEST PRACTICE: If you purchase a real signed certificate (e.g. Verisign), the stuff in the step above won't happen. Consider that a best practice (Microsoft is supportive of purchased real certificates).

10. The **Remote Web Workplace** logon dialog box appears (Figure 8-2). Type **NormH** in the **User name** field. Type **Purple3300** in the **password** field. Observe the other settings (using a public/shared computers, broadband connection). Click **Log on**.

BEST PRACTICE: Notice the Address line has switched to HTTPS. It's self-signed security certificate time, baby! Observe the little golden padlock on the lower right of IE. HUMOR ZONE: Back before July 2003 (when Microsoft went to stock grants), stock options for full-time Microsoft employees ("blue badges") have been referred to as the golden handcuffs, so this must be the origins of the golden padlock for IE in HTTPS mode!

Figure 8-2
The Remote Web Workplace logon page.

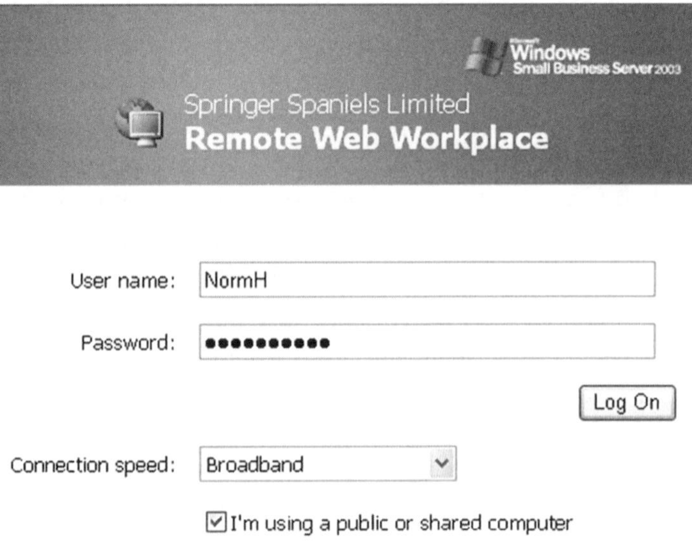

11. Observe the official Remote Web Workplace page that has four menu options by default (Figure 8-3). The first selection, Read my company e-mail, simply launches Outlook Web Access, which I'll discuss a little later in the chapter. The fourth option, Download Connection Manager, is also discussed later in the chapter. For now the focus is on the middle two options. So click **Connect to my computer at work**.

Figure 8-3

The infamous Remote Web Workplace welcome page. The ability to connect to your computer is only one of four options on this menu.

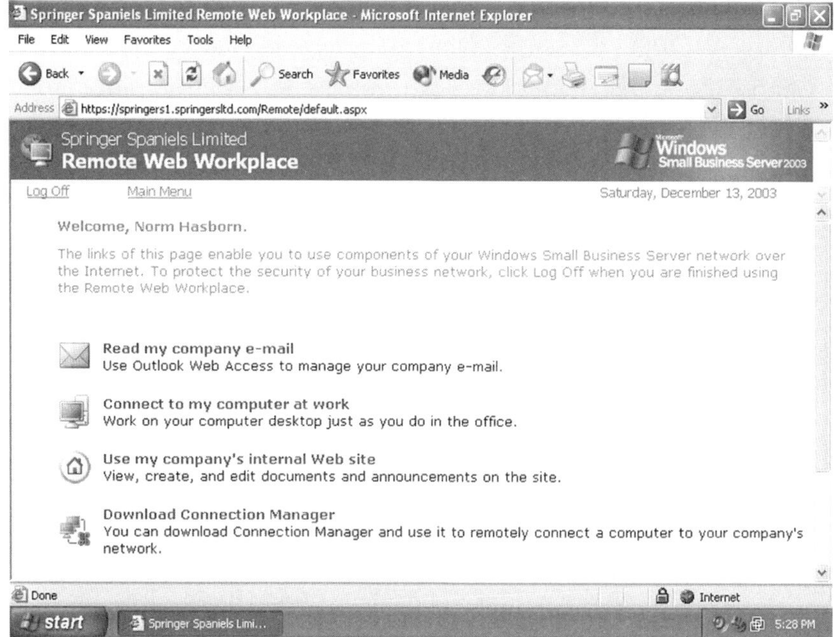

BEST PRACTICE: Exactly how does the RWW welcome page get built and know what options to display? In part, the RWW welcome page menu options are built from the options you select on the Web Services Configuration page in the EICW (refer to Figure 4-10). Another element is that an Active Directory query is run to look for computer objects. If none are found, the link to connect to desktop computers is suppressed. If you haven't completed the Remote Access Wizard from the To Do List in Server Manager, the Connection

Manager link is suppressed. That's what does it for mere mortals, but read on.

If you want to manually light up links in RWW, you can flip the DWORD value in the Registry for any menu link. Go to the following SBS 2003 Registry location in the Registry Editor (REGEDIT):

HKEY_LOCAL_MACHINE\SOFTWARE\Microsoft\SmallBusinessServer\RemoteUserPortal

and then drill into the two folders (AdminLinks, KWLinks) and look at the DWORD values (these line items list each RWW menu link). Choose the AdminLinks folder when you use RWW as Administrator. Select the KWLinks folder when you use RWW as a user who has Mobile User template membership or Power User template membership.

12. Click **Yes** when asked by the **Security Warning** dialog box to install the **Remote Destkop Active X control**. This control will install in the background. Note this is a one-time event that runs the first time you perform this procedure. You won't see it again.
13. Select **PRESIDENT** from the **Computers** list. Click the **Optional Settings** link and observe the settings. Select the **Enable files and folders to be transferred between the remote computer** and this computer and **Hear sounds from the remote computer on this computer**. The options you have just selected are self-explanatory. Your screen should look similar to Figure 8-4 (I realize the figure is slightly cropped). Click **Connect**.
14. Click **OK** after reading the **Remote Desktop Connection Security Warning** (Figure 8-5).
15. On the **Log on to Windows** dialog box that appears for the PRESIDENT client computer, type **NormH** as the user and **Purple3300** as the password. This step is identical to logging on to a Terminal Services server machine from a remote location, so it's likely within your comfort level.

Figure 8-4
Explore the options on the page where you select the computer you want to log on to remotely.

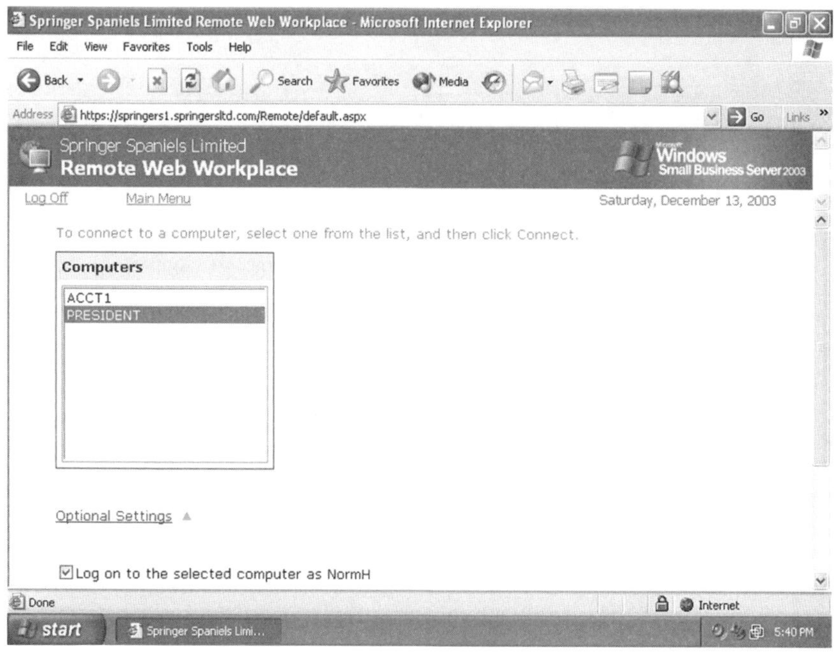

BEST PRACTICE: Hold the phone! Didn't you observe in step 13 that the RWW session had you log on as NormH yet you were challenged and had to log on as NormH in the Log on to Windows dialog box? This relates to the fact that user authentication credentials from the RWW sign on (step 10) aren't being passed on to step 15.

Technically speaking, here is what's up. The Remote Desktop ActiveX Control can only accept credentials in clear text before connecting to a client. Once you connect, the channel is encrypted, and passwords are sent securely. Microsoft could not allow people to have their credentials stored in clear text on a client ever, which is what would have to occur in order to automatically sign you in. It's too risky. Who knows? Maybe in the future this pass through will be securely perfected, saving that step. Good news, though. The step does preset your user name for you, saving you some typing (e.g., not having to type NormH again).

Figure 8-5
Approve this security warning which speaks towards local drive mappings.

16. You are now using the PRESIDENT machine at work as NormH. THIS IS SO COOL (NormH's exact words as he sipped a triple cappuccino at Starbucks!). Go ahead and perform a simple action such as launching his Outlook 2003 e-mail client from Start, E-mail and perhaps launch Microsoft Word from **Start**, **All Programs**, **Microsoft Office**, **Microsoft Office Word 2003** (the result would be similar to Figure 8-6).

BEST PRACTICE: Can anyone log on to any client computer on the SBS 2003 network using this RWW-based work from home or Starbucks approach? Nope! Remember back in Chapter 4 that the Add User Wizard process made the assigned user a local administrator and eligible to log on to the client computer via the Remote Desktop capability in Windows XP Pro (see from **Start**, right-click **My Computer**, select **Properties**, select **Remote** tab and explore the **Remote Desktop** section of the tab sheet). Bottom line: You have to be allowed to log on to a client computer.

Figure 8-6
Working remotely, Norm has hijacked his desktop machine back at SPRINGERS and typed a document in Word 2003. Cool!

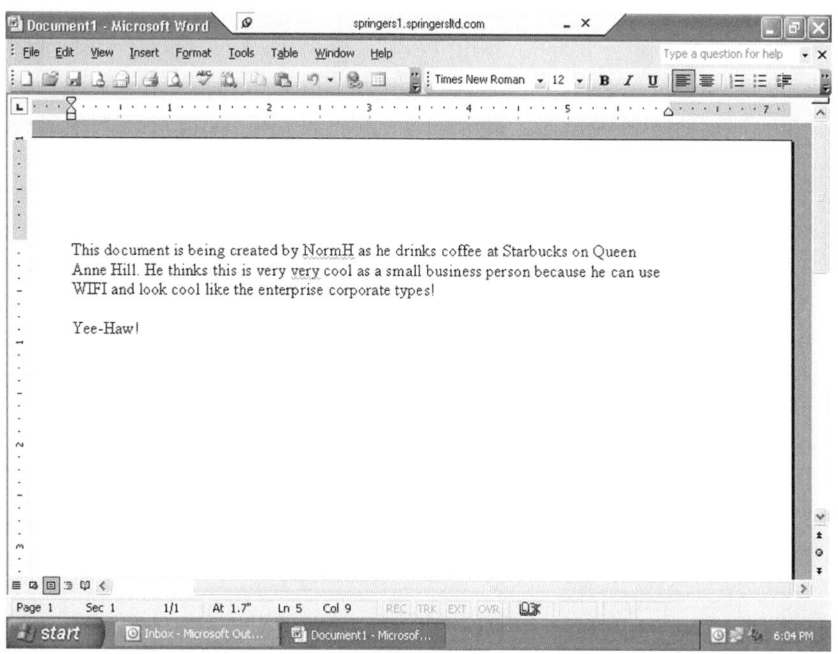

BEST PRACTICE: By the way, I remember a heated debate between individuals at the Fall 2003 Miami SBS 2003 hands-on lab regarding the Remote Desktop logon behavior in RWW. It was like witnessing a beer battle with one side claiming the brew was less filling, the other side insisting the brew tasted great. One party claimed that the auto-logoff that occurs, for example, on Norm's PRESIDENT machine (assuming it was logged on at the time back at the office) when Norm uses RWW to initiate a Remote Desktop session is a flaw. His point was someone could be working on PRESIDENT and receive no prior notification they are being logged off (work could be lost, etc.). The other party to the debate saw the situation much differently and claimed it was a feature! Performing this log off on the local desktop when a Remote Desktop session via RWW commenced enforced security and prevented snooping. So one man's flaw is another man's feature!

Oh-oh. Just one minor clarification to the story above. When Norm, who is working remotely, commences the Remote Desktop session, he will receive a notice that he's about to log off the local user (in this case we'll say Linda). It's Linda who doesn't receive the log off notification (Linda just finds herself being logged off).

17. Let's pretend you walked up to the counter and ordered another triple cappuccino. The line was long with worker bees and it was over 20 minutes before you returned to your remote session on your laptop (e.g., NormLap). You're greeted by Figure 8-7. Why? Because back in Step 9 at the RWW logon box, you told SBS 2003 that you were logging on from a public or shared computer. Knowing that, SBS 2003 will terminate your session after 20 minutes of idle time (a private or non-public computer has two hours). Note that you will always receive a RWW warning that you're about to time out at the remaining one-minute mark. Click on the **Return to the Remote Web Workplace** link.

Notes:

Figure 8-7
Oops. You took to much time getting the cappuccino and were logged off for security purposes!

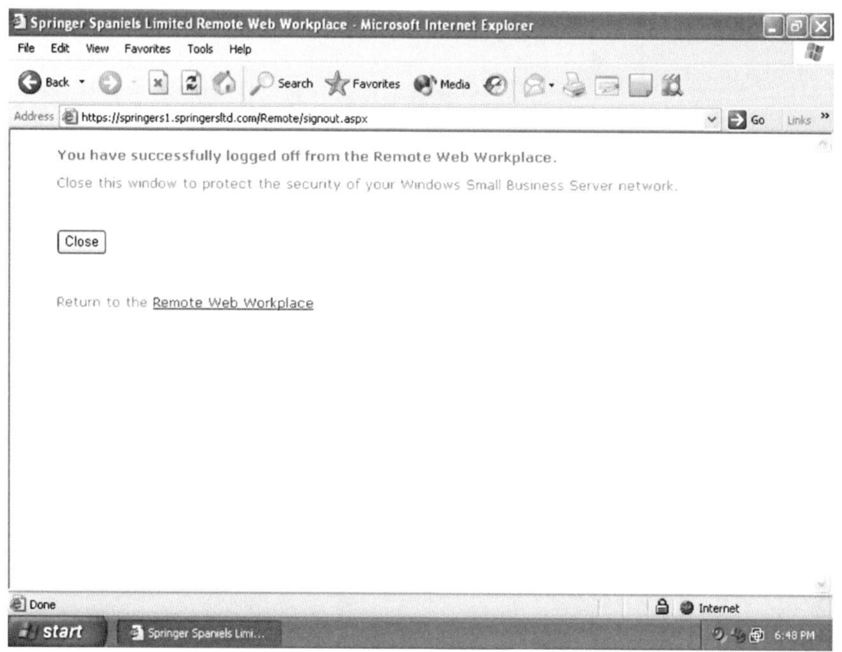

BEST PRACTICE: When you were auto-logged off, this wasn't just a termination of the Remote Desktop session with the PRESIDENT desktop machine. No sir! This was a total log out from RWW (that's going back a couple of steps there).

18. Complete the logon (again) to RWW in a manner similar to Step 10 above as **NormH**. Select **Connect to my computer at work**. Select **PRESIDENT** and click **Connect**. Log on as **NormH** using the **Purple3300** password. Whew! You're returned to the Word 2003 document shown in Figure 8-6. Yes Virginia, Windows XP Pro has session maintenance upon disconnect or forced logoff.

BEST PRACTICE: Note that RWW will display a list of Windows XP Pro machines with Remote Desktop and Windows 2000 Server/ Windows Server 2003 machines running Terminal Services in

Application Sharing Mode here. This is accomplished by a background query that pools network membership for machines that meet this specific criteria. This is an SBS 2003 feature and not found in the full Windows Server 2003 network. Yee-haw.

And by the way, if you connect to a server machine running Terminal Services in Application Sharing Mode via RWW, it will be over port 4125, not port 3389 (the traditional way). You read it here first.

19. You will now disconnect properly! Close Word 2003 (save the file if you like). Close Outlook 2003. Click **Start**, **Disconnect**. Select **Disconnect** when the **Disconnect Windows** dialog box appears. When you perform this step, a local user could log on to the machine again and commence working (e.g., Linda uses the desktop computer again).
20. You are returned to RWW's screen displaying computer names. Click the **Main Menu** link.
21. Click on the **Use my company's internal Web site link**.
22. Complete the connection dialog box that appears as **NormH** in the **User name** and **Purple3300** in the **Password** field.
23. The Windows SharePoint Services (WSS) Home page appears as seen in Figure 8-8.

Notes:

Figure 8-8
The WSS Home page as you left it in Chapter 7 but viewed via RWW.

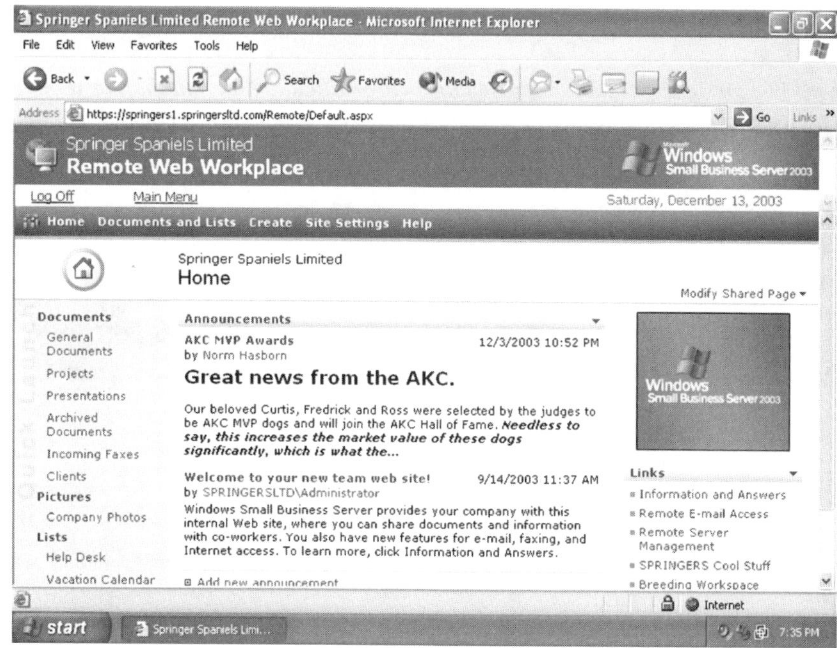

24. Select **Log Off**. Then click **Close**. When asked to close the window in the Microsoft Internet Explorer dialog box, click **Yes**.

You have now completed your exploration of RWW as NormH. Now perform the procedure to log on to RWW as the **Administrator** (password is **Husky9999!**). Your RWW screen should look like Figure 8-9.

Figure 8-9
The RWW experience as the Administrator is dramatically different than as a mere mortal user. Observe the different selections that you can make. Go ahead and play around with the RWW administrator options.

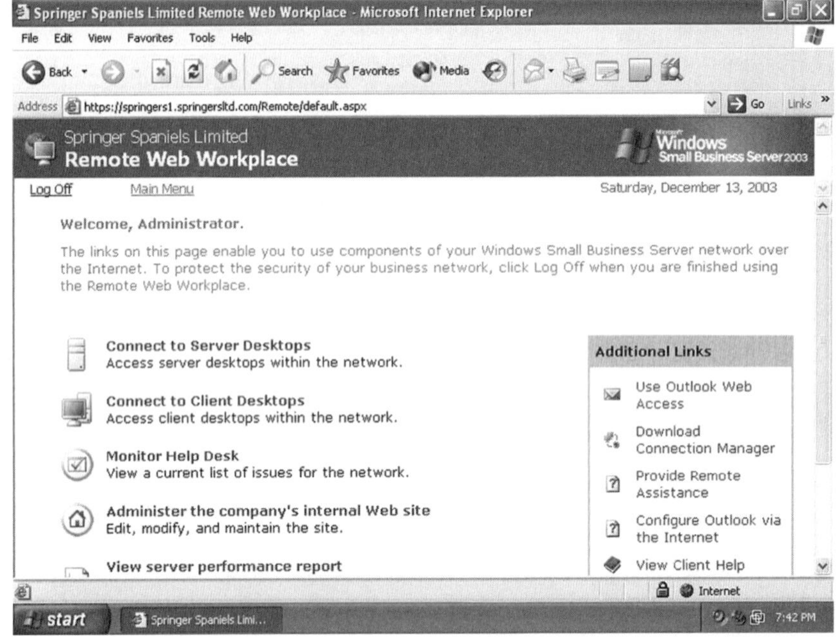

Under the Hood RWW Architecture

Specialists like specialist in the professional world, perhaps because there is an element of mutual respect. So when this SBS specialist (yours truly) needed some help digging deeper in this subject area, I went to fellow SBS 2003 hands-on lab instructor Beatrice Mulzer from Florida. Beatrice is an RWW nicher and provided the screen shots in this section showing a glimpse of how things work under the hood with RWW.

First off, it helps to see a Visio diagram that outlines the RWW architectural experience. This is shown in Figure 8-10.

Figure 8-10
This diagram outlines the RWW mechanics.

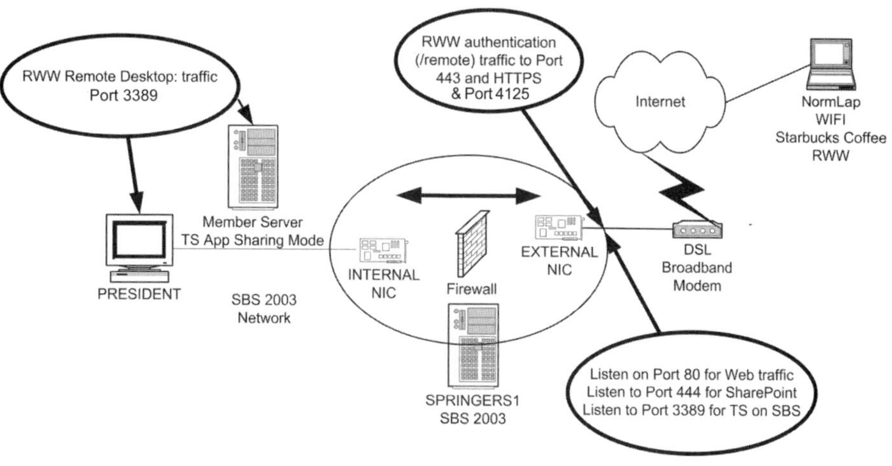

Now for the step-by-step figures that bring definition to the chart above.

Notes:

Figure 8-11

Initial connection to SBS 2003 external Web page over port 80. Note HTTP in the Address field of Internet Explorer.

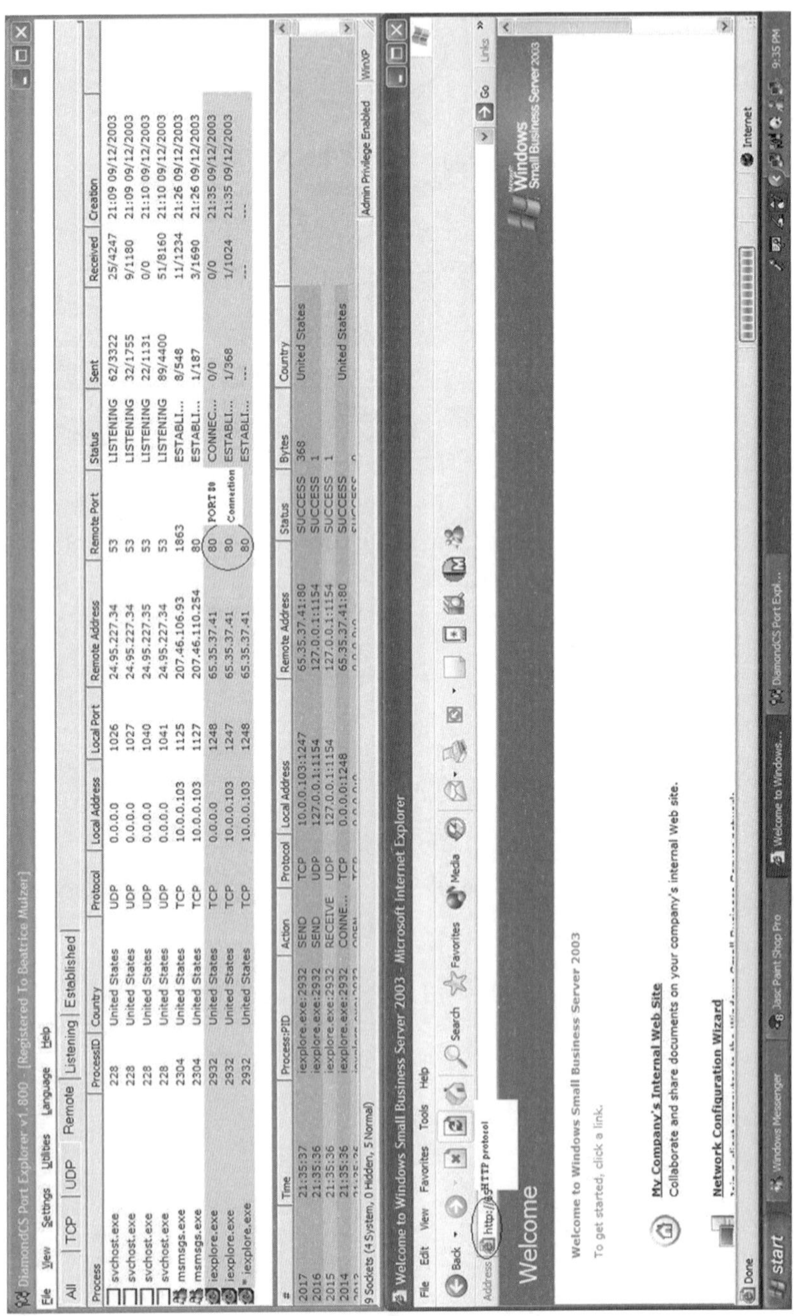

BEST PRACTICE: Note the above figure (Figure 8-11) assumes that you have selected the Business Web option on the Web Services Configuration page in the EICW. We did NOT do this back in Chapter 4 for the purpose of SPRINGERS. But please heed this advice, as imparted to me by the Microsoft program manager who owns this area. IN THE REAL WORLD, Microsoft discourages you from opening port 80 in the EICW via the Business Web selection. Rather, they'd rather have the address for RWW typed by external users be the FQDN followed by /remote (e.g., springers1.springersltd.com/remote). The /remote component of the address makes the external listening port become 443 and the address is appended to HTTPS.

Another real worldism for NOT opening port 80 if you can help it. Beside exposing your IIS root to the world (and Web search engine crawling), you also expose RWW to Web search engine crawling. This is something you probably don't want to do, as it might be the source of future vulnerabilities and attacks (as of this writing, this hasn't been exploited). A really interesting exercise to see this in action is to go to Google and search on the terms "remote web workplace" and view the results. You'll see pages of hits returned with Remote Web Workplace highlighted. These are SBS 2003 sites that have opened port 80 (again, likely via the Business Web selection on the Web Services Configuration page in the EICW). Stunning how many RWW sites you'll see.

Finally, if you must have port 80 open because you really do host a business Web site and you've accepted the risks, then please consider using a robots.txt file to restrict Web search engine crawling. Details on robots.txt at www.robotstxt.org/wc/robots.html and in Chapter 10.

Notes:

Figure 8-12

Approving the security certificate (SSL) pop-up to log on to Remote Web Workplace (this process started by selecting the Remote Web Workplace link). Note the port switch from port 80 to port 443. This would be the case when you've published your root page via the Business Web selection on Web Services Configuration in the EICW.

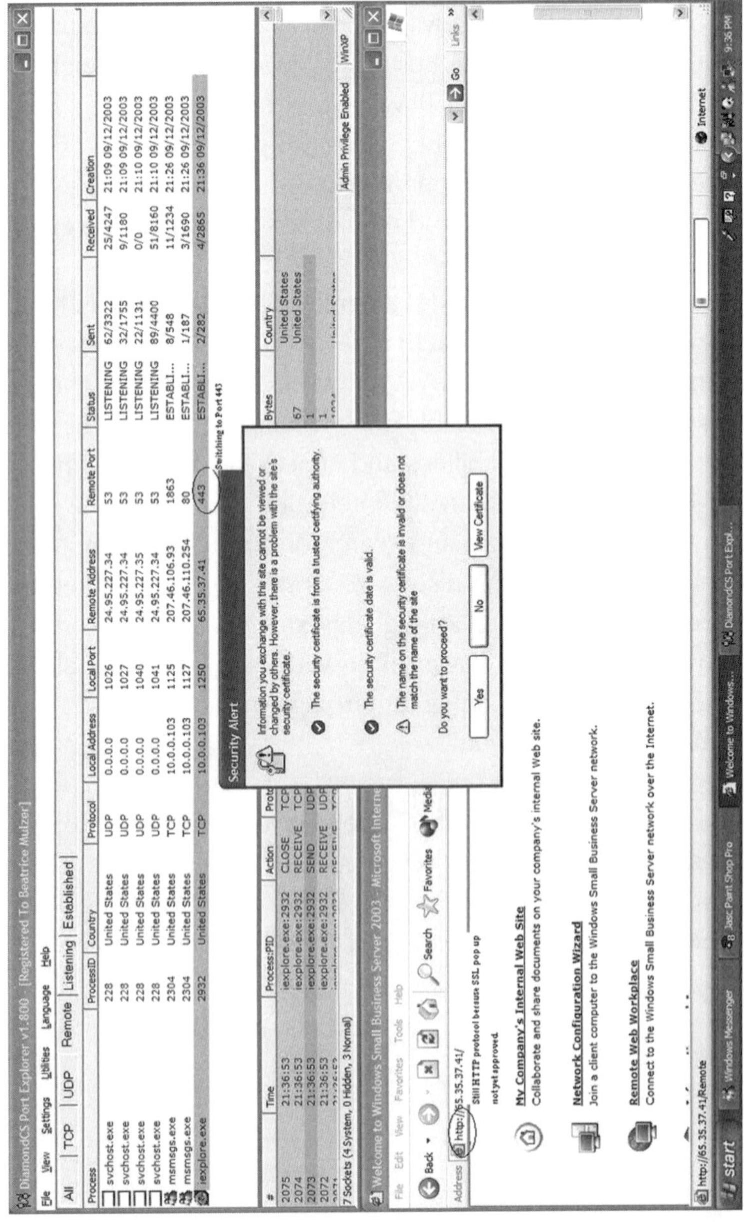

Figure 8-13

The SSL pop-up was approved and the RWW logon dialog box appears. Session traffic is over port 443 and the HTTP protocol has switched to HTTPS at this point.

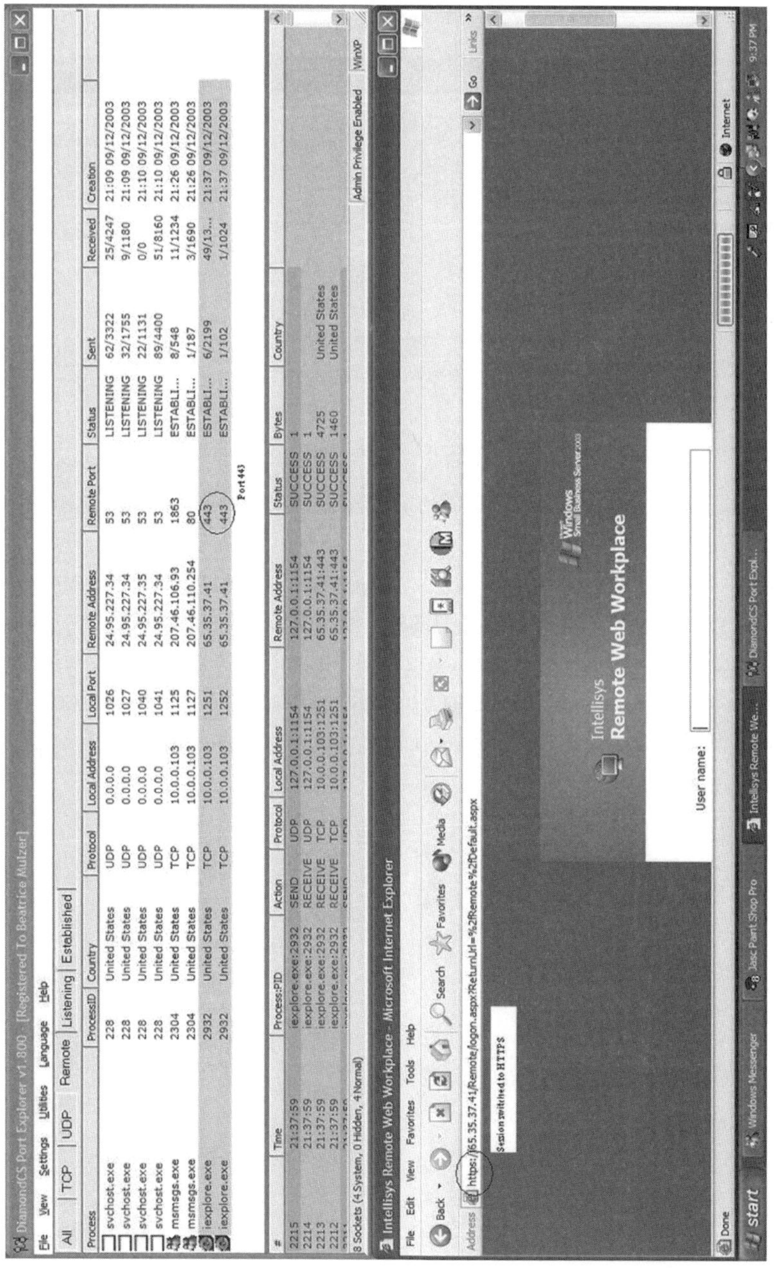

Figure 8-14
An RWW session underway with HTTPS and port 443.

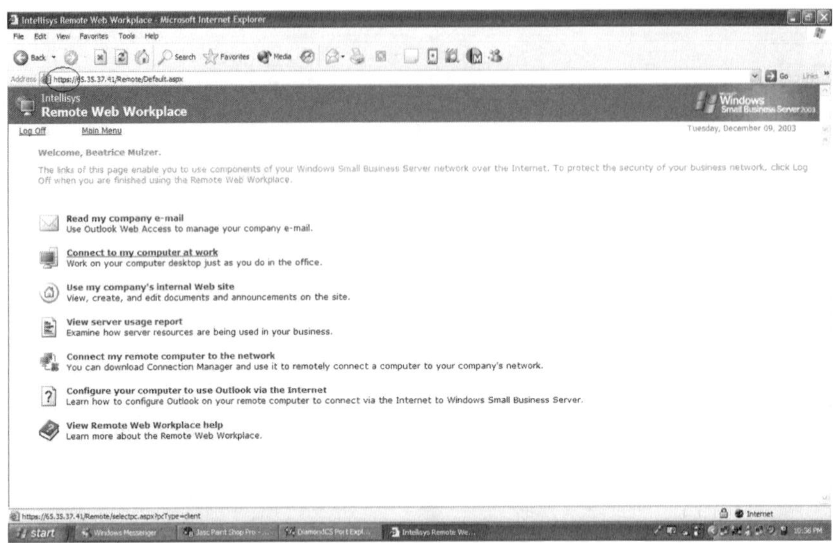

BEST PRACTICE: Did you look closely at the above figure and see the entry titled "View Server Usage Report"? How did that appear? If you have run the Monitoring Configuration Wizard (which you will do in Chapter 12) and the user (in this case Beatrice) has permission to view the server usage reports, this option will appear on the RWW page.

Figure 8-15
Internally accessing the WSS Home page (Intranet) over port 443 under RWW. Protocol is HTTPS. Note that external access to WSS is over 444 (which isn't being depicted in this figure).

Figure 8-16

*When you click the **Connect to my computer at work**, port 4125 is used for the Remote Desktop session traffic (note port 4125 doesn't become active and listen until you click this **Connect to my computer at work** button; listening actually occurs on port 443). This is in addition to port 443 that remains open (ports 4125 and 443 are simultaneously open under this scenario). At this juncture, some background voodoo is performed by SBS to authenticate you and prove you are who you say you are (that's about as well as I can explain it in this introductory text).*

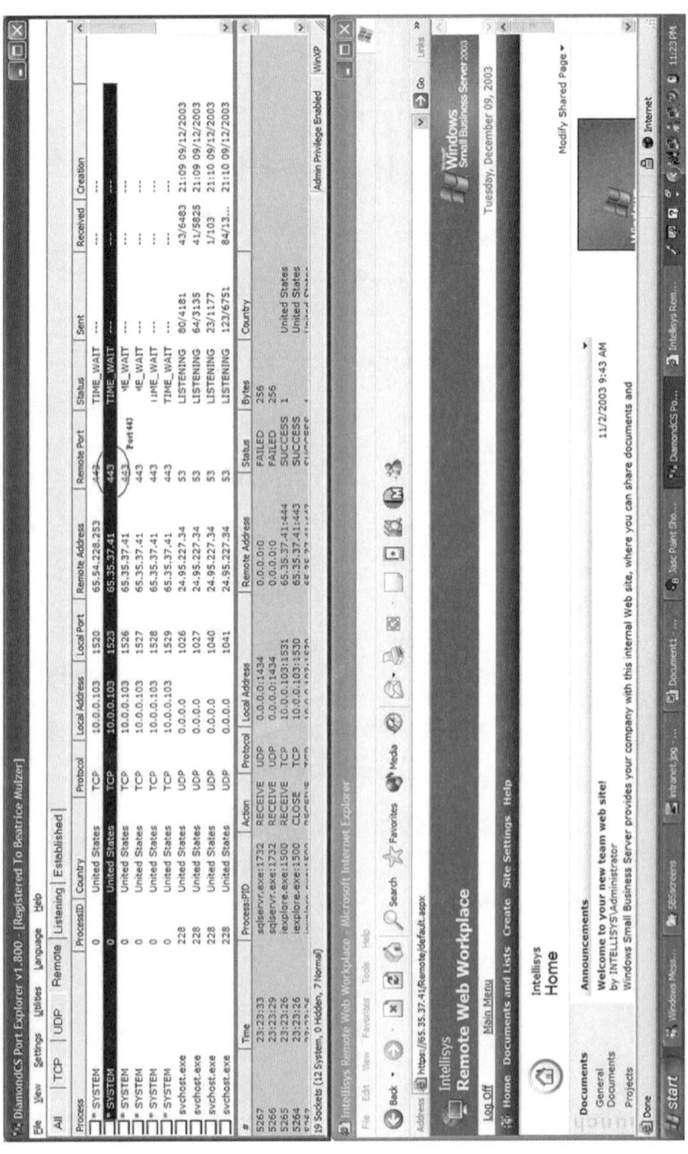

BEST PRACTICE: A common question in the Fall 2003 SBS hands-on labs related to which ports on a hardware-based firewall/router needed to be opened to allow RWW traffic through. RWW uses the following ports for its entire experience: 443, 444, 4125. Port 80 would be used if you published the root page (not recommended). And by the way, the other SBS-related port you'll need open is 1723 (VPN, which I discuss more later).

By the way, you can see the port 4125 setting for RWW in the Registry at:

HKEY_LOCAL_MACHINE\SOFTWARE\Microsoft\SmallBusinessServer\RemoteUserPortal and look at the Port key where the REG_DWORD value is 4125.

Another common question concerns whether you must first establish a VPN connection to drill down and take control of your Windows XP Pro workstation via Remote Desktop. The answer is no. You are using RDP over HTTP, not VPN tunneling to access the Windows XP Pro workstation.

So hopefully a few pictures here have saved over a thousand words. I thought that by starting with a diagram and then witnessing the port traffic, you could "feel" RWW first hand under the hood. More of this good stuff in my advanced SBS 2003 book in the second part of 2004.

RWW Security Summary

Before moving on and looking at Outlook 2003 remote approaches, oblige me and view the following RWW security summary:

- SSL connections required for access to the Web site.
- User authentication required for access to the Web site.
- Log out allows users to close sessions and clear any cached logon credentials.
- Timeout feature automatically closes sessions after a period of inactivity.

- Public or shared computer mode provides additional safety requirements in those environments (browser version checking, shorter timeouts).
- Web site is throttled through IIS.
- Web site files are strongly ACL'ed (governed by the Access Control List) to prevent unauthorized editing.
- Remote Desktop connections are encrypted and send only mouse clicks and keystrokes over the connection.
- Reduces or eliminated the need for VPN connections at the business.

BEST PRACTICE: Use the above list as "talking points" when talking about RWW.

Exploring RDP

Oops! I almost forgot some more stuff on RDP that I wanted to share (this has an advanced tone to it). RDP allows for separate virtual channels for carrying device communication and presentation data from the server, as well as encrypted client mouse and keyboard data. RDP uses its own video driver on the server-side to render display output by construction rendering information in network packets using the RDP protocol and sending them over the network to the client. On the client-side, it receives the rendering data and interprets them into the corresponding Win32 Graphic Display Interface (GDI) application programming interface (API) calls. On the input path, client mouse and keyboard messages are redirected from the client to the server. On the server-side, RDP uses its own virtual keyboard and mouse driver to receive these keyboard and mouse events.

Without encrypting the display protocol, it would be very easy to "sniff" the wire to discover the user's passwords as they log on to the system. Allowing an administrator to log on using a non-encrypted protocol exposes the entire domain resources that are now vulnerable to hackers, especially if connecting over a public network without a VPN. It is both darn interesting and important to note that protocols using "scrambling" to protect data are just as vulnerable to this sort of attack as protocols that send data using clear text.

The activity involved in sending and receiving data through the RDP stack is essentially the same as the seven-layer Open Standards Interconnection (OSI) model for the LANs on this planet. Data from an application or service to be transmitted is passed down through the protocol stacks, sectioned (sounds like a Ginsu knife commercial with slicing and dicing, eh?), directed to the channel (through MCS), encrypted, wrapped, framed, packaged onto the network protocol, and finally (really and truly) addressed and sent over the wire to the client. The returned data works the same way only in reverse, with the packet being stripped of its address, then unwrapped, decrypted, and so on (and on and on) until the data is presented to the application for use (Whew!). Key portions of the protocol stack modifications occur between the fourth and seventh layer, where the data is encrypted, wrapped and framed, directed to a channel and prioritized.

Lastly, every version of RDP uses RSA Security's RC4 cipher, a stream cipher designed to efficiently encrypt small amounts of varying data size. RC4 is designed for secure communications over networks and is also used in protocols such as SSL, which encrypts traffic to and from secure Web sites. By default, Windows XP Remote Desktop and Windows Server 2003 Remote Desktop and Terminal Services use high (128-bit) encryption to encrypt most data transmissions in both the client-to-server direction and the server-to-client direction.

> BEST PRACTICE: Don't forget the 128-bit encryption point raised here. It is frequently brought up in technology conversations about SBS.

Outlook Web Access

Meanwhile, back at the BBQ where the steaks are sizzling, another compelling SBS 2003 feature that "sizzles" in front of business decision makers (BDMs) is the massively improved Outlook Web Access (OWA). My infamous SBS customer, Bob in real estate, did back flips when I showed him the new OWA in SBS 2003. Why? For these reasons.

- **Look and feel.** The new OWA just looks more like "real" Outlook. That has been a major sticking point with Bob and other BDMs. It wasn't so much like reading an e-mail message in past OWA releases was that bothersome. Rather, things like calendar entries and contact records were downright rude!

- **Feature creature.** OWA, when compared to past OWA versions (apples to apples) and not compared to "real" Outlook (apples to oranges), is much richer. An example of improved features is the stronger integration with Outlook and its rules and options (such as Privacy and Junk E-mail Prevention options now accessible via OWA).

- **Sir Speedy.** This OWA version boogies. Older OWA releases were slow and seconds of delay felt like hours to Type-A businessmen like Bob. It was so bad in the past that I set up Outlook Express with IMAP as per Chapter 6 to workaround the OWA slowness.

- **Security improvements.** I felt honor-bound to show my customers, such as Bob the BDM, some improvements to security. As an SBSer in the early 21st century, I'm trying to use every opportunity to talk up security (and no, this isn't make-work or a self-employment act, but advice offered in a sincere way). See the security section below for details, but I'll share one now: OWA natively runs under HTTPS when you configure the default configuration of SBS.

BEST PRACTICE: So are there any limitations with the new OWA? Yes, there are a few. A bright student in Mumbai/Bombay India SBS 2003 hands-on lab correctly taught me (the instructor) that OWA doesn't display multiple mailboxes at the same time while real Outlook can. This is bothersome if you're a BDM that uses multiple e-mail aliases to look larger than life in the business community and you travel extensively and need to use OWA from Internet cafés or your laptop in a hotel room. With OWA and multiple mailboxes, you'd need to log on multiple times (as the different e-mail account) and view each mailbox separately (e.g., jobs@springersltd.com).

Another student at the San Francisco, California, SBS 2003 hands-on lab (October 2003) correctly pointed out that, when viewing a contact record in a public folder in the new OWA, the New Message to Contact toolbar button is disabled. Translation: You can't send an e-mail to a contact in a public folder with a single click using OWA. Rather, you have to manually copy and paste the SMTP e-mail address into a new message. He seemed really bothered by this (must have been having a bad SBS day).

Beatrice Mulzer from Cocoa Florida informs me that the search folder feature isn't available in OWA.

I personally noticed that, when entering a contact record in OWA in the SBS 2003 time frame, that the Address, City, State, Zip fields (ACSZ) are divided in the UI for OWA (you have separate fields for ACSZ). But, in real Outlook 2003, ACSZ is entered into a single field and then parsed in the background.

Meet OWA

Less talk, more look-see at this point. The new and improved OWA is presented in Figure 8-17 for your pleasure.

Notes:

Figure 8-17
Here is OWA in the SBS 2003 time frame. Notice in the Address that the URL identifies local host (running on the SBS server machine).

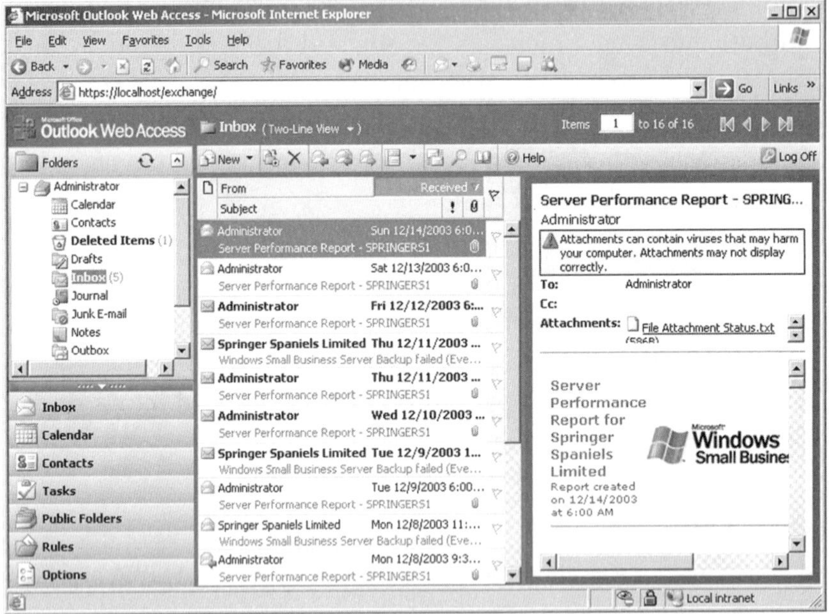

There are three ways to access OWA in SBS 2003.

- **Old-fashioned.** You're probably familiar with this approach. Type the fully qualified domain name (FQDN) appended with the term "exchange" for the external interface (that's the wild-side NIC card) on the SBS server machine) like springers1.springersltd.com/exchange. This approach assumes you have an "A" resource record registered in the DNS of your ISP that points to the wild-side NIC card. Of course, you could always point to the wild-side IP address in the following manner -207.202.238.215/exchange - and you'll start the OWA authentication process.

- **RWW.** If necessary, revisit the RWW discussion early in this chapter where you learned to authenticate over the Internet. The RWW menu has the Read my company e-mail link to launch OWA. From the outside, RWW is best accessed by FQDN/remote (springers1.springersltd.com/remote).

- **Local Host.** In Figure 8-17, I hinted at the use of OWA on the SBS server machine. This is possible with the localhost/exchange address. This is an excellent way to read e-mail messages et. al. on the actual SBS server machine and avoid the MAPI conflict I discussed in Chapter 6 (see Figure 6-26).

There are two types of OWA experiences:

- **Premium.** If ya want the good stuff, you need to select the Premium radio button on the OWA logon screen.

- **Basic.** While providing fewer OWA features, selecting the Basic radio button results in a session that runs faster and is recommended for slow links.

Notes:

I compare OWA Premium and OWA Basic on a deeper level (focused on security) in Table 8-1.

Table 8-1: Security: OWA Premium versus Basic

Capability	Description	OWA Premium	OWA Basic
Logon page	This has a new customized form for logging on to OWA. Includes cookie-based validation where OWA cookie is invalid after user logs out or is inactive for a predefined amount of time (or eats the cookie - just kidding).	Yes - and allows you choice to use OWA Basic	Yes - but only allows use of OWA Basic
Clear credentials cache on logoff	After logofff all the credentials in IE SP1 credentials cache are cleared automatically.	Yes	No
Public/Share computer and Private computer logon options	To provide SBSers with more protection, two logon page security options can be used. You can set the private logon page with a longer period before user is logged off because of inactivity.	Yes	Yes
"Web Beacon" blocking	Users can control options for blocking external content in e-mail.	Yes	Yes
Attachment blocking	Administrator options restrict access to some or all attachments in messages.	Yes	Yes
Junk mail filtering	Options to set up safe- and blocked-sender lists.	Yes	Yes
Encrypted/ signed mail	Sending and receiving encrypted and/or signed e-mail is supported.	Yes. IE 6 on Microsoft Windows 2000 or later.	No.

It's time for Norm Hasborn to check his e-mail via OWA.

1. Log on to the remote computer (in my example: NormLap). I'll assume you can log on as **NormH** (a local user) with the password **Purple3300**.
2. Launch Internet Explorer from **Start**, **Internet**. Type **springers1.springersltd.com/exchange** in the **Address** field. Note you can explore OWA via RWW on your own by repeating the RWW steps earlier in the chapter (from RWW, select **Read my company e-mail**). Here I want to expose you to the native OWA logon screen (RWW suppresses this screen, as I'll discuss in the security section).
3. Click **OK** at the two **Security Alert** dialog boxes that appear (a third such box may appear if you didn't install the SPRINGERS certificate earlier in the chapter and requires **Yes**).
4. Complete the OWA logon screen similar to Figure 8-18. **NormH** is the user with the password **Purple3300**. The **Client** is **Premium** and the **Security** is **Public or shared computer** (I discuss security in the next section). Click **Log On**.

Figure 8-18
Norm Hasborn is logging on to OWA here. The session has flipped to HTTPS at this point.

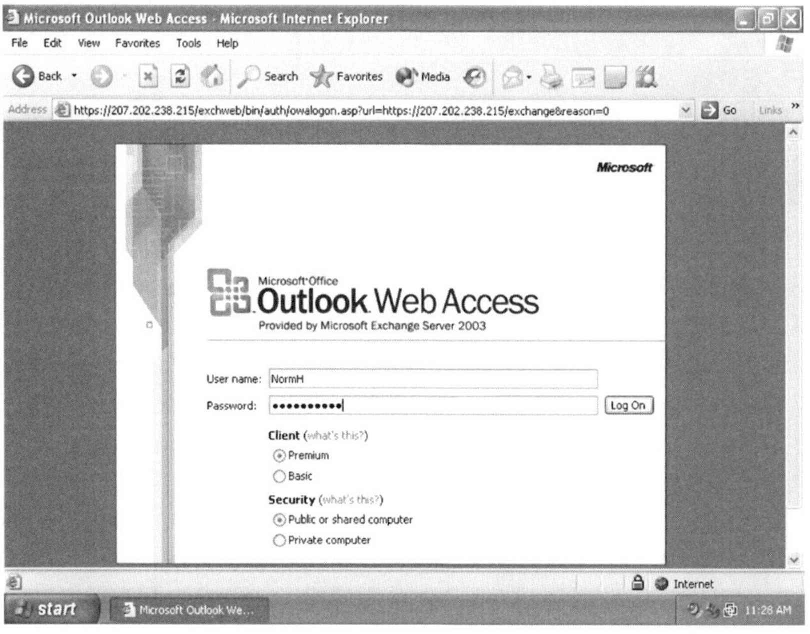

5. OWA can be seen for NormH in Figure 8-19. Notice the e-mail in the figure relates to the alert you configured in the prior chapter (Chapter 7 on WSS) relating to the Breeder1.doc document. Cool!
6. Go ahead and horse around with OWA for a few minutes. When you're done, log off via the Log Off button on the far right.

Figure 8-19
OWA time, baby!

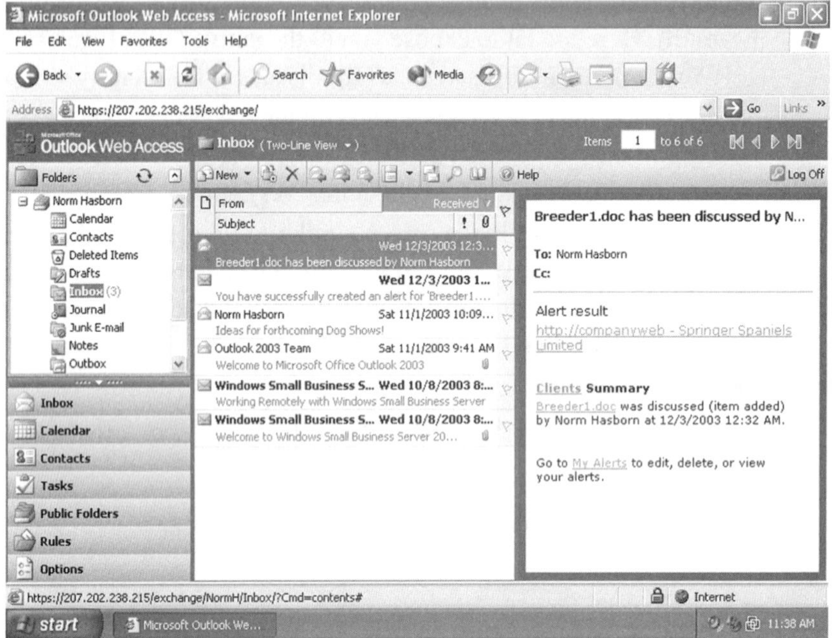

OWA Security

There are a couple of security matters relating to OWA.

- **Public vs. private computer.** In Figure 8-18, you can see the OWA logon screen. A public or shared computer has a shorter time-out period (akin to the same setting in RWW). A private computer informs the Exchange server to tolerate a longer period of inactivity before enforcing a log off.

- **HTTPS.** I mentioned earlier but I need to mention again. When you configured SBS properly (that is, run the EICW and create the self-signing certificate that is discussed in both Chapter 4 and 5), you'll always operate OWA under HTTPS. The translation for the BDM is that this is more secure and the data (in addition to the logon activity) is encrypted via PPTP. The port session related to this is shown in Figure 8-20.

Figure 8-20
Observe Port 443 making the OWA session operate under HTTPS.

- **Challenging.** When you log on the old fashioned way or the local host way, you must complete the OWA logon. In SBS 2000, a local host OWA session did not issue this logon challenge. When you access OWA via RWW, you are not challenged for an OWA-specific logon because RWW passes logon authentication to OWA.

BEST PRACTICE: Always have your SBS users properly log off OWA when they leave an OWA session. The logoff button is found on the far right of the upper OWA toolbar. Not logging off lays the foundation for sinister behavior, such as someone clicking **Back** several times in Internet Explorer to get to your mailbox! LOG OFF!

Outlook Mobile Access

Back in Chapter 6, I wrote about forwarding e-mails to your cell phone. The forwarding works, but an even better solution is to use the newly included feature of Exchange 2003 and SBS 2003 called Outlook Mobile Access (OMA). OMA is simply OWA for web-enabled phones and PocketPC browsers. The basic features of OMA were formerly offered in Mobile Information Server 2002 and also in third party devices - now they are free!

During the SBS 2003 launch events, I met Kim Walker in Columbus, Ohio. Everyone has a gadget that they can't live without and Kim's addiction is e-mail on her cell phone. She has been using and managing third-party add-ins for several years and is promoting the feature to her clients. Kim has offered up some OMA info and best practices. She's the OMA Momma and what follows in this section are her words! Go Kim!

Defining OMA

OMA offers a live text interface to your e-mail messages, calendars, tasks, and contacts. It replaces third-party add-ins at client computers or on additional servers. Therefore, it helps lower the total cost of ownership by reducing the need to deploy additional mobile server products in the corporate environment and by utilizing one mobile user device instead of multiple devices.

OMA supports Wireless Application Protocol (WAP) 2.x as well as XHTML browser-based devices, full HTML browsers and i-Mode devices such as mobile phones and personal digital assistants (PDAs).

OMA Server-Side

From the server-side, OMA setup is very simple. OMA is easier to manage than third party or desktop applications - everything is configured through Exchange System Manager. One important note is that in Standard Exchange Server 2003, OMA is disabled by default, but within SBS 2003 the default is OMA enabled (Figure 8-21).

Figure 8-21
The default Mobile Services Properties for Exchange has everything enabled.

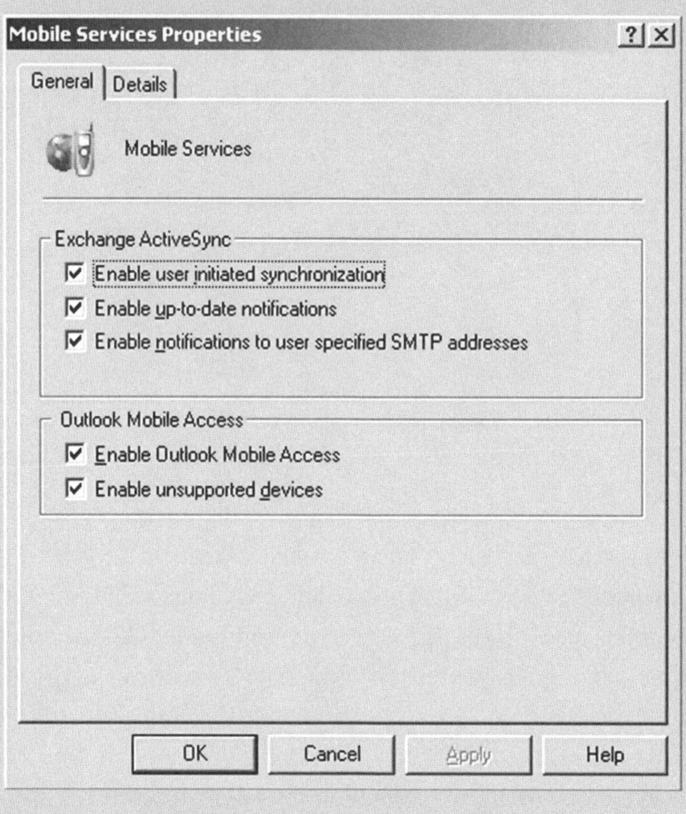

Notice the section titled **Enable unsupported devices**. Many devices have not been fully tested by Microsoft and are not on the supported device list. By default this box is checked, allowing a user to access Exchange on theses untested devices. The user gets an error that says: **The device type you are using is not supported**. Press **OK** to continue. This is shown in Figure 8-22. Once you press **OK** on the device, the service is generally available.

Figure 8-22
This is a screenshot from a mobile phone showing a failed connection.

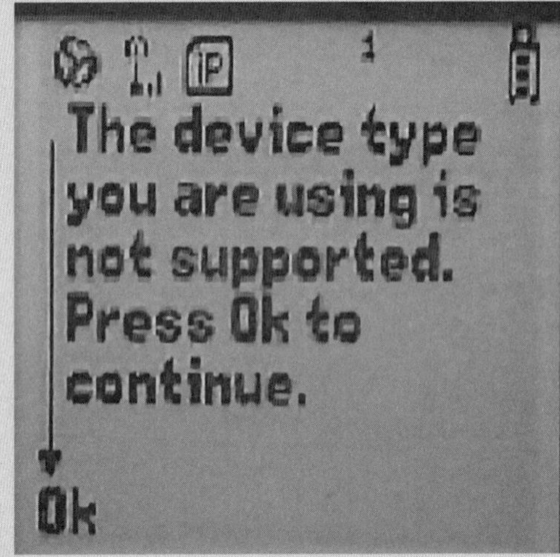

BEST PRACTICE: Keep the Enabled unsupported devices checkbox selected.

You can grant OMA access on an individual case-by-case basis. Say Norm Hasborn, owner of SPRINGERS, gets a new cell phone and doesn't tell you. If Outlook Mobile Access is disabled for him (see Figure 8-23), he might test out OMA and get an error. He won't have OMA access until he calls you, the SBSer, for support.

Figure 8-23
You can disable Mobile Services for individual user.

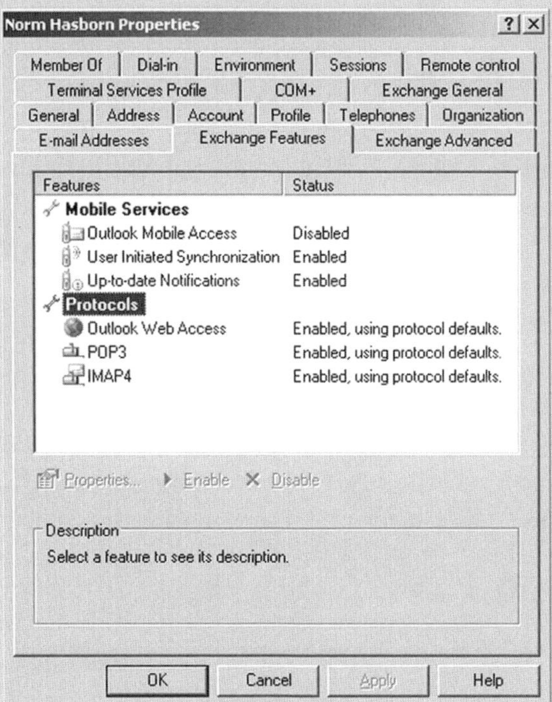

BEST PRACTICE: If you decide to manually add a user e-mail alias rather than run a custom recipient policy, your user will get an error accessing OMA: **Item no longer exists. The item you are attempting to access may have been deleted or moved.**

OMA Client-Side

From the client-side OMA is also fairly simple. It does not have all of the bells and whistles some third-party software has had, but it is definitely functional. OMA is customized for low-bandwidth high-latency type environments, but it still has the same feature set. Reply still means reply. Decline a meeting still means decline a meeting.

Time to use the SPRINGERS methodology where you will send an e-mail, enter contact records, and perform other such tasks from OMA. OMA can be accessed from a desktop computer as well - you don't have to have a mobile device. In fact, if you are using your laptop in a location with a very slow connection, OMA will get you to your e-mail without any OWA overhead.

Sending an E-mail

Time for some step-by-step to have NormH check his e-mail.

1. From the mobile device, point your browser to the following address: **http://springers1.springersltd.com/oma**.
2. At the **Authentication required screen**, type **NormH** in the **User** field and click **OK**.
3. On the **Password** screen, enter **Purple3300** and click **OK**.
4. If you get the **device type not supported error** (wording may vary), click **OK**.
5. You are taken to the **Exchange Mailbox** for the user (Figure 8-24). You can **scroll** (down arrow on cell phone) to see all of the **Mailbox** options (such as **Calendar**, **Contacts**, **Tasks**, etc.).

Figure 8-24
The OMA-based Mailbox on the mobile phone.

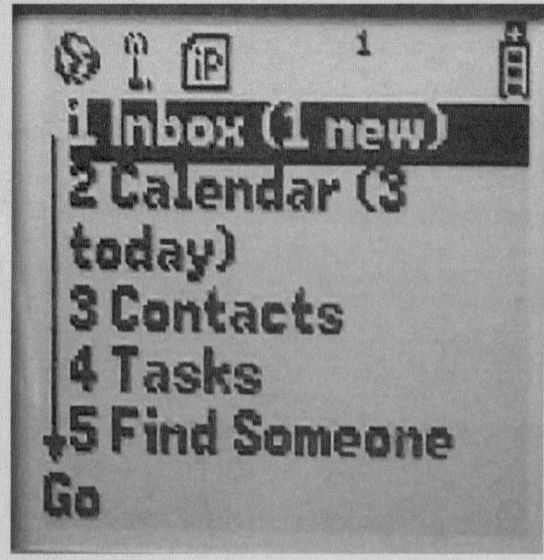

6. To read Norm's inbox, press the **1** or the **Go** menu button.. This will bring you to his Inbox listing (Figure 8-25).

Figure 8-25
This is an Inbox on a mobile phone.

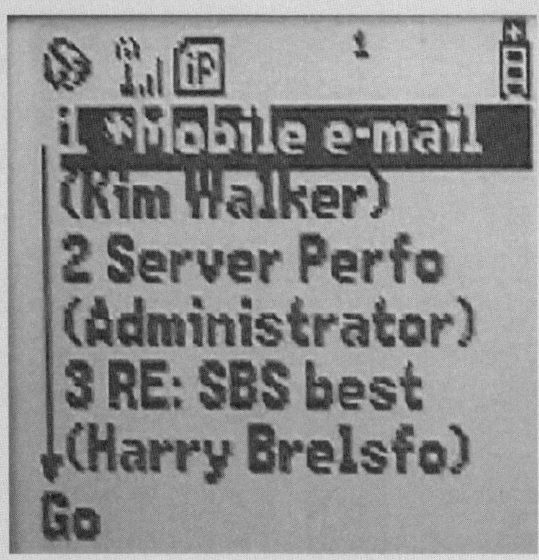

The asterisk on the first message in Figure 8-24 means that this is unread. Also notice the second message is the Standard SBS 2003 Server Performance report - it might take a little while to read through on the small screen, but in a pinch it's great. To read any message just select **Go** while highlighted or hit the corresponding number (there will not be numbers in standard Internet Explorer form a desktop). OMA provides full-featured e-mail functionality, including compose new, read, reply, reply all, forward, delete, flag, and mark as unread. From the details view of messages, you can browse to previous message or next message, close, or go home.

In the OMA calendar view, you can view today, next/previous day, or go to the day of your choice. For any OMA calendar item, you can accept, tentative, decline, reply, reply all, forward, delete, and view details.

Comparing OMA to Other Approaches

So how does OMA compare to cellular-provided desktop assistant programs? Functionality is similar, but the major advantage is that the phone now connects directly to the server. In order for one of the Desktop Assistant programs to function, the desktop must remain turned on with the forwarding program running. This places the failure point at the desktop and also uses both LAN and Internet bandwidth.

How does OMA on a standard cell phone compare to a SmartPhone or blackberry device? Generally cell telephones have smaller screens, but as you can see from the screen shots, if the phone is set to a small text, it is still readable. It is not as easy to type a reply, but it is possible and you can still check messages anywhere.

One important difference between OMA browser access and synchronization devices is that the information is only accessible when the user is in cellular coverage. The data does not get stored on the phone, but can be viewed only in the browser while the user is authenticated to the server.

As of this writing, I dearly miss some of the tricks that third party software offered. One of these tricks is a text message/page notification of mail - a rule that tells the user to check the mailbox rather than forward the message. For now, you can use the forward message from Chapter 6 for specific messages. In the past I have used notifications to page me when I received a message of high importance or a server message (based on words in the subject) or by sender. I check my e-mail frequently, but if I was in a meeting it would alert me to an issue that might be critical.

Daily OMA Use

I use OMA all of the time. Personally, I have a separate folding keyboard that attaches to my cell phone - I can send and receive e-mails without pulling up my laptop, but when I don't need it I still have a small form factor phone. Without a keyboard, you don't want to type long e-mails or replies, but you could send a short message saying "YES" (literal telephone pad keystroke sequence is: yes - Y - 999, E - 33, S - 7777 - it's the new Morse code). OMA is also great for checking calendar updates. While running from one meeting to another, you can quickly check to see if the upcoming meeting time or location has been moved.

Thanks, Kim, for the OMA expertise. Won't you consider speaking on this at the SMB Nation conference in Fall 2004? I can't resist sharing a photo from the Fall 2003 SBS hands-on lab tour where a student in San Francisco implemented OMA right in the class room (Figure 8-26).

Figure 8-26
Live from San Francisco! It's OMA and SBS 2003.

Exchange Server ActiveSync

Sync directly and with high levels of security to your Exchange mailboxes from Microsoft Windows powered devices such as Pocket PC 2002, the Pocket PC Phone, and Windows Powered SmartPhone. Stay in direct contact over the air with a server running Exchange 2003 so you can:

- **Work both online and offline.** Synchronize your e-mail messages, calendar, and contacts based on various settings from your device. Synchronization can be on-demand or scheduled. When coupled with Outlook Mobile Access, you can gain access to your Tasks list and the Global Address List.

- **Get up-to-date notifications.** Receive specially formatted short message service (SMS) messages from Exchange 2003 that wake up your Windows-powered device and prompt your device to initiate a synch.

This feature, new in Exchange 2003, enables you to set the conditions of these alerts by using your Inbox rules.

- **Choose your synchronization method.** Select from on-demand or scheduled synchronization. This includes remote access to your e-mail messages, calendar, and contacts list, and when coupled with Outlook Mobile Access, you can gain access to Tasks list and the Global Address List.

Those of you who have had Pocket PCs for a while are familiar with cradling the device at your desktop as you synchronize. You must have Outlook running on the desktop while you use Outlook to synchronize and connect to the Exchange Server, and as soon as you remove that device from the cradle, you're out of sync. That's not the case anymore with Exchange ActiveSync. You can still use the cradle, but you can also synchronize directly to Exchange over a wireless connection. Exchange ActiveSync does integrate with the desktop ActiveSync. So any settings you've created from your desktop translate over to the device and can be altered there. Any settings from the device translate over to the desktop.

Real Outlook 2003 Used Remotely

This section speaks to the ability to utilize your real Outlook 2003 client application across the Internet and connect to your SBS 2003 server machine. This might be used in lieu of OWA. There are two ways to make real Outlook speak to SBS 2003's Exchange Server 2003 messaging application: VPN and RPC over HTTP. The VPN method is fairly straightforward. You simply establish a VPN connection (discussed in the next section below) and launch your Outlook 2003 client application. Your mailbox is then presented to you.

But a more hip, cool, and exciting way to remotely connect your Outlook 2003 client application to SBS 2003 is to use RPC over HTTP. RPC, which stands for "remote procedure call," is how Outlook 2003 communicates over with Exchange Server 2003 on a local area network (LAN). The difference is that you are going to do it remotely over the Internet without having to first establish a VPN connection or present other authentication stuff like smart cards or security tokens. This allows a remote worker to use real Outlook 2003 and get through the firewall.

> BEST PRACTICE: Be advised there are some minimum requirements to using this cool messaging retrieval method. The client computer must be running Windows XP Professional with XP Service Pack 1 (SP1) and have the Microsoft Knowledge Base article 331320 updates installed. You must be running SBS 2003 (which includes Windows Server 2003 and Exchange Server 2003). The Exchange Server 2003 must be configured to allow connections via HTTP (fortunately, this is enabled by default in SBS 2003). You can see HTTP connection support in Exchange Server 2003 in SBS 2003 from **Start**, **Server Management**, **Advanced Management**, **SPRINGERSLTD (Exchange)**, **Servers**, **Springers1**, **Protocols**, **HTTP**, **Exchange Virtual Server**. Notice the virtual server is configured and running (compare this to the POP3 virtual server that is not).

Given the baseline prerequisites have been met, complete the following procedure.

1. On the remote client computer (**NormLap**), have **NormH** log on locally with the password **Purple3300**.
2. Launch Outlook 2003 from **Start**, **E-mail**. If this is the first time you've launched Outlook 2003, complete the configuration screens to configure Exchange e-mail to point to SPRINGERS1 for the user Norm Hasborn.
3. Click Tools, **E-mail accounts**. The E-mail accounts wizard commences.
4. Select **View or Change existing e-mail accounts** and click **Next**.
5. Select the **Exchange e-mail account** on the **E-mail Accounts** page and click **Change**.
6. Click **More Settings** and select the **Connections** tab on the Microsoft Exchange properties dialog box.
7. Under **Exchange over the Internet**, select **Connect to my Exchange mailbox using HTTP**. This is shown in Figure 8-27.

Figure 8-27
Selecting the option to connect over the Internet to your Exchange-based mailbox.

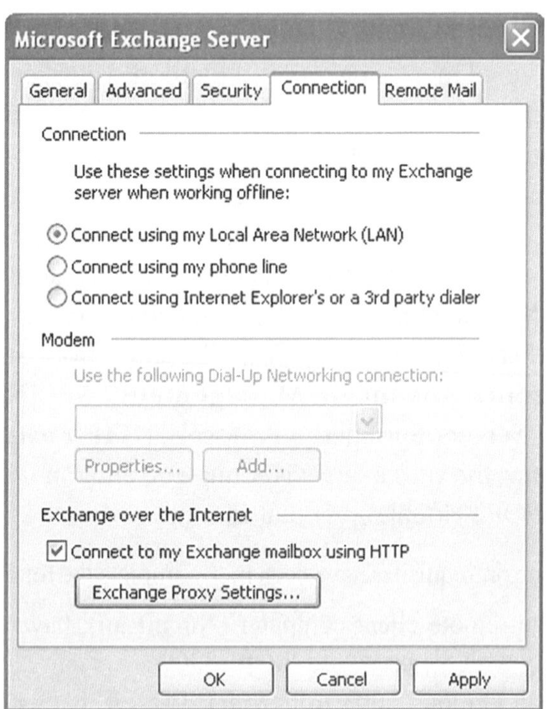

BEST PRACTICE: So let me guess. You don't see the menu option in Step 7 above. If that is the case, you didn't download and apply the patch specified above (331320). This can be found as www.microsoft.com/technet by entering **331320** in the **Search** field. The Microsoft search result should look similar to article page in Figure 8-28. Apply it now and restart the above procedure. See you back at Step 7, mate!

Notes:

Figure 8-28
Download and install this to complete the Outlook 2003 RPC over HTTP example.

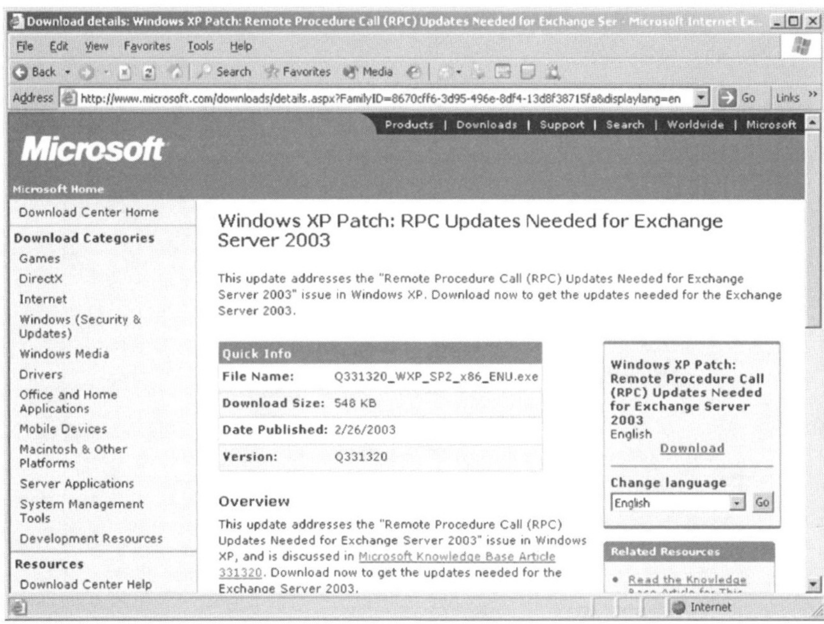

8. Click on the **Exchange Proxy Setting** button.
9. Complete the **Exchange Proxy Settings** screen with **https://springers1.springersltd.com** and verify the **Connect using SSL only** checkbox is selected. This is shown in Figure 8-29. Accept the default settings and click **OK**.
10. Click **OK** to close the **Microsoft Exchange properties** dialog box.
11. Click **OK** when notified you will need to restart **Outlook**.
12. Click **Next** on the **E-mail** Accounts wizard, followed by **Finish**.
13. Close and start Outlook again. Outlook 2003 will appear and ready for your use.

Figure 8-29
Completing the final RPC over HTTP steps for Outlook 2003.

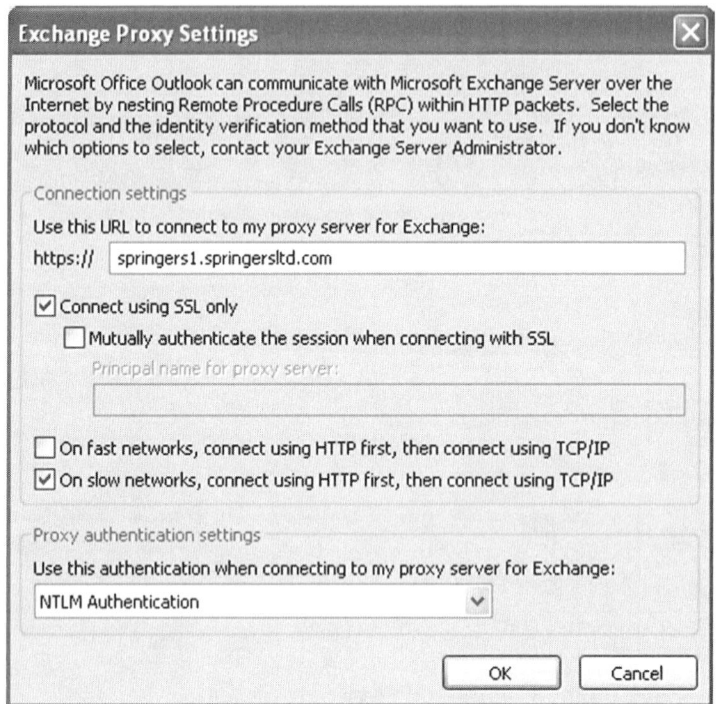

BEST PRACTICE: How 'bout a little bit more discussion on RPC over HTTP. Try on this advanced stuff for size. As you might have guessed, Outlook 2003 is capable of wrapping an HTTP/HTTPS header around each MAPI RPC request. This gives Outlook 2003 the capability of communication to the Exchange Server using direct HTTP or HTTPS. With the correct configuration (such as you did above), this feature allows a rich client experience to a corporate mailbox server over the Internet (as you know by now) where no RPC ports or VPN are required. Where Exchange front-end servers have been deployed in the DMZ, these act as RPC/HTTP proxy servers to the back-ends on the corporate network (oops - I just went beyond the scope of SBS there).

The Windows RPC over HTTP feature provides an RPC client (in this case, Outlook 2003) with the ability to establish connections across the Internet by tunneling the RPC traffic over HTTP. Because standard RPC communication is not designed for use on the Internet and doesn't work well with perimeter firewalls, RPC over HTTP makes it possible to use RPC clients in conjunction with perimeter firewalls (again, this is kinda beyond the scope of SBS). If the RPC client can make an HTTP connection to a remote computer running Internet Information Services (IIS), the client can connect to any available server on the remote network and execute remote procedure calls. Furthermore, the RPC client and server programs can connect across the Internet - even if both are behind firewalls on different networks.

So now for a real advanced issue! You and I have likely read popular trade journal media stories that the RPC stack on Windows (NT/2000/XP/2003) having been exploited by hackers (Blaster). Hell - you might have seen it! So is RPC over HTTP vulnerable to this type of attack? Nope would be the official reply. Nope because only authenticated users are allowed access to RPC over HTTP. That's why you're prompted to log on in again when you try to get Outlook to connect to the Exchange server using RPC over HTTP. The cited exploit could only use anonymous access to RPC.

And that's that!

VPN Connectivity

Building on the high-level VPN discussion we had in Chapter 5, this section is gonna do the step-by-step thing to have Norm Hasborn VPN in from his trusty HP Evo N800c laptop.

BEST PRACTICE: If you have run the Remote Access Wizard, you can then run the Connect My Remote Computer to the Network link in RWW to install Connection Manager on the mobile laptop or home computer. Here is the key point. Connection Manager automates the process of establishing a VPN connection to the SBS

2003 network. Connection Manager can be used across any type of connection (such as dial-up modem).

Connection Manager can be installed three ways:

- Add User Wizard/Setup Computer Wizard: You can specify that Connection Manager should be installed for a user on a machine. Revert to discussion in the latter part of Chapter 4 to refresh your memory on this. This approach will place a shortcut on the client computer desktop to run Connection Manager and initiate the VPN session.

- Connection Manager diskette. Yes, diskettes still exist in SBS 2003! This diskette can be created and given to an employee to take home to easily set up the VPN connection to the SBS 2003 network. Create the Connection Manager diskette from the Create Remote Connection Disk link on the Manage Client Computers page under Standard Management in the Server Management Console.

- RWW: Pick Download Connection Manager from RWW, which is what we'll do in the following procedure.

BEST PRACTICE: Connection Manager will only work with a FQDN that you've registered as a resource record with your ISP to point to the wild-side NIC card on the SBS 2003 server machine. If you want to use the wild-side IP address, you'll have to configure the connection manually.

VPN Step-by-Step Procedure

Time to have Norm VPN into SPRINGERS!

1. Log on locally as **NormH** using the password **Purple3300** on his laptop, NormLap.
2. Click **Start**, **Internet** to launch Internet Explorer.
3. Type **springers1.springersltd.com/remote** in the **Address** field.
4. Respond affirmatively to the security alerts (**OK**, **Yes**)

5. On the RWW logon screen, log on as **NormH** with the password **Purple3300**. But if you want to avoid the message in Figure 8-30, then deselect the **I'm using a public or shared computer** checkbox.

Figure 8-30
Microsoft will not allow Connection Manager to run on a public or shared computer.

6. Select **Download Connection Manager**. Click **OK** after reading the warning that you should ensure all users have strong passwords after you install Connection Manager.
7. Click **Open** on the **File Download** dialog box to open **Connection Manager** (sbspackage.exe).
8. Click **Yes** when asked if you want to install the connection to SBS 2003 in the **Connect to Small Business Server** dialog box. The installation process commences.
9. On the desktop, double-click on the **Shortcut to Connect to Small Business Server**.
10. Complete the **Connect to Small Business Server** logon box, as seen in Figure 8-31. Type **NormH** in the **User** name field, and **Purple3300** in the **Password** field. Click **Connect**. Your computer will be registered on the SBS network.

Figure 8-31
Simple stuff, Maynard! Connecting via the Connection Manager approach shields users from having to manually configure the VPN stuff on their computer.

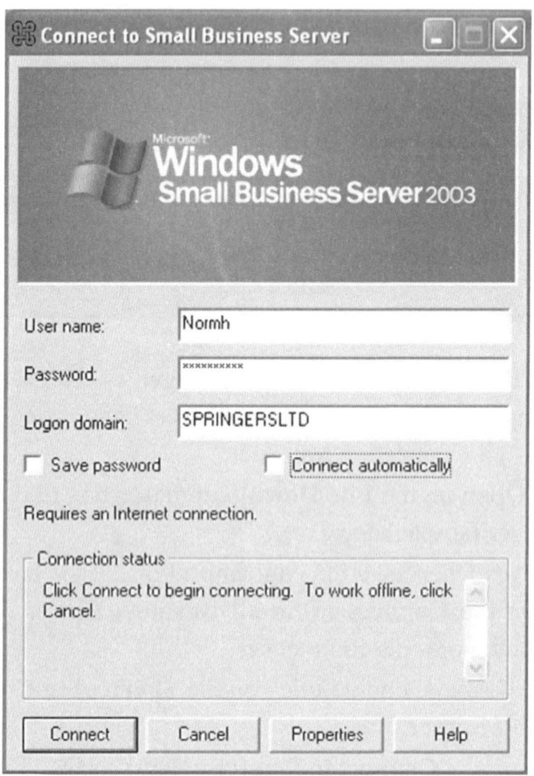

You have now established a VPN connection to the corporate network and the client computer acts as a "node" on the LAN at this point. The visual evidence of this will be a green dancing computer (connection icon) in the lower right corner of the screen. VPN connections are often appropriate to access network resources from afar and run business databases (where you truly need to be a network node).

Under the Hood: VPN

So what's the technical view of the VPN connection just made? Figure 8-32 shows the port-activity related to the VPN connection.

Figure 8-32

Observe that Port 1723 is being used for the VPN connection between a remote computer and SBS 2003.

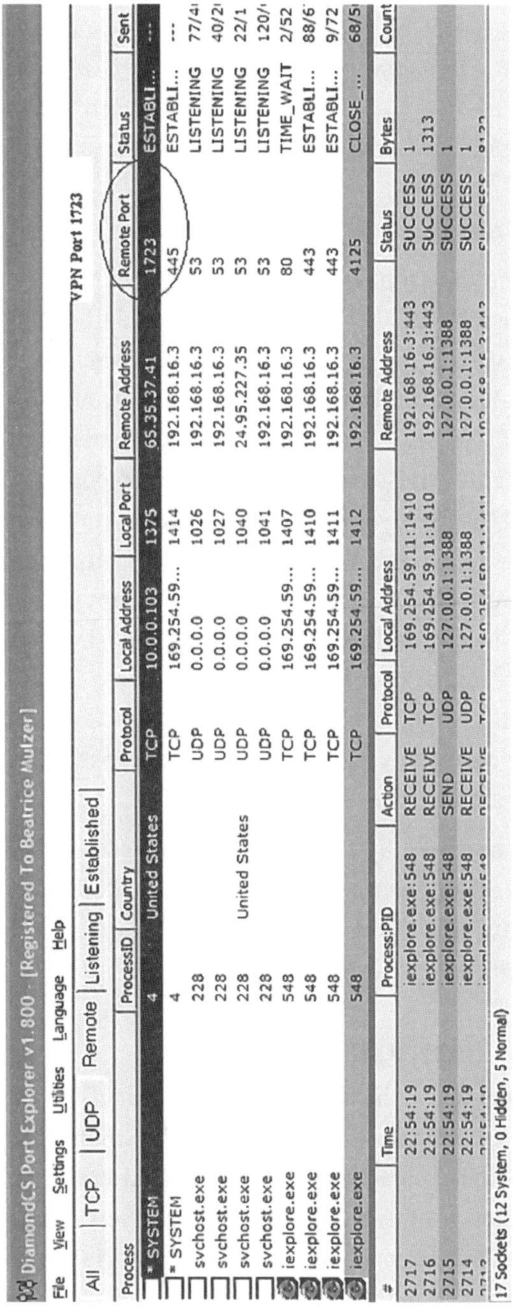

DiamondCS Port Explorer v1.800 - [Registered To Beatrice Mulzer]

File View Settings Utilities Language Help

All | TCP | UDP | Remote | Listening | Established

VPN Port 1723

Process	ProcessID	Country	Protocol	Local Address	Local Port	Remote Address	Remote Port	Status	Sent
* SYSTEM	4	United States	TCP	10.0.0.103	1375	65.35.37.41	1723	ESTABLI...	---
* SYSTEM	4		TCP	169.254.59...	1414	192.168.16.3	445	ESTABLI...	---
svchost.exe	228		UDP	0.0.0.0	1026	192.168.16.3	53	LISTENING	77/4
svchost.exe	228		UDP	0.0.0.0	1027	192.168.16.3	53	LISTENING	40/2
svchost.exe	228	United States	UDP	0.0.0.0	1040	24.95.227.35	53	LISTENING	22/1
svchost.exe	228		UDP	0.0.0.0	1041	192.168.16.3	53	LISTENING	120/
iexplore.exe	548		TCP	169.254.59...	1407	192.168.16.3	80	TIME_WAIT	2/52
iexplore.exe	548		TCP	169.254.59...	1410	192.168.16.3	443	ESTABLI...	88/6
iexplore.exe	548		TCP	169.254.59...	1411	192.168.16.3	443	ESTABLI...	9/72
iexplore.exe	548		TCP	169.254.59...	1412	192.168.16.3	4125	CLOSE_...	68/5

#	Time	Process:PID	Action	Protocol	Local Address	Remote Address	Status	Bytes	Count
2717	22:54:19	iexplore.exe:548	RECEIVE	TCP	169.254.59.11:1410	192.168.16.3:443	SUCCESS	1	
2716	22:54:19	iexplore.exe:548	RECEIVE	TCP	169.254.59.11:1410	192.168.16.3:443	SUCCESS	1313	
2715	22:54:19	iexplore.exe:548	SEND	UDP	127.0.0.1:1388	127.0.0.1:1388	SUCCESS	1	
2714	22:54:19	iexplore.exe:548	RECEIVE	UDP	127.0.0.1:1388	127.0.0.1:1388	SUCCESS	1	

17 Sockets (12 System, 0 Hidden, 5 Normal)

BEST PRACTICE: Regarding the day-to-day use of VPN connectivity in SBS 2003, I suggest you view this as a dial-on-demand approach. Whenever I've seen SBS sites that view the VPN area as full-time, 7/24 connectivity between branch offices, I've actively discouraged such thinking, because SBS isn't positioned as a branch office solution. But it's fine if a traveling Norm Hasborn needs to VPN into the SPRINGERS network to do some voodoo.

VPN and NAT-T

Finally, it's beyond the scope of this text and it's something I'll pursue in the advanced SBS book later (with step-by-step procedures), but be advised there is an issue with respect to having VPN connections when you place a hardware-based firewall router out in front of SBS 2003 and want to tunnel into the SBS network (especially if you're adhering to the best practice of a dual firewall). This area is NAT-T over IPSec across the firewall. Technically speaking, IPSec NAT Traversal (NAT-T) allows IPSec clients and server to work when behind a NAT. To use NAT-T, both the remote access VPN client and the remote access server must be IPSec NAT-T-capable. IPSec NAT-T provides UDP encapsulation of IPSec packets to enable Internet Key Exchange (IKE) and Encapsulating Security Payload (ESP)-protected traffic to pass through a NAT. IKE automatically detects that a NAT is present and uses User Datagram Protocol-Encapsulating Security Payload (UDP-ESP) encapsulation to enable ESP-protected IPSec traffic to pass through the NAT.

IPSec NAT-T is supported by the Windows Server 2003 family. As such, it's supported in SBS 2003. Your next step might be to delve deeper into the issue with the Microsoft Press Windows Server 2003 Resource Kit or look up some articles on TechNet.

Terminal Services

An oldie but a goodie in the world of mobility and remote connectivity is Terminal Services. Funny how times change. My Small Business Server 2000 Best Practices book had an entire chapter dedicated to Terminal Services. This book has a mere section of discussion, as Terminal Services has become a well-established remote management tool that doesn't warrant extensive discussion in the SBS 2003 time frame.

By default, Terminal Services is implemented in remote administration mode. This allows two users to connect remotely for administrative and management purposes without special licensing. Terminal Services has another mode called "application sharing mode" that is most commonly associated with a server machine (acting as a member server) dedicated to serving Terminal Services sessions to many remote mobile workers simultaneously.

BEST PRACTICE: I mentioned it early in the book and I'll do so again. Never ever place Terminal Services in application sharing mode on the SBS 2003 server machine. Microsoft doesn't give you the option to do this with SBS 2003 and please don't delve deep under the hood to try and figure out how to do it!

With Terminal Services, you enjoy a remote computing session with the server, with only screen activity passed to the remote client computer. This results in a very "fast" remote computing experience, but it's not as a network node. It's kinda like PCAnywhere just pushing screens! But remember that in its native form (remote administration mode) in SBS 2003, Terminal Services is designed to manage the server machine (again, an additional member server would be the way for everyone to enjoy Terminal Services).

BEST PRACTICE: I'd be remiss if I didn't honor the fact that Terminal Services has some funky licensing issues. Read the latest at www.microsoft.com/terminalservices.

You will work with Terminal Services again in Chapter 11 to manage the SBS 2003 network for SPRINGERS.

Advanced Topics

How 'bout an advanced bushel of "quick hitters" on mobility and remote connectivity before we move on to the next chapter? Cool!

- **VPN and Terminal Services expectation management.** Something I spend tons of time on in my SMB Consulting Best Practices book relates to VPN versus Terminal Services. An SBS customer will hear the VPN buzz word and ask you to come out to their house and set it up so that she can VPN into to SBS network back at the office. Upon completing your duties, she is disappointed that "nothing changed" and the only evidence is a dancing green computer in the lower right. Turns out many customers really want to use Terminal Services with its coolness of having a remote session, but they didn't know to ask for it.

- **HTTP compression is enabled by default.** One of the buzz words floating around building 43 in Redmond, where the Microsoft SBS development and marketing teams are housed, is HTTP Compression. HTTP compression speeds up OWA and is turned on by default in SBS 2003. To see for yourself, expand **Advanced Management** in the **Server Management** console. Expand **SPRINGERSLTD (Exchange)**, **Servers**, **SPRINGERS1**, **HTTP**. Right-click on **Exchange Virtual Server** and select **Properties**. Select the **Settings** tab. Observe that **Compression** is set to **High**.

- **Shared Modem Service removed.** I mentioned it earlier in the book and it's true. The Shared Modem Service, which facilitated outbound remote connectivity (such as dialing up a bulleting board system), can not be natively accomplished in SBS 2003. But leave it to Burl, the SBS consultant who works for me, to find a couple of third-party modem-sharing solutions: Spartacom (www.spartacom.com/products/modemshare.htm) and DialOut/Server (www.pcmicro.com/dialoutserver/).

BEST PRACTICE: So you're thinking about pulling a fast one, eh? Not so fast, pardner. When you upgrade from SBS 2000 to SBS 2003, you lose the Shared Modem Service. So the old upgrade switch-a-roo won't work, buddy boy. Sorry.

- **KBase article 821438.** As of this writing, you should put this on your SBS 2003 radar screen for RWW. This article, titled "FIX: Antivirus Programs May Cause Some Web Applications to Restart Unexpectedly," relates to SBS 2003 in that RWW might be affected by this (your antivirus program could impact RWW).

- **License Ticks.** This is an interesting question from SBS 2003 hands-on labs students, in nearly every town, related to RWW and licensing. Basically some folks were looking for a way to purchase few client access licenses (CALs) and have many folks log on remotely (essentially for free). The answer I received from a Microsoft product manager was "No and no!" The Windows authentication process during the RWW logon "ticks" against the SBS CAL count. You gotta pay full freight for the remote users.

- **Third-party.** Third-party mobile worker/remote connectivity solutions you could be aware of include Symantec's infamous PCAnywhere (version 11, $199.95). A popular grassroots solution is VNC (www.realvnc.com) shareware that relies on contributions, t-shirt sales, and mouse pad sales). Take a look at GoToMy PC, which was acquired by Citrix in late December 2003 (see the CRN article at www.crn.com/sections/BreakingNews/breakingnews.asp?ArticleID=46811). Also consider learning more about NetSupport 8.1 as a remote management tool (www.mcpmag.com/reviews/products/article.asp?EditorialsID=458). See Frank Ohlhorst's column in a moment.

Next Steps

You guessed it. Forward to dig deeper into the remote connectivity area. There are entire books on remote connectivity, VPN, and the like. A quick search at Amazon revealed several capable books on VPN computing, such as Stephen Northcutt's *Inside Network Perimeter Security: The Definitive Guide to Firewalls, Virtual Private Networks (VPNs), Routers, and Intrusion Detection Systems* (Que, ISBN: 0735712328).

Notes:

Guest Column

Beyond Remote Desktop, the path to remote control.

Frank J. Ohlhorst

Small Business Server 2003 does a wonderful job of bundling remote access capabilities, but there are some drawbacks to how the product goes about that. First off, there are some minimum requirements that must be met for those features to be viable, namely having Windows XP professional on the client PCs. That requirement leaves those using earlier operating systems out in the cold. Another limitation is that Microsoft's Remote Desktop Connection uses Terminal Services, in other words it is a remote session, not a remote control solution. That prevents sharing the desktop with a remote user, a key requirement for training or troubleshooting problems remotely.

To overcome those limitations, integrators can turn to several third party vendors for remote control packages, ranging from Symantec's PCanywhere to hosted services such as GoToMyPC.com, but selecting one of those products requires an additional expense, which can be a hard sell, especially as SBS2003 includes the "remote desktop connection" feature.

Savvy integrators can turn to a freeware/open source product called VNC (Virtual Network Computing), which can be downloaded from www.realvnc.com.

What makes VNC unique (beyond it being free) is that it is a multiplatform product, in other words you can control a windows system from a linux system or solaris system or vice versa and VNC is quite compact and easy to use. VNC is a two part product, there is a server component and viewer component. The server component is installed on the system to be controlled, while the remote user uses the viewer component to take control of a remote system. VNC is a barebones product, and just offers basic remote control capabilities, with that in mind there are a few tricks integrators need to know to use the product. First off, VNC will not search for a system on the network, you must know the destination system's IP address. Secondly, you will need access to the internal network to connect to a system. That can be a problem, but one easily solved by just using the included VPN server that comes with SBS2003. Once you have established a VPN connection, just input the IP Address of the target PC into the VNC viewer application, enter a password and the remote control session becomes active.

While third party products may offer more robust features, such as file transfer and search features, integrators will find that VNC fits the bill for most remote support needs and at a price that can't be beat.

Summary

I started the chapter emphasizing how important it is for mobile workers to have robust remote connectivity. SBS 2003 is positioned very well to support these individuals with services such as the amazing RWW and an impressive update to OWA. You were educated on other mobility matters such as VPN and Terminal Services. So now it's your moment to fly away and join the ranks of the upwardly mobile!

See you next chapter.

Chapter 9
Faxing

In working with SBS as both a user and consultant, I've noticed that the true value of some of its features can only be appreciated over time. SBS's faxing capability is one such feature.

The faxing topic is appropriately placed here, later rather than sooner, because it is usually one of those features my clients suddenly discover well after the installation and deployment of the SBS solution. Whereas the main priorities out of the gate for most SBS sites are Internet connectivity, e-mail, and being secure, faxing is usually something I can demonstrate when things settle down and I have the client's undivided attention. After other core SBS features, such as Outlook 2003, are accepted and widely used, the time is ripe to introduce faxing.

To balance my introduction of the faxing topic, full disclosure is necessary. I have some clients who view faxing as akin to religion. Implementing an electronic, network-based faxing solution, such as that found in SBS, acted as a key driver in their approval of the SBS network implementation project. And not only do I know this firsthand from selected clients, but I also know it from the e-mails you—the readers of my past SBS books—have sent me. Many of you commented at length how important faxing is in a small business environment networked with SBS. In fact, the dialog between reader and writer (that's me) revealed a couple of interesting points:

- Faxing, when used, is considered very important.
- In general, SBSers were disappointed with the reliability and capability of the faxing application in the SBS 4.x era (late 1990s).

- SBSers in the past (specifically, the SBS 4.x era) have opted to deploy third-party faxing solutions, such as GFI Fax, instead of using the native faxing capabilities inside SBS.

- Readers also reported that they truly got what they paid for in fax modems. Those who went with the low-cost modems (often included with workstations) frequently experienced poor performance. Contrast that with the experience of those who invested in a superior fax modem such as the external V.Everything modem. For an investment of about $250 USD, the folks using the V.Everything modem found that they could achieve five 9's or six sigma of reliability with the Shared Fax Service in SBS. It just flat out works!

The good news about the Shared Fax Service is that Microsoft listened over the years to the feedback on faxing within the SBS community. In the prior SBS 2000 release (the predecessor to SBS 2003), the fax application, is one area that received some of the greatest attention. And the results showed. Truth be told, it was actually a crack team of developers at Microsoft Israel who "rewrote" or reprogrammed the fax application from the ground up to take advantage of a more stable and robust Windows 2000 code base. This occurred in the summer of 2000. I share this historical insight with you because knowing how we got to where we're at with faxing in SBS 2003 makes you wiser about the faxing function offered in SBS. That is, I'm providing historical context for ya! More important, if SBS previously lost your trust with respect to faxing, I think this release will restore that trust.

BEST PRACTICE: It's the crime of the century. It's the Shared Fax Service caper. It's a big brother ripping off a little brother. What am I getting to? That the Shared Fax Service that was built for SBS 2000 just after the beginning of the new century was stolen by the Windows Server team for inclusion in the traditional Windows Server 2003 family. That's right! The Shared Fax Service perfected for SBS was soooo good that it's been, shall we say, borrowed for the other server products at Microsoft. In the world of intellectual property, there is certainly no greater compliment than theft, so the Fax Service developed for SBS being co-opted for the other Microsoft Servers operating systems is quite an affirmation of its value!

In the first part of the chapter, basic SBS faxing is defined as well as configured. You will also learn how to send and receive a fax. In the second half of the chapter, I discuss fax reporting and other advanced fax topics.

SBS Faxing Defined!

One of the first hurdles to overcome when generating excitement for the faxing function is to educate both yourself and the SBS users as to what faxing really is. In this secular world of atoms, bricks, and mortar, people have long known faxing as the capability to feed a page into a desktop device and send the contents of the page to another fax machine at a distant location. The SBS faxing function, shown in detail in Figure 9-1, includes:

- Sending and receiving faxes via the fax modem attached to the SBS server machine
- SBS's capability to save faxes to a folder titled Inbox (see the Inbox folder in Figure 9-1)
- SBS's capability to print faxes automatically to a network printer (see the Fax Printer in Figure 9-1)
- SBS's capability to e-mail the faxes to a designated recipient (see the SBS User Workstation in Figure 9-1)
- SBS's capability to save faxes in Windows SharePoint Services (WSS in Figure 9-1)

Notes:

Figure 9-1
Basic SBS faxing function.

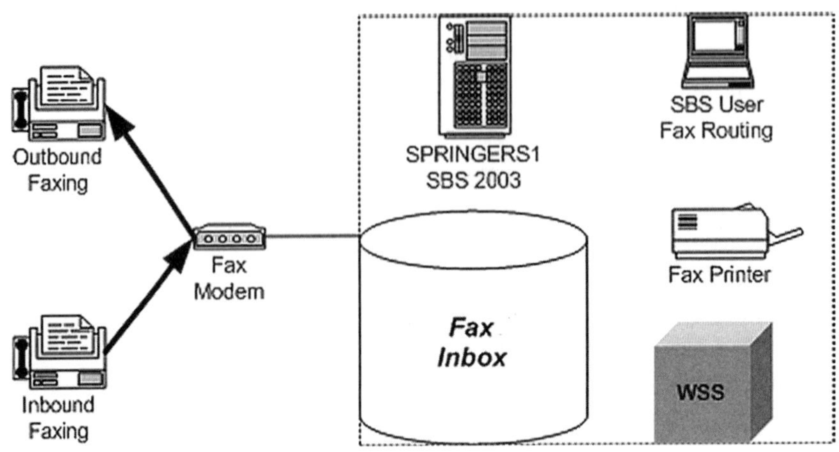

Outbound Faxes

One of the first questions SBS users ask regarding faxing is "How do you get the document into the computer?" This question, when unanswered, poses such a mental block that I've seen small businesses not embrace the powerful SBS fax capabilities. Here is the answer to this "fear of faxing" question. In reality, you will continue to use your existing fax machine for odd-sized outgoing documents, such as *Dilbert* comic strips that you're faxing to friends and family. You will likely continue to use the existing fax machine to transmit documents, such as letters, that need your signature (although later I'll show you how to scan your signature for your letters). And you'll probably use your fax machine to transmit handwritten notes. So there, I've now said it and clarified a major point of contention surrounding SBS faxing: You'll most likely continue to use your existing fax machine for very specific reasons.

But outbound faxing is in no way a total loser, either. Remember way back (in the first third of the book) when I discussed the landscaping company? The CEO saw his greatest potential with outbound faxing, targeted to his landscaping customers. His idea was to send out spring planting notices. Here, the outbound faxing capability would be integrated with his Outlook Contacts, something that is easily done. More important, this fine gentleman saw the business purpose of using the faxing capabilities in an SBS scenario. Bless his business heart!

BEST PRACTICE: Some progressive SBS sites are using low-cost scanners to scan in odd-shaped documents for use in outbound faxing scenarios. More firms will most likely use this approach in the near future as scanners become cheaper and enjoy greater acceptance. (But heck, you can already buy a color scanner for $100, so what are you waiting for?) I'll offer one word of caution with this approach: The scanned images that result when you scan odd-shaped documents are larger than you think. Even moderate scanning activity can result in over 100MB of scanned images. As you can see, you'll quickly eat up hard disk space that you might need. (Even so, hard disks are much cheaper than just a few years ago).

A few key benefits to outbound faxing include:

- Marketing announcements and flyers
- Form letters with a scanned signature
- Standard forms your customers might request
- Other documents appropriate for broadcasting

BEST PRACTICE: Understand that the capability to fax the same document to multiple parties via SBS faxing isn't true broadcasting. Fax broadcasting, in its pure form, is a service provided by a telco with lots and lots of extra fax lines (that is, burst capacity) with the ability to get your document out to tens or hundreds of parties within a few minutes. The telco uses a pool of lines to do this and charges you accordingly for such a wonderful service.

SBS's outbound faxing capability is, shall I say, linear. Given a list of parties who are to receive the same document, the SBS server calls each party in succession and transmits the fax. Such a linear approach can indeed take hours to complete, as each fax call is made one at a time. But fear not, the good news is that this activity is automatic, meaning you do not have to attend to the process (allowing you to go home and slow-cook a great meal, go out and play golf, go to your kid's dance recital, and so on).

Inbound Faxes

SBS faxing really shines where inbound faxes are concerned. Here the SBS server machine answers the fax line when an inbound fax is arriving (the telephone line generates a ring like a normal telephone line). The fax is received by the SBS server and processed as an image file in one or all of four possible ways: printed, saved to the server's hard disk, saved to a Windows Sharepoint Services (WSS) folder, or e-mailed to a single e-mail account (or an e-mail distribution group).

SBS does not facilitate automatic routing or distribution of faxes to additional e-mail accounts like high-end stand-alone fax applications can do. Other third-party faxing solutions with more advanced features (and, I'll warn you, a much more advanced price tag) include GFI Fax, WinFax PRO (Symantec), Fax Sr., and RightFAX.

The benefits of having the SBS server machine receive a fax include:

- The capability to forward a fax image to others via e-mail.
- The capability to store fax images on the SBS server for future use or as a permanent record. You'd be surprised how important this is when your firm becomes involved in litigation (or better yet, if you're a law firm that provides legal services in the litigation area).
- The capability to refax a document to another party without any loss of fax quality (with real fax machines, when you refax a document to someone else, you suffer a significant resolution loss). I like to refer to this in techno-babble as "non-generational loss of image quality."
- The capability to use your computer network laser printer as a plain-paper fax printer, thus eliminating the curly or heat-transfer fax paper

used by older fax machines (which a surprisingly high number of small businesses still use).

- The capability to view a fax on your computer display without printing it first. Under the SBS faxing model, when you receive junk faxes or faxes that simply aren't important, you can quickly glance at them with the SBS workstation fax viewer software (which I'll discuss in a moment) and then delete the fax, never sending it to a printer.

- The capability to read faxes remotely. When faxes received by the SBS server are either forwarded to me via e-mail or simply stored on the SBS server, I can dial in and read these faxes without having to cross the bridge and drive to the office just to retrieve my faxes. This feature alone has made a huge difference for me and my SBS clients, and we've all avoided a lot of unnecessary trips into the office to pick up faxes.

- The capability to scan graphics and signatures for use on your network. I'll show you how to do this later.

- Using a third-party text-scanning application, such as GFI Fax, to convert the faxed text into text that you can manipulate in your word processing application (a technology called "Optical Character Recognition" or "OCR"). This is still an immature technology that doesn't always work correctly as yet. You still have to proofread text that was converted. One more comment on this area: Other SBSers and I have already offered our feedback to Microsoft's SBS development team that OCR would be a desirable feature in the faxing application in future SBS releases. The good news is that the SBS development team is very good about receiving sincere feedback, so I'd rate it at even or better odds that you'll see OCR in future SBS releases!

More Fax Features

A few other cool features are included with the SBS Fax Server, many of which I'll discuss in more detail later:

- Fax Modem Pool Support.Like prior releases of SBS, the current SBS 2003 release is limited to four fax devices. That's because the underlying Windows Server 2003 standard edition operating system imposes this limit (other Windows Server 2003 SKUs don't have this limit)

BEST PRACTICE: This device limitation doesn't mean that the fax service ignores exceeding devices (such as having more than four fax modems). Rather, it only means that up to four fax devices can be used to send or receive faxes at any given time. Other devices will show up during that time (in the Fax-related user interface) but they will not send or receive faxes and can not be configured to do so.

Using the default modem pool actually supports limited group faxing on outbound faxing. That is, if everyone prints to the same fax printer from the desktop, the faxes can all be sent at the same time because each fax modem would use a separate fax line to initiate its call. This discussion is conceptually similar to printer pooling.

BEST PRACTICE: This fax modem pool capability also has a role for inbound faxing. When combined with a hunt-line capability from your telco, Microsoft Fax allows you to offer never-a-busy-signal-level services for your customers trying to fax your firm. Essentially, all your customers send faxes to a single published fax line, say 206-123-1235 for SPRINGERS. If a customer attempts to send a fax, and the first fax modem is occupied, the telco's hunt capability provides the capability to have the second, third, or fourth modem receive the inbound fax call. Cool, eh?

Theoretically, all four fax modems, assuming you have that many, could receive faxes at the same time. And because a small business would almost never receive more than four faxes simultaneously, you could advertise your business as never having a busy fax line!

I should also note that a fax modem pool also facilitates simultaneous inbound and outbound faxing operations, something many small businesses can enjoy only if they have truly separate fax machines. It's a tip worth mentioning to the small business owner seeking more information on how to use multiple telephone lines and a fax modem pool.

- Fax board support. Starting with the SBS 2000 launch in Atlantic City in February 2001, a collective "halleluiah" went up with the announcement of native SBS 2000 support for fax modem boards, such as the offerings from Brooktrout. Such support continues today with SBS 2003. In fact, a representative from Brooktrout was on hand to bask in his moment of glory and answer questions (Brooktrout support in the SBS 2003 time frame is shown in Figure 9-2). This is a long-requested capability in SBS, and those who take faxing seriously greatly appreciate this capability.

- Cover Pages. The SBS Fax Server also includes a set of fax cover pages for your use. You can also create your own fax cover pages via Fax Cover Page Editor or the Microsoft Fax Viewer software. Be advised that the use of a computerized faxing solution, such as the SBS Fax Server, eliminates the ability to use the popular Post-it Fax Notes (the physical kind you paste onto manual faxes). These tiny scraps of paper, with a sticky backing, are typically attached to the header of the first fax page when using an actual fax machine. Because you can't physically attach such as a Post-it Note to a computer-generated fax, you need to be content with using SBS Fax Server-based cover pages when transmitting. You manage cover pages via the Fax (Local) object under Standard Management on the Server Management console with the Manage Cover Pages link.

- Management Control. Via the Fax (Local) object under Standard Management in the Server Management console, you can manage the fax function for your small business in SBS 2003. By default, everyone can use the fax function, something I show later in my security discussion. Member of the Fax Operators security group may manage fax queues and fax cover pages. More on fax security and control later.

Figure 9-2

Because the Fax Service in Windows Server 2003 is exactly the same in SBS 2003, Brooktrout's support for SBS 2003 is unquestioned.

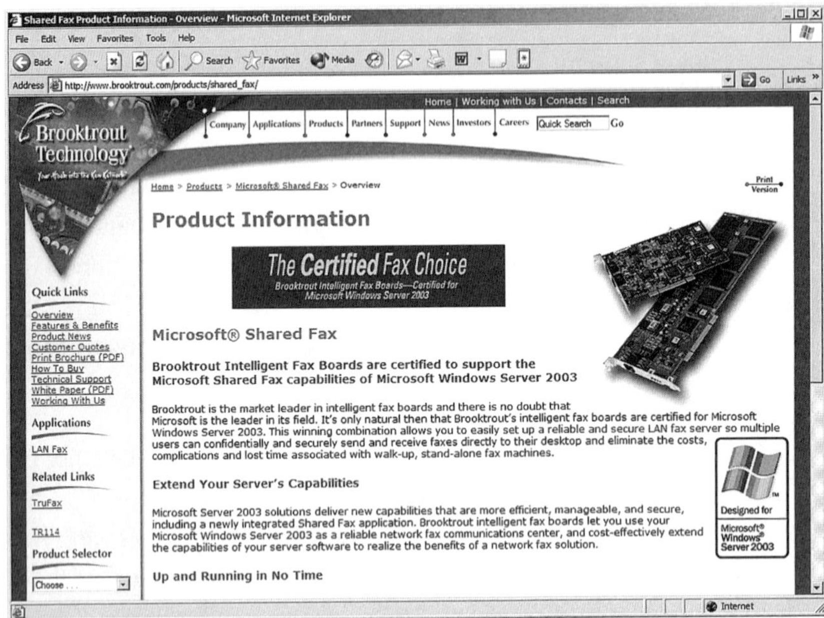

SBS Fax Components

SBS's fax capabilities can be divided into server and client components. First I'll discuss the server side, where basic configuration issues are addressed. On the client side, I'll show what components are installed on an SBS user's workstation.

> BEST PRACTICE: Before I go one sentence further, there is something you should know that was mentioned ever so briefly during the SBS setup discussion: YOU DON'T NEED TO HAVE A MODEM ATTACHED TO THE SBS SERVER MACHINE TO INSTALL AND CONFIGURE MICROSOFT FAX (I've used capitalization for emphasis – hope it worked). This is a huge improvement over prior releases of SBS and means you only need to physically attach a fax modem once you truly start to use the Microsoft Shared Fax.

The Server Side: Microsoft Fax

The actual faxing capability installed on the SBS server machine is known as Microsoft Fax. This server-side capability is installed automatically when you install SBS using the complete installation feature (which I recommend). It is comprised of the following three server-side components: Shared Fax Service Server, Shared Fax Service Manager, and Fax Console.

Shared Fax Service Server

This is the core server engine, and such a service it is (oy vay!). It is listed amongst other services (**Start**, **Server Management**, **Advanced Management**, **Computer Management (Local)**, **Services and Applications**, **Services**, **Fax**).

Shared Fax Service Manager

This is the "official" user interface to configure, manage, and monitor the Shared Fax Service. I show you this in Figure 9-3. This is accessed by clicking **Start**, **Server Management**, **Standard Management**, **Fax (Local)**.

Figure 9-3
The Shared Fax Services Manager as viewed in the Server Management console.

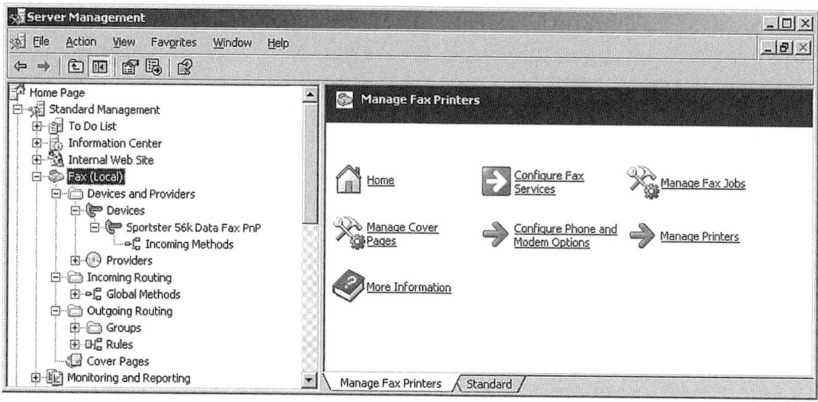

Later in the chapter I discuss the Microsoft Fax property sheet as the Swiss Army knife of faxing, where the real heavy lifting occurs. It is basically the property sheet accessed by right-clicking Shared Fax Services Manager.

Fax Console

This is more of a real-time user interface allowing you to view the sending and receiving of faxes as well as monitoring the fax queue and the all-important archiving function for sent and received faxes. This is useful for answering questions from business managers, such as “Did we receive that fax from the Ferguson Companies yesterday afternoon?” In the Fax Console, accessed from **Start**, **Server Management**, **Standard Management**, **Fax (Local)**, click the **Manage Fax Jobs** link, as shown in Figure 9-4.

Figure 9-4
Meet the Fax Console, a snap-in that runs in an MMC.

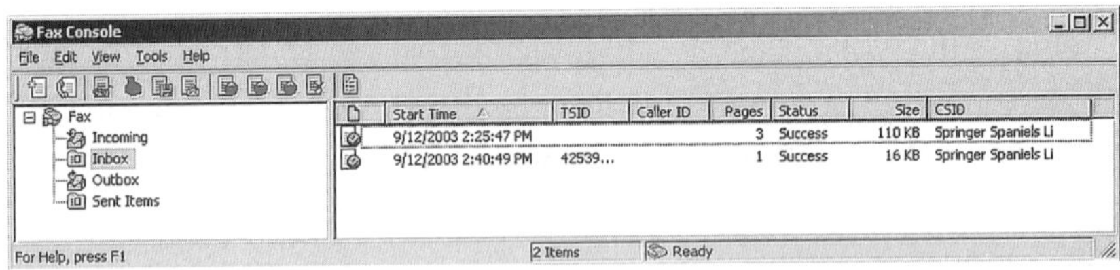

Note that there are other forms of fax reporting (to answer the “whether we got the Ferguson Companies’ fax” query) that I discuss later in the chapter.

Fax Modem

The installation of a fax modem device in SBS 2003 is truly automatic (continuing a positive trend that started in the predecessor SBS 2000 product). When you add a fax modem to the SBS server machine, it is automatically added as a device in the default fax modem pool. This fax modem is automatically configured to send but not receive.

You can also add a modem at a later date rather than when you install SBS 2003. This is a huge improvement over the first couple SBS releases (the SBS 4.x era), when fax modems had to be present and correctly detected during the installation of SBS (Chapter 3 of this book).

To see where the new fax modem was added as a device and to configure the Receive capability, simply look closely at Figure 9-3 above. Under **Fax (Local)** on the left side of the figure, observe the **Sportster 56k Data Fax PNP** modem device. You would right-click this device and notice the **Send** capability was selected, but you must select either **Auto Receive** or **Manual Receive**. You might be interested to note in SBS 2003 that the fax modem can be configured to **Manual Receive**. This wasn't possible in SBS 2000.

> BEST PRACTICE: Be sure to use high-quality fax modems with your SBS network. Assuming faxing is important to you, purchase high-quality fax modems instead of "el cheapo" modems. A favorite of many SBSers on the Yahoo-based SBS newslist (sbs2k@yahoogroups.com) is the US Robotics V.Everything fax modem. And don't forget that you can add multiple modems to support different variations of the faxing function in SBS 2003 (e.g., having one fax reserved for executives).

Fax Printer

The main Shared Fax Service functionality on the server-side that users will see is the printer called Fax. That's because said users will "print" to a device called "Fax" (the UNC path is \\SPRINGERS1\FAX) when they want to send a fax. Note that the fax printer is not used by the user to view faxes (that's handled via the Fax Console or by receiving a fax via e-mail or other methods such as WSS, which I discuss very soon!). To view the fax printer, click Start, Printers and Faxes, Fax. And for a real good time, right-click the Fax printer object, select Properties, and explore the various property sheets.

Notes:

Cover Page

You can select from several default cover pages that are sent along with the fax. The Cover Pages listing is shown in the Server Management console from **Start**, **Server Management**, **Standard Management**, **Fax (Local), Cover Pages**. Go ahead and open one of the cover pages by double-clicking it to launch the Fax Cover Page Editor. Figure 9-5 displays the Confident.cov cover page (this is the confidential cover page).

Figure 9-5

Cover page template (confident.cov).

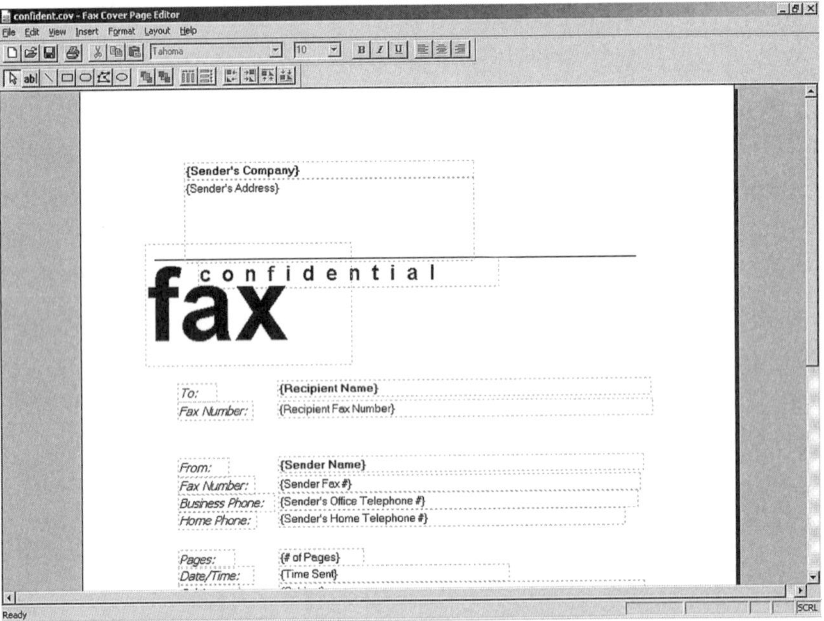

By default, a user is required to select from one of the listed cover pages when a cover page is used in a transmission.

> BEST PRACTICE: You can allow or prevent the use of personal cover pages (yes, the humorous ones) by selecting or deselecting the Allow use of personal cover pages on the Outbox tab of Fax (Local) Properties dialog box. See my discussion on the Swiss Army Knife later in the chapter for more on this topic.

The four default cover pages in SBS 2003 are stored at the following location (which is different from the SBS 2000 product):

%SystemRoot%\Documents and Settings\All Users\Application Data\ Microsoft\Windows NT\MSFax\Common Coverpages

> BEST PRACTICE: You can create a cover page for your company and have that cover page be the only fax cover page which can be used on the SBS network. To do this, right-click the **Cover Page** object beneath **Fax (Local)** and select **New**, **Cover Page** to launch the **Fax Cover Page Editor**. Create the cover page, with graphics if desired, and save the file with the *.COV extension. This new cover page you've created can now be used as a fax cover page on the SBS network. Be sure to delete the other cover pages so that your SBS users must use your new corporate fax cover sheet by default when they elect to send any cover page at all.

The Greatest Fax Improvement in SBS 2003

I've saved the best for last on the server-side discussion: the Configure Fax Services link! It's a long story, but the faxing functionality in the SBS 2000 time frame was left in the oven a few weeks longer than originally anticipated in order for it to be well done. But the chef—in this case the team at Microsoft Israel—didn't put the topping on the faxing application before delivering and presenting it at the dinner table. That is, the shared faxing application in SBS 2000 wasn't known for its attractive user interface and had to be configured manually from the property sheet discussed in the Swiss Army Knife section of this chapter (ouch!). That's changed in SBS 2003 with the Configure Fax link under Management Tasks on the To Do List. Let's run it now!

1. Log on as **Administrator** on **Springers1** with the password **Husky9999!**.
2. Launch **Server Management** from the **Start** button.
3. Select **To Do List** under **Standard Management**.
4. Click **Configure Fax**.

> BEST PRACTICE: Just revisiting one of the major methodologies of this book here. If you're tracking with me page by page, we've truly completed the To Do List in order as I've preached from early on.

Right now you will complete the Fax Configuration Wizard. In Chapter 11, you will complete the backup wizard by selecting the Configure Backup link from the To Do List. In Chapter 12, you will complete the server monitoring wizard by selecting the Configure Monitoring link from the To Do List.

5. Click **Next**.
6. Verify the information on the **Provide Company Information** page.

BEST PRACTICE: First, notice the default field information on the Provide Company Information has been taken from the company information you provided in Chapter 3 when you created the SPRINGERS1 server machine. Then notice the Company name field truncates at 20-characters, which doesn't fully spell out the full company title of Springer Spaniels Limited. Rather, it creates a funky variation of that name where "Limited" is truncated to "Li" which is unfortunate. I'd recommend that you append the Company name field to reflect something more meaningful like SPRINGERS, which I've done in Figure 9-6.

Figure 9-6
Complete the Provide Company Information screen similar to above.

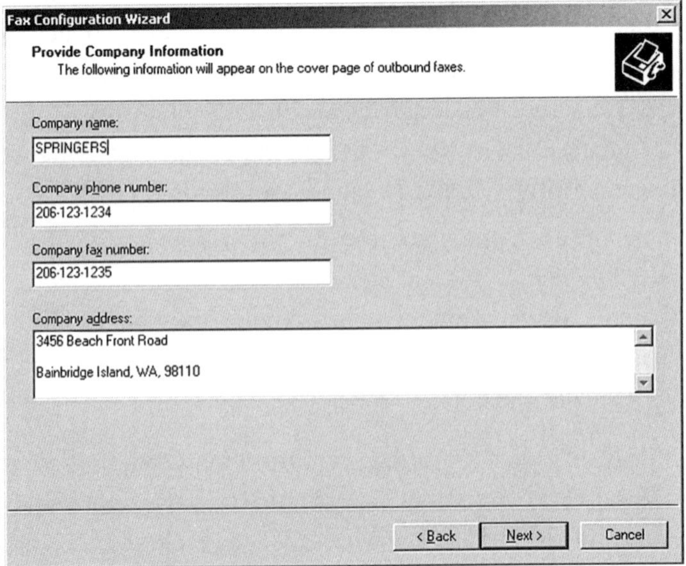

7. Click **Next**.
8. Select your fax modem on the **Outbound Fax Device** page. As seen in Figure 9-7, this is the **Sportster 56k Data Fax PnP**. Click **Next**.

Figure 9-7
The outbound fax device in the SPRINGERS methodology is a Sportster 56k Data Fax PnP.

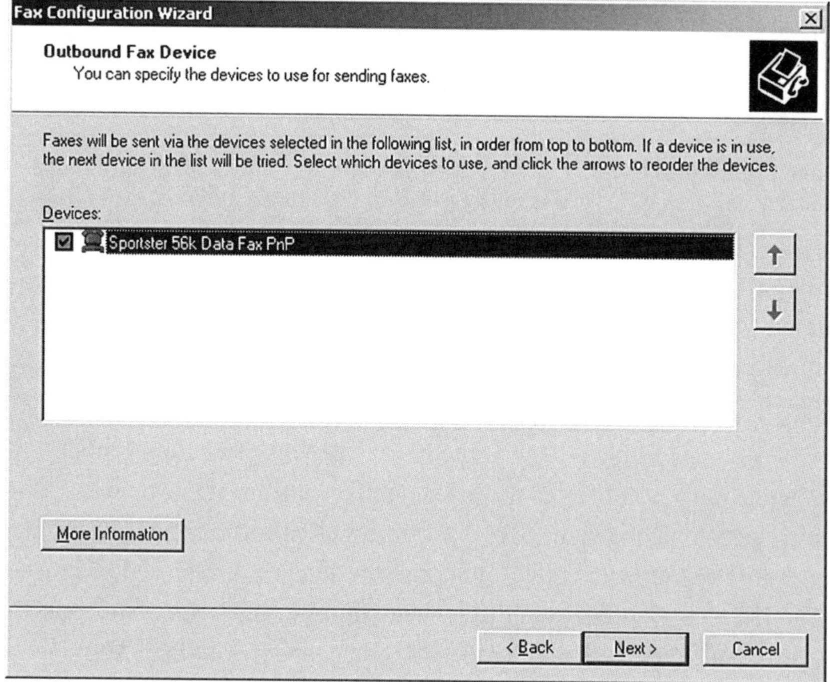

9. A similar-looking but different page to Figure 9-7 (you're eyes are not deceiving you), **Inbound Fax Device** will display the **Sportster 56k Data Fax PnP**. Accept the default setting of **Set routing destinations for all devices** and click **Next**.
10. The **Inbound Fax Routing** page appears. You will configure this extensively for SPRINGERS. Select and configure as per Table 9-1. After configuring, click **Next**.

BEST PRACTICE: This was the most difficult fax configuration to get right in the SBS 2000 time frame. That's because you had to manually configure routing from the property sheet for the fax service. We bless the Fax Configuration Wizard in SBS 2003.

Table 9-1: Inbound Fax Routing Configuration

Item	Configuration
Route through e-mail	**fax@springersltd.com**
Store in a folder	N/A (not applicable) to the Springers methodology. You will store your faxes in the Exchange public folder, not an NTFS-based folder. But if you are dying to know, the fax is stored in the Fax Store.
Store in a document library	Click the **Browse** button. You will be directed to the **CompanyWeb** (which is the SharePoint site). Select **Incoming Faxes** and click **OK** followed by another **OK**.
Print	Select **HP5** on the **Print** dialog box that appears (in the **Route incoming faxes to this printer** field). Click **OK.**

11. Save the information to your SBS network notebook folder on the completion page (click the **here** hyperlink) and click **Finish**.

You have now completed the Fax Configuration Wizard, the greatest improvement to faxing in the SBS 2003 time frame. And that, my friends, means your faxing capability is now functional for sending faxes (you will need to turn on the receiving fax capability when you right-click **Sportster 56k Data Fax PnP** modem beneath the **Fax (Local)** object under **Standard Management** in the **Server Management** console (drill down further into **Devices and Providers, Devices**).

The Client Side: SBS Faxing

On the client side, you handle the main configuration and observation activity via the Fax Console (the same one as discussed above and displayed in Figure 9-4). This tool is installed when Microsoft Shared Fax is installed.

With the Fax Console, you can send a fax (**File, Send a New Fax**), complete a User Information page, select a personal cover page (if you're allowed to), and view the server status of the computer running the Microsoft Shared Fax server-side service.

User Information

Selecting Sender **Information** from the **Tools** menu in Fax **Console** (which is launched from **Start**, **All Programs,Accessories**, **Communications**, **Fax** in Windows XP Pro; and **Start**, **Programs**, **Microsoft Shared Fax Client** in Windows 2000 Pro) allows you to complete the screen shown in Figure 9-8 so that basic user information is entered onto the fax cover pages. This, of course, would save the user time by not having to type basic identity information each time. Unfortunately, this information is not carried over from the same type of information you entered in Chapter 4 when you set up the user. Bummer.

Figure 9-8
Completing a meta-data user information screen that is used as part of the faxing process.

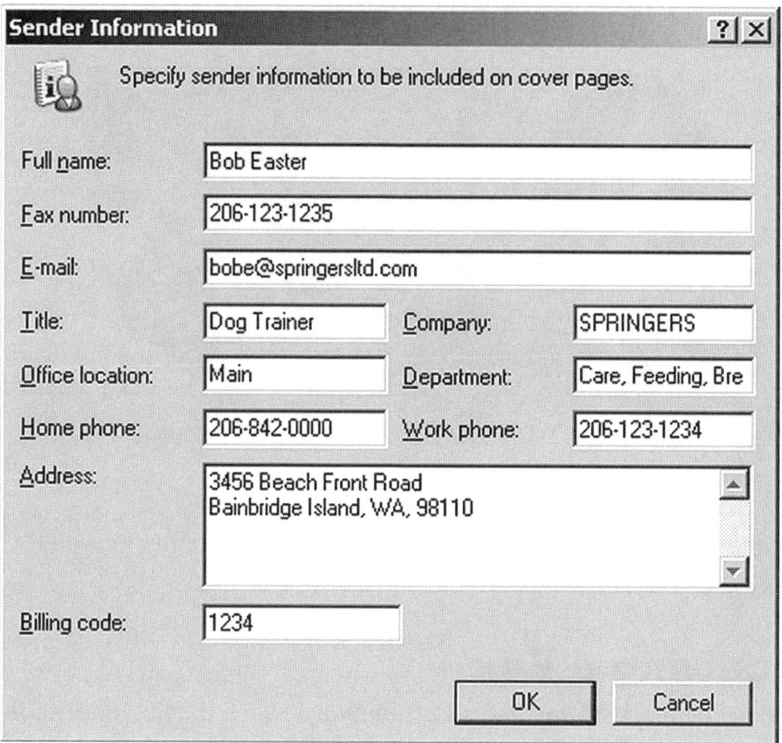

Cover Page

Select **Personal Cover Pages** from the **Tools** menu if you want to (and are allowed to) utilize personal cover pages. And just how do you create said personal cover pages at the workstation? On the **Personal Cover Pages** dialog box, click **New**, and the **Fax Cover Page Editor** will launch. You can create the fax cover pages you so desire, even adding TIF photos such as the one of Brisker and Jaeger, the two patriarchs of SPRINGERS (see Figure 9-9).

Figure 9-9
Creating a personal cover page on a less-than-serious note for SPRINGERS.

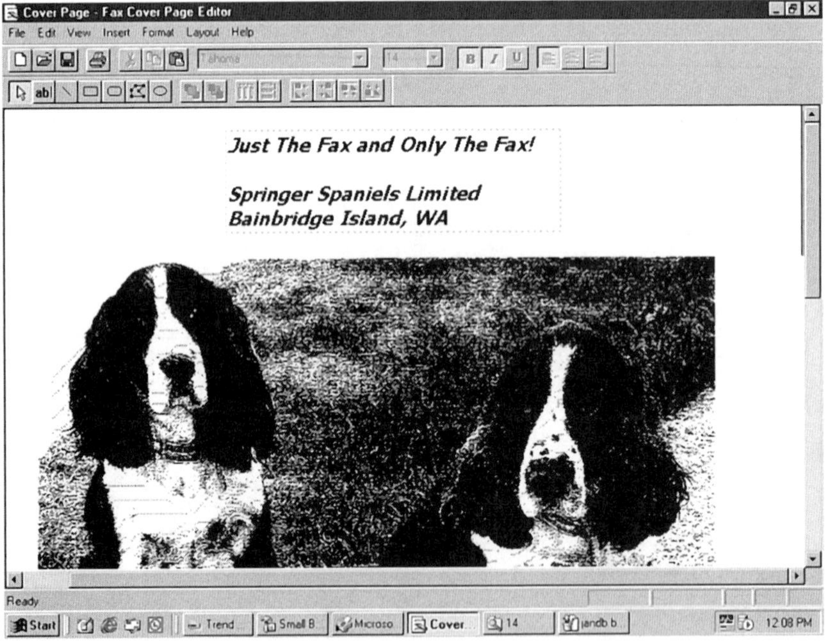

After the personal fax cover page is saved, it is listed in the **Personal Cover Pages** dialog box.

Receiving a Fax

A fax can be received any and all of four ways when the fax modem on your SBS server commences its reception: print the fax, store the fax in an NTFS folder, store the fax in Windows SharePoint Services, or e-mail the fax to an

SBS user or distribution group object (who typically redistributes or forwards the fax to the receiving party). This was discussed earlier based on the data in Table 9-1.

Viewing a Fax

Viewing a fax is truly a point-and-double-click exercise, assuming you don't want to print it out to hard copy but rather keep it in digital form. Whether you receive the fax as an attachment over e-mail or use the Fax Console at the workstation (or heck, you can even view a fax this way from the SBS server machine, but I wouldn't let your users work at the server machine), you simply double-click the ***.tif file** that represents the fax. And like magic, the application designated to view tagged information files (TIF) will display the fax. Previously, the application in a prior generation of SBS was the Kodak Viewer. In modern times, it's more likely to be the Microsoft Document Imaging Tool.

Typically a fax is viewed as an e-mail attachment (a TIF file) and I've encouraged you via the SPRINGERS methodology to send your faxes to a public folder called FAX.

Back at the SBS server machine, the SPRINGERS administrator must perform the following steps.

1. Click **Start**, **Server** Management c**onsole**.
2. **Right-click** on **Fax (Local)**.
3. Select **Properties**.
4. Click the **Security** tab.
5. Highlight **Everyone** in the **Name** field. Observe the default settings. It might be hard to believe in the SBS 2003 time frame, but fact of the matter is that the Everyone security group have limited permissions related to faxing. Therefore, we're going to grant additional fax-related permissions to Everyone to improve the functionality of the SBS faxing capability.
6. Click the **Advanced** button.
7. Select **Everyone** on the **Advanced Security Settings for Fax** dialog box and click **Edit**.
8. Select **View incoming messages archive** under **Permissions** for the purposes of viewing a fax from a workstation as part of the SPRING-

ERS methodology using the **Fax Console**. The correct permission setting is shown in Figure 9-10.

Figure 9-10

Setting the correct permission to allow a low-level user (member of the Everyone security group) to view a fax at the workstation-level.

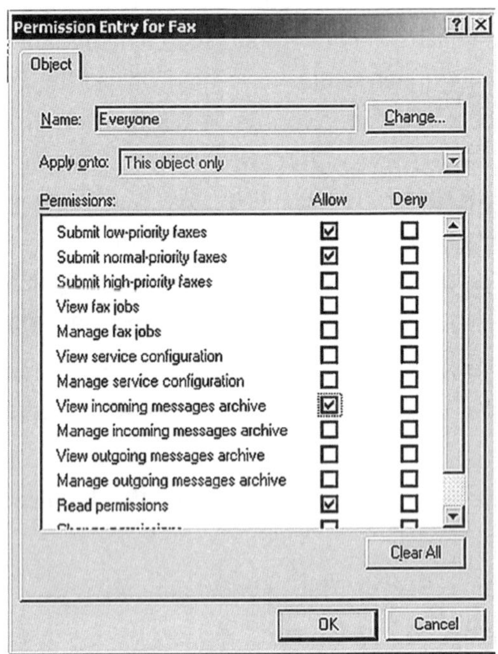

9. Click **OK**.

Now, the Fax Console, when launched at SPRINGERS users' workstations, will properly display faxes in the Inbox and the Outbox. This is a critical set of steps to perform for viewing received faxes. That's a good thing and such a fax viewed from the Inbox might appear as Figure 9-11.

Figure 9-11

Viewing an important received fax with the Fax Console. This is a tax form that was faxed to NormH and is being viewed at NormH's workstation.

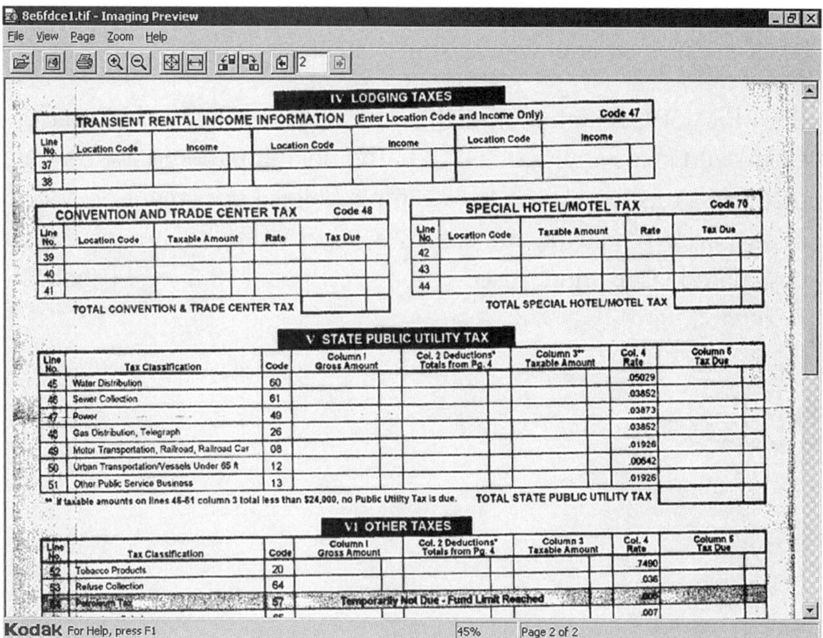

IV LODGING TAXES

TRANSIENT RENTAL INCOME INFORMATION (Enter Location Code and Income Only) Code 47

Line No.	Location Code	Income	Location Code	Income	Location Code	Income
37						
38						

CONVENTION AND TRADE CENTER TAX Code 48

Line No.	Location Code	Taxable Amount	Rate	Tax Due
39				
40				
41				
	TOTAL CONVENTION & TRADE CENTER TAX			

SPECIAL HOTEL/MOTEL TAX Code 70

Line No.	Location Code	Taxable Amount	Rate	Tax Due
42				
43				
44				
	TOTAL SPECIAL HOTEL/MOTEL TAX			

V STATE PUBLIC UTILITY TAX

Line No.	Tax Classification	Code	Column 1 Gross Amount	Col. 2 Deductions* Totals from Pg. 4	Column 3** Taxable Amount	Col. 4 Rate	Column 5 Tax Due
45	Water Distribution	60				.05029	
46	Sewer Collection	61				.03852	
47	Power	49				.03873	
48	Gas Distribution, Telegraph	26				.03852	
49	Motor Transportation, Railroad, Railroad Car	08				.01926	
50	Urban Transportation/Vessels Under 65 ft	12				.00642	
51	Other Public Service Business	13				.01926	

** If taxable amounts on lines 45-51 column 3 total less than $24,000, no Public Utility Tax is due. TOTAL STATE PUBLIC UTILITY TAX

VI OTHER TAXES

Line No.	Tax Classification	Code	Column 1 Gross Amount	Col. 2 Deductions* Totals from Pg. 4	Column 3 Taxable Amount	Col. 4 Rate	Column 5 Tax Due
52	Tobacco Products	20				.7490	
53	Refuse Collection	64				.036	
[illegible]	Petroleum Tax	57	Temporarily Not Due - Fund Limit Reached			[illegible]	
		[illegible]				.007	

BEST PRACTICE: You can't navigate to a shared fax folder on the SBS server machine in SBS 2003 like you could in SBS 4.5. You might recall that, in SBS 4.5, you could navigate from a workstation via Network Neighborhood (or My Network Places in Windows ME or Windows 2000) to the FaxStore shared on the SBS server machine and simply double-click the *tif file (representing the fax). There is no FaxStore share folder on an SBS 2003 server by default. Rather, faxes are stored in the unshared folder fax\archive that you designated when you set up SBS 2003 in Chapter 3. You'll recall we redirected the fax-related data to D: drive during setup.

> If for some reason you've got fax-sharing envy, you can easily share the fax folder on Drive D: by using Windows Explorer to navigate to the fax folder (D:\Fax), right-click, and select Sharing and Security. Select Share this folder on the Sharing tab and click OK. Now everyone could browse to this shared folder via My Network Places and read faxes (note that shares in SBS 2003 grant Everyone the Read permission by default).

When the fax is opened, you can rotate, shrink, resave, and otherwise manipulate the fax. You can even print faxes on different paper sizes.

> BEST PRACTICE: I mentioned this once early on, but I'll do so again. Odd-sized faxes are modified to fit the default paper in the printer that prints received faxes. For example, a legal document on legal-sized paper would be printed as a letter-sized document if the designated laser printer used letter-sized paper (8.5 by 11 inches) by default.

Notes:

Unusual Receive Uses

I've used the received faxes (as .TIF files) in two unusual ways. First, by having each SBS user proffer his or her signature on a piece of paper, which I fax to the SBS server machine, I effectively scan each SBS user's signature. These signature image files, which look similar to Norm Hasborn's signature in Figure 9-12, are then stored in a central location on the SBS server. In the future, when composing and faxing a letter from the desktop, all you do to add your signature to your letter is insert the signature image file. I discuss this approach in a moment under "Sending a Fax."

Figure 9-12
Scanned signature via SBS faxing.

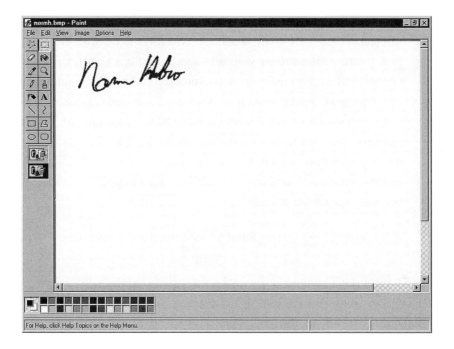

The second unusual use of fax reception is scanning artwork. Similar to scanning a signature into a .TIF file as described earlier, this function lets you also fax yourself maps, drawings, and photos. When received by the SBS fax server, the image is a .TIF image. The person receiving the fax can not only easily insert the image into word processing documents and Web pages, but can also modify and manipulate it with popular drawing applications.

Sending a Fax

Sending a fax from an SBS workstation is very simple. At its most basic level, sending a fax from an SBS workstation is nothing more than printing (via the Print command on the File menu in the application of your choice) the document you seek to fax somewhere. In other words, you simply print to the fax printer. Here's a quick list of all ways to send a faxes from an SBS workstation:

- File, Print command from a Windows-based application.
- Send To command in a Microsoft Office application.
- Microsoft Outlook e-mail. There are two ways to do this. When composing an e-mail message, you can select an Outlook Contact, Exchange Global Address List member (this is entered at the SBS server machine by creating a Contact via Active Directory Users and Computers found in the Small Business Server Administrator Console) or Personal Address Book listing with a fax telephone number. You can also fax directly by entering a fax number directly into the To: field using the following syntax: [fax:206-123-1235] (this is a sample telephone number, but you get the point).
- Fax Console by selecting Send a Fax from the File menu.

BEST PRACTICE: Many of these options give you the opportunity to send to ad hoc fax recipients. These are fax names and numbers that are entered on the fly. This type of ad hoc information is typically in a To: and Fax # field as the following step-by-step example demonstrates.

Here is a step-by-step example of how you send a fax. Norm Hasborn is sending a memo to Roni Vipauli, the lender at Small Business Savings who has loaned the money necessary for SPRINGERS to implement the SBS network.

Interestingly, you might recall from the list of SBS stakeholders in Chapter 2 that Roni's fax number is a vanity telephone number: 425-SBS-LEND. Note that SBS's faxing capability will not accommodate vanity telephone numbers; thus the number must be converted to its digital form (425-727-5363).

> BEST PRACTICE: While attempting to associate prefixes with a long distance call, I've found it is better to handle this capability manually, instead of attempting to configure such activity via the Dialing tab. Here's why. Many local prefixes really aren't dialed as an 11-digit long distance call (1-area code-telephone number) but rather as a ten-digit local call (area code-telephone number). Such oddities are best handled by SBS end users when a fax is sent.

To send a fax from a word processing program (such as Microsoft Word) using the wonderful SPRINGERS methodology:

1. At the SBS user's workstation, while working on the document you want to fax using a word processor such as Microsoft Word, select the **Print** command from the **File** menu. The **Print** dialog box is displayed.
2. In the **Select Printer** field, select **Fax** (located on SPRINGERS1) as the printer. Click Print.
3. The **Send Fax Wizard** starts. Click **Next** at the **Welcome to the Send Fax Wizard** page.
4. On the **Recipient Information** screen, complete the **To: Location:** and **Fax number:** field. You may also use an existing recipient name from the Exchange Global Address List by clicking the **Address Book** button (you will also have the chance to select **Personal Address Book** listings and **Outlook Contacts**). If you enter multiple names, these names will be listed in the **Recipient name** field. Click **Next**.
5. On the **Preparing the Cover Page** screen, click the **Select a cover page template with the following information** check box. Select the cover page of your choice, but I'll select the "dawgs.cov" personal cover page that I created while writing this book (you saw it in Figure 9-9). Click **Next**.
6. On the **Schedul**e screen, confirm that **Now** is selected under **When do you want to send this fax?** and Click **Next**. Note that there are options for sending during a discount period (which is defined by an administrator at the server level) or a specific time. You will also

note that the user in this example, NormH, can only select the Normal or Low faxing priorities. (By default, typically users such as NormH can not send a high-priority fax, so that option is grayed out, but the high-priority fax permission could be set on the Security tab displayed early in the chapter.).

7. Observe the summary information on the **Completing the Send Fax Wizard** and click **Finish**.

Assuming no problems are encountered, the fax will be sent. In Figure 9-13, the fax is awaiting transmission in the Outbox of the Fax Console.

Figure 9-13

Before you know it, this fax will be in the hands of George Sedoakes. When the fax modem successfully transmits, the fax will move from the Outbox to Sent Items.

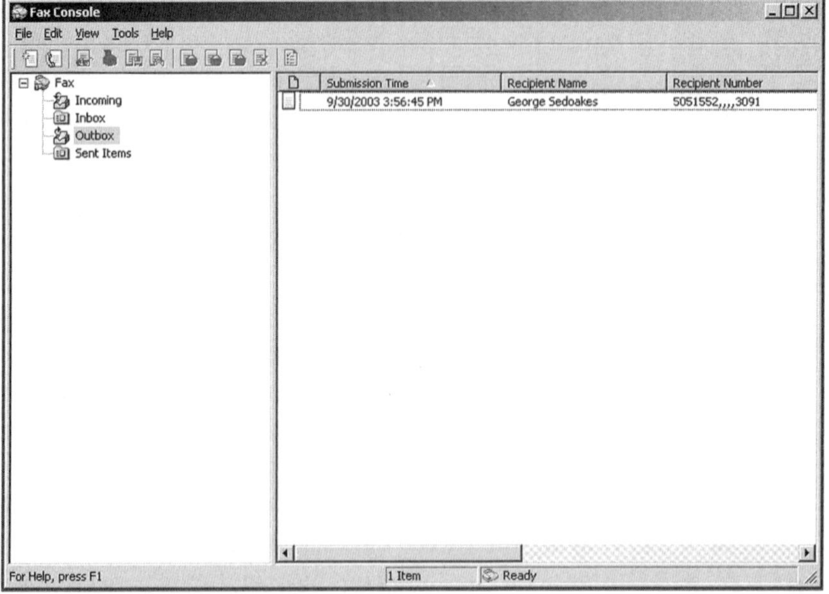

BEST PRACTICE: Back when "Windows" referred to glass panes set in the wall of a house or building, I had a client who used faxes like we used e-mail today – to send quick messages. This gentleman was a wealthy business owner who ran his business empire (he had several business entities in several states, including Alaska) in seclusion from his condo in Hawaii. He'd fax a one-line question on a fax cover page and have the recipient type out and fax the reply. There was rarely voice communication (much like business today with the use of e-mail). So, in memory of that client of long ago, I share with you a built-in tool on the client workstation side that does exactly what this gentleman did: fax a single cover page.

At a Windows XP Pro workstation on an SBS 2003 network, click Start, All Programs, Accessories, Communications, Fax, Send Fax Cover Page. A Windows 2000 Professional client would click Start, Programs, Microsoft Shared Fax Client, Send Fax Cover Page. The **Send Fax Wizard** starts (which you will need to complete each screen; click **Next** six times and click **Finish**). However, this version of the Send Fax Wizard only allows you to send a message on a fax cover page (this is described to you on the Welcome to the Send Fax Wizard screen). So, remember that when you're running your empire from a condo in Hawaii!

The Swiss Army Knife

Needless to say, I like the awesome faxing capability in SBS 2003. While it's similar to the faxing capability in SBS 2000, the setup and configuration of the Shared Fax Service is much better in SBS 2003. In fact, in my older "Small Business Server 2000 Best Practices" book, I spent a great deal of time in this section showing you how to manually configure faxing because no easy point-and-click wizards existed! Such dark days are behind us, and I can give you a quick overview of the Fax (Local) Properties property sheet.

First, perform the following steps at the SBS server machine while you are logged on as Administrator.

1. Click **Start**, **Server Management**.
2. Right-click on **Fax (Local)** under **Standard Management** and select **Properties**.
3. The **General** tab will be displayed by default. You will see tabs for Receipts, Event Reports, Activity Logging, Outbox, Inbox, Sent

Items, and Security (all of which will be shown and discussed in this section).

General

As seen in Figure 9-14, the **General** tab displays general in-progress information under **Activity**. However, this is not its great strength. What's really valuable is the ability to disable specific fax activities via the three disable check boxes. And why would you ever do this? I can think of one reason I've already used in SBS 2003: to add a new fax modem to the server. By disabling the function to send (**Disable transmission of outgoing faxes**) and receive faxes (**Disable reception of new faxes**), you could replace a broken modem or add a new one (an external modem I'm assuming) without affecting a user's ability to submit new faxes to be sent out when the faxing capability is restored via the fixed/ new modem. As long as the submission-related check box isn't selected (Disable submission of new outgoing faxes), users could continue to submit faxes to the default fax queue for transmission at a later time.

Figure 9-14
The General tab sheet is valuable for temporarily disabling faxing capabilities.

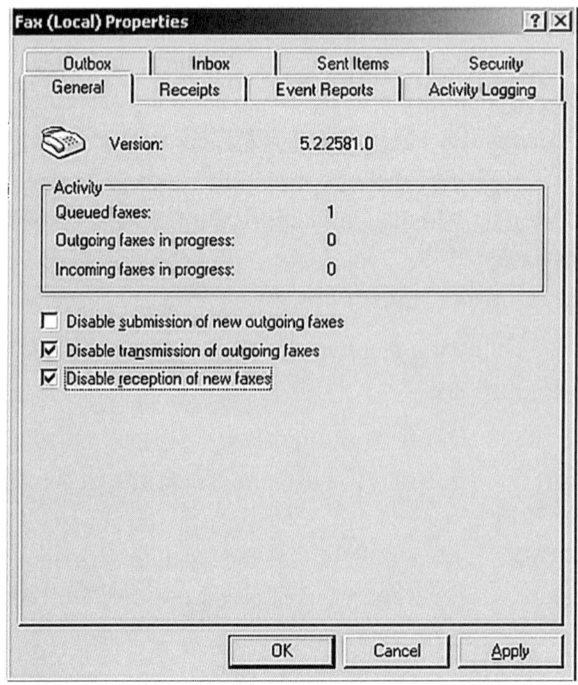

Receipts

Not surprisingly, the **Receipts** tab displays configuration selections for how delivery notification receipts should be handled. Under **Message Box**, the **Enable message boxes are receipts** check box is selected which allows users to elect how they would like to be notified when a receipt is sent.

More important, you can configure an SMTP e-mail box (either on the local SBS network or out on the wild side of the Internet) to receive delivery receipts. This occurs by completing the Fax Configuration Wizard (in SBS 2000 you have to manually configure the tab sheet). I thought you would enjoy seeing the Receipts tab before (Figure 9-15) and after (Figure 9-16) the Fax Configuration Wizard has been completed so that you could see exactly how said wizard configures the faxing function.

Figure 9-15
The Receipts tab before the Fax Configuration Wizard has been run.

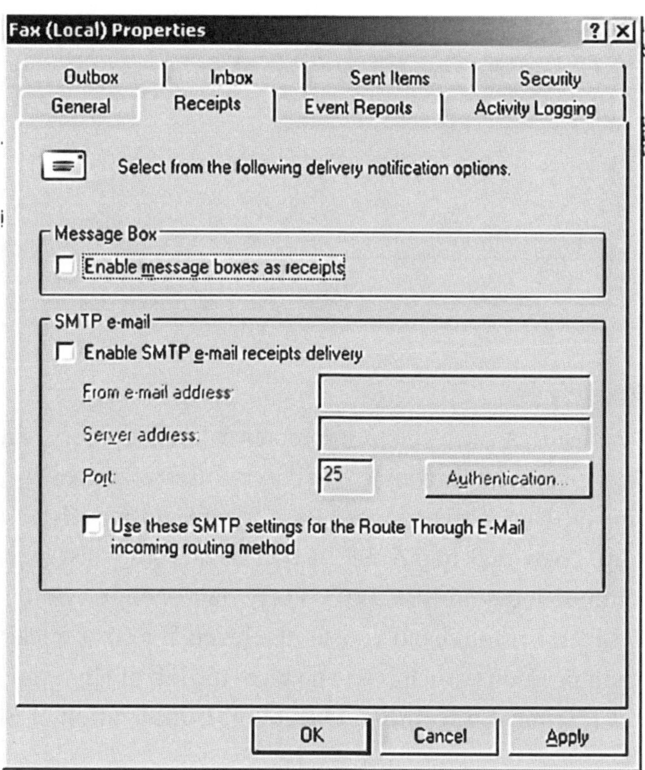

Figure 9-16
The Receipts tab after the Fax Configuration Wizard has been run.

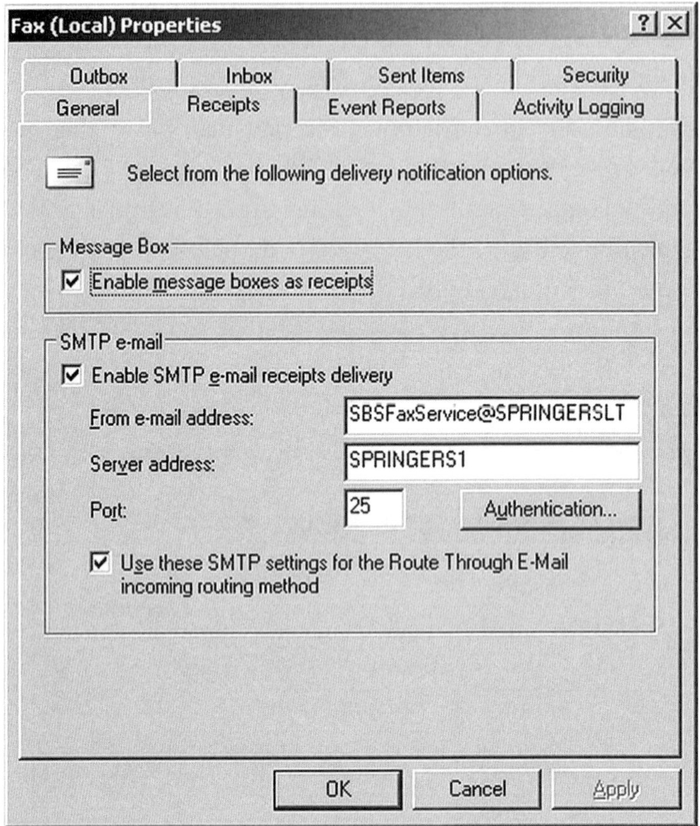

Event Reports

As they say in business, once you lose someone's trust, it is very hard to regain. Such is still the case with many SBSers who, twice burned by the faxing application in both SBS 4.x versions (4.0a, 4.5), are legitimately casting a wary eye toward the "new and improved" faxing capabilities that started in SBS 2000 and continue today in SBS 2003. Okay, fair enough. So on the **Event Reports** tab sheet, I recommend you set the levels for error tracking to **High** from the default position (which is one notch to the left of High) for each of the tracking areas (**General**, **Incoming**, **Outgoing**, **Initialization** or **Shutdown**).

That way, if you need to troubleshoot the faxing capability of SBS 2003, you'll at least be capturing all of the information you need.

Activity Logging

By default, the logging activity for incoming and outgoing fax activity is selected by default, as you can observe on the Activity Logging tab.

The logs are stored at:

%system root%\Documents and Settings\All Users\Application Data\Microsoft\Windows NT\MSFax\ActivityLog

> BEST PRACTICE: Note: To actually see the Application Data folder in the above string (fourth term from the left), your Windows Explorer file manager tool would need to be configured to display hidden files and folders.

The location can be changed by clicking the **Browse** button. The actual logs are text-based and reflect fax transaction activity.

> BEST PRACTICE: Take this fax logging discussion seriously. I've billed good hours to SBS clients having to go back in time and prove or disprove that faxes were sent or received in matters involving litigation. When the pedals hit the metal in the courtroom, it is often necessary to resolve a "he said, she said" argument by showing SBS fax logs.

One other way to view fax activity is to view Event Viewer in SBS 2003 with the following steps:

1. Assuming you are logged on to the SBS server machine as Administrator, click **Start**, **Server Management**.
2. Expand **Advanced Management**, **Computer Management (Local).**
3. Expand **Event Viewer.**
4. Select **System**.
5. To observe outgoing fax activity, look for an **Information** entry for Print that has an **Event ID** of **10**.

BEST PRACTICE: A Print entry #10 should be followed immediately by a Print entry #13 that confirms the document as deleted from the Fax queue after it was successfully sent. Also note that later in the book (Chapter 11) I speak to how to turn off Event ID 10 so your event log doesn't get full. You'll need to make the trade-off between tons of printer entries in your event log and receiving fax report information in this manner.

Now, viewing incoming faxes via Event Viewer is a slightly different procedure. Here you would look for at the Application event log in Event Viewer; for the Source equals Microsoft Fax, look for Event ID# 32008. This confirms the fax was received.

BEST PRACTICE: The Application event log will record Event ID # 32093 if the received faxed is archived and Event ID # 32081 if the received faxed is routed to an e-mail address.

Please refer to Chapter 12 and read the discussion on the Server Usage Report to learn about other ways to monitor and report faxing activity.

Notes:

Outbox

By default, several check boxes are selected for you on the **Outbox** tab sheet (see Figure 9-17). One that stands out in particular is that, by default, users can use personal cover pages. This is possible because the **Allow use of personal cover pages** check box is selected. But if you or your clients find this to be unacceptable, you should deselect this check box. Remember that personal cover pages can be silly and offensive in many business climates.

Figure 9-17
The default view of the Outbox tab sheet.

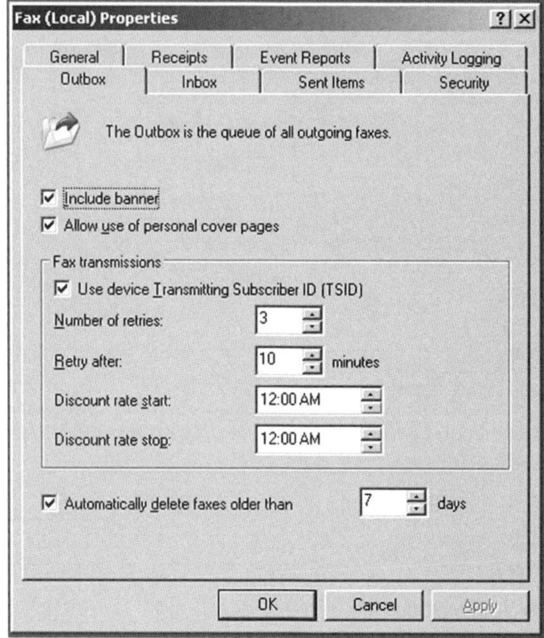

Note the Outbox tab sheet allows you to set some other important settings, such as number of times a fax call will be attempted (**Number of retries**), time between retries (**Retry after**), and setting the discount rate period (**Discount rate start**, **Discount rate stop**) that users can select when sending a fax. The **Automatically delete faxes older than 7 days** setting, selected by default, would indicate that older faxes that never successfully sent will be deleted.

Inbox

The **Inbox** allows you to make the selection that allows you to save incoming faxes (via the **Archive all incoming faxes to this folder** check box). This location was defined earlier in the chapter when I suggested you could create a shared folder on the SBS 2003 server called "SharedFax" for your users to browse. By default, the check box allowing Event log warning entries (**Generate warning in Event Log**) and deleting faxes over 90 days old (**Automatically delete faxes older than 90 days**) are selected. The Inbox is shown in Figure 9-18.

Figure 9-18
The Inbox tab sheet.

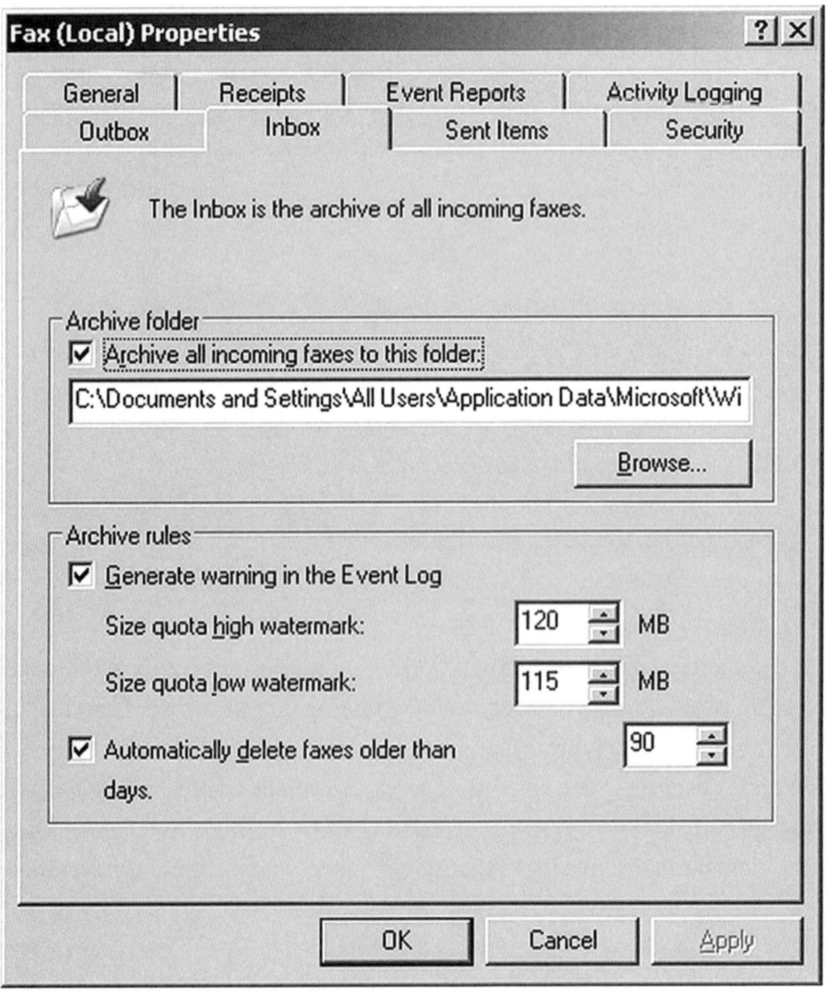

BEST PRACTICE: You might consider modifying to fewer days the **Automatically delete faxes older than 90 days** check box for one very important business reason. At this point in the chapter, you've used the Fax Configuration Wizard to tell SBS 2003 to save your faxes in a public folder named Faxes and in a WSS folder. That's where you'll store your faxes for historical purposes.

But there is another interesting tale to tell about the faxing Inbox. It was a sunny Seattle summer day when a program manager from Microsoft Israel both took me to school and lunch. Having read the chapter on faxing in my book, Small Business Server 2000 Best Practices, this gentleman wanted to bend my ear and set me straight on a few things. First, the Inbox in the Shared Fax Service is "transitory" in nature, so you shouldn't modify the quota (watermark) settings to stuff more faxes in the Inbox. Rather, use the other storage approaches allowed and just discussed a few sentences ago. Second, if your fax Inbox fills so rapidly because you're really using the inbound faxing capability, and you overstep the quota boundaries, you'd know that the Shared Fax Service will effective shut down until the Inbox is cleared. But here again, you wouldn't trade out your watermark settings, but lower the automatic fax deletion setting to keep that darn Inbox free!

Loyal readers will respectively notice that this is a reversal from my SBS 2000 book.

Notes:

Sent Items

The **Sent Items** tab sheet looks very similar to the Inbox tab sheet. You can make **Archive folder** and **Archive rules** selections. And again, you might deselect the **Automatically delete faxes older than 60 days** check box to preserve faxes indefinitely.

Security

We met the security tab sheet earlier in the chapter when we modified the permissions that allowed mere mortals to view faxes in the Fax Console. That said, Security is one of the more important tab sheets, and it is where you could use the Deny permission to prevent an individual user from using the faxing capabilities in SBS 2003.

Devices and Providers, Routing and Such!

In the prior SBS 2000 release, you really had to learn much about the nested settings beneath the Fax (Local) and shown in Figure 9-19 in order to fully utilize and appreciate the SBS faxing function. Such is not the case today with the wizard-based setup of the Shared Fax Service in SBS 2003 where all this stuff is basically handled for you. However, you're encouraged to poke and probe around the edges of the faxing function by drilling down into these settings and taking a look-see at how things work. In my advanced SBS 2003 text, due in mid-2004, I'll discuss this behind-the-scenes area much more. Until then!

Notes:

Figure 9-19
Delve deeper than you imagined with the child object beneath Fax (Local).

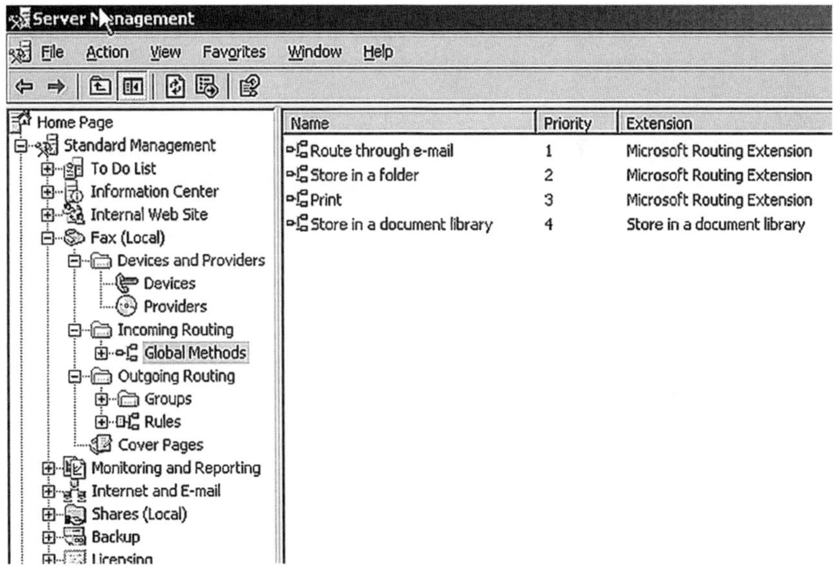

Faxing Alternatives

I want to quickly present an Internet faxing service that allows you to not use the faxing application in SBS 2003, but still have some of the benefits of computer-based faxing. This is a service I've used called OneBox at www.onebox.com (Figure 9-20). After completing a quick sign-up process, you will have free e-mail, voicemail (which is cool), and faxing tied to a regular telephone number in your area code and including a short telephone extension. So, when people want to fax to you, they enter the full telephone number followed by a few commas (pauses) and then your four-digit extension. The fax is received by OneBox and you're notified by e-mail that you have a fax waiting.

Notes:

Figure 9-20
OneBox is an Internet-based fax service that captures incoming faxes as a digital image.

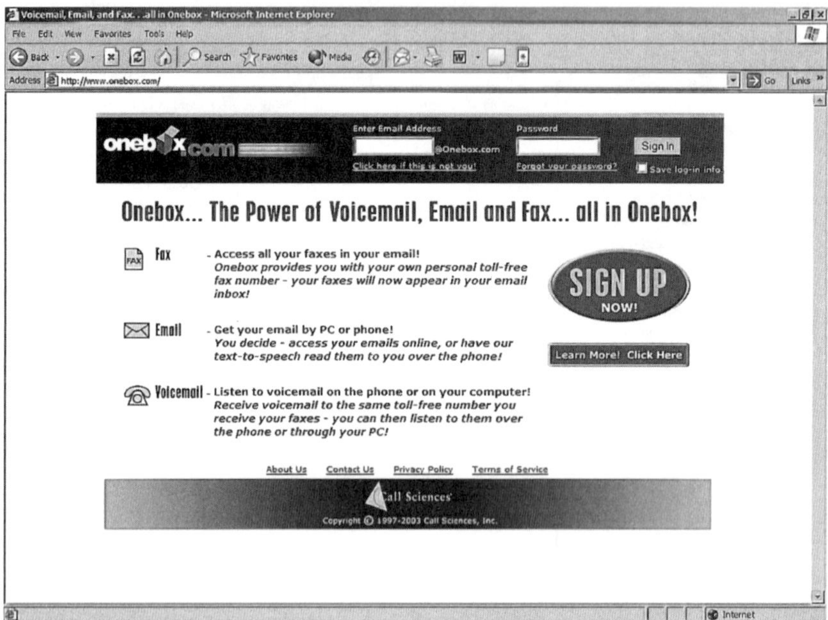

So, why in the world would you do this with the new faxing service so handy in SBS? I can think of two reasons.

- Carrot and stick. Set up a reluctant client on OneBox to turn them onto computer-based faxing and its benefits as a way to "hook" them. Then use that as leverage to implement the Shared Fax Service in SBS 2003.
- The "heck with it crowd." Perhaps the reading you've done in this chapter has actually scared you about SBS's faxing capabilities. You might find a service such as OneBox easier to use. Whatever works, as they say in business.

Summary

So you've decided to become an SBS fax organization: You've decided to make the fax function part of your SBS network and everyday business-world activity. You've possibly arrived at this decision, based on much of the discussion herein and by considering the following about SBS network faxing:

- Reduced hardware costs - Not only have you eliminated the need to purchase an expensive, modern fax machine, more important, you've eliminated the need to have each workstation equipped with its own fax modem and fax telephone line (I've seen it done). I've used the capability to eliminate multiple fax telephone lines in the past to help a firm justify the cost of an SBS conversion.

- Ease of use - Properly trained SBS users find sending certain types of documents and receiving any document to be easy with SBS network-based faxing. To read a typical fax, the user only needs to double-click to open the fax image. To send a fax, the user only needs to use the basic printing command.

- Monitoring and control - Again, depending on your unique situation, you might have an important need to control fax usage. That type of control is exceedingly difficult with a traditional fax machine, but with SBS, the network security model dictates who can use the fax service.

The next step to receiving and sending faxes is simple: Just do it!

Chapter 10
Internet and the Web

Here yesterday, here today, and here tomorrow. That would be a shorthand way to sum up SBS support for Internet connectivity and the Web. The ability to easily connect to the Internet is part of the SBS foundation. In this chapter, you will learn about how SBS "natively" interacts with the Internet, look under the hood at Internet Information Services, extend your SBS 2003 server machine out on the Web as an FTP server, and create a Web page as well as host it on bCentral.

I'll weave and bob the SPRINGERS storyline into this discussion as much as possible. Let's get started!

Going Native: SBS 2003 Internet Support

You'll recall configuring the Internet was an early task performed from the To Do List (the Connect to the Internet link) in Chapter 4 after you initially set up the SBS server machine. It was here you defined the inside and wild-side (outside) network adapter cards. You provided basic external IP address and DNS server information. A big assumption was made that you had acquired an external Internet-registered domain name from a firm such as Network Solutions (www.networksolutions.com).

So after the SBS 2003 setup and deployment is completed, much of your management of the SBS Internet connectivity will occur in two places. The first is the Manage Internet and E-mail page, as seen in Figure 10-1. The second is the Internet Information Services snap-in found under Advanced Management in the Server Management console (which I describe in the next section).

Figure 10-1
Manage Internet and E-mail page.

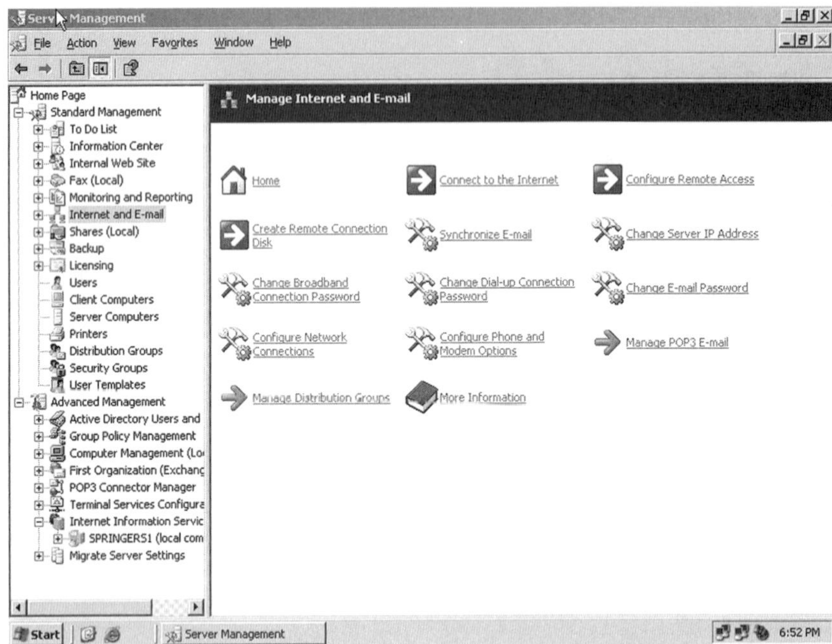

Specific to the Internet in SBS 2003, consider clicking on and learning more at these links:

- Connect to the Internet (this launches the E-mail and Internet Connection Wizard you completed in Chapter 4)
- Configure Remote Access (this launches the Remote Access Wizard you completed in Chapter 4)
- Create Remote Connection Disk
- Change Server IP address
- Change Broadband Connection Password
- Change Dial-up Connection Password

- Configure Network Connections
- Configure Phone and Modem Options
- More Information (strong online help you should peruse)

Under the Hood: Internet Information Server

Internet Information Services (IIS) is the Web-engine component that has its paws into more things than you might imagine. I'll highlight a few of those features in a moment. It's also something that, while assuming a larger IIS foreground role at the enterprise-level, where things like Web hosting (for external Web sites) make sense, such roles are deemphasized in SBS 2003. And you can't deny IIS has occasionally had something of a publicity problem, being best known for its susceptibility to worm attacks such as CODE RED, CODE RED II, NIMBA, and countless Microsoft security bulletins.

As spoken by Microsoft itself, "...IIS 6.0 provides a highly reliable, manageable, and scalable Web application infrastructure for all versions of Windows Server 2003." It is locked down by default as part of Microsoft's out-of-the-box experience and you effectively turn it on with some of the SBS Internet configuration options discussed immediately above.

> BEST PRACTICE: You are highly encouraged to visit the IIS site at Microsoft (Figure 10-2) and delve deeper into this product. Seriously! Grab a fresh soda and click over to www.microsoft.com/iis and read all the IIS news that's fit to print for at least 20 minutes. Catch the discussion on better memory management and steps taken to improve reliability (those are two "delta" points Microsoft is emphasizing).

Notes:

Figure 10-2

Instead of rewriting deep discussion on IIS in this chapter, I'd rather you went to this site.

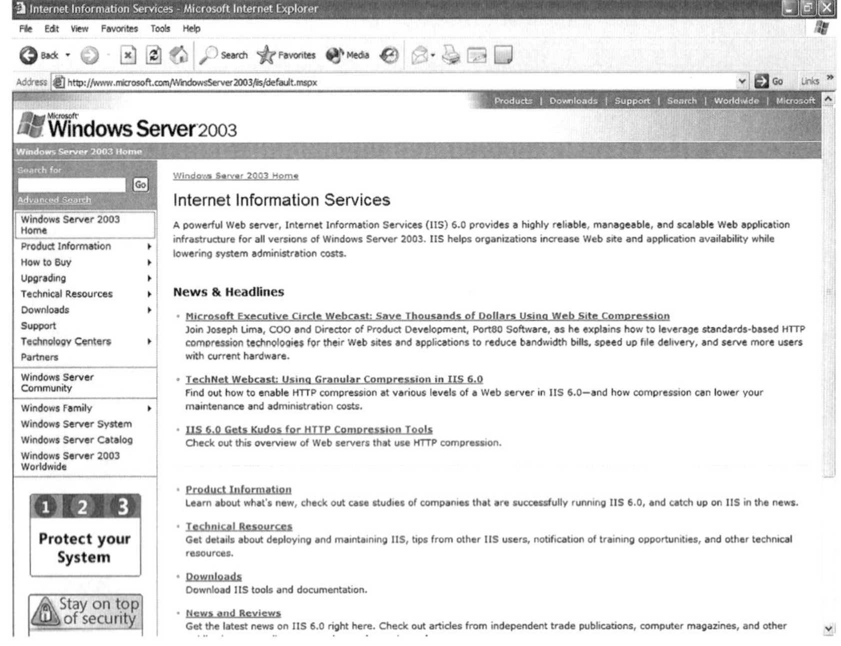

IIS is managed from the Internet Information Services snap-in seen in Figure 10-3.

Figure 10-3
Observe the default Web sites supported by IIS on a configured SBS 2003 server machine.

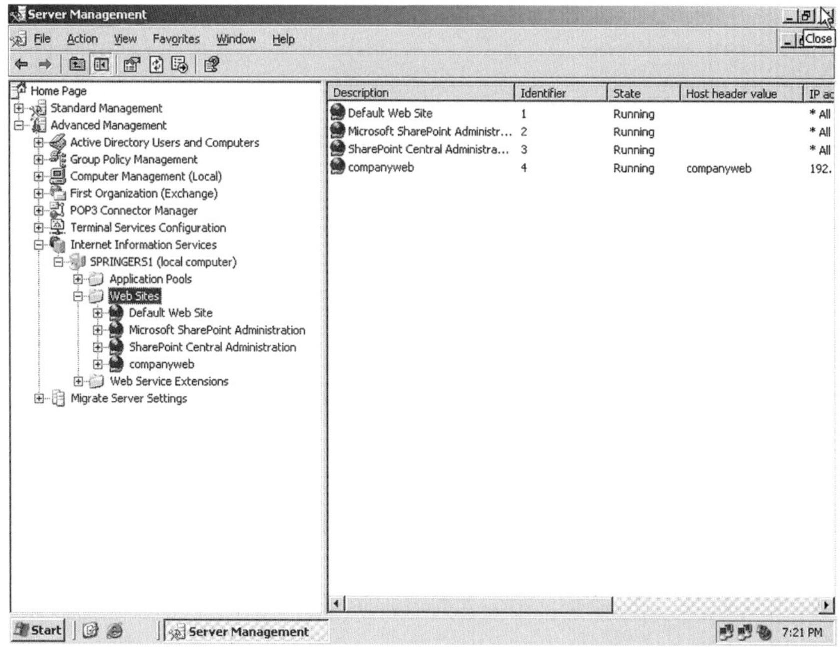

BEST PRACTICE: So how much will you interact directly with IIS on any given day? The answer is not much. IIS should basically run itself. But if you're bored, consider playing around with the memory recycling capabilities built into IIS 6.0. This can be found be selecting **Properties** (right click and select from the secondary menu) for any Application Pool (the DefaultAppPool is displayed in Figure 10-4). In SBS 2003, the default recycling period is 4:00am for work processes. Configure away, but I'll warn you. When I've lectured on this capability in the past, it's the enterprise-crowd running Web server farms that gets the most excited about this capability.

Figure 10-4

This is where you can recycle worker processes and memory on an application pool basis.

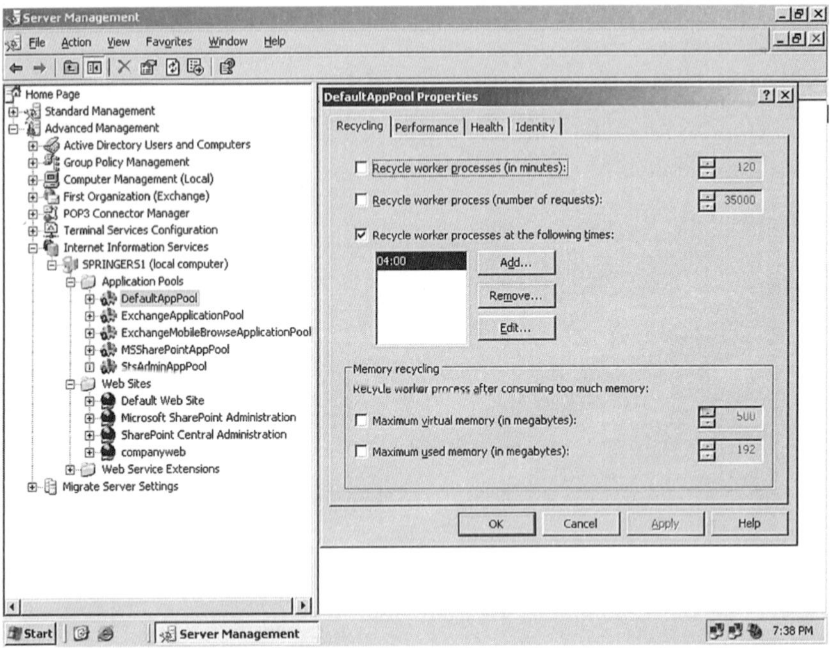

So how might IIS affect SBS 2003? How is IIS integrated with SBS 2003? One example is Figure 10-4 above where you can see the IIS application pools for Exchange and SharePoint on the left. You can also see the Web sites supported by IIS in SBS 2003 include CompanyWeb (this was discussed more appropriately in Chapter 7). Finally, consider how IIS support Exchange and SharePoint Web service extensions as seen in Figure 10-5.

Figure 10-5
Server extension support also glues SBS 2003 to IIS 6.0.

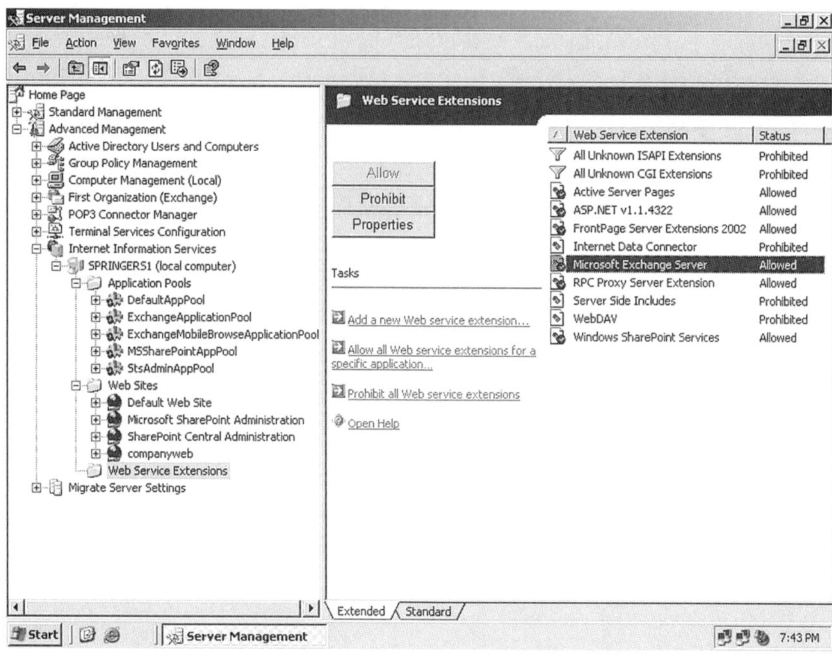

BEST PRACTICE: To be brutally honest and nothing less, it is possible that you'll never click the Internet Information Services snap-in. Seriously, you could operate just fine as an SBSer on an SBS network without ever interacting with IIS. That would assume that you're not going to implement much more than basic IIS functionality supported by the official SBS 2003 deployment approach.

Extending IIS in SBS 2003

It's SPRINGERS time! Let's implement the FTP server in the world of SPRINGERS to facilitate the efficient transfer of large document attachments that are realistically too large to send via e-mail. Then you'll download and use CuteFTP from a shareware site to test the FTP server you've implemented. You'll even learn how to make FTP more secure.

Installing FTP

There is a real-world need, more often than you think, to implement FTP. Why? Because many e-mail systems out there in real companies, including the Microsoft Corporation, have 5 MB attachment limits. This is a true hindrance when working with large files. Just ask my client, a traffic engineering firm that is making big plans (and I mean big AutoCAD plans) for Seattle's new light rail system. When you're dealing with 60 MB CAD drawings, e-mail doesn't cut it. You typically need to look to FTP as a solution.

> BEST PRACTICE: FTP, officially known as File Transfer Protocol, is really about creating and managing a storage space to facilitate large file transfers. To be honest, it's not very exciting, except when you surface the words "security" and "FTP" in the same sentence.
>
> The security issue is this: FTP passes the user name and password, as well as the files being transferred, in clear text. So an evil gremlin with a network sniffer could view your information in an unkind and insincere way.
>
> But hang on to your hat. Just a tad later, I'll make it so that you can secure FTP by binding it to the internal network adapter card and thereby force external users to establish a secure and encrypted virtual private networking connection (VPN) prior to using their FTP client.

Because the FTP service isn't installed by default in SBS 2003, we need to do that now.

1. Log on to **SPRINGERS1** as **Administrator** with the password **Husky9999!**.
2. Click **Start, Settings, Control Panel, Add/Remove Programs, Add/ Remove Windows Components**.
3. Select **Application Server** followed by selecting **Internet Information Services (IIS)**. Click **Details**.
4. Select **File Transfer Protocol (FTP) Service** in the **Internet Information Services (IIS)** dialog box (Figure 10-6) and click **OK**.

Figure 10-6
Installing FTP on the server-side.

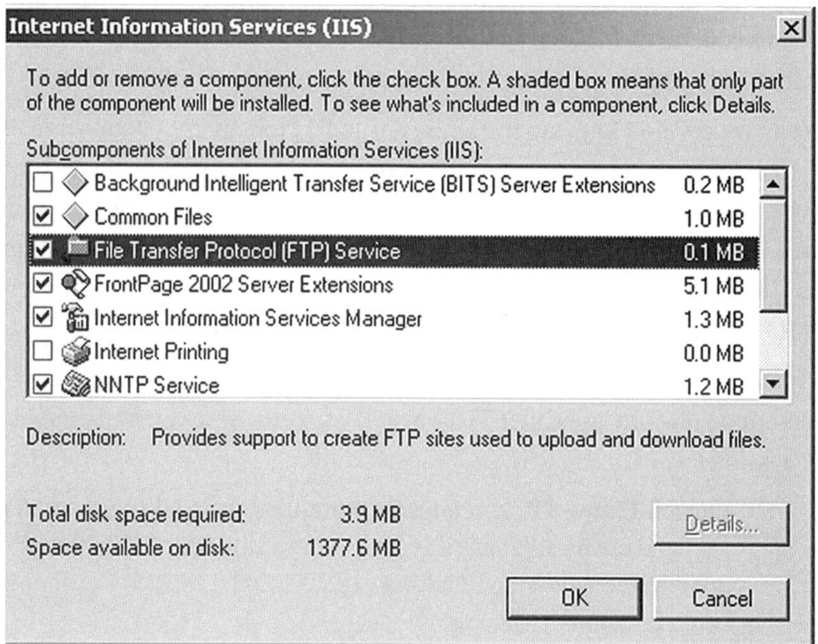

5. Click **OK** on the **Application Server** page followed by **Next** on the **Windows Components** page.
6. Insert SBS 2003 Disc 1 when requested.
7. Click **Finish** when the **Complete the Windows Components Wizard** page appears.
8. Close the **Add or Remove Programs** dialog box.

You will need to restart IIS for the FTP Sites folder to appear. This is easily accomplished by right-clicking on the **SPRINGERS1 (local computer)** object directly beneath the **Internet Information Services** object under **Advanced Management** in **Server Management** and selecting **Restart IIS** from the **All Tasks** item on the secondary menu. If you drill down into the **FTP Sites** folder that will now appear, the **Default FTP Site** is listed.

You will now use **Windows Explorer** on SPRINGERS1 (from **Start, All Programs, Accessories**) to view the FTP folder at **c:\Inetpub\ftproot** and create a sample document. When you navigate to this location, simply right-click in the right pane of **Windows Explorer** and select **New, Wordpad Document**. Name the file **"Springers Family Tree.doc"** and close **Windows Explorer**.

Next up is downloading and installing a true FTP client application and using it to transfer a file. First, on a machine connected to the Internet launch a Web browser and go to www.tucows.com (a popular shareware site). Search on **CuteFTP** and download the current version of this shareware application (as of this writing, that is CuteFTP 5.0.2 XP). Proceed to install **CuteFTP** on the REMOTE computer (double-click the CuteFTP setup file and complete its setup wizard).

So assuming that you got CuteFTP to install correctly now you will establish an FTP session to SPRINGERS1 and transfer a file.

1. Launch **CuteFTP**. If requested, complete the trial registration process and create a default selection entry titled SPRINGERS that will point to the wild-side IP address of 207. 202.238.215. Configure the entry for anonymous logon.
2. The FTP session will attempt to initiate (or you can force from **File, Site Manager**) and the connection will fail! Take a second to guess why before proceeding to the next step. (And no, SBS 2003 is not somehow flawed here.)
3. Perhaps you've guessed what the problem is. **CuteFTP** runs in "passive mode" natively and you will need to switch it to active mode. In CuteFTP, select **Edit, Settings, Connection, Firewall**, and de-select the **PASV** mode checkbox. Click **OK**.
4. Try the SPRINGERS connection again. This time the connection will work.
5. Highlight the text file discussed above (**Springers Family Tree.doc**) and drag it from the right pane to the left pane to copy it to the REMOTE1 workstation. This will copy the file to NormH's My Documents folder.
6. Close **CuteFTP** from **File, Exit**.

BEST PRACTICE: I've used CuteFTP as only an example herein. You could use the FTP client of your choice to complete the above example (but the keystrokes would be different). Heck - you can even use Internet Explorer as a rude and crude FTP client to complete this example. Ouch!

Hey - a bit of SBS trivia for you. Microsoft doesn't have a robust FTP client application, so whenever you read Microsoft documentation and books about use of FTP, they'll typically use either the command line (the rudest FTP client of all, let me tell ya!) or the IE Web browser.

BEST PRACTICE: You can make the FTP process even more secure by binding the FTP server service to the internal network adapter card and then requiring a user to VPN first into the SBS 2003 network. This will have the effect of not allowing plain text passwords to be passed.

To bind the FTP server service to the internal network adapter card, simply expand **Internet Information Service** beneath **Advanced Management** in the **Server Management** console, expand **SPRINGERS1** (local computer), expand **FTP sites**. Right-click on the **Default FTP Site** and select **Properties**. On the **FTP Site** tab of the **Default FTP Site Properties**, select **192.168.16.2** from the IP address drop-down as seen in Figure 10-7.

Notes:

Figure 10-7
Binding the FTP site to the inside NIC card of 192.168.16.2.

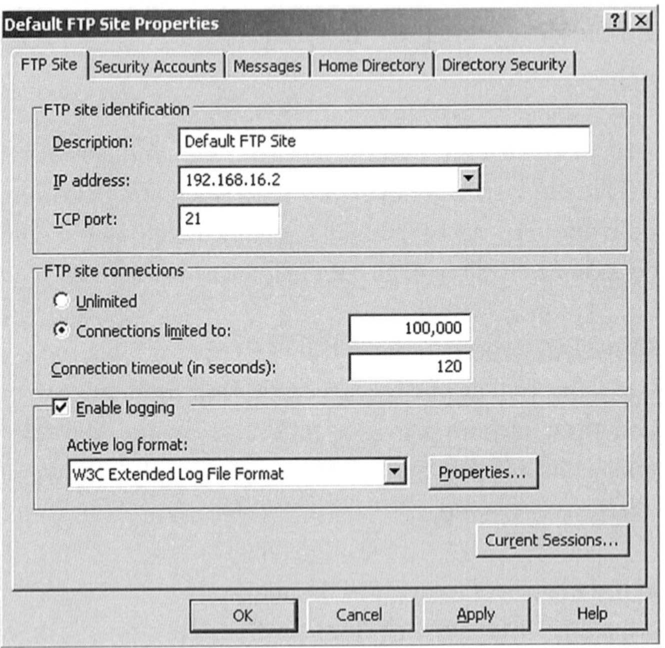

Notes:

Creating a Web Page in SBS 2003

In this section, you'll create a Web site using FrontPage 2003, learn about hosting a Web site externally using Microsoft bCentral, and then understand how to use Internet Explorer to visit a Web site related to SBS.

Obtaining and installing FrontPage 2003

You can obtain FrontPage 2003 two ways. It is part of SBS 2003 premium edition, where you receive a one-license version of this Web page development application (which is what FrontPage 2003 is). You may also purchase it separately for $199 USD as a standalone application.

> BEST PRACTICE: There is yet a third way to acquire FrontPage 2003: an Action Pack subscription. Action Pack, fully defined at www.microsoft.com/partner, is available to Microsoft Partners who aren't certified but otherwise are bona fide consultants, resellers, and system builders. Action Pack sells for $299 USD and includes over $25,000 USD worth of Microsoft server, client, and application software.

You will need to install FrontPage 2003 at this time to continue (this is a "normal" Microsoft application installation procedure).

> BEST PRACTICE: Be sure to learn more about FrontPage 2003 at www.microsoft.com/office and select the **FrontPage 2003** link.

Creating a Web Site

You will now create the Web page for SPRINGERS.

1. Log on to the client computer **PRESIDENT** as **NormH** with the password **Purple3300**.
2. Click **Start, Programs, Microsoft FrontPage**.
3. A blank Web page appears in the default view of Microsoft Front Page. Type and format the following text, shown in Table 10-1, such that it appears similar to Figure 10-8.

Table 10-1: Text input for SSL intranet Web page.

Text	Formatting
Springer Spaniels Limited	Bold, 18-point, Arial, left-alignment
Bainbridge Island, WA	Bold, 14-point, Arial, left-alignment
Web Site	Bold, 18-point, Arial, center-alignment
Jaeger and Brisker's Retirement Party - June 30th	Bold, Italic, 12-point, Times New Roman, left-alignment

Figure 10-8
SSL Web page after entering Table 10-8 information.

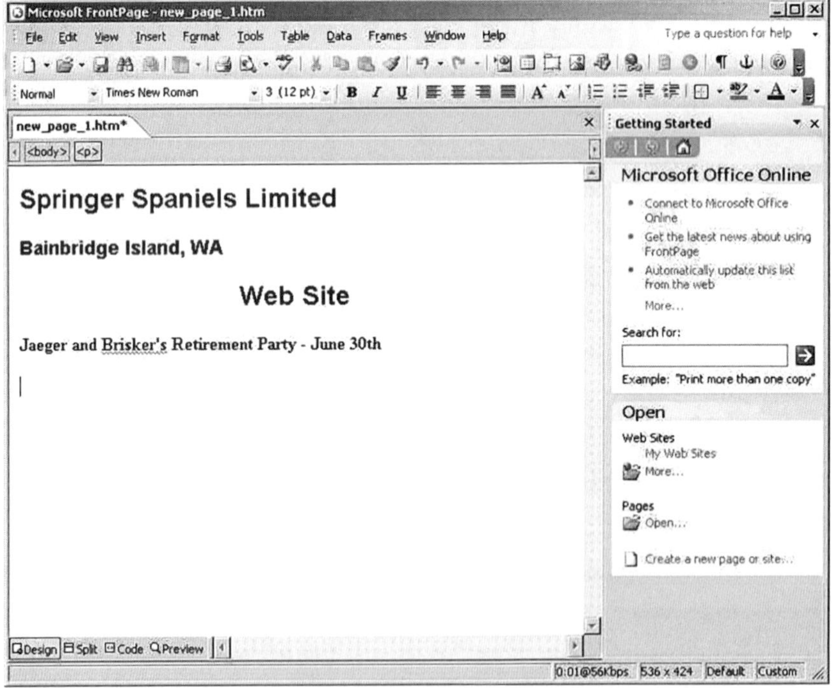

4. Let's take a moment to save the file we're working on. Click **File**, **Save** and accept the default file name (**springer_spaniels_limited.htm**). Click the **Save** button.
5. Click **OK** when the **Save Embedded Files** dialog box appears.

6. Click on the **Preview** tab. Your SPRINGERS Web page should look similar to Figure 10-9. If this is the case, proceed to the next section. Otherwise, make sure you haven't overlooked a step above in the creation of this Web page.

Figure 10-9
Your SPRINGERS Web site should now look similar to this.

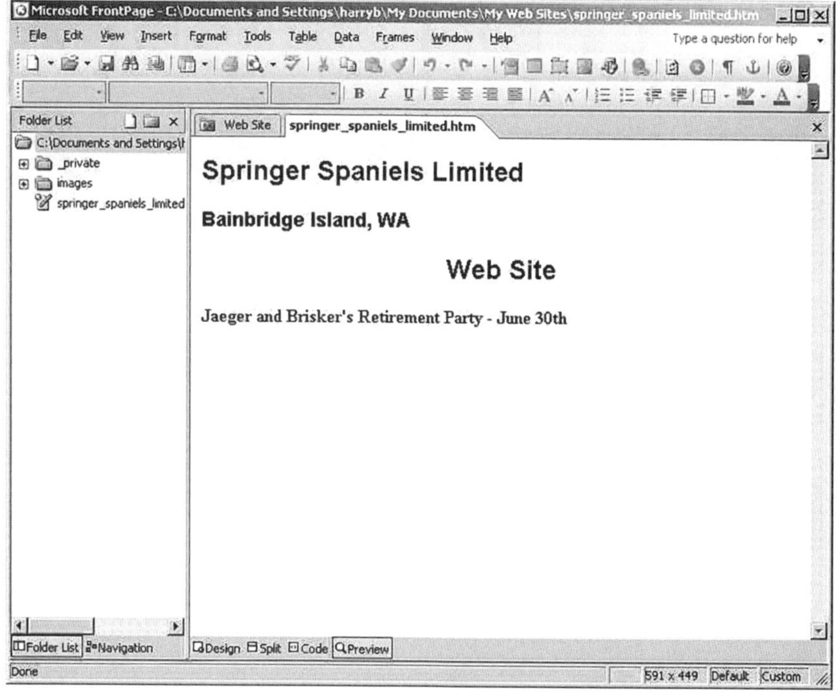

BEST PRACTICE: Clearly this example isn't intended to make you a great Web master. Rather, you are introduced to FrontPage 2003. You will want to retain a Web master to properly build a Web page worth its salt!

Externally Hosting a Web Site

Repeat after me: Never host your external Web site on an SBS 2003 server machine! That's because you're better off to select a Web hosting service with fatter Internet pipes, better backup batteries, and a just plain "better fit" for the

Web hosting duty. I recommend you consider contracting with Microsoft's bCentral services, seen in Figure 10-10, to host your Web page that you create with FrontPage 2003.

Figure 10-10
Services such as Microsoft's bCentral are better equipped to host your Web page (rather than your SBS 2003 server machine).

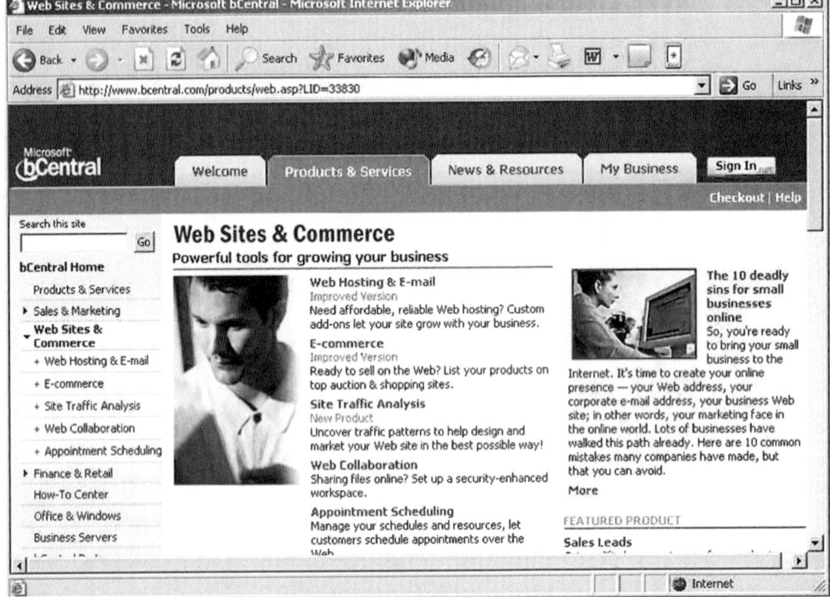

BEST PRACTICE: I've said it several times in the book (Chapter 4, Chapter 8 and here) and Microsoft concurs. Please don't use your SBS 2003 server machine for Web hosting unless necessary. But this time my rant takes a different tact. Port 80, opened by selecting the Business Web option on the Web Services page of the EICW, allows you to be crawled and sometimes worse.

If you must have port 80 open, please use a text file that slaps crawlers: robots.txt. Learn more about this approach at www.robotstxt.org/wc/robots./html and for a real good time, look (and learn) at a real robots.txt file such as www.cnn.com/robots.txt.

Visiting a Web Site

No chapter would be complete without launching Internet Explorer and visiting an interesting SBS-related Web site. So select **Internet** from **Start** on a personal computer attached to the Internet and wait for **Internet Explorer** to launch. Type www.smbnation.com in the **Address** field and press **Enter**. Your screen should look similar to Figure 10-11.

Figure 10-11
A shameless plug for the SMB Nation conference series that focuses on SBS. See you there!

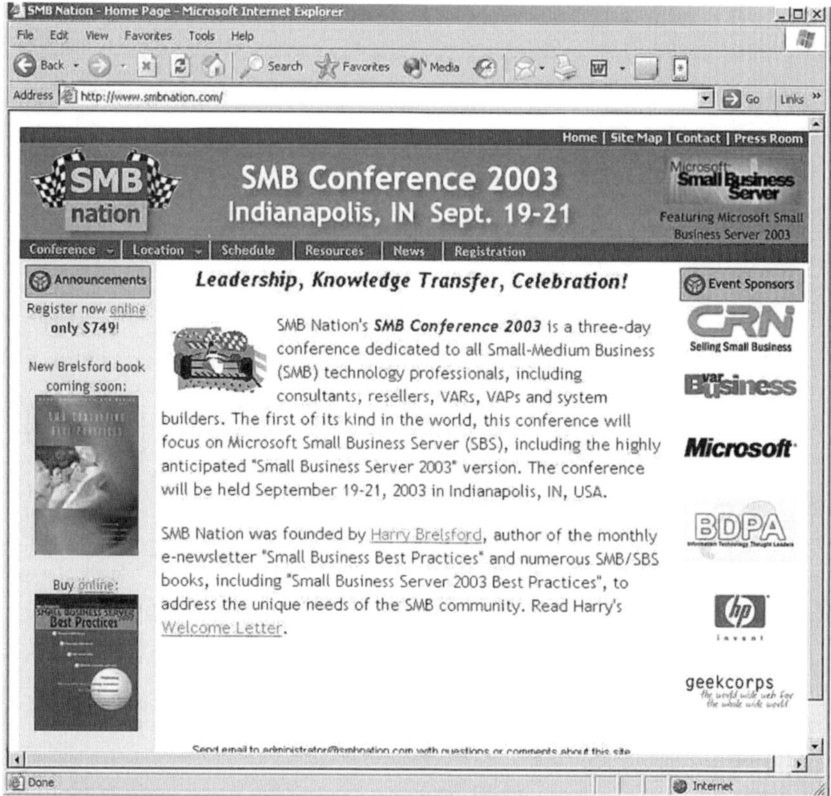

Notes:

Summary

And that's all folks when it comes to working with IIS, including using FTP and creating a Web site. If you read closely, you would have caught my stern endorsement that external Internet Web pages should be hosted with your ISP, not on your SBS server. The FTP exercise was not only real-world in nature, even to the point of using a third-party FTP client, but you learned one method for making FTP more secure (by requiring a VPN connection first). Finally, the SMB Nation conference series, a friend of the SBS community, was highlighted.

Section Three
SBS 2003 Administration

Chapter 11
Daily, Weekly, Monthly, Annual Tasks

Chapter 12
Monitoring SBS 2003

Chapter 11
Daily, Weekly, Monthly, Annual Tasks

This important chapter takes a very real-world view of SBS. You will find an assortment of tasks and duties you are likely to perform on your SBS network. Granted, the frequency with which you perform the tasks will depend on your unique situation. I'm assuming the tasks outlined here could be performed daily, weekly, monthly, and annually. You will likely have your own tasks to add to this list, such as performing some re-indexing job on a business accounting application.

It has been my observation that how and when SBS tasks are performed depend on the following factors. It might be that your skill level as an SBS administrator or consultant affects the tasks you perform. A newbie might perform minimal tasks and a guru might perform more tasks. The activity on your SBS network can determine which tasks you feel comfortable performing and when. Some tasks, such as those highlighted early in the chapter (backup, virus detection, spam blocking, spyware removal, etc.) are to be performed religiously, regardless of your SBS skill level.

Don't overlook how the computer knowledge of your users can determine what maintenance tasks are performed (especially the end-user support tasks). And believe it or not, physical stuff impacting the quality of your network from wiring to server brand can affect your task list too!

By this point, I assume that you've correctly set up a robust SBS network based on the SPRINGERS methodology used in this book (yes, it's that sample company Springer Spaniels Limited again). When you get to this point for real (that is, with your real SBS implementations) I hope that your SBS network is stable, functional and allows the time you need to perform other important work. (I understand that small businesses ask much of us and we often have several jobs, not just those of SBS guru.)

So, now that I've had my fuss, on with the SBS administration show using SPRINGERS!

Backup

Much improved in SBS 2003, the native backup program is to be taken seriously! It leads the pack in terms of administrative improvements in SBS 2003 time frame. Call it "most improved" compared to prior SBS releases. In this section you will configure a backup, recover a deleted e-mail item, learn about the importance of monthly and annual test restores, redirect My Documents, and be advised of third-party backup solutions for SBS.

Backup Configuration Wizard

Perform the following procedure to run backup.

1. Log on to **SPRINGERS1** as the **Administrator** with the password **Husky9999!**, then launch **Server Management** from **Start**.
2. Select **To Do List**.
3. Select **Configure Backup**.
4. Click **Next** on the **Welcome to the Windows Small Business Server Backup Configuration Wizard** page.
5. On the **Backup Location** page, select **Back up to a local hard disk or network share** and type **\\Springers1\Users** in the **Store backup files at this location** field. This is shown in Figure 11-1. For the purpose of the SPRINGERS methodology, I'm going to have you direct a backup job to a network share point. In the real world, you would likely consider a different approach, such as using a tape backup device, external high capacity hard disk, removable drives, etc. Click **Next**.

Notes:

Figure 11-1
Identifying the backup storage location.

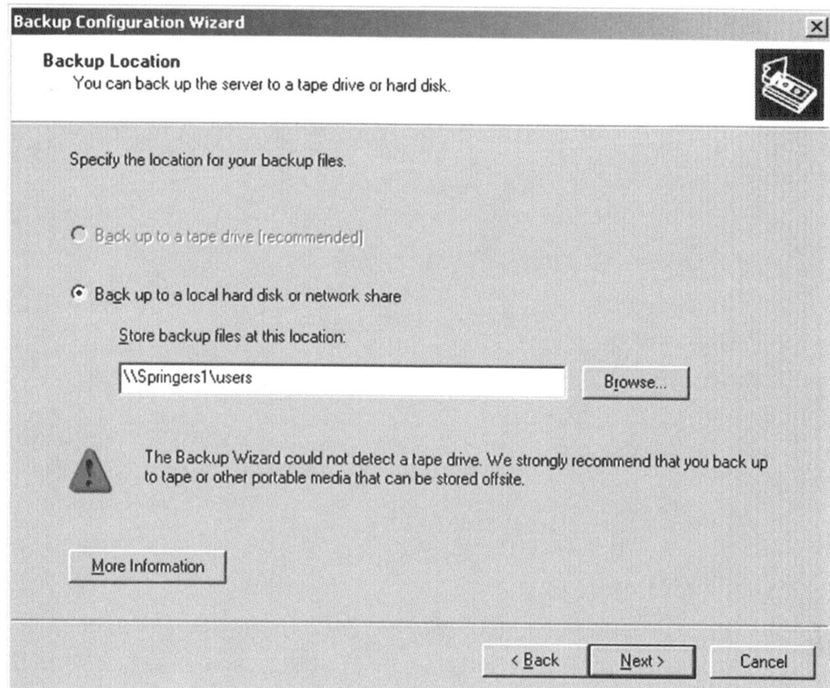

BEST PRACTICE: There is an SBS 2003 backup fix you should be aware of. SBS 2003 incorrectly identifies Travan tape devices as MiniQIC. You can clean up that malady by reading KBase article 831664 (search at www.microsoft.com/technet). Officially this is a hotfix that corrects the problem of NTBackup.exe incorrectly, choosing the backup tape type on a drive that supports multiple tape types. This hotfix was released November 24, 2003.

6. Carefully read the **Backup Summary** page and observe that all information necessary to perform a bare metal restore in being backed up (in my advanced SBS 2003 book, you will perform a bare metal restore). You could exclude folders if you so desired. Click **Next**.
7. Accept the default settings on the **Define Backup Schedule** page for each week night at 11:00pm and to store two backup copies (this is a modified overwrite command). See Figure 11-2.

Figure 11-2
The backup will commence late in the day (11pm).

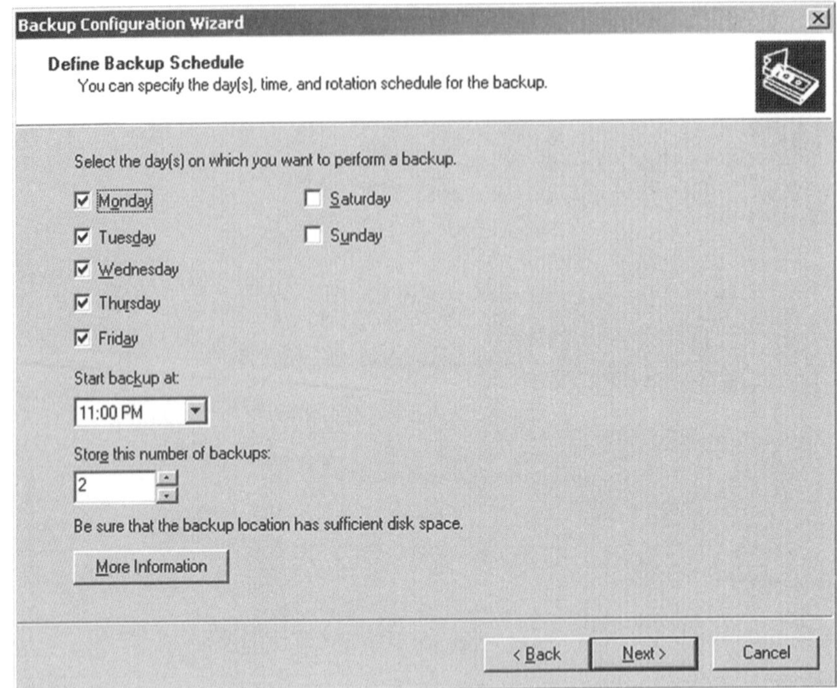

8. On the **Storage Allocation for Deleted Files and E-mail** page, accept the default setting to **Retain copies of the permanently deleted e-mail messages** but change the **Number of days** to **90**. Then select **Enable periodic snapshots of users' shared folders** (accept the default space allocation as shown in Figure 11-3). Click **More Information** to read some VERYGOOD INFORMATION on how the snapshots are made at 7:00am and 12:00 noon to effectively give users two data backups during the day between nightly 11:00pm back-ups. Another point here speaks to what happens when the users' shared folder is renamed or deleted (guess!). Click **Next**.
9. Click the **here** link to save this to your SBS Network Notebook (as you have done in past chapters).
10. Click **Finish**.

Figure 11-3
Configuring deleted files and e-mail settings.

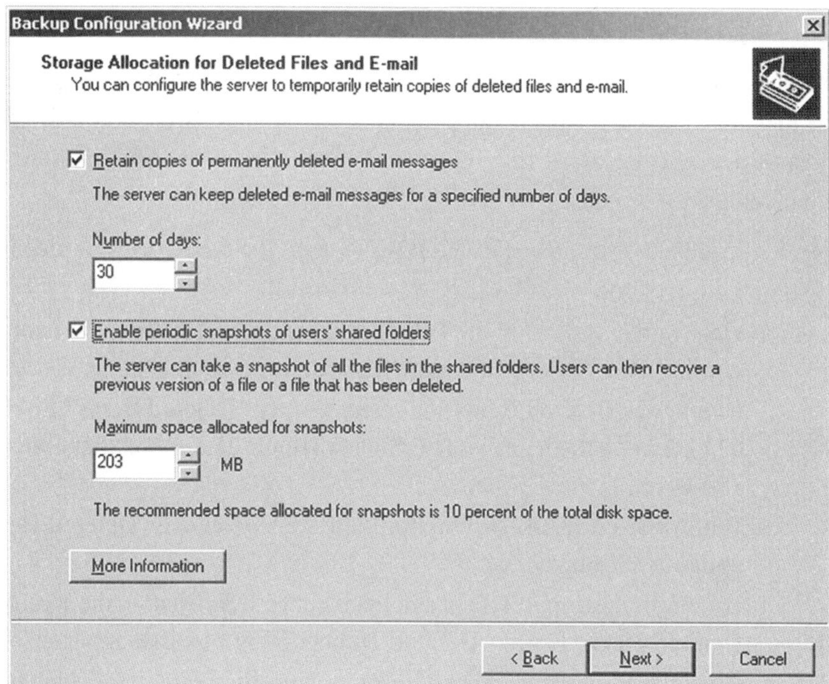

BEST PRACTICE: There are two hooks here that are very interesting as they relate to information in prior chapters. In Chapter 6, I spoke to Exchange's Deleted Item Retention capabilities already being set to 30 days. That is true and you are essentially affirming that setting on this page. However, I tripled it to 90 days, based on my real-world experience that a fiscal quarter is the best guide to retaining important e-mails.

In Chapter 3 during the SBS 2003 setup phase, I spoke to redirecting the data folders to another drive, such as drive D: (see Figure 3-21). That's because Volume Shadow Copy Restore triggers off of the drive where the data folders are located. Please revisit that discussion now if you want more information.

Note: See the discussion on the Automated System Recovery Wizard (ASRW) later in the chapter as a monthly/annual task.

Recovering Deleted E-mail

Now go ahead and give the deleted e-mail capability a test with this procedure. Note that there is great business value in this ability to rapidly recover individual pieces of e-mail (instead of relying on an Information Store-level restore via the native backup program).

1. Log on as **NormH** at **PRESIDENT** with the password **Purple3300**.
2. Launch Outlook 2003 from **Start**, **E-mail**.
3. Delete an e-mail from the **Inbox** (this could be the **"Ideas for forthcoming Dog Shows"** message that you created in Chapter 6).
4. Right-click **Deleted Items** and select **Empty "Deleted Items" Folder**. Click **Yes** on the **Microsoft Office Outlook** dialog box that appears. The e-mail is now gone.
5. With **Deleted Items** still highlighted, select **Recover Deleted Items** under the **Tools** menu.
6. Highlight the e-mail you just deleted beneath **Subject** in the **Recover Deleted Items From - Deleted Items** dialog box that appears.
7. Click the **Recover Selected Items** icon (yellow e-mail message with blue arrow on toolbar).
8. Notice the e-mail has been recovered to the **Deleted Items** folder. You could now copy it back to the **Inbox**.
9. Isn't that cool! It will save you HOURS as your manage your SBS 2003 network.

Monthly\Annual Test Restores

Once per month, restore a small file (such as a document) to a new location (don't overwrite the existing file) and open it, read it, print it! That's going to be the best assurance you could have that your backup process is sound! An annual test restore of the entire system to test server is highly recommended if you have the time and an extra server available (granted, this is very much a luxury).

The monthly test restore process commences from using the native NTBackup interface (**Start**, **All Programs**, **Accessories**, **System Tools**, **Backup**). This will launch the **Backup or Restore Wizard**. Click the **Advanced Mode** link to switch to native mode. The **Restore and Manage Media** tab is shown in Figure 11-4.

Figure 11-4
This is where you would select a file on which to perform a test restore.

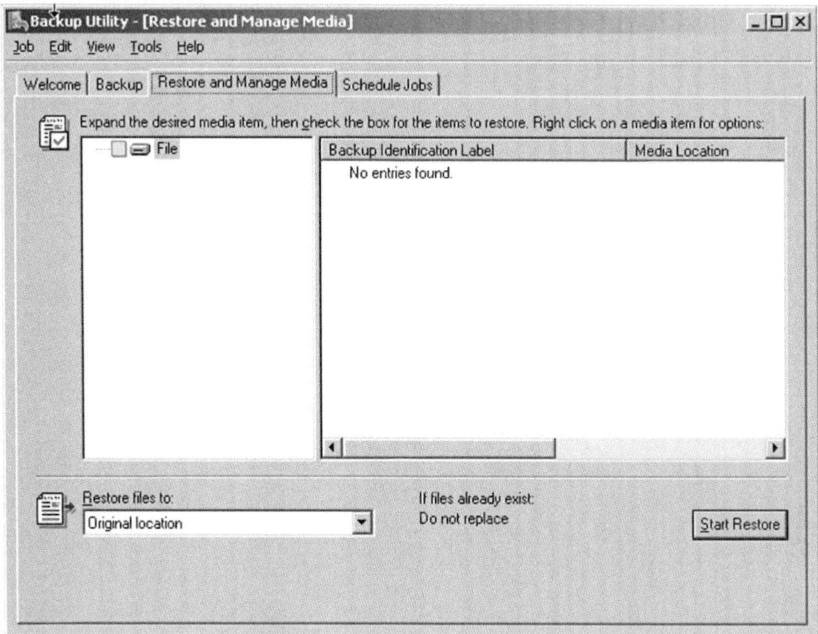

Your guidance for the annual test restore of a full server is documented right on the SBS 2003 server machine. In Server Management, under Standard Management, click **Backup** to display the **Manage Small Business Server Backup** page (Figure 11-5). The **Learn How to Restore the Server** link presents an article titled "Restoring Your Server." You will do exactly this in my advanced SBS 2003 book.

> BEST PRACTICE: Catch the note that you're instructed to check the Microsoft Web site to read the updated release notes for updates to this procedure. Good idea!

Figure 11-5

The Backup page in Server Management.

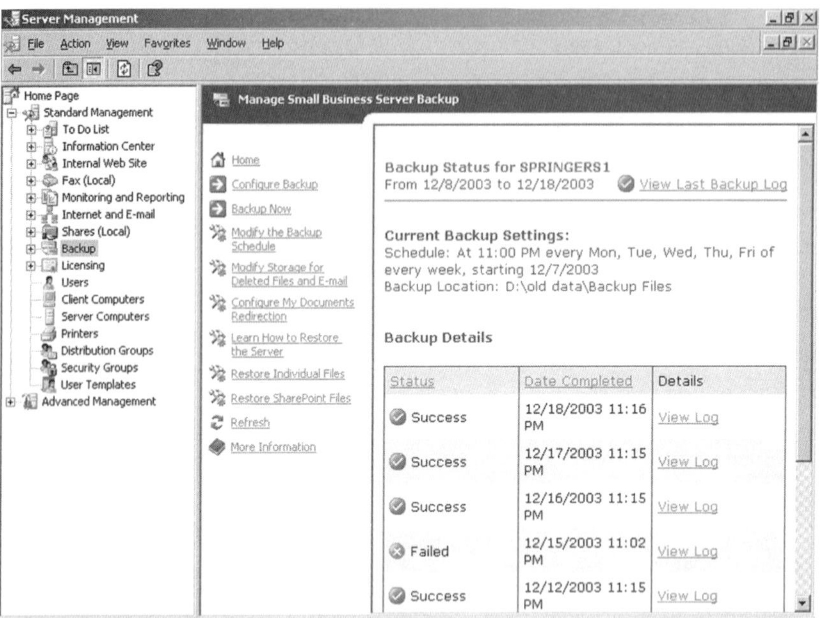

The Restore Individual Files link provides guidance on how to recover individual files via the Volume Shadow Copy Restore capability. The Restore SharePoint File link speaks to how to recover WSS data, including individual files.

Configure My Documents Redirection

The SBS development team views centralized storage of data as a part of the "best practices" in securing and protecting your data. I agree. So the Configure My Documents Redirection link displays the Client Document Redirection dialog box that allows you to use Group Policy to redirect data from user workstations up to individual user folders on the network. The data can then be backed up.

Figure 11-6
As ordered, this screen will configure data redirection. I'd highly recommend you click More Information and read all about this in detail.

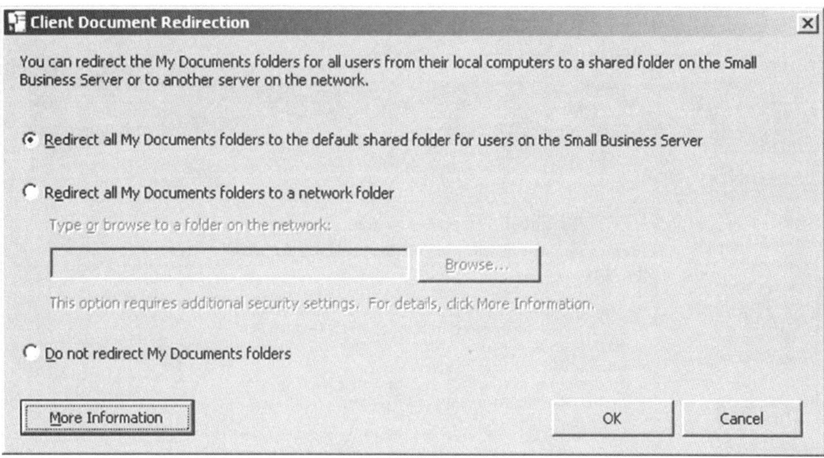

When you complete this process, the behavior you will observe is this: When you are finished working on your client computer and go to log off, a screen will appear showing the status of document being moved from your local My Documents folder to your shared folder on the network. There is no user interaction.

Third-Party Backup Solutions

The improved native data protection capabilities in SBS 2003 are not meant to be a "category killer" that would put ISVs out of business. Rather, the native tools are there for smaller firms that don't have sophisticated backup needs and perhaps can't afford a third-party backup tool. One such tool that I'm very familiar with is Veritas Backup Exec for Windows Servers version 9.1 (Figure 11-7).

Figure 11-7
Backup Exec 9.1 has robust SBS support as you can see here. Visit www.veritas.com.

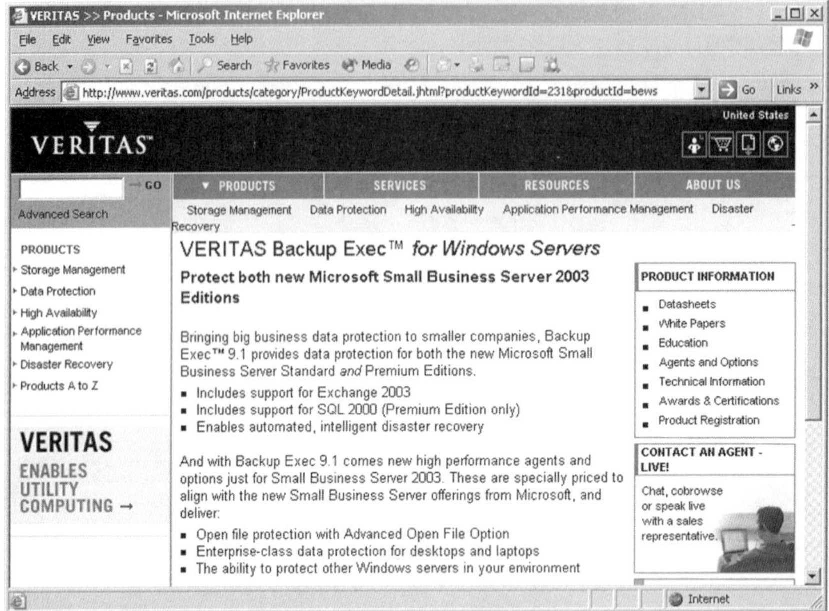

So why would you use Backup Exec in an SBS environment? Two possible reasons are the SQL Server agent for SBS 2003 premium edition and the brick-level e-mail backup and restore capability. But many good SBSers have opinions on this backup matter. One such SBSer is Traig Zeigler, who has posted for years in the SBS Yahoo! group (I had the great pleasure of meeting Traig at the SBS 2003 hands-on lab in Chicago). Traig participated in a newsgroup discussion thread on Veritas in mid-December 2003 where he questioned, "Why is Backup Exec really needed in SBS 2003 at all?" Traig is asking exactly the right question and in many cases (perhaps most cases), the use of third-party backup solutions is no longer a given in the world of SBS.

A little SBS backup trivia for you. In SBS 4.0, when you installed the Backup Exec SBS product, a Backup Exe button was placed on the SBS console (it modified the console). That was the only release in which the console modification occurred.

Virus Detection and Protection

This topic, covered in both Chapter 5 and Chapter 6, is revisited here appropriately as an administrative responsibility. It's likely we're all in agreement that you must implement virus protection. Perhaps the only question is "In what form?" These debates, frequently seen on the SBS newsgroups, are like religious wars and not easily solved (everyone seems to have their own favorite ISV). So let me add fuel to the fire and point you to my favorite virus protection ISV: Trend Micro.

Figure 11-8
Trend Micro (www.trendmicro.com) is a long-time citizen of the SBS community.

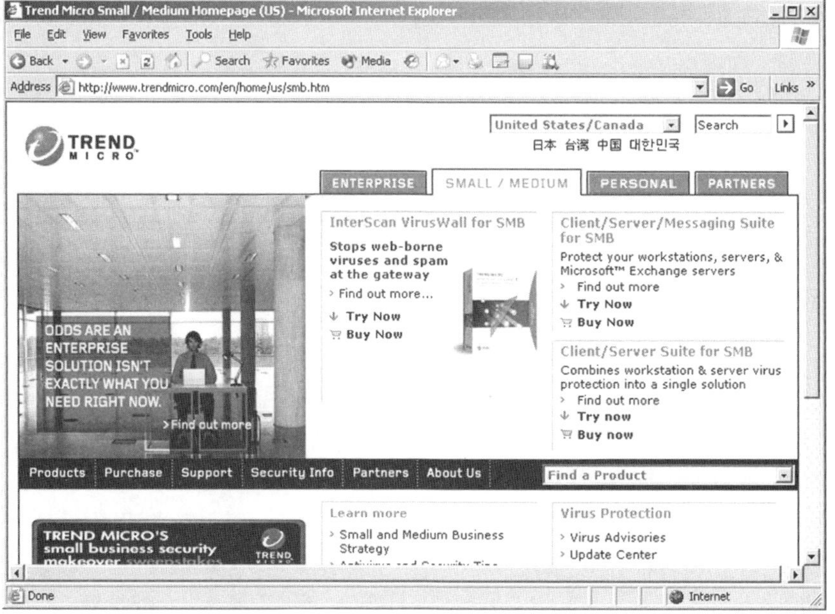

BEST PRACTICE: Some of you know that Trend Micro created a minor public relations nightmare in late 2002 when it removed its SBS-specific SKU and repositioned it as a SMB SKU. It was culturally offensive to long-time SBSers (as well as financially offensive, because the product price effectively increased). However, it's always a best practice to forgive and I've done so. But please, Trend Micro, don't do that again!

So I'd like you to move forward with SPRINGERS and complete two procedures here. First, download, install, and configure the Client/Server/Messaging Suite for SMB from Trend Micro (this is a 30-day version). Be sure to configure Trend Micro to update its virus data files hourly so you have the best protection regardless of when an outbreak hits!

After all that, I want you to download and install the trial version of Trend Micros's PortalProtect for SharePoint (we discussed this in Chapter 7). PortalProtect is displayed in Figure 11-9.

Figure 11-9
PortalProtect will work with WSS in SBS 2003.

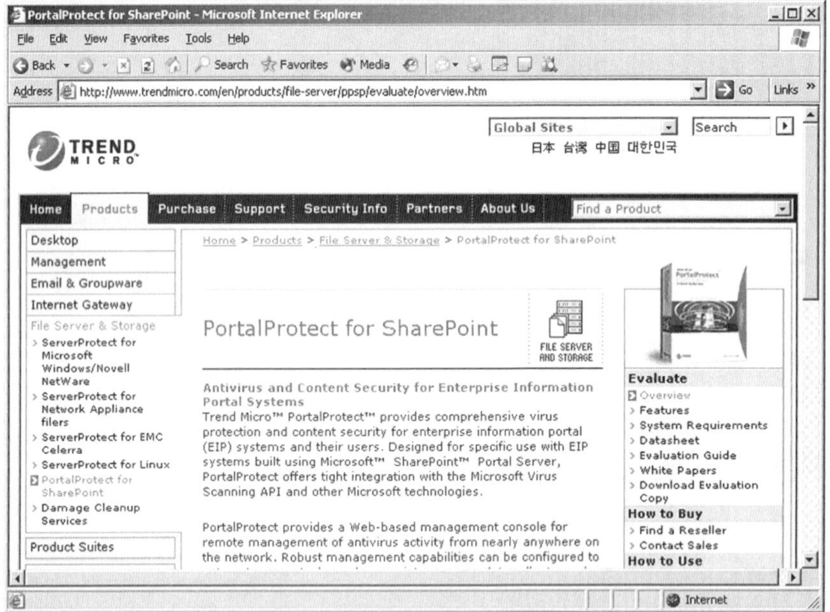

Late breaking news! Near the end of my writing this book, I was advised of Panda's Antivirus GateDefender that offers a hardware-based solution (www.pandasecurity.com). Very interesting!

> BEST PRACTICE: Subscribe to Trend Micro's *Weekly Virus Report* which keeps you up to speed on breaking news in the virus protection area. Visit www.trendmicro.com.

Spam Blocking

The best advice I've received in recent times about blocking spam messages was to use multiple spam blockers. That's good news for Sunbelt Software, creators of iHateSpam (Figure 11-10) and GFI with its MailEssentials (Figure 11-11), both of which I've used. The advice was given in the context that spammers are very creative in overcoming defenses, so you simply need more defenses!

Figure 11-10
iHateSpam (yes - I really do!).

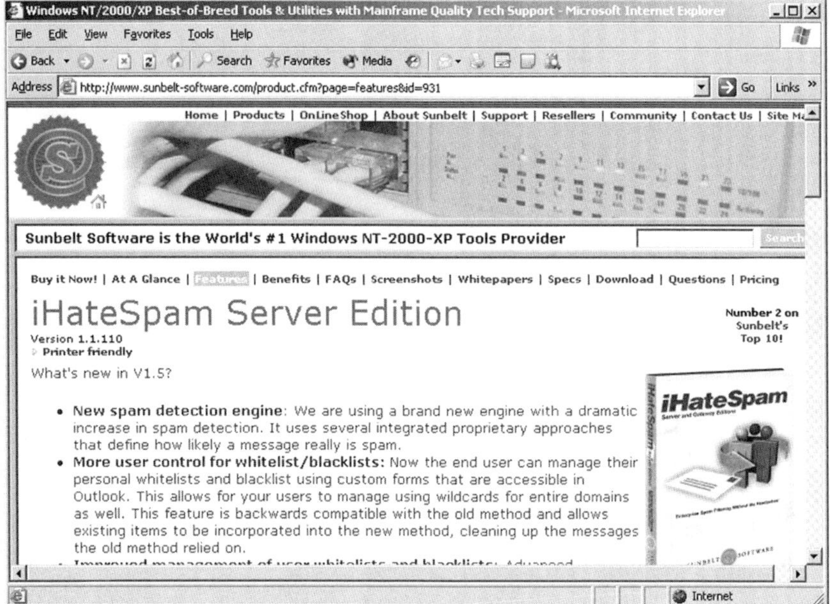

Figure 11-11

GFI's MailEssentials aggressively weeds out e-mails.

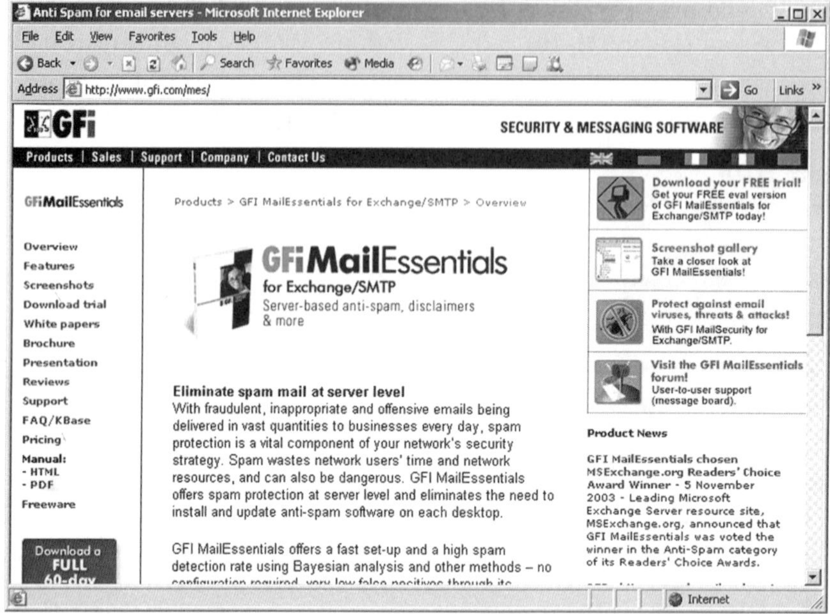

You guessed what's next! Download both products and install as part of the SPRINGERS methodology. Boring you say? Ah - just consider part of the SBS administration experience. Visit these sites to continue:

- iHateSpam at www.sunbelt-software.com
- MailEssentials at www.gfi.com

You'll recall that we have already discussed spam-related topics in several chapters of this book. In Chapter 4 you configured the e-mail attachment removal capability in the EICW (all right, some of you call it the CEICW). Chapter 5 viewed this topic properly from a security perspective. And Chapter 6 viewed it as a Exchange and Outlook topic.

BEST PRACTICE: It's probably never a best practice to talk politics, but what the hell, here goes. Spam fighting has become not just a technical matter, but a political one as well. In the course of one week in December 2003, President Bush signed federal anti-spam legislation and Microsoft teamed with New York Attorney General Elliott Spitzer to sue big-time spammers. I share this political moment with you so that you will view spam as a multi-dimensional issue.

Spyware Removal

As a kid, perhaps you watched the well-worn animated feature *Rudolph the Red-Nosed Reindeer*? If so, you might remember the scene whereby Yukon Cornelius tames the Abominable Snowman and turns that oversized creature into a humble bumble. In the world of SBS 2003 networks, there is one sure and quick way to become a humble bumble. Simply install and run a spyware application on your server and the workstations. You'll be tossin' cookies (the computer type) when you see the results. So this part of the SPRINGERS methodology demands that you visit www.bulletproofsoft.com (Figure 11-12) and download the trial version of the Spy Watch suite. Run the Spyware Remover application and make sure you're sitting down when you see the results. This will likely make you one humble bumble!

Figure 11-12
Home of the humbling-experience giver, BulletProofSoft.

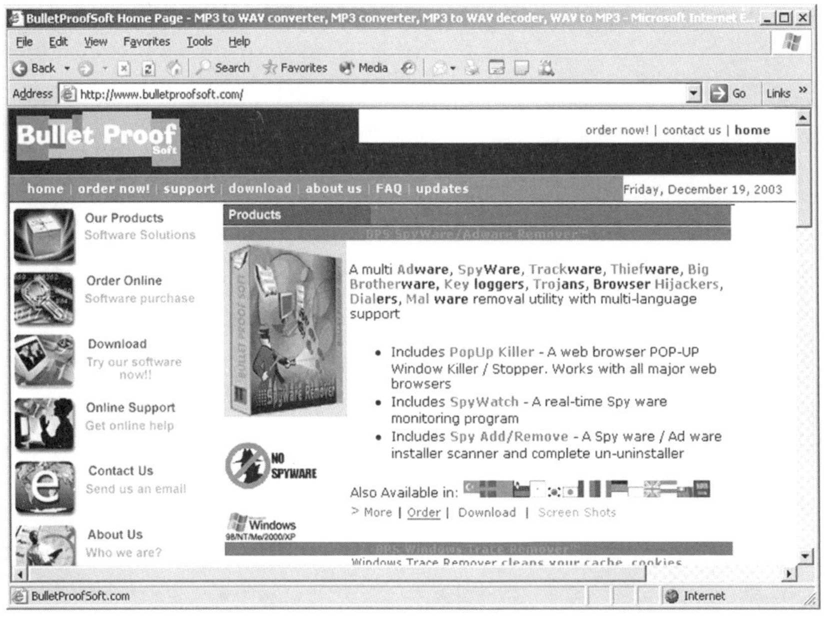

SBS 2003 Quick Hitters

By far the most popular SBS lecture I ever delivered was the "quick hitter" speech. I've given it to Gateway, IBM, and countless advanced SBS gatherings in the USA in 2003. The format is "cut to the chase" - less theory and tastes great! In this section, I'll give you some quick hitters on SBS administration topics.

- **Click through the SBS tools in Server Management.** Do yourself right and engage in a "daze and amaze" session where you explore the Server Management console. It's powerfully amazing.

- **Security quick hitter: permission upgrade.** Perform the following now to upgrade the permissions for Linda Briggs from user to mobile user. In **Server Management**, select **Users** under **Standard Management** and click on the **Change User Permissions** link. Click **Next** at the **Welcome to the Change User Permission Wizard** page. **Select Mobile User Template** on the **Template Selection** screen and click **Next** (make sure the **Replace any previous permissions granted to the users** check box is selected). Select **Linda Briggs** under **Users** and click **Add** (Linda will then appear under the **Change permissions for column** as seen in Figure 11-13). Click **Next**. Click the **here** link on the completion page to save the settings change to your SBS Network Notebook. Click **Finish** followed by **Close**.

Notes:

Figure 11-13
Elevating the permission of a user so that she can exploit the mobility features in SBS 2003 is a very common task.

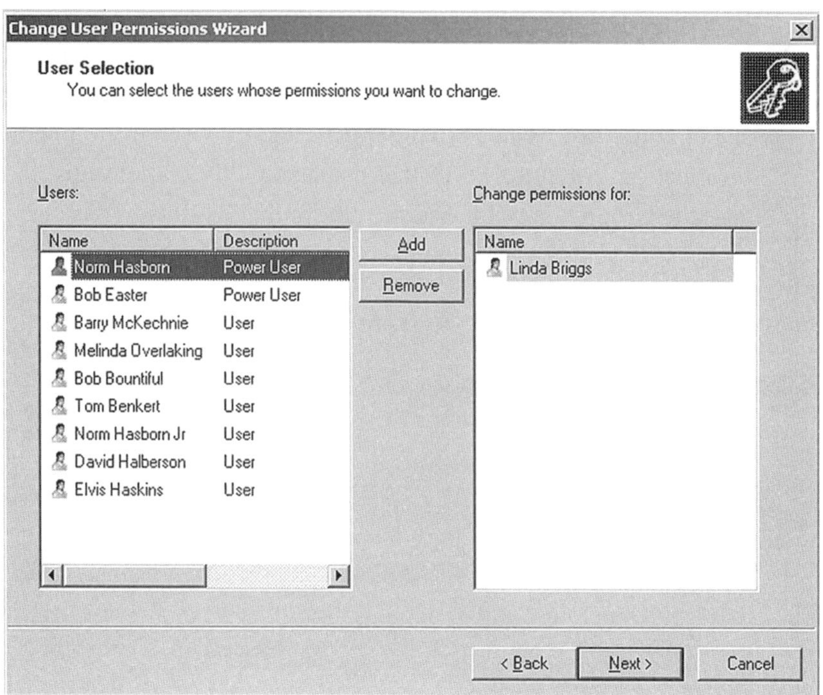

- **Active Directory - not enough said yet!** Just when you thought you'd escape this book without having to read about Active Directory (AD), I want to draw your attention to the built-in multiple organization units (OU) utilized extensively by SBS 2003 (note the single built-in OU wasn't really used in the SBS 2000 time frame - it was just test marketing!). Under **Advanced Management** in **Server Management**, select **Active Directory Users and Computers**. Expand **SpringersLtd.local** (the domain object). Expand the **MyBusiness** OU and peek into the child OUs (**Computers**, **Distribution Groups**, **Security Groups**, **Users**). You will find, for example, that user objects in SBS 2003 are placed in the SBSUsers child OU beneath the Users OU beneath MyBusiness, not the Users folder beneath the domain object in AD.

- **Group Policy Management.** Closely related to the AD discussion above is the object just below it in Advanced Management of Server Management: the Group Policy Management snap-in. This capability was highlighted extensively in the launch of Windows Server 2003 for its ability to give your Group Policy a "test run" before committing changes (the Group Policy Results tool). Select **Forest: SpringersLtd.local** and then select **Domains**. Select **SpringersLtd.local**. Observe the important information in Figure 11-14 that displays GPO relationships, in this case the Group Policy Inheritance tab for the SBSUsers.

Figure 11-14
Finally, an easy way to observe how GPOs are being applied!

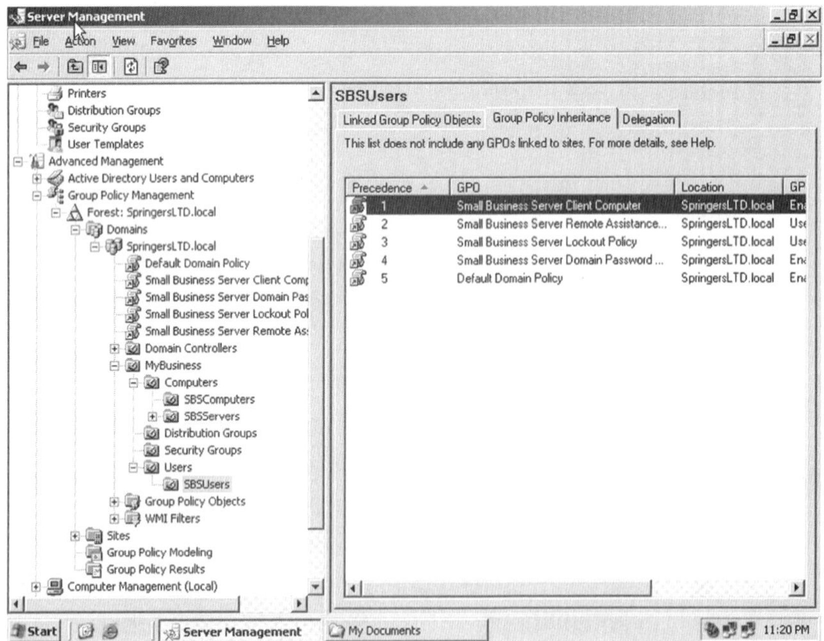

- **Migrate Server Settings Link.** Get to know the Migrate Small Business Server Settings page under Advanced Management in the Server Management console. I'm especially fond of the ability to export and import templates (this will be very helpful if you resell LOBs in which the custom template groups reflect LOB specific settings).

- **Sessions.** It's easy to find out who is logged on to the computer (the context being you've used the public address system asking all employees to log off before you reboot the server and you need to verify that everyone did so). You can simply select **Sessions** from the **Favorites**, **Advanced Management** menu in **Server Management**. (There is also a View Connected Users from the Manage Shared Folder page from the Shares (Local) link under Standard Management in Server Management.) Closely related to who is logged on would be the Security event log. Found under **Event Viewer** (**Server Management**, **Advanced Management**, **Computer Management** (Local), **System Tools**, **Event Viewer**), the Security event log tells you who has logged on and logged off! This is known as logon/logoff auditing

- **Computer Management (Local).** And speaking of the Computer Management (Local) snap-in, you really need to explore this tool. This is where many items housed in the Administrative Tools program group will appear in the Server Management console (it's how we SBSify many native Windows Server 2003 tools).

- **DNS Referral.** One difference between SBS 2003 RC code and the final "gold code" of the product was a fix to make the external NIC card use the local IP address as its primary DNS (e.g., 192.168.16.2) and then refer to the DNS Forwarders configuration to resolve queries. While you have Computer Management (Local) open, go to **Services and Applications**, **DNS**. Then right-click and select **Properties** on the server object (e.g., SPRINGERS1).

BEST PRACTICE: Some of the old-time SBSers will recall that you had to manually configure such DNS referrals (the wild-side NIC calling back to the internal DNS) in SBS 2000 using a TechNet article for guidance. This has now been automated.

- **System Health.** Time to sell you on the next chapter. Monitoring your server and using the system health tools from Monitoring and Reporting under Standard Management in Server Management is a uniquely SBS 2003 experience.

Daily and Weekly Administration Quick Hitters

In this section, I speak to the type of things you're likely to do on a daily or weekly basis. There are no hard and fast rules here, so please add to this list as you see fit.

- **Sharing Files and Folders.** Configure server-side shared folders from Shares (Local) under Standard Management in Server Management. Shares allow data to be easily accessed over the network (files can't be shared in the SBS 2003/Windows Server 2003time frame, something NetWare gurus notice as a difference immediately).

- **Mapping drives.** I'm assuming you're comfortable with the drive mapping and shared drive concepts. Typically you map a drive to a shared folder. An easy way to map a drive is to right-click **My Computer** and select **Map Network Drive**. Also consider accessing data by creating a "network place" (a concept explored in Chapter 7 on Windows SharePoint Services) from **My Network Places** (from the **Start** button).

- **UPS power levels.** If you believe all the APC ads you see in computer trade journals and consumer magazines, you'd believe that protection from power problems is important with your computers. It is! Not only should you have bona fide UPS devices and surge protectors in place, but you should monitor power levels with the software tools like PowerChute (this typically ships with an APC UPS). Power to the people, baby!

- **End-user support.** Even pious and haughty SBSers have to engage in end-user support. It's a two-pronged sword: technical support and customer service. (My *SMB Consulting Best Practices* book goes much deeper into this!) I didn't have to look far for an example of end-user support, as Figure 11-15 will attest. The situation here was my client, a large real estate company, has a secretary who is INFAMOUS for sending out an "I can't print" on late Friday afternoons, just as this SBSer is winding down his business affairs. Ya gotta love it.

Figure 11-15

True to form, Pat sends an "I can't print" on Friday afternoon just after 4:00pm. Note the date on the message. This is the Friday before the Christmas Holiday Week. CLASSIC!

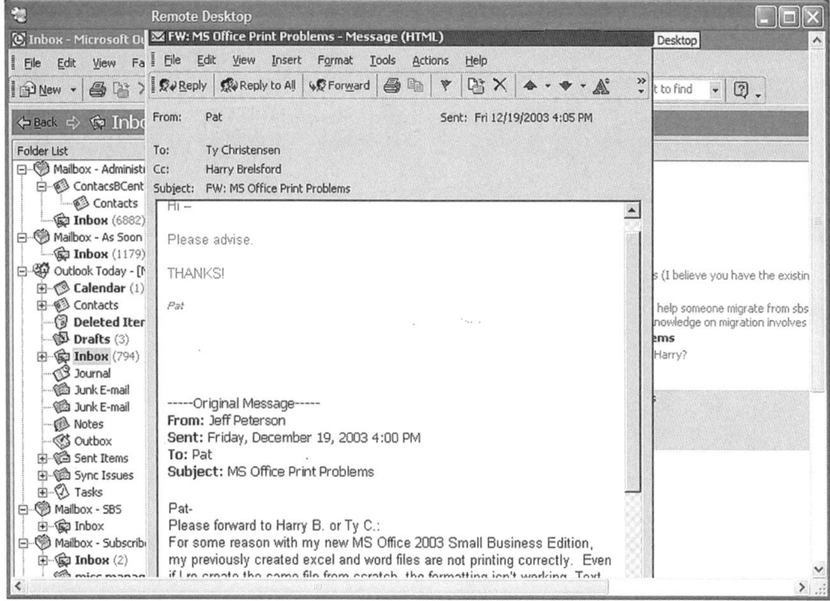

- **Remove Printer ID #10.** Something to free up entries in your System Event log is to remove Printer ID #10 from **Start**, **Printers and Faxes**, **File**, **Server Properties**, **Advanced** tab and deselect **Log spooler information events**. Consider deselecting the other printer events. Who needs printer event log entries when you have Pat in Figure 11-15 above?

- **Hard disk space management.** I discuss this more in Chapter 12, but for now, look at the Storage object in Computer Management (Local). Also see my reference to Raj's research and recommendations in the next section.

- **Patch management.** Talk about a business model. Continually protecting an SBS 2003 system from bad stuff is a lucrative career opportunity. In Chapter 4 you learned about Automatic Update and SUS. Here I want to point you to a really cool third-party tool, the Shavlik patch management program (www.shavlik.com) called HKNetChkPro. Go ahead and download it now from the site shown in Figure 11-16. See Frank Ohlhorst's column at the end of the chapter for more information on this tool and other sage advice on patch management.

Figure 11-16
Some grizzled and hardened SBS gurus I know live by Shavlik.

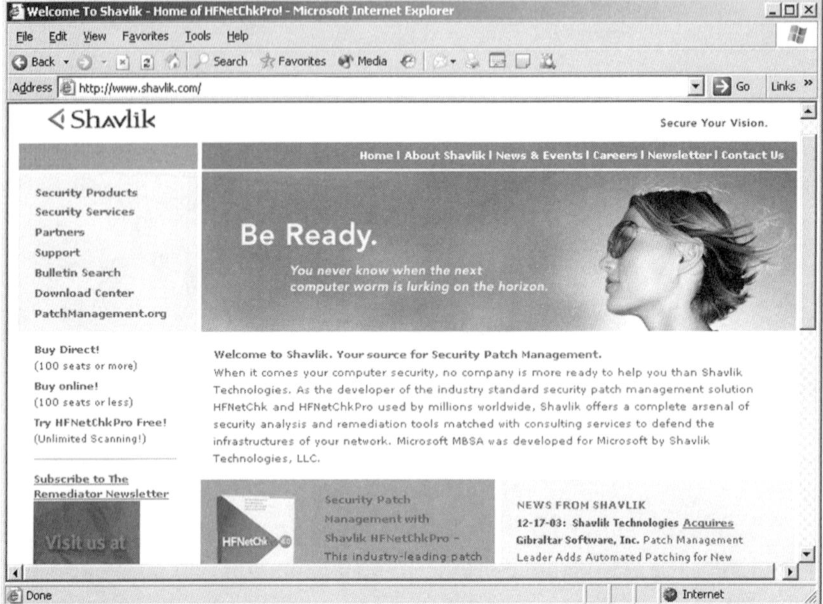

Monthly and Annual Quick Hitters

- **Raj's methodology papers.** There is a program manager at Microsoft named Raj who is the catalyst behind a series of SMB methodology papers that pay special attention to SBS 2003. These papers range from prescriptive guidance on how to implement the SBS networking infrastructure (present company excepted) to integrating Windows Storage Server in an SBS 2003 environment when you have large storage needs (my favorite paper). Download the Infrastructure Solutions for Small and Medium Business - Small IT Solution from http://members.microsoft.com/partner/solutions/infotech/default.aspx as seen in Figure 11-17.

Figure 11-17
Excellent methodology information here!

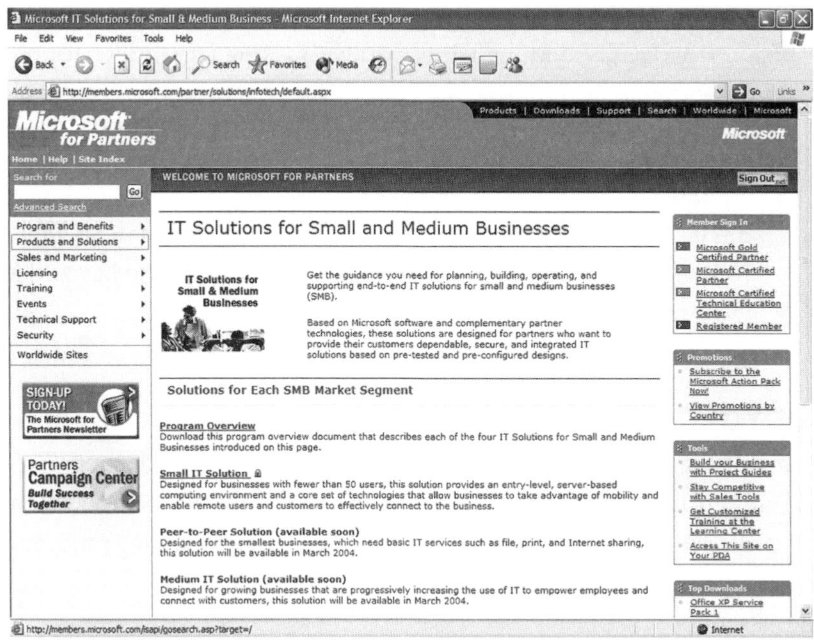

- **SBS 2003 Licensing.** Whew! Time to punt on this topic. You need to learn more about licensing the following two ways. First, visit the primary SBS 2003 Web sites mentioned in Appendix A (the Microsoft Partners site has the best licensing discussion!). Then attend a Microsoft TS2 event where licensing is explained (www.msts2.com).

- **Adding Value (CRM, Retail).** SBS 2003 is a platform that is the foundation for business solutions. So you can imagine it wasn't a huge leap for Microsoft to bundle some of its business solutions with SBS 2003. As of this writing, there are two such bundles: Microsoft Retail Management System and Microsoft CRM 1.2. Word has it that you'll see a plethora of such bundles going forward.

- **ERD and ASRW.** Just when you thought the emergency repair disk had gone the way of Microsoft Bob, you discover the NTBackup program (**Start**, **All Programs**, **Accessories**, **System Tools**, **Backup**) has a link on its Welcome tab for Automated System Recovery Wizard. This is central to your ability to recover a crashed SBS 2003 server machine.

BEST PRACTICE: Read the white paper "Backing Up and Restoring Windows Small Business Server 2003" accessed from the Technical Resources - Product Documentation link from the main Microsoft SBS site (links in Appendix A).

- **SMB Nation.** A shameless plug to encourage you to attend the SMB Nation annual conference that focuses on SBS 2003 and beyond! Visit www.smbnation.com.

Remote Management

The remote capabilities of SBS 2003 are best explored in Chapter 8 of this book, but here the spin is to use Terminal Services to perform remote management on the SBS 2003 server machine. You will complete the following procedure as part of the SPRINGERS methodology.

BEST PRACTICE: Terminal Services now uses 128-bit encryption and the screen resolution is much improved (both enhancements in the SBS 2003 time frame). The screen resolution improvement was a super big deal to the twins from Tyler Texas who attended the Dallas hands-on lab event.

1. Use the remote computer for this procedure, so have **NormH** log on locally to his laptop (which I've called **NormLap**) using the password **Purple3300**. It is assumed this laptop has an Internet connection.
2. Launch **Remote Desktop Connection** from **Start**, **All Programs**, **Accessories**, **Communications**.
3. Type **springers1.springersltd.com** in the **Computer** field and click **Connect**.
4. Complete the Windows logon dialog box to log on as **Administrator** with the password **Husky9999!** and click **Logon**.

5. You can now remotely manage the SBS 2003 server machine. Observe Figure 11-18, where you can see the Server Management console.
6. Repeat this exercise and log on as **NormH** for the Terminal Services session. Notice that, because he is a power user, Norm has access to the Power User Console and that's all!

Figure 11-18
Remotely administering your SBS 2003 server machine with Terminal Services.

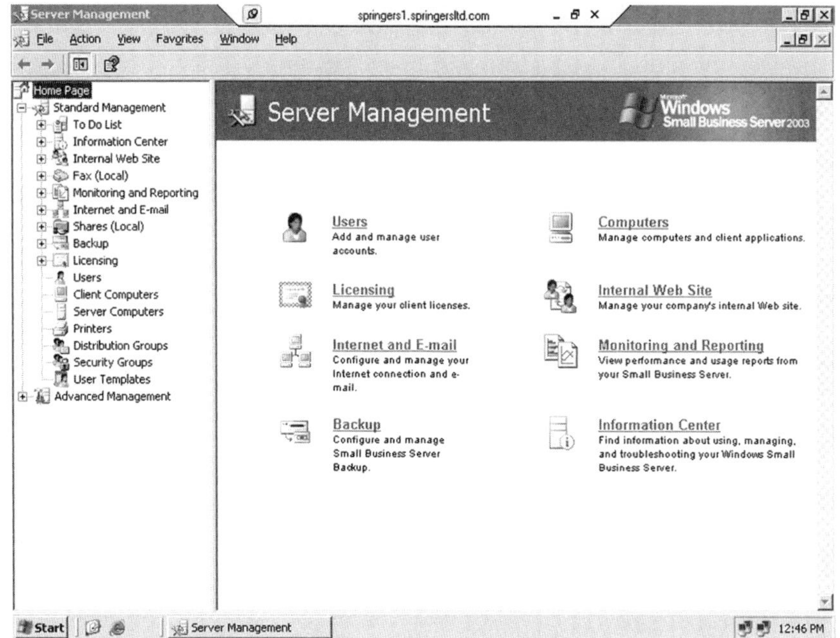

BEST PRACTICE: Terminal Services runs in Remote Administration mode in SBS 2003. Do not (and you can not) place it in Application Sharing mode in SBS 2003. If you need Terminal Services in Application Sharing mode, deploy a member server on your SBS 2003 network that will gladly handle that role. Period.

My SBS friend and inaugural SMB Nation attendee, Dick Davis, posted a very interesting Terminal Services (TS) licensing item on the SBS Yahoo! Group on the last possible day I could hijack it and place it in this book (thanks Dick!):

> FYI. Don't know if this was previously covered, if so forgive me. It won't hurt to be reminded to take advantage of the WXP Pro TSCAL (Device or User) Complimentary Transition plan.
>
> Go to the link: http://www.microsoft.com/windowsserver2003/howtobuy/licensing/tscaltransfaq.mspx?pf=true
>
> If you or your clients have any WXP Pro licenses (Volume, OEM or Retail) that were purchased on or before 4/24/03 pay attention to this: Microsoft will give you a complimentary (read free) W2K3 Terminal Services CAL for each WXP Pro license. That is worth about $150. This free transitional license offer is good until 12/31/05. After receiving the license you have until 12/31/05 to install it. So, even if you don't have W2K3 Server running now you may in the future and you may want to utilize W2K3 Terminal Services for your WXP Pro clients. A five pack of W2K3 TSCALs list for $749, a 20 pack is $2979.
>
> If you want to enroll the complimentary license in SA you must do that before 12/31/03.
>
> Dick Davis
> MCP, A+
> MIS
> Jif-Pak Manufacturing, Inc.

You can take remote management to the next level with HP's Remote Insights Lights-Out Edition (RILOE) card in your HP server (you'll recall SPRINGERS uses all HP gear). While delivering the SBS 2003 hands-on lab in Houston, Texas, I trotted over to HP's campus and was given a demo with a RILOE product manager. RILOE, seen in Figure 11-19, allows you to remote manage the server machine at the hardware level. This is a great tool in case the SBS network doesn't restart properly after a reboot (say from your patch management activities). You could connect to the failed server and work at the pre-operating system level. I will fully explore this functionality in my advanced SBS 2003 book.

Figure 11-19
Hello, RILOE! Details at www.hp.com.

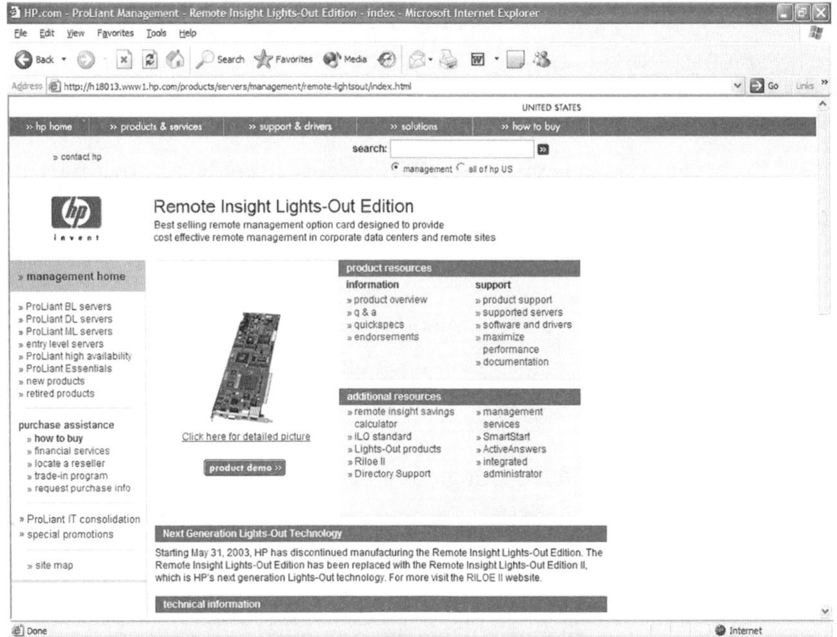

Working Smarter

Who doesn't want to work smarter each day with SBS? Of course, we all do! Here's a few hints starting with the simple and moving to the complex.

- **Rename network cards.** This is simple. Have your NIC cards icons displayed on the lower right of your SBS server machine (select **Show icon in notification area when connected** on the **General** tab of the NIC card property sheet). Then right-click the NIC card icon and select **Open Network Connections**. Right-click the NIC card in the **Network Connections** window that appears and select **Rename**. I'd recommend the inside NIC card be named **LAN 192.168.16.2** and the wild-side NIC card be named **Internet 207.202.238.215** in the SPRINGERS methodology (use your own IP addresses in the real world). Doing this allows you to monitor network activity at a glance and know which interface you're interacting with. Call it the WHOAMI command of NICs!

- **SBS Network Notebook.** Take a bow! If you've followed the SPRINGERS approach, you've already done this. You've built your network notebook across the pages of this book by clicking **here** at the end of each native SBS wizard.

- **TechNet.** A must have. Subscribe to it now from the Microsoft Partners site (Appendix A details). Note Technet is a Web site, a library of discs that are mailed to you monthly, and a seminar series.

- **Action Pack.** You are commanded to subscribe to Action Pack if you are an SBS consultant so you can acquire SBS on the cheap plus tons of other software. Order from the Microsoft Partners site.

- **The Web - Google It.** Google is a verb and something you need to do to stay current with SBS. Try this. Go to Google (www.google.com) and select the **News** tab. Type **Small Business Server** in the search field and click **Search News**. You'll be amazed at the number of SBS-related articles, all current, that are presented to you. Read 'em!

- **Update your toolkits (physical and mental).** Don't fall into the trap of not having a bona fide computer toolkit (you can easily order such a toolkit for under $50 USD at CDW: www.cdw.com). Build your mental toolkit by reading articles such as "Protecting Your Customers' Networks From Intruders" (Ed Tittel, VARBusiness, May 12, 2003).

- **Running your SBS consulting practice better.** This comment is directed to SBS consultants. Consider managing your consulting practice better so you can serve your SBS customers better. Cleanliness and all good things start at home. I highly recommend you consider

ConnectWise's PSA consulting practice management solution. It's something that I feature in my *SMB Consulting Best Practices* book. It's all part of working smarter as an SBS consultant. Figure 11-20 displays ConnectWise PSA.

Figure 11-20
Comprehensive SBS consulting practice management is part of the ConnectWise PSA solution. Visit www.connectwise.com.

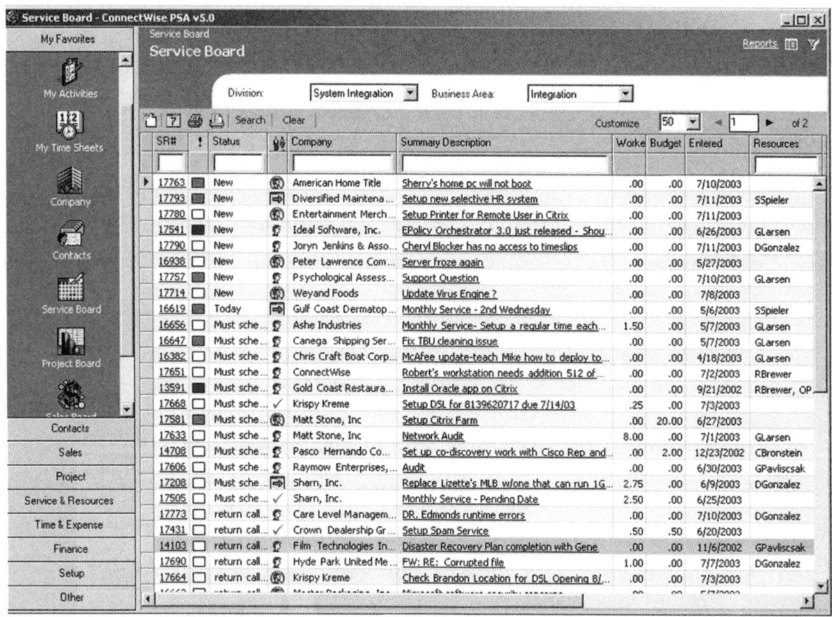

- **Time Synchronization.** Visit www.microsoft.com/technet and search on "Windows Time Service" to set your SBS server to an Internet time source.

Next Steps

The SBS 2003 administration area is one that I see evolving rapidly and changing often. Because of that, I'm committed to posting updates to this chapter at www.smbnation.com so you can stay current. Click over for the latest updates to this chapter! And don't forget to subscribe to my free SBS newsletter that will regularly feature administration articles.

Guest Column

Enhancing Security with Patch Management

Frank Ohlhorst

Keeping software up to date with patches is one of the most important tasks that can be performed when it comes to maintaining a secure and reliable network. Microsoft introduces several patches monthly for a variety of products and the importance of those patches can not be under estimated. The recent blaster worm outbreaks and a host of other security problems could have been prevented if systems had been properly patched. The problem is that applying patches is often overlooked or put off indefinably, mostly due to either ignorance or the chores involved.

Integrators have real opportunity with patch management, by automating and managing the process, integrators can both protect their customers and generate service revenue on a contractual basis or as part of an overall support plan.

The first step to effective patch management is to find an ally. That ally comes in software form. The primary job of a patch management product is to scan networked systems and determine if patching is needed. That is accomplished by examining a systems setup and comparing it to a known patch database. Furthermore, better patch management products keep a detailed history of patches applied and offer rollback and change management capabilities.

Many patch management solutions exist on the market from major players such as BigFix, Configuresoft and PatchLink, but those products are usually geared towards enterprise networks and can cost upwards of several thousand dollars. Those servicing the SBS market can turn to a free patch management product from Shavlik Software (www.shavlik.com). That company offers a 10 seat version of HFNetChkPro AdminSuite at no charge. Integrators will find HFNetCHKPro a powerful patch management solution. Shavlik's offering does a complete job of scanning both servers and workstations and determines what patches are needed, much of the process can be automated, yet provide detailed information on needed patches. The product also tracks when patches were applied and what each recommended patch does in detail.

Integrators will find patch management an important service for their SBS customers that can be included as part of an overall management and system maintenance service that protects SBS customers interests while providing on going revenue and piece of mind.

Summary

This chapter, which was probably more about “beginnings” than “ends,” provided you with sage advice and specific tools - many third-party - to manage your SBS 2003 network. Of course, the catch is that you’ve only just begun. SBS 2003 network management is an ongoing process which simply goes with the turf as an SBSer. Forward!

Chapter 12
Monitoring SBS 2003

This chapter concludes the SBS 2003 standard edition discussion in this text with a bang - namely the exciting area of performance monitoring. This is a special chapter to write as it brings back the thrill I felt 11 books ago when I wrote the first chapter of my first book on network performance monitoring. Hopefully, you'll pick up on this excitement and not treat it as a task area with the drudgery of auditing! No offense to my friends in the wonderful accounting profession.

So why get excited about performance monitoring? One reason is that performance monitoring includes both the "bits" and "biz" of technology. It's the hard core system statistics that MCSEs love. And it's trend-watching that the MBAs like. This mindset maps very closely to the SBS product position, as it's a product with both a technical and business dimension to it.

Past readers of my *SBS 2000 Best Practices* and SBS gurus might be asking, "Just what are some of the "delta" changes in the performance monitoring area with SBS 2003?" I've compiled a short list:

- Improved performance monitoring setup. Later in this chapter you will complete the wizard to implement the performance monitoring in SBS 2003.
- Improved Server Performance Report. The Server Performance Report (SPR), formerly called the Server Status Report, looks much better in its default state and doesn't need the special XML kit you added in the SBS 2000 time frame to get the same look.
- Emphasizing what's needed and de-emphasizing what's not needed. The SSR has gone on a diet and doesn't have too much fat. What you

receive is a report that's meaningful, baby! Health Monitor, while cool, has effectively been placed under the hood in SBS 2003 (accessed from the Administrative Tool program group) and is no longer an object on the consoles (Server Management, Power User).

- Server Status View changes. What used to be the main home page for the consoles in SBS 2000 is now a simplified view under Monitoring and Reporting under Standard Management in the Server Management console. It's now appropriately deemphasized to better reflect the interest level of the average SBSer.

- The Server Usage Report is new and cool. It reports on real-world features (not abstract performance monitor counters from MCSE land) that include specific Web activity, e-mail traffic reports, remote access activity, Outlook Web Access activity, and faxing details.

- The ability to fax server monitoring information was removed from SBS 2003. In SBS 2000 you could fax or e-mail or both! I lobbied hard to have "if...then..." logic inserted here in SBS 2003. If the server monitoring information couldn't be e-mailed (say the Exchange Server 2003 application was down), then the information would be faxed. As an SBS consultant, if I received a fax from the SBS customer site, I'd know something was amiss and New Delhi monkeys had unplugged the DSL computer cable again!

- The Reply e-mail address in the e-mail reports is no longer a "null" address but causes a replied message to revert back to the administrator. You can now specify what the return address should be and send the report reply back to your client.

- The ability to import and export Health Monitor settings between SBS 2003 machines. Note that you can't import/export report settings just Health Monitor). This is discussed later in the chapter.

You Are Already Doing It!

Here's an SBS confidence booster. You are already engaged in performance monitoring whether you know it or not. Sure, you're waiting with baited breath to complete the procedures to configure and implement native SBS monitoring. But that telephone call you got from a client (or user) today to complain a network is running slow IS PERFORMANCE MONITORING! Folks using your network will always be your number one performance monitor on a network, plain and simple. Don't believe me? Well, what if the power went out and the fancy network monitoring tools in SBS 2003 couldn't fire? But a user can easily reach you via mobile telephone to report those infamous words that "...the network is down." I rest my case.

As you work on an SBS network, you might be your own toughest critic (aka performance monitor). You're going to be the one who knows that something just isn't right! It's running slow. It's not running at all. It's running intermittently, etc. Consciously or unconsciously, you're already engaging in performance monitoring. All this chapter will do is add more tools to your toolkit and more arrows to your quiver.

Configuring Monitoring

A few 50,000 foot-level comments before installing the "good stuff," as a friend of mine in the Microsoft server clustering testing area would say (that's you, Jimbo!). On a plus note, it's now easy to implement the important performance monitoring function in SBS 2003. You'll do so in just a few seconds by completing the Monitoring Configuration Wizard. But on the other hand, Microsoft turned off the performance monitoring area by default. (I have recommended numerous times to the SBS development team that this be turned on out of the box.) So in completing the research for this book, I asked the product manager, "What's up with that?" He replied that turning on performance monitor by default was the subject of great debate and, in the end, it was all about adhering to Microsoft's modern paradigm that things should be turned off by default when you open the box of software (e.g., IIS is turned off by default in Windows Server 2003).

And in all fairness to Microsoft, if the feature set had to be turned off by default, it's a lot easier to turn on in the SBS 2003 time frame. So let's rock and roll and set up performance monitoring.

1. Log on as **Administrator** on **SPRINGERS1** with the password **Husky9999!** and open **Server Management** from the **Start** button.
2. Under **Standard Management**, select **Monitoring and Reporting** and then select **Set Up Monitoring Reports and Alerts**.
3. Click **Next** at the **Welcome to the Monitoring Configuration Wizard** page.
4. Select all checkboxes on the **Reporting Options** page to receive the daily performance report, the usage report, and the usage report every other week. This is shown in Figure 12-1. Click **Next**.

Figure 12-1
Selecting the basic reporting options for SPRINGERS.

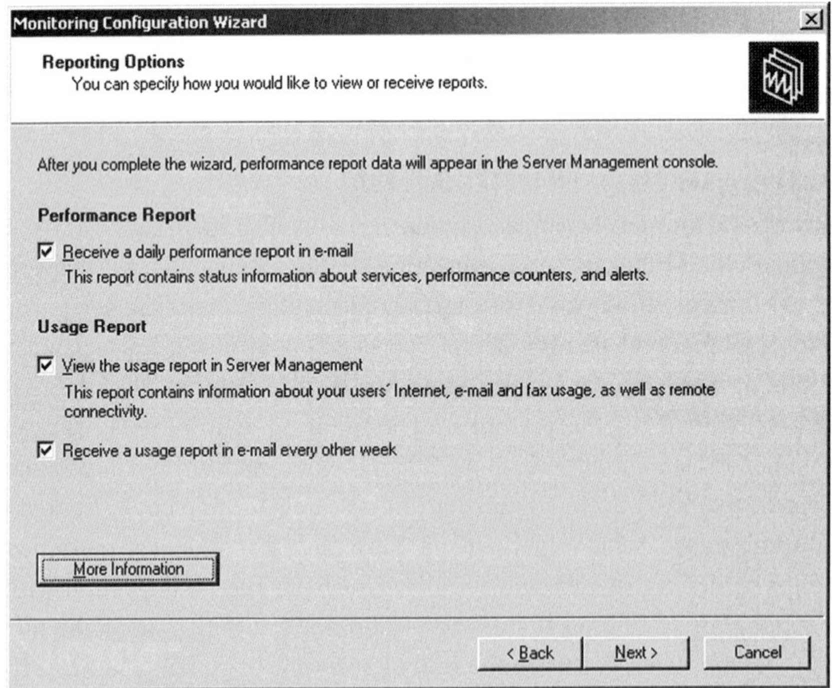

BEST PRACTICE: Reading the More Information screen from the Reporting Options page is especially meaningful and a great use of time. You'll find more details than I'll repeat here, about performance and usage. Read it now!

5. Type **normh@springersltd.com** in the **E-mail address** field on the **E-mail Options** page. Click **Next**.
6. Select **Norm Hasborn** and click **Add** on the **Business Owner Usage Report**, then click **Next**.

BEST PRACTICE: This is what I affectionately call the Bob Wallace report. Bob is my client in the Seattle area who has struck the balance between being very financially successful and very ethical, moral, and so on while still operating very much as a day-to-day president of his firm. You get the picture. Bob wants to receive the Business Owner Usage Report to see exactly what the heck is going on with his information infrastructure! Another client, Marc Sweet, also fits this profile. I'm sure you work with these types are well. Bless their hearts!

You really need to click the **More Information** button here to better understand how this is implemented. For example, you might be interested to know the usage report is accessed from http://springers1/monitoring.

Notes:

7. Complete the **Alerts** page by selecting the **Send me notifications of performance alerts by e-mail** checkbox and typing **administrator @springersltd.com** in the **E-mail address** field. Click **Next**. This is seen in Figure 12-2.

Figure 12-2
The Alerts page is easy to configure. but YOU MUST read the More Information button to better understand what the alerts actually are. Damn good online documentation here that explains everything from DHCP server alerts to the Kerberos Key Distribution Center to the World Wide Web Publishing performance monitor. You must read.

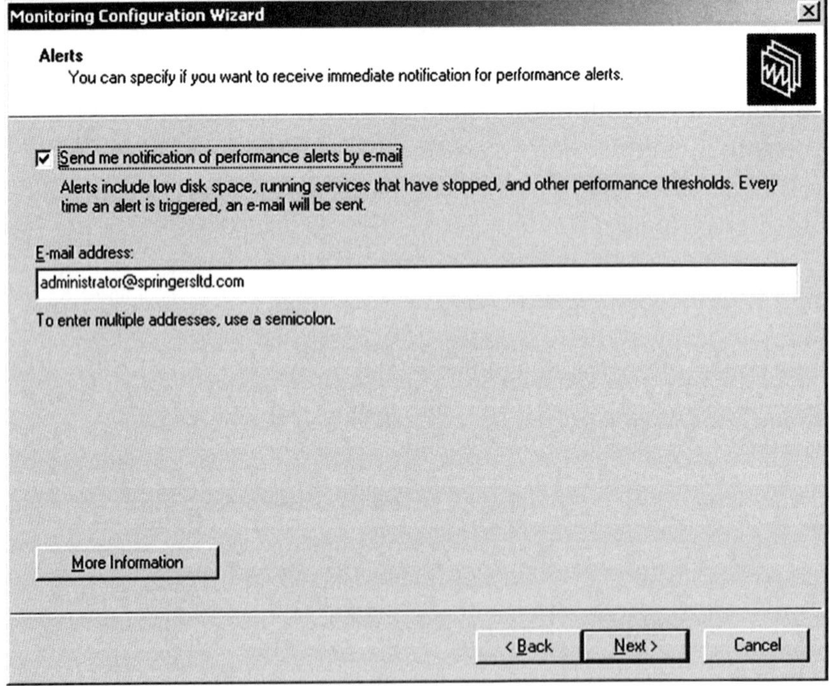

8. Click **here** on the information point reading to save this information to your network notebook on the **Completing the Monitoring Configuration Wizard** page.
9. The configuration information appears in Internet Explorer. Click **File**, **Save As** and save the Web page as **Monitoring Configuration.htm** under **My Documents** on the SBS server machine. Click **Save** and close Internet Explorer.

10. Click **Finish** and click **Close**. Note the configuration process can take over five minutes! Go get some coffee. Note that in the SBS 2003 hands-on lab in the fall of 2003, the image used required a reboot to continue. That's because the SBS 2003 hands-on labs used SBS 2003 Release Candidate code. Such wasn't the case on the HP ML-350, which I used to write this book because the reboot requirement was removed in the final "release-to-manufacturing" code in SBS 2003.

So another configuration issue is to attach more stuff to the SPR. You can attach logs that are native to Microsoft services and applications or from third-parties.

1. Assuming you are still logged on as **Administrator** on **SPRINGERS1** with the Server Management console appearing, click **Monitoring and Reporting**.
2. Select **Change Server Status Report Settings**.
3. On the **Server Status Reports** dialog box, select **Server Performance Report** under **Reports** (Figure 12-3) and click **Edit**.
4. Select the **Content** tab on the **Server Status Report Options** dialog box and select **SBS Backup Logs**. Note you could select the other logs shown in Figure 12-4.

Figure 12-3
Selecting the Server Performance Report.

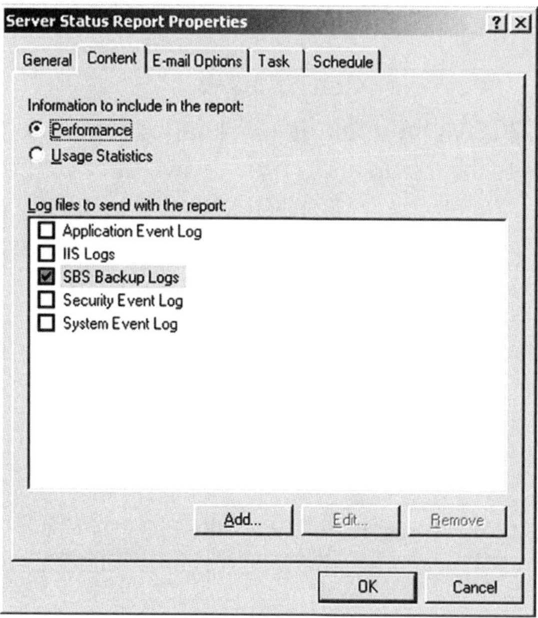

Figure 12-4
Selecting the SBS Backup Logs for the native backup program (NTBackup.exe). Note this was something you had to manually add this log (which was hidden 10 layers deep in c:\Documents and Settings...) in the SBS 2000 time frame. This is much better.

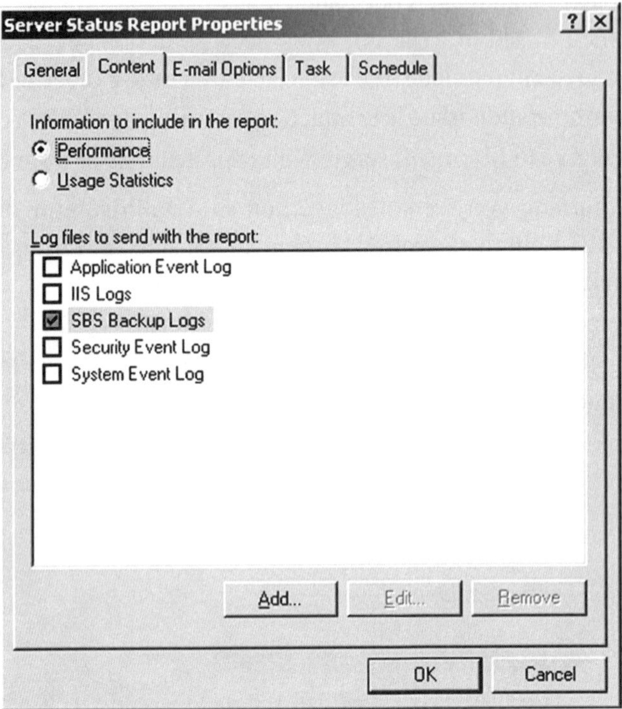

BEST PRACTICE: To add third-party reports, you would click **Add** and navigate to the logs to add. I provide two sample locations here:

- Trend Micro's OfficeScan Suite and its virus pattern file update log (default location): C:\Program Files\Trend\OfficeScan \PCCSRV\Log\update.log.
- Veritas Backup ExecSuite backup logs: C:\Program Files\Veritas\Backup Exec\NT\BEX*.*

So what gives with the star-dot-star wildcard sequence above? You might not have known that the SPR supports wild-carding in order to select the most current log each day. This is accomplished by typing *.* after the fixed portion of the log file name (the part that doesn't change) to accommodate for the variable naming portion. This effectively allows you to receive the log for the activity from the prior period, not all periods (you aren't sent all logs in the sub-directory each day). Very nice touch!

5. Click **OK** and then select **Send Now** on the **Server Status Report** dialog box. Click **OK** when notified that the **Server Status Report** has been sent.
6. Click **Close**.

Another configuration topic would be to point you to the links on the Monitor Small Business Server page in the Server Management Console. I'll discuss these more in the More Monitor Tools section at the end of the chapter.

BEST PRACTICE: This might be a good place to call it a night. Why you ask? Because by default the SPR is scheduled to send at 6:00am daily (Figure 12-5) and the Server Usage Report has a similar setting for 6:30am (although remember above that you told the Server Usage Report to send every two weeks).

Notes:

Figure 12-5
It's up and at 'em time for the SBS 2003 server monitoring function. Of course, 6:00am in my time zone (Pacific, GMT - 8) only means the night is young in Bangalore India (GMT + 5.5).

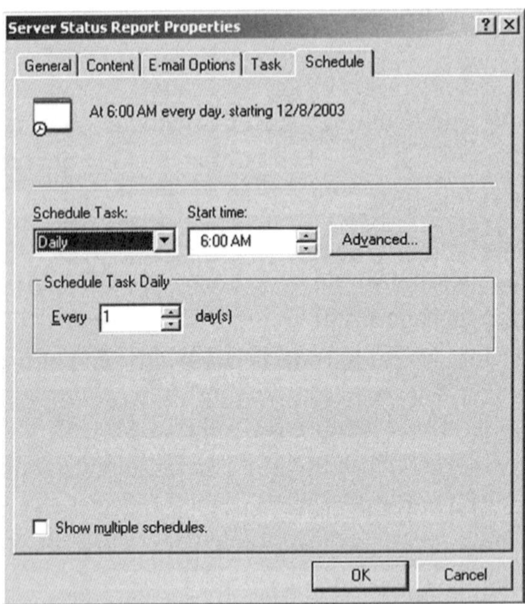

The beauty of setting the SPR to send at 6:00am is several-fold. First, it's late enough that things like the tape backup will have been completed (I know that if I start a tape backup at 11:00pm at a client site, it often completes around 2:00am) and an accurate backup log will have been generated. I also like the 6:00am time frame because I'm receiving the report shortly before the start of the business day. So I know that as of 6:00am, the SBS server machine was up and running. I also know the site had power, an Internet connection, and about five other things going for it (e.g., several Exchange Server 2003 services were functioning).

You wouldn't want to receive such information at 2:00am because you might believe all is well at the SBS site the next morning, but perhaps an unexpected windstorm knocked out power at 4:00am. Said 2:00am report wouldn't report that to you!

Interpreting Monitoring Settings

After you've configuring the native SBS 2003 monitoring capabilities, you've got to interpret the information. That's exactly what this section will do, starting first with the Server Performance Report and then looking at the Server Usage Report.

So here's how to interpret the Server Performance Report.

1. Log on as **Administrator** on the **PRESIDENT** workstation with the password **Husky9999!**
2. Launch Outlook 2003 from **Start**, **E-mail**. If necessary, configure Outlook for the Administrator using the Exchange e-mail server selection (past Outlook versions gave you a Corporate e-mail configuration option) and point it to the SPRINGERS1 server machine.
3. Notice that several reports have arrived. Some acknowledge the server monitoring configurations are complete. But hopefully you've received the true SPR as seen in Figure 12-6 Open this e-mail which should be labeled **Server Performance Report - SPRINGERS1**.

Figure 12-6

The improved daily server report in SBS 2003 is more attractive, relevant, and powerful.

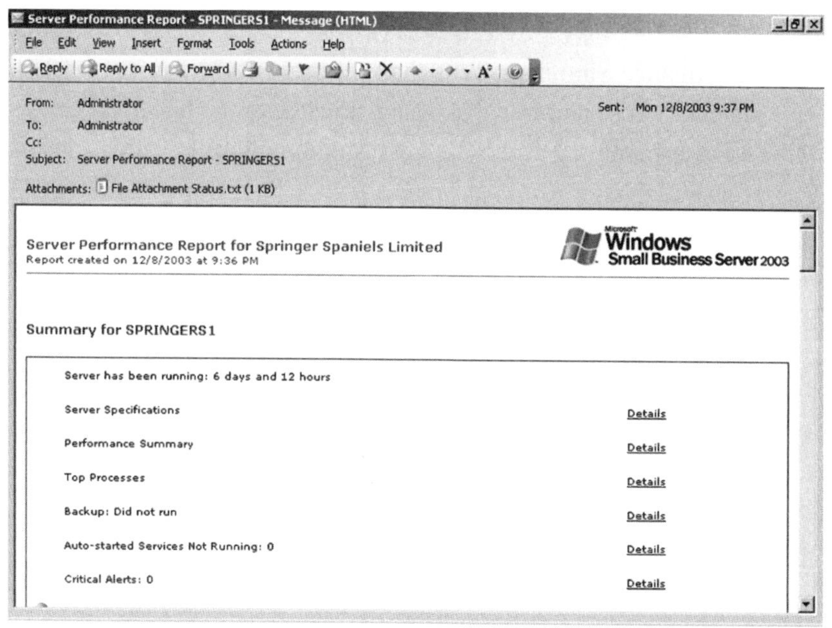

Let's take a moment to interpret the SPR in Figure 12-6. At the top of the report, there are several summary items at the top of the report, all of which can be easily expanded into more detailed categories by either clicking the Details link or simply scrolling down the body of the e-mail. The first line item in the Summary area, reflecting how long the server has been running, is a dramatic improvement over the report in SBS 2000 where you received uptime expressed in seconds (it's true). In Figure 12-6, you can see the server has been running for over six days.

Something else in the Summary area of interest is the fifth line discussing the backup function. In the fall 2003 hands-on labs, students objected to attaching the native backup log to the SPR when the backup status was clearly communicated as a report line item. They were curious what the intent of the exercise was. Here's the deal. The backup line entry is a great at-a-glance look at the success of the back-up function. However, many SBSers also like to delve deeper and peek at the backup logs to see specific backup activity. Heck, some SBSers don't take anyone's word for it and won't accept the fact a successful backup occurred until they've personally conducted a successful restore. Fair enough. And the SPR doesn't have a restore report line item if you missed that.

So go ahead and view each of the following major SPR areas:

- Performance Summary. Tells the information I like to see, including memory in use and free disk space. I just love the historical comparison to a month ago (see the Last Month column). This is shown in Figure 12-7.

Notes:

Figure 12-7
This is a very useful section of the SPR.

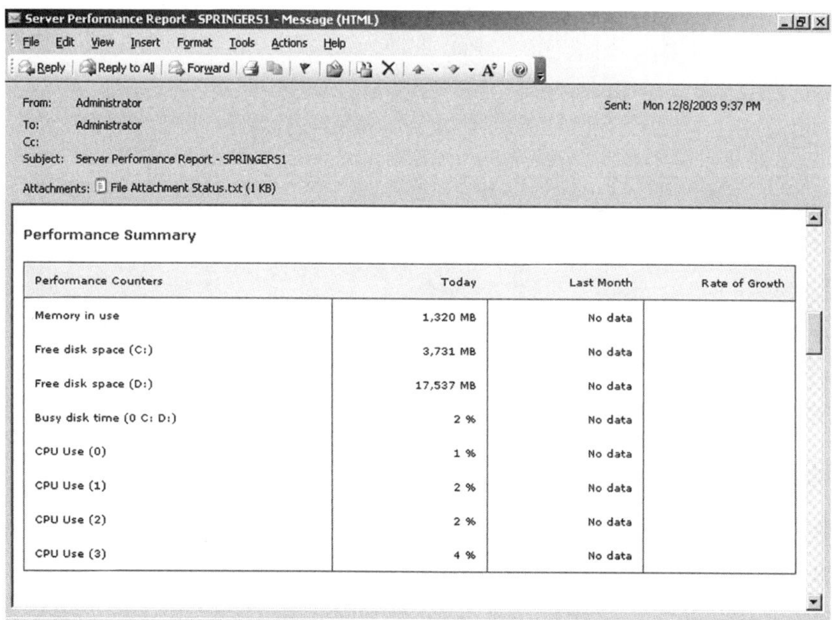
Server Performance Report - SPRINGERS1 - Message (HTML)

File Edit View Insert Format Tools Actions Help

Reply | Reply to All | Forward

From: Administrator
Sent: Mon 12/8/2003 9:37 PM
To: Administrator
Cc:
Subject: Server Performance Report - SPRINGERS1
Attachments: File Attachment Status.txt (1 KB)

Performance Summary

Performance Counters	Today	Last Month	Rate of Growth
Memory in use	1,320 MB	No data	
Free disk space (C:)	3,731 MB	No data	
Free disk space (D:)	17,537 MB	No data	
Busy disk time (0 C: D:)	2 %	No data	
CPU Use (0)	1 %	No data	
CPU Use (1)	2 %	No data	
CPU Use (2)	2 %	No data	
CPU Use (3)	4 %	No data	

- Top 5 Processes by Memory Usage. This tells which processes have been naughty and which have been nice in the memory consumption department!

- Top 5 Processes by CPU Usage. This would be good for finding an errant process that is consuming excessive processor time.

- Backup. Enough said already.

- Auto-started Services Not Running. This is an interesting way to view services with the start flag that have stopped (this could aide in troubleshooting performance matters). And as Eduardo (SBS 2003 program manager who owns the performance monitoring area) added, if an auto-start service has stopped, it's a good indication that something is amiss.

- Critical Alerts. This might reflect some intermittent performance nasties, such as processor queue buildup.

- Critical Errors in Application Log. Shown in Figure12-8, this often reflects some deep information that can greatly assist you in trouble-shooting the toughest problems.

Figure 12-8
This looks like a trip to the TechNet Disc to resolve: MAD Monitoring thread error.

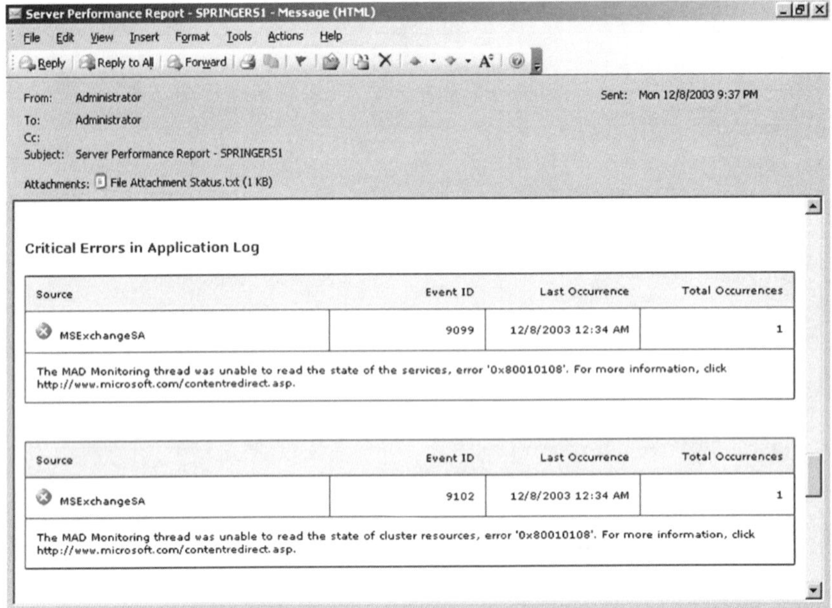

- Critical Errors in Directory Services Log, DNS Server log, File Replication Service Log, Security Log, and System Log.

BEST PRACTICE: What to do with all this data? The answer is to use common sense. A few time-tested rules known by many administrators (going back to the early Novell CNE days) are:

- Add more disk space when you have less than 20 percent free space. Also make sure disks are healthy and not excessively fragmented.

- A processor that exceeds 80 percent utilization over several days suggests a process upgrade is in order.

- RAM memory consumption should be monitored to make sure it doesn't grow excessively and you have sufficient free RAM memory (say 25 percent free).

- Network traffic. Watch for broadcast storms that could slow network traffic.

Because the performance monitoring area, such as specific settings, quickly ascends into the advanced category, I'll defer deeper discussion to my advanced SBS 2003 text. You can also consult Microsoft TechNet and my Windows 2000 Server Secrets (IDG) book for richer chatter on this.

Okay - this is the point where readers of my books and students of my SBS courses ask, "What do I do with this stuff?" or "Why am I here?" The concern expressed is about adding more value from the performance monitoring tool in SBS 2003. So here is your payoff. **YOU REPLY BACK TO YOUR SBS 2003 CUSTOMERS THAT EVERYTHING IS FINE!** The point I'm trying to make here, which I spend over 600-pages in my *SMB Consulting Best Practices* book doing, is that you need to reply each and every day to the SPR e-mail you receive.

If you simply click reply, it will revert to the Administrator account (that's you). But if you perform the following BEST PRACTICE, you'll direct the SPR reply to your customer. In this reply, you should add a few warm comments like "Good Morning" and "The tape backup reports were successful last night," you will be a bona fide hero. You've put the office manager at ease.

BEST PRACTICE: To facilitate this customer reply capability, select **Change Server Status Report** link from the **Monitor Small Business Server** page under **Monitoring and Reporting** in the **Server Management** console. **Select Server Performance Report** under **Reports** and click **Edit**. On the **Server Status Report Properties** dialog box that appears, select **E-mail Options**. In the **E-mail address**

for replies only field, type the SMTP-based e-mail address for your customer (e.g., Jeanette the office manager). Click **OK**. And now you've done it.

Note that by default, when you run the Monitoring Configuration Wizard, the reply address is set to the same address as the sent to address (in our case, that was administrator@springersltd.com).

It shouldn't be lost on you that you've "touched" each of the key stakeholders at each of your SBS customer sites each day with the suggested monitoring scenario here. That's how you get referrals and additional business in the whacky world of SBS consulting!

Oh-oh. A toot of ye' olde horn here. With Eduardo's permission, I'm proud as a peacock to let you know that I suggested the improved reply to customer functionality in the performance monitoring area and my suggestions were incorporated into SBS 2003. As previously mentioned, Eduardo is the hip program manager on the SBS 2003 development team who owns the performance monitoring area.

By the way, it's also acceptable to report that things are not well, such as the tape backup failed. SBS customers can handle bad news. It's more important that they receive it rapidly and straight up. Then you can go solve the problem.

SPRINGERS time: Go ahead and reply to the SPR e-mail you have in the Inbox. Tell NormH that all is well and life is good. Be the bearer of good news (a rarity for many technical professionals who only appear in public when trouble arrives).

As promised, let's also look at the Server Usage Report. You'll recall this was configured in the Configure Monitoring Wizard procedure (step 4 earlier in the chapter). You elected to have the report generated every two weeks at that time. The report, shown in Figure 12-9, is focused on real-world stuff (not deep MCSE-like statistics).

Notes:

Figure 12-9

The Server Usage Report can be viewed in both the Server Management console (shown) and e-mail. .

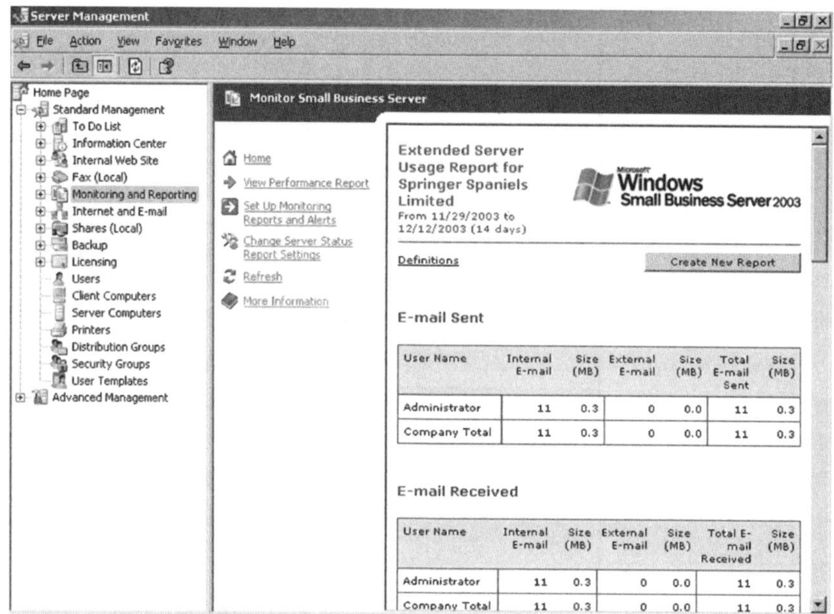

Table 12-1 provides specifics on what the Server Usage Report displays.

Table 12-1: Server Usage Report Details

Area Monitored	Specific Reading	Description
Web Activity by Computer	Computer Name	Lists the computers that made at least one connection to the Internet during the specified reporting period.
	Total Active Hours	Specifies the total number of hours spent on the Internet during the specified reporting period. Each five-minute time period of the day is counted as active if there are one or more hits during that time period.
	Average Active Hours per Day	Specifies the average number of hours spent on the Internet per day during the reporting period.
Web Traffic by Hour	Hour	Lists hourly intervals for the reporting period specified in the usage report.
	Total Connections	Specifies the total number of connections made, by hour, to the Web, during the reporting period.
	Average Connections per Day	Specifies the average number of connections made, by hour, to the Web each day.
E-mail Sent	User Name	Lists all user names that sent at least one e-mail during the reporting period.
	Internal E-mail	Specifies the total number and size of e-mail messages sent to an internal address during the specified reporting period.
	External E-mail	Specifies the total number and size of e-mail messages sent to an external address during the reporting period.

	Total E-mail Sent	Specifies the total number and size of e-mail messages sent during the reporting period.
E-mail Received	User Name	Lists all user names that received at least one e-mail during the reporting period.
	Internal E-mail	Specifies the total number and size of e-mail messages received from an internal address during the specified reporting period.
	External E-mail	Specifies the total number and size of e-mail messages received from an external address during the reporting period.
	Total E-mail Received	Specifies the total number and size of e-mail messages received during the reporting period.
Mailbox Size	User Name	Lists all user names with a mailbox.
	Starting Size (MB)	Specifies the size of a user's mailbox at the start of the reporting period.
	Ending Size (MB)	Specifies the size of a user's mailbox at the end of the reporting period.
	Rate of Change	Specifies the percentage of increase or decrease in the mailbox size from the start to the end of the specified date range.
Outlook Web Access Activity by User	User Name	Lists all user names that visited the Outlook Web Access site at least once during the reporting period.
	Visits	Specifies the number of visits a user made to an Outlook Web Access site during the reporting period. Each five-minute period of the day is

		counted as one visit if there are one or more hits during that time period. The list includes only users who sent at least one e-mail message during the reporting period.
	Average Visits per Day	Specifies the average number of visits per day, by user, to an Outlook Web Access site.
Outlook Web Access by Hour	Hour	Lists the hourly intervals for the reporting period specified in the usage report.
	Total Visits	Specifies the total number of visits to an Outlook Web Access site for all users during the specified reporting period.
	Average Visits per Day	Specifies the average number of visits per day, by hour, to an Outlook Web Access site. For each user, each five-minute period of the day is counted as one visit if there are one or more hits during that reporting period.
Remote Connection Activity by User	User Name	Lists all user names that established a remote connection to the server at least once during the reporting period.
	Total Connections	Specifies the total number of connections made to the server, by user, during the reporting period.
	Average Time	Specifies the average duration of connections made during the reporting period.
	Average Connections per Day	Specifies the average number of connections made to the server per day, by user.
Remote Connection Activity by Hour	Hour	Lists the hourly intervals for the reporting period specified in the usage report.

	Total Connections	Specifies the total number of connections made to the server, by all users, by hour, during the reporting period.
	Average Connections per Day	Specifies the average number of connections made to the server per day, by all users, by hour.
Faxes Sent	To	Lists all fax numbers to which at least one fax was sent during the reporting period.
	Total Faxes	Specifies the total number of faxes sent to a particular number during the specified time period.
	Average Size (Pages)	Specifies the average number of pages per fax sent to a particular phone number during the reporting period.
	Average Time	Specifies the average duration of each fax sent.
	Average Faxes Sent per Day	Specifies the average number of faxes sent per day to a particular number.
Faxes Received	From	Lists all fax numbers from which faxes were received during the reporting period.
	Total Faxes	Specifies the total number of faxes received from a particular number during the specified time period.
	Average Size (Pages)	Specifies the average number of pages per fax received from a particular phone number during the reporting period.
	Average Time	Specifies the average duration of each fax received from a particular phone number during the reporting period.

	Averages Faxes Received per Day	Specifies the average number of faxes received per day from a particular number.
Faxes Sent by User	User Name	Lists all user names that sent at least one fax during the reporting period.
	Total Faxes	Specifies the total number of faxes each user sent during the reporting period.
	Average Size (Pages)	Specifies the average number of pages per fax sent by each user during the reporting period.
	Average Time	Specifies the average duration of each fax sent.
	Average Faxes Sent per Day	Specifies the average number of faxes each user sent per day.
Fax Traffic by Hour	Hour	Lists the hourly intervals for the reporting period specified in the usage report.
	Total Faxes	Specifies the total number of faxes sent and received during the reporting period.
	Average Faxes per Day	Specifies the average number of faxes sent and received each day, by hour.

I close this interpretation section with a final thought. You'll be the best judge of what values are valid, germane, and correct as you work with SBS 2003 over time. You'll learn to detect false alarms along the way and you'll know a double-911 emergency when you see it. The point is to use these cool server monitoring tools in SBS 2003 and make 'em work for your individual situation. So go forth, dig into these cool reports, such as the business owner's report (log on as **NormH** at **PRESIDENT** and launch Outlook 2003 to view), use the usage reporting stuff (wait two weeks for this to be generated and then come back and take a look-see), and so on.

More Monitoring Topics

Forward we move. Here are some considerations in the SBS 2003 monitoring area.

Baselining

There are many good network performance monitoring white papers on the concept of baselining. This is the idea. You visit a client site and conduct a site survey (create an as-built drawing of the network layout, take initial baseline performance readings using a variety of tools, etc.). You then have a comprehensive baseline of the SBS 2003 network. At future dates, say quarterly, you revisit the SBS 2003 network and simply repeat the same performance measurements. Over time, you build up a hell of a data base, can track declines in performance with precision, and can lucidly plan for network enhancements based on solid performance data. If you're an SBS consultant, you can bill some great hours providing this valuable service for your customers.

More Monitoring Tools

There are more monitoring tools than you might imagine in SBS 2003 and the underlying Windows Server 2003 operating system. By order of popularity, these are:

Health Monitor

Clearly this is one advanced tool I'm going to do an injustice to in the introductory text. But I can point you to the best darn tome on Health Monitor you'll ever read: the online Health Monitor help system. Print it, read it, and use it. Configuring Health Monitor is very easy in SBS 2003 (you don't need to use the native Health Monitor snap-in which can be overwhelming). To configure Health Monitor alerts, simply select the **Change Alert Notifications** link on the **Monitoring Small Business Server** page (**Monitoring and Report** in the **Server Management** console) as shown in Figure 12-10.

Notes:

Figure 12-10
The most common monitor concerns are "pre-configured" for you in SBS 2003 and available when you use the performance monitoring function.

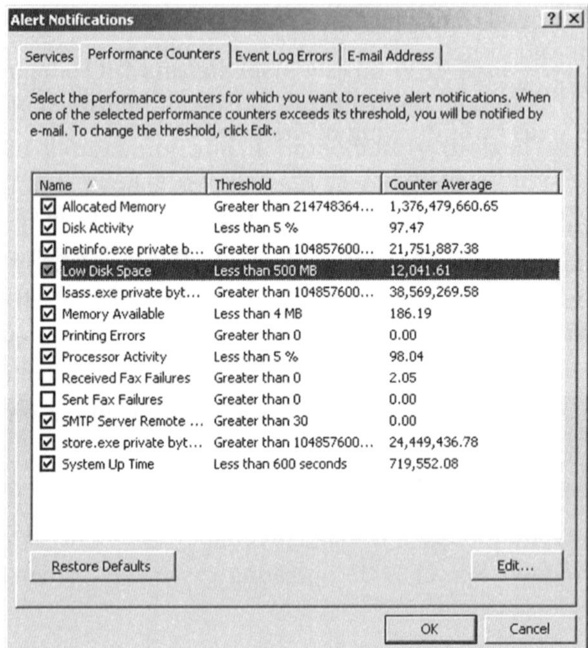

The idea behind the easy user interface to configure alerts was to encourage SBS customers to leverage the Health Monitor database and take advantage of the information being gathered. At the end of the day, it contributes to a smooth running SBS 2003 server machine!

By the way, the traditional view of the full Health Monitor application is no longer a part of the management console in SBS 2003. It's accessed from the Administrative Tools program group. You'll need to know that as you complete the following double-dare.

> BEST PRACTICE: Consider this a challenge or a double-dare now that you're nearing the end of this book and probably have developed some budding SBS skills. Using the online help system for Health Monitor, create an alert that fires to you when your SBS 2003 server

machine disk storage falls below 40 percent free space, 20 percent free space, and 10 percent free space. The idea behind these successive alerts is that the first alert gets you thinking about purchasing more storage. The second alert reminds you again to purchase more storage. And by the time you receive the third alert (10 percent free disk space), you are running out to the local electronics store to purchase hard disks! Good luck in your quest.

Task Manager

In the business world, at least until the fallout from Enron and Tyco, it was "understood" that a chief financial officer (CFO) always kept a few tricks in his hip pocket to boost quarterly earnings. On a technical note, I consider Task Manager to be a hip pocket tool I can use to quickly troubleshoot and help boost performance on an SBS server machine. To view Task Manager, simply right-click on the start bar on the server machine and select **Task Manager** (which is shown in Figure 12-11).

Figure 12-11
The Performance tab is perhaps the most useful part of Task Manager in glancing at processor utilization and memory consumption.

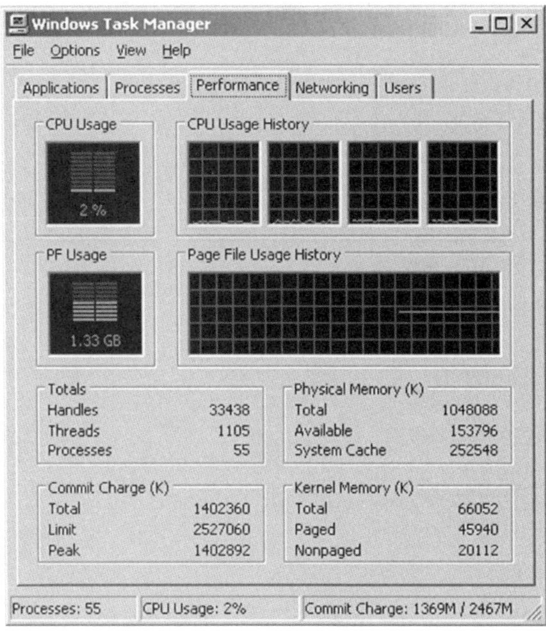

BEST PRACTICE: The Networking tab in Task Manager (new in the SBS 2003 time frame) is an excellent way to glance at network traffic when a user complains that the "network is running SLOOOOW!"

Disk Defragmenter

While I discussed disk defragmentation in the last chapter, I'm honor (that's honour in British Commonwealth countries) bound to repeat myself here. One of the fastest ways to boost SBS network performance is to run **Disk Defragmenter** from the **System Tools** program group (from **Start**, **All Programs**, **Accessories**). Note that the SPR doesn't provide information on the fragmentation of disks on the SBS 2003 server machine. You can only get that information using Disk Defragmenter and clicking either the **Analyze** or **Defragment** buttons.

Performance Monitor

Talk about a tool that's stood the test of time! Performance Monitor (also known as System Monitor) has been around since the earliest versions of SBS! It's found from **Start**, **All Programs**, **Administrative Tools**, **Performance**. Go ahead an open it now and observe in SBS 2003 that there are three performance counters configured by default (shown in Figure 12-12):

- Pages/sec
- Avg. Disk Queue Length
- % Processor Time

Notes:

Figure 12-12
It's free in SBS 2003 like other cool monitoring tools, so take Performance Monitor for a test drive. It's an excellent baselining tool with its ability to save data logs.

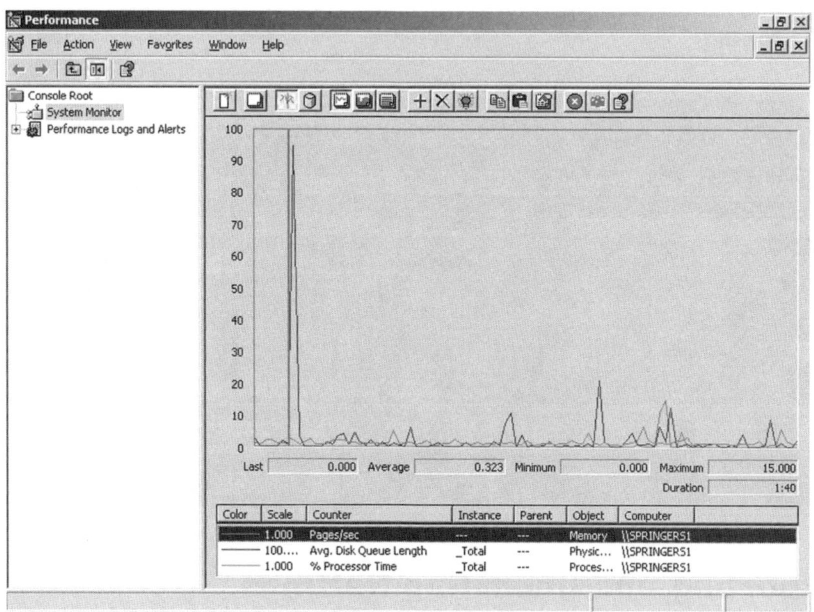

BEST PRACTICE: Two cool things you can do with Performance Monitor (amongst hundreds of cool things) are view the data as a histogram (Ctrl-B keystroke) and save the chart as a dynamic Web page that's cooler than a childhood in Alaska (right-click on the chart and select **Save As** from the secondary menu that appears). I'll now point you to one of the best darn Performance Monitor texts ever: *Windows 2000 Professional Resource Kit* (Microsoft Press). You read correctly (it's truly explored in the workstation, not server, resource kit!).

Command Line Stuff

Time to throw a bone to the SBS gurus again. Here's a bona fide command line-based performance monitor tool you can use to aid and assist your efforts to manage your SBS 2003 network. From the command line, simply type

netstat -o and observe the port scanning activity in real time that affects your SBS 2003 server machine. This is shown in Figure 12-13 below.

Figure 12-13
A quick (and also free) way to observe traffic by port is the netstat -o command. Bon appetite!.

```
C:\WINDOWS\system32\cmd.exe - netstat -o
(C) Copyright 1985-2003 Microsoft Corp.

C:\Documents and Settings\Administrator>cd\

C:\>netstat -o

Active Connections

  Proto  Local Address          Foreign Address        State           PID
  TCP    springers1:ldap        springers1.SpringerLTD.local:6141  ESTABLISHED
   944
  TCP    springers1:1024        springers1.SpringerLTD.local:6298  ESTABLISHED
   5632
  TCP    springers1:6141        springers1.SpringerLTD.local:ldap  ESTABLISHED
   336
  TCP    springers1:6298        springers1.SpringerLTD.local:1024  ESTABLISHED
   5556
  TCP    springers1:3191        kcwppub2.co.kitsap.wa.us:http  CLOSE_WAIT       3
868
  TCP    springers1:4045        a207-202-187-232.deploy.akamaitechnologies.net:h
ttp  CLOSE_WAIT       3868
  TCP    springers1:4145        209.120.213.227:http   CLOSE_WAIT      3868
  TCP    springers1:6318        209.181.88.187:http    CLOSE_WAIT      3868
  TCP    springers1:6319        209.181.88.187:3389    ESTABLISHED     4284
```

Exporting and Importing Settings

A hidden jewel in SBS 2003's performance monitor area is the ability to export your specific Health Monitor settings to another SBS 2003 server machine (which would import the settings). The reason I say it's hidden is that, if you look at Figure 12-14, you'll see this functionality is invoked via a set of links on the **Migrate Small Business Server Settings** page accessed under **Advanced Management** in the Server Management console. That's something you might not find early on in learning SBS 2003.

Figure 12-14
A very welcome SBS 2003 addition is the ability to export and import Health Monitor settings. Why? Because you create the perfect settings on one machine and then you can use these settings over and over again on other SBS 2003 networks!

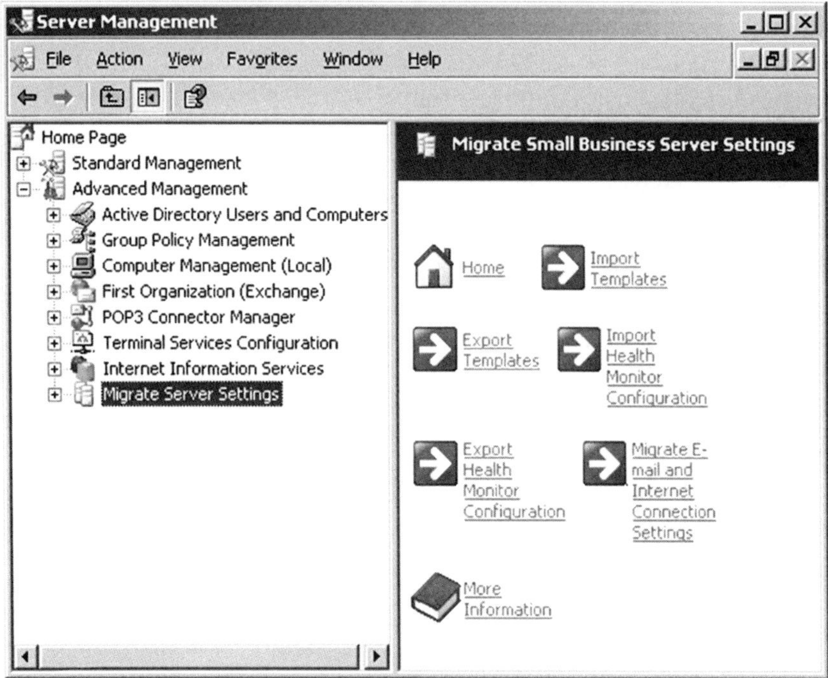

WMI and Mr. Performance Monitor

Something I truly don't completely understand is the Windows Management Interface (WMI) area that is tied to extending SBS 2003's performance monitoring tools. Perhaps it's because I have a limited programming/developer background.

So a tip of the performance monitoring hat to Grant Bedson, an Aussie from Victoria (that's Downunder, not up north in Canada). Grant is a software developer who has taken a keen interest in SBS. The pleasure was all mine to discuss the mystical powers of WMI and SBS performance monitoring when I delivered a three-day SBS training course in Melbourne, Australia, in late 2002. Grant, who is most comfortable with WMI, provided his unique insights to the SBS program manager who owns performance monitoring (Eduardo who hails from Brazil). Jeez - this underscores the international nature of SBS!

Back to business!

At the end of the day, many SBSers ask how something in SBS 2003 improves their life. With respect to having a network that purrs and hums, the performance monitor tools contribute greatly. With respect to SBS consultants, the gold standard is slightly different: It's based on gold. That is, how can you make money in the performance monitoring area with your SBS customers? There are many different business models out there. I'm aware of the following ways that SBS consultants are implementing the performance monitoring area into their service model:

- Fixed fee. You could charge $100 per month to continuously monitor the SBS 2003 network.

- Maintenance contract. You could charge $500 per month to maintain the SBS 2003 network and those services would include performance monitoring.

- Day rate. How 'bout a dollar a day for network performance monitoring, eh?

- Give away the milk, get the cow. This is actually my favorite. Provide the performance monitoring function for free and make it all up in extra work (because your superior customer service leads to great billable hours) and/or billable time you book to resolve problems. Don't laugh, as this approach deserves your serious second look.

BEST PRACTICE: A final dose of sage wisdom before the SBS 2003 premium edition chapters commence. The road to SBS consulting profitability travels through the performance monitoring area, irrespective of what your specific business model is. Why? Because performance monitoring will most assuredly result in better customer service. You'll be well aware of SBS 2003 maladies and performance-related matters before your customer will. You'll be "Johnny on the spot," already working on a solution when the customer calls with a problem. Better yet, you'll call the customer in advance of her discovering the problem. You read it here first!

Summary

It goes without saying, but then I'll promptly say it, that performance monitoring in SBS 2003 is one of the great opportunities to excel as an excellent SBSer! Use the launch pad provided in this chapter to implement the native performance monitoring in SBS 2003 and then go forth and take it to the next level. Consider performance monitoring to have a high return on investment. The hours you invest herein are returned many times over with an optimally performing network or the financial rewards that accrue to the SBS consultant amongst us. Bravo.

Section Four
SBS 2003 Premium Edition

Chapter 13
Premium Security: ISA Server 2000

Chapter 14
Database Management with SQL Server 2000

Chapter 13
Premium Security: ISA Server 2000

This chapter is dedicated to a security topic that will only affect readers who proceed to purchase the premium edition of SBS 2003 that contains Internet Security and Acceleration (ISA) Server 2000, and possibly ISA Server 2004. This is Microsoft's most robust firewall, caching, and Internet-related security software offering.

I'll weave in some SPRINGERS stuff, but understand that this is a tad beyond the scope of the book, which is dedicated to introductory and intermediate topics (surrounding the SPRINGERS methodology). As you've heard me say (so to speak) time and time again, look for my advanced SBS book in the second part of 2004, in which I'll delve much deeper into ISA Server 2000. Suffice it to say, I'll provide capable guidance here to get you started (and I also end the chapter by directing your attention to some excellent ISA Server 2000 books).

Why Use ISA Server 2000 in SBS 2003?

You might recall being teased in Chapter 5, which addressed standard SBS security, that I'd provide answers to this all-important question. ISA Server 2000 does more "stuff" in the security area. So that's not to say the firewall capability via Routing and Remote Access Services (RRAS) isn't adequate, because it is (please revisit Chapter 5 for that discussion). Rather, ISA Server does more "stuff" than just act as a firewall. Read on.

In the spring 2003, the Go To Market Hands-On Lab for Microsoft Partners toured the US and exposed students to ISA Server 2000 - and nothing but ISA Server 2000 - on the third day of the tour. There was one slide in the afternoon that appealed to me in describing what ISA Server 2000 does. This slide is shown in Figure 13-1 with my explanations to follow.

Figure 13-1
The five functions of ISA Server 2000.

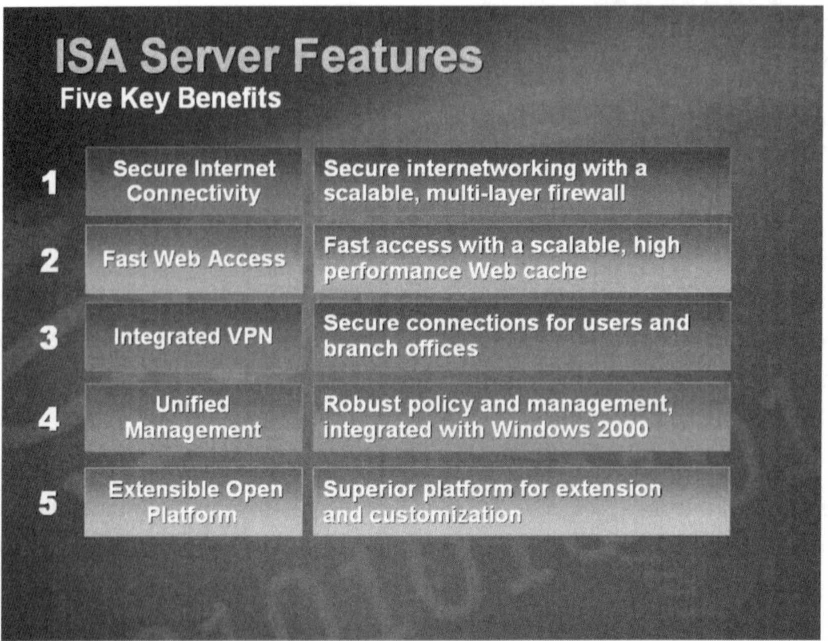

So, a few explanatory comments.

- **Secure Internet Connectivity**. ISA is a "smart" firewall that performs three levels of checks on Internet-related traffic. These are packet-level security (Figure 13-2), protocol-level security (Figure 13-3), and application-level security (Figure 13-4). The disparate concepts are integrated in Figure 13-5 at the end of the figure sequence here.

Figure 13-2
Understand the low-level packet layer relationship in ISA Server 2000.

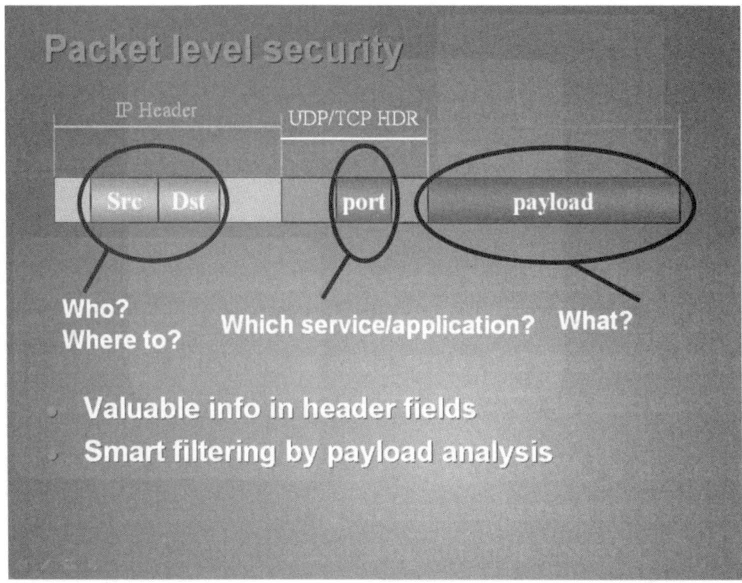

Figure 13-3
The middle protocol layer.

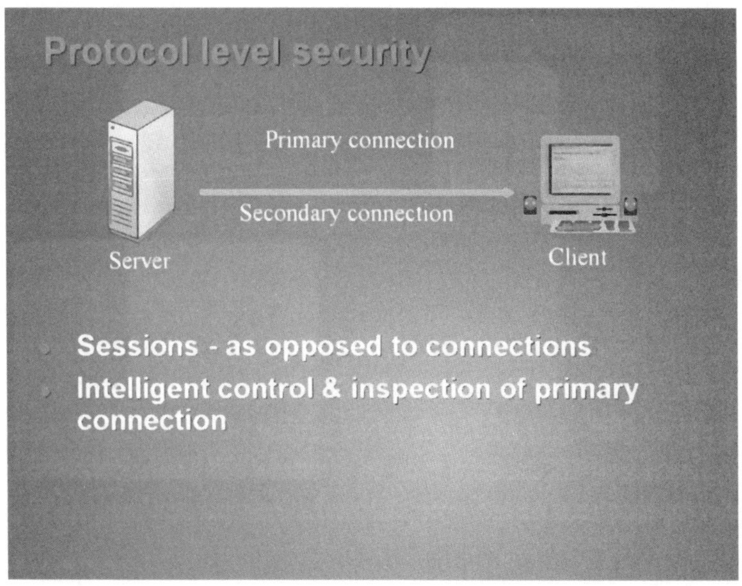

Figure 13-4
Something unique to ISA Server2000 and not replicated in hardware-based firewalls is the application-level inspection.

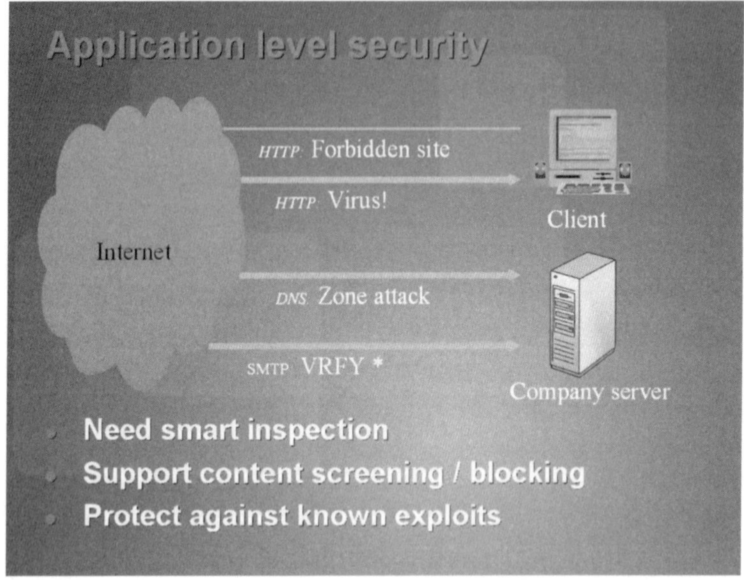

Figure 13-5
Using a stack chart to relate the prior three slides and their respective concepts to you.

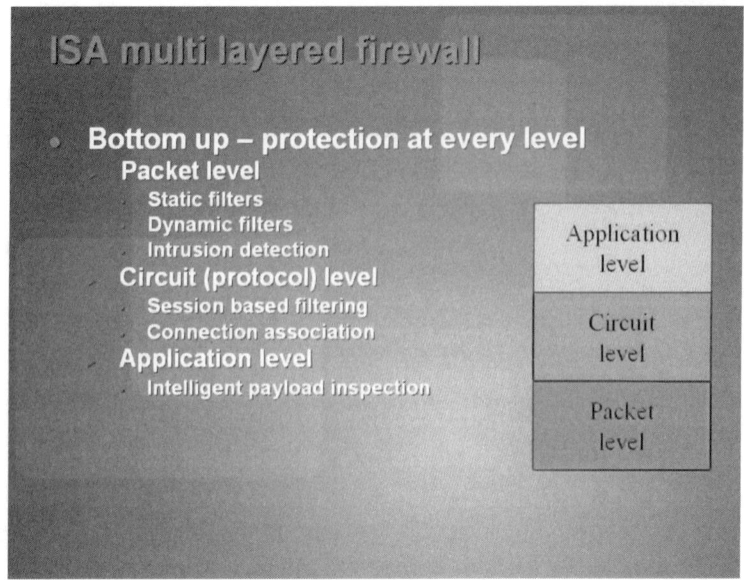

- **Fast Web Access**. This is a cool feature in ISA Server that allows for LAN-speed retrieval of frequently accessed Web sites "cached" on the server machine. When you install ISA Server 2000 on SBS 2003 (which I discuss in a moment), you will answer a setup wizard page (Figure 13-6) whereby you define the disk space allocated to the caching function.

Figure 13-6
By default, when installing ISA Server 2000, the caching directory selected will NOT be the system drive.

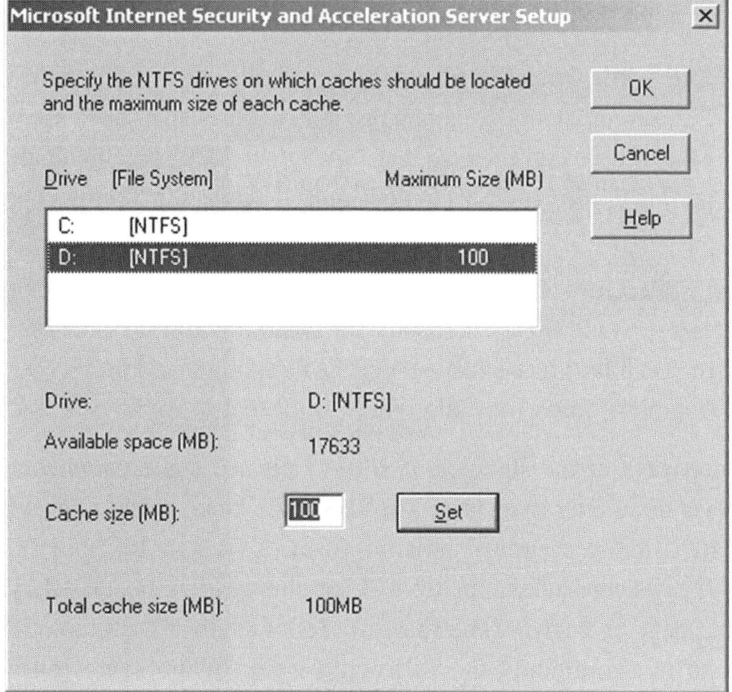

- **Integrated VPN**. Readers of my SBS 2000 book will recall the procedures I presented to allow ISA Server 2000 to configure the VPN functionality in SBS. Today we allow RRAS to manage the VPN function via the Configure Remote Access link on the To Do List. Ergo - this ISA 2000-based functionality isn't as foreground in SBS 2003 as it would be in a larger network using the full Microsoft Server SKUs.

- **Unified Management**. This is about things like Active Directory integration and the ability to invoke business management policies about who can use the Internet and how. I didn't "get it" on this point until a student in Denver, Colorado, who managed a medium-sized network for the county sheriff's department, jumped up and set me straight. His point was that managing stuff like Internet access was very important for this public agency that has a high profile in public. In fact, he used ISA Server 2000 only for its policy management capabilities (the sheriff's department actually used a hardware-based firewall for other Internet security roles).

- **Extensible Open Platform**. This is actually one of my favorite roles for ISA Server 2000. I'll explain this later in the chapter but tease you here: Most people don't realize that ISA Server 2000 is really all about supporting third-party ISVs to develop and extend the Microsoft product.

BEST PRACTICE: 'Cause I'm not going there, you should! Dig deeper into ISA Server 2000 at Microsoft's site: www.microsoft.com/isaserver. There you'll find more robust technical resources about ISA Server 2000 (albeit some of the discussion is more enterprise-oriented).

In the dog days of the summer of 2003, I penned some comments for the W2KNews newsletter that related to SBS 2003 being released as a "release candidate" in the standard edition form. This can be read in full at www.w2knews.com/index.cfm?id=433 (or simply click under **All Issues** on the home page at www.w2knews.com). Fellow author Dr. Thomas Shinder replied to my comments the following week in the same journal (see www.w2knews.com/index.cfm?id=434) and Figure 13-7 shows some of his "top reasons" for using ISA Server in an SBS environment. Note you should read the entire article to understand the context of these comments related, in part, to Dr. Tom's desire to see ISA Server 2000 placed on a second server in an SBS environment (which is "good news").

Notes:

Figure 13-7
Dr. Thomas Shinder responds to yours truly in the SBS security arena.

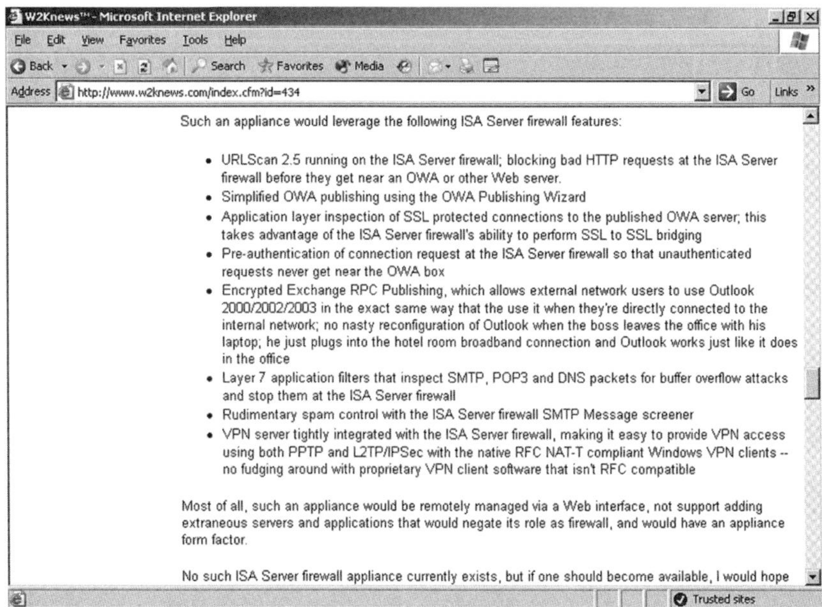

Such an appliance would leverage the following ISA Server firewall features:

- URLScan 2.5 running on the ISA Server firewall; blocking bad HTTP requests at the ISA Server firewall before they get near an OWA or other Web server.
- Simplified OWA publishing using the OWA Publishing Wizard
- Application layer inspection of SSL protected connections to the published OWA server; this takes advantage of the ISA Server firewall's ability to perform SSL to SSL bridging
- Pre-authentication of connection request at the ISA Server firewall so that unauthenticated requests never get near the OWA box
- Encrypted Exchange RPC Publishing, which allows external network users to use Outlook 2000/2002/2003 in the exact same way that the use it when they're directly connected to the internal network; no nasty reconfiguration of Outlook when the boss leaves the office with his laptop; he just plugs into the hotel room broadband connection and Outlook works just like it does in the office
- Layer 7 application filters that inspect SMTP, POP3 and DNS packets for buffer overflow attacks and stop them at the ISA Server firewall
- Rudimentary spam control with the ISA Server firewall SMTP Message screener
- VPN server tightly integrated with the ISA Server firewall, making it easy to provide VPN access using both PPTP and L2TP/IPSec with the native RFC NAT-T compliant Windows VPN clients -- no fudging around with proprietary VPN client software that isn't RFC compatible

Most of all, such an appliance would be remotely managed via a Web interface, not support adding extraneous servers and applications that would negate its role as firewall, and would have an appliance form factor.

No such ISA Server firewall appliance currently exists, but if one should become available, I would hope

BEST PRACTICE: To bolster your argument for the use of ISA Server 2000 via SBS 2003 premium edition, I recommend that you attend security-related hands-on labs regularly developed and delivered by Microsoft. In the US, visit www.msusapartnerreadiness.com for more information.

Deploying ISA Server 2000

The premium edition of SBS 2003, in some ways, kinda feels like an afterthought to the SBS 2003 standard edition. I can say that because, like many SBSers, I spent a lot of time with SBS 2003 standard edition in mid-2003. It wasn't until late 2003 that I was able to get my hands on the SBS 2003 premium edition and really dig into the remaining components. My expectations were to see a completely re-architected SBS setup process (remember the 42 steps in Chapter 3 for the standard edition?). Instead, all I really got in the SBS 2003 premium edition box was an extra CD-ROM disc that seemed like it was just thrown in there. The setup of the premium components (ISA Server 2000, SQL Server 2000, and FrontPage 2003) was essentially a manual setup without heavy SBS integration. This is underscored by Figure 13-8.

BEST PRACTICE: You will notice the ISA and SQL-related snap-ins are not inserted into the Server Management console. This again underscores a lack of integration with the premium components. Hang on, though. In a few moments, I'll show you how to add these snap-ins.

Figure 13-8
The "splash" screen for Disc 5 in the SBS 2003 premium edition SKU essentially directs you to manually install the premium components.

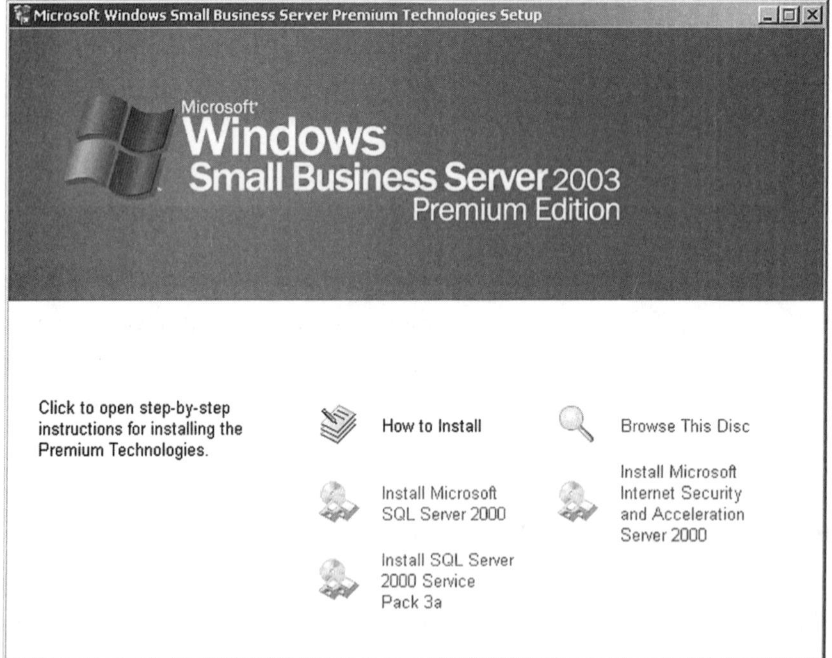

Installing ISA Server 2000

You will now install ISA Server 2000 on the server machine. On the figure above, you will notice the first link titled How to Install. This link launches a traditional read me file for setting up and configuring the SBS 2003 premium edition components. Go ahead, open (from How to Install) and read the file, "Completing Setup for Microsoft Windows Small Business Server Premium Technologies", as seen in Figure 13-9 and complete the ISA Server installation process. Do it now!

> BEST PRACTICE: Now is NOT a good time to be rebellious. You really need to study this document prior to installing the premium components. That is because the installation is slightly different from the standalone versions of these respective products in larger organizations.

Figure 13-9
Viewing the How to Install document is mission critical.

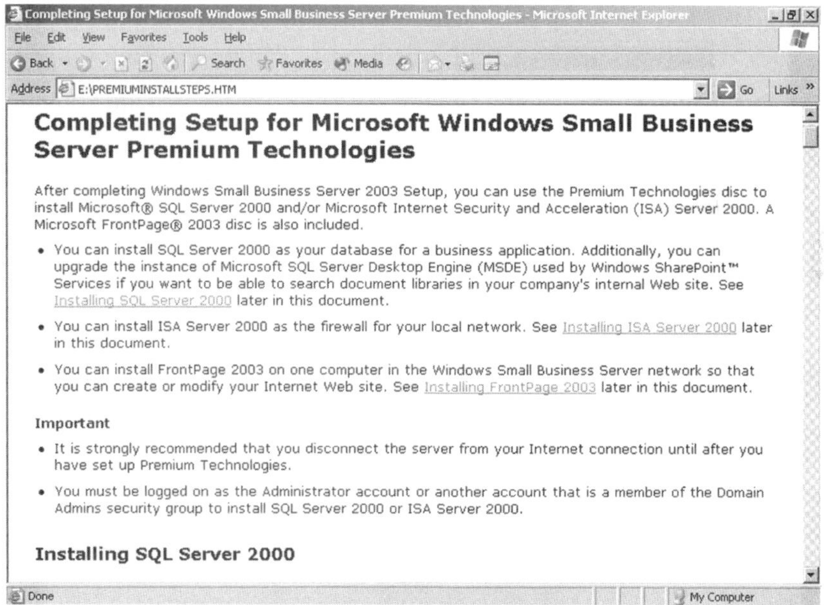

When you are completing the stepwise procedure to install ISA Server 2000, you will want to be aware of the following points.

- You will agree to a separate ISA Server license, but you do not need to enter a Product ID code.
- You will install ISA Server 2000 in integrated mode as per the setup instructions.

- The Local Address Table (LAT) creation process is much improved over the legacy SBS 2000 product (which by default added every known private IP address range on planet Earth). In SBS 2003, only the private IP address range discovered by querying the inside network adapter card is added.

This improved LAT table creation process prevents a mistake I used to lecture on in my spring 2003 advanced SBS tour, where I told the story of being "LATed out." I was creating a dual firewall scenario for a lumber yard on Vashon Island, Washington. The IP address range I correctly used was 10.0.0.x between the dual-homed SBS 2003 server machine and the hardware-based firewall. However, this being SBS 2000, the 10.0.0.x range was part of the LAT and resulted in end-users not being able to access the Internet (most noticeably, when they launched Internet Explorer and got a "page could not be displayed" error). No such problems exist in using a private IP address range in a dual firewall scenario with SBS 2003, because the LAT table isn't incorrectly populated with all private IP address ranges, as you can see in Figure 13-10. Whew!

Figure 13-10
This LAT reflects the internal SBS 2003 network as it should.

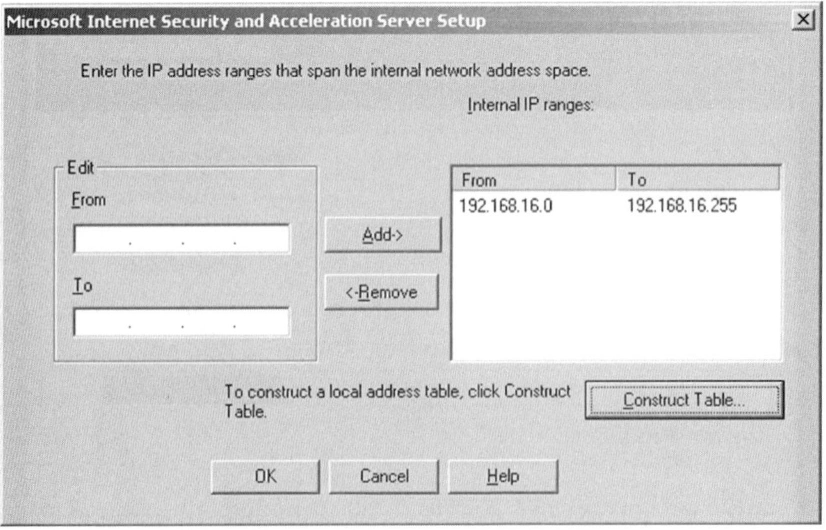

BEST PRACTICE: I recommend you select the option in Figure 13-11 to launch the Getting Started wizard in ISA Server 2000 to better configure security on your network.

Figure 13-11
ISA Server 2000's Getting Started wizard wasn't an option present in the SBS 2000 time frame but is with SBS 2003.

- Caching configuration. I already discussed this above but please note that you'll configure caching when you install ISA Server 2000.

Under the Hood Setup Stuff

Try as I might to position this book as being oriented toward the beginning and intermediate SBS crowd, I know that a few SBS gurus are reading it. Ergo, let' me throw them thar' gurus a bone and share a BAT file and some Visual Basic script.

Here's what occurs when you install ISA Server 2000 in the SBS 2003 premium SKU. A file titled configure_isa.bat (located at %SystemRoot%\Program Files\Microsoft Windows Small Business Server) runs with the following command line that essentially launches a VB script:

SystemRoot%\System32\csscript.exe //Nologo "%sbsprogramdir%\isaconfig.vbs

Then, the VBS script runs (located at %SystemRoot%\Program Files\Microsoft Windows Small Business Server\isaconfig.vbs). The first part (showing the well-commented section up top) is shown in Figure 13-12.

Figure 13-12
This VBS file is SBS 2003 premium edition-specific with respect to ISA Server 2000 being configured.

isaconfig.vbs - Notepad

File Edit Format View Help

```
' ISA Script
'
' TASKS:
'   1. Create "Internet Users" security group in "My Business->Security Groups" OU
'        a. SAM Name = SBS Internet Users
'        b. Should be Universal Security Group
'   2. Populate group with all currently defined SBS Users
'   3. Add ALL user templates for SBS to Internet Users group
'   4. Add Default Admin to Internet Users Group
'   5. Run "%sbsprogramdir%\networking\icw\icw.exe" when finished
'

' STRING TABLE TO BE LOCALIZIED
const L_LOGOFFMESSAGETITLE_TEXT = "Microsoft Windows Small Business Server 2003"
const L_LOGOFFMESSAGE1_TEXT = "The credentials for the account that you are currently logged on a:
const L_LOGOFFMESSAGE2_TEXT = "You can then verify whether the changes were successful by attempt
const L_INTERNETUSERSDESCRIPTION_TEXT = "Members of this group can access the Internet through IS
' END STRING TABLE

On Error Resume Next     ' set error handling property

Dim sGroupScope, sSAMacctName, sCName, sDescription      ' group parameter strings
Dim oDomain, sDomainDN, oNewGroup, wshShell              ' objects for other parameters
Dim bAdminFound, strSID, bytSID                          ' bool to indicate admin was found


Dim SBSProgramDir     ' expanded env var goes here
Dim oTxtstream        ' used by ChkErr to create a log file in %sbsprogramdir%\support\isalog.txt
Dim oFS               ' filestream object

Set wshShell = WScript.CreateObject("WScript.Shell")        ' create shell object
Set oFS = WScript.CreateObject("Scripting.FileSystemObject")
SBSProgramDir = wshShell.ExpandEnvironmentStrings("%sbsprogramdir%")


' ADSI errors
const ERROR_OBJECT_ALREADY_EXISTS = &h80071392

' Constants for group types
```

BEST PRACTICE: Time to integrate an earlier concept in this chapter with the above figure. If you look closely under Tasks, the first four tasks relate to exploiting ISA Server 2000's policy management (see the Unified Management bullet point a few pages ago). It is here that outbound access is being managed via Active Directory objects.

Run the E-mail and Internet Connection Wizard

So did you notice the last task in the above figure? It launches the E-mail and Internet Connection Wizard (EICW). Before I delved deep into the isaconfig.vbs file, I was simply going to write up this section to reflect that the EICW is run after installing ISA. But that would gloss over the mechanics of how it launches and what then occurs. After the EICW launches, you're presented with many of the same EICW screens you witnessed in Chapter 4. However, this time the firewall port openings are made in ISA Server 2000 and not the RRAS NAT/Basic Firewall. This is communicated in a unique screen (not seen when you run the EICW with SBS 2003 standard edition) that is shown in Figure 13-13.

BEST PRACTICE: Let's pretend for a moment that you previously ran the EICW after the initial SBS 2003 installation and before you installed the premium components. In such a case, you would effectively be "rerunning" the EICW and that would be a required step to switch the firewall protection function from RRAS NAT/Basic Firewall to ISA Server 2000.

Figure 13-13

This message, seen when the second network adapter card receives its IP address dynamically, refers to ISA Server 2000 providing the firewall services.

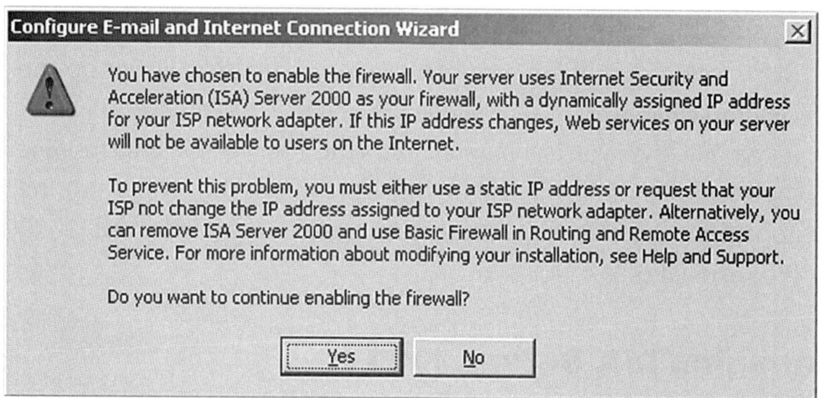

BEST PRACTICE: Let's talk VPN connectivity. In the baseline SBS case, you would proceed to configure VPN connectivity by completing the Remote Access Wizard (this hasn't changed from the SBS 2003 standard edition). The Remote Access Wizard is launched from the Configure Remote Access link on the To Do List.

However, you may recall that in SBS 2000 time frame, you were instructed on the Configure Remote Access link via the To Do List on the Small Business

Server Administrator Console to configure the VPN connections in ISA Server 2000. This is no longer the case and you may use either the RRAS VPN configuration (this is the baseline case) or the ISA Server 2000 VPN configuration (found from **Start**, **All Programs**, **Microsoft ISA Server**, **ISA Management**, **Servers and Arrays**, **SPRINGERS1**, **Network Configuration**, and clicking **Configure a Local Virtual Private Network (VPN)**, and then completing the wizard. My *SBS 2000 Best Practices* book presents the step-by-step procedure to complete this task).

Client Computer Setup

You will need to add the Firewall Client to each client computer to redirect traffic through ISA Server 2000 on the SBS 2003 network. You can do this by adding the Firewall Client software to the list of applications in the Setup Computer Wizard (which is chained to the Add User Wizard). The instructions for doing this are presented at the end of the How to Install document shown previously in Figure 13-9.

> BEST PRACTICE: If for some reason you have already set up the client machines prior to installing ISA Server 2000 on the SBS 2003 server machine, you can manually add the Firewall Client by running the setup file at: \\servername\Mspclnt\Setup.exe. This is also the approach to use for operating systems older than Windows 2000 Professional or Windows XP Pro.

Managing ISA Server 2000

By default, the ISA Management snap-in is not added to the Server Management console. You will want to do this when working with premium edition by completing the following procedure.

1. Log on as **Administrator** with the password **Husky9999!** on **SPRIGNERS1**.
2. Open **My Computer** from the desktop.
3. Navigate to **%SystemRoot%\Program Files\Microsoft Windows Small Business Server\Administration**.
4. Right-click **itprosbsconsole.msc** and select **Author**. This places the Server Management console in author mode.

5. Select **Add/Remove Snap-in** from the **File** menu.
6. Select **Add**.
7. Select **ISA Management** and click **Add**.
8. Select **Connect to local server** and click **OK** on the **Connect to dialog** box.
9. Click **Close** on the **Add Standalone Snap-in** dialog box.
10. Click **OK**. The ISA Management snap-in will now appear in the Server Management console. Be sure to save the Server Management console to save your hard work.

Extending ISA Server 2000

In this section, you'll learn two ways (among many) to extend the functionality of ISA Server 2000. Remember that my book will only take you so far (reader flames kindly ignored) with ISA Server 2000, and you need to purchase really thick books dedicated only to ISA Server 2000 (see the end of this chapter for some recommendations).

The two cool things you'll do with ISA Server 2000 are to create a custom port opening and create alerts. That's because these are tasks you might well perform in the real world of SBS.

Creating a Custom Port Opening

Much like the hostile student who might ask in the classroom, "why am I learning this?", you might be wondering why you need this section. There are at least two reasons why you might need to know of custom port openings in ISA Server 2000 on your SBS network:

- **Customer need.** I've had numerous customer situations where a port needed to be open in ISA Server 2000 to allow a line of business application to function. These customer scenarios included:

    - **Manufacturing.** This required a custom port opening to allow the manufacturer to access an Oracle-based enterprise resource planning (ERP) database being hosted by an application service provider (ASP). This required port 8000 to be opened.

- **Medical clinic.** This client required specific port openings that allowed access to a medical practice software solution (based on the HIPPA compliance matter in the US).

- **Accounting practice.** This accounting firm needed to extend basic terminal services functionality in conjunction with one of its client sites using Citrx MetaFrame. The issue here was to open MetaFrame-related ports (ports 1494, 1604 were opened; note port 3389 is opened in SBS when you elect to implement external Terminal Services functionality in the EICW).

- **Extending native SBS functionality.** This is a procedure that you'll complete to "make whole" an example we've created via the SPRINGERS methodology. You'll recall that I promoted the possible use of Internet Mail Access Protocol (IMAP) e-mail in the Exchange and Outlook chapter (Chapter 6). The context was the fussy executive who might need an alternative to Outlook Web Access (OWA) and would thus use Outlook Express with IMAP-based e-mail (don't laugh as I've seen this happen!). So please complete the following procedure to open port 143 to support IMAP version four (IMAP4).

1. Log on as **Administrator** using the password **Husky9999!** on **SPRINGERS1**.
2. Click **Start**, **Server Management** (assuming you added the ISA Management snap-in into the Server Management console as per above) and highlight **ISA Management**. Otherwise click **Start**, **All Programs**, **Microsoft ISA Server**, **ISA Management** to launch the ISA Management Microsoft Management Console (MMC).
3. Expand **Servers and Arrays**.
4. Expand **SPRINGERS1**.
5. Expand **Access Policy**.
6. Right-click **IP Packet Filters** and select **New**, **Filter**.
7. Type **IMAP Port Opening** in the IP packet filter name field on the **Welcome to the New IP Packet Filter Wizard** page. Click **Next**.
8. Select **Allow packet transmission** on the **Filter Mode** page. Click **Next**.

9. On the **Filter Type** page, select **Custom** and click **Next**.
10. Complete the **Filter Settings** page similar to Figure 13-14 where you have created a TCP port for both directions using port 143 for the local and remote fixed port. Click **Next**.
11. Select the **Default IP addresses for each external interface on the ISA Server computer** option on the **Local Computer** page and click **Next**.
12. Select **All remote computers** on the **Remote Computers** page and click **Next**.
13. Click **Finish** on the **Completing the New IP Packet Filter Wizard** page.

Figure 13-14
This page is where the heavy lifting occurs to open the custom port.

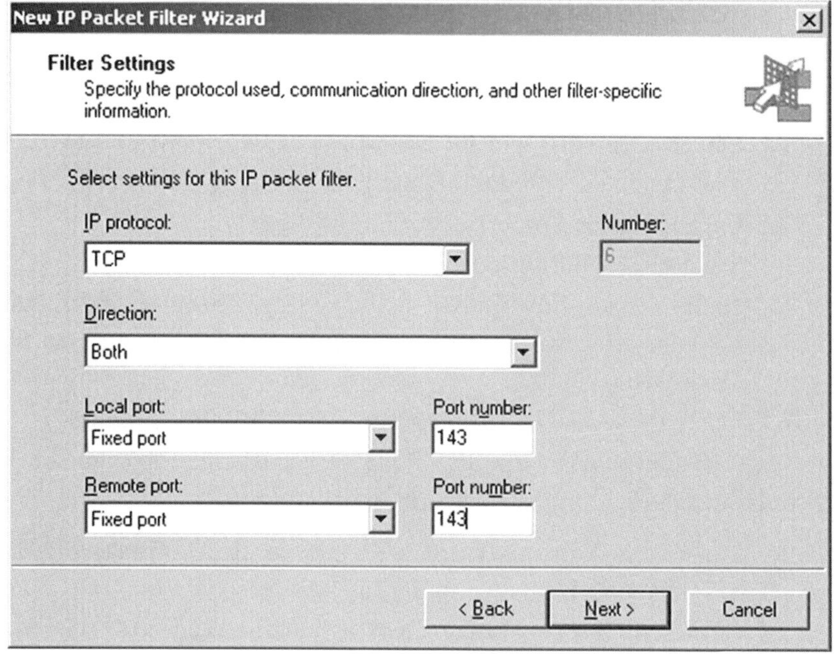

BEST PRACTICE: Because this wizard was native to ISA Server 2000 and not SBS 2003, there is no "here" link to add the configuration information (Step 13 above) to your network notebook. But you can select the text with your mouse and press Ctrl-C and then paste it to a text editor, such as WordPad with the Ctrl-V keystroke.

Creating Alerts

Another interesting configuration you can apply to SBS 2003 is the ability to send alerts to a public folder named "Security" so that you can monitor intrusion-related matters. I've found the business value of this to be that customers I serve as an SBS consultant can really see ISA Server 2000 at work. By sending the alerts to a public folder, the alerts are easily viewed from any client computer running Outlook. What I'm really saying here is you can add business value and be communicative with your SBS customers. The ISA Server 2000 alerts provide an opportunity to have dialog about how things are going (see my book, SMB Consulting Best Practices, for more of this discussion over 600 pages). So let's get started. You'll first create the public folder titled "Security" from the PRESIDENT machine. You will then log on to the server and configure the alerting capability in ISA Server 2000. It's jolly good fun.

1. Log on as **NormH** with the password **Purple3300** on **PRESIDENT**.
2. Start Outlook from **Start**, **E-mail**.
3. Expand **Public Folders** under **Folder List**.
4. Right-click **All Public Folders** and select **New Folder**.
5. On the **Create New Folder** dialog box, type **Security** in the **Name** field and select **Mail and Post Items** in the **Folder contains** field. Click **OK**.
6. Verify the security folder appears under **All Public Folders**.

Now you'll switch over to the SBS 2003 server machine to complete the following procedures to implement and test the alerting.

1. Log on as **Administrator** with the password **Husky9999!** on **SPRINGERS1**.
2. Click **Start**, **Server Management** (assuming you added the **ISA Management** snap-in into the Server Management console) and highlight ISA Management. Otherwise click **Start**, **All Programs**, **Microsoft ISA Server**, **ISA Management** to launch the ISA Management Microsoft Management Console (MMC).
3. Expand S**ervers and Arrays**.

4. Expand **SPRINGERS1**.
5. Expand **Access Policy**.
6. Right-click **IP Packet Filters** and select **Properties**.
7. Select **Enable Intrusion detection** on the **General** tab of the **IP Packet Filters Properties** dialog box.
8. Click the **Intrusion Detection** tab and select all attack detection options as seen in Figure 13-15. Also reduce to **1** (one) the values in both **Detect after attacks on** fields. Click **OK**.

Figure 13-15
This is an important configuration area to complete correctly to implement the intrusion detection capability.

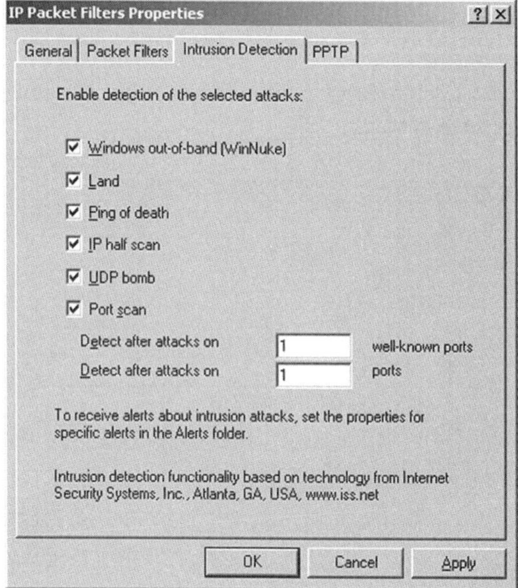

BEST PRACTICE: So why did you reduce the values in the detection occurrence fields down to one? That's simple. You want to generate a lot of traffic to show your customers they aren't alone out there in the big bad world. Small business clients often like to think no one knows they exist or cares about them. Filling the Security public folder with alerts is one way to thump 'em good and show that many folks are trying all the time to intrude!

This point also underscores the fact that the alerting capability is advisory in nature.

9. Proceed to expand the **Monitoring Configuration** object.
10. Expand **Alerts**.
11. Double-click the **Intrusion detected** alert.
12. Verify on the **General** tab of the **Intrusion detected Properties** dialog box that the **Enable** checkbox is selected.
13. Select the **Events** tab and check the **Number of occurrences before the alert is issued**. Set the value to **1** (one) to generate activity.
14. Complete the **Actions** tab similar to Figure 13-16 to configure where to send the alert e-mail to.
15. Click **OK**.

Figure 13-16
You will configure the alerts to send to the Security public folder on the SPRINGERS1 server machine.

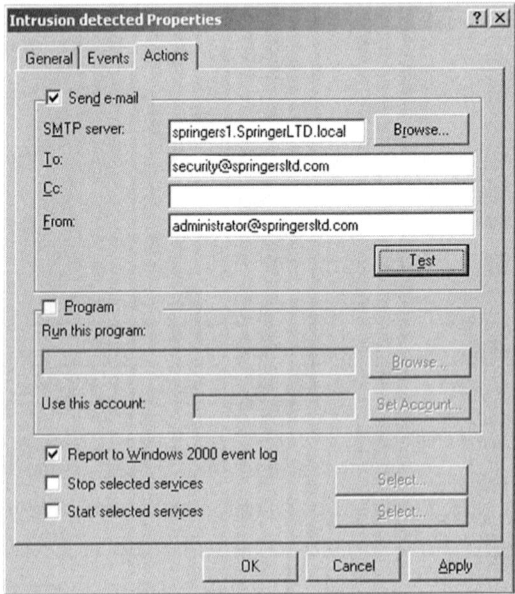

You would now proceed to "black hat" yourself (on the outside network adapter card) using a port scanner, such as GFI's Network Security Scanner (featured in Chapter 5). This will generate tons of intrusion detection traffic and fill the

Security public folder. In the real world, you'll be surprised how often intrusion detection alerts are fired to the Security public folder. A screenshot from a real customer site is shown in Figure 13-17.

Figure 13-17
Just when you thought it was safe to go out in the neighborhood again, the alerts fired to the Security public folder remind you that the world is an intense place.

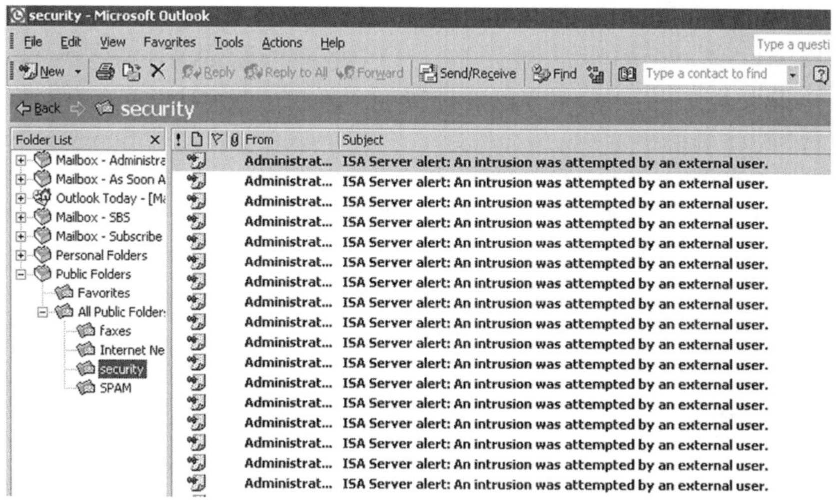

BEST PRACTICE: Perhaps you've heard the phrase or even worked with a super speedy secretary in the "old days" who could "type faster than the computer." You know what I mean. Back in the days of WordStar (even before the heyday of Word Perfect), a super speedy secretary could out-type the computer or get ahead of the characters appearing on the screen. We've got a little bit of that with respect to the above procedure. When you added the Security public folder, which is indeed SMTP e-mail-enabled by default, there is a propagation period whereby Active Directory needs a few minutes to catch up and make the Security public folder available for use. So if you're super speedy and you've completed the above procedure so fast that Active Directory is lagging behind you, take a ten-minute break and try the last exercise again where you create traffic to fire the alert.

BEST PRACTICE: Be sure to learn how to extend ISA Server 2000 with its Feature Pack 1 (details at www.microsoft.com/isa). Go for it!

Changing ISA Server 2000

In this section, you'll be exposed to a lot of ancillary stuff related to ISA Server 2000. Take it or leave it, but you'll likely find a gold nugget or two herein.

Hyper-active caching

One "delta" change from SBS 2000 to SBS 2003 is that active caching is now turned on by default. SBS 2000 was the only version in the life of SBS where active caching wasn't turned on by default (it was turned on automatically in the SBS 4.x era). You can see this by right-clicking **Cache Configuration** beneath SPRINGERS1 in the ISA Management snap-in. Select **Properties** and click the **Active Caching** tab. Your screen should look similar to Figure 13-18.

Figure 13-18
Note that you can select the ***Frequently*** *radio button to create a hyper-active caching scenario where much stuff is cached.*

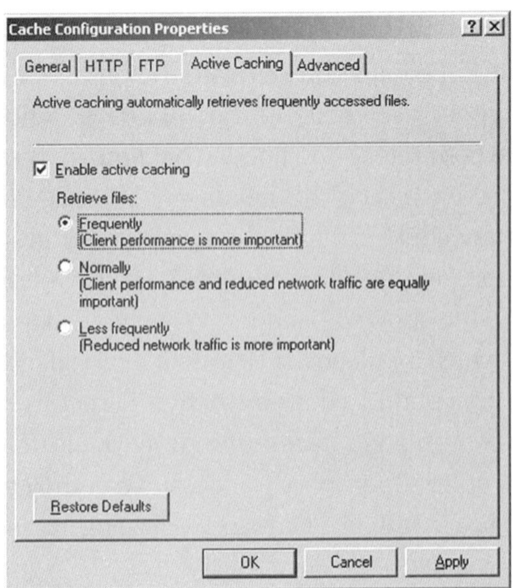

BEST PRACTICE: You'll recall that you set the caching file size when ISA Server 2000 was installed earlier in this chapter. You can modify that cache file size by selecting the **Drive** folder beneath **Cache Configuration**. Over time, you might want to increase the file size to cache more stuff.

BEST PRACTICE: One of the big complaints in the past regarding active caching was that it generated too many dial-out calls to the ISP via modem (where modems were the Internet connection approach). I well recall the day during the SBS 4.5 timeframe when I was called by a construction company client of mine who asked me to come out and explore "phantom" modem dial-ups. It turns out the active caching feature was updating cached Web pages with frequent dial-outs to the Internet.

More important, many international readers have written me complaining long and loud about active caching being something that actively drains their pocket books. In many foreign countries, telephone calls and connects to the Internet are billed by the minute, not a flat monthly fee. Thus active caching may be cost prohibitive.

Naughty Reports

Some of my SBS clients are control freaks and want to snoopervise users on Internet usage. Some are motivated by deeply held beliefs that viewing pornographic sites is simply wrong and immoral. Others have financial motivations that employees should work, not play, during business hours at their place of employment. With this second group of control freaks, they often don't care what you do with your own computer at home on your own time.

Granted, these reports were best presented in the SBS 4.x era as a button-click away via the management consoles, but as you'll see here, these reports, while hidden, can still be found and well used. What occurs is the reports are built using the nearly unreadable raw Internet activity data, shown below (Figure 13-19), and then the data is massaged and an attractive report is the result! Note that the SBS 4.x versions actually used a run-time version of Crystal Reports to render the naughty and nice reports.

Figure 13-19

The raw reports that hold the secrets as to who (individually) has been naughty or nice on the Internet. But, alas, the reports are hard to read.

WEBEXTD20010826.log - Notepad

File Edit Format Help

```
192.168.16.2    anonymous      Mozilla/4.0 (compatible; MSIE 5.01; Windows NT 5.0)    2001-08-2
192.168.16.2    anonymous      Mozilla/4.0 (compatible; MSIE 5.01; Windows NT 5.0)    2001-08-2
192.168.16.2    anonymous      Mozilla/4.0 (compatible; MSIE 5.01; Windows NT 5.0)    2001-08-2
192.168.16.2    anonymous      Mozilla/4.0 (compatible; MSIE 5.01; Windows NT 5.0)    2001-08-2
192.168.16.2    SPRINGERSLTD\Administrator    Mozilla/4.0 (compatible; MSIE 5.01; Windows NT 5.
192.168.16.2    SPRINGERSLTD\Administrator    Mozilla/4.0 (compatible; MSIE 5.01; Windows NT 5.
192.168.16.2    SPRINGERSLTD\Administrator    Mozilla/4.0 (compatible; MSIE 5.01; Windows NT 5.
192.168.16.2    SPRINGERSLTD\Administrator    Mozilla/4.0 (compatible; MSIE 5.01; Windows NT 5.
192.168.16.2    SPRINGERSLTD\Administrator    Mozilla/4.0 (compatible; MSIE 5.01; Windows NT 5.
192.168.16.2    SPRINGERSLTD\Administrator    Mozilla/4.0 (compatible; MSIE 5.01; Windows NT 5.
192.168.16.2    SPRINGERSLTD\Administrator    Mozilla/4.0 (compatible; MSIE 5.01; Windows NT 5.
192.168.16.2    SPRINGERSLTD\Administrator    Mozilla/4.0 (compatible; MSIE 5.01; Windows NT 5.
192.168.16.2    SPRINGERSLTD\Administrator    Mozilla/4.0 (compatible; MSIE 5.01; Windows NT 5.
192.168.16.2    SPRINGERSLTD\Administrator    Mozilla/4.0 (compatible; MSIE 5.01; Windows NT 5.
192.168.16.2    SPRINGERSLTD\Administrator    Mozilla/4.0 (compatible; MSIE 5.01; Windows NT 5.
192.168.16.2    SPRINGERSLTD\Administrator    Mozilla/4.0 (compatible; MSIE 5.01; Windows NT 5.
192.168.16.2    SPRINGERSLTD\Administrator    Mozilla/4.0 (compatible; MSIE 5.01; Windows NT 5.
192.168.16.18   anonymous      Mozilla/4.0 (compatible; MSIE 5.01; Windows NT 5.0)    2001-08-2
192.168.16.18   anonymous      Mozilla/4.0 (compatible; MSIE 5.01; Windows NT 5.0)    2001-08-2
192.168.16.18   SPRINGERSLTD\NormH    Mozilla/4.0 (compatible; MSIE 5.01; Windows NT 5.0)    2
192.168.16.18   SPRINGERSLTD\NormH    Mozilla/4.0 (compatible; MSIE 5.01; Windows NT 5.0)    2
192.168.16.18   anonymous      Mozilla/4.0 (compatible; MSIE 5.01; Windows NT 5.0)    2001-08-2
192.168.16.18   anonymous      Mozilla/4.0 (compatible; MSIE 5.01; Windows NT 5.0)    2001-08-2
192.168.16.18   SPRINGERSLTD\NormH    Mozilla/4.0 (compatible; MSIE 5.01; Windows NT 5.0)    2
192.168.16.18   SPRINGERSLTD\NormH    Mozilla/4.0 (compatible; MSIE 5.01; Windows NT 5.0)    2
192.168.16.18   SPRINGERSLTD\NormH    Mozilla/4.0 (compatible; MSIE 5.01; Windows NT 5.0)    2
192.168.16.18   SPRINGERSLTD\NormH    Mozilla/4.0 (compatible; MSIE 5.01; Windows NT 5.0)    2
192.168.16.18   SPRINGERSLTD\NormH    Mozilla/4.0 (compatible; MSIE 5.01; Windows NT 5.0)    2
192.168.16.18   SPRINGERSLTD\NormH    Mozilla/4.0 (compatible; MSIE 5.01; Windows NT 5.0)    2
192.168.16.18   SPRINGERSLTD\NormH    Mozilla/4.0 (compatible; MSIE 5.01; Windows NT 5.0)    2
192.168.16.18   SPRINGERSLTD\NormH    Mozilla/4.0 (compatible; MSIE 5.01; Windows NT 5.0)    2
192.168.16.18   anonymous      Mozilla/4.0 (compatible; MSIE 5.01; Windows NT 5.0)    2001-08-2
192.168.16.18   anonymous      Mozilla/4.0 (compatible; MSIE 5.01; Windows NT 5.0)    2001-08-2
192.168.16.18   SPRINGERSLTD\NormH    Mozilla/4.0 (compatible; MSIE 5.01; Windows NT 5.0)    2
192.168.16.18   SPRINGERSLTD\NormH    Mozilla/4.0 (compatible; MSIE 5.01; Windows NT 5.0)    2
192.168.16.18   SPRINGERSLTD\NormH    Mozilla/4.0 (compatible; MSIE 5.01; Windows NT 5.0)    2
192.168.16.18   SPRINGERSLTD\NormH    Mozilla/4.0 (compatible; MSIE 5.01; Windows NT 5.0)    2
192.168.16.18   SPRINGERSLTD\NormH    Mozilla/4.0 (compatible; MSIE 5.01; Windows NT 5.0)    2
192.168.16.18   SPRINGERSLTD\NormH    Mozilla/4.0 (compatible; MSIE 5.01; Windows NT 5.0)    2
192.168.16.18   SPRINGERSLTD\NormH    Mozilla/4.0 (compatible; MSIE 5.01; Windows NT 5.0)    2
192.168.16.18   SPRINGERSLTD\NormH    Mozilla/4.0 (compatible; MSIE 5.01; Windows NT 5.0)    2
```

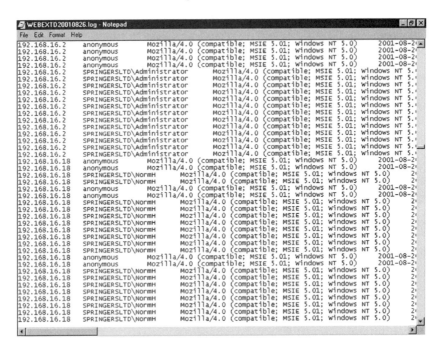

BEST PRACTICE: If you must, you can view the raw ISA Server logs at:: **%system drive%\Program Files\Microsoft ISA Server\ISALogs.** Rumor has it there are some great third-party parsing tools to present this raw data better. See the ISA Server 2000 Web sites I refer you to at the end of the chapter.

First, you must create a report job. Perform these steps.

1. Log on to **SPRINGERS1** as **Administrator** with the password **Husky9999!**.
2. Click **Start**, **Server Management**.
3. Expand the **ISA Management** snap-in (assuming you modified the console earlier in this chapter).
4. Expand **Servers and Arrays**.
5. Expand the **SPRINGERS1** server object.
6. Expand **Monitoring Configuration**.

7. Right-click the **Report Jobs** folder and select **New, Report Job**.
8. The **Report Job Properties** dialog box appears. Type **SPRINGERS Naughty and Nice Reports** in the **Name** field.
9. Select the **Period** tab and select **Monthly**.
10. Select the **Schedule** tab and select **Immediately**.

BEST PRACTICE: It is on the **Schedule** tab that you could have the report run every day at a specific time. You could elect to generate the report only once per month. For the SSL methodology, you have selected the option to generate the reports immediately so you can see your reports instantly.

11. Select the **Credentials** tab and complete the three fields that are displayed. In the **Username** field, type **Administrator**. In the **Domain** name field, type **SPRINGERSLTD**. In the password field, type **Husky9999!**.

BEST PRACTICE: In the **Domain** field of the **Credentials** page, you will type the internal NetBIOS domain name, not the external Internet domain name. This is very clear, but you can prove it by trying to type **SPRINGERSLTD.COM** and observing that the field isn't wide enough to accommodate this entry.

12. Click **OK** to close the **Report Job Properties** dialog box.

Next, surf to the naughty and nice Web sites of your choice. A nice site to consider is one of my favorites, www.smbnation.com. Then complete these steps to look at the naughty and nice reports.

1. Log on to **SPRINGERS1** as Administrator with the password **Husky9999!**.
2. Click **Start**, **Server Management**.
3. Expand the **ISA Management** snap-in.
4. Expand **Servers and Arrays**.
5. Expand the **SPRINGERS1** server object.
6. Expand **Monitoring**.
7. Expand **Reports**.

BEST PRACTICE: Even though the report job is displayed in the details pane when you click on Reports, you can't launch the naughty and nice reports from here. Move on to Step #8.

8. Expand **Summary** and double-click the **SPRINGERS Naughty and Nice Reports** entry. An IW Web browser is launched that displays the Array Summary Reports.
9. Click on the **Top Users** link on the left. As seen in Figure 13-20, NormH is the top user.

Figure 13-20
NormH just edged out the Administrator as the top user in this example.

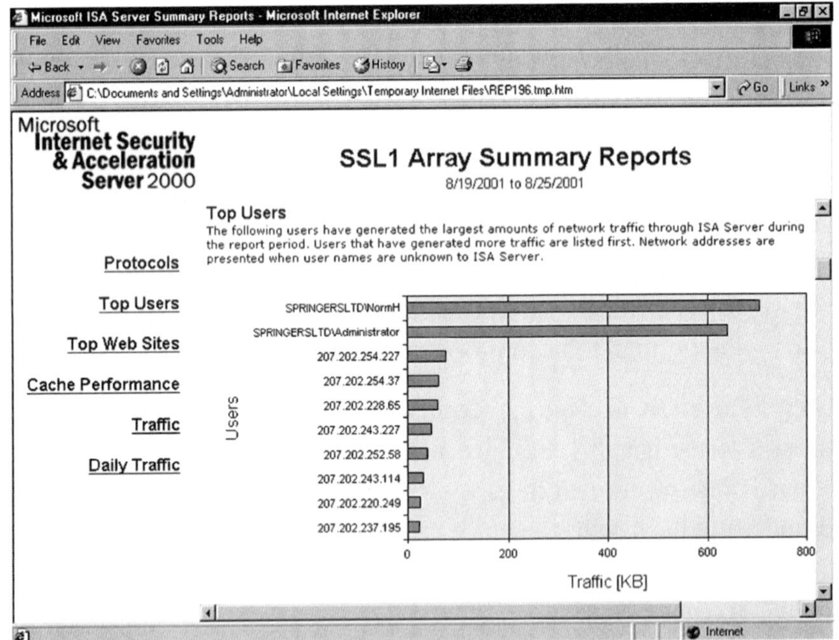

10. Click on the **Top Web Sites** link and compare to Figure 13-21. It appears some Web surfing has been nice, such as entries number two (www.microsoft.com) and number seven (www.cbsnews.com). However, some surfing has been naughty, as in entries number three (www.penthouse.com) and number ten (www.playboy.com).

Figure 13-21
Some SBS users have been naughty and some have been nice, if you look closely at the URLs of the Top Web Sites report.

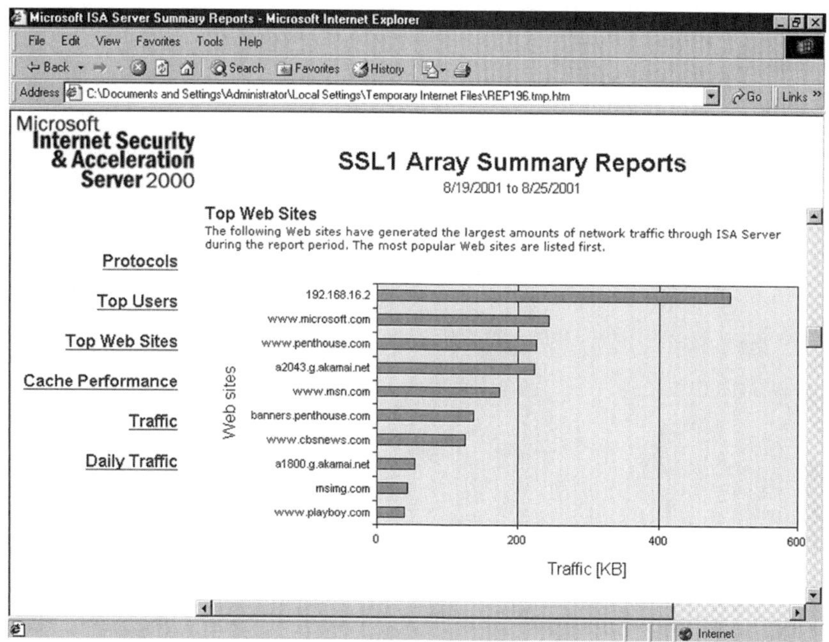

BEST PRACTICE: What the naughty and nice reports do not do is relate which user was naughty and which user was nice. That is, the Top Web Sites report shows total hits as an SBS network, not by individual. To find out which specific user has been naughty, you'd need to look directly at the ISA Server logs shown earlier in Figure 13-19.

11. Selecting the **Cache Performance** link shows a pie chart of how many hits are drawn from cache. This is displayed in Figure 13-22.

Notes:

Figure 13-22
In the case of SSL, the Cache Performance report indicates that most hits are returned from the Internet, not cache.

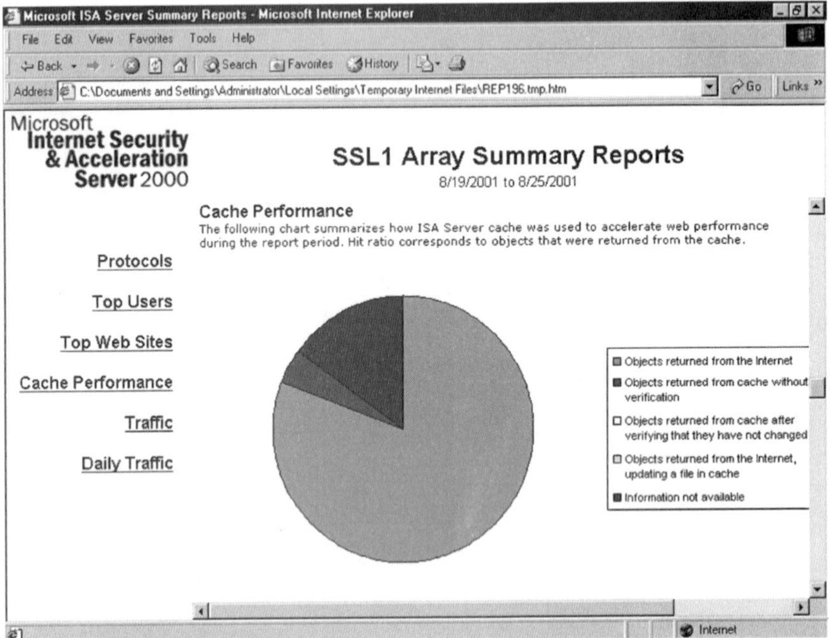

12. Click the **Traffic** link to display the **Traffic** report. This shows traffic over a range of dates.
13. Click **Daily Traffic** to observe traffic by time of day for a specific day. This is shown in figure 13-23.

Figure 13-23
The Daily traffic report is very valuable to observe when most of the Web surfing activity is occurring. For example, too much Web surfing over lunch might indicate horseplay by the employees at the firm.

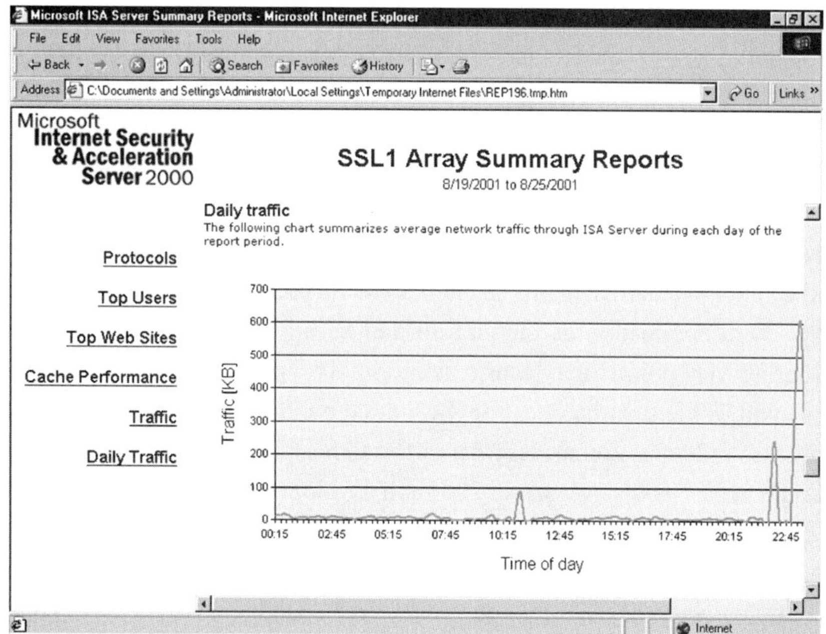

BEST PRACTICE: Matter of fact, I've used the **Daily traffic** report to exonerate the wrongly charged in organizations more than to obtain convictions for naughty behavior. Here's what I mean. An employee is suspected of surfing the Web for pornography on a company workstation. Perhaps this was determined by a supervisor viewing the History folder in Internet Explorer. But upon closer scrutiny, it might be revealed that the employee had left a workstation logged on each night and there was unusually high traffic at 1:00am when the janitors perform their work. I've now introduced reasonable doubt in the equation and allowed the shaken employee to retain his job. Whew!

Dual firewalls

Do me a favor and revisit Figure 5-12 in the earlier chapter on security in this book. That figure allows me the chance to reiterate and emphasize that a dual-firewall (ISA Server 2000 on the SBS 2003 machine and a hardware-based firewall out front on the perimeter) solution is perhaps the best form of security available to the small business. Speaking only for myself, I like the dual-firewall solution because it provides the utmost protection for my clients and myself (I look at it as being responsible and thus limiting my professional liability). Look for more of this discussion in my advanced SBS 2003 book (due the second half of 2004).

Third-party Development Platform

This section is a real treat in this chapter. So many people look at Microsoft's ISA Server 2000 application as the end all and be all of security. That is not an appropriate viewpoint. First, security is ever-evolving, so at best ISA Server 2000 is only part of the security equation. Second, the more healthy and holistic view of ISA Server 2000 is to consider what can be added to the core services it provides. In fact, Microsoft touts ISA Server 2000 as a development platform for its partners to add cool stuff on top. Vendors such as F5, Trend Micro, GFI, and others do exactly that, selling security-related applications that require ISA Server 2000 to operate. This was a key message during the GTM hands-on labs in the US during the spring of 2003. So remember that the oft-forgotten jewel in ISA Server 2000 is the ability to expand it with additional functionality provided by ISVs.

SBS Unlimited

Some folks just won't take no for an answer in the security field. They ask and ask again about separating ISA Server 2000 out from the SBS 2003 server machine and putting it on a separate server at the perimeter. Clearly I can't go on record suggesting you violate the inherent "per server" licensing in the SBS 2003 product. However, you might learn more about the SBS Unlimited SKU that allows the server applications to be placed on multiple servers (and allows you to have more than 75 CALs). You can learn more about this at www.microsoft.com/sbs.

BEST PRACTICE: The SBS Unlimited SKU is expensive, so don't tell me I didn't warn you!

Futurama!

This section of the chapter looks forward to ISA Server 2004, the next release of ISA Server from Microsoft. It's also a teaser for how you and I might meet again in my advanced SBS 2003 book down the road when I'll profile SBS 2003 in-depth.

First, as of this writing, it is not known when ISA Server 2004 will ship and how it will be offered to the SBS 2003 community. I give Microsoft credit for marching ahead with SBS 2003 and releasing it October 9, 2003, instead of waiting for ISA Server 2004. Why? Because based on the research I've done, ISA Server 2004 will likely benefit the enterprise sites with 5,000 users in its standalone product version versus greatly helping the ten-user SBS 2003 network. That's not to say SBSers won't be appreciative of ISA Server 2004 because they will. I'm just predicting that you'll find the delta changes to be smaller than you might have anticipated. Moving SBS 2003 forward with ISA Server 2000 was a good thing.

Second, exactly what is ISA Server 2004? According to WinBeta.org, ISA Server 2004 is a generational improvement to the ISA Server 2000 product. It'll incorporate improvements such as signature blocking and, borrowing from SBS-like thinking, have a simpler setup and configuration process. The public beta is anticipated in early 2004 (this book was written in the second part of 2003).

Third, what's my prediction on how it will integrate with SBS 2003 technically and from a marketing perspective? Clearly the setup process you saw for ISA Server 2000 in SBS 2003 premium edition is most likely how the setup process will work for ISA Server 2004. That is unless the SBS development team looks for a way to use the ISA Server 2004 release as a chance to refresh the SBS 2003 product with a new setup process (this could be accomplished with a simple wizard that accompanies ISA Server 2004 when shipped to registered SBS 2003 owners). The marketing side is in some ways more complex. Will Microsoft just give ISA Server 2004 to existing SBS 2003 premium edition owners? Will a discount be given on the purchase price? Will Microsoft not even emphasize ISA Server 2004 with the SBS 2003 premium edition product? Stand by!

Resources

How many times have I emphasized that (a) this book is an introductory and intermediate volume for the SBS 2003 product, (b) an advanced SBS 2003 book is forthcoming, and (c) you need to go forth and learn more about the individual rich applications, such as ISA Server 2000, by reading books, etc., dedicated specifically to the matter at hand. This book paints some broad and narrow strokes for each SBS 2003 component but can't hope to compete with individual texts dedicated to only one topic.

Books

I again feature my "fave" authors here: Roberta Bragg and Dr. Thomas Shinder. Consider books from either of these authors as a next step with ISA Server 2000.

Roberta Bragg offers the following ISA Server 2000 books (search on Roberta's name at Amazon to find these books):

- *MCSE Training Guide (70-227): Installing, Configuring and Administering Microsoft Internet Security and Acceleration (ISA) Server 2000*
- *Network Security: The Complete Reference*

Dr. Thomas Shinder offers the following ISA Server 2000 books (search on the good doctor's name to find these books):

- *Configuring ISA Server 2000*
- *Dr. Tom Shinder's ISA Server and Beyond: Real World security Solutions for Microsoft Enterprise Networks*
- *Configuring ISA Server 2000: Building Firewalls for Windows 2000*

Web Sites

Several sites I point you to here are great ISA Server 2000 and security resources. First and foremost would be www.isaserver.org, maintained by the good Dr. Tom! And you'll find Roberta's contributions in a monthly security column at www.mcpmag.com in her "Security Advisor" column. Don't forget

Microsoft's ISA Server site at www.microsoft.com/isa. And monitor www.microsoft.com/security and www.microsoft.com/technet for the latest updates related to security matters.

Courses

Perhaps you're like me and have attended Microsoft Official Curriculum courses that, to be honest, left you hungry. Such is not the case with the ISA Server 2000 three-day course titled *Deploying and Managing Microsoft Internet Security and Acceleration Server 2000* (Course 2159). I found this three day course to be excellent and worth the time and expense. Full details at www.microsoft.com/traincert.

Buddy Up!

A common concern in the SBS community is that you can't know it all (very true statement). You can hope to master one or two areas and then hang on for dear life with the remaining SBS applications. As I've traveled the world preaching the SBS gospel, I can say that many good folks (many of them readers of my books) are intimidated by the security area. So make sure you're sitting down for this next statement: You don't need to be an ISA Server 2000 guru to be an SBSer. Rather, do the best you can, read books on the topic, and keep the TELEPHONE NUMBER of a security guru handy. It's been said great technology consulting is knowing who to call to get the answer and such might be the case with you and your mastery of both security and ISA Server 2000.

> BEST PRACTICE: So I recommend that you periodically take your security buddy to lunch and talk shop. Might I suggest this pub on Bainbridge Island Washington (Figure 13-24), the home town of SPRINGERS!

Notes:

Figure 13-24
You'll find me out on the deck talking security and SBS at this Bainbridge Island eatery and watering hole!

Summary

Chapters like this scare me. Not only does this chapter revisit the wild and whacky world of security first discussed in Chapter 5 of this book, but you might have entered this chapter with the expectation of reading a full book on ISA Server 2000. That's not gonna happen with the limitations I have on page count (and when I have to present all SBS applications between the book covers, not just ISA Server 2000). However, I hope you leave this chapter knowing more about ISA Server 2000 and how it interacts with SBS 2000 than when you arrived. While I'm the first to admit a chapter on any security topic ages quickly, hopefully I've shared with you some foundation matters in ISA Server 2000 that will stand the test of time. And be sure to catch the page footers where you're encouraged to learn more about products such as ISA Server 2000 by continuously monitoring www.microsoft.com/technet and reading the latest articles. Go do it now!

Chapter 14
Database Management with SQL Server 2000

Talk about a career path. Not only can you find very good (and large) texts dedicated to the SQL Server 2000 database application (a database application helps you gather, organize, and report information), but more than one Microsoft Certified Professional (MCP) has made a good living doing the SQL thing. Studying SQL Server introduces you to one of the largest bodies of knowledge and know how contained within SBS 2003 (premium edition). Given this overwhelming perspective, I've made the decision to keep the SQL Server discussion germane, practical, and relatively brief (and, as always, with the SPRINGERS point of view). If you so desire, I can recommend a great SQL Server book from my fellow Seattle-area author, Richard Waymire: *Sams' Teach Yourself Microsoft SQL Server 2000 in 21 Days*, ISBN: 0-672-31969-1.

If I were to delve into the depths of SQL Server at the level of the aforementioned books, you and I would not only be here late into the night, but we'd be together for many days and nights forward. I can appreciate your interest in learning more about SQL Server (more than I can reasonably deliver in one chapter), so bear with me and consider this a sampler. Note that in the advanced SBS 2003 book I plan to write in mid-2004, I intend to show you more with SQL Server including importing a table from Microsoft Access.

After discussing SQL Server at a high level, this chapter has you create a database for SPRINGERS and then publish it to a Web site. Let's get started!

Clarifying SQL Server 2000

On the one hand, you can say SQL Server 2000 is a very important part of SBS 2003. Call it the revenge of the good old "It's the data, stupid" crowd. When you really think about it, the whole reason any of us technology professionals are here is because the underlying data drives business computing. Get it? No? Then consider how I interact with my clients on any given day. The property management firm I serve calls when they can't run payroll, not because some SBS event log entry looks interesting. A true story: The payroll program at the property management firm needed Internet access to obtain updated tax tables and forms before it would cut the paychecks. The solution was to open a port in the firewall to allow the traffic through. But understand that the call I received from the client was much more about the "data" than asking me to come over and open up a firewall port. So it truly is "the data, stupid!"

On the other hand, I can't deny that, in its natural state, SQL Server is one of the least used components in SBS 2003 (which is truly unfortunate). Part of that might be attributable to the fact that SQL Server 2000 is shipped only with the premium edition of SBS 2003, not the standard version. One interesting thought along these lines of SQL Server de-emphasis (and don't worry, I get to the "emphasis" argument in the next paragraph) relates to being an actual SQL language programmer. It's highly unlikely that, as an SBSer, you'll program inside of SQL Server (using the SQL programming language) at an SBS site. With respect to building custom applications and other SQL goodies (such as stored procedures), SQL Server is much more at home in development and enterprise environments. It's not my world, but I sure like the business applications that SQL Server developers create!

Now for some good news about SQL Server, starting with the old saying about having nothing to fear but fear itself (with all due respect to United States President Franklin Roosevelt). SQL Server has a very important role that I haven't even discussed yet: supporting business applications. To understand this supporting role, you'll learn the basics of SQL Server in this chapter. Such an understanding will aid greatly in supporting applications that run on top of SQL Server.

To understand SQL Server at an appropriate level for an SBS site, you'll spend the first part of the chapter creating a simple table to manage some information for SPRINGERS via SQL Server (yes, that never-ending SPRINGERS methodology is utilized yet again). Later in the chapter, the focus shifts to advanced SQL Server tidbits (such as publishing data as a Web page) that you need to know about to better manage SQL Server. I do want to manage your expectations: Today is not a day to master SQL Server; today is a day to meet and greet SQL Server.

BEST PRACTICE: In all seriousness, I hope I've managed your expectations to this point about what SQL Server is and isn't. More important, I want to emphasize that in no way, shape, or form is this chapter anything more than a SQL Server sampler. As stated previously, several thick books dedicated to SQL Server await your reading pleasure. And don't forget I intend to emphasize SQL Server in a future Advanced SBS 2003 text.

SQL Server Defined

At its heart, SQL Server is a database, but you likely already knew that from the introductory discussion. Did you know, however, that it differs from other databases you might have worked with in the past in that SQL Server is a client/server database? Perhaps you've worked with other databases, such as dBASE, which are relational databases (similar to SQL Server), but don't exploit the power of the network's server (the SBS server machine on an SBS network). Figure 14-1 shows how SQL Server works as a client/server database and how other databases (such as dBASE) work.

Notes:

Figure 14-1
SQL Server client/server versus other databases.

Client/Server Model
SQL Server 2000
Database Implementation
SQL Data
SPRINGERS1 running SQL Server 2000
SQL Server 2000 engine runs applications and stores data.
SBS 2003 User
Front-end client application send SQL queries for processing. Results returned to front-end client application.
Non-Client/Server Model
(other databases)
Server
Database files stored on server machine (may or may not be an SBS machine).
User
Data files completely downloaded for local processing.

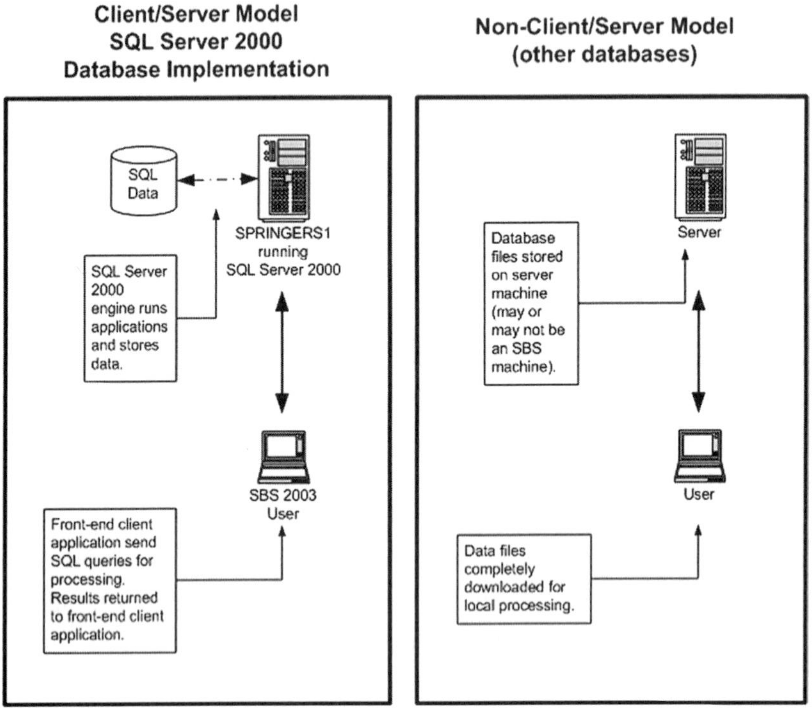

The Server Side

On the SBS server machine, the data resides not only in tables, but also is manipulated by the SQL Server engine. These SQL Server server-side capabilities include three functional areas: data warehousing, e-commerce, and line of business.

Data Warehousing

Microsoft has positioned SQL Server to act as a store of data for the organization. This is accomplished in several ways:

- **Comprehensive Analysis Services.** This speaks to SQL Server 2000's business analysis capabilities via online analytical processing (OLAP) and data mining.

BEST PRACTICE: The analysis services and data mining capabilities in SQL Server 2000 are damn cool. It was the focus of an afternoon in the four day GTM hands on lab in the spring of 2003. And at the ITEC trade show in Portland in December 2003, an attendee at a CRM presentation asked about using the data that CRM gathers. He wanted to know how to use that data to make better forecasts. Since Microsoft CRM is using SQL Server 2000, the answer was to data mine the CRM data!

- **Data Transformation Services.** These are the routines that automate the extraction and transformation of business data from multiple sources.

- **Web-enabled.** Not only can you publish your information to a Web page, but you can analyze data accessible from remote Web sites. You will publish a Web page at the end of this chapter with SPRINGERS data.

- **Meta-Data Services.** The idea here is that SQL Server supports the sharing of data between different tools and environments.

- **Indexed Views.** Microsoft is claiming that performance enhancements related to accessing your data can be gained by indexed views.

- **Microsoft Office Integration.** In Microsoft Excel, you can use the pivot table capabilities to manipulate SQL Server-based data.

- **English Query.** Here's something many SBSers, who don't claim to be SQL gurus, will like. In SQL Server 2000, there is greater support for posing queries in English versus SQL speak (or as Microsoft calls it, "Multi-Dimensional Expressions" - MDX for short).

E-Commerce

- **XML Support.** One of the more promising developments in the database world is that of the Extensible Markup Language (known as XML). This is the capability to parse data into a meaningful format. This is central to stuff like Office 2003 interoperability.

- **Web and Application Hosting.** SQL Server is clearly e-commerce-ready, with its ability to interact in real time with Web pages, and by collecting and providing data.

- **Distributed Partition Views.** This is the ability to distribute the workload over several servers (call it another fancy term for load balancing). This would be very important for an organization that has much Web activity, such as a Web retail storefront.

- **Database Administration.** Not surprisingly, the database administration area has improved with this release of SQL Server including automatic tuning and maintenance features.

Line of business

- **High Availability**. Short of getting the right data in the right hands, the other SBSer obligation to SQL Server is high availability. Consider the following. You're a king SBSer who knows infrastructure like no one else, and you've done a good job of advising your client or bosses on the use of a database. But without high availability, all of your credence might be shipped south. SQL Server 2000 is committed, as I can attest, to high-availability. One such way it demonstrates this is by its ability to make online SQL Server-based backups (say in the middle of the day) of critical databases.

- **Application support.** Ah, my favorite topic. Major line of business (LOB) software application vendors are committing to SQL Server 2000 (granted, these software vendors may have committed to Oracle first, but that's a whole different story and book).

- **Application hosting.** Interestingly, with Microsoft's ascension to the altar of application service providers (ASPs) with its .NET (called "dot-net") initiative, Microsoft is promoting the ASP paradigm shift in SQL Server 2000. So perhaps you can act as a line of business server to other businesses. Hmmmmmm...shall we say the possibilities are truly endless?

- **Replication.** I suspect you join me on this one, but I truly believe that having your data stored in more than one place is a business technology success factor. I shared with you the importance of replication in Chapter 6 in the context of PDA replication. SQL Server essentially has the same capability with its transactional and snapshot replication.

Primary server-side services

The main server-side services for SQL Server are:

- **MSSQLServer.** This is the SQL Server engine as you know it, the piece that processes the SQL statements (officially known as Transact-SQL). This service also allocates server resources (such as memory), manages the tables (for example, prevents collisions between users), and ensures the integrity of the data (via various tests).

- **Microsoft Distributed Transaction Coordinator.** This is a service which acts as a traffic cop, managing the sources of data that compose a transaction.

- **SQLServerAgent.** This is a service that manages scheduling activities and sends alerts.

- **Microsoft Search.** This is an indexing-related service used by SQL Server 2000 and other SBS 2003 components (such as the Find command in Windows Server 2003.

- **MSSQLServerOLAPService.** This service relates to the online analytical processing capabilities of SQL Server 2000. This service auto-starts when the underlying Windows Server 2003 operating system starts.

Notes:

The SQL Server 2000 Services are displayed and managed via the SQL Server Service Manager displayed in Figure 14-2.

Figure 14-2
SQL Server 2000 services can be stopped, started, and configured via the SQL Server Service Manager tool.

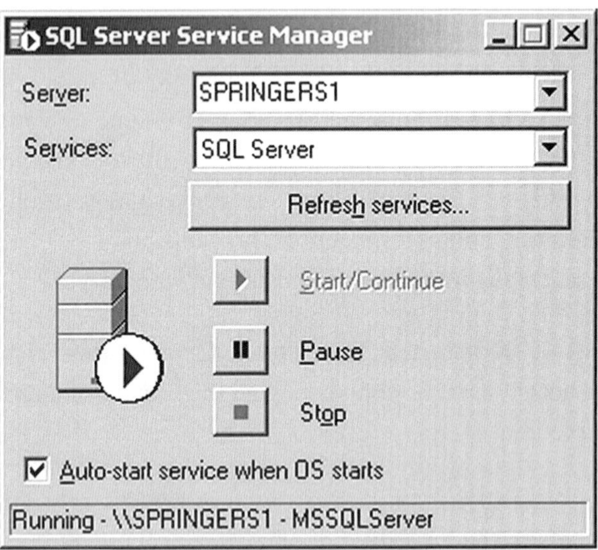

The following SQL Server system databases are automatically constructed when SBS 2003 installs SQL Server 2000:

- **Master.** This is the mother of all tables in SQL Server. Lose it (with no back up) and you'll die. Simply stated, it controls SQL Server operations completely (including user databases, user accounts, environmental variables, system error message, and so on). It is critical that you back up this database on a regular basis.

- **Model.** A template provides basic information used when you create new databases for your own use. This is akin to the metainformation you entered when you installed SBS 2003 (company name, address, fax, and telephone numbers) that reappears each time you add a user, via one of the SBS consoles, to your SBS network. You might recall that I defined *metainformation* early in this book in the middle of Chapter

3; it is information that is used globally by the computer system, not just in one place.

- **Msdb.** The SQLServerAgent uses this for scheduling and job history.
- **Tempdb.** This is another database that's very important to the operation of SQL Server. It's a temporary storage area used by SQL Server for working storage. This is akin to the paging file used by Windows Server 2003 (the underlying operating system in SBS).
- **Northwind.** Consider using this sample database as the prototype for developing your own company database. This is an addition in SQL Server 2000 that wasn't present in prior versions of SQL Server. This was the sample database in Microsoft Access and is the "standard" sample company used in Microsoft Official Curriculum (MOC) training courses for MCSEs.
- **Pubs.** Yet another database used in most of Microsoft's SQL Server manuals, including the wonderful online books!

Server-side management

This is where you will spend your time with SQL Server: using the management tools. You've already seen two of the management tools: the SQL Server Enterprise Manager and the SQL Server Service Manager. But there are various other SQL Server administration tools and wizards, as well as the books online. To introduce yourself to the full array of SQL Server management tools (which are technically considered client applications even though they run on the server), simply display the contents of the Microsoft SQL Server program group (found via the Start button, All Programs).

Notes:

The Client Side

The client side speaks to the wide range of applications that use SQL Server, including:

- Third-party applications, such as Microsoft Great Plains accounting software.
- Microsoft Access running on the SBS user's workstations.
- Microsoft Excel spreadsheets that link to databases housed on an SBS server machine running SQL Server.
- Microsoft Visual Basic-created applications that use SQL Server. These are typically homegrown applications written by either an employee at an SBS site or a consultant to use data stored and managed by SQL Server.
- Other applications. I've seen a wide range of applications, including Microsoft Excel, Word, and PowerPoint, that access a SQL Server database to extract and place data. The advanced pivot table feature in Microsoft Excel works very nicely with SQL Server-based data.

BEST PRACTICE: Client-side applications typically connect to SQL Server (running on the SBS server machine) via the following database application program interfaces (APIs):

- Open database connectivity (ODBC). ODBC is the connector by which many front ends running on the clients (a.k.a. client applications) connect to the SQL Server database. I'll show you ODBC in action shortly.
- Object linking and embedding (OLE). OLE, in English, is what I like to think of as copy-and-paste kept alive. When you paste data from one source to another and you change the data back at the source, it's automatically updated at the destination you created. With respect to SQL Server, imagine a Microsoft Excel spreadsheet containing financial information from a SQL Server-

based table. The financial information changes in the table and the Microsoft Excel spreadsheet is updated automatically. Plain and simple!

- ActiveX Data Objects (ADO). This is a connector that, among other things, provides record-level access to VSAM, AS/400, and PDS data
- Remote Data Objects (RDO). RDO provides a framework for using code to create and manipulate components of a remote ODBC database system.
- XML. Enough said!

Common Uses of SQL Server on SBS Networks

First and foremost, the greatest need I've seen for SQL Server 2000 on SBS networks is support for applications, such as Great Plains accounting software, and other narrow, vertical-market applications in the legal, medical, and instrument-repair industries (to name just a few).

Secondary uses for SQL Server 2000 on an SBS network include creating your own databases, importing databases from Microsoft Access, and learning SQL Server 2000 for MCSE certification purposes. (I'm just calling it like I see it.)

BEST PRACTICE: For more information on SQL Server 2000 specifics, I can send you to two free resources! First, visit Microsoft's SQL Server Web site at www.microsoft.com/sql. Second, read the SQL Server Books Online (installed as part of the complete SQL Server installation process). The SQL Server Books Online are excellent!

Notes:

SQL Server and SPRINGERS

No chapter on SQL Server, in any book, would be complete without having you create a database or a table or two, enter some data, and then display the data you've entered. This book is no exception. But again, understand that this exercise is almost an exception to the rule on SBS networks; you're far more likely to work with third-party applications that sit on top of the SQL Server 2000 engine.

That said, revisit your friends at SPRINGERS. Because no third-party software exists that explicitly tracks dogs, you'll create a database to accomplish this business purpose.

> BEST PRACTICE: Whenever considering the creation of a database, be sure you understand the purpose for undertaking this project. Poorly considered database projects are like poorly written books: difficult to read and soon ignored.

First, you will need to install SQL Server 2000 in SBS 2003. Please use the readme text accessed by clicking the How to Install link when you insert Disc 5 from SBS 2003 premium edition to install SQL Server 2000.

In a nutshell, the SQL Server process is broken into three parts:

- Installing SQL Server 2000
- Installing SQL Server 2000 Service Pack 3a (again, current as of fall 2003)
- Configuring the SQL Server Collation Settings

> BEST PRACTICE: So here is a chance to do as I say and not as I'll do for you. Heed the advice above and correctly install SQL Server 2000 based on the latest prescriptive guidance and return back to this spot to proceed with the chapter and create a database for SPRINGERS. See you back here in a little while.

Now get to work and create a database for SPRINGERS. Afterward, you will create a table and populate it with meaningful dog tracking information.

To create the database for SPRINGERS, perform the following steps:

1. Log on to the SBS server machine as **Administrator** with the password **Husky9999!**
2. Click **Start, All Programs, Microsoft SQL Server, Enterprise Manager**.
3. Expand the following objects in the left pane: **Microsoft SQL Servers, SQL Server Group, SPRINGERS1 (Windows NT)**.
4. Highlight **SPRINGERS1 (Windows NT)** and select **View, Taskpad** to display the taskpad in the right pane with the **General** tab initially displayed. Notice server and configuration information is displayed. The operating system is incorrectly identified as Microsoft Windows NT.
5. Click the **Wizards** tab and the resulting screen should look like Figure 14-3.

Figure 14-3
The Wizards page on the taskpage offers a wizard link to accomplish nearly any task.

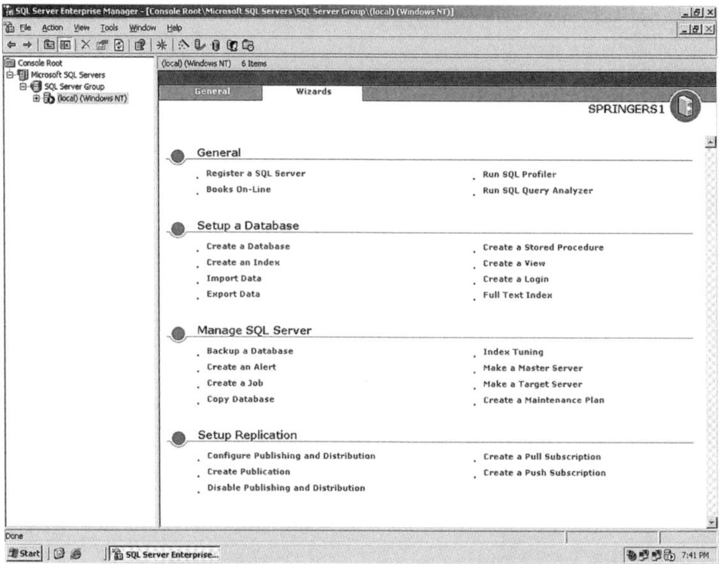

6. Select the **Create a Database** link under **Set up a Database** on the **Wizards** page of the taskpad. The **Create Database Wizard - SPRINGERS1** appears and the **Welcome to the Create Database Wizard** screen is displayed. **Click Next**.

7. The **Name the Database and Specify its Location** screen appears. In the **Database name: field**, type **SSLDOG**. Accept the settings for the database location in **Database** file location:. Accept the settings in the **Transaction log file location:** field. Your screen should look similar to Figure 14-4. Click **Next**.

Figure 14-4
Naming the database and accepting file locations on the Name the Database and Specify its Location screen.

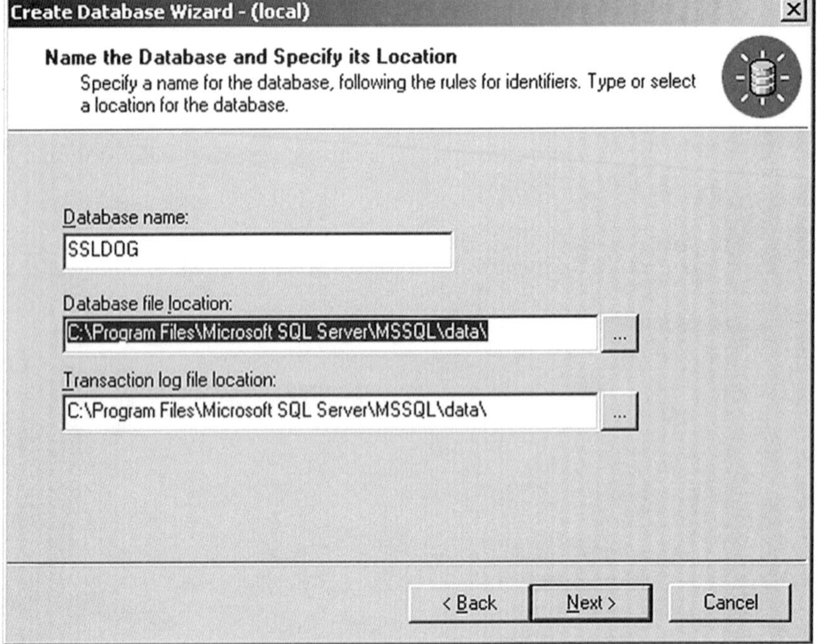

8. The **Name the Database Files** screen appears. Accept the default file name of **SSLDOG_Data** under **File Name** and type **10** under **Initial Size (MB)**. Click **Next**.
9. Accept the default settings on the **Define the Database File Growth** screen. Click **Next**.
10. Accept the default settings on the **Name the Transaction Log Files** and click **Next**. Note the initial size of the transaction log file will be 1 MB.

11. Accept the defaults on the **Define the Transaction Log File Growth** page and click **Next**.
12. Click **Finish** on the **Completing the Create Database Wizard page**.

BEST PRACTICE: Note because this is a native SQL Server 2000 wizard, it does not have a link to save, print, or e-mail your configuration settings (like you've seen in native SBS 2003 wizards).

But the completion configuration information can be selected via the mouse (hold down the right mouse button and drag across the text) and then copied by pressing **CTRL-C**. Open **Notepad** or some other text editor and paste this text. Then save the file as part of the SBS network notebook. With these simple steps, you will have the whole database configuration at a glance!

13. Click **OK** when the **Create Database Wizard** dialog box notifies you that you have successfully created the database.
14. You are asked whether you want to create a maintenance plan for the database SSLDOG on another **Create Database Wizard** dialog box. Click **Yes**.

BEST PRACTICE: It is critical that you set up a daily maintenance plan for your key databases (the master database and any databases you create). On more than one occasion, I've had to rely on the SQL Server-based database backups when a traditional backup tape failed me. A SQL Server-based database backup places a bona fide copy of your database on another part of the SBS server machine's hard disk. It's unbelievably valuable!

15. The Database Maintenance Plan Wizard launches. Click **Next** after reading the **Welcome to the Database Maintenance Plan Wizard** screen. Note that the **Welcome** screen tells you which tasks the Database Maintenance Plan Wizard will run, including running database integrity checks, updating database statistics, and performing database backups (inside of SQL Server 2000).
16. Select **master** and **SSLDOG** under the **Database** column on the **Select Databases** screen, as seen in Figure 14-5. Click **Next**. Kindly note that Figure 14-5 displays the SSLDOG database as being

selected in the Database column, but believe me that master is also selected. Given the constraints of the user interface for that dialog box, I can't get both selections to appear in a single figure (master is selected at the top of the databases list and has been scrolled out of the figure).

Figure 14-5
Select the master and SSLDOG databases on the Select Databases screen.

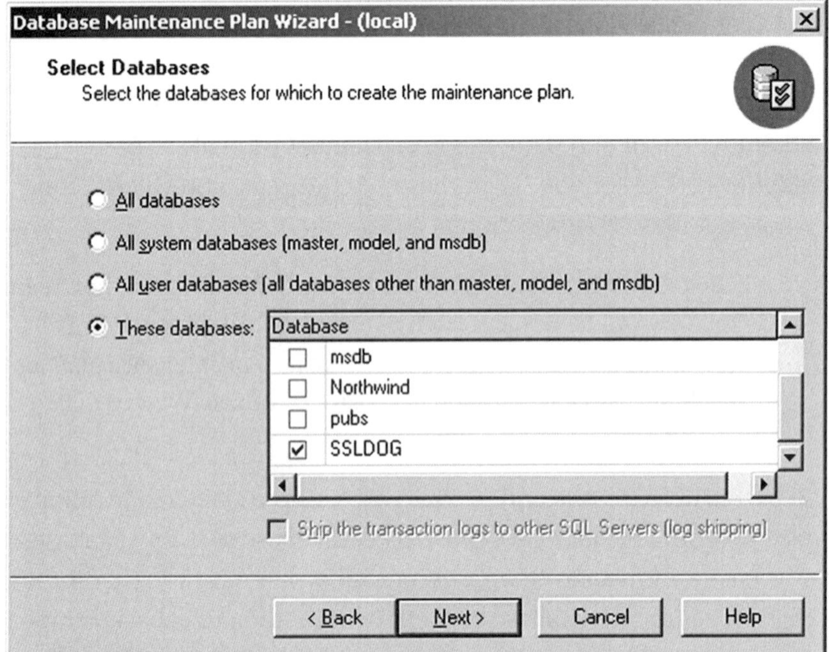

17. On the **Update Data Optimization Information** screen, select the **Reorganize data and index pages** check box. Select the **Change free space per page percentage to:** radio button and accept **10** in the numeric value field immediately to the right. Select the **Remove unused space from database files** check box and accept **50 MB** for the **When it grows beyond field:**. Accept **10 % of data space** in the **Amount of free space to remain after shrink:**. Accept the default schedule under **Schedule:** of **Occurs every 1 week(s) on Sunday, at 1:00:00AM** and click **Next**. Your screen should look similar to Figure 14-6. The selections you have made relate to managing disk space

from the SQL Server 2000 database perspective. And managing disk space on a computer is considered an important thing to do.

Figure 14-6

Your Update Data Optimization Information screen should look similar to this figure.

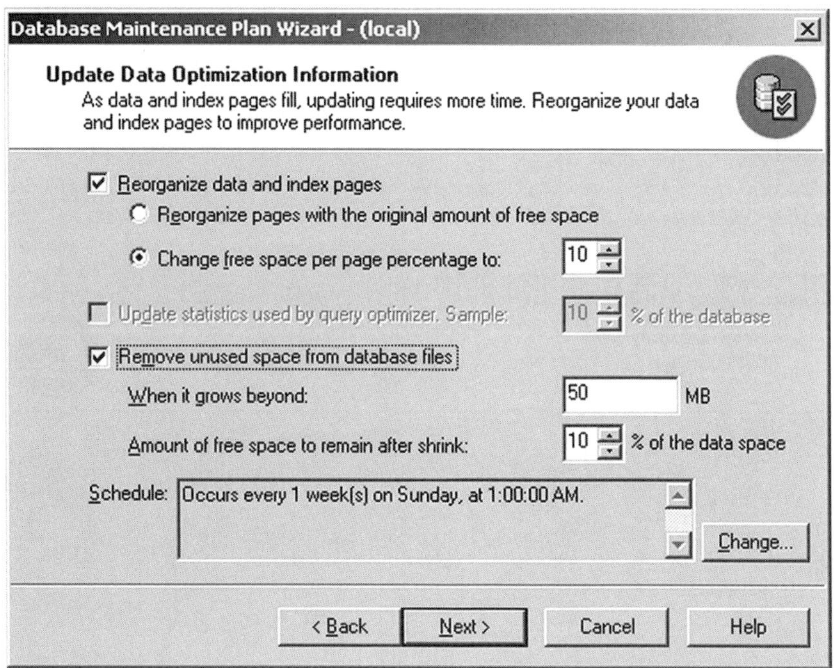

Notes:

18. On the **Database Integrity Check** screen, select the **Check Database Integrity** check box. Click the **Include indexes** radio button. Select the **Attempt to repair any minor problems** check box. Select the **Perform these checks before doing backups** check box. Your screen should look similar to Figure 14-7. Click **Next**. What you have just done is invoke the native SQL Server capability to maintain sound database integrity and to perform these actions before making an internal SQL Server backup.

Figure 14-7
The selections you make on the Database Integrity Check screen will allow you to keep your SSLDOG database healthy.

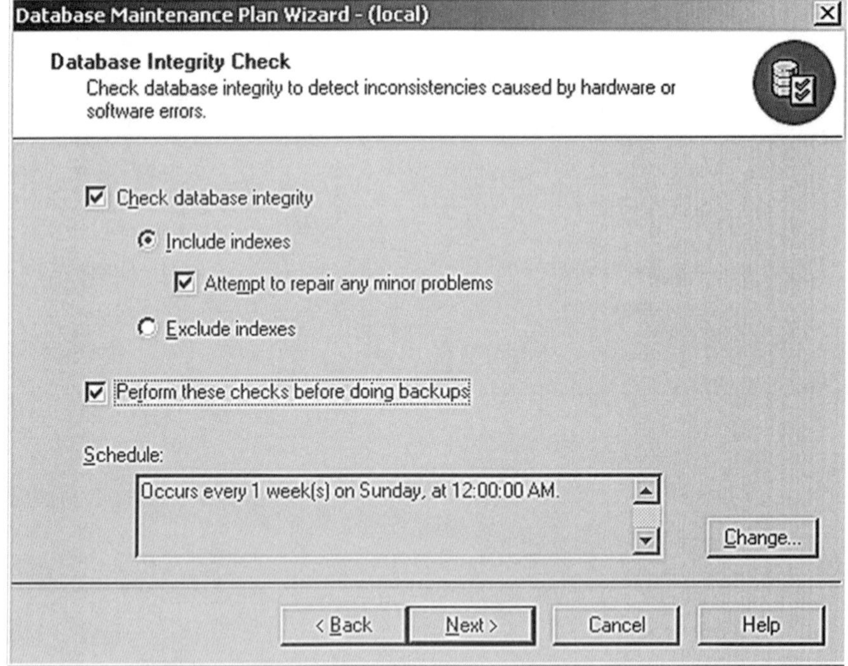

19. On the **Specify the Database Backup Plan** screen, select the **Back up the database as part of the maintenance plan** check box. Select the **Verify the integrity of the backup when complete** check box. Click the **Disk** radio button. Click the **Change** button and select **Daily** in the **Occurs** column when the **Edit Recurring Job Schedule** dialog box appears and click **OK**. You are returned to the **Specify the Database Backup Plan** screen. Click **Next**.

20. Accept the default select of **Use the default backup directory** on the **Specify Backup Disk Directory** screen. Click **Next**.
21. Select **Back up the transaction log as part of the maintenance plan** check box on the **Specify the Transaction Log Backup Plan** screen. Accept the default settings of **Verify the integrity of the backup when complete, Disk,** and the **Schedule:** that backs up the transaction log every week on numerous evenings. Click **Next**.
22. Accept the default selection of **Use the default backup directory** on the **Specify Transaction Log Backup Disk Directory** screen. Click **Next**.
23. Select the **Write Report to a text file in directory** check box on the **Reports to Generate** screen. Accept the default report storage folder (c:\Program Files\Microsoft SQL Server\MSSQL\LOG\). Select **Delete text report older than** and accept the default time period of **4 Week(s)**. Your screen should look similar to Figure 14-8. Click **Next**.

Figure 14-8
You can configure the text-based reports you want to generate.

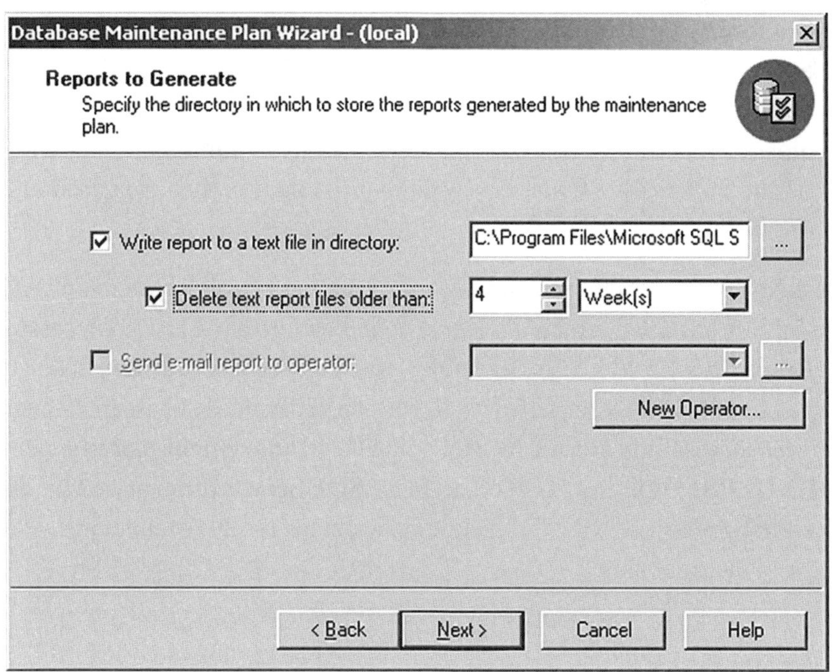

24. Accept the default settings of **Write history to the msdb.dbo.sysdb-maintplan history table on this server** and **Limit rows in the table to: 1000 rows for this plan** under Local Server on the **Maintenance History** screen and click **Next**.
25. The **Completing the Database Maintenance Wizard** screen appears. Accept the default plan name of **DB Maintenance Plan1** under **Plan name:**. Note you could select all of the configuration information in the text box using your mouse (by dragging) to copy it to the clipboard with the CTRL-C command and then paste it into a text editor such as Notepad for inclusion in your SBS network notebook. Click **Finish**.

BEST PRACTICE: You might receive an error message via the SQL Server Enterprise Manager dialog box that informs you that the SQL Server Agent service is stopped and must be started to complete this processing. If you receive this message, simply click the **Start** button from your SBS server machine desktop (you might have to hold the **CTRL-ESC** keys to display the Start button). Click **Start, All Programs, Microsoft SQL Server, Service Manager**. When the **SQL Server Service Manager** appears, select **SQL Server Agent** in the **Services:** drop-down field. Click the **green arrow button** next to **Start/Continue**. Close the S**QL Server Service Manager**. Click **OK** on the SQL Server Enterprise Manager dialog box that appeared at the beginning of this note.

You have now successfully completed the creation of a database maintenance plan for SPRINGERS. You will receive no indication that this was successfully created (in SBS 4.5 with SQL Server 6.5, you received a notification dialog box that you had to click OK on). However, you can verify the database maintenance plan was successfully created by expanding the **Management folder** under the **SPRINGERS1 (Windows NT)** object in the **SQL Server Enterprise Manager.** Click the **Jobs** object in the left pane and the details for DB Maintenance Plan1 appear in the right pane.

Creating the Tracking Table

You should always have a bona fide business purpose for creating a database and populating it with information. SPRINGERS is no exception. Here the underlying business purpose is clear: to use SQL Server to solve a problem. The problem is that, with the sheer volume of Springer Spaniels entering the world at SPRINGERS, you must have a method for tracking their whereabouts and exact origin. From the simple table here (a data dictionary) you'll create the Tracking table in SQL Server. This allows you to achieve the important business goal of tracking Springer Spaniels.

Table 14-1 shows the data dictionary that you will use to create the database.

Table 14-1: SPRINGERS Data Dictionary

Item (Column Name)	Description
SSLDOG	Database name
Tracking	Table name for tracking springer spaniels
DogName	Name of dog (column name, Data Type = char, Length = 30)
ShowName	Long name of dog for show purposes (column name, Data Type = char, Length = 50)
FatherDN	Father dog's name (column name, Data Type = char, Length = 30)
MotherDN	Mother dog's name (column name, Data Type = char, Length = 30)
DDOB	Dog's date of birth (column name, Data Type = datetime, Length = 8)
AKCNum	American Kennel Club (AKC) registration number (column name, Data Type = char, Length = 15)

Now commence the task of creating your Tracking table:

1. Log on to the SBS server machine as **Administrator** with the password **Husky9999!**

2. Click **Start, All Programs, Microsoft SQL Server, Enterprise Manager**.
3. Expand the following objects in the left pane: **Microsoft SQL Servers, SQL Server Group, SPRINGERS1 (Windows NT)**.
4. Expand **Databases, SSLDOG** and then right-click the **Table** icon in the left pane. Select **New Table** from the secondary menu.
5. The **New Table in SSLDOG on SPRINGERS1** screen appears. Create the table based on the information contained in Table 14-1. For example, enter the column name under the **Column Name** column. Enter the data type under the **Data Type** column. Enter the field length in the **Length** column. You will not modify the **Allow Nulls** column. The result should look similar to Figure 14-9.

Figure 14-9
Tracking table setup.

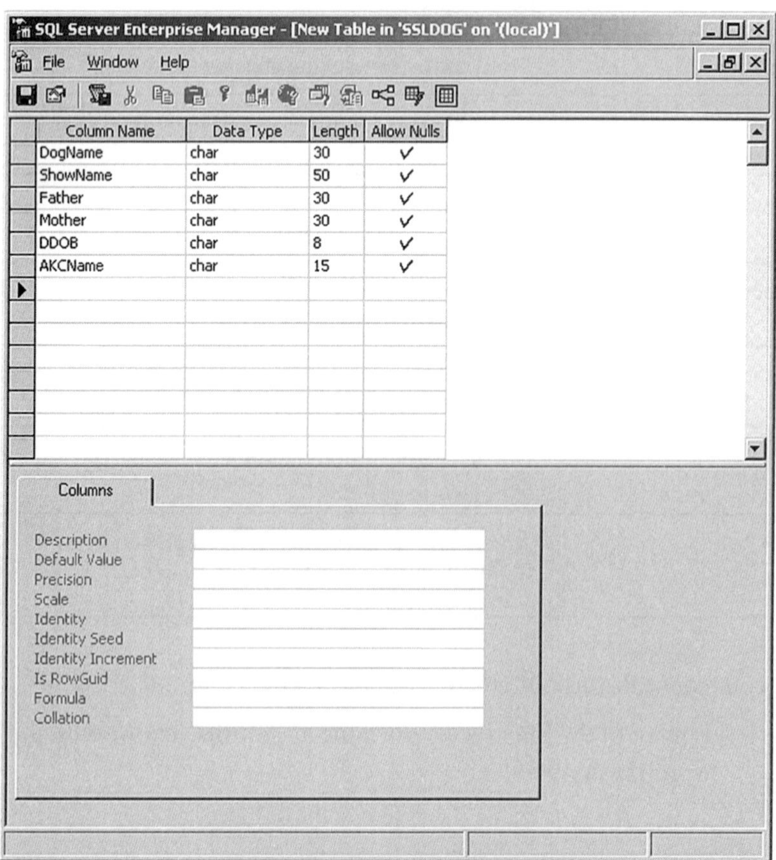

BEST PRACTICE: Move your cursor from field to field just like you would when using a spreadsheet. When your cursor is in the Data Type field, a down arrow appears. This is a drop-down menu containing the different types of data type fields you'll be working with (for example, datetime).

7. Click the **Save** icon on the left side of the toolbar (disk icon) on the **New Table in SSLDOG on SPRINGERS1** screen. Type **Tracking** in the **Enter a name for the table** field when the **Choose Name** dialog box appears. Click **OK**.
8. Close the **Tracking Table** window via the **X** in the upper-right corner of the screen.

If you look at the table listed for SSLDOG database in the SQL Server Enterprise Manager, you will see that the **Tracking** table is listed in alphabetical order right after the sysusers table.

Using Your SPRINGERS Database

You will now enter real business information into the Tracking table. Afterward, you will query the table to retrieve the data.

Data Entry

Time to enter data into the Tracking table. In Table 14-2, I've provided the data needed for two springer spaniels. You will use this information to populate the database.

Table 14-2: SSLDOG Data

Item	**Dog1**	**Dog2**
DogName	Brisker	Jaeger
ShowName	Sir David Brisker	Sir Jaeger Matthew
FatherDN	Pepper	Pepper
MotherDN	Maria	Maria
DDOB	8-15-93	8-15-93
AKCNum	WA98119A	WA98119B

1. Log on to the SBS server machine as **Administrator** with the password **Husky9999!**
2. Click **Start, All Programs, Microsoft SQL Server, Enterprise Manager**.
3. Expand the following objects in the left pane: **Microsoft SQL Servers, SQL Server Group, SPRINGERS1 (Windows NT)**.
4. Expand **SSLDOG**.
5. Expand **Tables**. The list of tables will appear in the right pane.
6. Right-click on the **Tracking** table. From the secondary menu, select **Open Table, Return All Rows**.
7. The **Data in Table 'Tracking' in 'SSLDOG' on 'SSL1'** window appears. Enter the information from Table 14-2 into this window. For example, in the case of Dog1, enter **Brisker** under **DogName, Sir David Brisker** under **ShowName, Pepper** under **FatherDN**, **Maria** under **MotherDN**, **8-15-93** under **DDOBB**, and **WA98119A** under **AKCNum**. (Note you can move between fields with your **TAB** key.)
8. Close the **Data in Table 'Tracking' in 'SSLDOG' on 'SSL1'** window by clicking the **X** on the upper-left corner of the window. You have successfully entered the data for two dogs in the table of a SQL Server database that you have created. Congratulations.

Query the Data

You will now query the SSLDOG database, much like a client application does. Why? Because in and of itself, a table populated with data is relatively worthless. For your relationship with SQL Server to have true value, you must use the information. That's an action verb, as in query. Thus, after populating a table with information, you will query it to return the information in a synthesized or value-added form. And that's essentially the database food chain.

1. Log on to the SBS server machine as **Administrator** with the password **Husky9999!**
2. Click **Start, All Programs, Microsoft SQL Server, Enterprise Manager**.
3. Expand the following objects in the left pane: **Microsoft SQL Servers, SQL Server Group, SPRINGERS1 (Windows NT)**.
4. Select and expand the **SSLDOG** database.
5. From the **Tools** menu, select **SQL Query Analyzer**. The SQL Query Analyzer program launches.
6. A **Query** window appears inside of the **SQL** Query Analyzer application. In the **SQL Query Analyzer** toolbar, confirm that **SSLDOG** appears in the database drop-down menu (upper right in Query window). If not, select **SSLDOG** from the database drop-down menu.
7. In the **Query** window, click the **blank space** in the upper-left part of the screen and type the following command: **select * from tracking**. This is shown in Figure 14-10.

Figure 14-10
Creating a select statement in SQL Server 2000 to query the SSLDOG database and, specifically, the Tracking table.

8. Select **Execute** from the **Query** menu (you can also press **F5** or click the **green right arrow** on the **Query** window toolbar). The contents of the Tracking table are returned to you, as seen in Figure 14-11.

Figure 14-11

Successful query against Tracking with result returned to the display.

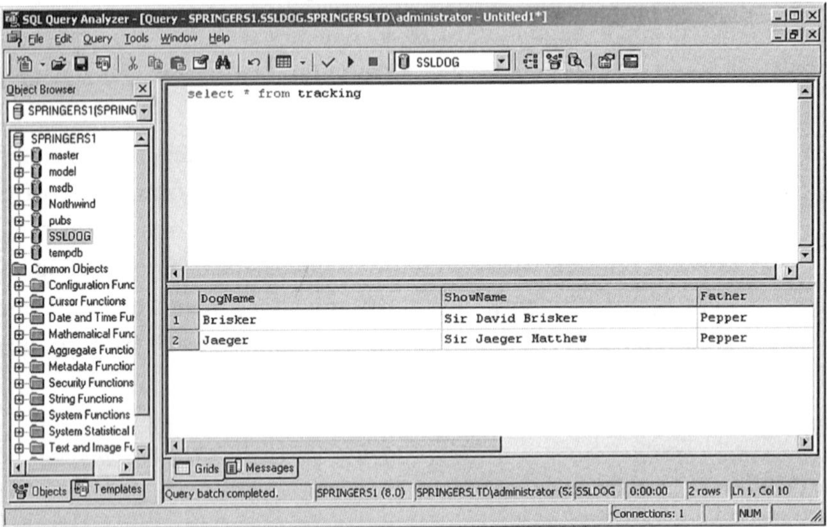

9. Close **SQL Query** by selecting **File, Exit**. Select **No** when the **SQL Query Analyzer** dialog box asks if you want to save the query (named **Untitled1** by default).

Success!

Enjoy your success. You've had a busy chapter so far performing the following SQL Server-related duties:

1. You learned SQL Server basics.
2. You created a SQL Server database title SSLDOG.
3. You created a table titled "Tracking" in the SSLDOG database.
4. You entered data for SPRINGERS in the Tracking table.
5. You queried (used) the data in the Tracking table by executing a simple SQL query.

I want to emphasize one final point before you move on: This short chapter on SQL Server is only a start, and you have a lot to learn about SQL Server 2000 if you so desire. In other words, for those readers who complain in posted reader reviews at Amazon and other online book sellers that I don't cover specific SBS components at the Ph.D. level, I hope I've sufficiently managed your expectations about the depth to which I can delve regarding individual BackOffice applications. No hard feelings, but there are many fine books (and large books at that) dedicated to individual applications, such as SQL Server 2000.

Advanced SQL: Publishing a Web Page

Now for some fun to wrap up this chapter on SQL Server 2000. Perhaps you didn't know-but you certainly will in just a few paragraphs-that your SQL-based data can easily be published as a Web page. This is actually one of the cooler features of SQL Server 2000 and very practical when you might want to publish information, such as real estate listings and product inventory sheets.

Publishing SPRINGERS data to a Web page

1. Log on to the SBS server machine as **Administrator** with the password **Husky9999!**
2. Click **Start**, **All Programs, Microsoft SQL Server, Enterprise Manager**.
3. Expand the following objects in the left pane: **Microsoft SQL Servers, SQL Server Group, SPRINGERS1 (Windows NT)**.
4. Select and expand the **SSLDOG** database.
5. From the **Tools** menu, select **Wizards**. The **Select Wizard** dialog box appears.
6. Expand **Management** under **Please select the Wizard you wish to use:**.
7. Select **Web Assistant Wizard** and click **OK**.
8. The **Welcome to the Web Assistant Wizard** screen of the **Web Assistant Wizard** appears. After reading the welcome notice, click **Next**.

9. On the **Select Database** screen, select **SSLDOG** in the drop-down list of databases in the **Database name:** field. Click **Next**. This is shown in Figure 14-12.

Figure 14-12
Selecting the SSLDOG database from the list of databases is an important step.

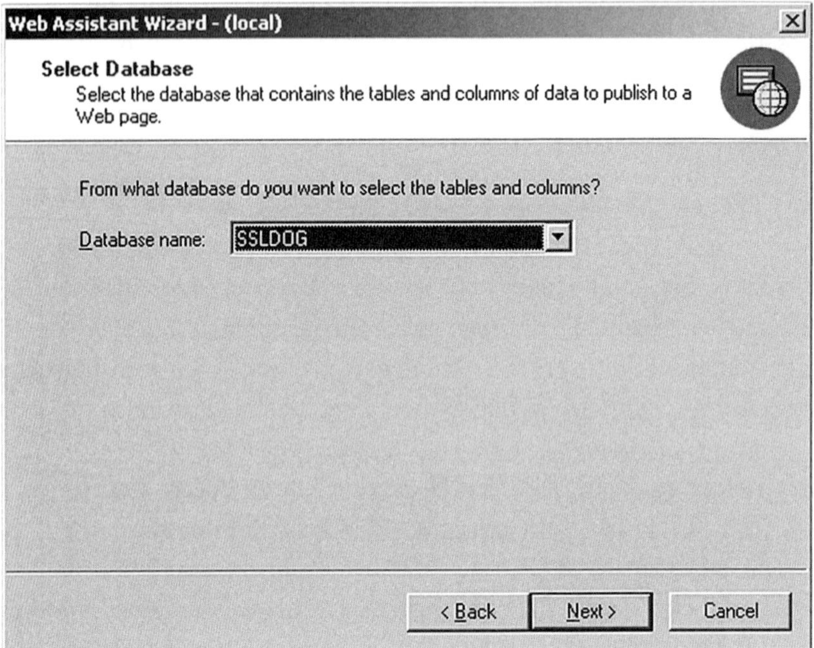

Notes:

10. On the **Start a New Web Assistant Job** screen (see Figure 14-13), accept the default database name of **SSLDOG Web Page** in the **What do you want to name this Web Assistant job?** field. Accept the default selection under **What data do you want to publish to the table on the Web page?** of **Data from the tables and columns that I select** (this is a radio button). Click **Next**.

Figure 14-13
Completing the Start a New Web Assistant Job.

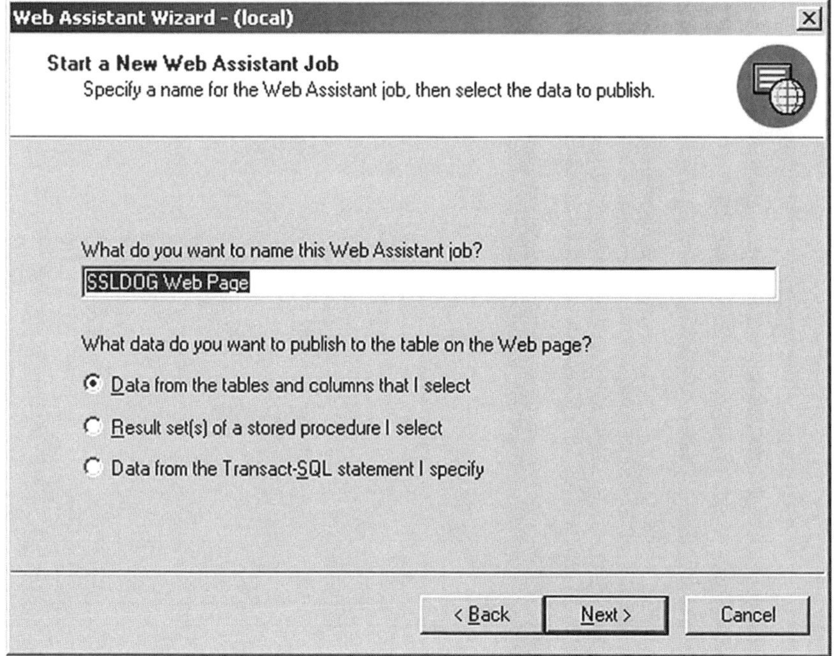

11. On the **Select a Table and Columns** screen, select the **Tracking** table (which is the default selection) in **Available tables**:. Click the **Add All** button so the columns initially listed under **Table columns** move over to **Selected columns**. Your screen should look similar to Figure 14-14. Click **Next**.

Figure 14-14
Selecting the table and columns to use in the Web page.

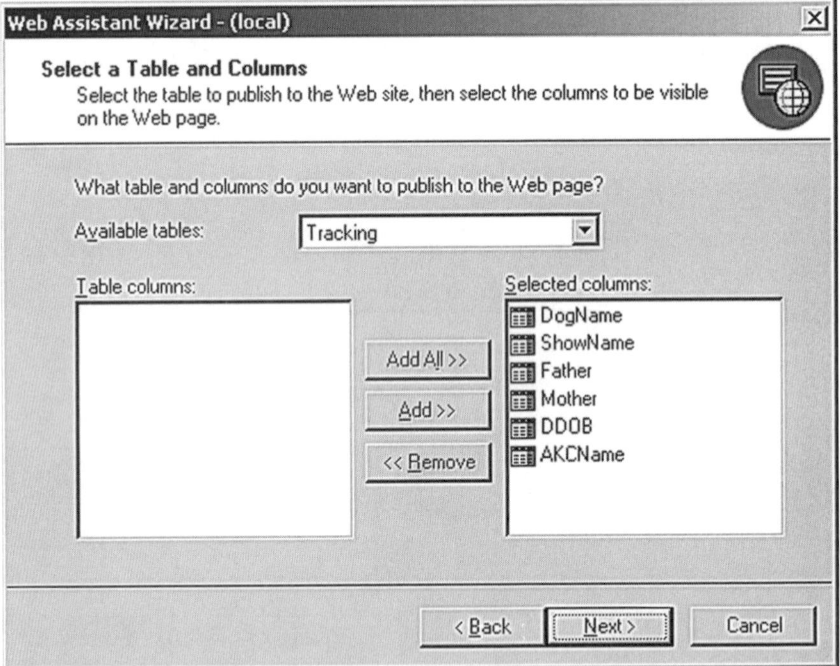

12. On the **Select Rows** screen, accept the default selection of **All of the rows** under **Which rows from the table do you want to publish to the Web page?**. Click **Next**.

13. On the **Schedule the Web Assistant Job** screen, accept the selection **Only one time when I complete this wizard** under **When should the Web Assistant update the Web page?** Note that this screen allows you to select the frequency the Web pages would be updated with data from SQL Server, as detailed in Figure 14-15. Click **Next**.

Figure 14-15
You can specify how often the Web page is updated with database information.

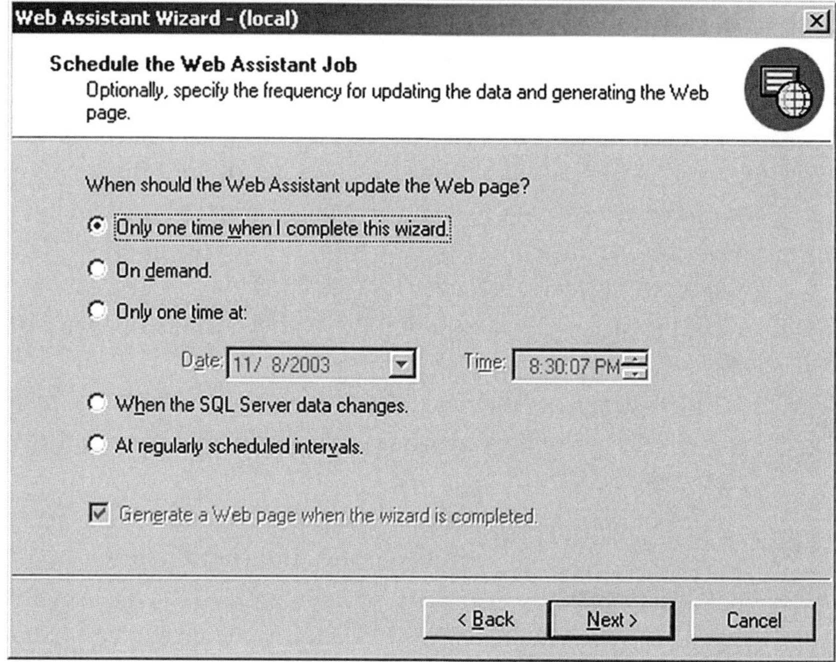

14. Accept the default file path and name of **C:\Program Files\Microsoft SQL Server\80\Tools\HTML\WebPage1.htm** in the **File name:** field of the **Publish the Web Page** screen. Click **Next**.
15. On the **Format the Web Page** screen, accept the default select of **Yes, help me format the Web page** and click **Next**.
16. The **Specify Titles** page appears. Under the **What do you want to title the Web page?** field, type **SPRINGERS Dog Registration Tracking Database**. Under the **What do you want to title the HTML table that contains the data?** field, type **AKC Registration**

Numbers. Accept the default setting of **H3 - Large** in the **What size should the HTML table title font be?** field. Click **Next**.

17. On the **Format a Table** screen, accept the default settings of **Yes** and display column names under **Do you want column names displayed in the HTML table?**. Accept the **Fixed** selection under **What font characteristics do you want to apply to the table data?** and keep the **Draw border lines around the HTML table** check box selected. Click **Next**.
18. On the **Add Hyperlinks to the Web Page** screen, accept the default selection of **No** under **Do you want to include hyperlinks on your Web page?**. Select **Next**.
19. The **Limit Rows** screen appears. Accept the default selection of **No, return all rows of data** under **Do you want to limit the total number of rows returned by SQL Server?**. Accept **No, put all data in one scrolling page** under **Do you want to limit the number of rows displayed on each Web page?**. Click **Next**.
20. Click **Finish** on the **Completing the Web Assistant Wizard** screen after reviewing the summary information.
21. Click **OK** when the **Web Assistant Wizard - SPRINGERS1** dialog box appears informing you that the **Web Assistant successfully completed the task**.
22. You will now view the Web page you just created. Launch Internet Explorer by clicking **Start, Programs, Internet Explorer**.
23. When Internet Explorer appears, select **File, Open**. Navigate by clicking the **Browse** button to the file location specified in Step 14 above. This file in the **File Name** field of the **Microsoft Internet Explorer** dialog box (which appears when you click Browse) should be: **C:\Program Files\Microsoft SQLServer\80\Tools\HTML\WebPage1.htm**. Click **Open**.
24. Click **OK** when you return to the **Open** dialog box.

Notes:

25. The Web page showing the AKC Registration Numbers for SPRINGERS appears, as seen in Figure 14-16. Close **Internet Explorer** after you've observed the Web page. Close the **SQL Server Enterprise Manager.**

Figure 14-16
Viewing SPRINGERS data in a Web browser.

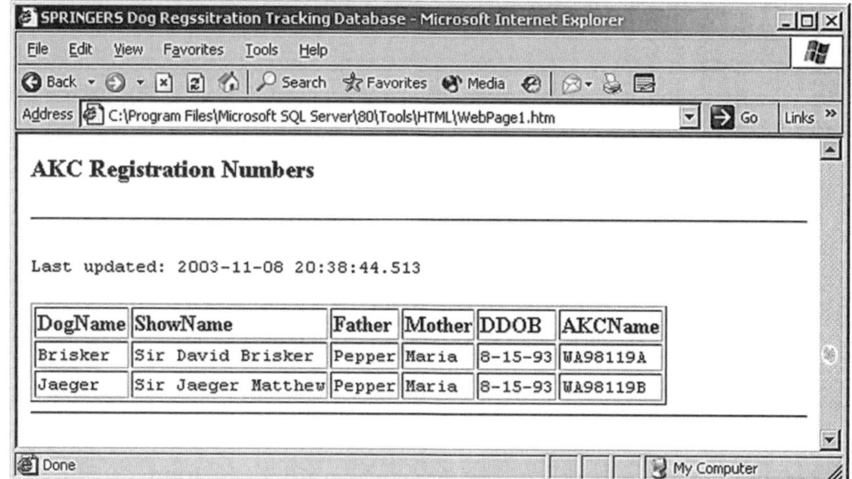

Next Steps - You've Only Just Begun

So you're still interested in learning more about SQL Server? That's great! It's a huge area where you can always grow; it has no upper knowledge limit. Aside from the advanced SQL Server books mentioned earlier today, there are several key areas to master as you continue in your quest to learn and use SQL servers. These study topics are:

- Learn SQL basics including these SQL commands: SELECT, UPDATE, INSERT, and DELETE.

- Learn the rules: how to define primary keys, secondary keys, and indexes, and how to normalize a database.

- Learn the power of stored procedures. Create a stored procedure of your own.

- Learn, inside and out, the tools that ship with SQL Server 2000 including SQL Server Enterprise Manager, SQL Query Analyzer, and Books Online (to name my three favorite tools).

- Learn and master client-side connectivity, especially ODBC.

- Learn how third-party applications use SQL Server 2000. Such third-party applications include Great Plains, the accounting application.

- Learn to connect sophisticated Web pages to SQL Server 2000 for online transactions (far more advanced than you learned in the last section). This is, of course, a very popular and in-demand skill set. It is the basis of many electronic commerce implementations.

- Learn to migrate data from Access to SQL Server 2000.

Summary

Today you worked with SQL Server 2000, the powerful database included with SBS 2003 (premium edition). I hope that the exercise in creating a database for SPRINGERS went a long way toward debunking the myth that databases are hard to use. If you followed the steps in this chapter, you not only created a database, but used it as well. That said, I emphasize the following point again: On an SBS network, your interaction with SQL Sever 2000 will likely be limited to installed third-party applications that use SQL Server 2000 as a database engine. If for some reason you decide to program SQL Server directly, as you did in creating the SSLDOG database table for SPRINGERS, remember to keep your databases simple and friendly, very much like you did today. That's my $0.25 USD advice to you. Good day.

Appendixes
Deploying SBS 2003

Appendix A
SBS 2003 Resources

Appendix B
Upgrading

Appendix C
Springers Information

Appendix D
Virtual PC and VMWare

Appendix E
Small Business Server 2003
OEM SKU

Appendix A
SBS 2003 RESOURCES

This appendix will list SBS 2003 resources that will be useful in your quest to better utilize SBS 2003. Many of these resources have previously been listed in the book, but many new resources are added here as well. Bottom line: All the SBS 2003 resources you need to move forward in one easy, at-a-glance location.

Microsoft Windows Small Business Server (SBS) Sites

- www.microsoft.com/windowsserver2003/sbs/default.mspx
- www.microsoft.com/sbserver
- www.microsoft.com/sbs
- Microsoft Learning SBS course: Designing, Deploying, and Managing a Network Solution for the Small and Medium-sized Business (three day SBS course): www.microsoft.com/traincert/syllabi2395afinal.asp
- Exam 70-282: Designing, Deploying, and Managing a Network Solution for the Small and Medium-sized Business: www.microsoft.com/learning/exams/70-282.asp.

Microsoft Partners-related Sites

- Microsoft Partner's SBS site: www.microsoft.com/partners/sbs
- Main Microsoft Partner site: www.microsoft.com/partner
- Microsoft SBS Partner Locator Tool: sbslocator.cohesioninc.com/apartnerlocator.asp

- Microsoft Certified Partner Resource Directory (how to find a Certified Partner): directory.microsoft.com/resourcedirectory/solutions.aspx
- Action Pack: members.microsoft.com/partner/salesmarketing/partnermarket/actionpack/default.aspx

Additional Microsoft or Microsoft-related Sites

- Microsoft TS2 Events: www.msts2.com
- Microsoft TouchPoint: www.connect-ms.com/mstps/ (or www.msbigday.com)
- Main Microsoft site: www.microsoft.com
- Microsoft TechNet: www.microsoft.com/technet
- Microsoft Office templates: officeupdate.microsoft.com/templategallery/
- bCentral small business portal: www.bcentral.com
- bCentral Technology Consulting Directory: directory.bcentral.com/ITConsultant/
- Great Plains: www.microsoft.com/greatplains
- Microsoft Visio: www.microsoft.com/visio
- Asentus: www.asentus.net
- Hands On Lab: www.handsonlab.com
- Granite Pillar: microsoft.granitepillar.com/partners/
- Entirenet: www.entirenet.net/registration
- Directions on Microsoft: www.directionsonmicrosoft.com

- Microsoft Solution Selling: www.solutionselling.com/mspartners/fusion.html
- Dr. Thomas Shinder's ISA Server Web site: www.isaserver.org
- Bill English's SharePoint Web site: www.sharepointknowledge.com

Third-party SBS-related sites

- Susan Bradley's Small Biz Server Links: http://www.sbslinks.com/ (and try www.sbslinks.com/really.htm for a really good time)
- Wayne Small's SBS Web site: www.sbsfaq.com
- Another SBS FAQ site: http://www.smallbizserver.net/

Newslists, User Groups, Trade Associations, Organizations

- SBS – Microsoft Small Business Server Support: http://groups.yahoo.com/group/sbs2k/
- Small BizIT "Small Business IT Consultants" newslist at Yahoo: groups.yahoo.com/groups/smallbizIT
- San Diego SBS User Group: www.sdsbsug.org
- CompTIA: www.comptia.com
- Network Professional Association: www.npa.org
- West Sound Technology Professional Association(Kitsap County, Washington): www.wstpa.org
- Adelaide Australia SBS User Group. For information, contact Dean Calvert: dean@calvert.net.au (also details at www.sbsfaq.com)
- Boston, MA, USA SBS User Group. For more information, contact Eliot Sennett: eliot@esient.com

- Cincinnati, OH, USA SBS User Group. This SBS group is a SIG that is part of a larger general user group. For more information, contact Kevin Royalty: kevin_royalty@yahoo.com

- Cleveland, OH, USA SBS User Group. For more information, visit http://www.gcpcug.org/ or contract Fredrick Johnson: fjohnson@rosstek.com

- Denver CO, USA SBS User Group. For more information, contact Lilly C. Banks: lilly@iSolutionsUnlimited.com.

- Omaha, NB, USA SBS User Group. For more information, contact Amy Luby: aluby@tconl.com. has started a user group in the Omaha, Nebraska area, 10 users

- Portland, OR, USA SBS User Group. For more information, visit http://pdxsbs.fpwest.com or contact Patrick West: patrick@west.net

- San Francisco/Bay Area, CA, USA SBS User Group. For more information, contact Ed Correia: ecorreia@sagacent.com

- Seattle, WA, USA SBS User Group. For more information, contact Steven Banks steve@banksnw.com

- Southern CA, USA SBS User Group. For more information, contact Donna Obdyke: DObdyke@prodigy.net

- Sydney, NSW, Australia SBS User Group. For more information, contact Wayne Small [wayne@correct.com.au] and visit http://www.sbsfaq.com

- Tampa/Palm Harbor/Largo, Florida SBS User Group. Rayanne M. Buchianico, rbuchianico@tampabay.rr.com, flsbsug@yahoogroups.com.

- Black Data Processing Association (BDPA): www.bdpa.org

Seminars, Workshops, Conferences

- SMB Nation: www.smbnation.com
- Microsoft TS2 events: www.msts2.com
- Microsoft Big Day/Business Solution Series: www.msbigday.com
- Microsoft Momentum Conference: http://www.microsoft.com/partner/events/wwpartnerconference/
- ITEC: www.goitec.com
- Guerrilla marketing and sales seminars: www.guerrillabusiness.com
- Who Moved My Cheese seminars: www.whomovedmycheese.com
- Myers-Briggs Type Indicator: www.apcentral.org
- Millionaire Mind / T. Harv Eker: www.peakpotentials.com
- TechMentor: www.techmentorevents.com
- SuperConference (accounting/technology): www.pencorllc.com

Business Resources

- US Small Business Administration: www.sba.gov
- Palo Alto Software for business planning: www.paloaltosoftware.com
- PlanWare: www.planware.org
- Outsourced accounting: www.cfo2go-wa.com
- US Federal Reserve Web site: www.federalreserve.gov
- Presentations: www.presentations.com
- CardScan: www.cardscan.com
- Plaxo: www.plaxo.com

Media

- Small Business Best Practices newsletter: www.nethealthmon.com/newsletter.htm
- CRN: www.crn.com
- SBS Maven Andy Goodman posts SBS-related articles at http://www.12c4pc.com.
- Small Business Computing: www.smallbusinesscomputing.com
- PC Magazine Small Business Super Site (www.pcmag.com/category2/0,4148,13806,00.asp)
- Mary Jo Foley's Microsoft-Watch: www.microsoftwatch.com
- NetworkWorldFusion SMB portal: www.nwfusion.com/net.worker/index.html
- Microsoft Certified Professional Magazine: www.mcpmag.com
- Certified Magazine: www.certmag.com
- Windows and .NET Magazine: www.winnetmag.com
- CRMDaily: www.crmdaily.com
- TechRepublic: www.techrepublic.com
- VAR Business: www.varbusiness.com
- Small Business Technology Report: www.smallbiztechnology.com
- Win2K News: www.w2knews.com
- SmallBizTechTalk: www.smallbiztechtalk.com
- Eweek: www.eweek.com
- ComputerWorld: www.computerworld.com

- Kim Komando Show: www.komando.com
- WinInformit: http://www.wininformant.com/
- Entrepreneur Magazine: www.entrepreneur.com
- INC Magazine: www.inc.com
- Fortune: www.fortune.com
- Bizjournals: www.bizjournals.com
- CNN: www.cnn.com
- Business Week: www.businessweek.com
- CBS MarketWatch: www.marketwatch.com
- USA Today: www.usatoday.com
- Money Magazine: www.money.cnn.com

SMB Hardware & Software Companies

- HP/Compaq: www.hp.com
- ConnectWise: www.connectwise.com
- Document Locator – Small Business Server edition: www.document-locator.com
- TimeSlips: www.timeslips.com
- QuickBooks: www.quickbooks.com

Miscellaneous

- Geekcorps – technology volunteers enabling communities worldwide: www.geekcorps.com
- Google search engine: www.google.com

- NPower, not-for-profit technology agency: www.npower.org
- eBay: www.ebay.com
- GeekSquad: www.geeksquad.com
- Geeks On Call: www.geeksoncall.com
- Soft-Temps: www.soft-temps.com
- Insurance for technology professionals: www.techinsurance.com
- Robert Half International salary survey: www.rhii.com
- AOL for Small Business: aolsvc.aol.com/small_biz
- eProject: www.eproject.com

Appendix B
Upgrading

Talk about serious errata time! I truly need to you visit my web site, www.smbnation.com, for the latest on the ability to upgrade to SBS 2003. The evidence as of this writing in late December 2003 is mixed. The SBS 2003 product has been released for a couple of months and folks are just starting to commence upgrade projects. Burl Carr, who works for me, will undertake a major upgrade for a San Francisco area cardiology clinic in early January 2004 which is past my press deadline but I'll gladly post the results at my web site.

If I were a stock analyst, I'd have to rate the official SBS upgrade scenarios as a "hold" or "neutral." There are mixed signals coming in from the real world on how well the upgrades are working. I can't commit to you on a suggested path and thus, I'll simply cop out!

In this Appendix, I'll present the official party line followed by real world feedback from readers.

Official Party Line

Follow Microsoft's prescriptive guidance at www.microsoft.com/windowsserver2003/sbs/upgrade/default.mspx and as seen in Figure B-1. It's that easy.

Notes:

Figure B-1
Microsoft has upgrade scenarios for SBS 2000 and SBS 4.5 plus the standard versions of Windows 2000 Server and Windows NT Server 4.0. Use it!

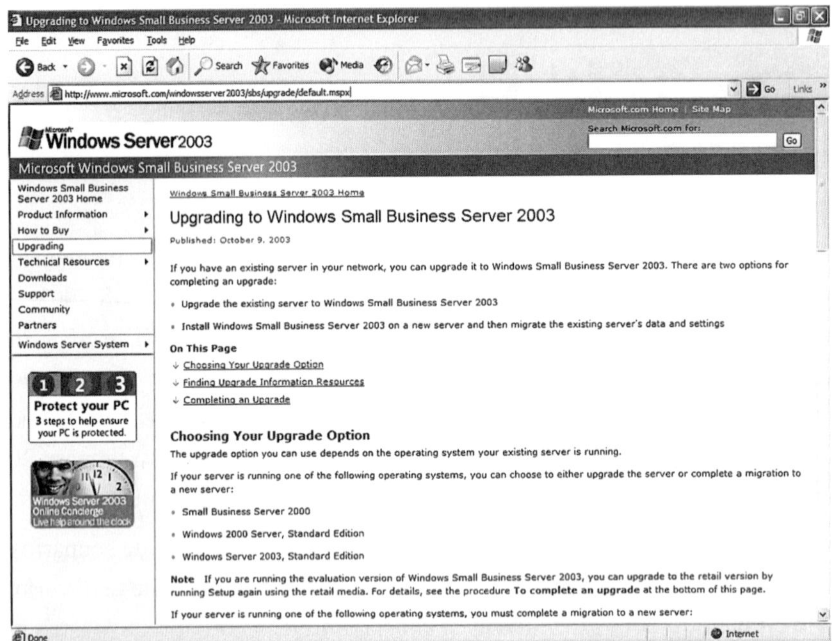

Real World

Three readers provide the following feedback, Richard, Karen and Beatrice.

Richard in Vancouver, BC

This is an e-mail from Richard to me:

Hi Harry,

I had no luck in upgrading the RC code to final code using the B2B wizard and the work around for the Share Point issue. I experienced various different behaviors each time I tried this. So I gave up and re-built the image from scratch with release code and then completed the work around for the Share Point issue. Now the machines are working in final code, I noticed some wording changes in the UI of some of the wizards.

I hated having to give up as it is not in my nature but a deadline was looming to have the machines upgraded to final code. I am going to keep a copy of the old image and see if I can puzzle out the challenges with this upgrade when I have some slack time.

The one comment I will add is when the B2B wizard asks you to back up your SBS server before running this process – DO IT !!!! This is a total commitment process with no way to role back the process.

If I don't speak to you before the holidays all the best to you and your family.

Cheers, Richard

Karen in Southern California

Karen was kind enough to take time out of her busy day and create an "In The Trenches" article for this Appendix.

Trials in the Trenches: A Real World Upgrade

By Karen Christian

North County Technology Group

www.nctg.com

This is a recap of an upgrade from SBS 2000 server with Service Pack 1a and ISA and SQL to Windows SBS 2003 Premium. We used Software Assurance media for the upgrade. The following steps are not all inclusive (or applicable to every network scenario) but they may be helpful to some who proceeds down this path. Be sure to review the Release Notes from CD1 and from the Premium Technologies CD (if applicable). They provide some excellent information that may help you get through or avoid some issues that may arise. Prior to this customer site installation, we had performed basically the same operation on our own production server: SBS 2000 with ISA but no SQL to Windows SBS 2003 Premium. The learning experience during that process was well worth the effort involved. As they say on the boards, YMMV (your mileage may vary).

1. Have a good backup before starting (highly recommended)
2. Log off all clients
3. Physically disconnect LAN clients and WAN DSL

4. Break mirrored drives if applicable (for extra caution you may want to physically disconnect the secondary drive to insure the integrity of the original data)
5. Stop all virus protection services and set to manual (our customer uses Trend Micro Client/Server/Messaging Suite and there are several services for OfficeScan, ScanMail and Trend ServerProtect)
6. NOTE: We recommend that you burn a CD of needed Service Packs and patches in advance as you will want to be disconnected from the Internet when the virus protection services are not running).
7. If you didn't install SBS 2000 Service Pack 1A already then you will need to do this http://www.microsoft.com/sbserver/downloads/sp1a.asp. It is available on a CD or via download.
8. Install ISA SP1 (that's Service Pack 1, not to be confused with ISA Feature Pack 1) if you haven't done this before (download at http://www.microsoft.com/isaserver/downloads/sp1.asp)
9. Install ISA Server 2000: Here you can get the required Updates for Windows Server 2003: http://www.microsoft.com/downloads/details.aspx?FamilyID=77d89f87-5205-4779-b1ab-fc338283b2d9&DisplayLang=en
10. Remove Windows 2000 Administration Tools located under Start, Control Panel, Add/Remove Programs
11. Install SQL SP3a from the Premium Technologies CD if you already have SQL 2000 installed. (We received the "Error running script SP3_serv-uni.sql(1)" during the installation process but after a reboot we were able to run the SP3a installation successfully)
12. **START THE OFFICAL UPGRADE TO SBS2K3**
13. Go through the installation CDs as requested and fill in or select items as appropriate
14. HEADS UP! Watch LAN/WAN NIC card assignments during upgrade process when you have two NICs (the program may name them incorrectly during process which can be confusing and tricky to fix later)
15. Connect to the Internet and be sure to update the virus patterns for your virus protection software
16. Check for updates from Microsoft Windows Update (In IE, Tools, Windows Update)

17. Reconnect clients and test connect to server, Internet, Intranet, network printer and custom SQL program access

Other problems and notes:

- We did not change the date on this server to circumvent the SharePoint issues related to installs after 11/24/03 with the original CD3 and installed the available patch after the installation was complete (http://www.microsoft.com/downloads/details.aspx?familyid=cb7e90a1-de9d-4a83-85f8-951e9f055bf0&displaylang=en).

- TrendMicro ServerProtect would not start after upgrade to SBS2003. This issue required a manual uninstall (documented on their website) and reinstall of the software to work. In the future we would recommend that this program be uninstalled before starting the upgrade to SBS2K3.

18. All Done…. but there was one loose end….

We ended up with a "Continue Setup" shortcut on the desktop. It should not appear when the installation is complete and all is done. Clicking the shortcut and continuing setup for the second time did not make it vanish and its presence was discomforting. Was the installation complete or not? The direction from Microsoft Product Support Services after some checking into the setup logs was to delete the shortcut. Why didn't we think of that? It turns out the setup had completed however the setup log showed 'Success' for all components except for 'Intranet' which indicated 'Failure'. This was related to the SharePoint issues that were fixed by the patch noted above. There was no indication of remaining issues like the lingering shortcut in any documentation available at the time. The phone support call was not ultimately charged to us (normally $245 per call) but the wait queue was almost two and a half hour long to talk to a support technician. This was quite unusual based on numerous calls we have placed to MS PSS in the past.

The bottom line here is that upgrades can be tricky even when you think you are well prepared. Do your homework in advance and plan your approach. The above work took several hours from start to finish and was done after work hours for the least impact on the customer's daily business operations.

The business owner was observing our work during the first couple hours and mentioned that he didn't understand why an upgrade from Microsoft for a

Microsoft product wouldn't go smoothly and without a hitch (perception… expectation… and then reality)? Is anyone from MS listening to this business owner? Maybe that just goes to show you how smart this business owner was in hiring a qualified company to do the job for him, a company like North County Technology Group that works with and specializes in Small Business Server products! (Harry told us we could pitch our business here at least once. Thanks Mr. bbbbb.)

We've now posted our SBS2K3 installation story as part of the 'Sweet Success with Windows SBS 2003 Server' campaign from Microsoft. We'd have to say it is a touch on the bittersweet side but that's the nature of this business sometimes. We anticipate that the next SBS2000 to SBS2003 upgrade project will go smoother.

Beatrice in Florida

Beatrice, true friend of the SBS community, shares the following:

In early December 2003 we (a 6 year MCSE vet and my newest aspiring MCSE student from the local college and new hire) were doing an upgrade on an existing SBS2000 network for an accounting firm here in the local Village. This client of mine is a special one, because after I initially installed the SBS2000 network, he decided that he didn't want to enter into a maintenance contract to save $$$.

After having instructed him on basic monthly server maintenance, I would get the occasional phone call to clean things up. Nothing out of the ordinary, a code red exploit due to failed AV definition downloads, mis-configured software, a non-working tape backup and other minor mishaps that only a 'we want to save money" philosophy can create.

So anyhow, the day we got there to do the upgrade, I figured about four hours to prep the server, worst case scenario. We started at 9:30 a.m and needless to say, numerous patches, updates and service packs later by 5:30 p.m, we were finally ready to roll out the SBS2003 upgrade. This wasn't so bad after all, and we felt good about going ahead.

We inserted disk 1 and things ran as smooth as a Porsche on the Autobahn.

Knowing about the SharePoint issue causing the install to fail during the WSS portion of the setup, (only for installs & upgrades after November 24th) we had downloaded the WSS patch and were ready for it. Btw., don't try to install the patch prior to the upgrade (as suggested by one member of the SBS team, I will refrain from mentioning names) because it will fail. (a very big Homer Simpson "Though" is in order here)

Low and behold, as anticipated on SBS2003 install disk 4, the installation failed as it was supposed to. Everything was going as planned!

With great anticipation we awaited the server reboot, feeling in control and groovy as only technical consulting administrators fueled by coffee for the past 12hrs can feel. We was flying high, baby, moving right along.

After the reboot, elated about the smooth progression of things, we entered the admin username and password, only to be greeted by the server with a friendly " The local policy of this system does not permit you to logon interactively." .....oops..... Allright, so yours truly is in the habit of setting up more than one admin account during upgrades and such (ha ha!), and proceeds to use the backdoor admin account, again, to be greeted by the same friendly server message. .....oh...oh

What had happened here? The admin account as a member of the schema and enterprise admin groups just lost its godliness, and a couple minor permissions not to mention. Logging on via the remote desktop of an XP client wasn't an option either, same friendly message. It was high time for a good brew.

There were these old fashioned two floppy ts client setup disks somewhere in my arsenal of weapons. Using the terminal services client interface, low and behold, we were able to log on to the server! First I checked the admin properties to find that the schema and enterprise group memberships were no longer in existence. Hmmm....

At this point we decided to run the server management option to migrate user accounts – now that the server management tools were installed, even though the installation wasn't quite finished yet.

To make a scary story short, after using the user account migration wizard, we were able to log on locally, applied the WSS fix, and were back on target like a surfboard in the pipe.

Do we have a clue what transpired here? Heck no, we can only guess, especially since the event logs only marked a non-fatal error, and the log file mentions that the full control ace was removed from the security descriptor on the account.

We have a GPO error and I will investigate all this personally, the first day we are snowed in – I promise.

Back to you Harry, and greetings from sunny Florida!

PS – Here's a few additional random SBS comments since I wrote the above story:

1. Using the OEM install, there was no WSS issue – we didn't have to apply the patch! Everything works like a charm
2. Used dyndns.org and it immediately took effect – check out iscflorida.dyndns.org, can only recommend it
3. Have NetGear router, then server w/2 NICs, then switch with DHCP assigned by server to clients. Opened port 80 on the router and pointed it to the server (one of the pics – Figure B-2) and you get right through. Have to open 442-445 as well as RPD and VPN ports. How sweet it is.

Figure B-2
Beatrice had to configure the NetGear router as per step two above.

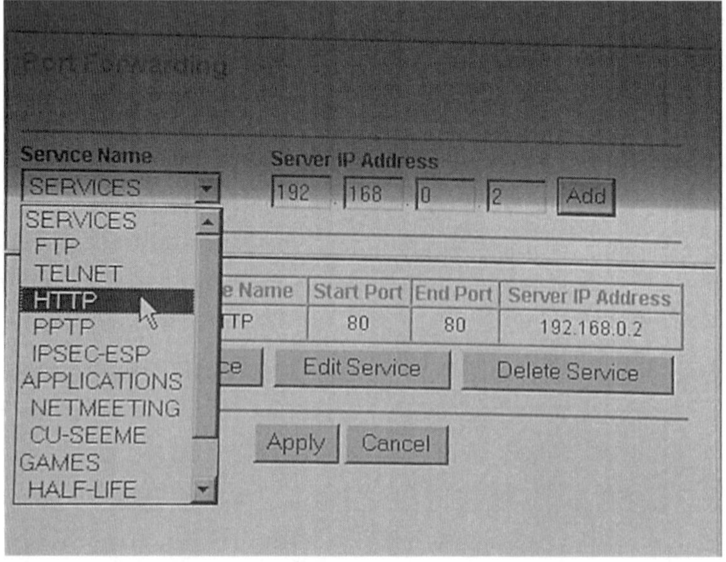

Thanks Bea!

BEST PRACTICE: Always test the upgrade on an imaginary network (e.g. SPRINGERS) before undertaking such activity in the real world. Also, when in doubt, make three complete and verifiable data backups (data, e-mail, Internet Explorer links, public folders, etc.) and then FDISK and start anew with a fresh SBS installation. I know that's an ouch but it is an assured outcome (granted, you'll have to re-install your line of business applications and so on).

Appendix C
Springers Information

As promised, here is your source of SPRINGERS information presented in a concise format to assist your input into SBS 2003. This information is divided into common and unique information.

Common Information

This information is common to all users

Item	Description	Completed
Server Name	SPRINGERS1	
Internal DNS Domain Name	SpingersLTD.local	
External Internet Domain Name	SPRINGERSLTD.COM	
Initial SBS Registration Name	Bob Easter	
Organization	Springer Spaniels Limited	
Installation Codes	Small Business Server (use from product ID sticker on disc sleeve)	
Area Code	206	
Address	3456 Beach Front Road	
City	Bainbridge Island	
State/Province	WA	
Zip	98110	
Country	United States of America	

Business Telephone	206-123-1234	
Business Fax	206-123-1235	
Initial Administrator Password	Husky9999!	
Hard disk	SBS operating system and applications partition is 10GB. Data partition is approximately 20GB. Both partitions are formatted NTFS. Server has a RAID-5 configuration. If you have only a single hard disk or mirrored drives (but not RAID 5), you may continue for the purposes of learning SBS 2003 via the SPRINGERS methodology. However, you'll want to consider RAID 5 or mirrored drives in the real world.	
Time Zone	Pacific	
User Accounts	Administrator (password= Husky9999!).	
Printers	Install new HP Color LaserJet 5M printer on network with HP5 share name.	
Registry	No known Registry modifications needed in SBS.	
Folders	Create additions folders on Data partition: **Accounting** (this is where Great Plains Dynamics will be installed along with the storage area for the accounting data) **Backup** (this folder will contain on-the-fly backups of company data between tape backups, such as internal SQL Server database backups)	
Shares	Create **ACCT** on the **Accounting** folder. Everyone allowed change rights. Full control rights to NormH, BarryM.	
Internal IP Addressing	Use the default 192.168.16.2 IP address and the 255.255.255.0 Subnet Mask.	
External IP Addressing	Use the following: IP: 207.202.238.215 Subnet Mask: 255.255.255.0 Default Gateway: 207.202.238.1 Primary DNS: 209.20.130.35	

	Secondary DNS: 209.20.130.33	
Misc.	Windows Server 2003 operating system to be installed on C:. SBS components (Exchange, etc.) to be installed on C:. Will approve all licensing questions with "Yes."	

Unique Information

This information is unique on a user-by-user basis

First: Norm
Last: Hasborn
User Name: NormH
Password: Purple3300
Job Title: President
Office: Executive
User Template: Power User
Computer Name: PRESIDENT

First: Barry
Last: McKechnie
User Name: BarryM
Password: 2Reedred
Job Title: Accountant
Office: Accounting
User Template: User
Computer Name: ACCT01

First: Melinda
Last: Overlaking
User Name: MelindaO
Password: Blue33
Job Title: Front Desk Reception
Office: Administration
User Template: User
Computer Name: FRONT01

First: Linda
Last: Briggs
User Name: LindaB
Password: Golden10
Job Title: Manager, Registration
Office: Registration and Scheduling
User Template: User
Computer Name: MANREG01

First: Bob
Last: Bountiful
User Name: BobB

Password: Bish4fish
Job Title: Breeding Manager
Office: Care, Feeding, Breeding
User Template: User
Computer Name: BREED01

First: Tom
Last: Benkert
User Name: TomB
Password: Whitesnow101
Job Title: Scheduler
Office: Registration and Scheduling
User Template: User
Computer Name: SCHEDULE01

First: Norm
Last: Hasborn Jr.
User Name: NormJR
Password: Yellowsnow55
Job Title: Sales Manager
Office: Sales and Marketing
User Template: User
Computer Name: SALES01

First: David
Last: Halberson
User Name: DaveH
Password: Grenadine2002
Job Title: Marketing Manager
Office: Marketing
User Template: User
Computer Name: MARKET01

First: Elvis
Last: Haskins
User Name: Elvis
Password: Platinium101
Job Title: Researcher
Office: Genealogy
User Template: User
Computer Name: GENE01

First: Bob
Last: Easter
User Name: BobE
Password: dogcatcher1
Job Title: Dog Trainer
Office: Care, Feeding, and Breeding
User Template: Power User
Computer Name: CAREFEED01

Appendix D
Virtual PC and VMWare

This appendix surfaces the discussion about using virtual machines to construct a sophisticated SBS 2003 network. I think you'll find the discussion interesting.

What is a virtual machine environment

Truth be told and pulling the drape back from the wizard in the Wizard of Oz, I largely wrote this book on two HP/Compaq laptops traveling the world. One laptop was used for writing and the other was used for running a virtual SBS 2003 network. I validated my work on a snappy and sassy HP/Compaq ML 350 server, but let's talk about the laptops for now. Going with the old "picture is work a thousand words" theory, please observe Figure D-1.

BEST PRACTICE: As you study the figure below, understand this is essentially how the SBS 2003 hands on labs were built (by yours truly). However, the naming convention was different (Woodgrove Bank).

Figure D-1

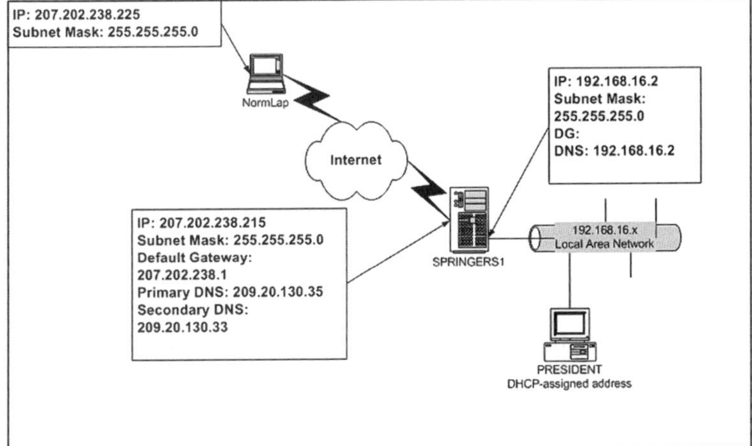

What has occurred here is that three virtual machines are running. Across this book, you've primarily worked with the SPRINGERS1 server machine and PRESIDENT client computer. This was done for simplicity even though you entered ten client computers as part of the SPRINGERS methodology (you're certainly welcome to create a test network with ten client computers attached but you might leave that for the real world).

Later in the book when remote connectivity was discussed, I suggested you add an external client computer to the mix (NORMLAP) in order to work with Remote Web Workplace (RWW).

> BEST PRACTICE: In your virtual environment, you can deploy what in effect is an external client computer by placing it on a separate IP address subnet. This technique is used all of the time with the hands-on labs.

So even if you've completed the SPRINGERS methodology on separate computers, consider re-doing this book again but virtualize everything. That'll provide a new twist on your second pass.

> BEST PRACTICE: Best thing since sliced bread! Running a complete SBS 2003 network on a laptop via virtualization is a great way to perform public demonstrations. For example, you can create THE PERFECT SBS 2003 NETWORK on your laptop and lock down the image. You typically do this by flipping a switch to "undo" so that, after each demonstration, the image reverts back to its perfect state. It's akin to having an image that is set to a baseline (say 9:00am). You then proceed to show off SBS 2003 by adding users, computers, running the EICW, etc. When you turn off the laptop, the image returns to 9:00am and you know exactly where it stands the next day when you meet with yet another customer.

Microsoft Virtual PC

Microsoft's entry into the virtual environment is Virtual PC (shown in Figure D-2). Long story short, but Microsoft acquired the technology from Connectix and never looked back. This acquisition, in the early spring of 2003, resulted from a breakdown in negotiations to purchase VMWare (see next section).

Figure D-2
Microsoft Virtual PC.

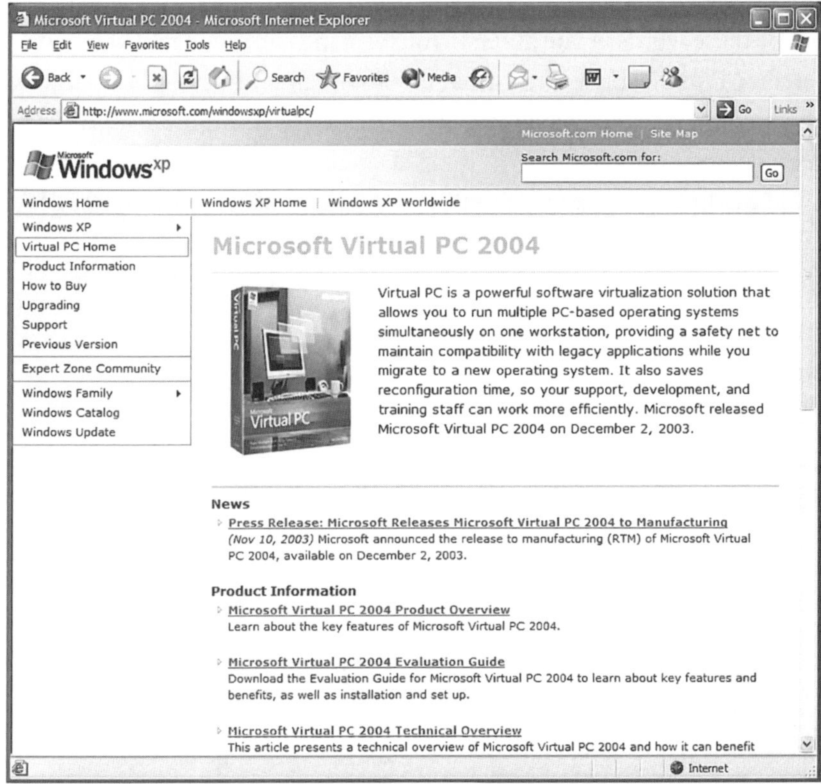

As these words are written, Microsoft has released the update to the version I've worked with (I worked with version 5.2). This new version, due in December 2003, is known as Virtual PC 2004. This release addresses one significant short coming in how the multiple network adapter cards were handled (poorly). I won't go into the history on multiple network adapter cards in the Virtual PC 5.2 era but you know what I'm talking about if you experienced it.

Learn more about Virtual PC at www.microsoft.com/windowsxp/virtualpc/default.asp.

BEST PRACTICE: Read the excellent white paper (Microsoft Virtual PC 2004 Technical Overview) from Jerry Honeycutt posted at the above site.

VMWare

As I type these words in late 2003, if you push me hard enough, I'll tell you that I prefer VMWare. This is the virtual environment product that I used to write the book with. It's a life saver because it demonstrated more maturity when I needed it. For example, VMWare has a great screen capture capability that allowed me to render many of the figures you've observe herein. VMWare's site is shown in Figure D-3. Highly recommended and something tells me that it'll have better native support for alternative operations systems (if you know what I mean).

Figure D-3

VMWare, was you can see in the upper left, was recently acquired by EMC2.

BEST PRACTICE: Carefully read the user manuals for either Virtual PC or VMWare so that you'll properly install SBS 2003. Things like configuring a virtual disk with sufficient size, enough RAM memory and proper operating system drivers are all areas of concern as you deploy SBS 2003.

Appendix E
Small Business Server 2003 OEM SKU

Something that has attracted a lot of attention in the SBS 2003 time frame is the much improved original equipment manufacturer (OEM) pre-installation stock keeping unit (SKU). This is the software version that ships when you order an HP ML-300 series server pre-installed with SBS 2003 standard edition.

> BEST PRACTICE: The configuration for the OEM SKU is built via the OEM Pre-installation Kit (OPK) that is available to system builders in the Microsoft Certified Partner program. It is similar to OPK for Windows XP that you might have seen demonstrated at a Microsoft TS2 event. The benefits to the OPK (again, used to build the OEM SKU) is that you can create the "perfect" configuration that you want to go out the door to your customers. Also, you can engage in branding and desktop icon placement. An example of branding might be to have your consultancy listed on the property sheet for the online help system so your client knows to call you.

Further discussion at the OPK is beyond the scope of this book but you can gather more information at www.microsoft.com/oem.

First Things First

You first need to decide if the OEM SKU makes sense for your situation. Are you looking to rapidly deploy SBS 2003 and benefit from the 15-minute pre-installation option. Are you willing to let the OEM (e.g. HP) be the product support provider during the warranty of your product. HP provides, as of this writing, 90-days of free support. Microsoft provides no such support when you purchase the retail SKU of SBS 2003 (all Microsoft support is paid support unless you use free options such as the newsgroups).

> BEST PRACTICE: Something to highlight in passing. Already a few folks in the newsgroups have grumbled that OEM support isn't as strong as Microsoft support. I'm not going to act as judge and jury on that matter here, but I can say this. With the OEM SKU, firms such as HP are providing a limited amount of free support via telephone. This is something that Microsoft, for all practical purposes, no longer does. Later, when the free support period expires, you would use other options such as the SBS newsgroups listed in Appendix A (purchasers of the OEM SKU can use the newsgroups, etc.). And another option for live support, which is the "default" when you purchase the SBS 2003 retail SKU and the post-free support period when you purchase the SBS 2003 OEM SKU, is the Microsoft paid support ($249 USD as of this writing).
>
> The point to take away from this best practice is that the support provided by the OEM SKU may actually be more cost effective than the retail SKU when you analyze the options closely.

One outcome of the OEM SKU in the early life of SBS 2003 has been the discovery that the simplified setup process only reinforces the structured SBS setup methodology discussed earlier in this book and does so with fewer screens. As you'll see in a moment, the SBS 2003 OEM SKU completes its basic setup process with 12 screens versus over 42 screens for the retail SKU. That helps prevent you from making errors in judgment when deploying SBS 2003 (fewer screens mean few potential errors, etc.).

> BEST PRACTICE: In the past, SBSers have been shy towards the OEM SKU because so many decisions were made back at the factory that it was felt your options were limited. For example, in the past, you might have inherited a system partition (C: drive) that was only 5 GB in size (far too small for successful long-term use). However, OEMs such as HP are offering the ability to order the partition sizes

of your choice when you order a server pre-installed with SBS. This is a great benefit.

Second Things Second

While the SBS 2003 OEM SKU clearly isn't part of the SPRINGERS storyline, it's interesting none the less to witness. The succession of screenshots below shows from the initial power on of the new server to the final setup reboot (after which you would be presented with the To Do List to complete).

Figure E-1
Start with the Welcome screen.

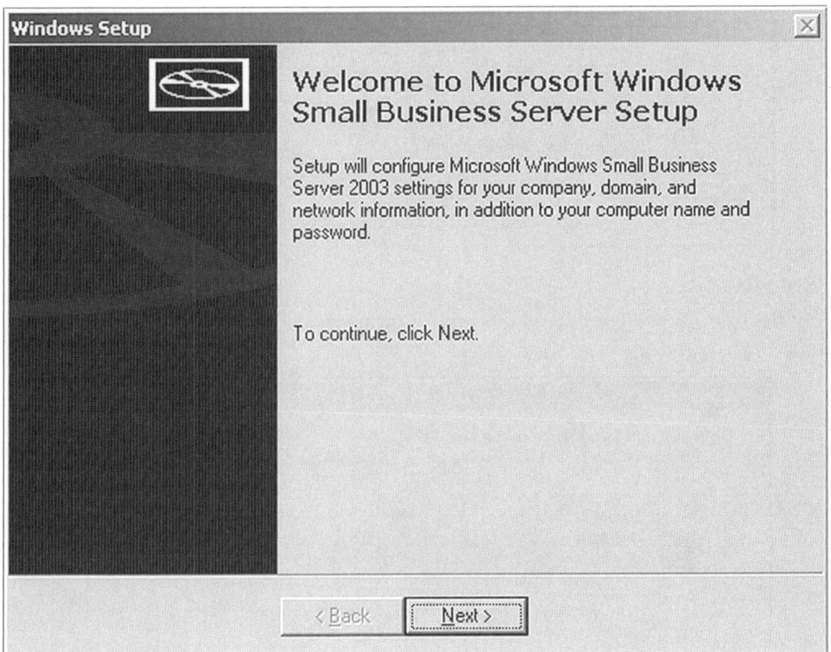

Figure E-2
Agree to the license. Note this was built with the 180-day evaluation edition, but in the real world, you'd see the full license presented.

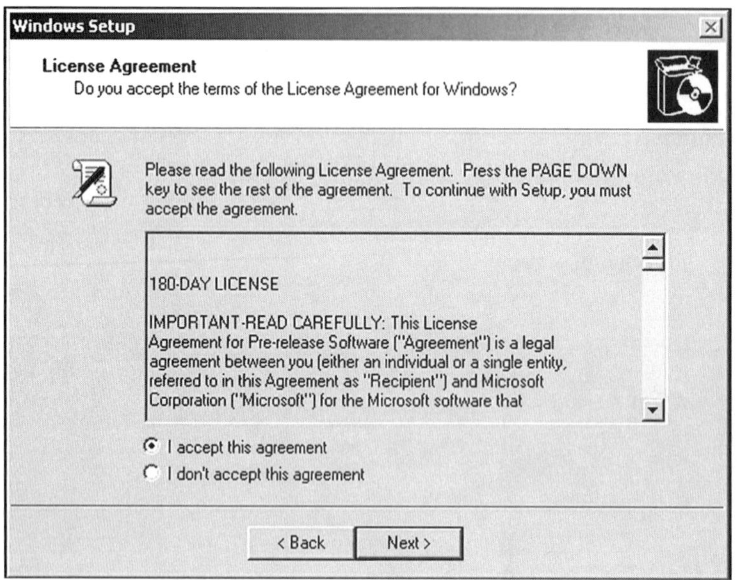

Figure E-3
Select the options for your language and region.

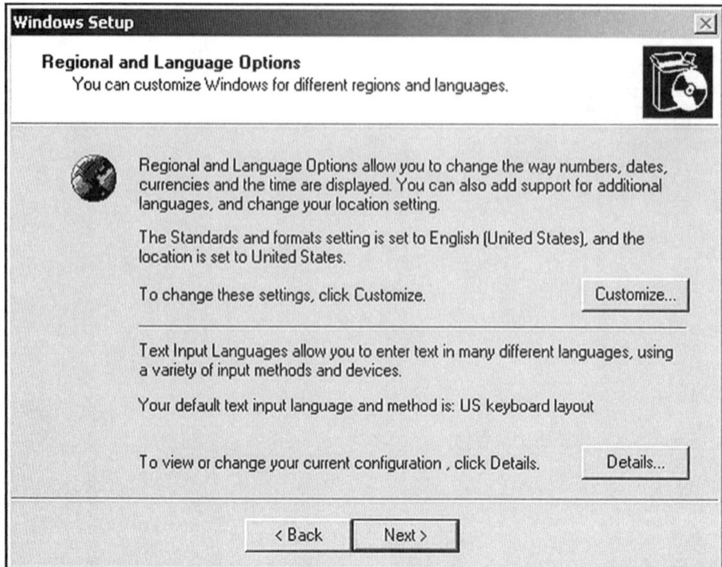

Figure E-4
Provide personalization information including name and organization.

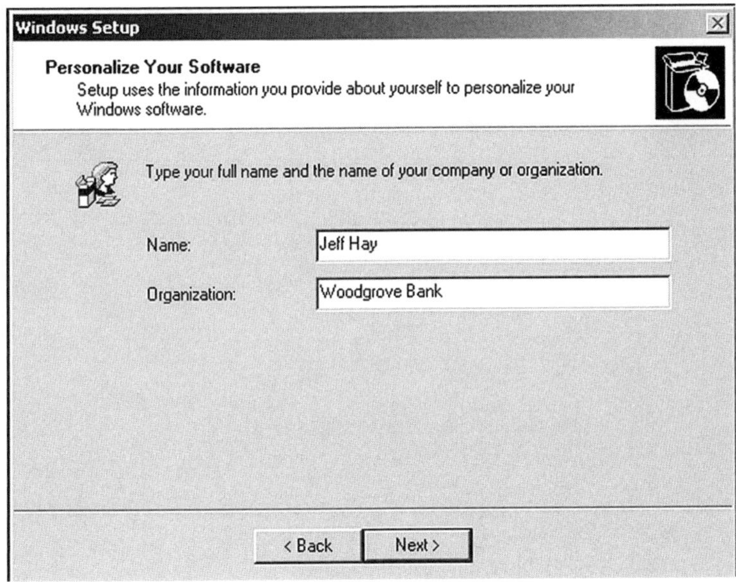

Figure E-5
Input your product key information.

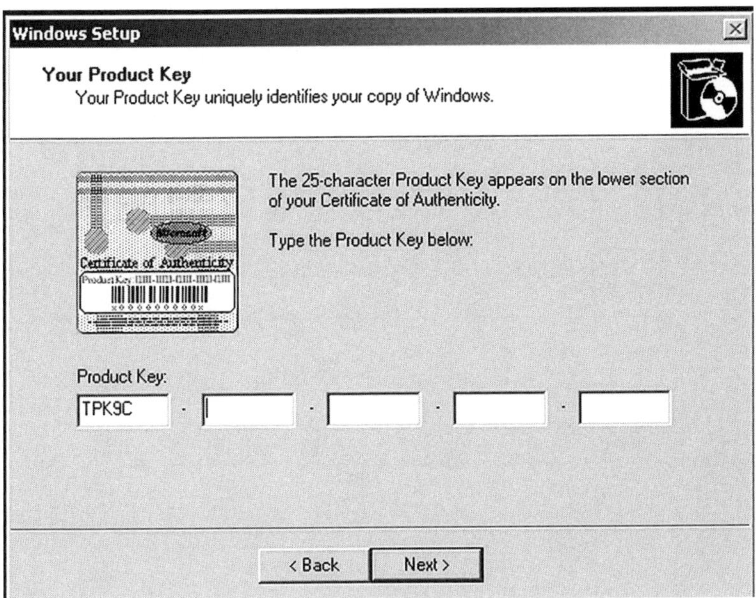

Figure E-6

Select your date, time and time zone. Note that this can be changed later via Control Panel, Date and Time.

Windows Setup
Date and Time Settings
Set the correct date and time for your Windows computer.
Date & Time
Friday , September 26, 2003
3:34:45 PM
Time Zone
(GMT-08:00) Pacific Time (US & Canada); Tijuana
Automatically adjust clock for daylight saving changes
< Back
Next >

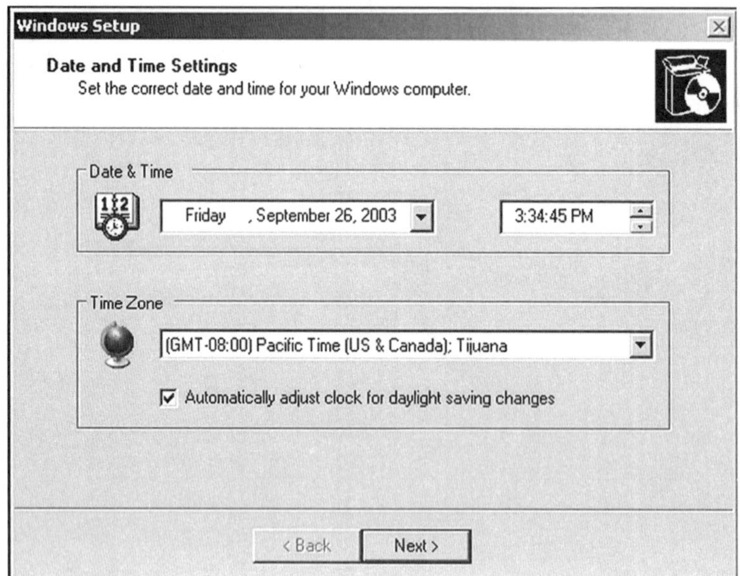

Figure E-7

Complete the company telephony and address information fields.

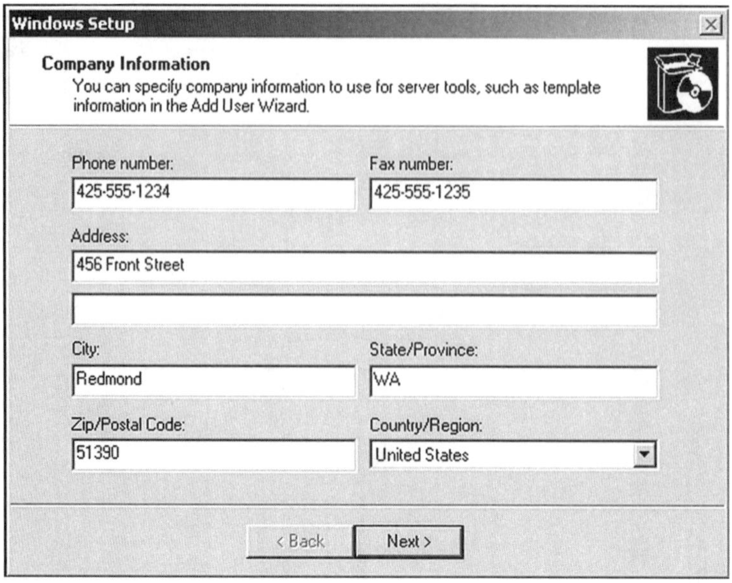

Windows Setup
Company Information
You can specify company information to use for server tools, such as template information in the Add User Wizard.
Phone number:
425-555-1234
Fax number:
425-555-1235
Address:
456 Front Street
City:
Redmond
State/Province:
WA
Zip/Postal Code:
51390
Country/Region:
United States
< Back
Next >

Figure E-8
Provide the computer name and the administrator password.

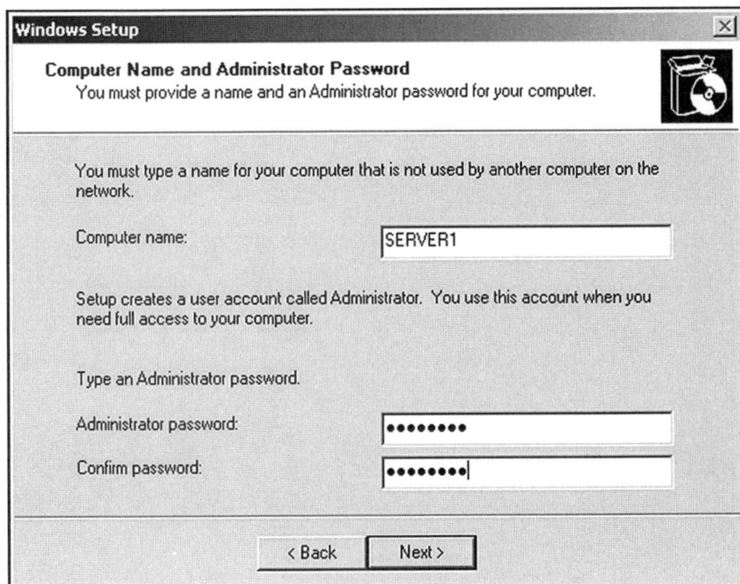

Figure E-9
Make your internal domain name choices.

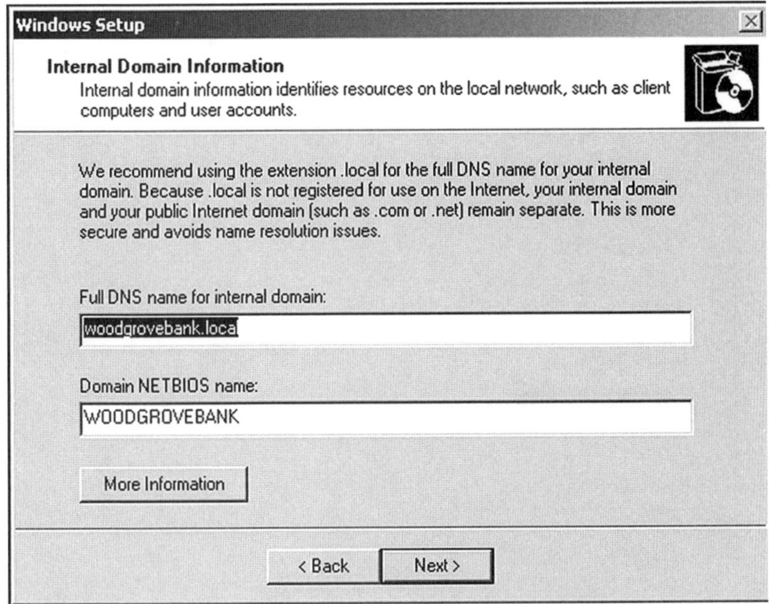

Figure E-10
Please accept the default IP addressing unless you have reasons not to.

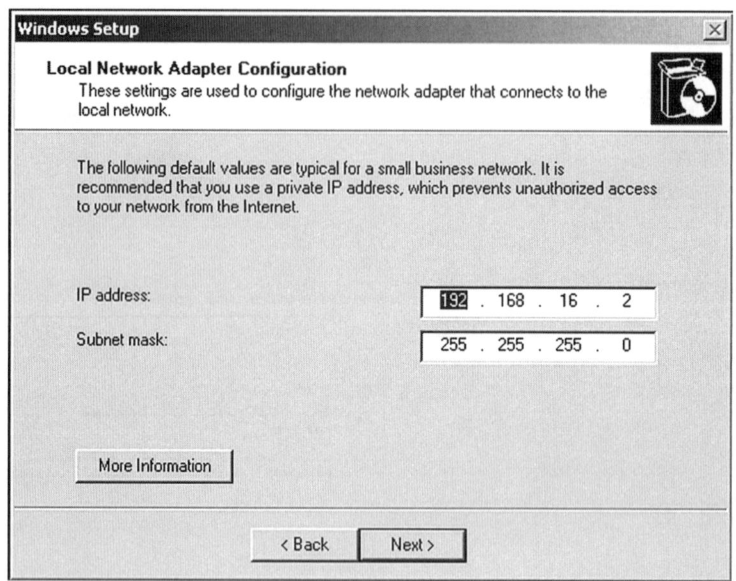

Figure E-11
Observe the final tasks are automatically being performed at this point.

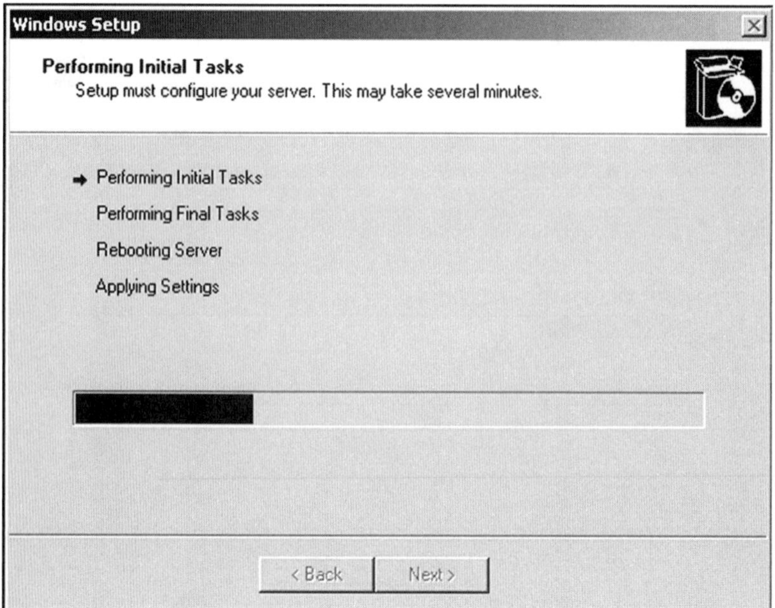

Figure E-12
After a reboot, a finish screen appears followed by the To Do List.

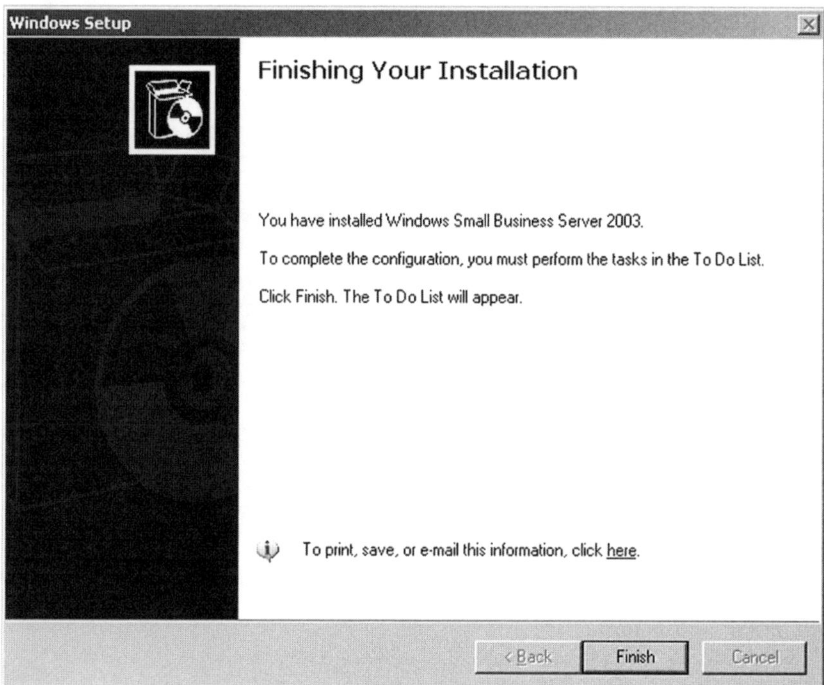

And there you have, a bona fide 12-step program to implement the OEM pre-installation setup approach. Note that the entire network setup doesn't take allegedly 15-minutes, just the steps shown above. You still have hours of work ahead to complete the To Do List and further maximize the use of your SBS 2003 network.

Index

A

B

Index

C

D

E

F

G

H

Index

N

O

P

Q

R

Index

T

U

V

Index

X

Y

Z

REGISTER THIS BOOK!

By registering this book with SMB Nation, you'll receive discounts on future SMB Nation book, conferences and workshops. You will automatically be registered for our free SBS e-mail newsletter.

SPECIAL OFFER

When you register this book with SMB Nation, you will receive a free PDF e-book version of Small Business Server 2003 Best Practices.

Complete the following information on this page and fax to 425-488-3646 or scan and e-mail to sbs@nethealthmon.com.

Name* ______________________________

Address* ______________________________

City* ______________________ **State*** __________

Country* ______________________ **Postal Code*** __________

E-mail address* ______________________________

Second e-mail address: ______________________________

(as a backup address)

Telephone: ______________________________

How did you hear about Small Business Server 2003 Best Practices?

__ Referral\Word of mouth
__ Advertisement
__ Newsgroup
__ Microsoft Web site
__ Other Web site
__ Search engine query

How did you purchase Small Business Server 2003 Best Practices?

__ Online directly from SMB Nation
__ Online from book seller (e.g. Amazon)
__ Off the shelf, national retailer (e.g. Barnes and Noble)
__ Off the shelf, local book reseller (e.g. San Diego Technical Books)
__ **Follow-up.** Please contact me about SMB Nation conferences, workshops, books, writing for SMB Nation Press, complete a follow-up survey, etc.

* Required

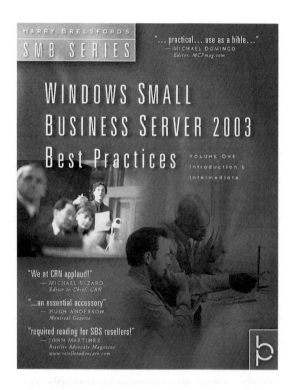

SUBSCRIBE TO FREE SBS NEWSLETTER!

Join over 5,000 readers who want to stay in touch bi-weekly via the SBS newsletter, *Small Business Best Practices*. This newsletter presents both technical and business topics surrounding SBS and other Microsoft SMB products.

Now in its third year, *Small Business Best Practices*, seen in the figure below, has build a reputation for delivering the most current news on SBS. This includes breaking news announcements such as product alerts!

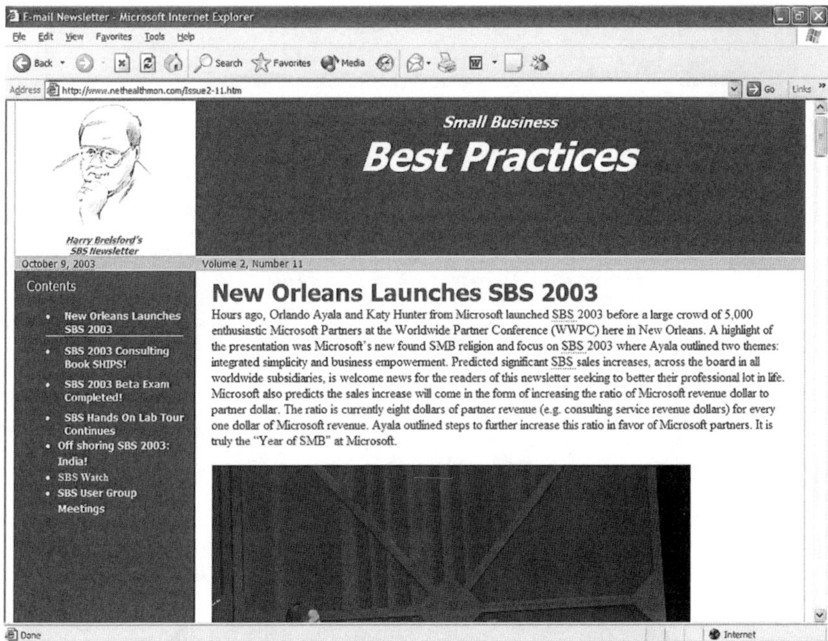

For your free subscription to *Small Business Best Practices,* visit the SMB Nation site at www.smbnation.com and sign-up!

Attend SMB Nation!

Plan on attending the annual SMB Nation conference that features SBS and other SMB technology solutions. In 2004, SMB Nation will be held in September 2004 in Seattle and Redmond Washington. You'll be able to interact directly with members of the SBS development and marketing teams, see the Microsoft campus and enjoy a day a Springer Spaniels Limited on Bainbridge Island for a retreat and concert! Good fun! Big fun!

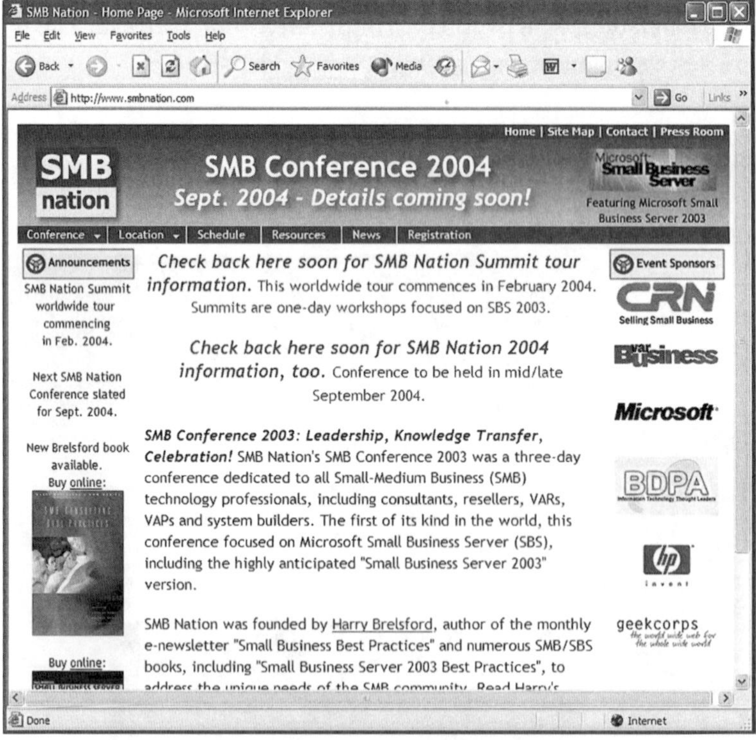

Visit the SMB Nation site to sign-up for the annual conference at www.smbnation.com

-AND-

Don't forget we have one-day SMB Nation Summits that travel worldwide! Information and sign-up at www.smbnation.com